Managing Stress

The Jones and Bartlett Series in Health Science

AIDS: Science and Society, Third Edition, Fan et al.

The Biology of AIDS, Fourth Edition, Fan et al.

Bloodborne Pathogens, Fourth Edition, NSC

Case Studies in Sport Psychology, Rotella et al.

Cases in Sport Marketing, McDonald/Milne

The Code of Ethics for the Health Education Profession: A Case Study Book, Greenberg

Community Health Education Methods: A Practitioner's Guide, Bensley/Brookins-Fischer

Community Health Promotion Ideas That Work, Kreuter et al.

Concepts of Athletic Training, Third Edition, Pfeiffer/Mangus

CPR, Fourth Edition, NSC

Cross Cultural Perspective in Medical Ethics, Second Edition, Veatch

Drug Abuse Prevention, Wilson/Kolander

Drugs and Society, Sixth Edition, Hanson/Venturelli

EMPOWER: Enabling Methods of Planning and Organizing within Everyone's Reach, Gold et al.

Essential Concepts for Healthy Living, Second Edition, Alters/Schiff

Essentials for Health and Wellness, Second Edition, Edlin/Golanty/McCormack Brown

Explorations in Women's Health: A Workbook, Howley/Edwards

Exploring the Dimensions of Human Sexuality, Greenberg/Bruess/Haffner

First Aid, Fourth Edition, NSC

First Aid and CPR, Third Edition, NSC

First Aid and CPR Essentials, Fourth Edition, NSC

Fostering Emotional Well-being in the Classroom, Second Edition, Page/Page

Health and Wellness, Sixth Edition, Edlin/Golanfy/McCormack Brown

Health Education: Creating Strategies for School and Community Health, Second Edition, Gilbert/Sawyer

Health Policy: Crisis and Reform in the U.S. Health Care Delivery System, Third Edition, Harrington/Estes

Healthy People, 2010, HHS

An Introduction to Community Health, Web-Enhanced, Third Edition, McKenzie/Pinger/Kotecki

An Introduction to Human Disease: Pathology and Pathophysiology Correlations, Fifth Edition, Crowley

Introduction to the Health Professions, Third Edition, Stanfield/Hui

Managing Stress: Principles and Strategies for Health and Wellbeing, Third Edition, Seaward

The Nation's Health, Sixth Edition, Lee/Estes

New Dimensions in Women's Health, Second Edition, Alexander/LaRosa/Bader

Nutrition, Insel/Turner/Ross

Physical Activity and Health: An Interactive Approach, McCormack Brown/Thomas/Kotecki

Physical Activity and Health: A Report of the Surgeon General, HHS

Recreation and Leisure in Modern Society, Sixth Edition, Kraus

Sport Marketing: Managing the Exchange Process, Milne/McDonald

Managing Stress

Principles and Strategies
for Health and Well-being

Third Edition

Brian Luke Seaward, Ph.D.

University of Colorado–Boulder

JONES AND BARTLETT PUBLISHERS

Sudbury, Massachusetts

BOSTON   TORONTO   LONDON   SINGAPORE

World Headquarters
Jones and Bartlett Publishers
40 Tall Pine Drive
Sudbury, MA 01776
info@jbpub.com
www.jbpub.com

Jones and Bartlett Publishers Canada
2406 Nikanna Road
Mississauga, ON L5C 2W6
CANADA

Jones and Bartlett Publishers International
Barb House, Barb Mews
London W6 7PA
UK

Production Credits:
Acquisitions Editor: Suzanne Jeans
Associate Editor: Amy Austin
Production Editor: Rebecca S. Marks
Editorial/Production Assistant: Amanda J. Green
Manufacturing Buyer: Therese Bräuer
Interior Design: Studio Montage
Composition: Shepherd, Inc.
Cover Design: Anne Spencer
Cover Photo: © Brian Luke Seaward
Printing and Binding: D.B. Hess Company
Cover Printer: D.B. Hess Company

Library of Congress Cataloging-in-Publication Data
Seaward, Brian Luke.
  Managing stress : principles and strategies for health and well-being / Brian Luke
Seaward.—2nd. ed.
    p. cm.
  Includes index.
  ISBN 0-7637-1462-3
  1. Stress management. 2. Stress (Psychology) 3. Mind and Body. I. Title.

RA785 .S434 2001
155.9'042—dc21   00-052059

Printed in the United States of America
05 04 03 02   10 9 8 7 6 5 4 3

Photo credits continued on page 509, which is a continuation of this copyright page.

To all my friends and family,
and to the many great people I have encountered
who have served as a dynamic inspiration in my own life journey.
Thanks for making this a better planet in which to live.

A portion of the royalty derived from the sale of
this book will be donated to several nonprofit
organizations dedicated to environmental conservation
and health promotion.

Great spirits have always encountered
violent opposition from
mediocre minds.
—Albert Einstein

Brief Contents

Contents

Foreword

"After ecstasy, the laundry!" This ancient saying can be applied to our current understanding of health and illness. During the past fifty years, we have discovered that, beyond doubt, the mind has an enormous impact on the body. Our emotions, thoughts, attitudes, and behaviors can affect us for good or ill. Now that we have glimpsed these lofty insights, it's time to get down to practicalities and apply them. It's time, in other words, to do the laundry. But the task isn't simple. How, exactly, can we bring mind and body into harmony? How can we alleviate the stressful effects of modern life? How can they be turned to our advantage? Can we learn to benefit from these changes? Can we become wiser and healthier in the process? Advice is not difficult to find: self-proclaimed experts abound. They shout the latest formulas for stress-free living and personal transformation from tabloids, talk shows, and a plethora of self-help books, giving the entire area of stress management a bad name.

It is refreshing, amid all this blather, to discover Dr. Brian Luke Seaward's *Managing Stress: Principles and Strategies for Health and Well-being.* In clear, uncluttered language, he takes us on a gentle walk through the territory of mind-body interaction. From cover to cover you will find that he is a very wise guide and possesses a quality almost always missing in stress-management manuals—humor. Dr. Seaward knows the field well—he has taught it and lived it—and he provides scientific documentation at every step. But perhaps most important, Dr. Seaward daringly goes beyond the usual approach to the subject to speak of the soul and of human spirituality because he realizes that stress management and maximal health are impossible to attain unless the questions of life's meaning are addressed.

Since *Managing Stress* first came out in 1994, the pace of life has certainly quickened, yet with this change, Americans have begun to embrace a host of complementary healing modalities, which underscores the importance of seeking a sense of inner peace from the winds of change.

As a physician who has long advocated the integration of mind and body for optimal health, I find it a pleasure and honor, therefore, to recommend this work. It is a fine contribution to the field of stress management and will serve as an invaluable guide to anyone seeking harmony in his or her life. A new day is dawning in medicine and health promotion, and Dr. Seaward has awoken early to watch and share the sunrise.

—Larry Dossey, M.D.
Executive Editor, *Alternative Therapies in Health and Medicine.* Author of *Reinventing Medicine* and *Healing Words.*

Students Praise *Managing Stress*

"The information I have learned from this book is definitely something I will remember and use the rest of my life. I found the exercises on breathing, yoga, and aromatherapy most beneficial."

—Christine S., University of Northern Colorado

"The chapter on time management was the best. Before this class I was extremely good at wasting time. Now I realize that time is an important resource that I need to make the most of. I do this by keeping a day-timer, prioritizing, and cutting out a lot of television. Thanks!"

—Jason A., Indiana University

"Just from reading the first chapter, I knew this was a book I wasn't going to sell back at the end of the semester. This book has been my saving grace. Thanks!!!"

—Bill G., Richland College, Dallas, Texas

"The most valuable thing I got out of the whole book was dealing with my anger. I never knew I was holding it in. I now know how to let it go and not let my feelings ruin my life. The chapters on music therapy and breathing were excellent."

—Melanie B., University of Northern Colorado

"By far the most significant aspect of this book was the chapter on Human Spirituality. Even though I had heard most of the information before, it has never been presented to me in such a broad yet concise manner. It refreshed my desire to continue to grow spiritually."

—Ivette B., University of New Mexico

"I had no idea how beneficial keeping a journal is to help ease the tension that occurs in everyday life."

—Emily B., University of Vermont

"It is a great comfort to know there is more than one way to deal with stress. Many times in college, I have found myself very stressed out and in need of relief. I now have many techniques to promote a less stressful lifestyle."

—Aspen V., University of Maryland

"Like most textbooks, I thought this one was going to be boring. Boy, was I wrong! I learned a great deal about my body, my mind, and my spirit. As an athlete, I now have skills for a lifetime. The chapter on humor therapy was the best! Keep those jokes coming."

—Will C., University of Utah

Preface to the Third Edition

In April of 1999 Littleton, Colorado, found itself in newspaper headlines and television sound-bites around the world. Although the impact of the shootings at Columbine High School affected everyone across the country, the ripples of stress from that event washed ashore in my life in January 2000, when I learned that several students in my stress management class at the University of Northern Colorado had been seniors at Columbine High School that spring; some of them had witnessed the shootings firsthand. One student wrote this on her course evaluation:

"My life was turned upside down last year. I never thought I would get it back together. This book has done more good than six months of therapy and counseling. Thanks a million."

The wonderful feedback I received about this textbook (as well as the accompanying journal workbook) from these students made it very clear how essential a holistic approach to dealing with stress really is. I continually receive cards, letters, and e-mails from students, nurses, social workers, psychologists, and health educators from around the country sharing similar sentiments as the former Columbine students.

I would like to say that since the first edition of *Managing Stress,* the world has become more relaxed and peaceful, but in truth, it hasn't. If anything, the "global village" we call home has become more stressed, which is all the more reason why this can make a difference in your life. As we begin a new century and millennium, I reflect on 1994, the year that this textbook was first published. Many of the ideas and concepts presented in the first edition of *Managing Stress,* such as T'ai Chi, art therapy, Chakras, and human spirituality were considered at the vanguard of health. Less than a decade later, many of these concepts, techniques, skills, and theories are now fully ingrained into American society, and I take great comfort in watching their acceptance grow.

Web exercises that support the information in each chapter can be found at www.jbpub.com/managingstress. I think you will find these interesting and entertaining (learning should be fun, right?). Feedback from my students has been nothing less than excellent. As they say, the Web exercises really help the learning process as the information is presented in a different way so as to reinforce the material.

Because so many people consistently say how well this book is referenced, I have included as many current references and resources at the end of nearly every chapter as room allowed.

As I continued to synthesize articles, books, and workshop presentations during the past three years, I knew I had to incorporate the highlights of this new material to which I was introduced. Like the second edition, new information has been added to nearly every chapter. Here are some highlights:

Chapter 1: A section titled Technostress has been added to highlight the problems that arise from the rapid pace of technology.

Chapter 2: Information regarding DHEA and other hormones involved with the stress response has been added as a sideline box.

Chapter 3: A section was included on the emerging topic of cell memory: particularly regarding people with organ transplants who retain memories of the organ donor.

Chapter 5: Some new ideas on anger and aggression were added as well as more information on depression.

Chapter 7: A section on Joseph Campbell and the hero's journey was added to the collection of luminaries regarding the power of myth and legend in human spirituality. Likewise, Joan Borysenko and Deepak Chopra have new insights on the topic from their recent books, which have been summarized in their sections as well.

Chapter 12. I included some new jokes and cartoons in the humor chapter.

Chapter 15. There are always new ideas about managing time, so I have included some of these here, particularly with a focus on technostress.

Chapter 16: With the interest in prayer research, several students (and professors) have asked to have this section expanded, and I have done so in chapter 16.

Chapter 28: I felt it was important to address the issue of genetically modified foods and include a few more herbs as well in this chapter.

Epilogue: Many people have asked if I would expand on this section of creating a personal stress management program, so I did.

Acknowledgments

When Maureen Stapleton won her Oscar for Best Supporting Actress in 1982 for her role in the movie *Reds,* she walked up to the podium and said, "I'd like to thank everyone I ever met." At times when I was writing this book, I felt much the same way. In fact, I would like to include many people whom I have never met. While I would like to share my gratitude with everyone—and you know who you are—there are some people who deserve special recognition for making this project a reality, from the seeds of inspiration to making the dream come true in my lifetime. My thanks, applause, and standing ovation are for all of you:

Dr. Joseph Pechinski, my undergraduate advisor, for inspiring me to enter the field of health promotion and wellness; Dr. Ben Massey, my graduate advisor, who encouraged me to follow my calling and be a free spirit; and Dr. Dave Clarke, my graduate advisor, who as my boss in the Lifeline Wellness program never once said no to any programming idea, including massage therapy. To my mentors, Drs. John Burt and Alan Fertziger, my appreciation for guiding me on the path of enlightenment during my years at the University of Maryland. I also want to express my thanks to Drs. Myrin Borysenko, Avery Spencer, Candace Pert, and Richard Gerber for taking the time to personally explain their theories to me. Thanks to Dr. Larry Dossey for his support and for sharing some great cartoons (we need more physicians like you!); to Carl Simonton, Roger von Oech, Tim Petersik, Alison Fisher, Cindy Conn, for allowing me to use their wonderful pieces of work in this book.

Thanks to Drs. Mike Felts, East Carolina University; Cathy Heriot, Medical University of South Carolina; Patricia Hogan, Northern Michigan University; Joan Keller-Maresh, Viterbo College; Mark Kittleson, Southern Illinois University, Carbondale; Emina McCormick, University of Vermont; Bob Russell, Southern Illinois University; Kathleen Zavela, University of Northern Colorado; and Bruce Ragon, Indiana University, who reviewed the entire manuscript and gave many excellent suggestions. Additional thanks to Patricia Norris, Steve Grebe, Teri Denunzo, Betsy Meholick, Andy Frank, Brien McCarthy, Steve Pearlman, Susan Luff, Bob Hetrick, Thomas Droege, Judian Breitenbach, Carolyn Nelka, Adam Dodge, and Brian Dalrymple, who read specific chapters to ensure accuracy within their areas of expertise. A hearty thank you to Martha Day at the University of Vermont, who helped me reference so many quotes and resources. Special thanks also go to Drs. Bernie Siegel and Larry Dossey for their wonderful endorsements; to my friends and colleagues at The American University, who learned a new meaning of the word *maverick* when they invited me to join the faculty of the Department of Health and Fitness; to Dr. Jo Safrit, who demonstrated an unyielding faith in my work; to Franka Van Allen and Jennifer Kakstis, who as my research assistants spent many hours assisting me in the search for research articles, books, verification of references, and copyright permissions; and to Guy Hadsall for his creative artwork. My appreciation as well to Nien Cheng, Bruce Laingen, Art Buchwald, Naomi Judd and her manager Laurie Kelley, James Owen Mathews, Patch Adams, Harley Goodbear, Susan Ulfelder, Mietek and Margaret Wirkus, Chris Flannagan, Ann Dieters, Anne Tongren, Roger Mursick, Sanford Markley, Suzie Hurley, Mary Ellen Metke, David Bergstein, and all the splendid guest lecturers who have come to my class, bringing to life what a textbook can never do justice to and making me look really good as a teacher in the process. For this third edition, I am ever so indebted to Amy Austin and Suzanne Jeans, my editors at Jones and Bartlett, who have helped groom this edition to its level of excellence. Special thanks to my assistant Marlene Yates and my research assistant Rita Bohn. Special thanks also to Jean Watson and Karen Holland at the Center for Human Caring at the University of Colorado-Denver, and to Carol Sheehy at the University of Colorado-Boulder. I would also like to acknowledge the extraordinary efforts of Linda Chapin and the entire staff of The National Wellness Institute in Stevens Point, Wisconsin; the Institute of Noetic Sciences in Sausalito, California; and the International Society for the Study of Subtle Energy and Energy Medicine in Golden, Colorado—thank you for being so supportive of my work. And finally, to all my students and clients, you have been marvelous teachers in your own right! Thanks!

Introduction

During the Renaissance, a philosophy shaping the direction of medicine in the Western world started taking hold. This philosophy, promulgated by René Descartes (1596–1650), stated that the mind and body are separate entities and therefore should be examined and treated differently. This dichotomy of mind and body advanced the understanding of the true human condition. Albert Einstein's revolutionary unified field theory, which at the time was regarded as ludicrous, began to lead Western science back to the ancient premise that all points (energy and matter) connect, each significantly affecting all others, of which the human entity (mental, emotional, physical, and spiritual components) is very much a part.

Only recently has modern science taken steps to unite what Descartes separated over 300 years ago. The unity of the body, mind, and spirit is quite complex, especially as it relates to stress management. But one simple truth is emerging from the research of the late twentieth century: the physical, mental, emotional, and spiritual aspects of the human condition are all intimately connected. Mental imagery, entrainment theory, *pranayama,* divinity theory, split-brain research, Jungian psychology, and beta endorphins all approach the same unity, each from a different vantage point, and each supporting the ancient axiom that "all points connect."

Stress is a popular topic in American culture today. Its popularity stems from the need to get a handle on this condition; to deal with stress effectively enough so as to lead a "normal" and happy life. But dealing with stress is a process, not an outcome. Many people's attitudes, influenced by their rushed lifestyles and expectations of immediate gratification, reflect the need to eradicate stress rather than to manage, reduce, or control their perceptions of it. As a result, stress never really goes away; it just reappears with a new face. The results can and do cause harm, including bodily damage. Studies now indicate that between 70 and 80 percent of all disease is strongly related to stress. So-called lifestyle diseases, such as, coronary heart disease and cancer, are leading causes of death; both seem to have direct links to the stress response. As the United States enters the twenty-first century, and with health care reform having become a major national issue, the ability of and the need for individuals to accept responsibility for their own health is increasing. But knowledge of the concepts of stress management alone is not enough. Continual application of this knowledge through both self-awareness and the practice of effective coping skills and relaxation techniques is essential for total well-being.

Thus, this book was written to acquaint you with the fundamental theories and applications of the mind-body phenomenon. More specifically, it offers fifteen coping strategies you can use as tools to deal more effectively with the causes of your stress, and eleven relaxation techniques to help you reduce or eliminate potential or actual symptoms associated with the stress response. It is my intention that collectively they may help you to reach and maintain your optimal level of physical, mental, emotional, and spiritual well-being in the years to come. For this reason, I would like to suggest that you revisit the book again and again as time goes by: what may appear today to be "some theory" to memorize for a final exam could one day take on great relevance in your life.

To the Instructor

In order to save time and aid the instructor in the teaching of the course, the publisher has provided instructor resources, which consist of the following: an Instructor's ToolKit CD-ROM with a Computerized Testbank, chapter outlines, PowerPoint presentations and teaching tips. This CD is free to all instructors who adopt the text for classroom use.

The computerized testbank consists of multiple choice, fill-in, matching, true-false, and essay questions. Also included is a list of additional multimedia resources and instructional materials.

For the student, each chapter of the text has a number of pedagogical devices designed to aid in the mastery of the material, including boxes, surveys, exercises, and checklists. Case studies entitled "Stress with a Human Face" illustrate how people deal with a variety of stressful situations. Each chapter concludes with a comprehensive summary of the main points in the chapter along with a list of key terms and references for further study. Key terms are also clearly defined in a handy glossary of terms at the end of the text, which can be useful in studying for examinations. In addition, at the end of almost every chapter there is a Self-Assessment to help relate the content to the reader's life.

Managing Stress: A Creative Journal, Second Edition, is also available as an optional supplement to the course. The journal contains more than 75 thought-provoking, soul-searching themes designed to engage the student in writing about personal stress, unresolved conflict, and tension-producing emotions. Journal writing has proven to be a formidable coping technique used by psychologists and health educators as an awareness tool for self-exploration and discovery. Also available to the student is a complimentary 60-minute audio CD that provides four relaxation techniques for stress reduction found in the back of each new book. Mental imagery, meditation, progressive relaxation, and autogenic training are taught with a professional mix of voice and restful music. Through listening to the CD, students are shown how to apply stress-reduction methods to their own lives.

Instructors and students using the third edition of this text can access the web site using the username: **bls3e** and the password: **managing stress.** The URL of the web site is www.jbpub.com/managingstress.

Part 1

The Nature of Stress

"Life is either

a daring adventure

or nothing at all."

-Helen Keller

$\mathcal{C}$hapter 1 The Nature of Stress

*I cannot and should not be
cured of my stress, but merely
taught to enjoy it.*

—Hans Selye

If you were to browse through any newspaper or magazine article prior to 1960, you would be hard-pressed to find the word **stress** in either the text or the headlines. The stress phenomenon, as it is referred to today, is quite new with regard to the history of humanity. Not even a household expression two decades ago, use of the word *stress* is now as common as the words *food* and *exercise*. In fact, however, stress in terms of physical arousal can be traced back to the Stone Age as a "survival mechanism." But what was once designed as a means of survival is now associated with the development of disease and illness that claims the lives of millions of people. Research now indicates that between 70 and 80 percent of all disease and illness is stress-related, most notably coronary heart disease, cancer, the common cold, migraine headaches, warts, some cases of female infertility, ulcers, insomnia, hypertension—the list goes on and on.

Government figures compiled by the National Center for Health Statistics in 2000 provide a host of indicators suggesting that human stress is indeed a health factor to be reckoned with. Prior to 1955, the leading causes of death were the sudden onset of illness by infectious diseases (e.g., polio, rubella, tuberculosis, typhoid, and encephalitis) that in most cases have since been eradicated or brought under control by vaccines and medications. The post-World War II era ushered in the age of high technology, which considerably altered the lifestyles of nearly all peoples of every industrialized nation. The introduction of consumer products, such as the washer, dryer, microwave oven, television, VCR, and cell phone, were cited as luxuries to add more leisure time to the work week. But as mass production of high-technology items increased, so too did the competitive drive to increase human effort and productivity, which in turn actually decreased leisure time, and thus created a plethora of unhealthy lifestyles.

Currently, the leading causes of death are dominated by what are referred to as lifestyle diseases, those diseases whose pathology develops over a period of several years, and perhaps even decades (Fig. 1.1). Whereas infectious diseases are treatable by medication, lifestyle diseases are, for the most part, preventable or correctable by altering the habits and behaviors that contribute to their etiology. Although it is suggested that stress is not the direct cause of these diseases, the influence of stress weakens the body's physiological systems, thus rapidly advancing the disease process. The most notorious lifestyle disease, coronary heart disease (CHD), continues to be the leading cause of death in the United States, far exceeding all other causes. The

Figure 1.1 Death rates for the ten leading causes of death per 100,000 population in the United States in 1900 and 1998. (National Center for Health Statistics, Washington, D.C., 2000.)

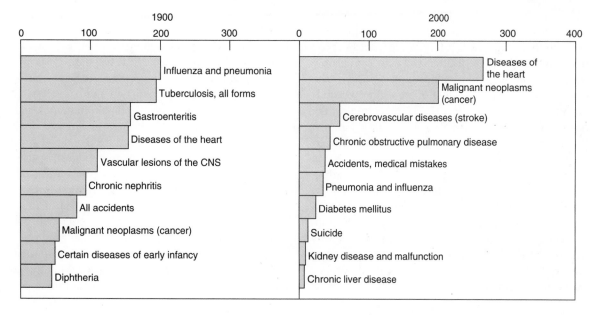

American Heart Association states that one person dies from heart disease every thirty-four seconds. And while the incidence of CHD has decreased over the past decade, cancer, in all its many types, continues to climb the statistical charts as the second leading cause of death. Currently cancer claims the lives of one out of every six people. By the year 2005 this rate is projected to be even higher. Alarming increases in suicides, child and spouse abuse, homicides, alcoholism, and drug addiction are only additional symptoms of a nation under stress. Today, research shows that people still maintain poor coping skills in the face of the personal, social, and even global changes occurring over the course of their lives. When put in perspective of the entire health care picture, where over $350 billion a year is spent on lifestyle and stress-related diseases, the whole health care system is put at risk of collapse. This has led to several national efforts for health care reform.

Originally, the word *stress* was a term used in physics, primarily to describe enough tension or force placed on an object to bend or break it. Relaxation, on the other hand, was defined as any nonwork activity done during the evenings or on Sunday afternoons when all the stores were closed. On rare occasion, if one could afford it, relaxation meant a vacation or holiday at some faraway place. Conceptually, relaxation was a value, influenced by several religions and represented as a day of rest. The word *stress* as applied to the human condition was first made popular by noted physiologist Hans Selye in his book *The Stress of Life,* where he described his research: to understand the physiological responses to chronic stress and its relationship to disease (dis-ease). Today, the word *stress* is frequently used to describe the level of tension people feel is placed on their minds and souls by the demands of their jobs, relationships, and responsibilities in their personal lives. Relaxation, meanwhile, has been transformed from an American value to a luxury many people find they just don't have enough time for. With the current economic expansion, some interesting insights have been observed regarding work and leisure. The average workweek has expanded from forty to sixty hours. The U.S. Department of Labor and Statistics reports that with more service-related jobs being created, more overtime is needed to meet the demands of the customers (as was observed in labor negotiations with United Airlines pilots and Verizon telephone operators in the summer

of 2000). Not only do more people spend more time at work, they spend more time driving to and from work (which is not considered work time). Moreover, leisure time at home is often related to work activities, resulting in less time for rest and relaxation. In a recent study by Anderson Consulting (Wong, 2000), it was observed that 80 percent of people who took a vacation in the summer of 2000 brought along their laptop computer and cell phone so they could stay in touch with the office. The "dividend" of high technology has proven to be an illusion that has resulted in a significant health deficit.

Definitions of Stress

In contemporary times, the word *stress* has many connotations and definitions based on various perspectives of the human condition. In Eastern philosophies, stress is considered to be an absence of inner peace. In Western culture, stress can be described as a loss of control. Noted healer Serge Kahili King has defined stress as any change experienced by the individual. This definition may be rather general, but it is quite correct. Psychologically speaking, stress as defined by noted researcher Richard Lazarus is a state of anxiety produced when events and responsibilities exceed one's coping abilities. Physiologically speaking, stress is defined as the rate of wear and tear on the body. Selye added to his definition that stress is the nonspecific response of the body to any demand placed upon it to adapt, whether that demand produces pleasure or pain. Selye observed that whether a situation was perceived as good (e.g., a job promotion) or bad (e.g., the loss of a job), the physiological response or arousal was very similar. The body, according to Selye, doesn't know the difference between good and bad stress.

However, with new psychoneuroimmunological data available showing that there are indeed some physiological differences between good and bad stress (e.g., the release of different neuropeptides), specialists in the field of **holistic medicine** have expanded Lazarus's and Selye's definitions as follows: Stress is the inability to cope with a perceived (real or imagined) threat to one's mental, physical, emotional, and spiritual well-being, which results in a series of physiological responses and adaptations. The important word to emphasize here is *perceived* (the interpretation), for what might seem to be a threat to one person may not even merit a second thought to another individual. For example, not long ago a raffle was held, with the winning prize being an all-expenses-paid one-week trip for two to a beach resort in Hawaii. Kelly, who won the prize, was ecstatic and already had her bags packed. Her husband, John, was mortified because he hated to fly and he couldn't swim. In his mind this would not be a fun time. In fact, he really wished they hadn't won. Each perceived the same situation in two entirely different ways. Moreover, with the wisdom of hindsight, our perceptions often change. Many episodes which at the time seemed catastrophic later appear insignificant, as humorously stated by Mark Twain when he commented, "I'm an old man and I have known a great many troubles, but most of them never happened." The holistic definition of stress points out that it is a very complex phenomenon affecting the whole person, not just the physical body, and that it involves a host of factors, some of which may not yet even be recognized by scholars and researchers. As more research is completed, it becomes increasingly evident that the responses to stress add up to more than just physical arousal; yet it is ultimately the body that remains the battlefield for the war games of the mind.

The Stress Response

In 1914 Harvard physiologist Walter Cannon first coined the term **fight-or-flight response** to describe the dynamics involved in the body's physiological arousal to survive a threat. In a series of animal studies, Cannon noted that the body prepares itself for one of two modes of immediate action: to attack or fight and defend oneself from the pursuing threat, or to run and escape the ensuing danger. What Cannon observed was the body's reaction to acute stress, what is now commonly called the "stress reaction." Additional observations suggested that the fight response was triggered by anger or aggression and was usually employed to defend territorial boundaries or attack aggressors smaller in size. The fight response required physiological preparations that would recruit power and strength for a short duration, or what is now described as short but intense anaerobic work. Conversely, the flight response, he thought, was induced by fear. It was designed to fuel the body to endure prolonged movement such as running away from lions and bears. In

many cases, however, it included not only fleeing but also hiding or withdrawal. The human body, in all its metabolic splendor, actually prepares itself to do both at the same time. In terms of evolution, it appears that this mechanism was so advantageous to survival that it developed in nearly all mammalian species.

In simple terms, there are four stages of the fight-or-flight response:

Stage 1. Stimuli from one or more of the five senses are sent to the brain (e.g., a scream, the smell of fire, the taste of poison, a passing truck in *your* lane).

Stage 2. The brain deciphers the stimulus as either a threat or a nonthreat. If the stimulus is not regarded as a threat, this is the end of the response (e.g., the scream came from the television). If, however, the response is decoded as a real threat, the brain then activates the nervous and endocrine systems to quickly prepare for defense and/or escape.

Stage 3. The body stays activated, aroused, or "keyed-up" until the threat is over.

Stage 4. The body returns to **homeostasis,** a state of physiological calmness, once the threat is gone.

It is hypothesized that the fight-or-flight response developed primarily against threats of a physical nature, those that jeopardized the survival of the individual. Although clear physical threats still exist in todays culture, they are nowhere near as prevalent as those threats perceived by the mind and, more specifically, the ego. In a theory put forward by a disciple of Selye's, Simeons (1961) suggested that, in effect, the fight-or-flight response is an antiquated mechanism that has not kept evolutionary pace with the development of the human mind. Consequently, the stress response becomes activated in all types of threats, not just physical intimidations. The physiological repercussions can, and do, prove fatal. The body enters a state of physical readiness when you are about to receive your final exam grades or walk into an important meeting late, just as it does when you sense someone is following you late at night in an unlit parking lot. Moreover, this same stress response kicks in, to the same degree and intensity, even when the threat is wholly imaginary, in reaction to everything from monsters hiding under your bed when you were four (Fig. 1.2), to the unsubstantiated idea that your boss doesn't like you anymore and is out to get you.

Figure 1.2

Cannon noted the activation of several physiological mechanisms in this fight-or-flight response, affecting nearly every physiological system in the body, for the preparation of movement and energy production. These are just a few of the reactions:

1. Increased heart rate to pump oxygenated blood to working muscles
2. Increased blood pressure to deliver blood to working muscles
3. Increased ventilation to supply working muscles with oxygen for energy metabolism
4. Vasodilation of arteries to the body's periphery (arms and legs) with the greatest muscle mass
5. Increased serum glucose for metabolic processes during muscle contractions
6. Increased free fatty acid mobilization as an energy source for prolonged activity (e.g., running)
7. Increased blood coagulation and decreased clotting time in the event of bleeding
8. Increased muscular strength
9. Decreased gastric movement and abdominal blood flow to allow blood to go to working muscles
10. Increased perspiration to cool body-core temperature

Unfortunately, the metabolic and physiological changes that are deemed essential for human movement in the event of attack, pursuit, or challenge are quite *ineffective* when dealing with events or situations that threaten the ego, such as receiving a parking ticket or standing in a long line at the grocery store, yet the body responds identically to all types of perceived threats.

Types of Stress

To the disbelief of some, not all stress is bad for you. In fact, there are many who believe that humans need some degree of stress to stay healthy. The human body craves homeostasis, or physiological calm, yet it also requires physiological arousal to ensure the optimal functioning of several organs, including the heart and musculo-skeletal system. How can stress be good? When stress serves as a positive motivation, it is considered beneficial. Beyond this optimal point, stress of any kind does more harm than good.

Actually, there are three kinds of stress: **eustress, neustress,** and **distress.** Eustress is good stress and arises in any situation or circumstance that a person finds motivating or inspiring. Falling in love might be an example of eustress; meeting a movie star or professional athlete may also be a type of eustress. Usually, situations that are classified as eustress are enjoyable and for this reason are not considered to be a threat. Neustress describes sensory stimuli that have no consequential effect; it is considered neither good nor bad. News of an earthquake in a remote corner of the world might fall into this category. The third type of stress, distress, is considered bad and often is abbreviated simply as *stress.* There are two kinds of distress: **acute stress,** or that which surfaces, is quite intense, and disappears quickly, and **chronic stress,**

Figure 1.3 The Yerkes-Dodson Curve illustrates that, to a point, stress or arousal can actually increase performance. Stress to the left of the midpoint is considered to be eustress. Stress beyond the midpoint, however, is believed to detract from performance and/or health status and is therefore labeled distress.

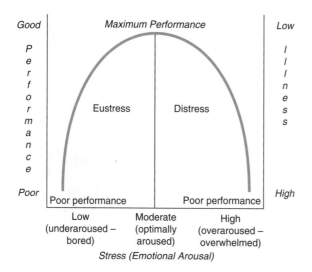

ples might include the following: being stuck for a whole semester with "the roommate from hell," a credit card bill that only seems to grow despite monthly payments, a boss who makes your job seem worse than that of a galley slave, living in a city you cannot tolerate, or maintaining a relationship with a girlfriend, boyfriend, husband, or wife that seems bad to stay in but worse to leave. For this reason, chronic stressors are thought to be the real villains, and it is this type of stress that is associated with disease, because the body is perpetually aroused for danger.

A concept called the **Yerkes-Dodson principle**, which is applied to athletic performance, lends itself quite nicely to explaining the relationship between eustress, distress, and health. As can be seen in Figure 1.3, when stress increases, moving from eustress to distress, performance or health decreases and there is greater risk of disease and illness. The optimal stress level is the midpoint, *prior* to where eustress turns into distress. Studies indicate that stress-related hormones in optimal doses actually improve physical performance and mental-processing skills, like concentration, making you more alert. Beyond that optimal level, though, all aspects of performance begin to decrease in efficiency. Physiologically speaking, your health is at serious risk. It would be simple if this optimal level was the same for all people, but it's not. Hence, the focus of any effective stress-management program is two-fold: (1) to find out where this optimal level of stress is for you so that it can be used to your advantage rather than becoming a detriment to your health status, and (2) to reduce physical arousal levels using both coping skills and relaxation techniques so that you can stay out of the danger zone created by too much stress.

or that which may not appear quite so intense, yet seems to linger for prolonged periods of time (e.g., hours, days, weeks, or months). An example of acute stress is the following. You are casually driving down the highway, the wind from the open sun roof is blowing through your hair, and you feel pretty good about life. With a quick glance in your rearview mirror you see flashing blue lights. Yikes! So you slow down and pull over. The police car pulls up behind you. Your heart is racing, your voice becomes scratchy, and your palms are sweating as you try to retrieve license and registration from your wallet while rolling your window down at the same time. When the officer asks you why you were speeding you can barely speak; your voice is three octaves higher than usual. After the officer runs a check on your car and license, he only gives you a warning for speeding. Whew! He gets back in his car and leaves. You give him time to get out of sight, start your engine, and signal to get back onto the highway. Within minutes your heart is calm, your palms dry, and you start singing to the song on the radio. The threat is over. The intensity of the acute stress may seem cataclysmic, but it is very short-lived.

Chronic stressors, on the other hand, are not as intense but their duration is unbearably long. Exam-

Types of Stressors

Situations, circumstances, or any stimulus that is perceived to be a threat is referred to as a *stressor,* or that which causes or promotes stress. As you might imagine, the list of stressors is not only endless but varies considerably from person to person. Acute stress is often the result of rapid-onset stressors—those which pop up unexpectedly—like a phone call in the middle of the night or the discovery that you have lost your car keys. Usually the body begins to react before a full analysis of the situation is made, but a return to a state of calm is also imminent. Chronic stressors—those that give some advance warning yet manage to cause physical arousal anyway, often merit more attention because their prolonged influence on the body appears to be more significant. Much research has been conducted to determine the nature of stressors, and they are currently divided into three categories: bioecological, psychointrapersonal, and social (Giradano, Everly, and Dusek, 1993).

Bioecological Influences

There are several biological and ecological factors that may trigger the stress response in varying degrees, some of which are outside our awareness. These are external influences, including sunlight, gravitational pull, and electromagnetic fields, that affect our biological rhythms. From the field of chronobiology we learn that these factors affect three categories of biological rhythms: (1) circadian rhythms, fluctuations in physiological functions over the course of a twenty-four-hour period (e.g., body temperature); (2) ultradian rhythms, fluctuations that occur over less than a twenty-four-hour period (such as stomach contractions and cell divisions); and (3) infradian rhythms, changes that occur in periods longer than twenty-four hours (e.g., the menses). These biological changes are influenced by such natural phenomena as the earth's orbit and axis rotation, which give us periods of light and darkness as well as seasonal differences (Fig. 1.4). A prime example of a bioecological influence is seasonal affective disorder (SAD), a condition affecting many people who live at or near the arctic circle. Many of these people become depressed when they are deprived of sunlight for prolonged periods of time. But technological changes are also included in this category, an example being jet lag as a result of airplane travel through several time zones. Electrical pollution, solar radiation, and noise pollution are other potential bioecological influences. In addition, some synthetic food additives may trigger the release of various stress hormones throughout the body. Note that there is a growing opinion among some health practitioners that increased stress levels in the twentieth century may be a direct result of our being out of touch with the *natural* elements that so strongly influence our body's physiological systems. In any case, some of these bioecological factors can be positively influenced by lifestyle changes, including dietary habits, exercise (see Chapter 28), and the regular practice of relaxation techniques, which bring a sense of balance back into our lives.

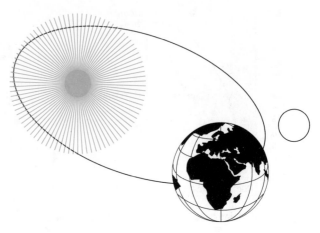

Due to the tilt of the earth's axis as it moves in its orbit around the sun, areas closest to the poles vary the most in the amount of daily sunlight they receive. Studies show that an inadequate amount of full-spectrum lighting is associated with depression, a phenomenon now known as seasonal affective disorder (SAD) or arctic winter madness.

Figure 1.4

Psychointrapersonal Influences

Our current understanding is that psychointrapersonal influences make up the greatest percentage of stressors. These are the perceptions of stimuli that we create through our own mental processes. Psychointrapersonal stressors involve those thoughts, values, beliefs, attitudes, and perceptions that we use to defend our identity or ego (see Chapters 4 and 5). When any of these are challenged, violated, or even changed, the ego is often threatened and the stress response is the outcome. Psychointrapersonal stressors reflect the unique constructs of our personality, and in the words of stress researcher Kenneth Pelletier, represent "the chasm between the perceived self and the ideal self-image." Because these influences are the most likely to cause stress, they are a major focus of this book and great emphasis is placed on helping you manage your stress through learning and practicing effective cognitive coping techniques that aim to resolve stress-related issues.

Social Influences

Social influences have long been the subject of research to explain the plight of individuals who are unable to cope with their given environment. Most

Figure 1.5 Weddings are thought to be joyous occasions; however, they can produce a lot of stress, especially when things don't go perfectly as planned.

notable is the issue of overcrowding. Studies conducted on several species have shown that when their numbers exceed the territorial boundary of each animal, despite an abundance of food and water, several seemingly healthy animals die off. This need for personal space appears to be universal in the animal kingdom, including humans, who likewise begin to show signs of frustration in crowded urban areas, traffic jams, long lines at checkout stands, or whenever their personal space is "invaded." The origin of this particular social influence may be instinctual in nature. Additional social causes of stress include financial insecurity, the effects of relocation, some technological advances, violation of human rights, and low socioeconomic status, to name but a few.

Social influences related to stress also include major life changes. Two researchers who made significant gains in understanding the relationship between stress and disease through life changes were Thomas Holmes and Richard Rahe. Based on the Life Chart theory of Adolph Meyer, Holmes and Rahe set out to determine what events in people's lives were most stressful. Surveying thousands of individuals, they created a list of circumstances that represent typical life stressors, or events that require some adaptation or readjustment to a situation. Their list, with a total of forty-three events, included several life events that, on the surface, appear to be positive, such as vacations, weddings (Fig. 1.5), and outstanding personal achievements, as well as traumatic ordeals such as the death of a child. Then they devised a system to weigh each event according to its stress potential. All events were assigned numerical values based on their degree of disruption of one's life and readjustment following the event. These values were called Life-Change Units or LCUs.

The result of their efforts was an inventory called the Social Readjustment Rating Scale (SRRS), which ranked the forty-three life events from most stressful to least stressful (Table 1.1). In further research using this assessment tool, Holmes and Rahe gave this inventory to several physicians and then compared their results with major health changes reported by the physicians. There was a significant correlation between life-event scores and personal health histories, with an LCU score of 150 being the point of demarcation between the exposure to major life stressors and health-related problems. With further analysis, they created categories based on LCU scores: 150–199 points suggested a mild life crisis, 200–299 points suggested a moderate life crisis, and any score over 300 points indicated a major life crisis. Based on the work by Holmes and Rahe, this survey and similar ones designed for special populations (e.g., college students) are now used to predict the likelihood of disease and illness following exposure to stressful life

Social Readjustment Rating Scale

Table 1.1

Rank	Life Event	LCU
1	Death of a spouse	100
2	Divorce	73
3	Marital separation	65
4	Jail term	63
5	Death of close family member	63
6	Personal injury or illness	53
7	Marriage	50
8	Fired at work	47
9	Marital reconciliation	45
10	Retirement	45
11	Change in health of family member	44
12	Pregnancy	40
13	Sexual dysfunction	39
14	Gain of a new family member	39
15	Business readjustment	39
16	Change in financial status	38
17	Death of a close friend	37
18	Change to different line of work	36
19	Change in number of arguments with spouse	35
20	Mortgage over $100,000	31
21	Foreclosure of mortgage or loan	30
22	Change in responsibilities at work	29
23	Son or daughter leaving home	29
24	Trouble with in-laws	29
25	Outstanding personal achievement	28
26	Spouse begins or stops work	26
27	Begin or end school	26
28	Change in living conditions	25
29	Revision of personal habits	24
30	Trouble with boss	23
31	Change in work hours or conditions	20
32	Change in residence	20
33	Change in schools	20
34	Change in recreation	19
35	Change in church activities	19
36	Change in social activities	18
37	Mortgage or loan less than $10,000	17
38	Change in sleeping habits	16
39	Change in number of family get-togethers	15
40	Change in eating habits	13
41	Vacation	13
42	Christmas	12
43	Minor violation of the law	11

CHECK OFF those events that currently apply to your life and add up the corresponding points or Life-Change Units. A score below 150 is thought to be within the range of normal stress. A score between 150 and 199 suggests a mild life crisis; between 200 and 299 points suggests a moderate life crisis; above 300 points is indicative of a major life crisis. (Reprinted by permission of the publisher from "The Social Readjustment Rating Scale" by T. H. Holmes and R. Rahe, *Journal of Psychosomatic Research*, vol. 11, pp. 213–218. Copyright 1967 by Elsevier Science Inc.)

events. It is important to note that a high LCU score does not predict illness for all people, and this fact has led to criticism of research. Evidence indicates that in the face of repeated disasters, some people, by nature of their personalities, appear immune to stress. (This is addressed in more detail in Chapter 6.) A modified version of the Social Readjustment Rating Scale has been defined for college student (Table 1.2).

While major life events like getting married or relocating for a new job may be chronic stressors to some, renowned stress researcher Richard Lazarus hypothesized in 1984 that the accumulation of acute stressors or daily life hassles, such as locking your keys in your car, playing telephone tag, or driving to work every day in traffic, is just as likely to adversely affect one's health as the death of a spouse (Table 1.3).

Table 1.2

Stress Units Associated with Common Life Changes Experienced by Students

Event	Life change units
Death of close family member	100
Death of a close friend	73
Divorce between parents	65
Jail term	63
Major personal injury or illness	63
Marriage	58
Fired from job	50
Failed important course	47
Change in health of family member	45
Pregnancy	45
Sex problems	44
Serious argument with close friend	40
Change in financial status	39
Trouble with parents	39
Change of major	39
New girlfriend or boyfriend	38
Increased workload at school	37
Outstanding personal achievement	36
First quarter/semester in college	35
Change in living conditions	31
Serious argument with instructor	30
Lower grades than expected	29
Change in sleeping habits	29
Change in social activities	29
Change in eating habits	28
Chronic car trouble	26
Change in number of family get-togethers	26
Too many missed classes	25
Change of college/change of work	24
Dropped more than one class	23
Minor traffic violations	20

SOURCE: I. G. Sarason, B. R. Sarason, and J. H. Johnson, "Stressful Life Events: Measurement, Moderators, and Adaptation," in Susan R. Burchfield, ed., *Stress* (Washington, D.C.: Hemisphere, 1985).

The Measurement of Hassles

Table 1.3

Recently psychologists have examined the role of minor stressors in the development of disease and illness. The following sample items from the Hassles Scale (Kanner et al.) indicate what might be perceived to be everyday hassles or petty annoyances.

1 = somewhat severe; 2 = moderately severe; 3 = extremely severe

Directions: Hassles are small irritants that can range from minor annoyances to fairly major pressures, problems, or difficulties. They can occur few or many times. Listed below are a number of ways in which a person can feel hassled. First, circle the hassles that have happened to you in the past month. Then look at the numbers to the right of the items you circled. Indicate by circling a 1, 2, or 3 how severe each of these circled hassles has been for you in the past month. If a hassle did not occur in the last month, do not circle it.

1. Not getting enough sleep	1	2	3
2. Job dissatisfaction	1	2	3
3. Use of alcohol	1	2	3
4. Inconsiderate smokers	1	2	3
5. Thoughts about death	1	2	3
6. Health of a family member	1	2	3
7. Not enough money for clothing	1	2	3
8. Concerns about owing money	1	2	3
9. Fear of rejection	1	2	3
10. Concern about weight	1	2	3

The Hassles Scale has over 118 items. These questions provide only a sample and thus it is not possible to evaluate your personal daily hassles from this set. The second part of this scale is referred to as the Uplift Scale, a series of 136 questions to determine what events promote joy and happiness. The following is a sample.

1. Being with younger people	1	2	3
2. Entertainment	1	2	3
3. Laughing	1	2	3
4. Being one with the world	1	2	3
5. Hugging or kissing	1	2	3

From S. Taylor, *Health Psychology* (New York: McGraw-Hill, 1998), pp. 10, 221. Reproduced with permission of McGraw-Hill.

These hassles are often based on unmet expectations that trigger an anger response of some type, whereas stressors of a chronic nature more often than not appear to have a greater association with fear and anxiety. Lazarus defined hassles as "daily interactions with the environment that were essentially negative." He also hypothesized that a balance of emotional experiences—positive emotions as well as negative ones—is necessary, and that people who have no exposure to life's "highs" or emotional uplifts are also susceptible to disease and illness. Further research by Lazarus (1983, 1984), Ornstein and Sobel (1989), and others has proved that his hypothesis has significant merit regarding stress and disease. As might be expected, the issue of lifestyle habits, changes, and hassles as social influences has come under attack by those who argue that perception or cognition plays an important role in the impact of stressors. Suffice it to say that all stressors, regardless of classification, are connected to human well-being in a very profound way.

The General Adaptation Syndrome

Following Cannon's lead early in the twentieth century, Hans Selye, a young endocrinologist who created a name for himself as a leading researcher in this field, studied the fight-or-flight response, specifically the physiological effects of chronic stress, using rats as subjects. In experiments designed to stress the rats, Selye noted that several physiological adaptations occurred as a result of repeated exposures to stress, adaptations that had pathological repercussions. Examples of these stress-induced changes included the following:

1. Enlargement of the adrenal cortex (a gland that produces stress hormones)
2. Constant release of stress hormones; corticosteroids released from the adrenal cortex
3. Atrophy or shrinkage of lymphatic glands (thymus gland, spleen, and lymph nodes)
4. Significant decrease in the white blood-cell count
5. Bleeding ulcerations of the stomach and colon
6. Death of the organism

Many of these changes were very subtle and often went unnoticed until permanent damage had occurred. He referred to these collective changes as the **general adaptation syndrome** (GAS), a process in which the body tries to accommodate stress by adapting to it. From his research, Selye identified three stages of the general adaptation syndrome:

Stage one: Alarm reaction. The alarm reaction describes Cannon's original fight-or-flight response. In this stage several body systems are activated, primarily the nervous system and the endocrine system, followed by the cardiovascular, pulmonary, and musculoskeletal systems. Like a smoke alarm detector buzzing late at night, all senses are put on alert until the danger is over.

Stage two: Stage of resistance. In the resistance stage, the body tries to revert back to a state of physiological calmness, or homeostasis, by resisting the alarm.

Because the perception of a threat still exists, however, complete homeostasis is never reached. Instead, the body stays activated or aroused, usually at a lesser intensity than during the alarm stage but enough to cause a higher metabolic rate in some organ tissues. One or more organs may in effect be working overtime and, as a result, enter the third and final stage.

Stage three: Stage of exhaustion. Exhaustion occurs when one (or more) of the organs targeted by specific metabolic processes can no longer meet the demands placed upon it and fails to function properly. This can result in death to the organ, and depending on which organ becomes dysfunctional (e.g., the heart), possibly the death of the organism as a whole.

Selye's general adaptation syndrome outlined the parameters of the physiological dangers of stress. His research opened the doors to understanding the strong relationship between stress and disease and the mind-body-spirit equation. In addition, his work laid the foundation for the utilization of relaxation techniques that have the ability to intercept the stress response, thereby decreasing susceptibility to illness and disease. Congruent with standard medical practice of his day (and even today), initial stress management programs were geared toward reducing or eliminating the *symptoms* of stress. Unfortunately, this approach has not always proved successful.

Stress in a Changing World

All you need do is glance at the covers of *Time, Newsweek, U.S. News, Psychology Today* or *Reader's Digest* to see and read what we already know: These are stressful times! But the stress we are encountering as a nation is not specific to being a world power. The problem seems to have reached every corner of the planet, permeating the borders of every country, province, and locale. In fact, after conducting several surveys on the topic of stress and illness, the World Health Organization came to the conclusion that stress is hitting a fever pitch in every nation. So alarmed were they by the results of their study, that they cited stress as "a global epidemic."

On the home front it appears that stress, like a virus, has infected the American population, and the symptoms are everywhere: Radio talk shows have become a national forum for complaining; political

Stress With a Human Face

SEAN'S BODY WAS A HUMAN BATTLEFIELD. To have an ulcer at age seventeen isn't unique, but it isn't common either. Most people who get ulcers are over the age of thirty; Sean was fourteen when he first developed his. A routine visit to the dentist signaled another problem: temporomandibular joint dysfunction (TMJ). It seemed that daytime skirmishes occurred in the stomach while nighttime combat maneuvers took place in the jaw. And when he didn't have migraine headaches, Sean was always coming down with a cold. Thinking back, Sean realized that the link between stress and the ulcer was more than obvious. The call to arms began when he was abused as a child, and flare-ups continued after a serious driving accident

in which manslaughter charges were pressed against him and then dropped after a year of litigation. Sean's body was in a constant state of exhaustion. A dream in which he was having a beer with the angel of death was enough to seek help. Sean enrolled in a stress management program and now, as he says in his own words, "The war's over, I have declared peace, and I am ready to reconstruct a new life." ✦

pundits repeatedly describe voter anger; headlines are filled with stories of people who have gone berserk with hostility, most notably road rage; television talk shows are reduced to airing personal catharses; workplace violence has escalated to several incidences per month in which co-workers are shot and killed; the American dream is out of reach for many; and psychologists describe a spiritual malaise that has swept the country. In 1995, a small but prophetic article titled *Bowling Alone,* by Harvard political scientist Robert Putnam, sent ripples throughout the nation. Years of research led Putnam to discover that communities are disintegrating, as are the civic institutions on which communities are based. And in the landmark book, *Emotional Intelligence,* author Daniel Goldman provides a dismal forecast with regard to the emotional state of this nation's children, a generation of youngsters raised on television violence. Yet where there is despair, there is also compassion. The Blizzard of '96 followed by the thaw of '96 (all in the same two-week period on the East Coast) brought out the best in some, as people came to the aid of their neighbors and strangers.

The sociology of stress can prove to be a fascinating study of interrelated factors that form a confluence of several recognizable stressors. Indeed, we encounter many social triggers daily, yet, at a closer look, the finger often points to our relationship with technology and our dependence on it. Whether it be faxes, cordless phones, email, overnight shipping, teleconferences, beepers, cellular phones, or laptop computers, there is a growing dependence on the convenience of high technology. Current estimates reveal that we spend more time at work, leaving less time to be at home with the family, and we are now accessible twenty-four hours a day. What's more, with several years of corporate downsizing and restructuring, Americans are realizing for the first time that there really is no such thing as job security.

Stress, it seems, knows no age, race, gender, religion, nationality, or socioeconomic class. For this reason, it is called "the equal opportunity destroyer," for when left unresolved, stress can undermine all aspects of your life. Although it may seem that stress becomes a critical mass in your life once you leave home and go to college, the truth is that the episodes and behaviors associated with stress start much earlier than the college years. Pressures in high school, even grade school, are well documented. Combined with the stress of high technology, the effects are exponential. First let's take a look at high tech stress and then focus on stress in the college setting, occupational stress, and finally stress and the retired population.

Technostress

As we begin the new decade, century, and millennium, a new term has taken hold in the American vernacular: technostress. It means to cope (or not cope) with the rapid pace of technology. The boom in the telecommunications industry and computer industry, pillars of the information age, have led to an overnight conversion of lifestyle change in the American (and global) society. In their book *Technostress,* authors Weil and Rosen suggest that the rapid pace of technology will only continue with greater speed in the coming years, giving a whole new meaning to the expression "24-7." They predict, as do others, that the majority of people will not deal well with this change. The result will be more stress, more illness and disease, more addictions, more dysfunction, and a greater imbalance to one's life. There is a general consensus that the rate of change with technology has far outpaced the level of responsibility and moral codes that typically accompany the creative process. The following are some aspects of technostress as they currently affect one's life and will continue to do so:

+ *Information overload:* Among a flood of emails, faxes, WWW advertisements,

magazines, and voice mail, it is easy to become overwhelmed with the inundation of information, particularly emails. The time spent reviewing and responding to a slew of emails and voice mails can set one back several hours.

+ *Boundaries:* Less than twenty years ago, there were clear-cut boundaries between one's personal and professional lives. Today the boundaries have dissolved to a point where it's hard to tell where one ends and the next begins. With cell phones, pagers, beepers, and palm computers, a person can be accessed every minute of the day. People feel compelled to take these devices to movie theaters, plays, restaurants, and even on vacations. While the expression 24-7 was first coined to refer to retail shopping, it now conveys nonstop accessibility (Fig. 1.6).

+ *Privacy:* With constant accessibility one forfeits privacy. However, with many purchases made on the WWW, each person develops a consumer profile, which then is sold to a host of other vendors. From "cookies" to markers, privacy has become a real issue in the information age. With advances in reducing the microchip to the size of a molecule, information storage will go from the smart card to biotech implants.

+ *Ethics:* As the Human Genome project nears completion, scientists produce the ability to identify persons likely to inherit genetic-based diseases. Fear arises when this information falls into the hands of insurance companies that revoke policies based on genetic profiling.

    While gene treatment therapy is currently in the experimental stages, another scientific breakthrough is genetic cloning, which carries with it many moral and ethical concerns, as does genetic research. Genetically modified foods (GMOs), where genes of pesticides, flounder, and nuts, for example, are placed in tomatoes, corn, and soybeans, are raising ethical issues as well.

+ *Less family time:* A recent study at Stanford University revealed that unlike television watching, which can be done as a family, surfing the Internet is a singular activity.

Figure 1.6 In a world where everything seems to be going digital, it is important to remember to balance your professional life with your personal life and have good boundaries between the two.

Thus, people are spending more time on their home computers and less time with each other.

✦ *Computer dating:* As people spend more and more time plugged into their computers, they find less time for social activities. Many people are now turning to chat rooms as a means to enter the realm of cyber dating.

✦ *Outdated technology:* What was once considered science fiction (cell phones on *Star Trek*) is now becoming a reality. It is suggested that with programs like MP3, music CDs will soon become obsolete. VCRs are giving way to DVDs, which in turn will give way to something else. The money spent on these "toys" often goes down the drain in a short time.

✦ *The ever-widening "digital divide":* The expression "The rich get richer and the poor get poorer" rings true for those who do not have a computer or who cannot keep upgrading their software. With computers becoming the cars of the twenty-first century, those without them will be at a disadvantage in terms of accessing the information superhighway.

College Stress

What makes the college experience a significant departure from the first eighteen years of life is the realization that with the freedom of lifestyle choices come the responsibilities that go with it. Unless you live at home while attending school, the college experience is one in which you transition from a period of dependence (on your parents) to independence. As you move from the known into the unknown, the list of stressors a college student experiences is rather startling. Here is a sample of some of the more common stressors that college students encounter.

✦ *Roommate dynamics:* Finding someone who is compatible is not always easy, especially if you had your own room in your parents' house. As we all know or will quickly learn, best friends do not make the best roommates, yet roommates can become good friends over

time. Through it all, roommate dynamics involve the skill of compromise and diplomacy under the best and worst conditions. And should you find yourself in an untenable situation, remember, campus housing does its best to accommodate students and resolve problems. However, their time schedule and yours may not always be the same.

✦ *Professional pursuits:* (What major should I choose?) Perhaps one of the most common soul-searching questions to be asked in the college years is, What do I want to do the rest of my life? It is a well-known fact that college students can change majors several times in their college careers and many do. The problem is compounded when there is parental pressure to move toward a specific career path (e.g., law or medicine), or the desire to please your parents by picking a major that they like but you don't.

✦ *Academic deadlines* (exams, papers, and projects): Academics means taking midterms and finals, writing research papers, and completing projects. This is, after all, the hallmark of measuring what you have learned. With a typical semester load of fifteen to twenty credits, many course deadlines can fall on the same day, and there is the ever-present danger that not meeting expectations can result in poor grades or academic probation.

✦ *Financial aid and school loans:* If you have ever stood in the financial aid office during the first week of school, you could write a book on the topic of stress. The cost of a college education is skyrocketing, and the pressure to pay off school loans after graduation can make you feel like an indentured servant. Assuming you qualify for financial aid, you should know that receiving the money in time to pay your bills is rare. Problems are compounded when your course schedule gets expunged from computer records because your financial aid check was two weeks late. These are just some of the problems associated with financial aid.

✦ *Budgeting your money:* It's one thing to ask your parents to buy you some new clothes or have them pick up the check at a restaurant. It's quite another when you start paying all your own bills. Learning to budget your money is a skill that takes practice. And learning not to overextend yourself is not only a skill, but also an art (most Americans owe an average of $5,000–8,000 on their credit cards). At some time or other, everyone bounces a check. The trick to avoid doing it is not to spend money you do not have.

+ *Lifestyle behaviors:* The freedom to stay up until 2 A.M. on a weekday, skip a class, eat nothing but junk food, or take an impromptu road trip carries with it the responsibilities of these actions. Independence from parental control means balancing freedom with responsibility. Stress enters your life with a vengeance when freedom and responsibility are not balanced.

+ *Peer groups and peer pressure (drugs and alcohol):* There is a great need to feel accepted by new acquaintances in college, and this need often leads to succumbing to peer pressure— and in new environments with new acquaintances, peer pressure can be very strong. Stress arises when the actions of the group are incongruent with your own philosophies. The desire to conform to the group is often stronger than your willpower to hold your own ground.

+ *Exploring sexuality:* While high school is the time when some people explore their sexuality, this behavior occurs with greater frequency during the college years, when you are away from the confines of parental control and more assertive with your self-expression. With the issue of sexual exploration come questions of values, contraception, homosexuality, bisexuality, AIDS, abortion, acceptance, and impotence, all of which can be very stressful. Although one does not come to college specifically to explore one's sexuality, many a student has left because sexual pursuits took priority over academic interests, resulting in poor grades.

+ *Friendships:* The friendships made in college take on a special quality. As you grow, mature,

and redefine your values, your friends, like you, will change, and so will the quality of each friendship. Cultivating a quality relationship takes time, meaning you cannot be good friends with everyone you like. In addition, tensions can quickly mount as the dynamics between you and those in your close circle of friends come under pressure from all the other college stressors.

+ *Intimate relationships:* Spending time with one special person with whom you can grow in love is special indeed. But the demands of an intimate relationship are strong, and in the presence of a college environment, intimate relationships are under a lot of pressure. If and when the relationship ends, the aftershock can be traumatic for one or both parties, leaving little desire for one's academic pursuits.

+ *Starting a professional career path:* It's a myth that you can start a job making the same salary that your parents make, but many college students believe this to be true. With this myth comes the pressure to equal the lifestyle of one's parents the day after graduation (this may explain why so many college graduates return home after graduation). The perceived pressures of the real world can become so overwhelming that seniors procrastinate on drafting a resume or initiating the job search until the week of graduation.

For the nontraditional college student, the problem can be summarized in one word: *balance!* Trying to balance a job, family, and schoolwork becomes a juggling act extraordinare. In attempting to satisfy the needs of your supervisor, colleagues, friends, spouse, children, and parents (and perhaps even pets), what usually is squeezed out is time for yourself. In the end everything seems to suffer. Often schoolwork is given a lower priority when addressing survival needs, and typically this leads to feelings of frustration over the inadequacy of time and effort available for assignments or exams. Of course, there are other stressors that cross the boundaries between work, home, and school, all of which tend to throw things off balance as well.

Occupational Stress

Stress doesn't end with college exams and research papers. It seems to continue and perhaps increase as one continues on a career path. Paul Rosch, M.D., director of the American Institute of Stress, notes that in American society today, job stress is at an all-time high. He defines job stress as "Occupational duties in which the individual perceives having a great deal of responsibility, yet little or no authority or decision making latitude."

In the first decade of the twenty-first century, more companies will merge, meaning more corporate restructuring. Companies looking to appease stockholders will look for ways to trim budgets, especially by letting go of senior employees and replacing them with a young eager workforce. Experts predict a high burnout rate factor coupled with poor work quality as workplace loyalty continues to diminish. Whether it is corporate mergers or keeping pace with technology, the Mitchum Report on Stress in the '90s confirms what several recent polls indicate. Nine out of ten people said they experience high levels of stress several times per week, and one out of four people indicated that they have high stress levels every day. While the Mitchum Report on Stress noted that common stressors in American society include urban crime, AIDS, and environmental problems such as the greenhouse effect, work-related problems—by far—constitute the critical mass of stress in our lives.

The cost of stress is not insignificant in terms of work productivity or the bottom line of corporate profits. Rosch noted that the fiscal consequences of occupational stress cost an average of $200 billion each year. Moreover, between 60 and 80 percent of all industrial accidents are stress induced, as are over 80 percent of all office visits to primary care physicians. Perhaps most striking is that workers' compensation claims associated with stress are skyrocketing, with 90 percent of claims being awarded in settlements.

What are some reasons for job stress? Although perceptions will vary from person to person, the following is a list compiled by the National Safety Council:

+ Too much responsibility with little or no authority
+ Unrealistic expectations, deadlines, and quotas
+ Corporate downsizing, restructuring, or job relocation
+ Inadequate training
+ Lack of appreciation
+ Inadequate time to complete job responsibilities
+ Inability to voice concerns
+ Lack of creativity and autonomy
+ Too much to do with too few resources
+ Lack of clear job descriptions
+ Commuting and traffic difficulties
+ Keeping pace with technology
+ Inadequate child care
+ Poor working conditions (lighting, noise, ventilation)
+ Sexual harassment and racial discrimination
+ Workplace violence

Rosch noted that in a recent study, the Public Health Service placed stress-management courses as its top priority in order to improve health standards at the worksite. However, Rosch, who surveyed several hundred existing stress-management programs in cooperation with the Office of Occupational Safety and Health, came to the conclusion that few stress-management programs currently taught in the corporate or industrial setting offer enough substance to make a positive influential change in lifestyle behaviors, because they are too narrow in focus or too brief in duration. Those programs he did find to be effective showed reduced illness and absenteeism, higher morale, and increased productivity.

Stress and the Retired Population

A gold watch at age sixty-five was once a coveted prize as one transitioned from the career path to the vacation path of retirement, but not anymore. Loss of corporate pensions and benefits, decreased Social Security funds, rising health care costs, and jeopardized Medicare benefits leave one quite vulnerable. Several studies reveal that the biggest concerns seniors have today are making ends meet financially and maintaining a quality of life comparable to what they had prior to retirement. Seniors do not take their retirement lightly. Any lawmaker will tell you that one of the biggest and most

Figure 1.7 Job disatisfaction often comes from feeling underappreciated. (Drawing by Modell: © 1985 The New Yorker Magazine, Inc.)

"I'd thank you Harrison, but, as you well know, yours is a thankless job."

powerful lobbying groups on Capitol Hill today is the American Association of Retired Persons (AARP), a strong voice for people who intend to make sure their voice is heard well after they retire from the workforce.

So serious is the threat to financial security that many people who reach retirement between the ages of sixty and sixty-five feel that they cannot retire. Although they may leave the company where they worked for years, quite often they search for another job to assure some degree of financial security. Those who do retire in financial comfort are not devoid of stress either. Studies of seniors reveal that those who place all their self-worth in their jobs, without any outside interests, leave their job structures and quickly fall prey to disease and illness. Added to the stress of financial insecurity are the ever-changing dynamics of increased health problems, the death of close friends, the death of a spouse, changes in living environments, and the realization of one's own mortality.

A Holistic Approach to Stress Management

When the stress response was first recognized, much attention was given to the physical aspects of the dynamics involved with fight-or-flight, specifically the symptoms of stress. As this field of study expanded to explore the relationship between stress and disease, it began to overlap, and to some extent even merge, with the fields of psychology, sociology, theology, physics, and clinical medicine. What was once thought to be a physical response, and then referred to as a mind-body phenomenon, is now suggested to be a complex, multifaceted, or holistic phenomenon involving the mental, physical, emotional, and spiritual components of well-being. Looking at stress from these four different perspectives may explain why there are so many definitions of it. Ironically, this new insight has produced some tension within the community of health care professionals.

Medical science is slowly experiencing a **paradigm shift.** A paradigm is a conceptual model used to understand a common reality. A shift is a change in the perception of that reality. For the past three hundred sixty years or so, Western culture has adopted a mechanistic model of reality, due in large part to the philosophy of René Descartes that the mind and body are separate, and to the laws of physics created by Isaac Newton, which are believed to have been inspired by Descartes. The mechanistic paradigm compares the universe and all its components to a large mechanical clock, where everything operates in a sequential and predictable form. When it was first developed, the mechanistic model, also called the reductionist model, seemed to logically explain nearly every phenomenon.

The field of medicine, strongly influenced by Newtonian physics, applied the mechanistic model to the human organism, comparing the body to a clock as well. This applied paradigm, during what Dr. Larry Dossey calles Era I medicine, focused on symptoms of dysfunction, and like a watch repairman, physicians were trained to fix or repair any parts that were broken. Drugs and surgery became the two primary tools forged in the discipline of clinical medicine. Prime examples of the fix-or-replace method include the prescription of penicillin and organ transplants, respectively. To no one's surprise, the application of this mechanistic model in medicine virtually stripped the responsibility of healing from the patient and placed it completely into the hands of the attending physician(s). There is no denying that many advances in clinical medicine have been nothing less than astonishing. Take, for example, heart and liver transplants and total hip replacements. Yet along with these magnificent achievements are significant limitations and hazardous side effects. Medicine is aptly

Figure 1.8

Sir Isaac Newton (along with René Descartes) is credited with what is now referred to as the mechanistic approach to scientific thinking, which is based on the idea that the universe operates like a large mechanical clock. Albert Einstein supported a different theory, called unified field theory, suggesting that the universe is a living web and validating the ancient whole systems theory in which everything is connected together and the whole is greater than the sum of the parts.

referred to as an art as well as a science, but in the mechanistic model of reality, anything that cannot be measured or quantified has been virtually ignored. Moreover, anything that cannot be scientifically explained by cause and effect is dismissed as superstition and regarded as invalid. What this medical paradigm failed to include was the dimension of the human spirit, an unmeasurable source of energy with a potential healing power all its own. The human spirit is now considered so important by the World Health Organization (WHO) that it issued a statement saying, "The existing definition of health should include the spiritual aspect, and that health care should be in the hands of those who are fully aware of and sympathetic to the spiritual dimension."

However, the Newtonian paradigm was viewed as the ultimate truth until the turn of the twentieth century, when a young physicist named Albert Einstein introduced his theory of relativity in 1905 (Fig. 1.8).

In simple terms, Einstein said that all matter is energy, and furthermore, all matter is connected at the subatomic level. No single entity can be affected without all connecting parts similarly being affected. From Einstein's view, the universe isn't a giant clock but a living web. New ideas are often laughed at, and old ideas die hard. But as new truths unfold, they gather curious followers who test and elaborate on the original idea. Initially mocked, the complexities of Einstein's theory have gained appreciation among physicists today, leading to the frontiers of the new field of quantum physics and a whole new understanding of our universe in what is now called the *whole systems theory*.

Although current medical technology is incredibly sophisticated, physicians for the most part still view the human body as a clock with fixable or replaceable parts. In other words, the basic approach to modern medicine in the Western world has not

Figure 1.9 Two different approaches to the wellness paradigm. In Model A, expounded by Elisabeth Kübler-Ross, all components are present in the human organism, but each holds specific dominance at different phases of the individual's growth cycle. The emotional aspect is the first to develop; the spiritual aspect is the last. In Model B each component is superimposed on the others in a holographic form, yet it is the spiritual component in which they are all contained.

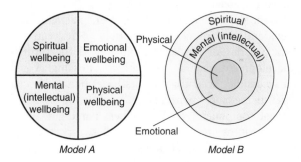

paradigm strongly paralleling Einstein's theory and called the **wellness paradigm.** This model suggests that total wellness is the balance, integration, and harmony of the physical, intellectual, emotional, and spiritual aspects of the human condition. These four components of total well-being are so closely connected and interwoven that it is virtually impossible to divide them. Although for the purposes of academic study these areas are best understood separately, in reality they all act as one interconnected living system, just as Einstein hypothesized about the universe.

The word *health* is derived from the Anglo word *hal,* meaning "to heal, to be made whole, or to be holy"; and throughout the ages wholeness has been symbolized by a circle. The wellness philosophy states that the whole is greater than the sum of the parts and all parts must be looked at as one system (Fig. 1.9). When applied to clinical medicine, this philosophy indicates that all aspects of the individual must be treated *equally* and each considered part of the whole. Regrettably, conventional medical practice still treats the physical component—the symptoms of stress— with drugs and surgery, often disregarding how the physical body connects with the mental, emotional, and spiritual aspects of well-being. Some physicians still refuse to acknowledge the link between stress and disease because they were trained in and are loyal to the mechanistic model. Nontraditional approaches (of which stress management is a part), specifically biofeedback, meditation, massage therapy, and mental imagery, are currently referred to as alternative medicine by the American Medical Association. Because the word *alternative* has a negative connotation to many practitioners in the field of holistic wellness, the words *complementary and integrative medicine* are now used to refer to additional healing modalities. Every technique for stress management falls within the domain of complementary medicine

Please note that healing and curing are two different concepts. Typically, the word *curing* means that the symptoms of a disease or illness are eradicated. While in some cases healing techniques may cure a person of disease or illness, the concept of healing really means bringing a sense of inner peace to someone's life, even in the face of death. From this vantage point you can see that a person can be healed and yet still be ill. In the age of high technology and instant gratification, expectations are often placed on

changed in over three hundred and sixty years. Furthermore, the mind and body, so completely separate in the theory of Descartes, are still treated separately, not as one living system. The idea of a mind-body connection (which in rare cases appears powerful enough to make cancers go into spontaneous remission) is still as foreign a concept to most physicians today as the idea of a Sony Discman would have been to the founders of the United States over 200 years ago. But new discoveries in the field of medicine have not fit so nicely into the concept of mechanical clock or reductionist theory. Instead, they mirror Einstein's concept of an intricate network of connecting systems. As a result, standard concepts regarding health and disease are slowly beginning to give way to a more inclusive reality or paradigm. As an example, very recently medical researchers have learned that emotions can suppress the immune system, an idea thought to be inconceivable and ludicrous only a decade ago. The body-as-clock mentality no longer seems to answer all the questions posed about the human organism; and thus some issues, like the placebo effect, are being completely reexamined.

But old paradigms are not abandoned until new conceptual models are created and established. Ironically, some new paradigms are actually old concepts that have been dusted off and resurrected. Such is the case with a very old but newly rediscovered health the curing aspects—eradicating the symptomatic problems—rather than the essence of true healing. This in itself has caused tension in the allied health fields because many health care professionals trained in the mechanistic paradigm use both terms interchangeably. But the tension doesn't stop there. In 1993 a study by David Eisenberg published in the *New England Journal of Medicine* announced that over one-third of the American population seeks methods of healing outside those accepted by traditional medicine because they are unsatisfied with the Western approach to health care. What makes this matter even more astounding is that most healing methods are not covered by medical insurance, meaning that people are paying for these services out of their own pockets. In the 1993 televised series entitled *Healing and the Mind,* creator and host Bill Moyers distilled the trend in this way: "There is a deep yearning for a human (whole) approach to medicine." Stress management techniques, which attempt to deal with the causes as well as the symptoms of stress, support and contribute to this holistic approach.

In a follow-up to his landmark study investigating the use of alternative medicine in the American culture, Eisenberg found that more than 42 percent of the American population used at least one form of complementary medicine in 1997, with an estimated $21.2 billion in out-of-pocket expenses paid to alternative health care practitioners. Eisenberg states that the magnitude of the demand for alternative therapy is noteworthy, in light of the poor reimbursement factor by insurance companies.

Let us take a closer look at the components of the wellness paradigm and the effects that stress has on them. **Mental** (intellectual) **well-being** is regarded as the ability to gather, process, recall, and exchange (communicate) information. Exposure to stress tends to overload the cognitive "circuits," decreasing the processing and recall abilities needed to make sound decisions. **Physical well-being** is described as the optimal functioning of the body's major physiological systems (e.g., cardiovascular, digestive, reproductive, etc.). From the observations documented in Selye's research, as explained in his book *The Stress of Life,* the inability to return to homeostasis can prove fatal to various organ tissues and eventually to the host organism. **Emotional**

well-being is defined as the ability to feel and express the full range of human emotions and to control them rather than be controlled by them. Anger and fear act as "umbrella" emotions that can collectively overload emotional circuits, resulting in mental paralysis and often leading to states of depression. **Spiritual well-being** is described as the maturation of higher consciousness through strong nurturing relationships with both the Self and others; the development of a strong personal value system; and a meaningful purpose in life. Stress can create a series of obstacles on the road to spiritual development, making the path to one's higher self inaccessible. Recently, scholars have included social well-being and environmental well-being as additional components of the wellness paradigm. Actually, what they have done is tease these aspects out of the mental, emotional, physical, or spiritual factors involved. If you take a closer look at the original four components, you will see that social well-being is a large factor of spiritual well-being. (This will be explained more clearly in Chapter 7.) And environmental well-being demonstrates how interwoven these four components really are, integrating aspects of physical and spiritual well-being. Although the major focus of this book is self-reliance—working from within to achieve inner peace—remember that our ability to harmonize with people within our collective environments is paramount to total well-being. Thus, from a holistic perspective, to effectively deal with stress, all areas of the wellness paradigm must be addressed and nurtured equally; the whole is greater than the sum of the parts.

Not long ago (and in some cases today), many stress management programs were based on the mechanistic model and focused solely on physical well-being. Upon initial recognition of the association between stress and disease, courses designed to intervene in this process emphasized techniques to decrease the physical symptoms of stress. These classes consisted primarily of teaching one or two relaxation techniques to help decrease the most obvious stress symptom: muscle tension. These techniques, addressing only the symptoms (the physical component), did nothing to relieve the causes of stress (the mental, emotional, or spiritual components). As a result, people often experienced a rebound effect;

their symptoms recurred. On a different front, coping skills (e.g., cognitive restructuring, time management, and journal writing) were taught by psychologists in private therapy sessions, and these coping strategies soon made their way into public awareness as well.

Through the efforts of advocates of the wellness paradigm, attempts have been made to unite the practice of both relaxation skills and coping skills for a holistic approach to stress management. This implies viewing each person as more than just a physical body and dealing with the causes of stress as well as the physical symptoms. The primary focuses in the application of the wellness model are on the prevention of disease and illness and the enhancement of health. Furthermore, the underlying current of this philosophy is to place the responsibility of healing back in the hands of the individual. Successful stress management therapy programs have now begun to adopt the wellness philosophy and holistic approach, supporting the concept that the whole is indeed greater than the sum of the parts. A sound stress management program does not attempt to merely reduce (fix or repair) stress but rather to manage it efficiently. This management process attempts to focus on all aspects of one's well-being. This philosophy is implemented by attempting to both resolve the causes *and* reduce or eliminate the symptoms of stress. It is imperative to remember that, as an intervention modality, the wellness paradigm does not preclude the use of medications or surgery. Rather, it strongly suggests that there be a collaborative integration of several therapeutic techniques to produce the most effective healing process (e.g., chemotherapy and visualization). Equally important as preventive measures, coping skills and relaxation techniques are also advocated to *maintain* inner peace.

Stated simply, effective stress management includes the following:

1. Sound knowledge of the body's reaction to perceived stress
2. Sound knowledge of mental, physical, emotional, and spiritual factors associated with stress
3. Utilization of several coping techniques to work toward a resolution of the causes of stress
4. Regular practice of relaxation techniques to maintain homeostatic balance of the body
5. Periodic evaluation of the effectiveness of coping skills and relaxation techniques

This book integrates all four components of the wellness paradigm. First, because it is so visible, we will look at stress from the physical point of view, including both the dynamics involved in fight-or-flight and the most current theories attempting to explain the relationship between stress and disease. We then focus on mental and emotional factors, outlining pertinent theoretical concepts of psychology: the stress emotions, anger and fear, as well as specific personality types that are thought to be either prone or resistant to stressful perceptions. (More cognitive aspects will be covered in Part III.) The much-neglected component of spiritual well-being will round out the first half of the book, showcasing selected theories of this important human dimension and its significant relationship to stress. The remainder of the book will focus on a host of coping strategies and relaxation techniques, and come full circle to the physical realm of wellness again, with positive adaptations to stress promoted through the use of physical exercise. As you will surely find, true to the wellness paradigm, where all components are balanced and tightly integrated, there will be much overlap between the physical, mental, emotional, and spiritual factors in these chapters, as these factors are virtually inseparable. And just as the word *stress* was adopted from the discipline of physics, you will see that some other concepts and theories from this field are equally important to your ability to relax. To understand the stress phenomenon accurately, it is important to see the human condition as one collective living system. Once this is understood, it becomes easier to manage stress effectively. It is my hope that the strategies in this book will enable you to access and enhance your inner resources, which in turn will enable you to design your own holistic stress management program. As Selye stated in his popular book, *Stress without Distress,* "I cannot and should not be cured of my stress, but merely taught to enjoy it." The enjoyment comes from the ability to manage stress effectively.

Summary

- The advancement of technology, which promised more leisure time, has actually increased the pace of life so that many people feel stressed to keep up with this pace.
- Lifestyles based on new technological conveniences are now thought to be associated with several diseases, including coronary heart disease.
- Stress is a term from the field of physics, meaning physical force or tension placed on an object. It was adopted after World War II to signify psychological tension.
- There are many definitions of stress from both Eastern and Western philosophies as well as several academic disciplines, including psychology and physiology. The mind-body separation is now giving way to a holistic philosophy involving the mental, physical, emotional, and spiritual components of well-being.
- Cannon coined the term fight-or-flight response to describe the immediate effects of physical stress. This response is now considered by many to be inappropriate for nonphysical stressors.
- There are three types of stress: eustress (good), neustress (neutral), and distress (bad). There are two types of distress: acute (short-term) and chronic (long-term), the latter of which is thought to be the more detrimental because the body does not return to a state of complete homeostasis.
- Stressors have been categorized into three groups: (1) bioecological influences, (2) psychointrapersonal influences, and (3) social influences.
- Holmes and Rahe created the Social Readjustment Rating Scale to identify major life stressors. They found that the incidence of stressors correlated with health status.
- Selye coined the term *general adaptation syndrome* to explain the body's ability to adapt negatively to chronic stress.
- Stress can appear at any time in our lives, but the college years offer their own types of stressors because it is at this time that one assumes more (if not complete) responsibility for one's lifestyle behaviors. Stress continues through retirement with a whole new set of stressors in the senior years.
- The rapid pace of technology may appear to make life simpler, but experts agree that the fallout, called technostress, will take its toll by increasing demands on both time and money, and decreasing personal time.
- Previous approaches to stress management have been based on the mechanistic model, which divided the mind and body into two separate entities. The paradigm on which this model was based is now shifting toward a holistic paradigm, where the whole is greater than the sum of the parts, and the whole person must be treated by working on the causes as well as the symptoms of stress.
- Effective stress management programming must address issues related to mental (intellectual), physical, emotional, and spiritual well-being.

Concepts and Terms

Acute stress	Holistic model	Social Readjustment Rating
Alarm reaction	Homeostasis	Scale
Alternative (complementary)	Lazarus, Richard	Spiritual well-being
medicine	Life-change units	Stage of exhaustion
Biological influences	Mechanistic model	Stage of resistance
Cannon, Walter	Mental well-being	Stress
Chronic stress	Newton, Isaac	Stress reaction
Einstein, Albert	Paradigm shift	Stress response
Emotional well-being	Physical well-being	Stressor
Eustress	Psychointrapersonal influences	Technostress
Fight-or-flight response	Seasonal affective disorder (SAD)	Wellness paradigm
General adaptation syndrome	Social influences	Yerkes-Dodson Principle

Self-Assessment

There are hundreds of surveys and questionnaires designed to assess one's level of stress. Most if not all of these are based on a mechanistic approach to health, not a holistic one (where the whole is considered greater than the sum of parts). The purpose of this self-assessment survey is to begin to have you look at your problems, issues, and concerns holistically.

1. **First, make a list of your current stressors and explain each one:**

    1. LOSS OF JOB - LITTLE MONEY GOMIN IN - BILLS
    2. SCHOOL - OUT OF THE HOUSE 4 NIGHTS PER WEEK - TIME
    3. RELATIONSHIP WITH OLDER DAUGHTER
    4. MOTHER - SICKLY - NEED TO COORDINATE TIME TO MASSAGE HER
    5. CHANGE IN LIVING - MOVING
    6. DISAPPOINTMENT - HOUSE GOING TO BUY IS FORECLOSING
    7. RELATIONSHIP - COMMUNICATION SKILLS
    8. CHILDREN - FEAR OF PROPER RAISING TECHNIQUES - STICK WITH THEM FOR LIFE - OR THEY BECOME LOSERS
    9. WEIGHT GAIN - INSPIRATION TO EXERCISE
    10. PHYSICAL DYSFUNCTION - NECK + RIGHT HIP

2. **Next, from the list you have just made, reorganize it into acute (short-term) stressors and chronic (prolonged) stressors.**

    Acute (lasting hours)
    1.
    2.
    3.
    4.
    5.

    Chronic (lasting days, weeks, or months)
    1.
    2.
    3.
    4.
    5.

3. **Now, from the first list you made, determine whether each stressor is mental, physical, emotional, or spiritual.**

Mental Overwhelmed/bored	**Physical** Injuries/sickness	**Emotional** Anger or fear based	**Spiritual** Relationships/Values/Purpose in life
1. SCHOOL	1. NECK + RIGHT HIP	1. JOB	1. COMMUNICATION SKILLS
2. DAUGHTER RELATIONSHIP	2.	2. CHILDREN - RAISING	2.
3. MOVING	3.	3. MOTHER	3.
4.	4.	4. WEIGHT GAIN	4.
5.	5.	5.	5.

References and Resources

Allen, R. *Human Stress: Its Nature and Control.* Burgess Press, Minneapolis, MN, 1983.

Cannon, W. *The Wisdom of the Body.* W. W. Norton, New York, 1932.

Carpi, J. Stress . . . It's Worse Than You Think, *Psychology Today* 29(1):34–41, 74–76, 1996.

Davis, J. B. The Ill Effects of the Toxic Office. Health and Fitness News Service, *Los Angeles Times News Syndicate,* February, 16, 1997.

Dossey, L. *Space, Time, and Medicine.* Bantam New Age Books, New York, 1982.

Eisenberg, D. et al. Unconventional Medicine in the United States, *New England Journal of Medicine* 328:246–252, 1993.

Eisenberg, D. et al. Trends in Alternative Medicine Use in the United States, 1990–1997: Results of a Follow-up National Survey, *JAMA,* 280: 1569–1575, 1998.

Gerber, R. *Vibrational Medicine.* Bear and Company, Santa Fe, NM, 1988.

Gibbons, V. Working, High Anxiety: Taking Charge of Your Career, *Smart Money,* August: 135–136, 2000.

Giradano, D., Everly, G., and Dusek, D. *Controlling Stress and Tension, A Holistic Approach.* Prentice Hall, Englewood Cliffs, NJ, 1993.

Girardet, E. One in Four Employees Angry at Work, *Indianapolis Star,* August 10, 1999.

Goleman, D. *Emotional Intelligence.* Bantam Books, New York, 1995.

Greenberg, J. *Comprehensive Stress Management,* 3rd ed. W. C. Brown, Dubuque, IA, 1990.

Holmes, T. H. and Rahe, R. The Social Readjustment Rating Scale, *Journal of Psychosomatic Research* 11:213–218, 1967.

Kanner, A. et al. Comparison of Two Modes of Stress Management: Daily Hassles and Uplifts versus Major Life Events, *Journal of Behavioral Medicine* 4(1):1–37, 1981.

Kaplan, A., ed. *Health Promotion and Chronic Illness,* World Health Organization, Geneva, 1992.

Kealey, T. Stress and Lack of Leisure Time, *New Scientist,* July 10, 1999.

King, S. K. Removing Distress to Reveal Health, in *Healers on Healing,* eds. Carlson, R. and Shield, B. Jeremy Tarcher Inc., Los Angeles, 1989.

Krohe, J. Workplace Stress, *Across the Board,* February 36–42, 1999.

Kübler-Ross, E. Keynote Address, American Holistic Health Association Annual Conference, Lacrosse, WI, 1981.

Kuhn, T. *The Structure of Scientific Revolutions.* University of Chicago Press, Chicago, 1970.

Lardner, J. et al. Overwhelmed by Technology, *U.S. News & World Report,* Law 15: 31–36, 2001.

Lazarus, R. and DeLongis, A. Psychological Stress, and Coping in Aging, *American Psychologist* 38:245–254, 1983.

Lazarus, R. Puzzles in the Study of Daily Hassles, *Journal of Behavioral Medicine* 7:375–389, 1984.

Lichetenstein, N. Workers Over Time, National Public Radio interview, September 3, 2000.

Manning, G., Curtis K., and McMillian, S. *Stress: Living and Working in a Changing World.* Whole Persons Associates, Duluth, MN, 1999.

Markes, J. Time Out, *U.S. News and World Report* 119 (23):84–96, 1995.

Meyer, A. *The Common Sense Psychiatry of Dr. Adolf Meyer: Fifty-Two Selected Papers.* Ayer, Salem, NH, 1948.

Mitchum Report on Stress in the '90s. Research and Forecast Inc., New York, 1990.

Moyers, B. *Healing and the Mind.* Doubleday, New York, 1993.

Moyers, B. *Healing and the Mind.* Public Broadcasting System, 1993.

Ornstein, R. and Sobel, D. *Healthy Pleasures.* Addison Wesley, Reading, MA, 1989.

Pelletier, K. *Mind as Healer, Mind as Slayer.* Dell, New York, 1977.

Putnam, R. Bowling Alone: America's Declining Social Capital, *Journal of Democracy* 6(1):65–78, 1995.

Rahe, R. et al. Simplified Scaling for Life Events, *Journal of Human Stress* 6:22–27, 1980.

Rosch, P. Is Job Stress America's Leading Adult Health Problem? A Commentary, *Business Insights,* 7(1):4–7, 1991.

Sapolsky, R. *Why Zebras Don't Get Ulcers.* W. H. Freeman & Company, New York, 1998.

Schor, J. *The Overworked American: The Unexpected Decline of Leisure.* Basic Books, New York, 1992.

Seaward, B. L. National Safety Council's Stress Management. Jones & Bartlett, Boston, MA, 1994.

Selye, H. *The Stress of Life.* McGraw-Hill, New York, 1976.

Selye, H. *Stress without Distress.* Lippincott, New York, 1974.

Simeons, A. T. W. *Man's Presumptuous Brain: An Evolutionary Interpretation of Psychosomatic Diseases.* E.P. Dutton, New York, 1961.

Taylor, S. *Health Psychology,* 2nd ed. McGraw-Hill, New York, 1998.

Washington Post. *Americans Are Working More Hours: Loss of Leisure Time Defies Predictions,* February 17, 1992.

Weil M. and Rosen, L. *Technostress: Coping With Technology @work, @ home, @ play.* John Wiley and Sons, New York, 1998.

Wong, M. Vacationing Americans have Given New Meaning to the Advertising Slogan, Don't leave home without it. Associates Press. Sept. 1, 2000.

World Health Organization (WHO) 525 23 St. N.W., Washington, D.C. 20037. (202) 861–3200.

Zarski, J. J. Hassles and Health: A Replication, *Health Psychology* 3:243–251, 1984.

Chapter 2 The Physiology of Stress

To understand the stress response, we must possess a fundamental knowledge not only of psychology but of physiology as well.

—George Everly

Hans Selye's discovery of a direct relationship between chronic stress and the excessive wear and tear throughout the body laid the foundation for a clearer understanding of how physiological systems work in an extremely complex and integrative way. Perhaps because of this discovery and the fact that physical deterioration is so noticeable, much attention has been directed toward the physiology of stress. This chapter will take you through some basic concepts that explain the physiological dynamics involved with the stress response, specifically, the immediate, intermediate, and prolonged effects on the body. These processes will be explained in terms of "pathways," which set in action the systematic and integrative steps of the stress response. Because physiology involves specific nomenclature outside the realm of your everyday vocabulary, you may find the nature of this chapter to be very specific and its contents very detailed. Most likely it will merit more than one reading to fully grasp, understand, and appreciate how the body responds to stress. The importance of a strong familiarity with human physiology as influenced by stressful stimuli becomes evident when the necessary steps are taken to effectively deal with the symptoms they produce, especially when using relaxation techniques. For example, it is important to know how the body functions when using specific imagery, visualization, music therapy, and biofeedback.

In many circles, this topic of study is referred to as psychophysiology. This term reflects the fact that a sensory stimulus that prompts the stress response must be processed at the mental level before it can cascade down one or more physiological pathways. In other words, the term *psychophysiology* suggests that there is a mind-body relationship and supports the theory that many diseases and illnesses are psychosomatic, meaning that their origins lie in the higher brain centers. Although the mind-body dualism suggested by Descartes is no longer a viable model for a complete understanding of human physiology, to hold an appreciation of the "whole person" we must first examine the parts in order to understand how they connect to that whole.

Three systems are directly involved with the physiology of stress: the nervous system, the endocrine system, and the immune system, all of which can be triggered by perceived threats. Because the immune system is so closely linked to the disease process, it will be dealt with separately in Chapter 3.

The Central Nervous System

The nervous system can be divided into two parts: the central nervous system (CNS), which consists of the brain and spinal cord; and the peripheral nervous system (PNS), comprising all neural pathways to the extremities. The human brain is further divided into three levels: the vegetative level, the limbic system, and the neocortical level (Fig. 2.1).

Figure 2.1 Three levels of the human brain: vegetative level, limbic system, and the neocortical level.

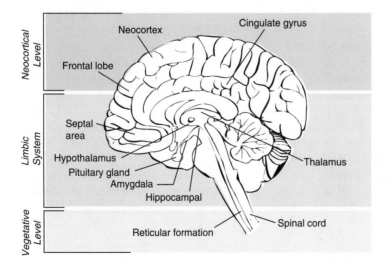

The Vegetative Level

The lowest level of the brain is comprised of both the reticular formation and the brain stem. The reticular formation, or more specifically the fibers that make up the reticular activating system (RAS), is the link connecting the brain to the spinal cord. Several stress physiologists believe that this is the bridge joining the mind and the body as one; this organ functions as a communications link between the mind and the body. The brain stem, comprised of the pons, medulla oblongata, and mesencephalon, is responsible for involuntary functions of the human body, such as heartbeat, respiration, and vasomotor activity. It is considered the automatic-pilot control center of the brain, which assumes responsibility for keeping the vital organs and vegetative processes functioning at all times. This level is thought to be the most primitive section of the human brain, as this portion is similar to those of all other mammals.

The Limbic System

The second or mid-level portion of the brain is called the limbic system. The limbic system is the emotional control center. Several tissue centers in this level are directly responsible for the biochemical chain of events that comprise the stress response Cannon observed. The limbic system is comprised of the thalamus, the hypothalamus, and the pituitary gland, also known as the master endocrine gland. These three glands work in unison to maintain a level of homeostasis within the body. For example, it is the hypothalamus that controls appetite and body-core temperature. The hypothalamus also appears to be the center that registers pain and pleasure; for this reason it is often referred to as the seat of emotions. The combination of these functions in the hypothalamus may explain why hunger decreases when body-core temperature increases in extreme ambient heat, or why appetite diminishes when you are extremely worried. When a threat is encountered, the hypothalamus carries out four specific functions: (1) it activates the autonomic nervous system; (2) it stimulates the secretion of adrenocorticotrophic hormone (ACTH); (3) it produces antidiuretic hormone (ADH) or vasopressin; and (4) it stimulates the thyroid gland to produce thyroxine. All of these will be discussed in greater detail later.

The Neocortical Level

The neocortex is the highest and most sophisticated level of the brain. It is at this level that sensory information is processed (decoded) as a threat or a non-threat and where cognition (thought processes) takes place. Housed within the neocortex are the neural mechanisms allowing one to employ analysis, imagination, creativity, intuition, logic, memory, and organization. It is this highly developed area of brain tissue that is thought to separate humans from all other species.

As Figure 2.1 illustrates, the positions of these structures are such that a higher level can override a lower level of the brain. Thus, conscious thought can influence emotional response, just as conscious thought can intercede in the involuntary control of the vegetative functions to control heart rate, ventilation, and even the flow of blood. This fact will become important to recognize when learning coping skills and relaxation techniques designed to override the stress response and facilitate physiological homeostasis.

Separate from the CNS is a network of neural fibers that feed into the CNS and work in close collaboration with it. This neural tract, the peripheral nervous system (PNS), is comprised of two individual networks. The first is the somatic network, a bidirectional circuit responsible for transmitting sensory messages along the neural pathways between the five senses and the higher brain centers. These are called the efferent (toward periphery) and afferent (toward brain) neural pathways. The second branch of the PNS is called the **autonomic nervous system** (ANS). The ANS regulates visceral activities and vital organs, including circulation, digestion, respiration, and temperature regulation. It received the name *autonomic* because this system can function without conscious thought or voluntary control, and does so most, if not all, of the time.

Research conducted by endocrinologist Bruce McEwen indicates that initially a stressful encounter is etched into the memory bank (so as to avoid it down the road), but that repeated episodes of stress decrease memory by weakening hippocampal brain cells. Chronic stress is thought to wither the fragile connection between neurons in this part of the brain, resulting in "brain shrinkage."

Until recently it was believed that, unlike the voluntary somatic system involved in muscle movement, the ANS could not be intercepted by conscious

Stress With a Human Face

PERHAPS NO SITUATION MORE CLEARLY triggers the fight-or-flight response than face-to-face combat. This was the situation for Geof Steiner, who found himself thrown into the turmoil of the Vietnam War in the late 1960s. Think of how fast your heart beats when you sense someone following you in an unlit parking garage. Then multiply this intensity by the duration of a whole year—a typical tour of duty overseas in wartime. This is the level and duration of stress Geof experienced. Long after his return to the States, Geof found that his memories of the war were still at his coattails, haunting him and ruining his life. It got so bad that the only viable option, he surmised, was suicide. His attempt on his life quickly brought him to a VA psychiatric hospital. But his problems didn't end there: he also battled chronic alcoholism and the ruins of a failed marriage. When all was said and done, all he had to his name was a trailer on a dirt road.

At first glance, the woods of Minnesota don't seem to have anything to do with the jungles of Vietnam. But the call of the forest lured Geof out of his trailer into the woods, where he began to find a peace in nature that had eluded him with his fellow man. It was this bond that gave him a vision and a purpose to live. Inspired by nature's life force, Geof bought open tracts of land near and around his trailer. On this land he vowed to plant a tree for every soldier that died on the soil of Vietnam. Today, in Cushing, Minnesota, stands the Living Memorial Forest, the only living tribute to those who fought in a war that Geof is still trying to understand. He believes that the forest has helped him and other veterans heal the emotional scars and find the inner peace symbolized by the life of each planted tree.◆

Figure 2.2 The sympathetic and parasympathetic systems. Internal organs are typically innervated by neural fibers from both sympathetic and parasympathetic divisions.

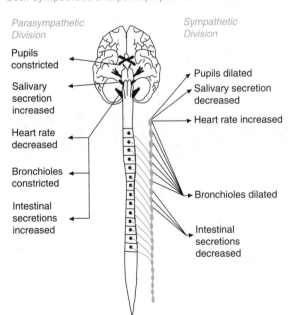

thought, but now it is recognized that both systems can be influenced by higher mental processes. (This will be discussed more in Chapters 25 and 26.) The ANS works in close coordination with the CNS to maintain a favorable homeostatic condition throughout the body. There are two branches of the ANS that act to maintain this homeostatic balance, the **sympathetic** and **parasympathetic** nervous systems, and these are activated by the hypothalamus. Most organs are innervated (stimulated) by nerve fibers of both the sympathetic and parasympathetic systems.

The Autonomic Nervous System

The Sympathetic and Parasympathetic Nervous Systems

The sympathetic nervous system is responsible for the responses associated with the fight-or-flight response (Fig. 2.2). Through the release of substances called catecholamines, specifically **epinephrine** (adrenaline) and **norepinephrine** (noradrenaline), at various neural synapses, a series of events occurs in several organ tissues to prepare the body for rapid metabolic change and physical movement. Sympathetic drive is associated with energy expenditure, a process known as catabolic functioning, where various metabolites are broken down for energy in preparation for movement. It is the release of epinephrine and norepinephrine that causes the acceleration of heart rate, the increase in the force of myocardial contraction, vasodilation of arteries throughout working muscles, vasoconstriction of arteries to nonworking muscles, dilation of pupils and bronchials, increased ventilation, reduction of digestive activity, released glucose from the liver, and several other functions that prepare the body to fight or flee. It is the sympathetic system that is responsible for supplying skeletal muscles with oxygenated, nutrient-rich blood for energy metabolism. Currently it is thought that norepinephrine serves primarily to assist epinephrine, as the ratio of these two chemical substances released at neural synapses is 5:1 epinephrine to norepinephrine during the stress response. The effects of epinephrine and norepinephrine are very short, lasting only seconds. Because of their rapid release from neural endings, as well as their rapid influence on targeted organ tissue, the effects of the sympathetic nervous system are categorized as immediate.

Just as the sympathetic neural drive is associated with energy expenditure, the parasympathetic drive is responsible for energy conservation and relaxation. This is referred to as anabolic functioning, during which body cells are allowed to regenerate. The parasympathetic nervous system is dominated by the tenth cranial, or vagus nerve, which in turn is influenced by the brain stem. When activated, the parasympathetic nervous system releases **acetylcholine** (ACh), a neurological agent that decreases metabolic activity and returns the body to homeostasis. The influence of parasympathetic drive is associated with a reduction in heart rate, ventilation, muscle tension, and several other functions. Both systems are partially active at all times; however, the sympathetic and parasympathetic systems are mutually exclusive in that they cannot dominate visceral activity simultaneously. These two systems allow for the precise regulation of visceral organ activity, much like the use of the accelerator and brake when driving. Sympathetic arousal, like a gas pedal pushed to the car floor, becomes the dominant force during stress, and parasympathetic tone holds influence over the body at all other times to promote homeostasis. In other words, you cannot be physically aroused and relaxed at the same time.

But there are exceptions to the dynamics of these biochemical reactions. For example, it is sympathetic nerves, not parasympathetic nerves, that release ACh in the sweat glands to decrease body-core temperature during arousal. And sympathetic and parasympathetic stimulation of salivary glands is not antagonistic; both influence the secretion of saliva. In addition, all blood vessels are influenced by sympathetic dominance, with the exception of the vasculature of the penis and clitoris, which is activated by parasympathetic innervation.

The Endocrine System

The endocrine system consists of a series of glands located throughout the body that regulate metabolic

---

Hormonal Imbalance

Box 2.1

The endocrine system is an amazing yet delicate system of chemical properties aligned to ensure physiological homeostasis. The stress hormone dehydroepiandrosterone (DHEA), for example, is secreted from the adrenal gland. DHEA is known as a sex hormone that decreases in both production and secretion throughout the aging process. Speculation suggests that supplementation of DHEA might increase stamina and memory, and may decrease the aging process in much the same way as antioxidants; beta-carotene, vitamin C, E, and selenium. Results of a host of studies revealed that no significant changes in these aspects occured in either animals or humans. Some scientists actually suggested that increased amounts of DHEA, above what the body normally produces, might actually promote cancer. Supplementation is recommended only on the advice of your physician.

Seratonin and melatonin are not stress hormones, yet they do seem to have an effect on mood. Decreases in both seratonin and melatonin are thought to be related to bouts of depression.

functions requiring endurance rather than speed. The endocrine system is a network of four components: glands, hormones, circulation, and target organs. Endocrine glands manufacture and release biochemical substances called hormones. Hormones are chemical messengers comprised of protein compounds that are programmed to attach to specific cell receptor sites to alter (increase or decrease) cell metabolism. Hormones are transported through the blood stream from the glands that produced them to the target organs they are called upon to influence. The heart, skeletal muscle, and arteries are among the organs targeted by hormones for metabolic change.

The glands that are most closely involved with the stress response are the pituitary, thyroid, and adrenal

Figure 2.3 The physiological response to stress.

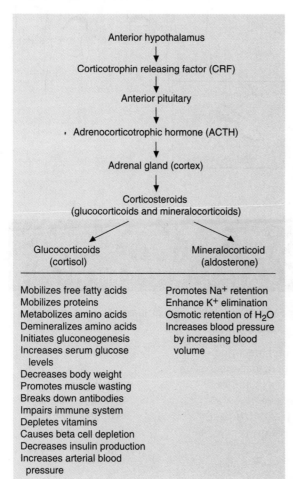

glands. The **pituitary gland** is called the master gland due to the fact that it manufactures several important hormones, which then trigger hormone release in other organs. The **hypothalamus** appears to have direct influence over it (Fig. 2.3). The thyroid gland increases the general metabolic rate. Perhaps the gland that has the most direct impact on the stress response, however, is the **adrenal gland** (Fig. 2.4). The adrenal gland, a cone-shaped mass of tissue about the size of a small grapefruit, sits on top of each kidney. The adrenal gland has two distinct parts, each of which produces hormones with very different functions. The exterior of the adrenal gland is called the adrenal cortex, and it manufactures and releases hormones called corticosteroids. There are two types of **corticosteroids:** glucocorticoids and mineralocorticoids. Glucocorticoids are a family of biochemical agents that includes cortisol and cortisone, with cortisol being the primary one. Its function is to help to generate glucose, through the degradation of proteins (amino acids) during a process called gluconeogenesis in the liver, as both an energy source for the central nervous system (the brain) and skeletal muscles during physical exercise. **Cortisol** is also involved in the process of lipolysis, or the mobilization and breakdown of fats (fatty acids) for energy. Recent clinical studies have linked increased levels of cortisol with suppression of the immune system. It appears that cortisol metabolizes (degrades) white blood cells. A metaphor to illustrate this process is the situation in which you resort to burning the furniture to keep warm once you exhaust your supply of firewood. As the number of white blood cells decreases, the efficiency of the immune system decreases, setting the stage for illness and disease. (This will be discussed in greater detail in Chapter 3.) It has also come to light that increased cortisol can direct excess amounts of cholesterol into the blood, thereby adding to associated artery plaque buildup and leading to hypertension and coronary heart disease. Mineralocorticoids, specifically aldosterone, are secreted to maintain plasma volume and electrolyte (sodium and potassium) balance, two essential functions in the regulation of circulation. (The exact mechanisms will be discussed later in this chapter.)

The inside of the adrenal gland is called the adrenal medulla. This portion of the gland secretes catecholamines (epinephrine and norepinephrine), which act in a similar fashion as those secreted at the endings of sympathetic nerves. The adrenal medulla releases 80 percent epinephrine and 20 percent norepinephrine. Under the influences of stress, up to 300 times the amount of epinephrine can be found in the blood compared to the amount in samples taken at rest.

The Neuroendocrine Pathways

Evolutionary adaptations have provided several backup systems to ensure the survival of the human organism. Not all pathways act at the same speed, yet the ultimate goal is the same: physical survival. First, not only does the hypothalamus initiate activation of the sympathetic nervous system to cause an immediate effect (Table 2.1), but the posterior hypothalamus has a direct neural pathway, called the sympathetic preganglionic neuron, that links it to the adrenal medulla. Next, upon stimulation by the posterior hypothalamus, the adrenal medulla secretes both epinephrine and norepinephrine. Once in the bloodstream, these catecholamines reinforce the efforts of the sympathetic drive, which has already released these same substances through sympathetic neural endings throughout the body. The release of epinephrine and norepinephrine from the adrenal medulla acts as a backup system for these biochemical agents to ensure the most efficient means of physical survival. The hormonal influences brought about by the adrenal medulla are called intermediate effects.

The adrenal gland, made up of the adrenal cortex and medulla, sits upon the top of each kidney, and is cone-shaped in appearance.

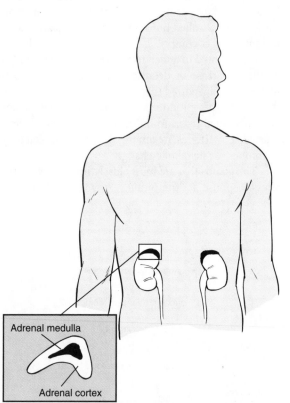

Figure 2.4

Adrenal medulla

Adrenal cortex

Pathways of Stress Response			
Effects	**Reaction**		**Time**

Table 2.1

The body has several backup dynamics to help ensure physical survival. Here, these dynamics are broken down into categories based on the duration of their metabolic reactions.

Immediate effects	Epinephrine and norepinephrine from the sympathetic nervous system	2–3 secs
Intermediate effects	Epinephrine and norepinephrine from adrenal medulla	20–30 secs
Prolonged effects	ACTH, vasopressin, and thyroxine neuroendocrine pathways	Minutes, hours, days, or weeks

From R. Allen, *Human Stress: Its Nature and Control* (Minneapolis, MN: Burgess, 1983).

Figure 2.5 The ACTH axis.

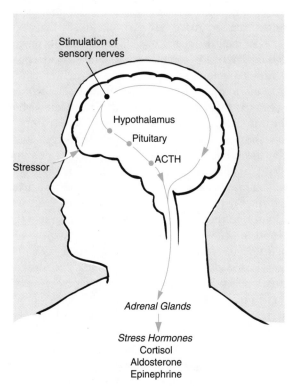

Stimulation of
sensory nerves

Hypothalamus

Pituitary

ACTH

Stressor

Adrenal Glands

Stress Hormones
Cortisol
Aldosterone
Epinephrine

The Stress Response
Increased neural excitability
Increased cardiovascular activity
 Heart rate, stroke volume,
 cardiac output, blood pressure
Increased metabolic activity
 Gluconeogenesis: turning
 glycogen into sugar for energy
 Protein mobilization
  Decreased antibody producer
  Muscle wasting
 Fat mobilization: for breakdown
 into sugar
Increased sodium retention (salt)
Increase in neurological sweating
Change in salivation
Change in GI system tonus and motility

Because their release is via the bloodstream rather than neural endings, travel time is longer (approximately twenty to thirty seconds), and unlike the release of these substances from sympathetic neural endings, the effects of catecholamines from the adrenal medulla can last as long as two hours when high levels of secretions are circulating in the bloodstream.

In addition, there is a third and potentially more potent system joining the efforts of the nervous and endocrine systems to prepare the body for real or perceived danger. Neural impulses received by the hypothalamus as potential threats create a chain of biochemical messages, which like a line of falling dominos cascade through the endocrine-system glands. Because the half-life of these hormones and the speed of their metabolic reactions vary in length from hours to weeks in some cases, this chain of reactions is referred to as the prolonged effect of stress.

The ACTH Axis

Physiologically speaking, a biochemical pathway is referred to as an axis. In this section we will discuss the ACTH axis. The other two axes, the vasopressin axis and the thyroxine axis, are covered in the following sections.

The **ACTH axis** (Fig. 2.5) begins with the release of corticotrophin releasing factor (CRF) from the anterior hypothalamus. This substance activates the pituitary gland to release ACTH, which travels via the bloodstream to in turn activate the adrenal cortex. Upon stimulation by ACTH, the adrenal cortex releases a set of corticosteroids (cortisol and aldosterone), which act to increase metabolism and alter body fluids, and thus blood pressure, respectively. The effects of hormones released by the adrenal cortex are considered to be prolonged because they activate their functions for minutes to hours. Note that increased secretions of cortisol in the blood act primarily to ensure adequate supplies of blood sugar for energy metabolism. However, when increasingly high levels of cortisol are observed due to chronic stress, this hormone compromises the integrity of several physiological systems.

The Vasopressin Axis

Vasopressin or antidiuretic hormone (ADH) is synthesized in the hypothalamus but is released by the pituitary through a special portal system. The primary purpose of vasopressin is to regulate fluid loss through the urinary tract. It does this in a number of ways, including water reabsorption and decreased perspiration. By altering blood volume, however, it also has a pronounced effect on stroke volume, or the amount of blood that is pumped through the left ventricle of the heart with each contraction. Consequently ADH has a pronounced effect on blood pressure. Under normal circumstances, ADH regulates blood pressure by either increasing blood volume (changing the concentration of water in the blood) should it be too low, or decreasing blood volume when it becomes too high. Under the influence of chronic stress, however, many regulatory mechanisms in the body lose their ability to maintain physiological homeostasis. Consequently, the increased secretions of vasopressin produced under duress will increase blood pressure even when someone already has elevated resting values; this is known as hypertension. The purpose of vasopressin as well as aldosterone, epinephrine, and norepinephrine is to increase blood pressure to ensure that active muscles receive oxygenated blood, but under chronic stress in a resting state this hormonal response—the abundance of stress hormones—is literally overkill, leading to hypertension and death due to CHD.

The Thyroxine Axis

Stimulation in the hypothalamus triggers the release of thyrothrophic hormone releasing factor (TRF). TRF is transported through a special portal system to the anterior portion of the pituitary where it stimulates the secretion of thyrotrophic hormone (TTH). Once in the bloodstream, TTH follows a path to the thyroid gland, which stimulates the release of two more hormones: thyroxine and triiodothyronine. The purpose of these two hormones is to increase overall metabolism, or basal metabolic rate (BMR). Thyroxine is powerful enough to double one's rate of metabolism. Note that the effects of this pathway are very prolonged. Because the production of thyroxine takes several days, it may be ten days to two weeks before visible signs manifest as significant symptoms through this pathway. This explains why you may come down with a cold or flu a week after a very stressful encounter rather than the day after. The metabolic effects of thyroxine released through this pathway are increased workload on the heart muscle, increased gastrointestinal activity (e.g., gastritis), and in some cases, a condition called cerebration or cerebral excitivity, which is associated with anxiety attacks and/or insomnia.

A Parable of Psychophysiology

A metaphor can be used to illustrate the three pathways discussed above (Fig. 2.6). Let us say that your life is in danger because of a classified CIA document you inadvertently stumbled across, and you now pose a threat to national security. You want to deliver a message and a copy of this document to your family, who lives a few hundred miles away, to let them know your life is in danger. This message is of course very important and you want to make sure your family gets it, so you use a couple of methods to ensure its delivery. First you immediately place a phone call to your parents' house because it is the quickest way to deliver the message, and the message is received instantaneously on their answering machine. This is like the action of the sympathetic nervous system. As a backup, you send a wire via Western Union in case no one listens to the answering machine. This form of communication is fairly quick, taking perhaps minutes to hours, and is equivalent to the preganglionic nerve to the adrenal medulla. And because you also need to send a copy of the document to further explain the contents of your message, you ship a package via overnight mail delivery. This means of communication allows more comprehensive information to be sent, but it takes much longer. It is like the neuroendocrine pathways. Similarly, our bodies are comprised of several communication systems, each with its own time element and function, the overall purpose being to prepare the body for physical survival. As illustrated by this story, there are many backup systems fast or slow, to get the message through.

Figure 2.6

Like communication networks that send and receive messages, the human body has several complex messenger systems, which not only see that the information gets through but ensure that the body will survive the perceived threat after the message is received.

Immediate effects	Intermediate effects	Prolonged effects
Phone call	Western Union telegram	Overnight delivery

In the short term, the combination of these various neural and hormonal pathways serves a very important purpose: physical survival. However, when these same pathways are employed continuously due to the influence of chronic stressors, the effects can be devastating to the body. In light of the fact that the body prepares physically for threats, whether they are of a physical, mental, emotional, or spiritual nature, repeated physical arousal suggests that the activation of the stress response is an obsolete mechanism for dealing with stressors that do not pertain to physical survival. The inability of the body to return to homeostasis can have significant effects on the cardiovascular system, the digestive system, the musculoskeletal system, and, research now indicates, the immune system. Organs locked into a pattern of overactive metabolic activity will eventually show signs of dysfunction. For instance, constant pressure and repeated wear and tear on the arteries and blood vessels can cause tissue damage to the inner lining of these organs. Numerous changes can also occur throughout the digestive system, including constipation, gastritis, diarrhea, and hemorrhoids. As was observed by Selye, the inability of the body to return to homeostasis can set the stage for signs and symptoms of disease and illness.

Summary

- Psychophysiology is a term to describe the body's physiological reaction to perceived stressors, suggesting that the stress response is a mind-body phenomenon.
- There are three physiological systems that are directly involved in the stress response: the nervous system, the endocrine system, and the immune system.
- The nervous system is comprised of two parts: the central nervous system (CNS), and the peripheral nervous system (PNS). The CNS is comprised of three levels, the vegetative, the limbic, and the neocortical.
- The limbic system houses the hypothalamus, which controls many functions, including appetite and emotions. The neocortical level processes and decodes all stimuli.
- The most important part of the PNS regarding the stress response is the autonomic nervous system, which activates sympathetic and parasympathetic neural drives. Sympathetic drive causes physical arousal (e.g., increased heart rate) through the secretion of epinephrine and norepinephrine, whereas parasympathetic drive maintains homeostasis through the release of ACh. The two neural drives are mutually exclusive, meaning that you cannot be aroused and relaxed at the same time.
- The endocrine system consists of a series of glands that secrete hormones that travel through the circulatory system and act on target organs. The major stress gland is the adrenal gland.
- The adrenal gland has two parts, each performing different functions. The cortex (outside) secretes cortisol and aldosterone, while the medulla (inside) secretes epinephrine and norepinephrine.
- The nervous system and endocrine system join together to form metabolic pathways or axes. There are three pathways: the ACTH axis, the vasopressin axis, and the thyroxine axis.
- The body has several backup mechanisms to ensure physical survival. These systems are classified as immediate, which lasts seconds (sympathetic drive); intermediate, lasting minutes (adrenal medulla); and prolonged, lasting hours if not weeks (neuroendocrine pathways). Each system is involved in several metabolic pathways.

Concepts and Terms

ACTH axis
Adrenal cortex
Adrenal medulla
Anabolic functioning
Catabolic functioning
Central nervous system (CNS)
Cerebration

Glucocorticoids
Hypothalamus
Immediate stress effects
Intermediate stress effects
Limbic system
Mineralocorticoids
Parasympathetic response

Prolonged stress effects
Psychophysiology
Reticular activating system (RAS)
Sympathetic response
Thyroxine axis
Vasopressin axis

Self-Assessment

As noted in this chapter, the stress response has immediate, intermediate, and prolonged effects. To reinforce your understanding of each type, reflect on how your body reacts to stress through these three processes.

1. What do you feel when immediately threatened?

	Yes	No
a. Tingling sensations	_____	_____
b. Sweating	_____	_____
c. Muscle tension	_____	_____
d. Rapid heart rate	_____	_____
e. Rapid breathing (or holding your breath)	_____	_____
f. Rush of blood to the head and face (feelings of being flushed)	_____	_____

g. Other _____

2. How would you best classify your body's intermediate (within hours) response to stress?

a. Tension headache

b. Stomachache

c. Sore neck and shoulders

d. Sore throat

e. Other _____

f. Other _____

g. Other _____

h. Other _____

3. What do you notice as long-term effects of prolonged (7–10 days) stress?

a. Cold or flu

b. Broken-out face

c. Herpes breakout (around lips)

d. Menstrual period

e. Other _____

f. Other _____

g. Other _____

h. Other _____

References and Resources

Allen, R. *Human Stress: Its Nature and Control.* Burgess Press, Minneapolis, MN, 1983.

Allen, R. *Psychophysiology of the Human Stress Response.* University of Maryland, College Park, 1990.

Bar-Tal, Y., Cohen-Mansfield, J., and Golander, H. Which Stress Matters? The Examination of Temporal Aspects of Stress, *The Journal of Psychology* 132(5):569–576, 1998.

Childre, D. L. *Cut-Thru.* Planetary Publications, Boulder Creek, CA, 1996.

Daniel, J. et al. Mental and Endocrine Factors in Repeated Stress in Man, *Studia Psychologica* 15(3):273–281, 1973.

Everly, G. and Rosenfeld, R. *The Nature and Treatment of the Stress Response.* Plenum Press, New York, 1981.

Greenfield, N. S. and Sternback, R. A. *Handbook of Psychophysiology.* Holt, Rinehart, & Winston, New York, 1972.

Guyton, A. C. *Textbook of Medical Physiology,* 5th ed. Saunders, Philadelphia, 1977.

Lacey, J. I. Somatic Response Patterning and Stress: Some Revisions of Activating Theory. Reprinted in Appley, H. H. and Trumbell, R. *Psychological Stress: Issues in Research.* Appleton-Century-Crofts, East Norwalk, CT, 1976.

Makara, G., Palkovits, M., and Szentagothal, J. The Endocrine Hypothalamus and Hormonal Response to Stress. In *Selye's Guide to Stress Research,* ed. H. Selye, Van Nostrand Rinehold, New York: 280–337.

McEwen BS, de Leon MJ, Lupien SJ, Meaney MJ. Corticosteroids, the aging brain and cognition. *Trends in Endocrinology and Metabolism,* 10:92–96, 1999.

Nemeroff, C. The Neurobiology of Depression, *Scientific American,* June 1998. www.sciam.com/1998/0698issue/0698nemeroff.html

Oatley, K. *Brain Mechanisms and Mind.* Dutton, New York, 1972.

O'Leary, A. Stress, Emotion, and Human Immune Function. *Psychological Bulletin* 108(3):363–382, 1990.

Pelletier, K. *Mind as Healer, Mind as Slayer.* Dell, New York, 1977.

Sapolsky, R. *Why Zebras Don't Get Ulcers.* W. H. Freeman & Company, New York, 1998.

Sapolsky, R. Stress and Your Shrinking Brain, *Discover,* March, 116–122, 1999.

Schnirring, L. DHEA: Hype, Hope not Matched by Facts, *Physician and Sports Medicine,* May 17, 1998.

Sherwood, L. *Human Physiology.* West, St. Paul, MN, 1989.

Usdin, E. et al. *Catecholamines and Stress.* Pergamon Press, Oxford, 1976.

William, D. Modernization, Stress and Blood Pressure: New Directions in Research, *Human Biology.* 71(4):583–605, 1999.

Chapter 3 Stress and Disease

By comprehending that human beings are energy, one can begin to comprehend new ways of viewing health and illness.

—Richard Gerber, M.D.

The association between stress and disease is not a new one. In fact, this relationship has been held to be intuitively valid for ages. But medical science does not take kindly to the use of intuition as a means of gaining knowledge. Well grounded in the mechanistic paradigm of the body as clock, medical researchers are trained to substantiate their beliefs with tangible, visible, and repeatable evidence. Despite the lack of concrete answers, however, some health professionals (and the clients they treat) are convinced of an intangible link between stress and disease. The seeds of clinical understanding were first planted with the observations made by Selye, giving rise to the general adaptation syndrome. Attention soon turned to the role of the central nervous system (CNS) and endocrine system, particularly with regard to the catecholamines and stress hormones responsible for elevated blood pressure, which have since been shown to lead to coronary heart disease. But, as further studies have now revealed, the CNS and endocrine system do not act alone. The current focus on the stress and disease phenomenon is directed toward the interactions of the immune system, the CNS, and human consciousness. Recently, traces of evidence scattered far and wide throughout the literature of the many allied health disciplines have finally begun to lend credence to the ageless intuition of holism. But when looked at from the traditional scientifical point of view, these traces raise more questions than they answer.

In 1977, stress researcher Kenneth Pelletier estimated in his book, *Mind as Healer, Mind as Slayer,* that between 50 and 70 percent of all disease and illness is stress related. By 1995, estimates were even higher, indicating that between 70 and 80 percent of health-related problems are either precipitated or aggravated by stress. The list of such disorders is nearly endless, ranging from the common cold to cancer.

To understand the relationship between stress and disease, you first must recognize that several factors act in unison to create a pathological outcome. These include the cognitive perceptions of threatening stimuli and the consequent activation of the nervous system, the endocrine system, and the immune system. In the past, these three physiological mechanisms were studied separately because they were thought to be independent systems. Today they are viewed as one network, and it is this current understanding that has given rise to the new interdisciplinary field of **psychoneuroimmunology** (PNI). As defined by Pelletier

(1988), psychoneuroimmunology is "the study of the intricate interaction of consciousness (psycho), brain and central nervous system (neuro), and the body's defense against external infection and internal aberrant cell division (immunology)."

There is a consensus among leaders in the field of psychoneuroimmunology that the expression "mind-body medicine" is rather limited in its scope, leading people such as Joan Borysenko, Deepak Chopra, Andy Weil, Gladys Taylor McGary, James Gordon, Larry Dossey, and others to call the approach to healing "mind-body-spirit healing."

Theoretical Models

There have been several research efforts that seek to explain the relationship between stress and disease. At best this relationship is still in the speculation stage, with no clearcut understanding of the complexities involved. After an attempt to synthesize a definitive model, based on his own work as well as on an exhaustive survey of over 300 research articles, Pelletier admitted that there is still not enough scientific information at the present time to create a substantiated stress and disease model. Nevertheless, some of the promising theories may in time provide medical science with the building blocks to create such a comprehensive model. Once this model is in place, the possibility of preventing and intercepting several disease processes will certainly take precedence over the current medical practice of relieving symptoms and fixing and replacing broken parts. The following are some of the most prominent theories regarding the mind-body-spirit relationship.

The Borysenko Model

In what is currently recognized as the most accurate description of the immune system, former Tufts University immunologist Myrin Borysenko (1987) outlined both a dichotomy of stress-induced dysregulation and a matrix describing the "immune balance" regarding four classifications of disease. The dichotomy broadly divides disease and illness into either **autonomic dysregulation** (overresponsive autonomic nervous system), or **immune dysregulation** (Table 3.1).

He suggests that when the autonomic nervous system releases an abundance of stress hormones, several physiological repercussions can result, among them, migraines, ulcers, and hypertension. The notion that

Table 3.1	Borysenko's Stress and Disease Dichotomy	
	Autonomic Dysregulation (Overresponsive ANS)	**Immune Dysregulation**
	Migraines	Infection (virus)
	Peptic ulcers	Allergies
	Irritable bowel syndrome	AIDS
	Hypertension	Cancer
	Coronary heart disease	Lupus
	Asthma	Arthritis

the nervous system is responsible for several symptoms of illness and disease through the release of stress hormones (epinephrine, norepinephrine, cortisol, and aldosterone) was first postulated by Cannon, then established through the pioneering research of Selye.

No less important, however, are the repercussions of a dysfunctional immune system, which can precipitate infection, allergies, and perhaps cancer. In order to understand how the immune system can become dysfunctional or suppressed, let us first take a look at the current perception of this unique physiological system. The purpose of the immune system is to protect the body from pathogens, either externally generated (e.g., bacteria) or internally manufactured (e.g., mutant cells), which impede the proper functioning of the body's regulatory dynamics. Pathogens are comprised of certain molecules (antigens) that have the capacity to interact at various receptor sites on several types of immune system cells, which in turn attempt to detoxify them. Metaphorically, the immune system acts like the collective branches of the armed services to ensure national security by protecting the country from both invading forces and internal insurrection. Like all other physiological systems, the immune system begins to develop in the fetus and matures at about the time of birth, when the body becomes vulnerable to external pathogens.

The immune system is a network of several organs. These include the bone marrow, which throughout life supplies the lymph tissue with stem cells, the precursor to lymphoid cells; the thymus, a gland below the throat that allows stem cells to mature into T-lymphocytes; the bursa equivalent (described by Borysenko as the appendix and gut tissue), which promotes the maturation of stem cells into B-lymphocytes

after their release from bone marrow; and the lymph nodes, spleen, and gut-associated lymphoid tissue into which T-cells and B-cells migrate and are occasionally housed. Upon completion of their maturation process, both T-cells and B-cells migrate throughout the body, ready to encounter their respective antigens.

The lymphocytes are one of three types of leukocytes in the family of cells in the immune system. They work together with granulocytes, another group of leukocytes, in a process called phagocytosis, to engulf various pathogens as well as release histamines. Macrophages, the third type of leukocytes, circulate in the blood and seem to collaborate with T-cells and B-cells to help identify antigens for destruction.

T-cells and B-cells may appear morphologically similar, but their function is different. T-lymphocytes are primarily responsible for cell-mediated immunity, that is, the elimination of internally manufactured antigens (e.g., mutinous cells) in organ tissue. It is currently believed that the human body produces one mutant cell approximately every couple of hours. In an action similar to scanning a grocery store product for its bar code, each T-cell travels throughout the body to scan all other cells for a match between their DNA structure and its own. If a cell's structure doesn't match, the T-cell considers it foreign substance and proceeds to destroy it. Examples are a cancerous cell and transplanted tissue (i.e., organ transplant). In the laboratory where T-cells were observed performing this function, they were called "killer cells" for their search-and-destroy missions. T-cells have been observed to destroy mutinous cells either through direct attack, in which they engulf the bad cell, or to release nonspecific substances called lymphokines, which assist in the elimination process. B-cells, by contrast, are responsible for humoral immunity.

This means the antibodies they discharge circulate throughout various body fluids, primarily blood, and combine with foreign antigens to deactivate the agents that make them a threat. Antibodies are a special type of protein that are found in the globulin of plasma and are typically referred to as immunoglobins (Ig). The function of B-cells is primarily the elimination of pathogenic microorganisms that contribute to infectious diseases, including viruses and bacteria. While T-cells and B-cells have their own specific functions, they often work together. In fact, in some cases, B-cells depend on T-cells for their function.

A closer examination of T-cells indicates that there are three subgroups of this crucial leukocyte, plus one additional immune cell that collaborates with the cytotoxic T-cell (Fig. 3.1). Each has a unique molecular configuration and function, as follows:

1. *Cytotoxic T-cells,* the basic T-cells that with the help of specific neuropeptides (interleukins) become sensitized to identify endogenous antigens for destruction. In addition, with the help of macrophages they attack and destroy tumorous cells.
2. *T-helpers.* Clinically labeled as T4, these cells appear to increase the production of antibodies released by T-cells. T-helpers are thought to manufacture interleukin.
3. *T-suppressors.* Clinically labeled as T8, these cells appear to decrease the production of antibodies necessary to assist T-cells in attacking and killing endogenous antigens. T8 is believed to keep cytotoxic T-cells in check so that they do not attack self-proteins and thereby cause degeneration of healthy tissue. A reduction in T8 is thought to be associated with arthritis and lupus. (Borysenko notes that clinical tests show a 2:1 ratio of T4:T8 to be normal, whereas a ratio less than this is a signal that this aspect of the immune system is deficient.)
4. *Natural killer (NK) cells.* Unlike cytotoxic T-cells, these immune cells appear to have an innate ability to detect endogenous antigens without the help of any neuropeptides to sensitize them. NK cells collaborate with cytotoxic T-cells to destroy mutant cells.

Research on the relationship between the stress response and immunofunction has yielded less than

The family of T-lymphocytes is comprised of three cells: cytotoxic T-cells, T-helpers (T4), and T-suppressors (T8). The natural killer (NK) cells collaborate with the cytotoxic T-cells.

Figure 3.1

absolute results. Studies investigating the effect of catecholamines and stress-related hormones have reported questionable integrity of the immune system when excess levels of these substances were found in the blood. Increases in epinephrine and norepinephrine have been observed to promote the release and redistribution of lymphocytes yet at the same time decrease their efficiency. Some types of stress (e.g., exercise) cause the release of neuropeptides (endorphins), which not only enhance immunofunction, but produce an almost euphoric state of mind. Injections of norepinephrine in mice have been shown to enhance NK cell activity. During chronic stress, however, the increase of cortisol and other glucocorticoids has been linked to a marked decrease in T-cells, reducing their ability to locate and destroy mutant cells. The effects of acute and chronic stress on B-cells are yet unknown but are speculated to be similar to those on T-cells. What all this means is that the integrity of the immune system is thought to be greatly influenced by stress.

In Borysenko's model, when the immune system is operating normally it is said to be precisely regulated. However, when the immune system is not working as homeostatically intended, the result is immunological overreaction, underreaction, or perhaps both. In any case, disease and/or illness are certain (Table 3.2). The causes of overreactions can be exogenous, as in an allergic reaction created by a foreign substance; or endogenous, as when lymphocytes begin to attack and destroy healthy body tissue. Similarly, in an exogenous underreaction, foreign substances outmaneuver and undermine the ability of the B-cells to prevent infection; and in endogenous underreactions antigens are left undisturbed by T-cells, which may then develop into neoplasms (cancerous tumors).

In Borysenko's opinion, it is psychological stress that throws this precisely regulated mechanism out of balance. Stress is the catalyst that exaggerates the direction in which your immune system is headed,

Table 3.2	**Borysenko's Immune Activity Matrix**		
		Over-reactions	Under-reactions
Exogenous activity		Allergies	Infections (colds & flu) Herpes
Endogenous activity		Arthritis Lupus	Cancer

Figure 3.2 From Pert's observations the sixty known neuropeptides appear to have a single molecular structure. The subtle differences among them may be the rate at which each molecule oscillates.

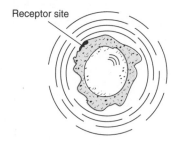

Receptor site

precipitating an over- or underreaction. Note that you can have an allergic reaction (overreaction) and a cold (underreaction) at the same time because they are produced by different dynamics. Borysenko adds that despite the differences among these aspects, the same relaxation techniques work to reinstate precise regulation of the immune system. In other words, regular practice of a relaxation technique, such as meditation or mental imagery, can bring the entire immune system back into homeostatic balance.

Although Borysenko (1991) believes that "stress alters the vulnerability of the immune system to both exogenous and endogenous antigens," the connection between the mind's ability to perceive situations as stressful and the consequent changes in the integrity of the immune system he left to speculation. New discoveries indicate that the physiological systems are more complex than was once believed. For example, formerly described as specialized lymphocytes, T-helpers and T-suppressors may in fact be "double agents" working for the CNS as well.

The Pert Model

Until recently it was thought that there was no direct link between the nervous system and the immune system; virtually all physiologists believed that these two systems acted independently. But researchers have now isolated neural endings connecting the CNS to the thymus, lymph nodes, spleen, and bone marrow. In addition, the tonsils, adenoids, and Peyces cells of the small intestine have been found to be innervated by sympathetic nerve fibers.

A second and perhaps more important link indicates that neuropeptides (messenger hormones) produced in the brain are able to fit into receptor sites of lymphocytes, like keys fit into a lock, thus altering their metabolic function. This communication system is altogether different from the efferent/afferent system observed between neuromuscular tissue and the brain. The codes of neuropeptide information are "spoken" through receptor sites of various lymphocyte cells located throughout the body, and their language is apparently influenced by emotional responses.

It was Candace Pert (1985, 1986, 1987), former Chief of Brain Chemistry at the National Institute for Mental Health, who discovered that immune cells have built-in receptor sites for neuropeptides, with similar findings reported by Edwin Blalock (1985). The identification of neuropeptides themselves is a recent discovery. In trying to uncover the dynamics in the brain associated with chemical addictions, scientists were surprised to find that the brain produces its own (endogenous) opiates, neurotransmitters that have a similar effect to those manufactured externally, such as morphine. The most publicized neuropeptide is beta-endorphin, but so far about ninety neuropeptides have been identified. They are thought to be associated with mood changes and immune regulation. Pert further suggested that there may actually be only one neuropeptide molecule which, like a chameleon, changes its configuration as a result of emotional influences (Fig. 3.2). Pert hypothesized that this spontaneous change may be accounted for by the wavelike oscillations or vibrations of the electrons in each neuropeptide molecule.

Because the hypothalamus has the greatest preponderance of neuropeptide receptors, it was first believed that these substances, produced by the brain, were involved in the biochemical mediation of emotional responses. Pert discovered, however, that neuropeptides are not produced solely by the brain. Her research revealed that throughout the body immune cells not only have receptors for neuropeptides but can manufacture them independently themselves. Furthermore, immune cells seem to have a kind of memory that enables them to adapt to specific emotional responses. Thus neuropeptides are believed to be the means of communication between the brain and T- and B-cells, and it is a bidirectional pathway: immune cells speak to the brain and vice versa. Pert's discovery has given credence to the supposition that some emotions may suppress the function of lymphocytes while others may act as immunoenhancers.

Today the scientific literature is loaded with studies that clearly document the association between the stress response, emotional regulation, and their respective influences on the immune system. The following are some of the landmark studies that gave PNI an established foundation of validity in the medical community.

Jermott et al. (1983) looked at the influence of academic stress on the rate of secretory immunoglobin (S-IgA) in Tufts University dental students. S-IgA is thought to be the first line of defense against upper respiratory diseases. Subjects were administered a personality profile to identify a specific personality trait called power motivation (control), and based on this trait they were divided into two groups. Saliva samples, used to measure S-IgA, were taken five times during the academic year. The results were that mean S-IgA values were significantly reduced during stressful periods, particularly in the students who demonstrated high power motivation.

In another study, Kiecolt-Glaser and her colleagues (1984) reported a decreased number of lymphocytes in Ohio State University medical students during their first day of exams, as compared with samples taken prior to and after the exam period.

Studies investigating the relationship between emotional stress and immunosuppression have also been conducted using animals as subjects (Bovbjerg et al., 1984). For example, when rats were subjected to foot shocks they could not control, a significant reduction in immune function (i.e., decreased lymphocyte proliferation) was detected (Launderslanger et al., 1983). The suppression of the immune system was considered a *conditioned* response. The researchers concluded that a helpless-hopeless attitude, initiated by an inability to control factors of the environment, can pave a path toward illness.

Immunosuppression has also been observed in individuals during bereavement. A study by Bartrop et al. (1977) indicated that people manifested lower lymphocyte proliferation within eight weeks of the loss of a spouse. Similar findings were observed by Schleifer et al. (1983) in men whose wives had died of breast cancer, with results showing a significant reduction in lymphocyte proliferation. These studies have led some to suggest that humans, like rats, can also be conditioned to suppress their immune systems by means of emotions and/or thought processes.

One of the most interesting studies regarding the effects of relaxation and coping techniques on immunoenhancement was conducted by Esterling et al. (1994). In this study, the effect of various stress management skills on natural killer (NK) cell activity was investigated among nursing home patients. Subjects were divided into three groups: (1) those who were taught relaxation techniques, (2) those who were provided with abundant social contact, and (3) those who received no special techniques or contact. Results revealed that after a one-month period, the NK count was significantly higher in those subjects who received stress management therapy than in the controls. Other studies, inspired by the work of Norman Cousins, have also been conducted to determine the relationship between positive emotions and changes in the immune system (see Chapter 12).

In her book *Molecules of Emotion,* Pert highlights the journey of discovery that brought her to the realization that the body is not a machine. "What is this energy that is referred to by so many alternative healers, who associate it with the release of emotion and the restoration of health? According to Western medical terms, energy is produced strictly by various cellular metabolic processes, and the idea that energy could be connected to emotional release is totally foreign to the scientific mind . . . It is my belief that this mysterious energy is actually the free flow of information carried by the biochemicals of emotion—the neuropeptides and their receptors."

What all these studies seem to indicate is that there is a strong relationship between emotional responses and the biochemical changes they produce, specifically with regard to constituents of the immune system. Whereas before Pert's findings, it was believed that cortisol played the crucial role in immunosuppression, it is now thought that structural changes in neuropeptides, influenced by emotional thought, play the most significant role in immuno-incompetence. Currently, the search is underway for other neurotransmitters produced and secreted by the brain that may be responsible for producing the emotional thoughts, which in turn synthesize specific neuropeptides to influence the immune system. Pert is of the opinion that this type of search is fruitless. In the *Noetic Sciences Review* (1987) she writes, "I think it is possible now to conceive of mind and consciousness as an emanation of emotional information processing, and as such, mind and consciousness would appear to be independent from brain and body." It is this point of view that has led her and others (e.g., Joan Borysenko,

Larry Dossey, Deepak Chopra, and Bernie Siegel) to look beyond the physical to the fields of parapsychology and metaphysics for answers to the puzzling relationship between stress and disease. Blazing a trail to this doorstep is radiologist Richard Gerber, M.D.

The Gerber Model

Until now, clinical researchers, influenced by the reductionist theory, have designed studies based on the assumption that the mind and the brain are one, in that all thoughts are merely the result of biochemical reactions occurring within the neurons and synapses of the brain's gray matter. Yet, in many clinical circles, human consciousness is referred to as "the ghost in the machine," an intangible entity. In his books *Vibrational Medicine* and *Vibrational Medicine for the 21st Century,* reviews of hundreds of studies, Dr. Richard Gerber takes an empirical look at the alternative hypothesis—a holistic or systems-theory approach—that mind as conscious and unconscious thoughts exists as energy that surrounds and permeates the body, influencing a host of corporal biochemical reactions. From this perspective, stress-related symptoms that appear in the physical body are the manifestation of "problems" that have occurred earlier as a result of a disturbance at a "higher energy level."

Gerber cites several studies that have begun to scientifically measure and validate the existence of what is now called the human energy field. While these efforts are embryonic at best, Gerber is confident that the end result will be findings that consciousness is indeed comprised of subtle energy—a frequency band of oscillations that surrounds and permeates the body—and like Pert suggested, will show that human consciousness is independent yet tightly integrated with the physical body. Gerber describes the human energy field of subtle matter as consisting of several layers of consciousness (Fig. 3.3): the etheric, that closest to the body; the astral, which is associated with emotional thought; the mental, three tiers of consciousness including instinct, intellect, and intuition; and the outermost layer, the causal, which is associated with the soul. Each of these layers of the energy field is associated with a specific vibrational frequency and state of consciousness. Gerber points out that in a state of optimal health all frequencies are in harmony like a finely tuned piano. A disruption in the harmony

Figure 3.3 The human energy field, also called the electromagnetic field and the auric field, is hypothesized to have many layers, each representing a state of consciousness. Each may also have a subtle vibrational frequency associated with it. (Reprinted from *Vibrational Medicine* by Richard Gerber, copyright © 1988, Bear & Co. Inc., P. O. Drawer 2860, Santa Fe, NM 87504.)

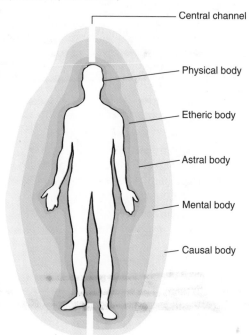

- Central channel
- Physical body
- Etheric body
- Astral body
- Mental body
- Causal body

of frequencies is said to eventually lead to illness and disease. According to this model, a specific thought (e.g., "This grade will put me on academic probation") coupled with an emotion (e.g., fear) cascades through the energy levels, resulting in an effect on some aspect of the body (e.g., a suppressed immune system). Based on Einstein's theory of relativity, which asserts, among other things, that matter and energy are interchangeable, Gerber builds a convincing argument that the mind and the brain are two distinct yet tightly intertwined elements of the human condition.

Since the beginning of recorded healing powers, shamans and medicine men have alluded to a multilayered body of energy that surrounds the physical body. This energy has gone by several names, including *Chi, Prana, breath,* and *spirit.* In academic circles today, this has come to be referred to as **subtle energy,** with the layer closest to the body termed the etheric energy level or bioplasma. Because subtle energy is comprised of matter that appears different (less dense) than that of the physical body, it is often associated in the esoteric literature with the spiritual nature or higher consciousness. While some people claim to actually see this energy field, which they may describe as an aura, it remains virtually invisible to the naked eye. The human energy field remained undocumented until 1940, when an ingenious photographic technique created by Russian researcher Semyon Kirlian, detected traces of this energy field. Using a high-frequency, high-voltage, low-amperage electrical field, electrophotography, or **Kirlian photography** as it is now known, measured the electromagnetic field—the etheric layer—around small living objects. What was revealed through this process appeared very similar to the corona around the sun during an eclipse.

In simple terms, when Kirlian placed a photographic plate between an object—a leaf, say—and a specially designed electrode emitting a specific frequency (Hz), the movement of billions of charged electrons radiating from the object was captured on the film (Fig. 3.4). When the film was processed, brilliant colors and "spark patterns" became evident, creating an electromagnetic image similar to the leaf that was photographed. Surprisingly, if a partial (torn) leaf was photographed, an aura representing the entire leaf still appeared on film. In repeated experiments photographing human hands, Kirlian observed marked dif-

A Kirlian photograph of a leaf. The aura surrounding the leaf is said to be comprised of tiny particles observable through the electromagnetic film process.

Figure 3.4

ferences in the colors and spark patterns between those of healthy people and those diagnosed with cancer.

Among Asian cultures, thoughts and feelings are believed to pass through the many layers of the human energy field through two unique systems comprising what is referred to as our subtle anatomy. The first system is a series of energy vortices that align themselves vertically down the front of the body. These "doors" of energy, called **chakras** (Sanskrit for spinning wheel pronounced shuck-ra), interface with the physical body at various points corresponding to specific organs of the endocrine, and to a lesser extent, central nervous systems. Invisible to the naked eye, these chakras act as transducers between the various layers of subtle energy.

Currently there is much interest in the human energy field in consciousness and its relationship to the chakras. In her collaborative book with Norm Shealy, *The Creation of Health,* author Carolyn Myss states that the chakras are the vital link to understanding the dynamics between health and disease. Myss, a clinical intuitive who can see the initial stages of disease in the auric field, with a 93 percent accuracy rate, believes that illness does not happen randomly. Rather, she is convinced that the majority of disease and illness result from an overload of unresolved emotional, psychological, and spiritual crises. Gifted with the ability to see the human energy field and the chakras themselves, Myss has teamed up with several physicians, most notably the founder of the American Holistic Medical Association, Norm Shealy, to explore the mind-body connection with the use of intuitive skills. Myss's work, which substantiates the Gerber model of stress and disease, has proven quite remarkable as the health care paradigm slowly shifts from a mechanistic to a holistic approach. Myss is not alone. Physician Christiane Northrup, author of *Women's Bodies, Women's Wisdom* and former president of the American Holistic Medical Association, discusses the relationship between chakras and various disease states. In Northrup's words, "When we have unresolved chronic emotional stress in a particular area of our life, this stress registers in our energy field as a disturbance that can manifest in physical illness." As part of the subtle anatomy, the chakras are a multidimensional network that influences behavior at both the organ and cellular levels. The concept of the chakras may begin to explain why two people with the exact same stressor manifest different symptoms of disease, as their thoughts and emotions are processed energetically through the layers of subtle energy and the chakra system.

The following is a synthesis of interpretations from the works of both Gerber and Myss regarding the chakra network system.

First chakra.   The first chakra is commonly known as the root chakra and is located at the base of the spine. The root chakra is associated with issues of safety and security. There is also a relationship with our connectedness to the earth and feelings of groundedness. The root chakra is tied energetically to some organs of the reproductive system, as well as the hip joints, lower back, and pelvic area. Health problems in these areas, including lower-back pain, sciatica, rectal difficulties, and some cancers (e.g., prostate) are thought to correspond to disturbances with the root chakra. The root chakra is also known as the seat of the Kundalini energy, a spiritually based concept yet to be understood in Western culture.

Second chakra.   The second chakra, also known as the sacral chakra, is recognized as being associated with the sex organs, as well as personal power in terms of business and social relationships. The second chakra deals with emotional feelings associated with issues of sexuality and self-worth. When self-worth is

viewed through external means such as money, job, or sexuality, this causes an energy distortion in this region. Obsessiveness with material gain is thought to be a means to compensate for low self-worth, hence a distortion to this chakra. Common symptoms associated with this chakra region may include menstrual difficulties, infertility, vaginal infections, ovarian cysts, impotency, lower-back pain, sexual dysfunction, slipped disks, and bladder and urinary infections.

Third chakra.   Located in the upper stomach region, the third chakra is also known as the solar plexus chakra. Energetically, this chakra feeds into the organs of the GI tract, including the abdomen, small intestine, colon, gallbladder, kidneys, liver, pancreas, adrenal glands, and spleen. Not to be confused with self-worth, the region of the third chakra is associated with self-confidence, self-respect, and empowerment. The wisdom of the solar plexus chakra is more commonly known as a gut feeling, an intuitive sense closely tied to our level of personal power, as exemplified in the expression, "This doesn't feel right." Blockages to this chakra are thought to be related to ulcers, cancerous tumors, diabetes, hepatitis, anorexia, bulimia, and all stomach-related problems. Gerber points out that many illnesses related to this chakra region are the result of what he calls "faulty data of old memory tapes" that have been recorded and programmed into the unconscious mind during early portions of the individual's life. Myss adds that the enculturation of fears and issues of unresolved anger are deeply connected to organic dysfunction in this body region.

Fourth chakra.   The fourth chakra is affectionately known as the heart chakra and it is considered to be one of the most important energy centers of the body. The heart chakra represents the ability to express love. Like a symbolic heart placed over the organic heart, feelings of unresolved anger, or expressions of conditional love work to congest the heart chakra, which in turn has a corresponding effect on the organic heart.

Anathema to the Western mind so firmly grounded in the mechanistic model of reality, anatomical symbolism may seem to have no place in health and health care. But the ties between a symbolic and organic heart became abundantly clear through the research of cardiologist Dean Ornish. To date, Ornish is the only one known to have scientifically proven the reversal of atherosclerotic plaque. While diet, exercise, and support groups are factors in Ornish's regime, it is the practice of meditation (what Ornish calls the "open heart meditation" to open the heart chakra) which seems to be the critical factor in the reversal of coronary heart disease.

The heart, however, is not the only organ closely tied to the heart chakra. Other organs include the lungs, breasts, and esophagus. Symptoms of a blocked heart chakra can include heart attacks, enlarged heart, asthma, allergies, lung cancer, bronchial difficulties, circulation problems, and problems associated with the upper back and shoulders. Also, an important association exists between the heart chakra and the thymus gland. The thymus gland, so instrumental in the making of T-cells, shrinks with age. Gerber notes that this may not be so much an age factor, but rather a reflection of the state of the heart chakra.

Fifth chakra.   The fifth chakra lies above and is connected to the throat. Organs associated with the throat chakra are the thyroid, parathyroid glands, mouth, vocal chords, and trachea. As a symbol of communication, the throat chakra represents the development of personal expression, creativity, purpose in life, and willpower. The inability to express oneself in feelings or creativity, or to freely exercise one's will inevitably distorts the flow of energy to the throat chakra, and is thought to result in chronic sore throat problems, TMJ, throat and mouth cancers, stiffness in the neck area, thyroid dysfunction, migraines, and cancerous tumors in this region. In her book *The Creation of Health*, Myss points out that self-expression and creativity are essential to one's health status. She adds that the inability to express one's feelings, whether they be joy, sorrow, anger, or love, is similar to pouring concrete down your throat, thus closing off the energy needed to sustain the health of this region.

Sixth chakra.   The sixth chakra is more commonly known as the brow chakra or the third eye. This chakra is associated with intuition and the ability to access the ageless wisdom or bank of knowledge in the depths of universal consciousness. As energy moves through the dimension of universal wisdom into this chakra it promotes the development of intelligence and reasoning skills. Directly tied to the pituitary and pineal gland, this chakra feeds energy to the brain for information processing. Unlike the solar plexus chakra, which is responsible for a gut level of

Figure 3.5

Nearly one-half of the American population now partakes in some form of complementary medicine on a regular basis, and most people have a better understanding of it than do their primary care physicians.

"You've been fooling around with alternative medicines, haven't you?"

intuition with personal matters, the wisdom channeled through the brow chakra is more universal in nature with implications for the spiritual aspect of life. Gerber suggests that diseases caused by dysfunction of the brow chakra (e.g., brain tumors, hemorrhages, blood clots, blindness, comas, depression, and schizophrenia) may be caused by an individual's not wanting to see something that is extremely important to their soul growth.

Seventh chakra.   If the concept of chakras is foreign to the Western mind, then the seventh chakra may hold promise to bridge East and West. Featured most predominately in the Judeo-Christian culture through paintings and sculptures as the halo over saintly beings, the seventh chakra, also known as the crown chakra, is associated with matters of the soul and the spiritual quest. When the crown chakra is open and fully functioning, it is known to access the highest level of consciousness. Although no specific disease or illness may be associated with the crown chakra, in truth, every disease has a spiritual significance.

According to Elliot Dacher, M.D., author of *PNI, the Ageless Wisdom and Esoteric Literature,* the insight of chakras can be found in many cultures and disciplines, most notably in the Western culture through the field of psychology with Maslow's hierarchy of needs (see Chapter 4). Beverly Rubik, director of the Center for Frontier Sciences at Temple University, states that although clinical research findings exist regarding various aspects of subtle anatomy and subtle energies, they remain outside the mainstream of Western medicine because they challenge the dominant biomedical model by defying conventional scientific theory. But she notes that just as Einstein opened the doors of thought that challenged Newtonian physics, the principles of energy and information exchanged through energy will gain validity and acceptance in Western science through the doors of quantum physics.

Similar to the chakras is the meridian system: a network of hundreds of interconnected points throughout the body, which allows for the passage of energy between the physical and subtle bodies of the energy field. The meridian system of energy is used in the practice of *shiatsu* massage and Chinese acupuncture.

To most Western physicians, the theoretical concepts behind Chinese acupuncture may seem completely unrelated to the dynamics responsible for the immune system, but to Gerber they are all very much related. If these subtle energy pathways are blocked or congested, the organs they supply may go into a state of dysfunction. Acupuncture is a healing practice that attempts to unblock congested energy pathways, thus allowing a freely flowing current of energy. This healing technique first gained national recognition during President Nixon's trip to China in 1974. At that time, one of his advisors was stricken with acute appendicitis. Rushed to the nearest hospital, he was successfully treated, without anesthesia, to the amazement of the White House officials. Scientists and physicians trained in the Western tradition were quick to ridicule this healing practice, but now studies show that there appears to be a connection, albeit small, between the points designated as meridian gates (acupuncture points) and neuroimmunological crossroads.

The most clinically sound studies to determine the anatomical link between the etheric and physical bodies have been performed by Dr. Kim Han, of Korea, as reported by Rose-Neil in 1967. By injecting a radioactive isotope of phosphorus (P32) through acupuncture needles at traditional points of insertion, he discovered that traces of the isotope followed a fine ductlike tubule system not related to the circulatory, lymphatic, or nervous systems; rather, they paralleled the acupuncture meridian system. Dr. Han's work has been validated by Dr. Pierre de Vernejoul in 1985, who used radioactive technetium (^{99m}Tc) to follow the lines of the ancient acupuncture meridians. When samples of the isotope were injected randomly into the skin, no particular pathways were reproduced.

The human energy field has also been studied with regard to the healing power of touch. Several studies by Bernard Grad and Dolores Krieger, involving both plants (to avoid the placebo effect) and people, have demonstrated that "healing thoughts" in the form of energy produce statistically significant changes in chlorophyll and red blood cells, respectively. Similar studies by Drs. Leonard Laskow and Glen Rein have shown that conscious thoughts can decrease the growth rate of cancer cells in the laboratory. This conscious energy transfer is said to show properties similar to those observed with electromagnetic fields. Investigations into the subtle anatomy of the chakras have also been initiated by a handful of other researchers, including Dr. Elmer Green at the Menninger Clinic in Topeka, Kansas, Valerie Hunt at UCLA, and Dr. Hiroshi Motoyama at the California Institute for Human Science.

To date, Hunt shows the most promise in detecting electromagnetic frequencies associated with the chakras. Her work began with biofeedback studies of muscle tension, but soon shifted to electrical activity in the seven regions associated with the primary chakras, where she noted a difference in frequency many times higher (1600 cps) than could possibly be explained by electrochemical tissue of the heart and brain (0–250 cps). So inspired was Green by the concept of the human energy field that he created the International Society for the Study of Subtle Energy and Energy Medicine (ISSSEEM), which now publishes its own research journal, *Subtle Energies and Energy Medicine.*

How does the mind-body lose its harmonic equilibrium? Two possibilities have been suggested. The first faults bioecological influences, that is, repeated exposure to those energy frequencies, natural (ultraviolet rays) or man-made (high tension power lines), with a rhythm greater than 7.8 Hz, which distort some aspect of the human energy field.

In order to understand this relationship from Gerber's perspective, we need to first understand some additional concepts of the physical world elucidated by Einstein. First, the smallest particle within an atom is comprised of energy, and energy and mass are interchangeable; thus, each object gives off a unified rhythm or series of oscillations. These oscillations are depicted in units of measurement called Hertz (Hz), or oscillations per second. In turn, objects that oscillate, including the human body, create a magnetic energy field. Through processes known as sympathetic resonance and sonic **entrainment,** a vibration can resonate from one object to another, as observed with tuning forks. An object with a lower or weaker frequency of oscillations will alter its own frequency to entrain with (match) that of an object emitting a higher or stronger frequency of oscillations. In humans, the result over time if several organs are influenced to entrain at a higher than normal frequency is a decreased ability to return to homeostasis, resulting in metabolic dysfunction or possibly irregular cell division in those organs.

In support of this hypothesis is the work of Dr. William Becker. Becker, who was twice nominated for a Nobel Prize in medicine, researched the relationship between the incidence of cancer and radiation emitted from various electrical sources, including power lines, microwave ovens, electric blankets, and video display terminals (VDTs). Becker concluded that an unequivocal relationship exists between extremely low frequencies (ELF)—the range in which electrical current oscillates (60Hz)—and the development of diseases in people who are repeatedly exposed to them. Becker is of the opinion that oscillations of a higher frequency are somehow absorbed through the human energy field (what he calls the human electromagnetic field), resulting in alterations to the genetic makeup of cells at the atomic level.

Speculation that the human body had magnetic properties that could be enlisted as a healing mechanism was first suggested by Austrian physician Anton Mesmer in the late 1800s; it was dismissed as nonsense. But in 1992, geobiologist Joseph Kirschvink discovered that human brain cells do indeed synthesize a magnetic-like substance called magnetite. Like

Becker, Kirschvink speculated that exposure to various electrical impulses can alter the integrity of magnetite and affect the cell's health or rate of activity. Disturbances produced by electrical interference can result in mutations at the cellular level, which may then become cancerous tumors.

Compounding the problem is the fact that T-lymphocytes are also affected by ELFs. Becker cited a study by Dr. Daniel B. Lyle of Pettis Memorial Hospital in Loma Linda, California, in which in vitro T-lymphocytes exposed to a 60-Hz energy field significantly reduced their cytotoxic ability against foreign antigens over a forty-eight-hour period. Becker also suggested that energy currents may affect mood and emotions, which are thought to be associated with the astral and mental layers of the human energy field.

In his book *Cross Currents,* Becker concludes:

> At this time, the scientific evidence is absolutely conclusive: 60-Hz magnetic fields cause human cancer cells to permanently increase their rate of growth by as much as 1600 percent and to develop more malignant characteristics. These results indicate that power frequency fields are cancer promoters. Cancer promoters, however, have major implications for the incidence of cancer because they increase the number of cases of causing agents in our environment, ranging from carcinogenic chemicals to cosmic rays. As a result, we are always developing small cancer cells that are recognized by our immune system and destroyed. Any factor that increases the growth rate of these small cancers gives them an advantage over the immune system, and as a result more people develop clinical cancers that require treatment. (Becker, 1990)

While the hazards of high tension power lines have fallen off the radar screen of national attention, the dangers of prolific cell phone use have surfaced as a new health care risk as reported in the *Washington Post* and the *International Journal of Radiation Biology and Environmental Health Perspectives.* Several reports highlight incidences of headaches, memory loss, and brain tumors with excessive use, due to the close proximity of the microwaves (ELFs) to the head.

Regrettably, Becker's findings have largely been either ignored or denounced by the medical community and federal government. For many reasons,

Becker's research is very controversial. For one thing, many people find the idea of electrical pollution hard to believe because it cannot be detected through the five senses. If you find this concept difficult to grasp, think of the TV commercial in which the vibrations of Ella Fitzgerald's voice shatter a crystal goblet. Neither a nervous system nor an immune system is necessary to feel the effects of vibrational energy.

The second explanation for the loss of mind-body equilibrium is that *self-produced* emotional disturbances congest the energy field at the astral (emotional) layer and precipitate a host of physical maladies. Toxic thoughts that go unresolved, often referred to as emotional baggage, may in fact translate into physical ailments that serve as a reminder of these issues. Gerber believes that, in essence, that which comprises our human energy field can be thought of as a sixth (and in his opinion underdeveloped) sense. As examples, he suggests that people who have the power of clairvoyance (clear vision) are able to access various levels of the human energy field in themselves and others; out-of-body experiences and near-death experiences may be explained in the same way.

Thoughts, perceptions, and emotions, according to Gerber's theory, originate in the various layers of subtle energy, cascade through the mind-body interface, and are decoded at the molecular level to cause biochemical changes in the body. He states, "Thoughts are particles of energy. [Negative] thoughts are accompanied by emotions which also begin at the energy levels. As these particles of energy filter through from the etheric level to the physical level, the end result is immunoincompetence" (Gerber, 1988).

It is fair to say that human consciousness is the part of psychoneuroimmunology that is the least understood. As specialists examine the mind-body relationship more and more, though, they are beginning to look beyond the conventional scientific wisdom of a mind within a body and consider the alternative idea, a body within a mind. Gerber's theory may test the limits of your credibility. However, given his careful documentation and the support of a growing body of empirical research from members of ISSSEEM and the Institute of Noetic Sciences, the possibility of this phenomenon cannot be completely ruled out. Gerber reminds us that Nobel laureates Lister and Pasteur, who were once mocked for their theories of "invisible bacteria" as causes of infectious disease, were vindicated after

years of research. Ultimately, what Gerber is saying is that the medical community is beginning to experience a paradigm shift in its approach to health, and this change is meeting with much resistance.

The Pelletier Premodel

As mentioned earlier, Pelletier is yet to be convinced that sufficient medical evidence has been collected to substantiate a definitive stress-disease model. Nevertheless, his comprehensive research article entitled "Psychoneuroimmunology toward a Mind-Body Model," brings to the attention of the allied health professions some valid points he believes must be considered and understood before such a comprehensive model can be constructed. Some intriguing findings in the medical literature approach the fringes of parapsychology and metaphysics, areas that Pelletier hints should be taken a little more seriously and investigated empirically to develop a stress-disease model. The following highlight some of these findings:

1. *Multiple personality disorder.* Braun (1983) cites people diagnosed as having multiple personality disorder (MPD) whose different personalities manifest different illnesses. For instance, a patient may be a diabetic under the influence of one personality, yet show no signs of this disease in the presence of another. Similarly, one personality may require prescription glasses or have asthma or severe allergies, whereas the remaining personalities show no traces of these symptoms. These disease states disappear within the individual when another personality becomes dominant. In most cases of MPD, the patient experienced some incredibly traumatic event as a child. Stress is thought to be strongly associated with the etiology of disease, yet its appearance and disappearance from personality to personality has medical experts baffled.

2. *Spontaneous remission.* Perhaps even more baffling to the medical community is the notion of spontaneous remission—the sudden disappearance of diseased tissue—most often observed with cancerous tumors but acknowledged with other diseases as well. What makes these reports so remarkable is that

Stress With a Human Face

IN 1980, HANS POULSEN, A CHILDREN'S folk singer, was diagnosed with testicular cancer. Before he could begin treatment, it was discovered that the cancer cells had metastasized to his lungs. A second series of tests revealed over twenty tumors throughout his body. For better or worse, his physician told him he should try to get various aspects of his life together as time was of the essence; at most, he had six months to live.

Chemotherapy is no picnic, as Hans attested to—nausea, vomiting, loss of hair, the recounted stories that have become all too commonplace yet no less disturbing in the fight against the beast called cancer.

Well, that was over twelve years ago, and Hans is still composing and singing songs for children of all ages. A miraculous recovery? Hans would definitely say yes! His team of physicians just scratched their heads, never once asking him what therapy he might have done on his own to complement the chemotherapy. If they had asked, they would have discovered that Hans went through a conversion, you might say. Soon

after the discovery of the multiple tumors, he lay down to rest in what he thought might be his last trip to bed. But in thinking over his choices, he made a decision to live and fight rather than be a victim. He learned and practiced positive affirmations, mental imagery, art therapy, and several other complementary healing techniques to assist in his healing process.

I had the chance to meet Hans in the summer of 1992. He glowed with enthusiasm as he shared his story and songs with a group of us who sat around him. Although cases of spontaneous cancer remission are far from common, the remarkable stories of Hans Poulsen and others like him are being taken more seriously by those beginning to appreciate the concepts of complementary healing practices and the emerging wellness paradigm, where the whole is greater than the sum of its parts. ✦

the people who were spontaneously cured were originally diagnosed as terminally ill. There are now even two documented cases of HIV remission. Typically, the first reaction of members of the medical community is denial, with the standard explanation that the patient was misdiagnosed. But a closer look into the matter reveals that in documented cases, some people who were given weeks to live seemed to go through an "about-face attitude" resulting in a "spontaneous cure." These people end up living years, if not decades, beyond their estimated time of departure. The Institute of Noetic Sciences began to document cases of spontaneous remission in the mid 1980s. They found over 3,000 cases of spontaneous

remission in the medical literature, 15 percent of which occurred with no clinical intervention (e.g., radiation or chemotherapy) at all.

In a review of these findings, Jaylene Kent et al. (1989) noted several cases that today are still unexplained. For instance, they examined the results of the International Medical Commission of Lourdes (CMIL), a body of medical professionals that investigates the clinical cases of people who visit the shrine of St. Bernadette at Lourdes, France. Of thirty-eight cases of "cures" examined by the commission since 1954, nineteen were found to be medically and scientifically inexplicable. Kent and her colleagues are quick to point out that evidence of spontaneous remission is rare, yet its existence cannot be ignored. To date, however, it *has* been ignored, in part because the findings are "anecdotal" and cannot be replicated in controlled laboratory studies.

3. *Hypnosis.* When the powers of the unconscious mind are accessed through hypnosis, documented physiological changes have been observed that also prove baffling. Hypnosis can create a state of increased suggestibility that appears able to influence the biochemical mechanisms responsible for healing. According to Pelletier, the following illnesses have been shown to be cured by hypnosis: warts, asthma, hay fever, contact dermatitis, and some animal allergies. Case studies of icthyosis, a congenital skin disease, have also been successfully treated with hypnosis (Dossey, 2000). Pelletier notes that although hypnosis can produce a very relaxed state in which the stress hormone ACTH may be suppressed, enhancement of immune responses alone cannot account for these hormonal changes.

4. *Placebos and Nocebos.* Placebos fall in the realm of faith healing, where a person so strongly believes that the medication he or she received will cure the illness that a healing effect occurs even when what was ingested is no "real" medication at all. The fact that a person suffering from an illness can be cured by taking a sugar pill may sound ludicrous, but indeed this is often the case. In fact, the Food and Drug Administration (FDA) insists that new medicines must produce a cure rate of greater than 35 percent—the demarcation of the placebo effect—in clinical studies before they can be approved. But some placebos have a cure rate of 70 percent. In his book *Love, Medicine, and Miracles,* Dr. Bernie Siegel cites several examples of patients who were healed by their "faith" in medicine even when it wasn't really "medicine," particularly when their attending physicians were very supportive. This type of faith healing is an aspect of clinical medicine not fully understood. What was once thought of as a fluke in modern medicine, however, is now considered a part of the mystery of the stress-disease phenomenon.

Nocebos is a name given to explain the phenomenon when a medication that has been proven to be extremely effective is given to a patient who is told that it is experimental and most likely it won't work. In many cases, the result is that the medication does nothing despite its proven effectiveness.

5. *Cell memory.* With the development of medical technology that has made organ transplants possible, a critical mass of case histories has revealed that cells of various organ tissues hold an energetic memory pattern that transfers to the next recipient. In the book *The Heart's Code,* author Paul Pearsall cites several case studies where people with transplanted organs began to have memories of events in which they took no part (yet the organ donor did). One remarkable story is that of Claire Sylvia who, upon having a heart transplant, began to have dreams of a young blond-haired man named Tim, wearing a motorcycle jacket. Although a vegetarian and a connoisseur of wine, Claire had cravings for chicken McNuggets and beer—the last food Tim had before he died hours later from a motorcycle accident. These and other stories like them suggest that cells retain some level of consciousness that is then passed on to the recipient of the organ. Similarly, some people who, while in the therapy, recount memories of childhood physical abuse, begin to manifest bruises in the places where they were beaten decades earlier.

6. *Subtle energy.* Another area of scientific investigation that merits attention is the concept of subtle energy. Pelletier (1988) states "Mind-body interaction clearly involves subtle energy or subtle information exchange. . . . Given that mind-body interactions involve an exchange of subtle energy, principles of physics may be appropriately applied to issues of health and disease." Pelletier advocates the use of magnetic resonance imaging (MRI) and the superconducting quantum interference device (SQUID), which are based on the concept of subtle energy, for clinical diagnosis of disease and illness. He also suggests that researchers in the field of psychoneuroimmunology try to understand and apply the principles of quantum theory and astrophysics.

7. *Immunoenhancement.* Pelletier points out that if a suppressed immune system can, by way of conscious thought, influence the progression of tumors and other disease processes, psychological factors (e.g., mental imagery, meditation, and cognitive restructuring) may also be able to *enhance* the immune system to create an environment conducive to spontaneous remission and other healing effects. Pelletier cites two studies opening the door to this possibility. In addition to the study by Kiecolt-Glaser et al. (1985) with nursing home residents discussed earlier, he points to the findings of McClelland and Kirshnit (1989) in which subjects watched an inspirational movie about Mother Teresa. Salivary IgA samples were collected before and after viewing the film, and it was observed that values increased afterward, regardless of the subject's opinions of Mother Teresa's work.

In his review of the medical literature, Pelletier has found that most of the evidence collected so far has been anecdotal, meaning that, in his opinion, controlled studies cannot yet prove that positive emotions can enhance immune function. But he suggests that this is a prime area for research. In particular, Pelletier raises the following questions:

1. Is immunoenhancement merely a return to existing baseline levels of the constituents of this precisely regulated system?
2. Are some constituents of the immune system suppressed (e.g., T8) to create an *illusion* that the entire system is enhanced?
3. Could stressors produce a rebound effect, causing elements of the immune system to increase above baseline levels once the stressor is removed?
4. Can the immunological responses actually be increased above baseline?

These are questions he feels need to be answered in order to better understand what immunoenhancement really is. Pelletier's scientifically trained, analytical side is skeptical about the probability of the healing powers of the mind, but his intuitive side allows for the possibility of immunoenhancement. He writes, "Speculations concerning the ultimate role of beliefs, positive emotions, and spiritual values in organizing and transcending biological determinism might seem like philosophical speculation if the answers to these questions were not so critical to our survival as a species balanced between health and illness, life and death."

Pelletier does not specifically use the word *spirituality* with regard to stress and disease, but we can infer that he believes spiritual well-being has been largely ignored by clinical medicine, which leaves the stress-disease model incomplete. He suggests that the only logical approach to understanding the stress-disease/mind-body phenomenon is to take the whole systems approach, in which the individual is greater than the sum of its physiological parts. Until a viable model explaining the relationship between stress and disease is complete, we must work with the information we have. And what is known through the current medical model is that physical symptoms arising from stress can wreak havoc on physical health in specific regions of the body. Over the years, Pelletier has not changed the premise of his stress and disease premodel. However, his interest has taken him further into the exploration of mind-body healing, specifically in the realm of complementary medicine (Pelletier, 2000).

Target Organs and Their Disorders

Looking back at Borysenko's model, we can begin to see how disease and illness can arise from either an overresponsive autonomic nervous system (elevated stress hormones) or a dysfunctional (suppressed) immune system. The importance of understanding how these physiological systems work, as well as the pathways leading to disease, is considered by Borysenko, Pert, Gerber, and Pelletier to be the first step in the healing process. Borysenko, Gerber, and Pelletier also advocate the use of relaxation techniques, including meditation and mental imagery, as supplemental aids in any recovery process. In fact, some healing methods now take a multimodal approach, combining standard Western medical practices with healing methods that employ the powers of the mind. Although this approach is now entering the mainstream of the American health care system, many physicians still remain "doubting Thomases," in part because they have received no formal training in these areas; others perceive the multimodal approach as a threat. While there has been no predictive correlation between a specific stressor (e.g., divorce) and a physical outcome (e.g., ulcers), several studies have shown relationships between the inability to express emotions, the personalities most closely associated with this characteristic, and the incidence of some illness and disease. For instance, the expression of hostility is a behavioral trait of the Type A personality and is commonly associated with coronary heart disease (see Chapter 5).

For some unexplained reason, during various stages of acute and chronic stress, certain regions of the body seem more susceptible to excessive metabolic activity than others. The organs that are singled out or targeted by increased metabolic activity are called **target organs.** Any organ can be a target organ: hair, skin, blood vessels, joints, muscles, stomach, colon, and so on. In some people one organ may be singled out, while in others several organs may be targeted. Genetics, emotions, personality, and environmental factors have all been speculated as possible explanations for target organs, without conclusive evidence to support any of them. In fact, it is likely that they may all contribute to the disease process. The following are some of the more common disorders and their respective target organs, which are now known to be influenced by the stress response. Using Borysenko's model, they have been divided into two categories: nervous system-related disorders and immune system-related disorders.

Nervous System-Related Disorders

In the event of perceived stress, organs that are innervated by neural tissue or acted upon by the excessive secretion of stress hormones increase their metabolic rates. When denied the ability to rest, organs may begin to dysfunction, much like a car engine that overheats on a very hot day. Several states of disease and illness first appear as stress-related symptoms that if undetected or untreated, may result in serious health problems. The following are descriptions of the more common ones.

1. *Bronchial asthma* is an illness in which a pronounced secretion of bronchial fluids causes a swelling of the smooth-muscle tissue of the large air passageways (bronchi). The constriction of these passages produces a choking effect, where the individual feels as if he or she cannot breathe. Asthmatic attacks can be severe enough to send someone to the

hospital and, in some cases, are even fatal. Several studies have linked the onset of asthmatic attacks with anxiety; others have linked it with an overprotective childhood. Currently, drugs (e.g., prednisone) are the first method of treatment. However, relaxation techniques, including mental imagery, autogenic training, and meditation, may be just as effective in both delaying the onset and reducing the severity of these attacks.

2. *Tension headaches.* Tension headaches are produced by sympathetic-mediated contractions of muscles of the forehead, eyes, neck, and jaw. Tension usually builds as the parasympathetic inhibition of muscular contraction gives way to sympathetic drive, increasing the state of muscular contraction. Increased pain results from increased contraction of these muscles. Lower back pain can also result from the same process. Although pain relievers such as aspirin are the most common source of relief, tension headaches have also been shown to dissipate with the use of meditation, mental imagery, and biofeedback.

3. *Migraine headaches.* Unlike a tension headache, which is produced by nervous tension in the facial muscles, a migraine headache is a vascular headache. The word *migraine* literally means "half a skull," and usually when a migraine occurs, the sensation of pain occupies either the right or left side of the head but not both. Migraines are thought to be the result of a sympathetic response to the baroreceptors of the carotid artery, which undergo a rapid constriction (prodrome) followed by a rapid dilation. During the dilation phase, blood quickly moves in from the periphery to flood the cerebral vasculature. The change in vascular pressure combined with humoral secretions is considered the cause of the intense pain so often associated with migraines. Symptoms can include a flash of light followed by intense throbbing, dizziness, and nausea. It is interesting to note that migraines do not occur in the midst of a stressor, but rather hours later. Migraines are thought to be related to the inability to express anger and frustration. Although several medications are prescribed for migraines, current research

indicates that biofeedback and mental imagery can be equally effective, with fewer side effects.

4. *Temporomandibular joint dysfunction.* Excessive contraction of the jaw muscles can lead to a phenomenon called temporomandibular joint dysfunction or TMJ (Fig. 3.6). In many cases, people are unaware that they have this illness because the behavioral damage occurs during sleep. But when they make a trip to the dentist, they find that they are showing signs of clenching and grinding their teeth (bruxism). Other symptoms include muscle pain and clicking or popping sounds when chewing, as well as tension headaches and earaches. Like migraines, TMJ is often associated with the inability to express feelings of anger. However, other behaviors are also associated with this symptom, including excessive gum chewing, resting one's chin on a hand, even nail biting. Severe cases require that a mouth brace be worn at night. Relaxation techniques, including biofeedback and progressive muscular relaxation, have been shown to be effective in decreasing the muscular tension associated with TMJ.

5. *Irritable bowel syndrome.* IBS is characterized by repeated bouts of abdominal pain or tenderness, cramps, diarrhea, nausea, constipation, and excessive flatulence. It is often considered a result of excessive sympathetic neural stimulation to one or more areas of the gastrointestinal (GI) tract. While symptoms may vary from person to person, this stress-related disorder is most commonly associated with anxiety and depression. One reason IBS is considered so closely related to stress is that the hypothalamus, which controls appetite regulation (hunger and satiety), is closely associated with emotional regulation as well. Various diets and medications may be prescribed, depending on the nature of the symptoms. Several recent studies have employed various types of relaxation and cognitive skills, including thermal biofeedback, progressive muscular relaxation, mental imagery, cognitive reappraisal, and behavior-modification techniques to reduce existing levels of anxiety. All had promising results.

There are many forms of TMJ, including clicking of the jaw and grinding one's teeth during sleep. Experts suggest that twenty percent of the American population has some form of TMJ.

Figure 3.6

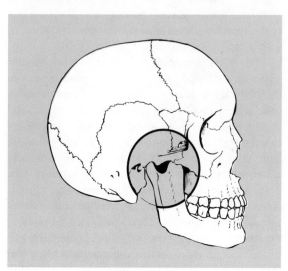

6. *Coronary heart disease.* There are two major links between the stress response and the development of coronary heart disease, which the American Heart Association now estimates kills one person every thirty-two seconds. The first link is elevated blood pressure, or hypertension. In an effort to shunt blood from the body's core to the peripheral muscles in the event of physical movement during the fight-or-flight response, several stress-related hormones are released into the bloodstream. Sympathetic arousal releases epinephrine and norepinephrine from neural endings as well as from the adrenal medulla. These agents increase heart rate and myocardial contractility in order to cause the heart to pump a greater supply of oxygenated blood to the body's muscles for energy production. These catecholamines are also responsible for constricting blood vessels of the gastrointestinal tract while at the same time dilating vessels to the body's periphery, causing an overall change in total peripheral resistance. Aldosterone, secreted from the adrenal cortex,

increases blood volume by increasing water retention. Vasopressin, or ADH, also acts to increase blood volume. The net effect of these stress hormones is to "jack up" blood pressure far above resting levels in order to transport blood to areas where it is needed. Ironically, stress provokes the same physiological response, even when there is no conscious attempt to physically move.

When pressure is increased in a closed system, the risk of damage to vascular tissue due to increased turbulence is significantly increased. This damage to the vessel walls appears as small microtears, particularly in the intima lining of the coronary heart vessels, which supply the heart muscle (myocardium) itself with oxygen. As a way of healing these tears, several constituents floating in the blood bind with the damaged vascular cell tissue. Paradoxically, the primary "healing" agent is a sticky substance found floating in the blood serum called cholesterol.

The second link between coronary heart disease and the stress response is the release of cortisol from the adrenal medulla. One of the many functions this stress hormone performs is to increase the level of free fatty acids carried by lipoproteins from the adipose (fat) tissue sites

into the blood, to be used by the working muscles for energy production. An abundance of cholesterol in the blood makes it readily available for use in the attempt to repair damaged vascular cell tissue. However, what may seem like a protective mechanism actually becomes a major hindrance to the efficiency of the heart muscle, causing coronary heart disease.

The three stages of coronary heart disease are atherogenesis, atherosclerosis, and arteriosclerosis (Fig. 3.7). With **atherogenesis,** the initial stage, a fatty streak appears on the inner lining of the artery wall. Some evidence suggests that this can occur as early as age five. As this fatty streak continues to circumnavigate the perimeter of the artery as well as travel its length, it creates a buildup of plaque, which narrows the inside of the artery. The stage at which the passage narrows due to thickening of plaque is referred to as **atherosclerosis.** As this fatty plaque accumulates, it attracts other constituents in the blood, including calcium, causing increased resistance to blood flow and increased blood pressure. With age, plaque hardens, making the artery walls like lead pipes that are no longer able to constrict or dilate. This compounds the effect of high blood pressure,

Figure 3.7 Coronary heart disease can start as early as age five when turbulent blood flow may cause damage to the inner lining of the artery wall. Cholesterol deposits, which attempt to heal damaged tissue, actually thicken the passage, thus decreasing the diameter of the vessel for blood to pass through. The greater the thickness, the greater the chance for an occlusion to that vessel—and an ensuing heart attack.

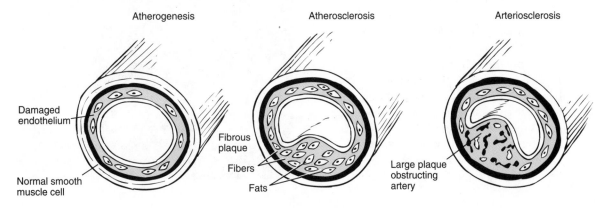

which is one reason resting blood pressure increases with age. At the third stage, **arteriosclerosis,** the arteries themselves become hard, and possibly occluded from the flow of blood. If blood flow is impeded, the heart muscle may show signs of oxygen deprivation (ischemia) resulting in either angina (chest pain) or death of myocardial cell tissue. The end result is a heart attack, or myocardial infarction (MI). The degree of coronary artery blockage determines the severity of the heart attack, the most extreme result being death. Similar etiology may occur with tears in the carotid arteries (located on either side of the vocal cords) that supply oxygenated blood to the brain. Strokes, like coronary heart disease, are the result of blocked arteries creating an inadequate oxygenated blood supply, in this case to the brain.

Immune System-Related Disorders

As mentioned previously, emotional stress appears both to alter the molecular structure of biochemical agents or neuropeptides and to suppress the number and functions of various key leukocytes. Stress hormones (cortisol) may also decrease the effectiveness of leukocytes. With this process underway, protective mechanisms are less efficient and the body becomes more vulnerable to exogenous and endogenous antigens. As previously discussed, diseases that are the result of immune dysfunction can be classified as (1) exogenous-underreactive, (2) exogenous-overreactive, (3) endogenous-underreactive, and (4) endogenous-overreactive. The following are examples of some diseases in each of these categories:

1. *The common cold and influenza (exogenous underreaction).* In 1991, a study (Cohen, Tyrrell, and Smith) published by the prestigious *New England Journal of Medicine* supported the hypothesis that colds are unequivocally related to undue stress. The results made headlines across the country. From Borysenko's model of the immune system, we can see that as B-lymphocyte numbers decrease, the body becomes more vulnerable to the influences of the viruses that produce the common cold. Colds and influenza fall into the category of exogenous underreaction in Borysenko's immune activity matrix because there are insufficient B-lymphocytes to combat the exogenous antigen.

2. *Allergies (exogenous overreaction)* (Fig. 3.8). An allergic reaction is initiated when a foreign substance, or antigen (e.g., pollen, bee venom, dust spores, etc.) enters the body. In response to this intrusion, granulocytes secrete antibodies called histamines. When histamines encounter the antigens they form inactive complexes, in essence neutralizing their toxic effect. In an overreactive immune response to exogenous antigens, the excess of histamines causes swelling of mucus-membrane tissue, in the case of inhaled antigens; or of skin tissue, in the case of infection. Some studies have shown that the introduction of foreign antigens isn't necessary to trigger an allergic reaction. Borysenko suggests that B-lymphocytes have the capacity of memory that may induce the production of histamines and other antibodies (immunoglobins) without direct contact of an antigen. In some people, allergic reactions can occur just by thinking about the stimulus that provoked a previous attack. Several

The list of allergy-producing substances is nearly endless. *Figure 3.8* Pollen and dust are two of the most common ones.

studies have also shown that allergic reactions are more prevalent and severe in subjects prone to anxiety. Over-the-counter medications containing antihistamines and allergy shots are the most common approaches to dealing with allergies. New data suggest that relaxation techniques also minimize the effects of external antigens.

3. *Rheumatoid arthritis (endogenous overreaction).* Tissue swelling may also occur from inflammation produced by an overreactive immune system responding to cells perceived to be (endogenous) antigens. In this case, constituents of the immune system begin to attack apparently healthy tissue, mistaking it for a foreign substance. Rheumatoid arthritis, a joint and connective tissue disease, occurs when synovial membrane tissue swells, causing the joint to become inflamed. In time, synovial fluid may enter cartilage and bone tissue, causing further deterioration of a joint. Severe cases of rheumatoid arthritis are most evident in deformed finger joints. A substance identified as rheumatoid factor, a protein found in the blood, is thought to be associated with this disease. There is speculation that rheumatoid arthritis has a genetic link. It also has an association with stress, as it has been noted that the severity of arthritic pain is often related to episodes of stress, particularly suppressed anger. The treatment for this disease varies from pain relievers (e.g., aspirin) to steroid injections (e.g., cortisone), depending on the severity of pain and rate of joint deterioration. Relaxation techniques are now being recommended as a complementary treatment to help reduce symptoms.

4. *Ulcers and colitis.* Ulcers are often described as a hole in the stomach, and this depiction is not far from the truth. The series of events that lead to the destruction of this organ tissue begins with an excessive sympathetic neural drive. Increased secretions of norepinephrine are thought to cause a constriction of the vasculature in the lining of the stomach. This in turn is believed to decrease mucus secretions produced by the inner lining of the stomach wall. The purpose of

mucus is to protect against the strong digestive enzymes that break down foodstuffs in the stomach. If the balance of mucosal fluid and digestive enzymes (hydrochloric acid) is thrown off, the inner lining becomes susceptible to these enzymes. The stomach may actually begin to digest itself, producing a hole in the stomach wall. Ulcers were one of the first diseases associated with undue stress; Selye noted this in his earliest studies with rats. Similarly, physicians immediately noticed an association between anxiety and the symptoms of ulcers in their patients, most notably sharp pains in the stomach.

The colon, situated below the stomach along the gastrointestinal tract, is also prone to ulceration, with a similar etiology producing colitis, or inflammation of the inner lining of the colon. Stress in the form of anxiety is thought to be strongly associated with colitis as well. Relaxation techniques are usually recommended, in conjunction with a special diet to minimize the symptoms of this disease. Some techniques, including mental imagery, have even helped to heal ulcerations in the stomach wall.

For years, if not decades, it was thought that stress was the primary reason for ulcers. But in 1981, Barry Marshall, M.D., of Perth, Australia, proved that over 75 percent of ulcers are caused by a bacteria known as *Helicobacter,* a carcinogen (Ubell, 1995). Clinical studies showed that this bacteria can settle in the lining of the stomach, creating an open wound that stomach acids then worsen, resulting in moderate to severe ulceration. Previously, it was thought that microbes such as *Helicobacter* could not survive in an acid-rich environment, but Marshall discovered this not to be the case. Treatment with antibiotics is now shown to be highly effective for a large percentage of people who have ulcers, yet two questions remain: What makes some people more vulnerable to the *Helicobacter* virus than others? and Why are antibiotics only effective in 75 percent of the cases of people with ulcers?

5. *Cancer (endogenous underreaction).* Cancer has proved to be one of the most perplexing diseases of our time, affecting one out of every three Americans. To date there is still no cure short of prevention and early detection. The American Cancer Society defines cancer as "a large group of diseases all characterized by uncontrolled growth and spread of abnormal cells." In other words, there are many types of cancer and the specific etiologies are still not completely understood. There are also many theories that attempt to explain the development of cancer. The most prominent and well-accepted one suggests that somewhere in the DNA structure there is a gene, called an **oncogene,** that produces an abnormal or mutant cell. Whether this gene can be inherited or is somehow externally triggered is yet to be determined; there are arguments both ways. The production of an abnormal cell in the body by itself is not uncommon. Some research suggests that the body produces about six mutant cells per day. In a precisely regulated immune system, T-cells and NK cells keep such endogenous antigens in check.

When a cell does mutate, that is, its genetic structure deviates from that of normal cells, it is regarded as an endogenous antigen and becomes subject to destruction by the cytotoxic T-lymphocytes, or T-cells. T-lymphocytes, you will remember, have a commando mission to search for and destroy malignant cells. If for some reason their ability is suppressed, the likelihood of a cancerous tumor is increased. While the life span of a mutinous cell is markedly shorter than that of normal cells (this process is called *relative inviability*), if undetected it proliferates much more quickly than a normal cell, producing a tumor. Because of their structural inability to manufacture various enzymes necessary to perform normal cellular functions, cancerous tumors rob healthy cells of their nutrients. Unlike normal organ tissue, too, cancer cells are not self-contained and thus are able to detach from their original site and move to other areas throughout the body. This spread of cancerous tumors is referred to as metastasis, and at this advanced stage prognosis for recovery is not good.

Explanations for the manifestation of oncogenes are still speculative. Research has shown that external factors called carcinogens (e.g., ultraviolet rays, benzopyrene in cigarettes, asbestos, etc.) produce tumorous growths in both laboratory rats and humans. Medical researchers are still looking for endogenous factors that may also play a role in this disease process. At the same time, attention has been given to personality characteristics, and some traits have been found to be common among those who develop cancer. Although it is hard to put one quarter of the American population into the same personality category, several studies show that the incidence of cancer appears higher among people who have a hard time expressing their emotions, have low self-esteem, and experience feelings of rejection. By no coincidence, these same traits are said to comprise the codependent or addictive personality (Chapter 6).

The treatments for cancer include drugs, radiation, and surgery. However, thanks to the work of O. Carl Simonton, Elisabeth Kübler-Ross, Bernie Siegel, Joan Borysenko, and Jeanne Achterberg, coping skills involving cognitive restructuring, art therapy, and relaxation techniques including mental imagery and meditation are being used as complementary healing methods. While these methods are not a cure for cancer in themselves, in some cases they seem to have a pronounced effect when used in combination with traditional medicine.

Much attention is currently being given to the relationship between stress and disease in America. As lifestyles appear to become more stressful, the incidence of several illnesses that appear to be closely linked with stress is also increasing. Although stress is not a direct cause of disease and illness, the association between them is too significant to be considered mere coincidence. With the continued work of people like Borysenko, Pert, Gerber, Pelletier, and others, some answers may be uncovered shortly.

Summary

- There has been an intuitive association between stress and disease for centuries, but the link has only come to be accepted scientifically in the last decade or so. Scientists from several disciplines have come together to form a whole new field of study called psychoneuroimmunology.
- Recently the immune system has been discovered to be greatly affected by prolonged bouts of stress.
- Pelletier states that there is still not enough data to substantiate a definitive stress-disease model that would help us to understand the relationship between the two.
- Borysenko's model outlined both a dichotomy of autonomic dysregulation and immune dysregulation, and an immune activity matrix, which classifies diseases in one of four categories: (1) exogenous overreaction, (2) endogenous overreaction, (3) exogenous underreaction, and (4) endogenous underreaction.
- Pert's model cites research findings linking the nervous system with the immune system. Various cell tissues comprising the immune system can synthesize neuropeptides just as the brain can. Pert believes that all neuropeptides are really one molecule that undergoes a change at the atomic level brought about by various emotional states or energy thought forms.
- Gerber's model states that the mind consists of energy (bioplasma) surrounding and permeating the body. Disease, then, is disturbance in the human energy field, which cascades through the levels of the subtle energy to the body via chakras and meridians.
- Pelletier's pre-model states that a number of issues must be addressed and understood before a stress-disease model can be developed. These issues include disease states in people with multiple personality disorders, spontaneous remissions, hypnosis, placebos, subtle energy, and immunoenhancement.
- Based on Borysenko's model, stress-related diseases were placed into one of two categories: those related to an overresponsive autonomic nervous system (e.g., migraines, ulcers, and coronary heart disease) and those associated with a dysfunctional immune system (e.g., colds and cancer).
- Research shows that several relaxation techniques are effective as complementary strategies in decreasing the symptoms of stress-related illness.

Concepts and Terms

Atherogenesis
Atherosclerosis
Arteriosclerosis
Autonomic dysregulation
B-cells
Bioplasma
Borysenko model
Chakras
Endogenous overreaction
Endogenous underreaction
Entrainment
Etheric energy
Exogenous overreaction

Exogenous underreaction
Gerber model
Human energy field
Immune dysregulation
Immunoenhancement
Kirlian photography
Leukocytes
Lymphocytes
Meridians
Natural killer cells
Neoplasms
Neuropeptides
Nocebos

Oncogene
Pelletier premodel
Pert model
Placebos
Psychoneuroimmunology
Spontaneous remission
Subtle energy
Sympathetic resonance
Target organs
T-cells (cytotoxic T-cells)
T-helpers (T4)
T-suppressors (T8)

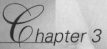
Self-Assessment

Physical Symptoms Questionnaire

Look over this list of stress-related symptoms and circle how often they have occurred in the past week, how severe they seemed to you, and how long they lasted. Then reflect on the past week's workload and see if you notice any connection.

	How Often? *(number of days in the past week)*	How Severe? *(1 = mild, 5 = severe)*	How Long? *(1 = 1 hour, 5 = all day)*
1. Tension headache	0 1 2 3 4 5 6 7	1 2 3 4 5	1 2 3 4 5
2. Migraine headache	0 1 2 3 4 5 6 7	1 2 3 4 5	1 2 3 4 5
3. Muscle tension (neck and/or shoulders)	0 1 2 3 4 5 6 7	1 2 3 4 5	1 2 3 4 5
4. Muscle tension (lower back)	0 1 2 3 4 5 6 7	1 2 3 4 5	1 2 3 4 5
5. Joint pain	0 1 2 3 4 5 6 7	1 2 3 4 5	1 2 3 4 5
6. Cold	0 1 2 3 4 5 6 7	1 2 3 4 5	1 2 3 4 5
7. Flu	0 1 2 3 4 5 6 7	1 2 3 4 5	1 2 3 4 5
8. Stomachache	0 1 2 3 4 5 6 7	1 2 3 4 5	1 2 3 4 5
9. Stomach/abdominal bloating/distention/gas	0 1 2 3 4 5 6 7	1 2 3 4 5	1 2 3 4 5
10. Diarrhea	0 1 2 3 4 5 6 7	1 2 3 4 5	1 2 3 4 5
11. Constipation	0 1 2 3 4 5 6 7	1 2 3 4 5	1 2 3 4 5
12. Ulcer flare-up	0 1 2 3 4 5 6 7	1 2 3 4 5	1 2 3 4 5
13. Asthma attack	0 1 2 3 4 5 6 7	1 2 3 4 5	1 2 3 4 5
14. Allergies	0 1 2 3 4 5 6 7	1 2 3 4 5	1 2 3 4 5
15. Canker/cold sores	0 1 2 3 4 5 6 7	1 2 3 4 5	1 2 3 4 5
16. Dizzy spells	0 1 2 3 4 5 6 7	1 2 3 4 5	1 2 3 4 5
17. Heart palpitations (racing heart)	0 1 2 3 4 5 6 7	1 2 3 4 5	1 2 3 4 5
18. TMJ	0 1 2 3 4 5 6 7	1 2 3 4 5	1 2 3 4 5
19. Insomnia	0 1 2 3 4 5 6 7	1 2 3 4 5	1 2 3 4 5
20. Nightmares	0 1 2 3 4 5 6 7	1 2 3 4 5	1 2 3 4 5
21. Fatigue	0 1 2 3 4 5 6 7	1 2 3 4 5	1 2 3 4 5
22. Hemorrhoids	0 1 2 3 4 5 6 7	1 2 3 4 5	1 2 3 4 5
23. Pimples/acne	0 1 2 3 4 5 6 7	1 2 3 4 5	1 2 3 4 5
24. Cramps	0 1 2 3 4 5 6 7	1 2 3 4 5	1 2 3 4 5
25. Frequent accidents	0 1 2 3 4 5 6 7	1 2 3 4 5	1 2 3 4 5
26. Other	0 1 2 3 4 5 6 7	1 2 3 4 5	1 2 3 4 5
(please specify)_____			

Score: Look over the entire list. Do you observe any patterns or relationships between your stress levels and your physical health? A value over 30 points may indicate a stress-related health problem. If it seems to you that these symptoms are related to undue stress, they probably are. While medical treatment is advocated when necessary, the regular use of relaxation techniques may lessen the intensity, frequency, and duration of these episodes.

References and Resources

Achterberg, J. Imagery and Medicine: Psychophysiological Speculations, *Journal of Mental Imagery* 8(4):1–14, 1984.

Ader, R. Developmental Psychoneuroimmunology, *Developmental Psychobiology* 10:251–267, 1983.

American Cancer Society. 1599 Clifton Rd., N.E., Altanta, GA 30329.

American Heart Association. *1991 Heart and Stroke Facts,* National Center, Dallas, TX, 1991.

Austin, J.A. et al. Complementary and Alternative Medicine Use among Elderly Persons: One Year Analysis of a Blue Shield Medicare Supplement, *Journal of Gerontology* 55(1):M4–9, 2000.

Bartrop, R. W. et al. Depressed Lymphocyte Function after Bereavement, *Lancet* 1:834–836, 1977.

Becker, W. *Cross Currents.* Tarcher Press, Los Angeles, 1990.

Blalock, J. E., Harbour-McMenamin, D., and Smith, E. Peptide Hormones Shared by the Neuroendocrine and Immunologic Systems, *The Journal of Immunology* 135(2):858s–861s, 1985.

Blanchard, E. B. et al. Biofeedback and Relaxation Treatments for Headaches in the Elderly: A Caution and a Challenge, *Biofeedback and Self-Regulation* 10(1):69–73, 1985.

Borysenko, M. Personal Communication, December 10, 1991.

Borysenko, M. Psychoneuroimmunology, *Annals of Behavioral Medicine* 9:3–10, 1987.

Borysenko, M. *Stress and the Immune System,* paper presented at the Sheraton Hotel, Washington, D.C., October 25–26, 1991.

Bovbjerg D., Ader, R., Cohen, N. Acquisition and Extinction of Conditioned Suppression of Graft-vs.-Host Responses in the Rat, *Journal of Immunology,* 132:111–113, 1984.

Braun, B. Psychophysiological Phenomena in Multiple Personality and Hypnosis, *American Journal of Clinical Hypnosis* 26(2):124–137, 1983.

Brennen, B. A. *Hands of Light: A Guide to Healing through the Human Energy Field.* Bantam, New York, 1987.

Brody H. (with Daralyn Brody) *The Placebo Response.* Cliff Street Books. New York, 2000.

Clark, W. *The Experimental Foundations of Modern Immunology,* 4th ed. Wiley, New York, 1991.

Cohen S., Tyrrell, D., and Smith, A. P. Psychological Stress and Susceptibility to the Common Cold, *New England Journal of Medicine,* 325:606–612, 1991.

Cohen, S., and Williamson, G. M. Stress and Infectious Disease in Humans, *Psychological Bulletin* 109:5–24, 1991.

Collinge, W. *Subtle Energy: Awakening to the Unseen Forces in Our Lives.* Warner Books, New York, 1998.

de Vernejoul, P. et al. Etude des Meridiens, D'Accupuncture par les Traceurs Radioactifs, *Bull Acad Natle Med* 169 (Oct):1071–1075, 1985.

Dacher, E. A Challenge to Healers: An Integrated Healing Model, Fifth Annual ISSSEEM Conference, Boulder, CO, June 26, 1995.

Dacher, E. *PNI: The New Mind-Body Healing Program.* Marlowe & Company, New York. 1992.

Dossey, L. *Reinventing Medicare.* Harper-San Francisco, San Francisco, 1999.

Eden, D. *Energy Medicine.* Tarcher /Putnam Books, New York, 1998.

Eskola, S., Ylipaavalniemi, P., and Turtola, L. TMJ-Dysfunction Symptoms among Finnish University Students, *Journal of American College Health* 33(4):172–174, 1985.

Esterling, B.A., Kiecolt-Glaser, J. K., Bodnar, J. C., Glaser, R. Chronic Stress, Social Support, and Persistent Alterations in the Natural Killer Cell Response to Cytokines in Older Adults, *Hlth Psychol* 13:291–299, 1994.

Ferguson, M. Electronic Evidence of Aura, *Chakras* in UCLA Study, *Brain/Mind Bulletin* 3(9):1978.

Gerber, R. Personal Communication, November 25, 1991.

Gerber, R. *Vibrational Medicine.* Bear and Co., Santa Fe, NM, 1988.

Gerber, R. *Vibrational Medicine for the 21st Century.* Eagle Brook; Harper Collins, New York, 2000.

Gordon, J. *Manifesto for a New Medicine*. Addison Wesley, Reading, MA, 1996.

Grad, B. Healing by the Laying on of Hands: A Review of Experiments. In *Ways of Health: Holistic Approaches to Ancient and Contemporary Medicine*, ed. D. Sobel. Harcourt Brace Jovanovich, New York, 1979.

Green, E. Presidential Address, Second International ISSSEEM Annual Conference, Boulder, CO, June 26–28, 1992.

Greenberg, J. *Comprehensive Stress Management*. W. C. Brown, Dubuque, IA, 1995.

Harman, W., and Clarke, J. *New Metaphysical Foundations of Modern Science*. Institute of Noetic Sciences, Sausalito, CA, 1994.

Henri-Benitez, M. et al. Autogenic Psychotherapy for Bronchial Asthma, *Psychology Psychosomatica* 11(6):11–16, 1990.

Hirshberg, C. and Barasch, M. *Remarkable Recovery*. Riverhead Books, New York, 1995.

Horrigan, B. and Ornish, D., M.D. Healing The Heart, Reversing the Disease, *Alternative Therapies* 1(5):84–92, 1995.

Horrigan, B. and Pert, C., Ph.D. Neuropeptides, AIDS, and the Science of Mind-Body Healing. *Alternative Therapies* 1(3):70–76, 1995.

Hunt, V. *Infinite Mind: Science of the Human Vibrations of Consciousness*. Malibu Publishing Co., Malibu, CA, 1996.

Hunt, V. et al. A Study of Structural Integration from Neuromuscular, Energy Field, and Emotional Approaches, paper presented at the University of California at Los Angeles, 1977.

Jermott, J. B. Psychoneuroimmunology: The New Frontier, *American Behavioral Scientist* 28(4):497–509, 1985.

Jermott, J. B. et al. Academic Stress: Power Motivation and Decrease in Saliva Immunoglobin-A Secretion Rate, *Lancet* 1:1400–1402, 1983.

Justice, B. *A Different Kind of Health: Finding Well-being Despite Illness*. PeAk Press, Houston, TX, 1998.

Kent, J. et al. Unexpected Recoveries: Spontaneous Remission and Immune Functioning, *Advances* 6(2):66–73, 1989.

Kiecolt-Glaser, J. et al. Psychosocial Modifiers of Immunocompetence in Medical Students, *Psychosomatic Medicine* 46(1):7–14, 1984.

Kirlian, S. and Kirlian V. Photography and Visual Observations by Means of High-Frequency Currents, *Journal of Scientific and Applied Photography* 6:145–148, 1961.

Kirschvink, J. et al. Magnetite in Human Tissues: A Mechanism for the Biological Effects of Weak ELF Magnetic Fields, *Bioelectronics Supplement* 1:101–114, 1992.

Krieger, D. Healing by the Laying on of Hands as a Facilitator of Bioenergetic Change: The Response of In-Vivo Hemoglobin, *International Journal of Psychoenergetic Systems* 1:121, 1976.

Krieger, D. The Response of In-Vivo Human Hemoglobin to an Active Healing Therapy by Direct Laying on of Hands, *Human Dimensions* 1 (Autumn):12–15, 1972.

Krieger, D. Therapeutic Touch: The Imprimatur of Nursing, *American Journal of Nursing* 75:784–787, 1975.

Laskow, L. *Healing with Love*. HarperCollins, San Francisco, CA, 1992.

Laudenslanger, M. L. et al. Coping and Immunosuppression: Inescapable Shock Suppresses Lymphocyte Proliferation, *Science* 221:568–570, 1983.

Learner, M. *Choices in Healing*. The MIT Press, Cambridge, MA, New York, 1995.

Levenson, J. L. and Bemis, C. The Role of Psychological Factors in Cancer Onset and Progression, *Psychosomatics* 32(2):124–132, 1991.

McClelland, D. C. and Kirshnit, C. The Effect of Motivation Arousal through Films on Salivary Immunoglobin A, *Psychology and Health* 2:31–52, 1989.

Miller, R. Bridging the Gap: An Interview with Valerie Hunt, *Science of Mind*, October 12, 1983.

Mitchell, M. C., and Drossman, D. A. Irritable Bowel Syndrome: Understanding and Treating a Biopsychosocial Disorder, *Annals of Behavioral Medicine* 9(3):13–18, 1987.

Moran, M. Psychological Factors Affecting Pulmonary and Rheumatological Diseases: A Review, *Psychosomatics* 32(1):14–23, 1991.

Moriyama, Y., Kishimoto, A., and Mastushita, T. The Relationship between Stress and the Onset of Gastrointestinal Diseases: Questionnaire Survey of Patients with Gastric Cancer and Gastric Ulcers, *Kyushu Neuropsychiatry* 34(3–4):282–288, 1988.

Motoyama, H. and Brown, R. *Science and the Evolution of Consciousness*. Autumn Press, Brookline, MA, 1978.

Motz, J. *Hands of Life*. Bantam Books, New York, 1998.

Myss, C. *Anatomy of the Spirit*. Harmony Books, New York, 1996.

O'Leary, A. Stress, Emotion, and Human Immune Function, *Psychological Bulletin* 108(3):363–382, 1990.

Ornish, D. *Dr. Dean Ornish's Program for Reversing Heart Disease.* Random House, New York, 1990.

Pare, W. P. Stress Ulcer Susceptibility and Depression in Wistar Kyoto (WKY) Rats, *Physiology and Behavior* 46(6):993–998, 1989.

Pearsall, P. *The Heart's Code.* Broadway Books, New York, 1998.

Pelletier, K. The Best Alternative Medicine: What Works? What Does Not? Simon & Schuster, New York, 2000.

Pelletier, K. Between Mind and Body, Stress, Emotions and Health in *Mind Body Medicine,* ed. Goleman, Daniel. Consumer Reports Books, Yonkers, N.Y., 1993.

Pelletier, K. Life with a New Roommate: Alternative Medicine Moves in with Conventional Medicine. *Healthcare Forum Journal,* November/December, 35–37, 41, 1998.

Pelletier, K. *Mind as Healer, Mind as Slayer.* Dell, New York, 1972.

Pellietier, K. Personal Communication, September 20, 2000.

Pelletier, K. *Toward a Science of Consciousness.* Celestial Arts, Berkeley, CA, 1985.

Pelletier, K. and Herzing, D. Psychoneuroimmunology: Toward a Mind-Body Model, *Advances* 5(1):27–56, 1988.

Pert, C. B. Neuropeptides: The Emotions and Bodymind, *Noetic Sciences Review* 2:13–18, 1987.

Pert, C. B. Personal Communication, December 18, 1991.

Pert, C. B. The Wisdom of the Receptors: Neuropeptides, the Emotions, and Bodymind, *Advances* 3(3):8–16, 1986.

Pert, C. B. *Molecules of Emotion: Why You Feel the Way You Feel.* Scribner, New York, 1997.

Pert, C. B. et al. Neuropeptides and Their Receptors: A Psychosomatic Network, *Journal of Immunology* 135 (2 suppl.): 820s–826s, 1985.

Pert, C. B. Dreher, H., and Ruff, M. The Psychosomatic Network: Foundations of Mind-Body Medicine. *Alternative Therapies in Health and Medicine* 4(4):30–40, 1998.

Pfaffenrath, V., Wermuth, A., and Pollmann, W. Tension Headache: A Review, *Fortschritte der Neurologie Psychiatrie* 56(12):407–422, 1988.

Rabin, B. et al. Bidirectional Interaction between the Central Nervous System and the Immune System, *Critical Review Immunology* 9:279–312, 1989.

Rein, G. As Reported in Vibrational Medicine for the 21st Century by Richard Gerber. Eagle Brook, New York, 2000. Page 375.

Rose-Neil, S. The Work of Professor Kim Bong Han, *Acupuncturist* 1:15, 1967.

Roundtree, R. with Carol Coleman. *Immunotics.* Putnam Books, New York, 2000.

Rubik, B. Energy Medicine and the Unifying Concept of Information, *Alternative Therapies.* 1(1):34–39, 1995.

Saibil, F. *Chron's Disease and Ulcerative Colitis.* Firefly Books, New York, 1997.

Schleifer, S. et al. Suppression of Lymphocyte Stimulation Following Bereavement, *JAMA* 250(3):374–377, 1983.

Schwartz, J. Cell Phones May Have Cancer Link, The Washington Post, Saturday, May 22, 1999.

Seaward, B. L. Alternative Medicine Complements Standard, Health Progress 75(7):52–57, 1994.

Shealy, C. N., and Myss, C. *The Creation of Health.* Stillpoint Press, Walpole, NH, 1993.

Siegel, B. *Love, Medicine, and Miracles.* Perennial Library, New York, 1986.

Smith, E. M., Harbour-McMenamin, D., and Blalock, J. E. Lymphocyte Production of Endorphins and Endorphin-Mediated Immunoregulatory Activity, *Journal of Immunology* 135:779s–782s, 1985.

Spiegel, D. Healing Words; Emotional Expression and Disease Outcome, *JAMA* 281(14):1328, 1999.

Sternberg E. *The Balance Within:* The Science Connecting Health & Emotions. W.H. Freeman, New York, 2000.

Straley, C. Is Stress Hurting Your Skin? Parents Magazine, Nov.: 93, 1999.

Talbot, M. *The Holographic Universe,* HarperCollins, New York, 1990.

Tasner, M. TMJ, *Medical Self-Care,* November/December: 47–50, 1986.

Tecoma, E., and Huey, L. Psychic Distress and the Immune Response, *Life Sciences* 36(19):1799–1812, 1985.

Temoshok, L. Personality, Coping Style, Emotion, and Cancer: Towards an Integrative Model, *Cancer Surveys* 6:545–567, 1987.

Tucker, L., Cole, G., and Freidman, G. Stress and Serum Cholesterol: A Study of 7000 Adult Males, *Health Values* 11: 34–39, 1987.

Ubell, E. Soon, We Won't Have to Worry About Ulcers, *Parade Magazine,* April 2: 18–19, 1995.

Part II
The Mind and Soul

"To thine own

self be true."

-William Shakespeare

Chapter 4 Toward a Psychology of Stress

Modern man is sick because

he is not whole.

—Carl Gustav Jung

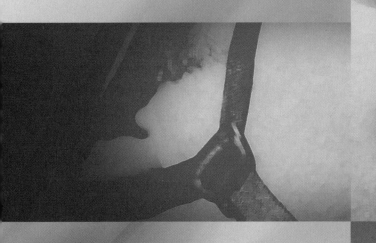

For centuries scientists have debated the relationship between the mind and the brain. Is the mind a function of the brain, a series of biochemical reactions, or is the mind a complex dynamic of consciousness: a separate entity unto itself that uses the brain as its primary organ of choice? This question has polarized researchers to believe either that all thoughts and feelings can be explained as neurochemical messages transmitted from brain cell to brain cell; or that the mind exists separately from the brain yet somehow is housed and fused with it. This one question, perhaps more than any other, initiated the discipline of psychology at the turn of the twentieth century. As the mind-body connection is more closely examined with regard to the stress response, it becomes increasingly clear that the mind is a very complex phenomenon, and not merely a by-product of neurochemical interactions. The interactions of thoughts, emotions, behaviors, and personality traits—the mind is held accountable for all of them. In this chapter, we will look at how the mind perceives stress so that the "antiquated" stress response can be updated or recircuited, highlighting some specific aspects of the psychology of stress. (Chapters 5 and 6 will address the stress emotions and stress-prone and stress-resistant personalities in more detail.)

Since the advent of the discipline of psychology, many notable figures have made significant contributions to the understanding of the mind, specifically, those regarding personality, emotions, perceptions, and a whole realm of human behaviors. From these individuals have come a host of theories attempting to interpret the complexities of emotional wellbeing on which stress has so great an influence. These theories have been inspired by such questions as, Why does the mind perceive some events as threatful? and, What cognitive mechanisms are used to deal with psychological stress? Although no one theorist seems to explain the psychological aspects of stress in its totality, together these theories at least begin to address several issues involved. The following psychiatrists, psychologists, and therapists offer some of the greatest insights into the mind's role in the psychology of stress.

Freud and the Egg

Because of their profound influence on the field of psychology (perhaps more than those of any other individual), the works of Sigmund Freud are chosen by many scholars as the reference point from which all other psychological theories emanate. Most recognized for his concepts of conscious and unconscious thought and their associations to sexual drive, Freud established the groundwork for understanding human behavior. Specifically, he made tangible the abstract concepts of emotional thought processes and the constructs of

Figure 4.1 Sigmund Freud

personality. From Freud's perspective, humans operate from an instinctual nature, or those biological and physiological impulses he referred to as the id. These impulses aim to satisfy the body's immediate needs. In Freud's opinion, there is a constant instinctual tension between body and mind as the mind attempts to cater to these impulses in socially acceptable ways. This internal tension can be decreased, but because of the power of human instincts, it is never fully extinguished. Consequently, Freud believed that humans have some degree of *innate* stress.

Freud developed a wonderful metaphor to illustrate the intangible complexities of the human psyche. He compared the mind's innermost thoughts, memories, and feelings, components that make up one's identity, to an egg (Fig. 4.2). Like the contents of an egg, the human psyche is extremely delicate and fragile. And like an egg it is enclosed and protected by a sturdy yet quite vulnerable shell. According to Freud, the primary purpose of the ego is to seek pleasure and to avoid pain with regard to our biological impulses (a function now thought to be similar to that of the hypothalamus). That is, the ego is primarily responsible for controlling the flood of impulses from the id. The ego is also vulnerable to perceptions of outside stimuli, which constantly threaten the stability of the contents within. This too, he observed, produces tension.

The metaphor of the egg and Freud's theory of the function of the ego have been useful to comprehend the environmental balance of the mind, specifically in terms of cognitive stress-management strategies. Understanding that stress or anxiety is aroused simultaneously by internal impulses and perceived outside stimulation (threats) means that the protection of identity (ego) is critical to survival. As if a missile were headed for the White House, anxiety triggers the mind's alarm system, signifying imminent danger to the existence of the ego. Defense systems are immediately activated. Should these defenses fail to function properly, panic and disaster ensue. Through his work with mentally and physically ill patients, Freud observed enough stress-related behaviors to credit excessive anxiety (unknown fears that penetrate the ego's shell and produce pain) and inadequate defenses with the primary roles in the development of neurotic and psychotic behavior.

According to Freud, the mind's defense system consists of a host of thought processes, or **defense**

Figure 4.2

Freud compared the abstract human psyche to an egg. Instinctual tension is always present, Freud believed, because the id constantly releases impulses. These, along with external stimuli, threaten the integrity of the ego, which must protect itself with what Freud termed defense mechanisms.

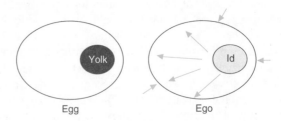

mechanisms, to aid in the protection of the ego's fragile contents. They act to shield the contents from harm by minimizing the impact of perceived threats. From his perspective, defense mechanisms are a collection of coping strategies to deal with stress. Because of both constant inner tension produced by instinctual impulses and stressfully perceived external stimuli, Freud believed that defense mechanisms must always be in operation to some extent. Thus, he was convinced that all behavior is defensive in nature. Freud theorized that all defense mechanisms share two characteristics: (1) they are denials or distortions of reality, and (2) they operate unconsciously. Furthermore, an individual rarely uses just one defense mechanism. Rather, each person employs a variety of ego-protecting mechanisms overall, and usually several at the same time. Freud postulated a number of defense mechanisms, including denial, repression, projection, rationalization, reaction formation, regression, displacement, sublimation, and humor. The following are most commonly used in the defense of stress-produced anxiety:

1. *Denial.* When people are confronted with circumstances they find to be a threat, they often deny association or involvement with any aspect of the situation. Young children are often caught in the act of lying (denial) when they are accused of eating cookies right before dinner or making a mess in the bathroom. Examples in adulthood include denying a drinking or gambling problem. Any stimulus perceived to be a threat to the integrity of one's

identity can push the button to deny involvement or knowledge. At a conscious level, the person truly believes he or she is innocent and sees nothing wrong with the behavior.

2. *Repression.* Repression is the involuntary removal of thoughts, memories, or feelings from the conscious mind. It differs from suppression, wherein painful experiences are intentionally forgotten, in that the conscious mind is unaware of this process. Freud referred to repression as an unconscious denial of something that brings emotional discomfort or pain. Examples are memories of unpleasant family holidays, child abuse, or embarrassing moments you cannot seem to recall even when friends and family tell you in fine detail what you did.

3. *Projection.* Projection is a process in which an individual defends the ego by attributing unacceptable feelings, impulses, and behaviors to other people—or objects such as dogs, tennis racquets, swim goggles, or the weather. In this way, when an impulse or emotion is manifested, it is now less threatening because its source appears to be generated externally rather than from within. Ownership of painful feelings is minimized. According to Freud, projection is most prevalent in response to feelings of sexual desire, insecurities, and aggression. An example of projection is oversleeping, getting a late start for work, getting caught in traffic, and then blaming every dumb driver for your lateness.

4. *Rationalization.* Rationalization is the reinterpretation of the reality of one's behavior or circumstances. It's a manipulation of the truth. Rationalization can be described as a filtered lens that makes emotional pain more acceptable, even appealing, to one's emotional vision. Actions or thoughts that are perceived to be threatening are quickly reinterpreted in terms of another, more acceptable, rational explanation. For example, someone who has been fired from a job he loved might rationalize this outcome by saying, "It was an awful job and I'm glad to be done with it." Another example would be when your

boyfriend breaks up with you and you tell friends you wanted to break it off because the relationship was too great a time commitment.

5. *Displacement.* When something that causes pain to the ego is inaccessible or otherwise cannot be responded to directly, the painful feelings can be transferred to an unrelated person or object. This is what Freud called displacement. Displacement involves transferring emotional pain and its related behavior from an unacceptable object (e.g., an authority figure) to a nonthreatening object (usually children and pets). For example, your boss is a jerk and you would love to choke him, but instead you go home and shoo away the cat who begs for attention. Even though feelings of anger and aggression are most commonly cited as those that are displaced, it is also possible to displace feelings and behaviors associated with joy and love to those you perceive to be most receptive to them, rather than those you believe would not respond favorably.

6. *Humor.* Later in his career, Freud began to study the psychology of humor and jokes. Reviewing the works of several humorists, he was at first perplexed at the phenomenon but soon saw it as a device for the body to release sexually repressed thoughts through laughter. This is the rationale he proposed to explain the popularity of "dirty" jokes. Humor, remarked Freud, is a unique defense mechanism unlike the others. It simultaneously decreases pain and increases pleasure, making it the most advanced of all the defense mechanisms (see Chapter 12).

These are but six of the many defense mechanisms Freud believed are most commonly used in response to anger and fear. Each mechanism, used to protect our identity, is a camouflage of reality. The ego perceives uncamouflaged threatening stimuli as attacks on the existence of our innermost feelings, perceptions, values, beliefs, and attitudes, so protection is often necessary, especially for children in the early stages of growth and development. However, overprotection of the ego can ultimately be as dangerous to the maturation process as lack of adequate protection. Overprotection usually results in the inhibition of emotional growth and maturation of the individual's mental and emotional boundaries, a situation analogous to a houseplant rootbound by too small a pot. When anxiety or a perceived threat enters the walls of the ego, emotional pain results. With a less defensive attitude, however, this pain can enable the individual to expand his or her self-awareness and personal growth. In this case, the result is an expansion of the ego. Each time this "space" grows, therein lies an opportunity to expand one's capabilities and enhance one's human potential. It may not seem that stress always involves the ego, but in truth, it really does. Our ego is *our identity,* and whether it is fear or anger that triggers the stress response, things that cause stress typically attack the integrity of our identity and perceptions of self-worth. Freud's coping mechanisms are the front-line defense. The degree to which defense mechanisms are innate or learned behavior has yet to be decided. Perhaps because Freud understood anxiety to be an inseparable part of the individual, he left no substantial advice on minimizing it, short of psychoanalysis. Despite varying opinions of his work, Freud's theories of personality have become so well acknowledged, if not respected, it is not uncommon to find strong parallels in the concepts of other theorists.

Jung and the Iceberg

The theories of Freud inspired many physicians to investigate the new clinical field of the psyche and human behavior. One such physician was Carl Gustav Jung of Switzerland, who was hand-picked by Freud to be his "heir apparent" and champion his theories. During the close collaboration of the two, Jung began to voice disagreement with some of Freud's theoretical concepts. As a result, their professional (as well as personal) relationship quickly eroded. Although Jung and Freud parted company in their opinions of the mysteries of the mind, Jung has become respected as the second greatest influence on modern psychological thought. His theories involving introversion and extroversion, personality types (inspiring the Myers-Briggs Type Inventory), midlife crisis, synchronicity, anima-animus, archetypes, the shadow, and the spiritual nature of humankind sowed many seeds in the human potential movement (see Chapter 7), and his

Figure 4.3

Carl Gustav Jung *Figure 4.4*

following continues to grow both within and outside the field of psychology.

Unlike Freud, who postulated that humans act by instincts, biological forces, and childhood experiences, Jung theorized human personality as a process

Figure 4.5 Jung compared the mind to an iceberg. That which is above the water represents the conscious mind, while that below represents all unconscious thought processes. Despite the fact that the unconscious mind may appear dormant at the conscious level, Jung theorized that it is perpetually active.

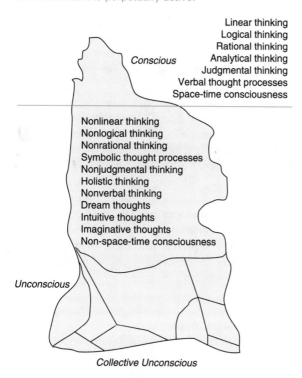

Conscious

Linear thinking
Logical thinking
Rational thinking
Analytical thinking
Judgmental thinking
Verbal thought processes
Space-time consciousness

Nonlinear thinking
Nonlogical thinking
Nonrational thinking
Symbolic thought processes
Nonjudgmental thinking
Holistic thinking
Nonverbal thinking
Dream thoughts
Intuitive thoughts
Imaginative thoughts
Non-space-time consciousness

Unconscious

Collective Unconscious

while Freud placed less importance on aspects of the unconscious mind, Jung focused his life work on this construct, particularly in his empirical research on dreams as a means to enhance the individuation process.

Jung likened the human mind to an iceberg (Fig. 4.5). Metaphorically speaking, the conscious mind is represented by the tip above the water, while the unconscious, the greatest percentage of the mind, lies below the water. (To Jung's credit, scientists now believe that people use only 10 percent of their mental capacity, about the same proportion as that of an iceberg above the water.) The conscious mind, with its limited awareness, focuses on specific thoughts, which compete for attention (e.g., What should I have for dinner tonight? How will I be able to afford a new car? What time is it? Will he ask me to the formal?). The unconscious mind is the receptacle for ideas, images, and concepts the conscious mind has no room to hold, as well as repressed thoughts, memories, and a host of undiscovered thoughts of enlightenment. Jung divided the unconscious mind into two levels. The first layer, the level he referred to as the personal unconscious, is the repository of the thoughts, perceptions, feelings, and memories of the individual; everything dropped from the attention of the conscious mind. However obscure these ideas, feelings, and perceptions may be, they do not cease to exist, and in fact continue to influence conscious thought and behaviors. The second level Jung called the **collective unconscious**, a profound and potentially inexhaustible reservoir of human thoughts and ideas integrated with ancient wisdom, which he claimed is essentially passed down from generation to generation, not unlike physical characteristics genetically passed down through generations of humanity. Jung believed that although this level was more difficult to access, the resources in this reservoir were invaluable in aiding the self-discovery process.

Jung believed that the passage of thoughts from the conscious to the unconscious mind is quite easy when compared to the difficult migration of intuitive or suppressed thoughts and dream images trying to surface to conscious attention. From Jung's viewpoint, consciousness naturally rejects anything unknown and unfamiliar. Consequently, the threshold of consciousness, like the membrane of a cell,

of self-discovery and realization, a concept he referred to as **individuation.** Individuation involves not only the culmination of childhood experiences but a spiritual life force that shapes one's being and life direction. Jung was convinced that self-awareness and a quest for a greater understanding of the self enhance the process of individuation, helping one navigate through the difficult passages of life. This ability to soul-search, to wrestle with personal issues, and to further the understanding of one's life purpose, he believed, augmented psychological health. On the other hand, reluctance, avoidance, and indolence contribute to self-ignorance and perpetuate the stress associated with underutilized inner resources. Jung also disagreed with Freud's notion that human behavior is driven primarily by sexual impulses. And acts as a barrier, censoring material from the uncon-scious mind that seems irrelevant, incoherent, inane, or ego-bruising.

From the analysis and interpretation of his own dreams as well as thousands of dreams of his patients, Jung discovered that the conscious and unconscious minds speak two different languages. The conscious mind communicates through very linear, rational, analytical, and verbal processes. Conversely, the processes of the unconscious mind are nonlinear, irra-tional, intuitive, and non-time-oriented processes rep-resented through dreams in symbols and vivid colors. (It is interesting to note that Nobel Prize–winning research by Roger Sperry et al. has documented a sim-ilar division of cognitive functions in the left brain and right brain, respectively.) If you reflect on some of your own dreams you may recall images that seem absurd—swimming in red air, a herd of elk grazing in the attic, or a conversation with a college buddy and a highschool sweetheart who in real life are thousands of miles apart and have never even met.

In Jung's view, daily stress is compounded by internal tension between the seemingly incompatible thought processes of the two minds. Contrary to pop-ular belief, the unconscious mind is not dormant dur-ing the waking hours of conscious thought. It is open to sensory stimulation and thought processes, just as the conscious mind is. Moreover, the unconscious mind acts as a navigator for the driver of the conscious mind. Yet in many cases the two are worlds apart in the front seat of the same car, with the conscious mind in a dominant role, charting its own course. In the dream state, however, the unconscious mind both navigates and drives, working to resolve issues raised in the course of the day. Confusion arises when the unconscious presents resolutions in dream symbols that the conscious mind passes off as ludicrous or unimportant. To the conscious mind, dreams hold lit-tle significance if there is no overt understanding, yet in Jung's opinion they continually offer impeccable insight to the problem-solving process.

To understand the concept of the unconscious bet-ter, imagine that while driving in a foreign country you become lost and stop to ask directions from people who speak no English. You do not speak a word of their native tongue either. They try to warn you that the road you are on is unsafe, but even their pantomimes are unclear. You proceed and encounter the same situation with more natives a mile down the road. Baffled and discouraged, you shake your head, ignoring the warn-ings and continuing to drive on into potential danger.

Similarly, Jung proposed that internal tension develops at the interface of the conscious and uncon-scious minds due to the inability of these two entities to communicate effectively. In an attempt to minimize this tension, Jung explained that the conscious mind acts as a censoring mechanism that limits access to unconscious thought processes trying to bubble up from below. This explains why many people initially cannot recall their dreams, nor make sense of them if they do remember them. Although the censoring process may seem effective in the short term, the inability to decipher the language of the unconscious perpetuates internal stress in the long run.

New languages may be difficult to master at first, but with practice comes fluency. According to Jung, the conscious mind can be trained to interpret the dream symbols created by the unconscious mind by manipulating and playing with these images. Based on five decades of dream analysis, Jung made the follow-ing observations about dreams:

1. Dreams should be treated as fact, not as fabrications of the mind.
2. Dreams have a definite and purposeful idea or theme expressed in unique symbols.
3. Dreams make sense when time is devoted to understand their meaning.
4. Recurring dreams may represent a traumatic life event, an attempt to compensate for a personal defect in attitude, or signal an event of importance in the future.
5. Dream interpretation is individualistic in that no dream symbol can be separated from the person who dreams it (e.g., the meaning of a plane crash is specific to the person who dreamed it).
6. Dream interpretation is essential to the resolution of stress and anxiety. In his last published book, *Man and His Symbols,* Jung wrote, "For the sake of mental stability and even physiological health, the unconscious and the conscious minds must be integrally connected and thus move in parallel lines."

Jung's concept of individuation emphasized the importance of self-reflection: quality time spent in

Stress With a Human Face

PATTIE IS A MIDDLE-SCHOOL TEACHER WHO is currently working on her master's degree in psychology at the University of Northern Colorado. One day, after hearing a lecture on dreams and dream therapy, she became very intrigued with the notion of accessing the wisdom of the unconscious mind through dream interpretation. It didn't take long for her to decide the focus of her term paper for this course. It would be on the study of dreams and dream therapy.

Like most people, Pattie confides that she doesn't remember her dreams, yet knowing that all people have dreams, she was curious to learn more about herself and what wisdom would be revealed to her by making a more concerted effort to remember her dreams. The research paper became a catalyst for self-exploration.

Based on information she researched, Pattie knew that it was possible to train the conscious mind to remember dreams and uncode the language of dream symbols. She bought a notebook specifically to record her dreams and made a habit of practicing a relaxation technique before she went to bed, a technique she noted as an important step in the dream therapy process. Just as one would learn any skill, the first few attempts to record dreams were fruitless, but Pattie persisted.

One night, after listening to a relaxation tape, Pattie fell asleep. When she awoke, she recalled having a dream so vivid, so real, that she remembered the entire dream sequence. Taking pen in hand, Pattie recorded the dream in her notebook.

"I dreamt I was in my classroom and a student came by and popped her head in the door and smiled. She was much older than my typical students and, although I didn't recognize her, I knew her. In analyzing the dream, I came to understand that she was actually a composite of several former students, and her appearance in my door was a message. She had come back to tell me that my teaching had had a positive influence on her life, and her smile to me was an acknowledgment of her gratitude. I interpreted her visit as a vote of confidence in my teaching skills and the dream served as a reminder that my job is worthwhile, and my work is having a positive impact on my students.

"Through my research I really learned how valuable dream therapy is to people with post-traumatic stress disorder (PTSD), and through my own experience I learned how valuable dream interpretation is. It has had a positive impact on my life."

In describing her dream experience, she added, "I would like to pass along a quote from Carl Jung: 'No dream symbol can be separated from the individual who dreams it, and there is no definite or straightforward interpretation of any dream.'" ✦

---

solitude dedicated to expanding one's conscious awareness as well as learning the language and wisdom of the unconscious mind. His travels to the Orient, during which he studied the concepts behind meditation, reinforced his belief that self-reflection was essential to mental health. Jung was convinced that when you take the time to examine the depths of your own mind, a unity of conscious and unconscious thought processes occurs, which helps you to resolve personal issues and leads to a greater sense of inner peace. This unity he called **psychic equilibrium**.

To assist his patients toward the goal of psychic balance, Jung employed what he called **active imagination**. This is a process where, during a conscious yet relaxed state, an individual uses creativity to manipulate dream fragments and complete the dream experience. This technique is most useful with recurring dreams, where the dreamer gives a desired ending to the neglected issues represented in these unfinished stories. Active imagination has been adapted to many coping and relaxation techniques alike, including mental imagery, journal writing, and art therapy. Jung was of the firm opinion that sickness, both mental and physical, was the result of the inability to bridge the gap between conscious and unconscious minds as a way to share knowledge to resolve inner tensions. In fact, he was once quoted as saying, "Modern man is sick because he is not whole," with wholeness being a peaceful union of the conscious and unconscious minds.

Jung suggested that each individual become introspective and dive below the waters of the conscious mind to gain insight into the causes of specific anxiety and stress. Once this awareness is gained, the source of anxiety can be confronted and handled at the conscious level, where it can lead to resolution and strength of the spirit. Throughout his life Jung was devoted to the development of human potential, which begins with self-awareness. Many of Jung's followers have augmented and developed his concepts for application to psychotherapy, specifically dream therapy. All in all, Jung's theories are quite profound, and they invite us to continue the exploration of the mysteries of the mind.

With the groundwork established by Freud and Jung, other theories have been added throughout this century to the collective body of psychological knowledge. With each new insight we gain a stronger grasp of the psyche, particularly the influence that stress has on it. The following theories only begin to touch on aspects of emotions, behavior, and personality. Yet when combined with those of Freud and Jung, they give a wider perspective on the factors associated with the psychology of stress.

Elisabeth Kübler-Ross *Figure 4.6*

Elisabeth Kübler-Ross—The Death of Unmet Expectations

When the Social Readjustment Rating Scale was designed, it became obvious to its creators that the death of a spouse is the most stressful event a person can experience. The death and dying process, be it your own or that of someone you are close to, is very traumatic. Similarly, the death of any expectation is stressful. One person who brought the issue of death to the forefront of human consciousness is Elisabeth Kübler-Ross. A Swiss psychiatrist, Kübler-Ross stepped onto the global stage in 1969 with her pioneer work studying and counseling terminally ill cancer patients. Through her work she taught the world about the emotions and mental processes associated

with death. Her work was inspired by her experiences as a teenager assisting in first-aid stations in Poland and Russia after World War II with survivors of Nazi concentration camps. From the carnage of the war and the concentration camps, Kübler-Ross realized that humankind had a great need to understand and cope with the problems of death and dying. She soon learned that the fear of death is universal, and that the death and dying process brings with it an abundance of emotional baggage. Not only grief, but guilt, shame, fear, and anger are all associated with the death experience.

Relocating to the United States after earning her degree in psychiatry, she was asked to join a group of physicians conducting a research seminar involving interviews and counseling sessions with terminally ill cancer patients. In the course of this work, she noted similarities in the patterns of emotional behaviors among the patients, which led her to outline a process of mental preparation for death applicable to everyone.

In her most acclaimed book, *On Death and Dying,* Kübler-Ross refers to these stages as the psychological stages of grieving. Although these stages were observed among dying cancer patients, the same stages apply to any type of loss, including the death of unmet expectations. The following is a description of the five stages with examples she observed among her cancer patients. Also included are examples of how each stage applies to the death of an unmet expectation—a more common stressor—the discovery that one's wallet has been stolen.

1. *Denial* is the refusal to accept the truth of a situation; a rejection of the truth. Kübler-Ross observed denial in her patients who, upon learning of their diagnosis, were often heard to exclaim, "I don't have cancer. This isn't happening to me. It cannot happen to me. I'm too young to die. I won't let it happen." Denial is also described as shock. In the case of a stolen wallet, the comparable reaction would be observed, "My wallet must be at home. I couldn't have misplaced it. Perhaps it's in my other pants (pocketbook)."

2. *Anger.* The anger stage is a fit of rage that may include yelling, pounding, crying, and/or deep frustration manifested in a physical and emotional way. In this stage, anger is the physical expression of hostile feelings. Kübler-Ross typically saw anger directed not only at clinicians and family members but also toward a "higher power," even in those people who claimed not to believe in one. Similarly, a stolen wallet can provoke an outward expression of anger, where everyone becomes a suspect in its disappearance.

3. *Bargaining.* Kübler-Ross described this phase as a very brief but important one. Bargaining is an agreement between the conscious mind and the soul involving an exchange of offerings; primarily, a negotiation for more time to live. With cancer patients it may be expressed as, "If you let me live, I'll never smoke again." In the case of the stolen wallet, the negotiations would be something along the lines of, "Go ahead and take the money—but please don't use my credit cards."

4. *Depression.* Kübler-Ross divides the depression stage into two categories: reactive depression,

when a patient grieved for a specific anatomical loss resulting from surgery (as with breast or bone cancer), and preparatory loss, feelings of impending losses related to the cancer, including personal freedom, time, family, and perhaps one's own life. Preparatory-loss depression is best described as a quiet or passive mood of uneasiness while feeling overwhelmed with thoughts and responsibilities at the same time. With depression there is very little, if any, perceived hope. In the case of the wallet, not only is there depression over the missing article but also a feeling of being overwhelmed by having to arrange the replacement of its contents.

5. *Acceptance.* If and when a person has moved through the previous stages of the grieving process, then and only then can he or she arrive at the final stage, acceptance. Acceptance is an approval of existing conditions; a receptivity to things that cannot be changed. Acceptance is *not* giving in or giving up. It is *not* a surrender to the circumstance. Rather, it is acknowledgment of the particular situation in which you find yourself. Acceptance allows you to move on with your life. With acceptance comes hope. For those cancer patients who arrive at this stage, their frame of mind can be described as, "Ok. So this is the way it is. I'm going to keep living my life as best I can. I'm going to put up a good fight." In the case of the stolen wallet, "So I lost my wallet. I'll get a new license, credit cards, ATM card, and a new wallet." In the acceptance stage there is no trace of anger or pity. Kübler-Ross indicates that this stage is very difficult to arrive at; and in fact, many people never reach this stage in the course of their grieving.

Kübler-Ross states that these stages are experienced by virtually every terminally ill patient. By no coincidence, these same stages are observed, to a greater or lesser degree, among people who go through other losses, including relationships (the end of a romantic relationship, divorce, or separation), identity (unemployment, retirement, new location, or new job), possessions (a lost/stolen wallet, damaged car, or fire-damaged house), as well as less tangible items (a failed exam, poor athletic performance, etc.). Actually, it could be the loss of anything significant. This mental-preparation-for-death process happens hundreds of times in one's lifetime. As Kübler-Ross explains, the stress associated with the mental stages is a catalyst to provide a greater mental awareness of several or all unresolved emotions. As an individual passes from one stage to the next, he or she enters a deeper level of mental awareness. In recent years, Kübler-Ross has amended her original theory to suggest that, in some cases, one of the first four stages may be skipped. She has devoted her whole life mission to assisting people so that they may complete this final stage peacefully.

To paraphrase Kübler-Ross, acceptance is your ability to acknowledge the emotional chains that bind you to your primary cause of stress, and acceptance allows you to free yourself from their bondage. Complete, unconditional acceptance, a full resolution without any resentment, animosity, or pity associated with these emotional potholes, leads to what Kübler-Ross calls essential inner peace. The process of acceptance, resolving pent-up feelings or frustrations, is not an easy one. In fact, it can be quite emotionally painful. In her work, she observed some people with a stubborn streak who would rather leave matters unresolved than face the fear of this process. Others were unsure how best to resolve these emotions and eventually became hostage to them.

Typically, individuals repress or rationalize painful feelings that are perceived to be a threat to their inner self. As Kübler-Ross notes, the defense mechanisms of the ego serve, function, and manipulate well on a short-term basis but cause utter chaos in the long run. Through repression and rationalization, unresolved feelings, like phases of the moon, come full circle and ultimately resurface to haunt the conscious mind. To leave these emotional debts unresolved is what she refers to as the unfinished business of the soul. Kübler-Ross suggests that the process of addressing and completing unresolved feelings should not be delayed; rather, it should take top priority on a daily basis. The best way to initiate this resolution process, she says, is to grant yourself some quality "alone time" to learn to recognize unresolved feelings between yourself and others, and perhaps most importantly within yourself, then attempt to resolve them. There may be several strategies for resolution,

including accepting a situation that is unchangeable and continuing to live with this fact. In any case, without a doubt, unconditional acceptance promotes inner peace.

Viktor Frankl—A Search for Life's Meaning

Stressors come in all shapes and sizes. Little problems, like small potholes on a dirt road, are easily avoided, but major stressors obstruct your progress in the journey of life and can stop you dead in your tracks. Whatever the events in your life you perceive as stressful, few, if any, can match the intensity of the suffering experienced by psychiatrist Viktor Frankl as a Nazi concentration camp prisoner and survivor. Frankl's experiences prior to and during his three years in Auschwitz led him to the development of a form of psychoanalysis he refers to as **logotherapy,** an existential analysis simply defined as a search for the meaning of life.

In his most acclaimed book, *Man's Search for Meaning,* Frankl illustrates the depth of human suffering in the Nazi concentration camps. From this basis of personal experience and observation, he augmented his understanding of the human quest for the meaning of existence. Having been stripped of every possible possession including clothes, jewelry, even hair, camp prisoners were left with what Dr. Frankl calls the last human freedom: "the ability to choose one's attitude in a given set of circumstances." Of the prisoners who were fortunate enough to avoid the gas chambers and crematoriums, Dr. Frankl noted that it was largely the ability to choose one's attitude that ultimately distinguished those who lived from those who later perished from disease and illness in the concentration camps. Those who found and held onto a reason to live were able to survive the ghastly conditions, while those who saw no substantial meaning for living became physically and spiritually weak and succumbed to death.

Much of Frankl's psychological theories center around the concept of human pain and the meaning of suffering. Unequivocally, suffering is a direct consequence of profound stress. One does not have to experience the horrors of Auschwitz to feel suffering. Any experience that promotes feelings of emotional trauma, according to Frankl, contains the essence of a

Figure 4.7 Viktor Frankl

purposeful meaning. The death of a child, severe illness, retirement, a change of jobs—these are all candidates for inducing personal suffering. Frankl was convinced that suffering is as much a part of life as happiness and love, and that like love, suffering has a purpose in the larger scheme of things. From his own observations, Frankl realized that suffering is a universal experience. Therefore, he reasoned, it must have some significant value to the advancement of one's human potential or spiritual evolution. In *Man's Search for Meaning* he writes, "If there's meaning in life then there must be meaning in suffering. Suffering is an ineradicable part of life, and death. Without suffering and death, human life would not be complete." Frankl did not advocate avoiding suffering, but rather suggested that the cause of emotional pain be examined to try to make some rational sense out of it; to find a meaningful purpose in suffering. This search for meaning is not a defense mechanism, a rationalization

of pain, but the search for a truthful understanding. In fact, writes Frankl, meaning is not a fabrication of the mind, but a truth uncovered by the soul.

A tool to augment the search for meaning, as defined by Frankl, is **tragic optimism.** Tragic optimism he defined as the ability to turn suffering into a meaningful experience, and to learn from this experience with a positive perspective on life's events. The history of humanity is filled with inspiring examples of people who completed their grieving by finding meaning in their stressful suffering. One such person was Candy Lightner, who after losing her young daughter to the recklessness of a drunk driver, assembled her creative energies and formed the national organization Mothers Against Drunk Drivers (MADD). Another example is Jim Abbott, who overcame the mental anguish of a birth defect (no right forearm or hand) to earn a position as a pitcher on the 1984 Olympic baseball team. In fact, many contemporary heroes and role models are individuals who overcame obstacles of biblical proportions, and soon became the epitome of human potential in action for others to emulate.

Finding meaning in a painful experience is not easy. Frankl notes that many people in contemporary society look upon victimization as more prestigious than personal achievement. Quite often people tend to wallow in self-pity beyond the point where it serves any beneficial purpose. So how does one begin a quest for the meaning of one's own life? Dr. Frankl suggests that the best time for this to occur is when you feel mental anguish or emotional suffering of any kind. When these conditions surface, you must journey into the garden of your soul and examine your conscious mind. A mental examination quite often leads to questioning your ideals and values, and testing your will to fulfill or abandon them. Dr. Frankl notes that the will to find meaning in most people is *supported* by something or someone, not based on faith alone. It is also important to note that each person must find his or her own unique meaning, not a universal one, nor can one be borrowed or adopted from others. In fact, as people age there will be many different meanings to be searched for and recognized in their lifetimes. And suffering awaits in between the periods of life's meanings.

Frankl was convinced that, to an extent, stress plays an important role in mental health. Like Freud and Jung, Frankl believed that internal tension was inevitable among humans, but he held that mental health is dependent on the tension that exists between past accomplishments and future endeavors. A lack of tension (boredom) is what he called an existential vacuum, a state of tension where the current meaning to life is as yet undiscovered. In his experience, this reason outnumbered all other reasons combined for bringing people to psychotherapy and counseling. Frankl coined the term "Noo-dynamics" to describe a process to resolve this existential vacuum by using the tension of boredom to search for life's meaning. Whereas Freud placed emphasis on childhood experiences, Frankl was concerned with the present and future as if to say, "So, what happened, happened. What are you going to do with your life now? Where are you headed from here? What new contribution can you make to humanity?" In logotherapy, Frankl advocates the concept of goal-setting to aid in the search for personal meaning in one's life. Setting and accomplishing goals involve creativity to visualize where you are going, and stamina, the energy to get you there. The fundamental purpose of personal goals, Frankl states, is to enhance one's human potential. Furthermore, pleasure should be a consequence of meaning, not a purpose in and of itself. Frankl also suggests that a quest for true meaning has a spiritual quality to it (*logos* in Greek translates not only as "meaning" but "spirit"). In this case, however, the term *spirituality* has less of a formal-religious connotation; rather, it refers to the human dimension of inner balance between faith in self-reliance and individual will. Spiritual health is imperative in the search for one's own meaning in life and in dealing with the suffering brought about by various life experiences, regardless of their cause. In his autobiography, Frankl spoke of those who, in the midst of a crisis, lost their belief in the future, in themselves, and their spiritual hold. Without spiritual health they were subject to mental and physical deterioration and eventual premature death.

Although Frankl's theories may seem rather abstract, the fundamental messages are clear: (1) one must continually search from within for life's meaning to achieve inner peace, and (2) in the absence of everything but one's body, mind, and soul, one has the ability to choose one's attitudes; in so doing one either perpetuates or resolves each circumstance. He writes, "We had to learn from ourselves and we had to teach despairing men that it did not matter what we expected from life, but rather what life expected from us."

Learning to live in the present moment. (Reprinted with special permission of King Features Syndicate.) *Figure 4.8*

Wayne Dyer—Guilt and Worry

Relaxation is said to be achieved when the present moment is fully experienced and appreciated; this belief has been passed down for over 2,000 years by wise people of all cultures (Fig. 4.8). Yet for many people, the present moment is a scary and insecure place to be. Feelings of discomfort, boredom, and inadequacy arise. In the earliest years, all a child knows is the present moment. But as the child matures into adulthood, the ability to enjoy the present moment seems to become ever more elusive. Instead, the mind becomes willingly preoccupied (often paralyzed) with either past or future events. The fact that many people spend their conscious thought processes in either the past or future has not gone unnoticed. Psychotherapist Wayne Dyer has observed this phenomenon in virtually all his clients. His most present works integrate the mind and the soul, but his earliest work is as solid today as it was decades ago

In his best-selling book, *Your Erroneous Zones*, Dyer states that to be occupied with the past or

Figure 4.9 Wayne Dyer

The Sin of Guilt

Dyer defines guilt as the conscious preoccupation with undesirable past thoughts and behaviors. Guilt feelings surface in our internal but conscious dialogue in the form of "should haves." Guilt feelings can easily be produced by thinking about something you said or did just as easily as by something you didn't say or do but feel you should have. Dyer is of the opinion that guilt contains a perplexing element of cultural respect, like that recorded by those who fled religious persecution in Europe to become this nation's earliest settlers. Three hundred years later, guilt, he observes, is still a socially acceptable way to express the responsibility of caring. Yet true, productive caring, Dyer believes, should never be confused with this immobilizing emotion. When guilt is the overriding emotion, all thoughts and behaviors are influenced by it. Guilt is so powerful an emotion that it can have a paralyzing effect on all other thoughts and feelings and prevent a positive behavior or action from taking place. According to Dyer, guilt experienced to any extent can result in mild to severe depression. He states that, for the most part, guilt is fruitless because no amount of it can change the past. While guilt appears to be a "natural" human emotion, Dyer is convinced that it serves no functional purpose beyond fostering recognition of important lessons to be learned and issues to be resolved. If and when these lessons are learned, guilt disappears.

From observations he made counseling his clients, Dyer created a dichotomy of guilt. **Left-over guilt** he describes as remnant thought patterns originating in early childhood, primarily through parental disciplinary tactics as, for example, shame imposed by an authority figure for naughty or unapproved behaviors. What worked as an inspirational force during childhood (approval seeking to avoid guilt), however, produces significant stress when carried into adulthood, yet the same unhealthy behaviors are usually continued. By contrast, **self-imposed guilt** is described as the guilt placed on oneself when an adult moral or ethical behavior, based on the constructs of one's personal value system, has been violated. Examples are missing church on Sunday or saying yes to something because it seemed like the right thing to say, then later regretting having agreed to it because you were never committed to it. Dyer notes that guilt is also used as a conventional tool for

future can diminish, even extinguish, our appreciation of the present moment, thus robbing us of the ability to relax and be at peace with ourselves. The zones Dyer describes highlight certain stress-prone emotional responses; those unhealthy defensive processes learned very early in life as cognitive survival skills. In his theory of unproductive emotions and their related behaviors, Dyer states that one of two emotions, guilt or worry, is associated with virtually every stressor perceived by people in America. Guilt is an expression of self-anger; worry, a manifestation of fear. When these emotional responses are triggered, they tend to immobilize rational thought processes, resulting in clouded thinking, delayed reactions, and poor decision making. Dyer goes as far as to say that guilt and worry are in fact the most ineffective coping techniques for stress management because they perpetuate the avoidance of stress-related issues needing resolution.

manipulating other people's thoughts, feelings, and actions, a behavior that inappropriately transfers stress to others. He advocates avoiding using guilt and shame on others, and most important, avoiding using it on yourself.

The Art of Worrying

While guilt, like Dickens's Ghost of Christmas Past, is associated with keeping the mind hostage with thoughts and behaviors in the past, worry infiltrates the mind to immobilize thought processes regarding events yet to come. Dyer defines worry as the immobilization of thinking in the present moment as a result of preoccupation with things that may, or may not, occur in the future. Like guilt, Dyer notes that worry is looked on by many as an act of compassion. In reality, it too immobilizes cognition, clouds rational thought processes, and cultivates stress. The practice of worrying, like guilt, can lead to severe depression.

Dyer believes it is essential for everyone to distinguish the difference between worrying about the future and planning for the future. Worrying paralyzes and overrides present-moment thought processes and dilutes self-control. Then the imagination goes wild, creating a series of worst-case scenarios, all of which can seem very real and threatening. Dyer is convinced that worrying tends to produce a rebound effect, first resulting in a less effective means to deal with a given situation, which then produces more worry. Ironically, Dyer notes that people typically worry about matters over which they have no control. In addition, many seemingly insurmountable worries are later regarded as quite trivial (the making-a-mountain-out-of-a-molehill syndrome). Unfortunately, the knowledge of hindsight is ignored when worrying thoughts surface again. Unlike the worrying process, the constructive thought process of planning contributes to a more effective and productive future, minimizing potential stressors. Planning for the future, for example, by setting goals, making a strategy, and evaluating progress, provides a sense of empowerment.

To illustrate this difference, consider a person who worries about finding a job after graduation: he sits and stews about not finding a job and the hazards of being unemployed. Conversely, planning involves drafting a résumé, making phone calls, writing cover letters, networking, following up with contacts, and

Figure 4.10

making appointments. Although planning a strategy of options for future events does not guarantee a "smooth ride," it does provide a base of security, whereas worrying leaves one in the driver's seat with no keys, gas, or tires.

As mentioned earlier, Dyer suggests that American culture breeds the emotion of worry by equating it with caring and love. He discovered that many of his clients emphatically prove their love by demonstrating the worry process. Several other psychotherapists note a similarity between this characteristic and the stress-prone codependent personality (see Chapter 6).

What the emotions of guilt and worry share is the *distraction* of one's present mental processes. Both guilt and worry are what Dyer calls negative or nonproductive emotional states of cognition, and he confirms that these emotions are a waste of energy. As a therapist, Dyer counsels that the first step to removing these two erroneous zones is the awareness that they are used as ineffective coping techniques. When the practice of employing guilt or worry enters your awareness as a result of perceived stress, Dyer suggests removing guilt or worry by reframing your perception either to find the lessons to be learned from the past, or to start planning strategically for future events that are occupying your attention. Like other leading psychologists, Dyer advocates acceptance of past events as an important stress-management strategy to enable you to move on with your life. Dyer is in the company of several prominent psychologists and scholars who concur with his theories of guilt and worry, two emotions responsible for more visits to psychologists' offices than all others combined.

Since his first book, *Your Erroneous Zones,* Dyer has written several other best-selling books that focus on the theme of moving from a motivation of fear to a motivation of love. In his book *Your Sacred Self,* Dyer continues the theme of erroneous zones, with guilt and worry both manifestations of fear. Ultimately, Dyer says, the ego is the cause of these two "erroneous zones," and the sooner the ego is tamed, the sooner we move to a place of love.

Leo Buscaglia—The Lessons of Self-Love

Of all the psychological theories developed over the past century, most, if not all, have been influenced by anxiety as the primary force of human motivation. This narrow focus has eclipsed several equally motivating emotions, particularly love. By and large, science has remained reticent on this subject. To paraphrase the words of psychologist Abraham Maslow, "It's amazing how little time the empirical sciences have to offer on the subject of love." One might assume that the concept of love has been perceived to be either unimportant or too complex an emotion to adequately define and study. Both assumptions hold elements of truth. In the past, love was left to poets, philosophers, actors, and songwriters to be explored, explained, and elaborated; psychology maintained a hands-off approach. While this approach still continues today, love as a viable motivational force and healing tool has recently moved out of the anthologies of poetry and Hollywood cinema and into classrooms, corporate board rooms, and operating rooms. Upon taking a closer look at the theory and application of this enigmatic emotion, love is now recognized as a powerful inner resource much too important to ignore. In simple terms, love is the epitome of eustress; its absence, distress.

One man to bring the theoretical concept of love into the respectable forum of academia was Dr. Leo Buscaglia. Buscaglia developed an experimental undergraduate course at the University of Southern California in the late 1960s called the "love class."

Through his investigations, he brought forth some simple yet profound concepts of this elusive emotion, with many implications for both eustress and distress. Furthermore, he gave credibility to a component of emotional wellbeing that had been long overlooked.

Buscaglia is quick to admit that love is very difficult to define. First and foremost, he states, "Love is a response to a learned group of stimuli and behaviors." An infant learns to love primarily through contact with his or her parents in the home environment. Love—specifically, self-love—is not innate, but taught. Yet, unlike many other subjects, it is taught neither in school nor in church. Buscaglia notes that as children we are taught to control our emotions (e.g., don't cry, stop laughing, wipe that smile off your face). As a result, the ability to express our emotions fully is denied, including the emotion of love. The emotional pain of rejection, or denied love, only compounds this inability. That is, ego defenses strengthen to prevent or minimize recurrences. As a child matures to adulthood, love often diminishes to the point of dormancy. Sadly enough, Buscaglia indicates, most of us never really learn to love at all. This, he believes, can have dangerous repercussions later in the growth process, when one forms lifelong relationships. And this may be the reason, he explains, why the divorce rate is hovering around 50 percent.

One reason why love is so hard to define, Buscaglia admits, is that so many people equate it with related concepts: sex, romance, attraction, needs, security, and attention. Love is also perceived to be comprised of a wide spectrum of feelings, including ecstasy, joy, irrationality, dissatisfaction, jealousy, and pain. In Buscaglia's opinion, however, there may be many degrees of love, from joy to grace, but there is only one love, that which leads to the positive growth process of self-discovery. Love is love, he proclaims. In his best-seller, *Love,* he writes, "for love and the self are one, and the discovery of either is the realization of both." Love brings with it change, and change requires adaptation, which like other types of stress can produce either pleasure or pain. Despite fairy-tale endings in which love conquers all with relative ease, Buscaglia repeatedly states that love takes much work, continuous work. There is much responsibility with love. Left unattended and unnurtured, it will evaporate and disappear. Buscaglia also compares love to knowledge, which you must have before you can teach it. Likewise, you must feel and experience love before you can share it. There are no exceptions.

In Buscaglia's words, "To love others, you must first love yourself," and this is no small feat. As youngsters, we experience some degree of love from our parents, yet self-love is rarely taught and thus remains a foreign concept to many people. In fact, self-love is misrepresented as egotistical selfishness and is strongly discouraged. Humbleness is advocated, but often at the risk of sacrificing self-love. The Christian ethic commands that you "love your neighbor as yourself"; however, Buscaglia observes that this equation is rarely balanced. Through his research, Buscaglia has found that most people are deficient in their capacity to love themselves unconditionally; and that they are restrained from expressing self-love by their low self-esteem. Moreover, he cites several deterrents to self-love. The greatest of these are the conditions we place on ourselves for self-acceptance, primarily physical appearance and capabilities; in short, everything that prevents perfection. A recurring pattern of "not completely liking myself because . . . " creates a negative-feedback system that perpetuates a lifetime of unhappiness. This phenomenon is more descriptively referred to as chronic stress, and it is associated with low **self-esteem.**

Buscaglia offers an alternative to this self-defeating attitude. He suggests that you take an honest look at yourself from within. Be prepared to openly accept all that there is to see, for better or worse, exclude nothing. From this honest look, begin to accept yourself as you really are. This means accepting all those qualities you cannot change (e.g., height, hair color, parents, etc.) while pushing the limits of those qualities that allow room for growth (e.g., creativity, humor, intellect, and love). Then, take the initiative to enhance those qualities that will help you reach your highest potential. In addition, Buscaglia emphasizes the need for each individual to focus on his or her individuality rather than aiming for conformity by comparing oneself to others. He coined the term the **X-factor** to symbolize a prized quality that makes each person special and unique. People need to focus on this quality to move toward unconditional self-acceptance and unconditional self-love.

In Buscaglia's quest for love, he has searched for every color of love's rainbow to comprehend and share his understanding of this often misused, misunderstood, and misacknowledged emotion. His attempts to understand the fundamental concepts of love have taken him to the shores of nearly every continent. Unlike the approach of Western culture, which is geared toward the achievement of happiness through external pleasures, Buscaglia has turned toward the East, adopting a philosophy that supports unconditional self-love. The philosophy of many Eastern cultures is one in which the individual focuses inward to understand him- or herself; and the continuous journey toward self-understanding yields inner peace. Inner peace, in turn, creates universal harmony. Harmony, in turn, promotes happiness. And happiness nurtures love. Buscaglia illustrates this concept with the Hindu greeting *namaste,* which literally translated means, "I honor the place in you where, if you are at peace with yourself, and I am at peace with myself, then there is only one of us."

Buscaglia argues that for love to be an inner resource it cannot lay dormant. It must be acted out and acted on continually. And for love to exist there must be a will or desire to love. The will to love is an attitude of choice. Poets, film directors, and song writers often make love seem too dynamic, distant, or elu-

Leo Buscaglia

Figure 4.11

sive, sometimes even unattractive. But love of the self begins and grows with positive feelings toward the self, which each person is capable of creating. Buscaglia's message of self-love is directly tied to self-esteem, for we value only those things we love and feel positively about. When we do not love ourselves completely, or place conditions on our self-love, our self-esteem is compromised and thus deflated. And low self-esteem makes us vulnerable to, and almost defenseless against, the perceptions of stress.

From all his research, Buscaglia makes six hypotheses regarding love as a motivating influence:

1. One cannot give what one does not possess. To give love you must possess love.
2. One cannot teach what one does not understand. To teach love you must comprehend love.
3. One cannot know what one does not study. To study love you must live in love.
4. One cannot appreciate what one does not recognize. To recognize love you must be receptive to love.

5. One cannot admit what one does not yield to. To yield to love, you must be vulnerable to love.
6. One cannot live what one does not dedicate oneself to. To dedicate yourself to love, you must be forever growing in love.

Buscaglia's attempt to validate love as a crucial component of human motivation has been met with both enthusiasm and apathy. His work is accepted by many professionals who implement his concepts in counseling and therapy with their clients, but for the most part, the topic today remains ignored by researchers. Be that as it may, the focus on love in psychology is slowly gaining momentum as the field of psychospirituality begins to unfold (see Chapter 7).

Abraham Maslow—The Art of Self-Actualization

Perhaps the most optimistic of all psychologists who have made contributions to modern psychology is Dr. Abraham Maslow. While his predecessors and contemporaries studied mentally ill, emotionally disturbed, and maladjusted individuals to form the basis of their theories of human behavior, Maslow chose to study examples of men and women who epitomized the height of human potential, individuals exhibiting the unique combination of creativity, love, self-reliance, confidence, and independence. Despite the atrocities of World War II, Maslow was convinced of the existence of a brighter side of human nature, and he became committed to the development of a theoretical construct to support this hypothesis of a humanistic approach to psychology. Maslow's faith in humankind led him to believe that by understanding individuals with positive personality characteristics and admirable traits, he could devise a framework to serve as a model for others to follow in their pursuit of self-improvement. Unlike other psychologists, who attempted to describe how personality and behavior are affected by stress, Maslow placed emphasis on personality traits, those reflections of inner resources that seem to help people cope with stress and achieve psychological health. In other words, certain personality traits he observed in this special collection of people combine to act as a buffer in personal confrontations with stress.

Figure 4.12 Abraham Maslow

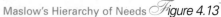

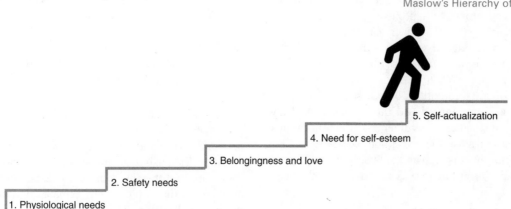

5. Self-actualization

4. Need for self-esteem

3. Belongingness and love

2. Safety needs

1. Physiological needs

Maslow's concept of behavior and personality is referred to as the **theory of motivation** for the nature of the characteristics he studied. This theory suggests that human beings operate on a hierarchy of needs that influence behavior. When the needs at one level are met, then needs at higher levels can be addressed in a linear, stair-step approach. In this hierarchy, the more advanced needs will not appear until lower needs have been acknowledged and addressed. In addition, when lower needs, such as hunger, reappear, all higher needs momentarily vanish.

This hierarchy of needs consists of five tiers or levels. Once described in terms of climbing a ladder, it is now usually illustrated as a series of steps (Fig. 4.13). The first tier is comprised of the most basic physiological needs to ensure survival of the human organism. These include food, sleep, and sex (and, in some cases, the need for drugs or alcohol when chemical dependency is involved). The second tier, safety needs, also contributes to survival and are those factors that provide security, order, and stability, including clothing, money, and housing. Maslow called these first two tiers lower, or deficit, needs, while the remaining levels of the hierarchy he referred to as growth needs. Affection and strong bonding relationships comprise the third stage, belongingness and love needs. The fourth tier he called personal esteem needs, or the need and desire to seek or prove self-worth. The final level Maslow called the need for self-actualization, a stage of personal fulfillment in which ego boundaries and attachments are virtually eliminated, and a feeling of oneness with the universe is experienced, thus allowing one to maxi-

mize one's human potential. Ideally, self-actualization is the fulfillment of one's highest human potential and capabilities. Maslow writes in *Religions, Values, and Peak Experiences,* "Self-actualization is the point where one is ultimately at peace with oneself."

According to Maslow, to progress from one level to the next, each area or need must be fulfilled and satisfied. What is important to note is that there is often fluctuation between levels when needs in the lower levels reappear. Even a person who has reached the level of self-actualization does not stay there indefinitely. What makes the level of self-actualization so challenging to attain is the requirement that one lower the walls of the ego and explore the unknown with anticipation, not fear. In fact, Maslow states that the need to know (curiosity), and a desire to take risks and actively pursue an understanding of oneself are essential to reaching self-actualization.

In his quest to understand this highest level of needs, self-actualization, Maslow studied the lives of thousands of people, including students, acquaintances, public figures (Albert Einstein, Eleanor Roosevelt, and Albert Schweitzer), and historical figures (Thomas Jefferson, Jane Addams, and Abraham Lincoln), finding a number he considered both healthy and prime examples of quality human beings. From his research, cited in *Motivation and Personality,* Maslow noticed many characteristics common to people he identified as being self-actualized. It is this collection of characteristics that appear to contribute to the resilient nature of people who possess psychological health. To the untrained eye, these people appear to have no stress in their lives, but upon closer scrutiny of the makeup of their personalities, they do in fact have stress but know how to deal with it effectively. According to Maslow, self-actualized people display the following characteristics:

1. *A highly efficient perception of reality.* Self-actualizers are individuals who are able to maintain a clear and objective perspective on themselves and others. Their perceptions are not clouded or disturbed by egotistical influences. Rather, they are unbiased by prejudice and supposition. Maslow found that these people had a strong sense of qualitative judgment.

2. *Acceptance.* People in this class of individuals are aware of not only their strengths but their weaknesses as well. Like everyone else, they have faults and imperfections. But they harbor no guilt, animosity, or shame about the failings or shortcomings in themselves or others. These people accept their shortcomings and do not victimize themselves with their less-than-desirable traits. They work to move beyond them.

3. *Naturalness and spontaneity.* Self-actualizers are themselves, and they feel very comfortable with themselves. They display no false facade, nor are they rigid in their mannerisms. They are open, frank, and present natural, unfiltered behavior in most, if not all, situations and circumstances. Most importantly, they go with the flow and are unthreatened and unfrightened by the unknown. They can think on their feet and react favorably to changes in a spontaneous fashion. They are not easily stressed when plans or circumstances change abruptly.

4. *Problem centering.* People who exhibit the traits of self-actualizers have a strong sense of commitment and dedication to their jobs and other responsibilities. They see themselves as part of the whole, not the whole. When problems arise, these people do not get bogged down in petty personal issues. They confront issues, not people. Due to this strong sense of commitment and purpose in life, self-actualizers work very hard, yet they derive

much pleasure from their work. Maslow was once quoted as saying, "If the only tool you have is a hammer, you tend to see every problem as a nail." Self-actualizers have many tools for problem solving.

5. *Solitude and independence.* Self-actualized people can find as much pleasure in being by themselves as in the company of friends, without feeling lonely. They like their moments of privacy and make time for them. Solitude is considered a blessing, often a time to recharge. Satisfaction is derived from within, as opposed to being dependent on others. Alone-time is often a time of reflection and a time to draw on inner strengths. There is a strong element of autonomy and free-spiritness.

6. *A continual freshness of appreciation.* Grasshoppers, falling leaves, the Big Dipper; these people "stop and smell the roses" along the way. Not only do self-actualizers continually find unexpected wonder and awe in the simplest of surroundings, but like children they typically face daily living with freshness and a bigger-than-life attitude. These people know how to live in the present moment, minimizing feelings of guilt and worry. Rarely do they take anything for granted, and they count their blessings regularly.

7. *Creativity.* Self-actualizers are highly creative individuals who bring imagination, inventiveness, originality, and energy to the thought process. They are able to conceive an idea, visualize it, and then implement it. They are inquisitive and open to new possibilities in their thinking. They are not afraid to fail because they know that failure leads to success. In his book *The Farther Reaches of Human Nature,* Maslow writes, "My feeling is that the concept of creativeness and the concept of the healthy, self-actualized, fully human person seem to be coming closer and closer together, and may perhaps turn out to be the same thing."

8. *Interpersonal relationships.* To be self-actualized does not mean one has hundreds of friends. Rather, the circle of friends is small, but those in this circle are very similar in interests and compatible. Self-actualizers develop closeness

to individuals who stimulate them and who contribute to their own growth and human potential. Relationships are selective and based on the ability to inspire rather than influence.

9. *Human kinship.* Self-actualizers appear compelled to assist in social and moral causes, and they are willing to help all levels of humanity. According to Maslow, they take on a brother or sister role toward other people. Above all, these people have a genuinely unselfish desire to help the human race.

10. *A democratic character.* People who display this characteristic find they have something to learn from everyone. They do not come across as condescending or "uppity." These people have the ability to relate to people from all walks of life.

11. *Strong sense of ethical values.* Maslow found that people he considered self-actualized consistently demonstrated knowledge of right and wrong in their own terms. "These people," wrote Maslow, in the book *Motivation and Personality,* "rarely show the confusion and inconsistency, or the conflict that are so common in the average person's ethical dealings."

12. *Resistance to enculturalization.* Self-actualizers are their own people. They are not likely to conform to or follow trends of fashion or politics. While they may greatly appreciate aspects of other cultures, they do not adopt them as their own. They are directed more by their own nature rather than by the influences of cultural tides.

13. *A sense of humor.* Self-actualizers possess the ability to appreciate the flood of incongruities and ironies in life as well as laugh at their own foibles and mistakes. A light and happy heart is a common trait; these people do not employ sarcasm or hostility in their repertoire of humor. There is a strong spontaneous and playful nature to their sense of mirth.

14. *Mystical or peak sensations.* A peak experience is considered by Maslow to be the climax of self-actualization. A peak experience is any experience of real excellence, real perfection, or of moving toward a perfect justice or perfect values. He found that people who described a peak experience often analogized it to spiritual orgasm. It is a very spiritual moment when you feel one with the world and very much at peace with yourself.

If all of this sounds like the Wonderful World of Disney, it is, because there are very few people who completely fit this description. Maslow estimated from his research that approximately 1 percent of the human population has ever reached this level with any great frequency. And even then, people who do fulfill this need don't tend to stay at this level for their entire lives. Most of the people he classified as self-actualizers were over thirty years old. Teenagers, he found, were too busy polishing their identity to reach this level in high school, or even college. What Maslow came to realize is that individuals are not born self-actualizers. Instead, they must evolve through a multitude of human experiences, smooth the rough edges, and polish the surface of their personal existence. Those who succeed have developed a remarkable human potential and, in the process, a healthy example for others to follow. Yet, to be sure, people who show the traits of self-actualization don't *always* exhibit these characteristics. Maslow noted that, on occasion, they get angry, bored, depressed, selfish, and perhaps even rude. They too, have ups and downs, and must address the other needs of their existence as well. Overall, though, it is their desire to be all they can be that puts them in this select group of individuals. Self-actualizers are not angels, messiahs, or prophets. They have imperfections and flaws like the rest of Earth's inhabitants. But unlike other people, they don't dwell on them. Basically, self-actualizers are people with a strong positive outlook on themselves and life in general. They hold a tremendous amount of faith in themselves and their work. They live life with a passion, not a grudge. They know themselves inside and out, and without a doubt, they are their own best friend.

It is interesting to note that Maslow often talked about the relationship between emotional states and

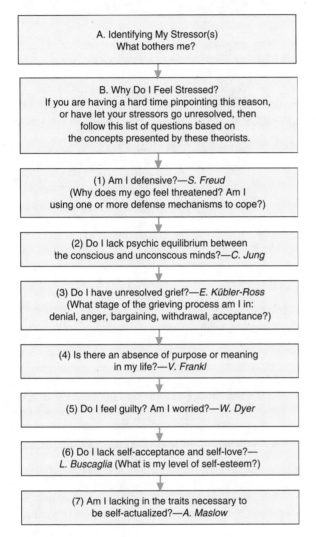

Figure 4.14 Stress awareness chart. Select a problem you are confronted with and ask yourself the questions suggested by each theorist.

and we are all capable of becoming self-actualized. Unfortunately, Maslow states, we limit our capabilities, and these limits stifle our evolution to self-actualization. We place barriers (defense mechanisms) around ourselves for emotional protection. But the barriers around emotional security often cause us to stagnate and eventually inhibit the growth of this remarkable human potential. Self-actualizers have learned to collapse the barriers, lower the walls of the ego, and welcome the opportunity for growth. In a society where stress is becoming more and more apparent, Maslow's theory is an illuminating torch in the field of psychology, so much so that several psychologists have taken his lead and advocated his "hardy" characteristics as being among those conferring the ability to resist the effects of stress.

Some Theoretical Common Ground

From these theories, we can see that the mind creates several strategies to deal with stressful stimuli. Many of these strategies fall in the realm of defenses used to protect the mind from the threat of painful or dangerous events in our lives. Whether these defenses are as specific as those described by Freud and Jung, or more general, as described by Kübler-Ross, Frankl, Dyer, and Buscaglia, they appear to be a very real, if primitive, part of the coping process to deal with stress. When one looks at these theories, it becomes evident that self-awareness is a critical process to move beyond defensive action into the realm of resolution (Fig. 4.14). In fact, the premise of psychotherapy is to put the client back on track through the process of self-awareness, as painful as it may be. Moving from a stance of defensive thoughts and actions toward more positive coping styles based on the strength of our inner resources is thought to be the most effective strategy to deal with stress. It is these inner resources that Maslow began to identify with his theory of self-actualization. His theory indicates that we all have the potential to move beyond the primitive defense mechanisms outlined by Freud, which stunt our human potential.

disease. In a presentation to a group of people at the Esalen retreat center in California, he spoke of the concept of *meta-disease,* where disease and illness are the results of unresolved emotional states of consciousness.

The exciting aspect of Maslow's theory of self-actualization is that we all have this potential. We all have the ability to access our inner resources,

Summary

- Many theories attempt to explain the psychological nature of stress, or more specifically, how humans attempt to deal with the problems they face. These theories are based on the many aspects of psychology, including personality, emotional responses, perceptions, and a wide range of human behaviors.

- Freud believed that humans maintain a level of (instinctual) tension that arises from both internal sources (instinctual impulses) and external sources that attack our ego or identity. The ego copes with stress through the use of a host of defense mechanisms, including denial, repression, projection, rationalization, displacement, and humor.

- Jung also suggested that there is a certain level of innate tension, psychic tension, which exists due to the language barrier between the conscious and unconscious minds. This tension can be reduced through the process of individuation, a continual soul searching that builds a bridge of understanding between the conscious and unconscious minds. Jung advocated self-awareness through dream analysis because he believed that the unconscious mind works to resolve issues and problems, but the conscious mind, which does not understand the language of symbols presented in dreams, tends to ignore them.

- Stress can also be aroused through the death of unmet expectations, which produces a series of mental processes described by Kübler-Ross. These are denial, anger, bargaining, depression, and acceptance. Resolution of emotional baggage leads one to the final stage, acceptance, which in turn enhances inner peace.

- Viktor Frankl's logotherapy was founded on the belief that for life to be complete there must be suffering, but that there must also be a search for the meaning of the suffering to resolve the issues of emotional stress.

- Stressors fall into two categories, according to psychologist Wayne Dyer: guilt and worry, which are two emotional states that immobilize the thought processes, distract one from the present moment, and thus make one unable to conquer stress and attain inner peace.

- Self-love is the critical inner resource described by Leo Buscaglia to cope with life's hardships. Self-love is unattainable, however, without unconditional acceptance of who you are (self-acceptance). To share love, you must first possess love.

- People who are able to achieve self-acceptance and self-love are what Abraham Maslow called self-actualized people. They are well-centered, balanced, and enjoy an unparalleled appreciation of life, proving self-acceptance and self-love to be sound tools to deal effectively with stress. This chapter listed fourteen characteristics Maslow found to be common among self-actualized people. These characteristics seem to allow them to interpret situations in a non-stressful manner and buffer themselves against undue stress.

- Common themes among the theories are the concepts of self-awareness and self-acceptance, two inner resources that become the most important coping skills to manage personal stress effectively.

Concepts and Terms

Active imagination

Collective unconscious

Defense mechanisms

Denial

Displacement

Ego

Hierarchy of needs

Humor

Individuation

Instinctual tension

Leftover guilt

Logotherapy

Love

Meta-disease

Mystical (peak) sensation

Noo-dynamics

Personal unconscious

Problem centering

Projection

Psychic equilibrium

Rationalization

Repression

Self-actualization

Stages of grieving

Theory of motivation

Tragic optimism

X-factor

Chapter 4

The Psychology of Stress

Self-Assessment

The following questions are based on the theories of this chapter to help you become more aware of your perceptions, attitudes, and behaviors.

1. **In hindsight, do you find that you use one or more defense mechanisms to protect your ego? Reflecting on your behavior, which of the following do you see as *common* behaviors in your psychology of stress?**

	Yes	No
1. Defensiveness	_____	_____
2. Rationalization	_____	_____
3. Projection	_____	_____
4. Repression	_____	_____
5. Displacement	_____	_____
6. Humor	_____	_____
7. Other	_____	

2. **Carl Jung was adamant that we need to listen to the wisdom of our dreams. Please answer the following questions based on Jung's theories related to stress.**

   1. How often do you remember your dreams? _____
   2. Do you try to understand your dreams and *the dream symbols?* _____
   3. Do you have any recurring dreams? *yes no.* If yes, describe them. _____
   4. Have you ever had a dream of an event that later came to pass? *yes no.* _____
   5. Briefly describe a dream you had recently and try to explain it from all vantage points. _____
      _____
      _____

3. **Are you currently experiencing the death of a significant expectation?**   Yes   No

   Describe the situation: _____
   _____
   _____

4. **Refer back to your list of stressors in the self-assessment in Chapter 1. If it has been a while since you looked at this list, update it. After having done this, list your stressors under the categories of anger or fear, distinguishing anger-based fears from those which are fear-based.**

Anger-based stressors	Fear-based stressors
1. _____	1. _____
2. _____	2. _____
3. _____	3. _____
4. _____	4. _____
5. _____	5. _____

References and Resources

Briggs Myers, I. *Gifts Differing*. Consulting Psychologists Press, Palo Alto, CA, 1980.

Buscaglia, L. *Born for Love: Reflections on Loving*. Fawcett Columbine, New York, 1992.

Buscaglia, L. *Living, Loving, and Learning*. Fawcett Books, New York, 1982.

Buscaglia, L. *Love*. Fawcett Crest, New York, 1972.

Campbell, J., ed. *The Portable Jung*. Viking Press, New York, 1971.

Dyer, W. *Pulling Your Own Strings*. Avon Books, New York, 1978.

Dyer, W. *Your Erroneous Zones*. Avon Books, New York, 1976.

Dyer, W. *Your Sacred Life*. Harper, New York, 1995.

Dyer, W. *Your Sacred Self? Make the Decision to Be Free*. HarperPaperback Books, New York, 1995.

Dyer, W. *Wisdom of the Ages*. Harper, New York, 1998.

Frankl, V. *Man's Search for Meaning*, 3rd ed. Pocket Books, New York, 1984.

Frankl, V. *The Doctor and the Soul*. Knopf, New York, 1965.

Freud, S. *Standard Edition of the Complete Psychological Works of Sigmund Freud*. Hogarth Press, London, 1986.

Freud, S. *Jokes and their Relationship to the Unconscious*. Norton, New York, 1960.

Hall, C. *A Primer of Freudian Psychology*. Mentor Books, Harper & Row, New York, 1982.

Jung, C. G. *Memories, Dreams, Reflections*. Vintage Books, New York, 1963.

Jung, C. G. *Man and His Symbols*. Anchor Press, New York, 1964.

Jung, C. G. *Modern Man in Search of a Soul*. Harvest Books, New York, 1933.

Jung, C. G. *The Undiscovered Self*. Mentor Books, New York, 1958.

Kübler-Ross, E. Death Does Not Exist. In *The Holistic Health Handbook,* ed. E. Brown et al. And/Or Press, Berkeley, CA, 1981.

Kübler-Ross, E. *Death, the Final Stage of Growth*. Simon & Schuster, New York, 1988.

Kübler-Ross, E. *On Death and Dying*. Macmillan, New York, 1969.

Kübler-Ross, E. *On Life after Death*. Celestial Arts, Berkeley, CA, 1991.

Kübler-Ross, E. *The Wheel of Life: A Memoir of Living and Dying*. Scribner, New York, 1997.

Kübler-Ross, E. Personal Conversation, Scottsdale AZ Jan 14th, 2000.

Kübler-Ross, E. and Kessler, D. *Life Lessons*. Scribner, New York, 2001.

Maslow, A. H. *The Farther Reaches of Human Nature*. Penguin Books, New York, 1976.

Maslow, A. H. *Motivation and Personality*, 3rd ed. Harper & Row, New York, 1987.

Maslow, A. H. *Religions, Values, and Peak Experiences*. Penguin Books, New York, 1964.

Maslow, A. *Self-Actualization*, Esalen Lecture Series, Big Sur Tapes, Tiburon, CA, 1966 and 1972.

Maslow, A. H. Self-actualization and Beyond. In J. F. T. Bugental, ed., *Challenges of Humanistic Psychology*. McGraw Hill, New York, 1967.

Maslow, A. H. *Toward a Psychology of Being*, 2nd ed. Van Nostrand Reinhold, New York, 1968.

Schultz, D. *Theories of Personality*, 4th ed. Brooks/Cole, Pacific Grove, CA, 1990.

Sperry, R. The Great Cerebral Commissure, *Scientific American* 174:42, 1964.

Ursin, H., Baade, E., and Levine, S. *Psychology of Stress*. Academic Press, London, 1978.

Chapter 5 The Stress Emotions: Anger and Fear

"To be free is not merely to cast off one's chains, but to live in a way that respects and enhances the freedom of others."

—Nelson Mandela

Emotional well-being, as defined in the wellness paradigm, is the ability to feel and express the entire range of human emotions and to control them, not be controlled by them. This sounds like a tall order, yet it is not impossible. It takes some unlearning, relearning, and implementation. At an early age, we are socialized to behave in a certain way. We are told to calm down, chill out, never talk back, not cry, and to wipe that smile off our face. The message that we receive is that it is not socially acceptable to exhibit various emotions. Consequently, as adults we carry a lot of unresolved emotional baggage with us. Many health-related problems are thought to be directly tied to our inability to recognize and appropriately express our emotions. There are two primary emotions especially associated with the stress response: anger, which produces the urge to fight, and fear, which promotes the urge to run and hide (Fig. 5.1). Each of these emotions has many shades and layers, which often overlap each other and allow them to coexist in the same situation. This chapter will look at both anger and fear, what dangers await those who do not recognize these emotions consciously, the problems associated with mismanaging or being controlled by these emotions, their relationship to depression, and finally, some helpful strategies to gain control of them.

The Anatomy of Anger

As the story goes, Cain killed his brother Abel in a fit of jealous rage. Since this early case of blatant, hostile aggression, the expression of anger has haunted men and women alike as perhaps the most uncomfortable of all human emotions. It is uncomfortable because the feelings are powerfully real, yet at the same time the hazards of expressing them can be very serious. Anger is equally uncomfortable, perhaps, because mixed messages abound as religious dogma and society's ethic advocate turning the other cheek in the face of aggression, while recent voices in the field of psychology advocate the benefits of ventilating it. Only in the past two decades have researchers begun to uncover the importance of this dark and powerful emotion and its potential relationship to coronary heart disease, as well as other serious maladies. And only recently have new behaviors been suggested as effective ways to creatively ventilate anger and thus bring about a clear resolution of frustrations in order

to promote inner peace. This is a good thing because anger has escalated to a national issue, including Road Rage, Air Rage and Sports Rage.

In its most basic form, anger is a survival emotion common to all animals. Darwin referred to this as the **rage reflex.** He believed that this aggressive nature was essential to the survival of all species. While animals act instinctually to defend and protect themselves, their territory, or their young, humans have engineered the ability to combine conscious thought with the rage reflex to produce a hybrid of anger unparalleled in the animal kingdom. In that sense, human anger is a unique phenomenon. Humans are the only species that can process anger into delayed revenge and behave aggressively for seemingly inexplicable reasons. Freud, in his study of the human psyche, wrote off the rage reflex as an immutable instinct. Although he and his protégés pondered acts of human aggression, Freud focused most of his attention on anxiety, an emotional state he believed could be more greatly influenced by psychotherapy. For the better part of a century, due in large part to Freud's influence, anger was considered to be uncontrollable by conscious thought. Hence, little research was conducted in this area. Even today, in the *Diagnostic and Statistical Manual of Mental Disorders* (DSM-IVR), the diagnostic bible for psychiatrists and psychologists, there are no diagnoses specifically addressing anger or aggression.

Stressful situations can promote feelings of either anger or fear, or in some cases both.   *Figure 5.1*

In the last decade, researchers have uncovered some myths and simple truths about this baffling emotion. One of the first myths to be revealed is that while anger is apparently a universal emotion, aggressive behavior is not instinctual in nature, that is, not a part of the genetic makeup of humans. For example, the Semai people of Malaysia are reported to show no aggressive behavior toward each other; rather, they display passive behavioral responses thought to be a result of resolving issues through informal group dream analysis. From this and other research reports the so-called Seville Statement was drafted in Seville, Spain, in 1986 by twenty prominent researchers from twelve countries, and endorsed by the American Psychological Association. This document proclaimed that aggression is neither genetically nor biologically determined in humans. A second myth about anger regards a theory presented by Dollard et al. in 1939, which stated that aggression is a direct result of frustration. Contrary to this hypothesis, two cultures in the South Pacific—the Kwoma of Papua New Guinea and the Balinese of Bali—demonstrate withdrawal, avoidance, and fasting, not aggression, in the face of frustration. These recent findings reveal that aggressive behavior is only one of several possible responses to feelings of frustration.

Recent studies of anger in the United States indicate that the average person experiences approximately fifteen anger situations per day. Most of these episodes were found to be based on violations of expectations, such as long lines at a checkout stand, car problems, a game of telephone tag, or a rude driver on the way to or from work. When one considers the many emotions related to anger, including rage, hostility, frustration, jealousy, prejudice, resentment, guilt, impatience, even fear, it becomes clear that fifteen anger episodes per day is not a high number. It was also revealed that the expression of anger is influenced by the source of provocation, with a predominantly passive style toward figures of higher authority, and a more active style with people of equal or lower status.

Typically, the manifestation of the anger response reveals the dark underside of civilization rather than the height of human achievement. Newspaper headlines and newscast sound bites are repeatedly filled with stories pointing a finger at the dangers of uncontrolled aggression. Yet despite its negative reputation, anger has a place in human interactions. First and foremost, anger is a form of communication. It reveals information about one's values and personal constructs of importance. Like other species of animals, humans communicate territorial boundaries through the expression of anger. But with humans, these territorial boundaries represent the ownership of the ideas, perceptions, values, and beliefs that constitute one's identity or ego, as well as the ownership of material possessions. In addition, the expression of anger is used to assert authority as well as strengthen or terminate relationships. Anger also provides an incredible source of energy and physical strength that remains unparalleled when compared to the influences of other emotions. The hormonal and other metabolic processes that occur during feelings of aggression have spared several lives in the face of death, and reportedly even fueled the performance of many athletes to Olympic medals (in which case it is called "controlled aggression").

Jane Middelton-Moz is a nationally recognized therapist and author of the book *Boiling Point*. She explains that anger is a force to be reckoned with in the American culture. Road rage, sky rage (disgruntled airline passengers), and children who shoot children are just the tip of the iceberg of the anger phenomenon. It is her contention that one reason for the heightened level of anger is the loss of connection, a result of technology, poor community relations, and the illusion of the American dream (Fig. 5.2).

"Raising Cain" is an expression to connote making trouble, but it's also the title of a book that explores the emotional life of boys. Authors Kindlon and Thompson suggest that due to social pressures, boys are not encouraged to get in touch with their emotions. Episodes of violence, which typically involve men (and sadly young boys and teenagers too), are traced back to a series of episodes where boys learn to mask and hide their true feelings. While boys may transfer their aggression in sports activities, not all boys take up sports. In their research, Kindlon and Thompson have found that a growing number of boys are hurt, sad, afraid, angry and silent–not due to protective mothers, male programming, or testosterone, but rather to the emotional miseducation of boys. Like many others, Kindlon and Thompson are advocates of "emotional literacy," a term used to describe the awareness of emotional well-being: the ability to feel and safely express the entire range of human emotions and to control them, rather than be controlled by them.

Anger knows no gender difference, yet women have been socialized not to display anger because it contradicts the image of femininity.   *Figure 5.2*

Gender Differences

In her book *The Dance of Anger,* Harriet Lerner discusses the gender differences and inequities between male and female anger styles (Fig. 5.2). From her research, Lerner concluded that social mores allow men to express their anger openly and freely in public, and even encourage them to express aggression in some sports (e.g., ice hockey and football). Women, on the other hand, have been denied the same opportunity. The inability of women to express their feelings of anger has fueled much personal frustration and depression over the decades, if not centuries. According to social mores, women are supposed to be pleasant and happy, not angry, aggressive, or violent. When "temperament" is displayed by a woman, it is perceived by men (and some women) to be unfeminine, unladylike, sexually unattractive, and symbolic of evil. As a result of such cultural influences, women are less likely to express their anger. The ramifications can be dangerous to their health. In addition to the more obvious anger-related symptoms (e.g., ulcers, migraines), a study by Greer and Morris (1975) found that breast cancer is related to unresolved anger. In other surveys and questionnaires designed to study the phenomenon, virtually all women said that they feel uncomfort-able, and even guilty and afraid, when anger feelings surface. Lerner also points out that even when men are cursed for their bad behavior with names such as "son of a bitch" or "bastard," it is the female gender that ultimately takes the blame, as these names indicate. Observations made by psychologist Mary Kay Biaggio (1988) indicate that men feel more comfortable with aggressiveness and tend to project their feelings onto the person who provoked them. Women, she noted, are more likely to feel shame, or direct their anger inward, which often manifests itself in physiological symptoms. Lerner states that the greatest problem for many women is to recognize feelings of anger, as these feelings are often ignored, avoided, or suppressed. Until anger can be recognized and validated, she adds, it cannot be expressed correctly.

A significant finding by Kessler and McLeod presented in 1984 revealed not only that men and women respond to the same types of stressors differently, but also that the two genders also have different stressors. It was observed that women, for example, carry an additional burden of responsibilities—and stress—in their roles as mothers and wives. The Framingham study investigated various aspects of anger in both women and men. Using a specially designed

Figure 5.3 (Copyright, 2001, Duane Powell. Distributed by the Los Angeles Times. Reprinted by permission.)

Physiological Responses

As might be expected, sensory stimuli that are interpreted as aggressive threats produce physiological arousal, or the stress response. Research into the physiology of anger first suggested that it triggered the release of norepinephrine, because large amounts were once found in the blood during moments of intense aggression. More recent studies, however, show that norepinephrine in urine and blood samples appears in conjunction with several emotional states, not solely anger. Past attention was also focused on the role of the hypothalamus, which was thought to control emotional responses. But again, recent studies have revealed that the hypothalamus is not solely responsible for the feelings and responses associated with anger; indeed, there are several interactions involved between the hypothalamus and the higher cognitive centers of the brain.

Early studies by Albert Ax in 1953 showed that while most of the physical responses to anger and fear are similar, some are different, specifically, peripheral vasodilation. Anger produces a flushed face—a greater percentage of blood flow to the skin of the face and neck. Fear produces the opposite effect, causing the face to become pale. Studies designed to investigate the relationship between stress and disease, more specifically, emotional response and manifestations of the stress response, found that migraine headaches, ulcers, colitis, arthritis, and hypertension were a few of the ailments significantly associated with anger. But the most startling finding, presented by Friedman (1980) and Rosenman (1985), was that hostility was directly linked to the development of coronary heart disease, making this the most prominent disease-related behavioral trait.

Even though perceptions that arouse sensations of anger may bend the limits of reality, the feelings produced by those perceptions are very real. The current focus of anger research and therapy suggests that anger is within the normal range of human emotions and that feelings of anger should be recognized and validated as legitimate. Along with this validation, however, comes the responsibility to diffuse anger sensations in a healthy fashion. Problems arise when feelings of anger are either suppressed or expressed violently. Anger is considered by many psychologists to be healthy only when expressed or ventilated correctly. Yet it is now documented to be unhealthy, perhaps fatal, when improperly expressed. Herein lies the myth of anger ventilation.

questionnaire, the Framingham Anger Scales Inventory, researchers measured anger-in (anger withheld and internalized), anger-out (the physical expression of anger toward others), anger discussed (confiding to a friend about anger), and anger-related symptoms (physical symptoms possibly brought on by anger episodes). The results were that women scored higher than men in both anger-in and anger-related symptoms. In a similar study conducted in 1991, Thomas and Donnellan observed that the manifestation of anger-related symptoms in middle-aged women was strongly associated with a high number of daily hassles and less-than-adequate social support system. Paradoxically, they also reported that, like women who suppress their feelings of hostility, women who habitually expressed their anger did not escape anger-related physical symptoms, specifically breast cancer. Several other empirical studies designed to uncover variations in the expression of anger between men and women show no overt differences, yet there is still a consensus that differences exist due to strong cultural influences. Whatever is the case, the topic of inequities of anger expression between men and women is now gaining attention as a major focus with regard to women's health issues. Just how these emotions influence the body's physiological systems and pave the path toward dysfunction is also under clinical investigation.

The Myth of Catharsis

In perhaps the most comprehensive review of the subject of anger, social psychologist Carol Tavris described the difference between effective and noneffective catharsis, dispelling yet another myth about anger. To ventilate anger randomly is no longer thought to be therapeutic. The term **catharsis**, used by Freud to mean "purification," is a concept to describe the emptying of emotional reservoirs, such as by crying, laughing, yelling, and in some cases, exercise. Citing several studies in which subjects were encouraged to ventilate anger as a therapeutic catharsis, Tavris concluded that randomly released feelings of anger and ventilated frustrations did not produce a healthy catharsis. To the contrary, not only did the random release of pent-up emotions not relieve feelings of aggression, but it validated them, in effect reinforcing anger and causing even greater emotional arousal. In a study by Ebbesen, Duncan, and Konecni (1975), 100 aerospace engineers were interviewed after losing their jobs prior to the end of their three-year contract. Their responses were compared to those of engineers who left voluntarily with no apparent grievances. Results showed that both responses to questionnaires and the chance to ventilate during interviews by those who were laid off proved to be an ineffective catharsis, resulting in greater hostility toward management. To the surprise of many psychologists, these and similar findings by psychologist Edward Murray (1985) indicate that random, hostile expression of anger is not a suitable means to emotional composure, despite popular belief to this effect.

As someone who has spent a great deal of time studying the connections among anger, Type A behavior, and health, Redford Williams, M.D., cautions against feelings of unresolved anger. Williams predicts that at least 20 percent of the American population has levels of hostile anger that can produce serious health problems, with another 10–20 percent teetering on the edge of anger-health-related issues. In his book *Anger Kills*, Williams underscores the significance of the connection between unreconciled anger and a plethora of symptoms associated with it, from ulcers to coronary heart disease. Williams notes that hostile people, as a rule, tend to be loners or lack a strong social support network, thus making their plight even more difficult. Many thoughts and feelings can surface as sarcasm, cynicism, and pessimism, and the use of these behaviors is a sure sign of unresolved issues. One way Williams recommends to deal with anger is to first make yourself aware of your thoughts, feelings, and behaviors through journaling, including the time and date of the anger episode, the thought, feeling, action, and involvement, so that patterns of behavior can be tracked and modified.

Taking note of the strong association between anger and heart disease, Joseph Sundram and colleagues at the Institute of Heart Math in Boulder Creek, California, have designed several studies to develop an understanding of the effect on the heart of the connection between stress and disease. Their findings, many of which can be found in the book *Cut-Thru* by Doc Lew Childre, speak to the importance of love, compassion, and empathy as the most effective means to defuse the anger response and reverse the physiological parameters maladapted by a closed heart.

To generate a healthy catharsis of anger, certain criteria must be met. In her book *Anger—The Misunderstood Emotion*, Tavris made the following recommendations regarding effective catharsis, all of which should be used simultaneously to resolve anger conflicts:

1. *The expression of anger must be cast in the direction of the provocation.* Tavris observed that for anger feelings to be resolved, they must be vented directly at the person or object that is perceived to violate personal space, values, or identity, not randomly. The ventilation of anger at third parties or at unrelated inanimate objects provides temporary relief but no lasting resolution.

2. *The expression of anger must restore a sense of self-control.* For anger to feel resolved, there must be a sense of justice, a vindication of the personal violation you felt, whether this means just explaining your side of the story or seeing that someone is tried in a court of law for his or her misconduct. Self-esteem must be reinstated, but not at the expense of the person you feel did you an injustice. In other words, revenge is not a viable option in anger resolution.

3. *The expression of anger must change the behavior of the provoker or provide insight to create personal resolution.* When feelings of anger are verbalized, drawn, or written out in a journal,

new insights are often revealed, which can explain and give a wider perspective on the problem. Conversation with friends who act as sounding boards is also beneficial when this means of communication invites objective viewpoints. The most beneficial conversations, however, are with the person(s) with whom you share a grievance and ultimately influence toward a common understanding. In the words of Tavris, "such repeated expressions, without illumination, are not cathartic." Insight provides understanding, and understanding cultivates forgiveness (resolution).

4. *Anger must be expressed in understandable language.* When animals communicate anger there is no doubt about it; their language is direct. Humans, however, can be less than direct in their expressions of anger. Frustrations can be candy-coated and passed over, exaggerated, or masked in deceptive retaliation, none of which is beneficial. The ventilation of anger verbally causes an immediate defensive reaction in those who are nearby. For this reason, anger must be communicated clearly but diplomatically. Psychologists suggest the use of "I" statements (e.g., I am angry because I . . .) rather than "you" statements (e.g., You really made me mad when you . . .), which are less effective in bringing about resolution. In situations where verbal communication is not possible (as with a deceased parent), some type of communication (e.g., an unsent letter) is advocated.

5. *The expression of anger must not provoke retaliation.* For a catharsis to be beneficial, it must put an end to feelings of anger on all sides. Retaliation to one or more outbursts of anger will result in ongoing battles that only perpetuate the anger cycle, making the problem(s) more difficult to resolve.

A review of the literature regarding the expression of anger shows that holding anger in is not the answer, yet neither is yelling to the wind. The expression of anger, like love, requires direct and diplomatic contact, two elements that seem rather distant if not absent when most people get angry. Rarely is anger managed correctly.

Anger Mismanagement Styles

What has become obvious from research on anger is that those who mismanage their feelings of aggression far outnumber those who express it effectively. In his acclaimed book, *Make Anger Your Ally,* describing the expression of anger, Neil Warner categorizes people into four classic anger-mismanagement types based on the behaviors they typically employ. They are somatizers, self-punishers, exploders, and underhanders.

1. **Somatizers.** Somatizers, as the name implies (soma = body), present a passive behavior style which takes its toll on the body. Somatizers are individuals who choose not to express their feelings of anger overtly, but rather suppress them for fear of rejection or loss of approval by those who have caused a grievance. This management style promotes the role of martyr for those who choose it. Somatizers can also be distinguished from those employing other mismanagement styles by the fact that their suppressed anger may soon manifest as physical symptoms such as migraine headaches, ulcers, colitis, arthritis, and temporomandibular joint dysfunction (TMJ).

2. **Self-punishers.** A second passive mismanaged-anger style involves those who channel their anger into guilt. These people often get angry with themselves for getting angry at others. As a result, they deny themselves the proper outlet or catharsis of their anger. Instead, they punish themselves with control measures which, in effect, lower self-esteem. For example, overeating or deliberate starvation, excessive drinking, and sleeping and shopping, can all deflate self-esteem and are displayed by self-punishers.

3. **Exploders.** Exploders represent the stereotype of uncontrolled aggression. These are the people who express their anger in a hostile manner, either verbally or physically, and like a volcano they erupt, spreading their hot lava in a path of destruction toward anyone around them. Exploders hold in their feelings of anger and then often erupt at people or objects that have nothing to do with the cause of their frustration. Explosive behavior is sometimes displaced onto others, as when feelings of anger toward the provoker are suppressed,

Stress With a Human Face

BRIAN HAD JUST COMPLETED HIS SOPHOMORE year and, like every other college student, he was looking forward to summer vacation. The Boston waterfront is the place to be on hot summer nights, and there were many that year. But this particular summer was hot in another way, too, the likes of which Brian had never experienced. Things just seemed to get out of control. First, his summer job working construction fell through. Second, and more important, his father, to whom he was very close, was diagnosed with terminal cancer. He was given two months to live, a prognosis that turned out to be right on the button. Brian got angry that his summer plans, and for that matter his life plans, didn't go as expected.

To Brian, this just wasn't how it was supposed to turn out. The whole dynamics of his life changed, and there was resentment in every corner of his heart. When I saw Brian the first day of school I barely recognized him, for he seemed to have doubled his body weight in muscle mass, and his typical smile was absent. Right away he told me how difficult it can be to lose a father and become the head of a household while still a teenager. Brian was in a lot of pain. After a few minutes I thought I would change the subject and

inquire about his new and improved physique. But Brian didn't want to change the subject.

"Well," he said, "I started lifting weights to take out my aggression. I'd go down to the gym every night and try to release it somehow."

"It must have worked," I replied, "Just look at you." "Yeah!" he answered. "I was really pissed." Then he paused for a moment and added, "You know, it didn't solve my problems, but it did help work through them."

Brian had directed his feelings of anger in a way that literally augmented his strength to deal with the situation in which he found himself. ◆

then released onto innocent bystanders such as employees, spouses, and children. In many cases, explosive anger is used as a form of intimidation (e.g., swearing, yelling) to maintain control over a situation or other people's emotions. Road rage is explosive behavior. It is this behavior that is considered by psychologists to be indicative of Type A personality, and the factor most closely associated with coronary heart disease.

4. **Underhanders.** Like the exploder, the underhander exhibits an active style of mismanaged anger that inflicts mild abuse on individuals in his or her proximity. What

separates underhanded behavior from the explosive style is that underhanders usually target their aggression toward the cause of the threat, but indirectly—in what they perceive to be socially acceptable ways (passive-aggressive behavior). Underhanders seek revenge for injustices to their egos and try to sabotage their "enemy" with little acts of aggression that are somewhat socially acceptable. Examples include walking into a staff meeting late and sarcastic comments (verbal sabotage) that demonstrate the need to gain control of the aggressor. Underhanders see themselves as life's victims, and although their anger is often directed at the proper cause, resolution is rarely accomplished.

Warner points out that we each tend to employ all of these mismanagement styles at some time, depending on the situation and people involved. One style, however, becomes the dominant behavior in our personality and is used most extensively in daily interactions. It should be pointed out that none of these four behavior patterns is healthy; that is, to switch from being a somatizer to an exploder is not recommended. Warner suggests that we begin to recognize our feelings of anger, and then channel them into more creative outlets.

Creative Anger Strategies

Human anger is thought to be comprised of conscious thought, physiological changes, and some form of consequent behavior. Therefore, the most successful strategies to deal with anger involve cognitive coping strategies, relaxation techniques, and behavior modification to deal with these three components. Anger *should* be dealt with and reconciled. But there are both effective and noneffective ways to deal with the various shades of this emotion. The best approach is to learn a variety of ways so that one or more are available when various situations trigger the anger response in you. Based on the works of Carol Tavris (1982) and Harold Weisinger (1985), and in the spirit of twelve-step self-help programs to modify behaviors, the following suggestions are provided to help you learn to manage your anger more creatively:

1. *Know your anger style.* Is your anger style predominantly passive or active? Are you the type of person who holds anger in, or are you the kind of person who explodes? Are you a somatizer, exploder, self-punisher, or underhander? Become aware of what your current style of anger is. Take mental notes of what ticks you off and how you react when you get angry.

2. *Learn to monitor your anger.* Keep track of your anger in a journal, or even on a calendar. Write down the times that you get angry and what precipitates it. Are there predictable trends to your anger feelings? Ask yourself why. After several entries, look for patterns of circumstances or behaviors that lead to the "critical mass" or "boiling point" of your anger.

3. *Learn to deescalate your anger.* Rather than show an immediate response, count to ten, take a walk around the block, get a drink of water, try some deep breaths, use some mental imagery to relax; but calm down. Research shows that the anger response is initially quick, then followed by a long simmering process. Give yourself ten to twenty seconds to diffuse, to collect and regroup your mental faculties. No rational conversation can take place while you are shouting in anger. So take a "time out," by removing yourself from the scene momentarily to cool off. Time-outs are very helpful to validate your feelings, and at the same time get a full perspective on the circumstances. Remember, though, that a time-out must be immediately followed by a "time in."

4. *Learn to out-think your anger.* What are some ways to resolve this feeling in a constructive way so that you and everyone involved feel better? Anger carries with it much energy. How can you best utilize this energy? Learn to construct rather than destruct.

5. *Get comfortable with all your feelings, and learn to express them constructively.* People who are most vulnerable to stress-related disease and illness are those who are unable to express their feelings openly and directly. In other words, don't ignore, avoid, or repress your feelings. Anger, especially, is like acid; it needs to be neutralized. And it is neutralized by creative (constructive) expression.

6. *Plan ahead.* Some situations can be foreseen as potential anger provocations. Identify what these situations are, and then create viable options to minimize your exposure to them. Interactions with people (e.g., family get-togethers, traffic, long lines at the post office) are especially likely to trigger anger. Try to plan your time wisely and work around situations you think will light your fuse.

7. *Develop a support system.* Find a few close friends you can confide in or vent your frustrations to. Don't force a person to become an ally; rather, allow him or her to listen and

perhaps offer an insight or objective perspective your anger blinds you to. By expressing yourself to others, you can begin to process bits of information, and a clearer understanding of the situation will usually surface.

8. *Develop realistic expectations of yourself and others.* Many moments of anger surface because the expectations we place on ourselves are too high. Anger also arises when we place high expectations on others and these are not met. Learn to reappraise your expectations and validate your feelings before your top blows off. Learning to assess a situation by fine-tuning your perceptions is essential to minimizing anger episodes.

9. *Learn problem-solving techniques.* Don't paint yourself into a corner. Implement alternatives to situations by creating viable options for yourself. To do this you must be willing to trust your imagination and creativity. You must also take risks with the options you have created and trust the choices you have made. But remember that problem-solving techniques do not include retaliation (see Chapter 14).

10. *Stay in shape.* Staying in shape means balancing your mental, emotional, physical, and spiritual components of well-being. Studies show that people who are in good shape bounce back from anger episodes more quickly than those who are not. Exercise has been proven to be beneficial as one step in the catharsis process, to validate feelings of anger. Eat well, exercise on a regular basis, give yourself alone-time or solitude, and learn to laugh more. Laughter is a great form of stress reduction, and it gives you a better perspective on the situation at hand. Remember, though, that while laughter is the best form of medicine, anger vented in sarcasm is neither creative nor healthy for anyone (see Chapter 12).

11. *Turn complaints into requests.* Pessimists tend to complain, whine, and moan. Anyone can complain. Complaining is a sign of victimization. When frustrated with a co-worker or family member, rework the problem into a request for change with the person(s) involved. Seek opportunities rather than problems. Take a more optimistic outlook on how you perceive situations. This will most likely aid in the request process.

12. *Make past anger pass.* Learn to resolve issues that have caused pain, frustration, or stress. Resolution involves an internal dialogue to work things out within, and an external dialogue to work things out with others, done of course in a diplomatic way. Most important, learn to forgive both yourself and others. Forgiveness is an essential part of anger management. Set a "statute of limitations" on your anger, and hold to it.

There are some who say that anger and fear are two very different sides of the same coin. There are others who believe that anger is really just another shade of fear, inspired by that which generates a sense of uneasiness inside of us. Whether they are two entirely different emotions, or derived from the same source but expressed differently, they are both very real.

The Anatomy of Fear

Like anger, fear is an element of survival. In its most primitive form, fear stimulates a physical response to flee and hide from threats that are intimidating, overwhelming, and sometimes fatal. Often described as a state of anxiety, fear comes in many shades, including embarrassment, prejudice, anxiety, despair, worry, arrogance, doubt, intimidation, and paranoia, to name a few. This aspect of human behavior spurred extensive inquiry long before Freud recognized it as a purpose for therapy. Perceptions of what is intimidating or fatal are extremely individual to the person who experiences them. A large black dog, for example, can be perceived as either friendly or dangerous. Freud's theories substantiated the need to deal with human fears, and his work has paved the way to a host of anxiety-reduction therapies. According to Freud, anxiety is an unknown fear, meaning that the individual is unaware of his or her reason for feeling anxious. More recently, many psychologists and other health professionals have used the terms *fear* and *anxiety* interchangeably, which is how they are used in this chapter as well. Like anger, chronic anxiety produces physiological adaptations created by the stress response, with a strong involvement of the immune system. Repeated episodes of fear are thought to be associated with colds, flus, warts, impotence, and, according to some research, cancer.

The current school of thought suggests that fears are not instinctual. Rather, they are a learned response from one or more exposures to an event (e.g., a third-degree burn, the death of a loved one, a poor exam grade, being jilted) that resulted in some amount of physical or emotional pain. Exposures can be either direct, as in getting stung by a wasp; or indirect, by learning through another's experiences, as in listening to horror stories or even watching TV. These exposures create a conditioned response, from caution and apprehension, to paralysis in the presence of the event that initiated it. After one or more experiences, fear can be manufactured and replicated by the imagination, and it can seem as real as any face-to-face confrontation. For this reason, anxiety is categorized as either rational (useful) or irrational (useless). Useful fears are stimulated by real events that are life threatening and require a response to survive or avoid the threat. Conversely, useless fears are imagined, exaggerated, or distorted threats that override cognitive processes in the higher brain centers, resulting in some degree of mental, emotional, physical, or spiritual paralysis. Useless fears are illusions created in the mind. Illusory fear is the target of therapy and treatment in stress management.

In his groundbreaking book *Emotional Intelligence,* author Daniel Goleman synthesizes a plethora of research and information about the emotional aspect of the human condition. As Goleman explains, while mental intelligence (as measured in IQ) is praised and rewarded, our emotional intelligence, the ability to feel and express the full range of human emotions, suggests a higher level of intellect than that measured by mere brain power alone. Emotions offer a different, if not superior, level of intelligence, and our ability to use our emotional skills to our greatest advantage will separate those who live a healthy life from those who are prone to disease.

As one of the basic human emotions, fear tends to dominate the emotional palette; Goleman refers to this as "emotional highjacking." Neuroscientists now indicate that one portion of the brain, the amygdala, is responsible for registering and acknowledging any fear-based stimulus. In a complicated network, neural transmissions quickly travel from one or more sensory

ports (e.g., eyes) to the thalamus and on to a specific area of the cerebral cortex. Yet another impulse goes from the thalamus directly to the amygdala, which itself can arouse the stress response before the cortex can even decipher the cause of fear.

Whereas with anger there is a rush of adrenaline and with it a surge of energy, fear is a very draining emotion. The urge to hide serves as a metaphor for pulling in one's energy rather than radiating it, for whatever purpose. Worries that become chronic in nature tend to become self-defeating, says Goleman. In other words, problems, issues, and concerns do not get resolved through worry or fear. Rather, they are perpetuated by the emotional energy put into them. And Goleman is one of many people who are convinced of the stress and disease connection. He is convinced that learning to identify, empathize, and resolve our feelings (e.g., anger, anxiety, depression, pessimism, and loneliness) is in itself a necessary form of disease prevention.

Basic Human Fears

Virtually anything can trigger fear. However, events or situations that elicit anxiety tend to fall into one of six categories: (1) failure, (2) rejection, (3) the unknown, (4) death, (5) isolation, and (6) loss of self-dominance. The complexity of anxiety, as Freud and his followers discovered, lies in the fact that many of these basic fears tend to overlap and intertwine, making the origin of some stressors difficult to isolate. But if attention is paid to identifying stressors that trigger anxiety, one basic fear will usually become evident. That is, typically one basic fear tends to dominate our perceptions of specific threats. The six categories of fears are all associated with the inability to access and utilize inner resources, resulting in low self-esteem. The following provides a description and some examples of each category:

1. **Fear of failure.** Fear of failure is associated with low self-esteem or the potential loss of self-esteem. People are more apprehensive about and less likely to try new ventures or repeat their efforts at a previously defeating task when their self-value is low. Fear of failure is a conditioned response from a past experience wherein one's performance did not

meet one's own expectations. When people perceive that they have failed at something, their confidence, and thus their self-value and self-acceptance, decreases. This can become a cyclical process, paving the way for repeated failures. A bad experience in the past inhibits a person from attempting an identical or similar task again. Examples include public speaking, using a computer, taking an exam, even marriage. Maslow called this the *Jonah complex,* and it means that one is afraid to maximize one's potential. Fear of failure sets the stage for the self-fulfilling prophecy: if a person thinks he or she will not succeed at a given task, chances are he or she will not. If for some reason someone does succeed, chance and fate are given credit, not his or her own resources and talents. Failure is often associated with lack of achievement, when in reality it is due to lack of effort–not giving something your all when called upon to do so. The flip side of fear of failure is fear of success. This occurs when people achieve success and then become frightened of "defending the title," fearing they cannot match their previous success.

2. **Fear of rejection.** Fear of rejection is also associated with low self-worth, but this fear involves your perception of how others perceive and accept you, while fear of failure is based solely on self-acceptance. The seeds of this fear are sown early in life, when a child seeks the approval and love of parents and figures of authority. At a young age, however, children cannot distinguish between disapproval for acts for which they are responsible (e.g., breaking a lamp) and nonrelated incidents (a parent's bad day at the office); rejection appears identical in both cases. As one matures, fear of rejection manifests itself during daily interactions with family, friends, bosses, coworkers, and acquaintances in one's environment. Circumstances in which fear of rejection may surface include negotiating a raise, asking a woman or man for a date, applying for a job, pursuing an intimate relationship, exchanging presents, submitting manuscripts to publishers, and remarrying into families with stepparents and/or stepchildren. Fear of rejection also goes by other names, including fear of intimacy and fear of commitment. Rejection becomes anxiety only when lack of approval or acceptance supports one's inner feelings of low self-esteem. Dyer associated fear of rejection with feelings of guilt and worry.

3. **Fear of the unknown.** There is great comfort in the familiar, and there can be tremendous apprehension of and intimidation by the unknown. This is one reason why many battered women stay in bad relationships and why many people stay in jobs they hate. It may seem paradoxical, but there is some degree of comfort and security even with the undesirable, while there appears to be intolerable tension with the unknown. Jung called this *misoneism,* the fear or hatred of anything new. At its worst, fear of the unknown is paralyzing. With all other basic fears, there are "known quantities" to work with and manipulate; this fear produces shades of panic due to a lack of information. Other fears give you a visible "enemy"; fear of the unknown makes you feel defenseless. When details and sources are unavailable, security of the ego begins to evaporate. Examples of this fear include vacationing in new corners of the globe, graduating from college, getting married, becoming pregnant, or getting lost while driving. In the case of a battered wife, fear of the unknown entails how to survive financially without the support of a husband. Fear of the unknown is a black hole in the wall of the ego. It may appear difficult to create a comfortable strategy for dealing with situations unknown, but it is not impossible. Methods include gaining information about the situation, and employing the inner resources of faith and self-reliance.

4. **Fear of death.** Fear of death falls into the domain of useful fears when danger is present and survival is jeopardized. But this fear becomes a useless fear when the danger is exaggerated or "fabricated out of whole cloth." The fear of death includes many phobias where death seems imminent, such as acrophobia (heights), claustrophobia (small spaces), and

Do Not Stand at My Grave and Weep

Do not stand at my grave and weep
I am not there. I do not sleep.
I am a thousand winds that blow.
I am the diamond glint on snow.
I am the sunlight on ripened grain.
I am the gentle autumn rain.
When you wake in the morning hush
I am the swift, uplifting rush
of quiet birds in circling flight.
I am the soft starlight at night.
Do not stand at my grave and cry
I am not there. I did not die.

Joyce Fessen

hydrophobia (water). In a more general sense, this fear is coupled with fear of the unknown when one contemplates the existence of an afterlife and reaches no comfortable answers. The conscious mind can't fathom life without itself, and the thought of nonexistence is less than comforting. Psychologists indicate that many people who demonstrate fear of death are excessively cautious, typically have many unresolved issues in their lives, and have many personal regrets. They may also acquire many possessions as a base of security, and feel naked without them. This fear inhibits the ability to take calculated risks. Kübler-Ross felt that fear of death was universal, but also conquerable (Box 5.1).

5. **Fear of isolation.** Fear of isolation is the fear of being left alone, and may very well be the first fear developed in life. From the moment we enter this world, we are nurtured in the company of care givers who address all our needs. In a baby, the absence of this nurturing presence elicits crying. Later, in adulthood, lack of quality social contact through support systems results in anxiety and depression. Just as people need quality alone time for self-reflection, they also require human interaction and support to feel connected to other members of their community. Buscaglia notes

that the absence of love does not produce fear of rejection so much as it cultivates fear of loneliness. Moreover, Harold Benjamin, founder of the Wellness Community, in his book *From Victor to Victim,* believes that this fear and fear of the loss of self-dominance are the two significant fears of cancer patients.

6. **Fear of the loss of self-dominance.** This fear is exhibited when one feels the loss of control over major events and circumstances in one's life. In other words, this is a fear of loss of personal freedom. This is a predominant fear of people with substance addictions, battered wives and children, nursing home patients, and even the nation's homeless. It also surfaces when individuals contract prolonged illnesses such as cancer or AIDS. This fear is also prevalent in people whose personality type is described as learned helpless-hopeless, people who feel they have little control of their lives.

Strategies to Overcome Fear

Because of the complexity of anxiety, several types of therapy exist to help people overcome specific fears and phobias. Although no therapy holds dominance over another, what they all have in common is the premise that the fear must be confronted at some level. Using a pure psychoanalytical approach (Freud's approach), attention is focused on uncovering childhood experiences (e.g., child molestation) that have been suppressed or repressed in the unconscious mind and are thought to be the cause of the anxiety. The length of this type of therapy is dependent on the type and severity of the anxiety. A second option is called behavioral therapy, based on the work of behavioral psychologist John B. Watson, where an individual engages in coping (cognitive reappraisal) and relaxation (mental imagery) techniques to desensitize himself or herself to the stressor(s) (Wolpe, 1988). Additional work by Joseph Wolpe (1973) helped clients to create a mindset that would be conducive to modifying behaviors. Referred to as **systematic desensitization** and exposure desensitization, clients are repeatedly exposed to their stressors, first at small and tolerable levels, then with a systematic progression toward face-to-face confrontation with the stressor (see Chapter 20). In essence, people are taught to overcome their fears by piecemeal steps at which they always feel in control of their tolerance level.

Lufthansa Airlines offers a very successful program based on this technique for potential passengers who have fear of flying. Such people take a course in airflight anxiety-reduction, which includes visiting an airport terminal and waiting for a plane; boarding a mock plane, sitting for a short duration, and deplaning without flying; and then progressing to very short flights. Another type of behavior therapy is assertiveness training, the goal being to increase self-esteem. The greatest success with these therapies comes from awareness of the fear(s) and the stressors that produce them, proficiency in applicable coping and relaxation techniques, and the ability to confront stressors peacefully, emerging the victor, not the victim.

Depression: A By-Product of Anger or Fear?

It would be false to assume that anger and fear are the only two emotions associated with stress. There are, in fact, several others, but they all appear to be linked, either directly or indirectly, to anger and/or fear. One emotion that surfaces as a result of unresolved stress is depression.

Overwhelming sadness. The blues. Eternal darkness. Shuffling underwater. Prolonged grieving. Deep heaviness. Melancholy. Just like anger and fear, depression goes by several names and descriptions. With estimates that over one-third of the American public is on medications for depression, this topic certainly merits more attention than a passing comment. Depression is the silent face of stress. And depending on who you talk to, there seem to be many causes of mood swings, from high carbohydrate diets and traumatic childbirth, to hormonal imbalances and poor brain chemistry. What is often overlooked are stressful events that precede each bout of depression.

While it's true that no one word seems to adequately describe this emotional state, many of the following symptoms are common to those who share this feeling:

+ Persistent sadness or empty moods
+ A loss of interest or pleasure in activities
+ Lethargic moods with decreased productivity
+ Loss of appetite and weight loss or overeating and weight gain
+ Difficulty concentrating, remembering, or making decisions
+ Pervading hopelessness in personal and professional lives
+ Alcohol and drug use to cope with problems
+ Thoughts of death and suicide to "resolve" issues.

Depression is a lot more than just brain chemistry. And while Prozac, Paxil, and Zoloft may work to alleviate the imbalance in seratonin, norepinerphrine, and dopamine levels in the brain, in the words of author Susan Skog, "a chemical cure cannot heal emotional wounds." For many people pharmacological aids have worked wonders; however, given the complexity of depression, the best approach is a holistic one.

Those who have studied this emotion describe depression "as anger turned inward." It is unresolved anger issues, however long they have been lingering in the psyche, that experts now agree are essential to resolve for the clouds of depression to lift and clear.

While it is common to feel down in the dumps at times, to be locked into this emotion for prolonged periods, to the exclusion of all others, is neither normal nor healthy. Some type of intervention is needed to reestablish a balance between the positive and negative feelings generated by daily life in order to regain emotional wellbeing. Psychotherapeutic intervention to treat depression includes many coping and relaxation techniques. For example, several studies have shown that physical exercise results in a less depressed state of mind. In a study conducted by Egil Martinson (1985) to determine the effects of exercise on depression, it was concluded that "Exercise is associated with an antidepressive effect in patients with mild to moderate forms of unipolar depression." In an article titled "Exercise and Depression" (1998), authors Artal and Sherman state that exercise plays a significant role in the treatment of depression. Similar results have been observed following the use of Saint-John's-wort, nutrition therapy (decreasing simple sugars), music therapy, art therapy, and humor therapy. These same techniques are equally effective for individuals who find themselves occasionally "under the weather" after a stressful day, and may in fact help move them toward a peaceful resolution of their stress.

Summary

+ Anger and fear are two sides of the same coin. Both emotions are triggered by stimuli perceived to be a threat at a physical, mental, emotional, or spiritual level, or perhaps a combination of these.

+ Feelings of anger initiate the fight response to defend oneself and the components that constitute one's identity.

+ Fear triggers the flight response, which makes one want to run and hide.

+ Both emotions are thought to be survival emotions, yet when conscious thoughts are combined with these innate reflexes, feelings are magnified rather than resolved, leading to an unbroken cycle of stress.

+ Social factors may play a significant role in the different anger-management styles of men and women. Women are often flooded with feelings of guilt after tempers flare; men demonstrate anger in more overt ways.

+ There are several myths regarding the emotion of anger, the most common being that any type of ventilation producing a catharsis is healthy. However, research reveals that undirected ventilation only validates and perpetuates feelings of anger.

+ People who do not ventilate anger correctly are categorized as one of four mismanaged-anger types: somatizer, self-punisher, exploder, or underhander.

+ Current stress-management programs are introducing courses in creative anger management to change anger-generated thoughts and feelings into constructive energies which work toward peaceful resolution.

+ Fear is based on an actual or vicarious exposure to physical or emotional pain. Those fears which enable a person to avoid life-threatening situations are called useful fears, while those which are exaggerated and immobilize the individual are deemed useless fears. It is the latter, irrational fears that are targeted for change.

+ Basic human fears include failure, rejection, the unknown, death, isolation, and loss of self-control. Most anxieties can be placed in one of these categories.

+ The most effective way to dissolve fear is to confront it. One way to do this is through a technique called systematic desensitization, where the stressor is confronted piecemeal to build a psychological immunity to it.

+ The road to resolution for both anger and fear is not difficult, yet it is often avoided, resulting in mismanaged styles of anger and fear and consequent physical ailments.

+ Left unresolved, both anger and fear can sow the seeds of depression, an emotional state that may require therapy.

+ Several strategies, involving both coping and relaxation techniques, are recommended to express anger and fear in a healthy fashion, and to control these emotions for optimal wellbeing.

Concepts and Terms

Behavioral therapy
Catharsis
Conditioned response
Creative anger strategies
Exploders
Exposure desensitization
Fear of death
Fear of failure

Fear of isolation
Fear of loss of self-dominance
Fear of rejection
Fear of the unknown
Jonah complex
Misoneism
Myth of catharsis
Passive-aggressiveness

Rage reflex
Self-punishers
Seville Statement
Systematic desensitization
Somatizers
Underhanders

Anger Recognition Checklist

The following is a quick exercise to understand how anger can surface in the course of a working day and how you may mismanage it. Put a check in front of any of the following that apply to you when you get angry. Next, if applicable, try to identify your most common mismanaged anger style.

_____ anxious

_____ depressed

_____ overeat

_____ start dieting

_____ trouble sleeping

_____ excessive sleeping

_____ careless driving

_____ chronic fatigue

_____ abuse alcohol/drugs

_____ explode in rage

_____ cold withdrawal

_____ headaches

_____ sarcasm

_____ hostile joking

_____ accident-prone

_____ guilty & self-blaming

_____ high blood pressure

_____ frequent nightmares

_____ harp/nag

_____ intellectualize

_____ stomach upsets (e.g., gas, cramps, colitis)

_____ muscle tension (e.g., shoulders, leg, fist)

_____ name call

_____ cry

_____ threaten others

_____ buy things

_____ frequent lateness

_____ never feel angry

_____ tight, clenched jaw

_____ bored

_____ nausea, vomiting

_____ skin eruptions

_____ easily irritable

_____ sexual difficulties

_____ backache

_____ busywork (clean, straighten)

_____ sulk, whine

_____ hit, throw things

Mismanaged Anger Styles

When I mismanage my anger, I typically express myself in the following way (check one):

_____ 1) Exploder

_____ 2) Self-punisher (guilt)

_____ 3) Underhander (revenge, sarcasm)

_____ 4) Somatizer (suppress anger feelings)

My average number of anger episodes per day is _____.

References and Resources

Ax, A. F. The Physiological Differences between Fear and Anger in Humans, *Psychosomatic Medicine* 15:433–442, 1953.

Archer, J. *The Behavioral Biology of Aggression.* Cambridge University Press, Cambridge, 1988.

Artal, M. and Sherman C. Exercise Against Depression. *Physician and Sports Medicine* Oct pp 55–60, 1998.

Baumeister, R., Smart, L., and Boden, J. Relation of Threatened Egotism to Violence and Aggression: The Dark Side of Self-Esteem, *Psychological Review* 103(1):5–33, 1996.

Benjamin, H. *From Victim to Victor.* Dell Publishing, New York, 1987.

Biaggio, M. *Sex Differences in Anger: Are They Real?* Paper presented to the American Psychological Association, Atlanta, Georgia, 1988.

Bramson, R. *Coping with Difficult People.* Anchor Press/Doubleday, New York, 1981.

Buscaglia, L. *Love.* Fawcett Crest, New York, 1972.

Childre, D. L. *Cut-Thru.* Planetary Publishing, Boulder Creek, CA, 1996.

Dalai Lama. *Healing Anger—The Practice of Patience from a Buddhist Perspective.* Snaw Lien Publishers, New York, 1997.

Dentan, R. K. *The Semai—A Nonviolent People of Malaysia.* Holt, Rinehart, & Winston, New York, 1968.

Dollard, J. R. et al. *Frustration and Aggression.* Yale University Press, New Haven, CT, 1939.

DuPont, R. *Phobia.* Brunner/Mazel, New York, 1982.

Ebbesen, E., Duncan, B., and Konecni, V. Effects of Content of Verbal Aggression on Future Verbal Aggression: A Field Experiment, *Journal of Experimental Social Psychology* 11:192–204, 1975.

Esler, G. *United States of Anger: The People and the American Dream.* Penguin Books, New York, 1997.

Friedman, M. *Overcoming the Fear of Success.* Seaview Books, New York, 1980.

Goldstein, A. *Agress-less: How to Turn Anger and Aggression into Positive Action.* Prentice Hall, New York, 1982.

Goleman, D. *Emotional Intelligence; Why It Can Matter More Than I.Q.* Bantam Books, New York, 1995.

Goodwin, D. *Anxiety.* Oxford University Press, New York, 1986.

Greer, S., and Morris, T. Psychological Attributes of Women Who Develop Breast Cancer: A Controlled Study, *Journal of Psychosomatic Research* 19:147–153, 1975.

Handly, R., and Neff, P. *Beyond Fear.* Fawcett Crest, New York, 1987.

Harbin, T.J. *Beyond Anger: A Guide for Men: How to Free Yourself from the Grip of Anger and Get More Out of Life.* Marlow & Co., New York, 2000.

Haynes, S. et al. The Relationship of Psychosocial Factors to Coronary Heart Disease in the Framingham Study, I. Methods and Risk Factors, *American Journal of Epidemiology* 107:362–383, 1978.

Jung, C. G. *Man and His Symbols.* Anchor Press, NY, 1964.

Kessler, R., and McLeod, J. Sex Differences in Vulnerability to Understand Life Events, *American Sociological Review* 46:443–452, 1984.

Kindlon, D. and Thompson, M. *Raising Cain: Protecting the Emotional Life of Boys.* Ballantine Books, New York, 2000.

Kübler-Ross, E. *Death: The Final Stage of Growth.* Touchstone Books, New York, 1988.

Lerner, H. G. *The Dance of Anger.* Harper & Row, New York, 1985.

Martinsen, E. W. Benefits of Exercise for the Treatment of Depression, *Sports Medicine* 9(6):219–231, 1985.

Maslow, A. H. *The Farther Reaches of Human Nature.* Penguin Books, New York, 1976.

McKay, M., Rogers, P., and McKay, J. *When Anger Hurts: Quieting the Storm Within.* New Harbinger Publications, Oakland, CA, 1989.

Middelton-Moz, J. *Boiling Point: The High Cost of Healthy Anger to Individuals and Society.* Health Communications, Inc., Deerfield Beach, FL, 1999.

Middelton-Moz, J. *Boiling Point: The Workbook.* Health Communications, Inc., Deerfield Beach, FL, 2000.

Mogg, G. *Creative Anger Management.* The American University, Washington, DC, 1992.

Murray, E. Coping and Anger. In *Stress and Coping,* eds. T. Field, P. McCabe, and N. Schneiderman. Erlbaum, Hillsdale, NJ, 1985.

Neale, R. E. *The Art of Dying.* Harper & Row, New York, 1973.

Nuckols, C., and Chickering B. *Healing an Angry Heart: Finding Solace in A Hostile World.* Health Communications, Inc., Deerfield Beach, FL, 1998.

Reich, J. The Epidemiology of Anxiety, *Journal of Nervous and Mental Disease* 174(3):129–136, 1986.

Rosenman, R. H. Health Consequences of Anger and Implications for Treatment. In *Anger and Hostility in Cardiovascular and Behavioral Disorders,* eds. M. A. Chesney and R. H. Rosenman. Hemisphere, Washington, DC, 1985.

Schimelpfening, N. Depressed Women at Greater Risk for Breast Cancer, http://depression.about.com/health/depression/library/weekly/aa100300.htm

Schwartz, G. E., Weinberger, D. A., and Singer, J. A. Cardiovascular Differentiation of Happy, Sad, Anger, and Fear Following Imagery and Exercise, *Psychosomatic Medicine* 43:343–364, 1981.

Segal, J. *Living without Fear.* Ballantine Books, New York, 1989.

Shekelle, R. et al. Hostility and Risk of CHD, and Mortality, *Psychosomatic Medicine* 45:109–114, 1983.

Skog., S. *Depression: What Your Body's Trying to Tell You.* Avon: Whole Care Books, New York, 1999.

Sundram, J. *Re-Engineering the Human System: The Physiology of Conscious Evolution.* Institute of Noetic Sciences, 5th Annual Conference, Boca Raton, FL, July 18–21, 1996.

Sussman, V. To Win, First You Must Lose, *U. S. News and World Report,* January 15, 1990.

Tavris, C. *Anger–The Misunderstood Emotion.* Simon and Schuster, New York, 1982.

Thomas, S. P., and Donnellan, M. M. Correlates of Anger Symptoms in Women in Middle Adulthood, *American Journal of Health Promotion* 5(4):266–272, 1991.

Thomas, S. and Jefferson, C. *Use Your Anger Wisely: A Woman's Guide to Empowerment.* Simon & Schuster, New York, 1996.

Warner, N. *Make Anger Your Ally: Harnessing Our Most Baffling Emotion.* Simon and Schuster, New York, 1983.

Weisinger, H. *Weisinger's Anger Work-Out Book.* William Morrow, New York, 1985.

Williams, R. B. et al. Type A Behavior, Hostility, and Coronary Atherosclerosis, *Psychosomatic Medicine* 42:539–549, 1980.

Williams, R. and Williams, V. *Anger Kills.* Harper-Perennial, New York, 1994.

Wolpe, J. *The Practice of Behavior Therapy.* Pergamon Press, New York, 1973.

Wolpe, J., and Wolpe, D. *Life without Fear.* New Harbinger Publications, Oakland, CA, 1988.

Wood, C. The Hostile Heart, *Psychology Today* 20:9, 1986.

Zane, M., and Milt, H. *Your Phobia.* American Psychiatric Press, Washington, D.C., 1984.

Chapter 6 Stress-Prone and Stress-Resistant Personalities

"When I was 25, I got testicular cancer and nearly died. I don't know why I am still alive. I can only guess. I have a tough constitution and my profession taught me how to compete against long odds and big obstacles."

—Lance Armstrong

In the summer of 1966, at the age of fifty-five, Nien Cheng (Fig. 6.1) was placed under house arrest in her private home in Shanghai. It was the dawn of the Cultural Revolution in Mao Tse-Tung's communist China. Thousands of innocent people found themselves incarcerated, political prisoners accused of being enemies of the state. Educated in London, employed by Shell Oil as a management advisor, and widow of a former official of Chiang Kai-shek, Nien Cheng quickly became the target of several communist indictments. She was soon moved from house arrest to solitary confinement, in a cell no bigger than a walk-in closet, at the Number 1 Detention House for political prisoners. Convinced she had committed no crime, she defended her innocence despite hunger, disease, intimidation, terror, and humiliation. Many innocent prisoners perished from the torture of the communist Red Guards, yet Nien Cheng was determined not only to survive but to prove her innocence. Upon her release in 1972, after six and a half years in solitary confinement, she was declared a victim of false arrest. At this time, she frantically sought the whereabouts of her only daughter. What she discovered about the fate of Meiping Cheng made it impossible for her to remain in her homeland. In 1980, Nien Cheng emigrated to North America, whereupon she wrote of how she prevailed over this tumultuous experience in her stirring autobiography, *Life and Death in Shanghai.* As a guest speaker in my Strategies for Stress Reduction class, Mrs. Cheng was asked what it was that allowed her to survive such a harrowing ordeal. Gracefully, she answered, "I saw my stay at the detention house as a challenge, and with the grace of God, I was committed to proving my innocence." Nien Cheng left no doubt that she demonstrated a special personality in surviving her ordeal.

While almost everyone has a concept of what personality is, scholars in the field of psychology have yet to agree on a definition of the term. The word originally derives from the Latin word *persona,* meaning mask, as in the masks used by actors in ancient Greek plays. In more contemporary times, personality has come to mean a conglomeration of the several characteristics—behaviors, expressions, moods, and feelings—that are perceived by others. The complexity of one's personality is thought to be shaped by genetic factors, family dynamics, social influences, and a wealth of personal experiences. Just as there are many definitions, there

Nien Cheng was imprisoned at age 56 for six and a half years. She is now 85 and the fortitude that allowed her to survive her ordeal keeps her going strong.

Figure 6.1

are also many theories of personality, which attempt to explain the differences in the psychological make-up from one person to another. The basis of many of these theories centers on whether these traits and behaviors are primarily innate or learned—the nature versus nurture question. No clear-cut answers have emerged, and whether personality can actually be changed is still being argued. The research findings are fascinating but quite inconclusive. Currently, growing opinion suggests that the most likely component of personality to be alterable is behavior, rather than specific traits, and it is this opinion that has led to the formation of and emphasis on behavior modification classes in health promotion programs, including stress management.

The story of Nien Cheng is a remarkable testimony to the strength of the human spirit. It is this characteristic, as well as many others, that psychologists and psychiatrists have attempted to study to determine which personality types are prone to the effects of stress, and which seem to be immune or resistant to it. Although the search has not been easy, researchers have identified specific personality traits and behaviors, classified as personality types, which have begun to shed some light on the relationship between personality and disease. They include Type A behavior, codependent personality, helpless-hopeless personality, hardy personality, and sensation seeker or Type R personality. As people strive to learn more about themselves, these labels have now become household words in North America. What follows is a look at these personality types and the factors that separate stress-prone from stress-resistant traits and behaviors.

Type A Behavior

In the late 1950s, coronary heart disease emerged as the number one killer in the country, claiming the lives of many men and women, including several politicians, physicians, and executives of the nation's leading corporations. Unlike infectious diseases initiated by viruses and bacteria, this disease was attributed to factors associated with specific lifestyle behaviors and thus, recognized as potentially preventable. During the Eisenhower and Kennedy administrations this "epidemic" was given national attention, and federal funds were appropriated for research to understand the nature of this disease. Like detectives at the scene of a murder, federally funded researchers searched for potential clues that might lead to the development of this killer disease. Studies conducted at Harvard University and the Framingham Study in Massachusetts revealed several factors that were believed to place an individual at risk for coronary heart disease, including cigarette smoking, hypertension, elevated levels of cholesterol and triglycerides, inactivity, diabetes, obesity, and family history of heart disease. Surprisingly, data also revealed that several heart attack victims had few, if any, of these risk factors. So the search went on.

Although assumptions had previously been made about the seemingly obvious relationship between emotional responses and health status, it was the initial work of cardiologists Meyer Friedman and Ray Rosenman, whose research in 1964 added one more significant risk factor to the list: **Type A behavior,** or a rushed or hurried lifestyle. As the story goes, they stumbled upon this insight while having their office furniture reupholstered, during which they discovered that their patients literally sat on the edge of the chairs while waiting to be seen. This tip led them to look at the psychological profiles of their patients, as well as the usual physical assessments. From their research, they developed an assessment tool to diagnose Type A behavior, called the Structured Interview. This interview process between the trained physician and patient was designed to measure the intensity, frequency, and duration of several criteria associated with Type A behavior. Later, a second assessment questionnaire, based on Friedman and Rosenman's work, was developed by psychologist David Jenkins and called the Jenkins Activity Questionnaire (JAQ). Because of its simplicity—individuals can fill it out on their own—the JAQ has been used more often than the Structured Interview to assess Type A behavior. Examples from both instruments are shown in Box 6.1.

Initially, Friedman and Rosenman referred to Type A as the "hurried sickness." In several research studies, the behavioral traits of "tense" individuals were compared to others who were regarded as "laid back" and called Type B individuals. Striking evidence was observed by Rosenman et al. (1964) in the landmark Western Collaborative Groups Study, which examined over 3,500 subjects over an eight-year period. Results revealed that Type A behavior was in fact a greater predictor of heart disease than all other risk factors combined. Physiologically speaking, research shows that Type A individuals are more prone to sympathetic arousal (i.e., increased secretion of catecholamines), hypertension, and elevated levels of cholesterol and triglycerides, placing these people at greater risk for several stress-related disorders, but especially coronary heart disease (Rice, 1992). Based on years of research by Rosenman, Friedman, and others, the following personality traits may identify Type A behavior. As you will see, many of these traits are interrelated. Friedman and Rosenman felt that it only took one of these traits to be classified as Type A, though in truth Type As have been found to share many of these characteristics.

1. *Time urgency.* Type A people were found to be preoccupied, if not obsessed, with the passage of time and appeared very impatient. Typically

Sample Items from Jenkins Activity Survey and Structured Interviews

The Jenkins Activity Survey* measures Type A behavior by asking people about their typical responses to life's situations, either pleasant or troubling, where some element of challenge is perceived to be present. The following are two examples of items that appear on that survey.

1. When you listen to someone talking and this person takes too long to come to the point, how often do you feel like hurrying the person along?

   _____ Frequently

   _____ Occasionally

   _____ Almost never

2. Would people who know you well agree that you tend to do most things in a hurry?

   _____ Definitely yes

   _____ Probably yes

   _____ Probably no

   _____ Definitely no

The following assessment tool is adapted from Friedman and Rosenman's *Structured Interview*† (1974) as a means to determine Type A behavior. This is an awareness tool used to help a person become more cognizant of behaviors that are strongly associated with Type A. Read the following questions and check the appropriate boxes. If you find that you have checked yes to the majority of questions, you may demonstrate behaviors highly associated with Type A.

1. _____ yes _____ no: Do you tend to accentuate (explode) some words in speech and hurry the last words in your sentences?

2. _____ yes _____ no: Are you in the habit of always moving, eating, and walking quickly?

3. _____ yes _____ no: Do you find yourself generally impatient and irritated when things do not move fast enough for you?

4. _____ yes _____ no: Do you typically direct or dominate the topic of conversation toward your own interests?

5. _____ yes _____ no: Are you repeatedly involved with more than one activity at a time (e.g., shaving or putting on makeup while driving)?

6. _____ yes _____ no: More often than not, are you unaware of new changes in your environment?

7. _____ yes _____ no: Are you more impressed with having things rather than just being?

8. _____ yes _____ no: Does the idea of taking time to relax bring with it a sense of guilt?

9. _____ yes _____ no: Do you usually have a sense of time urgency, where you have more responsibilities than time to do them in?

10. _____ yes _____ no: Do you express yourself in nervous movements (muscle twitching, jaw clenching) or overemphatic gestures (e.g., pounding the table to emphasize a point) when engaged in conversation?

11. _____ yes _____ no: Do you believe that your success is based on your ability to get things done quickly?

12. _____ yes _____ no: Do you find yourself threatened when a colleague or peer seems to be making greater progress than you in career or school?

13. _____ yes _____ no: Do you measure success in life in terms of numbers (e.g., sales, cars, money)?

*From the Jenkins Activity Survey. Copyright, 1965, 1966, 1969, and 1979 by The Psychological Corporation. Reproduced by permission. All rights reserved.

†Based on M. Friedman and R. H. Rosenman, *Type A Behavior and Your Heart* (New York: Knopf, 1974).

these individuals hate to wait in lines, honk at the car in front when the light turns green, and show incredible impatience with others who are too slow with tasks that threaten their own work schedule or personal responsibilities. Type As feel uncomfortable or guilty about relaxing when there is no set agenda. They rarely take

vacations. Everything in the course of a working day—eating, walking, talking—is done with speed. Time itself becomes a major stressor.

2. *Polyphasia.* Polyphasia is engaging in more than one thought or activity at one time. Today it's called multi-tasking. It can lead to sensory overload as the mind juggles thoughts

competing for attention. An example of polyphasia is the following: driving to work, talking on the car phone, putting on makeup or shaving, and listening to the radio, all at the same time. Polyphasia is related to the sense of time urgency in that these people feel that they must do many things at once because their time is so limited.

3. *Ultra-competitiveness.* Type As are very self-conscious in that they compare themselves with others of similar social status. This trait is exhibited by working extra hours, working on several projects at one time, and vying for top recognition at work. All colleagues or peers at the same status level are perceived as personal threats. Type As may also appear to be egocentric, perceiving that they are more important than others with regard to their work. Moreover, Type As are found to be more concerned with quantity of work than quality of work, despite what they may say. The ultra-competitiveness may carry over into nonwork-related events, such as sporting activities, also. This manifests itself when Type As are in the presence of other people who exhibit a similar competitive drive.

4. *Rapid speech patterns.* Type A people are found to raise their voices in normal conversations, and use explosive words to influence, control, or intimidate others. During conversations, Type As often finish sentences for people who take their time expressing or articulating their thoughts.

5. *Manipulative control.* Manipulative control is a trait symbolic of a person who is very ego-driven. This behavior results from a desire to influence, and even intimidate, co-workers, family members, and acquaintances. Control is achieved through either direct intimidation, or circuitously, in a passive-aggressive way. As one might expect, this attitude of dominant control is maintained to promote feelings of one-upmanship. Type As assert control when they feel threatened.

6. *Hyperaggressiveness and free-floating hostility.* Type As have a need to dominate other people. They not only strive for high goals, but walk over people to get to the top, showing little or no compassion. These people are very aggressive and may even come across as abrasive. Type As are also noted to have what is now called free-floating hostility. Free-floating hostility is explained as permanently indwelling anger that erupts at trivial occurrences like traffic lights, long lines at the supermarket, or broken photocopy machines. At closer range, Type As seem to have an inability to express anger in a creative fashion. In many cases, they momentarily suppress feelings of anger and then later explode. Hostility of this nature is also observed to be unfocused, free-floating, and often unresolved. Type As typically display annoyance with circumstances that would seem barely noticeable to Type Bs.

One factor that all these traits share is low self-esteem, here meaning the perception of self-worth based on both how one perceives oneself and how one perceives others' perceptions of oneself. People classified as Type A are also preoccupied with how they are perceived by others regarding material possessions and social status. (The issue of self-esteem will be explained in more detail at the end of this chapter.)

Demographic Analysis of Type A Behavior

Friedman and Rosenman (1974) estimated that over half of the U.S. male population could be classified as Type A. They postulated that in the American culture, these traits were deemed enviable and perhaps even necessary to climb the ladder of success. In the early 1960s, when this behavior was singled out as a risk factor, the workforce was primarily male, so Type A behavior was considered primarily a male trait. In the 1970s and 1980s as more and more women entered the workforce, it became evident that Type A personality was not gender-specific. In fact, when socioeconomic factors were taken into account, it was discovered that women showed as great a frequency of Type A behavior as men. Studies headed by Baker (1984) and Sorenson (1987), for example, indicated no gender differences between males and females with regard to Type A behavior. More specifically, it was noted that for both men and women, long working hours, high occupational mobility, and nonsupportive interactions with co-workers were indicative of Type A behaviors. With regard to coronary heart disease (CHD), women who were classified as Type A were twice as likely to suffer from this disease as those who were not. But unlike men, who report their first symptom of CHD with a heart attack, women are more likely to be aware of earlier symptoms, including chest pain (angina pectoris). Gender may not have much to do with the development of Type A behavior, but Friedman and Rosenman felt that urban living, more so than rural, was conducive to fostering Type A behaviors. In fact, they suggested that over 75 percent of all people living in cities exhibit traits associated with Type A behaviors. In addition, a study by Shekelle, Schoenberger, and Stamler (1976) revealed that Type A behaviors are closely associated with socioeconomic status, with Type A behaviors more prevalent as income levels increase. Perhaps for this very reason, Type A as a risk factor for CHD is more closely associated with white-collar than blue-collar occupations. But as later studies revealed, Type A behavior as a whole was not as important a consideration in predicting CHD as one specific factor of it: hostile aggression.

Hostility: The Lethal Trait

Originally, time urgency was considered the most critical factor associated with Type A and heart disease, and it was this trait that was thought to be directly related to hypertension. Upon closer examination, several people classified as Type A exhibited neither hypertension nor coronary heart disease, leaving doubt as to whether this criterion merited further research. More recent investigations by Rosenman (1990) and others suggest that the most important, even dangerous, component of Type A behavior is hostile aggression. Work in this area now supports the idea that this factor alone is more responsible for the strong correlation to coronary heart disease than are all the other traits classified as Type A behavior.

With the suspicion that hostile aggression was the most important predictor of CHD, new ways to assess aggressive behavior were considered. To date, the most popular method is the Cook-Medley Hostility Index, also referred to as the Ho Scale (Cook and Medley, 1954). This index was developed from questions on the Minnesota Multiphasic Personality Inventory (MMPI) to measure hostility. Using this and other assessment tools (e.g., Potential for Hostility Scale, or PoHo), several studies have begun to show a strong correlation between hostility and the development of CHD. In one study by Williams et al. (1980), for example, it was found that hostility was correlated with coronary blockage, suggesting that hostile aggression could be used as a predictor for CHD. Studies by Barefoot et al. (1983, 1987) also indicated a strong correlation between hostility and increased risk of heart disease. Using the Ho Scale, Barefoot and colleagues studied a group of physicians over a twenty-five-year period. Those who scored high on the aggression index showed a fourfold greater incidence of CHD than those who scored low.

Hostility is an expression of anger, and as we saw in Chapter 5, anger can surface in many ways, including cynicism, sarcasm, intimidation, and various other aggressive behaviors. It should be noted that impatience is also a form of anger, and although it may not seem as potent as hostility, Friedman and Rosenman were not far off when they cited time-consciousness as the cornerstone of the Type A personality and its relationship to CHD. It may be that impatience festers into what they referred to as free-floating hostility, which in turn snowballs into mismanaged anger. Whatever the case, hostility and aggression are thought to be the most important factors with regard to heart disease, rather than the collection of Type A behaviors as a whole.

Behavior Modification for Type A Behavior

Since the identification of Type A personality, much research has been designed to determine if its traits and behaviors can be changed or modified to reduce the risk of coronary heart disease. Friedman et al. (1984), for example, placed over 500 post–heart attack patients in an education/behavior modification program, including twenty-nine counseling sessions, for a three-year period. Those who participated in this program showed a 44 percent decrease in Type A behaviors as measured by questionnaires and personal interviews. Many individuals also reduced the incidence of recurring heart attacks. The findings of this and other studies have led many health specialists to develop intervention programs that can alter negative health behaviors and improve health status. The same study also indicated that although the totality of personality will not change, components of it can be favorably influenced and altered to improve one's health status. Currently, behavior modification programs focus on the creative release of anger. It is the findings of Friedman and associates that led to current behavior modification programs in anger management.

Social Influences on Type A Behavior

Several researchers have speculated on the origins of Type A behavior, and the nature (genetics) versus nurture (environment) issue surfaces again. It is well accepted that children model their behavior on that of parents and other figures of authority, including aggressive behaviors. But researchers seem to agree that Type A behavior is a product of broader social and cultural factors as well. Many of the behaviors associated with Type A are often rewarded in our society as positive attributes leading toward success in one's career. Based on the work of Friedman and Rosenman, Schafer (1992) lists these as the following:

1. *Material wealth.* Part of the American dream is to have the freedom to own a house, car, and a number of consumer goods. In a free-market economy, people seem caught up in the accumulation of material goods. This fact became most evident in the 1980s, when sociologists noted a veritable obsession with material possessions.

2. *Immediate gratification.* The ability to drive up to a window and receive service immediately, whether for food, liquor, money, or videos, has had a big impact on our expectations for virtually all goods and services. In general, the pace of life has quickened in tandem with the pace of technology. In keeping pace with technological advancements, people have come to expect immediacy in everything.

3. *Competitiveness.* Competition for grades, salary increases, and sales are just three examples of the ways people feel pressured to become successful and get ahead. There is constant pressure to keep up with the Joneses. Friedman and Rosenman referred to this as "the excess of the competitive spirit," where more never seems to be enough.

4. *People as numbers.* Bureaucratic policies and procedures often make one feel like a number rather than a person. To be identified by your Social Security number for class registration, auto insurance, or taxes decreases the personal aspect of human interaction. This lack of personal attention is thought to contribute to an overall sense of alienation from oneself and others.

5. *Secularization.* As people become less and less involved with spiritual issues and growth, a vacuum is created, leading to a decline in self-reliance, self-esteem, and social connectedness.

6. *Atrophy of the body and right brain.* Reliance on technology to carry out functions humans used to do can make us physically sedentary. Moreover, there is a general consensus that our society encourages left-brain thinking processes, such as analysis and judgment skills, over right-brain thinking processes, which in excess can lead to increased tension and frustration.

7. *Television watching.* Studies show that the average person watches between twenty and forty hours of television per week. Many of the qualities and behaviors observed in Type As are the same ones illustrated in television programming. The rise in violent crimes, for example, is thought to be significantly correlated to the preponderance of violence seen on TV. The sheer number of violent acts on television programs implies condonement of this behavior.

It should come as no surprise that the behavioral traits associated with Type A personality precipitate the stress response. When left unmanaged, these create a vicious cycle of perceived stress-related problems spiraling into physiological responses. The pressures of time, threats of competition, and unresolved anger generate a modus operandi of perpetual stress.

Codependent Personality

The concept of **codependency** was introduced by psychologists in the 1980s to describe individuals who, in simple terms, are dependent on making other people dependent on them as a means of self-validation. In layman's terms, this label has been used to describe people who "love (conditionally) too much." Codependency is also referred to as an addictive personality because the behaviors associated with it are similar to those observed with other process addictions ("addictions" to behaviors rather than substances). The term *codependency* was first coined by a handful of counselors and therapists who were themselves recovering from chemical and process addictions. It evolved primarily from the study of individuals participating in alcohol rehabilitation programs. Originally, these programs focused solely on the addict. Over time, however, it was found to be imperative to include the spouses and children for greater success of the recovery process of the addict. When family members were introduced into the therapy process, it was learned that many of these individuals "enabled" the alcoholic to continue his or her addictive habits by covering up for them, allegedly out of concern, loyalty, and love, but in fact to act out their need to be needed. Thus, these individuals were labeled **enablers**, and strangely enough, it was observed that many of their own personality traits and related behaviors were of an addictive nature as well. Further studies on this group of people, many of whom were adult children of alcoholics (ACOA), led researchers to redefine the parameters of the enabler personality type and the traits associated with it.

Codependency, as defined by Melodie Beattie in her book *Codependent No More,* is "an addiction to another person(s) and their problems or to a relationship and its problems." This personality first became evident among children of alcoholics. But now, three criteria have been established as precursors to the development of this personality: having alcoholic parents or guardians, having divorced parents, or having emotionally repressive parents. A fourth criterion suggests that codependent traits are simply a product of American social mores. Regardless of one's background, codependent traits and their related behaviors are thought to develop early in childhood, in a lifestyle or environment that is chaotic, unpredictable, or threatening. Children are believed to unknowingly adopt various codependent behaviors as survival skills in their developmental years, usually to win approval and love from the parents and elders who most influence their lives, as well as to cope with family stress on a day-to-day basis. In many cases, these children assume adult responsibilities long before they reach high school. As they mature, they carry these survival skills—many

inappropriate—into adult relationships as excess baggage. Nevertheless, these skills remain the first line of defense in their attempt to deal effectively with others and themselves, yet the nature of these characteristics only perpetuates the stress cycle of threatening perceptions and consequent physical arousal.

Psychologist Ann Wilson Schaef (1986) describes codependency as a **process addiction** because each behavior is like a "fix" to acquire self-validation. But like the effects of a chemical addiction, the "high" is only short-lived so these behaviors are continually repeated. The traits associated with this personality type are many and have been criticized by some (Katz and Lieu, 1991) as being so widespread that they include nearly everyone living in the United States. Perhaps because the identification of this personality style emerged from psychotherapy and not clinical medicine, it has not been researched to the same extent as Type A personality. Regardless, there are several key traits that stand out as indicative of individuals who validate their own existence through the approval and manipulation of others. It should be pointed out, first, that codependent people are extremely nice and very well liked because they like to please others. (Many gravitate to the health care industry; Schaef points out that 83 percent of all nurses are first-born children of alcoholics.) Either individually or collectively, the traits associated with codependency are not considered bad; in fact, many of them are looked on as being quite admirable. However, it is the habitual exhibition of these traits, in an obsessive-compulsive manner, that defines the codependent personality. These traits include the following:

1. *Ardent approval seekers.* Codependent people know how to say the right things, wear the right clothes, and do the right things to draw other people to them and to avoid rocking the boat. Often they ask for an opinion or feedback on their performance and appearance, looking for approval from others.
2. *Perfectionists.* These people are extremely well organized and are in the habit of going beyond a quality job every time. They do, however, get caught up in details, spending extra time on every project or activity to make everything just right. They get very stressed (either annoyed or worried) when things aren't perfect.

3. *Super-overachievers.* This trait means being involved in an abundance of activities and obligations—school, sports, social functions—and receiving stupendous recognition for all of these (Fig. 6.2). These people do it all, and they do it all extremely well.

4. *Crisis managers.* Perhaps because of the environment in which they were raised, codependents thrive on crisis. They constantly try to make order out of chaos and, for the most part, are successful at it. They rush to take control in time of crisis and show that they can be counted on to be there and steer the ship back to a safe harbor.

Figure 6.2 People with a codependent personality are typically super-overachievers. They take on many responsibilities and do them all extremely well.

5. *Devoted loyalists.* Codependents are extremely loyal to friends and family, despite their addictions and abusive behavior. It has been suggested that extreme loyalty may be shown for fear of rejection and abandonment.

6. *Self-sacrificing martyrs.* People who express this personality put everyone else first, before their own needs, to the point of sacrificing their own time, values, property, and even life goals.

7. *Manipulators.* Unlike Type As, who use intimidation and dominance to manipulate others, codependents manipulate others through acts of generosity and "favors." They feel that the ability to express their own emotions and control their own lives is nowhere as easy as doing these for other people. Control and manipulation are performed in a humbling fashion. Codependents adopt what Schaef calls the illusion of control, wherein they try to control others and their environment to compensate for the fact that they cannot maintain self-control (e.g., of emotions, perceptions, etc.).

8. *Victims.* In tandem with repeated acts of martyrdom, these people perceive that they never receive enough gratitude or credit for self-sacrifice. These people find it impossible to say no but feel taken advantage of after the fact when feeling used sets in. Both crisis management and simple charitable tasks are unconsciously described by the codependent individual as "I've been wronged."

9. *Feelings of inadequacy.* Simply stated, codependents have a black cloud of inferiority over their heads, despite the fact that they are overachievers. (Remember, every action is a "fix" of self-validation.) They feel that the quality and quantity of work done is never to their satisfaction, that more is always expected of them. By being dependent on others for approval, they forfeit self-reliance, the ability to turn inward for strength, faith, and confidence. Self-reliance is the ability to be inspired from within, not motivated solely by external factors. And feelings of inadequacy dissolve self-reliance.

10. *Reactionaries.* Codependent individuals tend to overreact rather than respond to situations. At

a young age, their reactions of concern and worry were perceived as expressions of love. But as noted in Chapter 4, worrying is an immobilizing emotion that inhibits the ability to respond adequately to a given situation. When small problems arise, overreacting makes them appear catastrophic, which in turn makes them all the more important to address.

Schaef elaborates on several behaviors that appear to be hallmarks of the codependent personality in her book *Co-Dependence: Misunderstood, Mistreated.* The manifestation of codependent traits includes the following behaviors:

1. *External referencing.* This is a process whereby an individual gains feelings of importance from external sources. Codependents often doubt their own intrinsic value, so the greatest percentage of their self-validation is derived externally. An example of this behavior is trying to live up to other people's expectations.
2. *Lack of emotional boundaries.* This means that an individual takes on other peoples' emotional feelings—sadness, happiness, fear, or whatever people around them are feeling or thinking. Codependents often cannot delineate where their feelings end and where the feelings of others begin.
3. *Impression management.* Codependents are always trying to be good people, and they believe they can control the perceptions of others by their good deeds. Their main goal in life is to try and figure out what others want and then deliver it to them. They develop amazing abilities to learn about the likes and dislikes of other people. They truly believe that if they can just become what others want, they will be safe and accepted. When things go unexpectedly wrong, they often use the words, "I'm sorry," to win sympathy and approval.
4. *Mistrust of one's own perceptions.* Codependents tend to ignore their own perceptions of situations unless or until they are verified externally by others. Even though they might have a very clear impression of a person or a situation, they often dismiss it as being crazy or mistaken. They have learned not to trust their own intuition.

5. *Martyr syndrome.* There is a difference between helping people in need and living their lives for them. Codependents will help anyone (most often their immediate families), and they help them with everything. They say yes because they don't know how to say no. They are afraid that saying no will mean permanent rejection. Martyrs actually perpetuate chaotic situations by accepting responsibility for spouses, parents, and other family members to keep the household together, rather than blowing the whistle on inappropriate behavior.
6. *Lack of spiritual health.* Codependents adopt a mode of dishonest behavior (lying) to survive. The habit of lying begins as white lies in order to appease people. In this process, they also lie to themselves, hiding their own feelings. In the opinion of Schaef, "Lying does not keep with our deepest spiritual self. Lying to ourselves is always destructive to the self, and it is always destructive to others." According to Schaef, this is a form of spiritual destruction. The mental, emotional, and often physical imbalances spill over into a spiritual imbalance as well.

Estimates by Larsen (1983), Wegscheider-Cruse (1984), and Schaef (1987) suggest that the codependent personality is so prevalent in the United States that it has become "the American personality," with over 96 percent of Americans exhibiting traits of codependency (and leading to what Schaef calls "an addictive society" as a whole). This number is quite likely inflated, but research does indicate that approximately 25 million Americans are alcoholics, and that their addictive habits can and do negatively effect family members and coworkers. (Some estimates are that each alcoholic negatively affects between ten and twelve people, thus surpassing the country's population.) In many families where one or both parents are alcoholics, children often assume the role of an adult, handling many parental responsibilities. These children learn to react to family crises by taking charge in hopes of winning love and approval. Like Type A behavior, codependency is not gender-specific, and both personality types include the inability to recognize and express emotions. But unlike Type A individuals, who operate on the energy of misdirected and unresolved anger, codependents are motivated by fear, most notably, fear of rejection, fear of the unknown, and fear of failure. The codependent personality has many similarities to what medical researchers have identified as the cancer-prone personality (Type C personality), which is described as a people-pleasing and emotionally repressed personality.

Helpless-Hopeless Personality

The helpless-hopeless personality, while less defined by various traits than the Type A or codependent personality, nevertheless is a stress-prone personality based on low self-esteem. Seligman (1975) was the first to study this personality and to derive the theory of what he called learned helplessness. Seligman described people with this personality as those who have encountered repeated bouts of failure, to the point where they give up on themselves in situations where they clearly have control. That is, repeated failure becomes a learned response. Seligman noted that the signatures of learned helplessness are (1) poor self-motivation, where no attempt is made at self-improvement; (2) cognitive distortion, where perceptions of failure repeatedly eclipse prospects of success; and (3) emotional dysfunction, where repeated failures result in chronic depression.

Dr. Arthur Schmale (Locke and Colligan, 1986) has also studied individuals whom he classifies as the helpless-hopeless personality. These individuals, he found, perceive that their problems are beyond the range of their own resources and ultimately give up. Schmale defines the helpless-hopeless personality as "Feelings of frustration, despair, or futility perceived as coming from a loss of satisfaction for which the individual himself assumed complete and final responsibility by a sense of frustration that one has failed miserably at accomplishing anything in life." In a study reported by Locke and Colligan (1986), Schmale and Iker surveyed the personalities of fifty-one women using psychological tests and personal interviews to detect an intrinsic state of hopelessness. Based on the analysis of these tests and interviews, eighteen women were predicted to contract cancer, and these predictions held true.

Perhaps the characteristic that best identifies the helpless-hopeless personality is referred to as external **locus of control** (Box 6.2). This concept was developed by psychologist Julian Rotter in the early 1960s. Rotter theorized that behavior is normally influenced by both internal and external sources. A preponderance of external factors reinforcing behavior constitutes what Rotter defined as an external locus of control. Examples of external factors might include other

---

Box 6.2   ## Sample Items from the I-E Locus of Control Scale

1. _____ a. Many of the unhappy things in people's lives are partly due to bad luck.

   _____ b. People's misfortunes result from the mistakes they make.

2. _____ a. One of major reasons why we have wars is because people don't take enough interest in politics.

   _____ b. There will always be wars, no matter how hard people try to prevent them.

3. _____ a. In the long run, people get the respect they deserve in this world.

   _____ b. Unfortunately, an individual's worth often passes unrecognized no matter how hard he or she tries.

4. _____ a. The idea that teachers are unfair to students is nonsense.

   _____ b. Most students don't realize the extent to which their grades are influenced by accidental happenings.

5. _____ a. Without the right breaks, one cannot be an effective leader.

   _____ b. Capable people who fail to become leaders have not taken advantage of their opportunities.

6. _____ a. No matter how hard you try, some people just don't like you.

   _____ b. People who can't get others to like them don't understand how to get along with others.

(From J. B. Rotter, Generalized Expectancies for Internal versus External Control of Reinforcement, *Psychological Monographs* 609:80, 1966. 1966 by the American Psychological Association. Reprinted with permission.)

people, luck, the weather, chance, or even astrological influences. Conversely, people who demonstrate internal locus of control feel responsible for their own actions as derived by the internal resources of self-confidence, faith, intuition, and willpower.

Rotter observed that those individuals identified as having an internal locus of control were, on the whole, healthier and more productive individuals. They were observed to be information seekers and goal-directed, and to obtain a sense of mastery to cope with problems. Individuals who were identified as having an external locus of control often showed signs of apathy and complacency. The helpless-hopeless personality is the epitome of external locus of control. Such attitudes and behaviors appear to have been learned early in life, when failure with tasks was a common occurrence. The lack of success, coupled with less-than-desirable environmental factors, shapes the individual's personality to feel helpless in stressful situations and give up productive attempts to overcome the circumstances perceived as stressful. Rotter believed that although many features of personality were fixed entities, locus of control was not an absolute; it could be changed to the advantage of the individual. This is the premise of many drug- and alcohol-treatment programs, wherein patients are taught to capitalize on aspects of their lives they do in fact have control over in order to beat the chemical dependency.

Extreme examples of individuals with the helpless-hopeless personality type include alcoholics, drug addicts, abused children, abused wives, the aged, and some of the nation's homeless. Although these examples may seem distant from the average person, everyone experiences moments of hopelessness. However, repeated bouts of failure at any time in one's life could allow shades of this personality to manifest. Because of the failure-control issues involved, the helpless-hopeless personality is considered synonymous with an on-going stress response.

Hardy Personality

Using the framework of the mechanistic medical model, many researchers in the 1960s and '70s were trying to find a relationship between personality traits and the top leading killers in the country, coronary heart disease and cancer. Growing evidence suggested

a link between mind (negative thoughts) and body (physical symptoms), and this in turn spurred the pessimistic suggestion that the greater the stress level, the greater the chance of disease and illness.

But one group of researchers, headed by Dr. Suzanne Kobasa, became interested in individuals who despite stressful circumstance appeared *resistant* to the psychophysiological effects of stress. Kobasa et al. (1979, 1981, 1982, 1983) studied several hundred AT&T employees during the period of federal deregulation when scores of executives were laid off or transferred to other positions. In this study, over 700 executives were given a version of the Holmes and Rahe stress inventory and a checklist of physical symptoms and illnesses. While hundreds of executives showed physical symptoms of stress, under the same circumstances several did not. When this smaller group of individuals was studied further, it became quite obvious that what distinguished them from those who succumbed to the stress were specific personality traits enabling them to cope with their perceptions of stress. Kobasa et al. found three specific personality traits that collectively acted as a buffer to stress and contributed to what she called the **hardy personality** (Box 6.3). These three traits were:

1. *Commitment.* The dedication to oneself, one's work, and one's family that gives the individual a sense of belonging. Commitment involves an investment of one's values and life purpose to the growth of one's human potential and is a direct reflection of one's will-power.
2. *Control.* In this case, control means a sense of personal control, a sense of causing the events in one's life rather than a feeling of helplessness. Self-control, or empowerment, helps one overcome factors and elements in one's environment so that one does not feel victimized.
3. *Challenge.* The ability to see change and even problems as opportunities for growth, rather than threats to one's existence. Challenge, in Kobasa's mind, symbolized a hunger of the heart that serves as an inspiration. Challenge can also be viewed as a sense of adventure.

The results of this and similar studies with lawyers, housewives, and other groups, revealed that the traits of the hardy personality were not limited to

Box 6.3   How Hardy Are You?

Below are twelve items that appear in the hardiness questionnaire. Evaluating hardiness requires more than this quick test, but this exercise should give you some idea of how hardy you are. Write down how much you agree or disagree with the following statements.

0 = strongly disagree, 1 = mildly disagree, 2 = mildly agree, 3 = strongly agree

_____ **A.** Trying my best at work makes a difference.

_____ **B.** Trusting to fate is sometimes all I can do in a relationship.

_____ **C.** I often wake up eager to start on the day's project.

_____ **D.** Thinking of myself as a free person leads to great frustration and difficulty.

_____ **E.** I would be willing to sacrifice financial security in my work if something really challenging came along.

_____ **F.** It bothers me when I have to deviate from the routine or schedule I've set for myself.

_____ **G.** An average citizen can have an impact on politics.

_____ **H.** Without the right breaks, it is hard to be successful in my field.

_____ **I.** I know why I am doing what I am doing at work.

_____ **J.** Getting close to people puts me at risk of being obligated to them.

_____ **K.** Encountering new situations is an important priority in my life.

_____ **L.** I really don't mind when I have nothing to do.

Scoring: These questions measure control, commitment, and challenge. For half the questions a high score indicates hardiness; for the other half, a low score does. To calculate your scores, fill in the numbers of your responses as specified on the lines below. Then subtract the totals in the second line from those in the first and write in the results on the bottom line. Add your scores on commitment, control, and challenge together on the bottom line to get a score for total hardiness. A total score of 10–18 shows a hardy personality; 0–9, moderate hardiness; below 0, low hardiness.

$$\overline{A} + \overline{G} = \_\_\_\_$$

minus:

$$\overline{B} + \overline{H} = \_\_\_\_$$

_____
Control +

$$\overline{C} + \overline{I} = \_\_\_\_$$

minus:

$$\overline{D} + \overline{J} = \_\_\_\_$$

_____
Commitment +

$$\overline{E} + \overline{K} = \_\_\_\_$$

minus:

$$\overline{F} + \overline{L} = \_\_\_\_$$

_____
Challenge = ____

Total Hardiness Score

white, upper-middle-class, executive males employed by AT&T, but were found in people from both genders and all races and religions. In addition, Kobasa concluded the following:

✦ A hardy personality may override a genetic disposition to illness.

✦ A person can exhibit several Type A traits without risk of heart disease.

✦ Inner resources are more important than strong family support during high-pressure jobs.

✦ Some people observed as hardy showed signs of Type A personality minus feelings of hostility. These people enjoyed life so much they would often hurry with some tasks to enjoy others.

Kobasa and a colleague, Sal Maddi (1982), are of the opinion that while the hardy personality appears to be innate, the traits of commitment, control, and challenge can be learned as well. In a study to determine the efficacy of teaching hardiness skills to Illinois Bell executives over an eight-week period, sixteen executives experiencing stress-related health problems were divided into two groups: a treatment group to learn hardiness skills, and a control group. The skills taught to the treatment group were (1) focusing, or recognizing the body signals of stress (e.g., muscle tension); (2) reconstruction, reinterpretation of a stressor, and viable options to resolve it; and (3) compensation, turning control of personal talents into abilities that accent strengths rather than foster helplessness. After exposure to the new behavior skills, the treatment group scored higher on the hardiness scale, and even demonstrated a decrease in resting blood pressure, while the control group showed no change. The several research findings of Kobasa et al., which closely parallel the theories of Abraham Maslow and his concept of self-actualization, led them to believe that commitment, control, and challenge were necessary traits to maintain a buffer against the effects of stress, and that a hardy personality contributed to overall good health.

Calculated-risk taking is what separates sensation seekers from those who choose to sit on the sidelines. To accomplish a goal under these conditions is thought to augment self-esteem, which in turn enables one to deal more effectively with stress.

Figure 6.3

Sensation Seekers

Another personality identified as stress resistant is called the sensation seeker or Type R (risk taker), terms Zuckerman (1971) coined to describe those people whose personality appears dominated by an adventurous spirit (Fig. 6.3). Studies by both Zuckerman (1971) and Johnson, Sarason, and Siegel (1979) found that people who are inclined toward activities providing intense sensation, like rock climbing, sky diving, windsurfing, hang gliding, and exotic travel, are better able to cope with life events than those who are more inclined to avoid taking risks. It is hypothesized that in their intentional exposure to "approachable stress," or sensation activities, they calculate the risks involved. This prepares them for unexpected stressful events, which they also approach in a calculated manner. In other words, sensation seekers think through their strategies rather than reacting impetuously. They are spontaneous, yet calculating. An additional hypothesis suggests that the inner resources required to perform sensation activities (e.g., confi-

dence, self-efficacy, courage, optimism, and creativity) are the same qualities used as coping skills to deal effectively with stress. These hypotheses do not imply that sensation seekers do not have stress; rather, they try to meet it head on and aim to overcome it.

In a questionnaire designed to assess this characteristic, Zuckerman focused on four specific traits—adventure seeking, experience seeking, disinhibition, and susceptibility to boredom—to define the parameters of sensation seeking. Results suggested that individuals who had a low stimulation threshold are more vulnerable to stressful life events. Perhaps for that very reason, many outdoor education programs, including Outward Bound, Project Adventure, and National Outdoor Leadership School (NOLS), use the concept and application of calculated-risk taking in their activities, in order to build "survival skills" that will carry over into the everyday lives of adolescents and corporate executives alike.

Figure 6.4 A High level of self-esteem is vitally important to effective stress management. (ZIGGY © 1984 ZIGGY AND FRIENDS, INC. Reprinted with permission of UNIVERSAL PRESS SYNDICATE. All rights reserved.)

Self-Esteem: The Bottom-Line Defense

There are many traits common to all individuals, which makes distinguishing among personality types and their related behaviors difficult at times. Level of **self-esteem**, however, appears to be a critical factor in how people respond to stress, regardless of personality type. Low self-esteem is the common denominator in stress-prone personalities, as can be seen in Type A, codependent, and helpless-hopeless types. High self-esteem is a prerequisite for creating stress-resistant personalities, as it is directly linked to the accessibility of one's internal resources. Self-esteem is often described as self-value, self-respect, even self-love. It is reflected in the things we say, the clothes we wear, and perhaps most evidently in our behaviors. Self-esteem has also been described as the harmony or discrepancy between actual self-image and ideal self-image, where high self-esteem is harmony between the actual and ideal, and low self-esteem is the distance between the two.

When we place little or no value on our self, we become quite vulnerable to the perceptions of stress. Conversely, with high self-esteem, problems and worries tend to roll off one's back and might even go unnoticed. Self-esteem is continually fed by the thoughts, feelings, actions and even memories that contribute to our identity. Self-esteem, however, is a variable entity; it rises and falls, like ambient temperature, over the course of a day. But these variations remain within a specific range where the core of one's self-value resides. Individuals with stress-resistant personalities typically have a high level of self-esteem. For this reason, it is the construction and maintenance of high self-esteem that is the goal of many behavior modification programs involving recovering addicts, battered wives and children, and juvenile delinquents.

In his book *The Six Pillars of Self-Esteem,* Nathaniel Branden calls self-esteem the immune system of the consciousness. The author of several books on the topic of self-esteem, Branden highlights what he calls the six pillars of self-esteem, the internal resources that guide us on the human journey. They are:

1. *The focus on action,* expressing our free will so that we may reach our highest potential.
2. *The practice of living consciously,* living in the present moment, rather than confining yourself to past or future events, and being mindful of each activity you are engaged in.
3. *The practice of self-acceptance,* the refusal to be in an adversarial relationship with yourself.
4. *The practice of self-responsibility,* choosing to acknowledge responsibility for one's feelings, such as saying, I am responsible for my own happiness, rather than surrendering your feelings to the whims of those you are in a relationship with.
5. *The practice of self-assertiveness,* honoring one's wants, needs, and values, and seeking appropriate ways in which to satisfy these.
6. *The practice of living purposefully,* getting out of the thought processes of hoping and wishing, and instead, doing what you need to do to make your goals happen.
7. *The practice of personal integrity,* working to achieve congruence between your values and actions.

Researchers are now beginning to strongly advocate ways to raise self-esteem as the primary goal in stress-management therapy programs. As might be expected, prevention is more effective than rehabilitation, and for this reason, a special task force was created in California to incorporate self-esteem lesson plans into classroom curricula at the primary- and secondary-education levels. It is too early to know any results from this curriculum change, but it is hoped that, by giving attention to this crucial element of human potential, significantly fewer problems with drug and alcohol addiction, divorce, and homelessness will result in the coming decades. According to child psychologists Harris Clemes et al. (1990), the seeds for self-esteem are planted early in childhood and comprise four basic elements: connectedness, uniqueness, power, and models. All four of these factors need to be present, and cultivated continuously, to ensure a high sense of self-esteem. And these four characteristics are essential for self-esteem not only in early childhood development but in all developmental stages throughout one's life. They are defined as follows:

1. *Connectedness.* A feeling of satisfaction that associations and relationships are significant, nurturing, and affirmed by others.
2. *Uniqueness.* A feeling that the individual holds qualities that make him or her special and different, and that these qualities are respected and admired by others as well as oneself.
3. *Power.* A sense that one can access inner resources as well as use these resources and capabilities to influence circumstances in one's life.
4. *Models.* A mentoring process by which reference points are established to guide the individual on his or her life journey by sharing goals, values, ideals, and personal standards.

Individuals with low self-esteem often feel powerless, are easily influenced by others, express a narrow range of emotions, become easily defensive and frustrated, and tend to blame others for their own weaknesses. Individuals with high self-esteem promote their independence, assume given responsibilities, approach new challenges with enthusiasm, exhibit a broad range of emotions, are proud of accomplishments, and tolerate frustration well. Because high self-esteem is central to the stress-resistant personality, much attention is now placed on ways to increase self-esteem in people of all ages. Among the many ways to raise and maintain self-esteem, Clemes gives the following suggestions:

1. Disarm the negative critic. Challenge the voice inside that feeds the conscious mind with put-downs and negative comments. A critic taking only one side is unbalanced and dangerous to your self-esteem.
2. Give yourself positive reinforcements and affirmations to remind yourself of your good qualities. Write these down, and look at the list when you're feeling down.
3. Avoid "should haves," where you place a guilt trip on yourself for unmet expectations. Learn from the past, but don't dwell on it. Look for new opportunities for growth.
4. Focus on who you really are, your own identity, and your role models or mentors.
5. Avoid comparisons with others. Respect your own uniqueness, and learn to cultivate it.
6. Diversify your interests. Don't put all your eggs in one basket. Diversify so that if one aspect of your life becomes impaired, other areas can compensate to keep you afloat. (For instance, if you see yourself solely as a student and you do badly on an exam, this will pull down your self-esteem like a rock.)
7. Improve your connectedness. Widen your network of friends, and find special places in your environment that recharge your energy and strengthen your social bonds.
8. Avoid self-victimization. Martyrs may be admired, but begging for pity and sympathy gets old and the effects are short-lived.
9. Reassert yourself and your value before and during a stressful event.

Is there a difference between self-esteem and self-image? Yes! Self-image, how you perceive yourself and self-esteem, how you value yourself, are related, yet two different concepts. Self-image is recognized as being a by-product of one's level of self-esteem. This difference between self-esteem and self-image became quite clear in the early 1960s through the work of Maxwell Maltz, author of the book *Psycho-Cybernetics.* In his work as a plastic surgeon, Maltz was intrigued to learn that after performing scores of nose jobs and facelifts, his clients didn't seem all that much happier with their new appear-

Box 6.4 **And Still I Rise**

You may write me down in history,
With your bitter, twisted lies,
You may trod me in the very dirt,
But still, like dust, I'll rise.

Does my sassiness upset you?
Why are you beset with gloom?
'Cause I walk like I've got oil wells
Pumping in my living room.

Just like moons and just like suns,
With the certainty of tides,
Just like hopes springing high,
Still I rise.

Did you want to see me broken?
Bowed head and lowered eyes
Shoulders falling down like teardrops
Weakened by my soulful cries?

Does my haughtiness offend you?
Don't you take it awful hard
'Cause I laugh like I got gold mines
Diggin' in my own back yard.

You may shoot me with your words,
You may cut me with your eyes,

You may kill me with your hatefulness
But still, like air, I'll rise.

Does my sexiness upset you?
Does it come as a surprise?
That I dance like I got diamonds
At the meeting of my thighs?

Out of the huts of history's shame
I rise.
Up from a past that's rooted in pain
I rise.
I'm a black ocean, leaping and wide
Welling and swelling, I bear in the tide.

Leaving behind nights of terror and fear
I rise.
Into a daybreak that's wondrously clear
I rise.
Bringing the gifts that my ancestors gave,
I am the dream and the hope of slave.
I rise.
I rise.
I rise.

—Maya Angelou

ance. After scores of interviews with patients, he came to the realization that before any external changes take place, the real change first has to take place inside. In other words, if people change their physical image, but their self-image remains poor, no amount of surgery will change how one feels about oneself. The changes have to come from within first, changes that nurture and cultivate our inner resources such as confidence, courage, love, compassion, and willpower. If your level of self-esteem is low, so, too, will be your self-image. Through his principles of psycho-cybernetics, Maltz suggests that we first work within before changing external features. Working within means focusing on our positive aspects; shedding old beliefs, attitudes, and perceptions that trap us in the mindset of low self-esteem; and learn to use our inner resources to move out of crisis into creative opportunity.

High self-esteem is considered the best defense against stress; strategies used to combat stress are useless without a strong feeling of self-worth or self-value. Although an abstract concept, your self-esteem should be attended to regularly, every day, like brushing your teeth and eating. It is that important.

Summary

+ Personality is thought to be comprised of several traits, characteristics, behaviors, expressions, moods, and feelings as perceived by others.
+ Personality is thought to be molded at an early age by genetic factors, family dynamics, social influences, and personal experiences.
+ Personality is thought to be a fixed entity, not subject to significant changes; however, the most likely part of personality to change is behavior.
+ Personalities can be classified as either stress-prone (seeming to attract stress) or stress-resistant (providing a buffer against various stressors).
+ Type A, codependency, and helpless-hopeless are three personalities that have been associated with both acute and chronic stress. They have one common factor: low self-esteem.
+ Type A, "the hurried sickness," was first observed by cardiologists Rosenman and Friedman as a major risk factor for heart disease. Later studies revealed that the trait of hostility is most closely linked with hypertension and coronary heart disease.
+ Type A behavior is not gender-specific; as many females demonstrate Type A behavior as males. However, desire for higher social status is thought to be strongly correlated with Type A behavior.
+ Codependency, first observed in the spouses and children of alcoholics when recovery programs began to include family members, is now thought to apply as well to children of broken homes and those with emotionally repressive parents. Codependents are people who validate their existence by serving others at their own expense. Codependents typically operate from fear of rejection, failure, and fear of the unknown.
+ The helpless-hopeless personality develops as a result of repeated bouts of failure over time, to the point where individuals no longer feel competent to try things they really do have control over. Low self-esteem and an external locus of control appear to be significant factors in this type of personality.
+ The hardy personality and the sensation seeker are two personalities currently believed to be stress-resistant. The commonality between the two is high self-esteem.
+ The hardy personality was coined by Kobasa and Maddi, who observed that some people under severe stress did not succumb to stress-related ailments while others did. People who showed a strong sense of commitment, control, and challenge were labeled hardy personalities.
+ Zuckerman identified the sensation-seeking personality as those people who seek thrills and sensations but take calculated risks in their endeavors.
+ Self-esteem is a crucial cornerstone of personality. Low self-esteem attracts stress; high self-esteem seems to repel it. Clemes states that self-esteem is comprised of four components: connectedness, uniqueness, power (control) and models. The strength or weakness of these components is highly correlated with level of self-esteem.

Concepts and Terms

Codependency
Compensation
Enablers
Focusing
Hardy personality
Helpless-hopeless personality

Illusion of control
Locus of control (internal and external)
Polyphasia
Process addiction
Reactionaries

Reconstruction
Self-esteem
Sensation seekers
Substance addiction
Time urgency
Type A personality

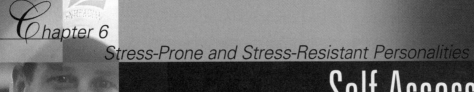

List the characteristics you feel you employ to deal with stress based on the concept of the hardy personality:

1. _____ 2. _____ 3. _____

List any other aspects that help you get through tough times.

1. _____ 3. _____

2. _____ 4. _____

Do you have any attributes in common with Type A behavior? If so, list them here.

1. _____ 3. _____

2. _____ 4. _____

Assuming that the codependent personality is quite prevalent in American society, do any of the traits and characteristics of codependency surface when you become stressed, or perhaps experience a precursor to stress? If so, list them.

1. _____ 3. _____

2. _____ 4. _____

To nurture our self-esteem and keep it at a high level, we need to address these four areas: uniqueness, power, role models, and connectedness. In the columns below, list (1) five things about yourself that make you feel special and unique; (2) five areas in which you feel you are in control or are self-empowered; (3) five people and the one or more characteristics they exhibit that you wish to emulate, include, or stengthen in your own personality; and (4) five people (you may also include animals) with whom you share a sense of belonging.

Uniqueness	Control	Mentorship	Connectedness
1. _____	1. _____	1. _____	1. _____
2. _____	2. _____	2. _____	2. _____
3. _____	3. _____	3. _____	3. _____
4. _____	4. _____	4. _____	4. _____
5. _____	5. _____	5. _____	5. _____

References and Resources

Associated Press. Attention-Deficit Drug OK'd, *Denver Post,* August 2, 2000.

Baker, L. J., Dearborn, M., Hastings, J. E., and Hamberger, K. Type A Behavior in Women: A Review, *Health Psychology* 3:477–497, 1984.

Barefoot, J. C., Dahlstrom, W. G., and Williams, R. B., Jr. Hostility, CHD Incidence, and Total Mortality: A 25-Year Follow-Up Study of 255 Physicians, *Psychosomatic Medicine* 45:59–63, 1983.

Barefoot, J. C. et al. Predicting Mortality from Scores on the Cook-Medley Scale: A Follow-Up Study of 118 Lawyers, *Psychosomatic Medicine* 49, 210 (abstract), 1987.

Barry, C. R. *When Helping You Is Hurting Me: Escaping the Messiah Trap.* HarperCollins, New York, 1989.

Beattie, Melody. *Beyond Codependence.* Harper/Hazelton Press, New York, 1989.

Beattie, Melody. *Codependent No More.* Harper/Hazelton Press, New York, 1987.

Branden, N. *The Power of Self-Esteem.* Health Communications, Inc., Deerfield Beach, FL, 1992.

Branden, N. *The Six Pillars of Self-Esteem.* Bantam Books, New York, 1994.

Cheng, N. *Life and Death in Shanghai.* Penguin Books, New York, 1986.

Clemes, H., Bean, R., and Clark, A. *How to Raise Teenagers' Self-Esteem.* Price Stern Sloan, Los Angeles, 1990.

Cook, W. and Medley, D. Proposed Hostility and Pharisaic-Virtues Scale for the MMPI, *Journal of Applied Psychology* 38:414–418, 1954.

Friedman, M. Type A Behavior Pattern, *Bulletin of the New York Academy of Medicine* 53:593–603, 1977.

Friedman, M. and Rosenman, R. H. *Type A Behavior and Your Heart.* Knopf, New York, 1974.

Friedman, M. and Ulmer, D. *Type A Behavior and Your Heart,* 2nd ed. Knopf, New York, 1984.

Friedman, M. et al. Alteration of Type A Behavior and Reduction in Cardiac Recurrences in Post-myocardial Infarction Patients, *American Heart Journal* 108:237–248, 1984.

Holmes, T. H. and Rahe, R. H. The Social Readjustment Rating Scale, *Journal of Psychosomatic Research* 11:213–218, 1967.

Jenkins, D. et al. Development of an Objective Test for the Determination of the Coronary Score Behavior Pattern in Employed Men, *Journal of Chronic Diseases* 20:371–379, 1967.

Johnson, J. H., Sarason, I. G., and Siegel, J. M. Arousal Seeking as a Moderator of Life Stress, *Perceptual and Motor Skills* 49:665–666, 1979.

Katz, S. and Lieu A. *The Codependency Conspiracy.* Warner Books, New York, 1991.

Kobasa, S. Commitment and Coping in Stress Resistance among Lawyers, *Journal of Personality and Social Psychology* 42:707–717, 1982.

Kobasa, S. Stressful Life Events, Personality, and Health: An Inquiry into Hardiness, *Journal of Personality and Social Psychology* 37:1–11, 1979.

Kobasa, S., Maddi, S. and Courington, S. Personality and Constitution as Mediators in the Stress-Illness Relationship, *Journal of Health and Social Behavior* 22:368–378, 1981.

Kobasa, S., Maddi, S., and Kahn, S. Hardiness and Health: A Prospective Study, *Journal of Personality and Social Psychology* 42(1):168–177, 1982.

Kobasa, S. and Puccetti, M. Personality and Social Resources in Stress Resistance, *Journal of Personality and Social Psychology* 45(4):839–850, 1983.

Kristol, E. Declarations of Codependence, *American Spectator,* June 20–23, 1990.

Larsen, E. *Basics of Codependency.* E. Larsen Enterprises, Brooklyn Park, MN, 1983.

Leftcourt, H. M. *Locus of Control: Current Trends in Theory and Research.* Hillsdale, NJ, Earlbaum, 1976.

Locke, S., and Colligan D. *The Healer Within.* Mentor Books, New York, 1986.

Maltz, M. *Psycho-Cybernetics.* PocketBooks, New York, 1960.

McKay, M. *Self-Esteem.* New Harbinger Publications, Oakland, CA, 1987.

Minchinton, J. *Maximum Self-Esteem: The Handbook for Reclaiming Your Sense of Self-Worth.* Arnford House Publishers, Vanzant, MO 1993.

Ragland, D. and Brand, R. J. Type A Behavior and Mortality from Coronary Disease, *New England Journal of Medicine* 318:65–69, 1986.

Rice, P. *Stress and Health,* 2nd ed. Brooks/Cole, Pacific Grove, CA, 1992.

Rosenman, R. H. Type A Behavior Pattern: A Personal Overview, *Journal of Social Behavior and Personality* 5:1–24, 1990.

Rosenman, R. H. et al. A Predictive Study of Coronary Heart Disease: The Western Collaborative Groups Study, *Journal of the American Medical Association* 189:15–22, 1964.

Rosenman, R. H. and Friedman, M. Modifying Type A Behavior Pattern, *Journal of Psychosomatic Research* 21:323–331, 1977.

Rotter, J. B. Generalized Expectancies for Internal versus External Control of Reinforcement, *Psychological Monographs* 609:80, 1966.

Schaef, A. W. *Codependence–Misunderstood, Mistreated.* Harper & Row, San Francisco, 1986.

Schaef, A. W. *When Society Becomes an Addict.* Harper & Row, San Francisco, 1987.

Schafer, W. *Stress Management for Wellness,* 2nd ed. Harcourt Brace Jovanovich, Fort Worth, TX, 1992.

Schmale, A., and Iker, H. Hopelessness as a Predictor of Cervical Cancer, *Social Science and Medicine* 5:95–100, 1971.

Schultz, D. *Theories of Personality,* 3rd ed. Brooks/Cole, Pacific Grove, CA, 1990.

Seligman, M., Happy Days (Positive Psychological Movement), *Psychology Today* 33(3):32, 2000.

Shekelle, R. B., Schoenberger, J. A., and Stamler, J. Correlates of the JAS Type A Behavior Pattern Score, *Journal of Chronic Disease* 29:381–394, 1976.

Seligman, M. E. *Helplessness: On Depression, Development, and Death.* Freeman, San Francisco, 1975.

Seligman, M. *Learned Optimism: How to Change Your Minds and Life.* PocketBooks, New York, 1990.

Smith, E. Fighting Cancerous Feelings, *Psychology Today* 22(5):22–23, 1988.

Sorenson, G. et al. Relationships among Type A Behavior, Employment Experiences, and Gender: The Minnesota Heart Survey, *Journal of Behavioral Medicine* 10:323–336, 1987.

Staffenhagen, R. *Self-Esteem Therapy.* Praeger, New York, 1990.

Staffenhagen, R. *The Social Dynamics of Self-Esteem: Theory to Therapy.* Praeger, New York, 1987.

Taylor, S. E. *Health Psychology.* Macmillan, New York, 1998.

Turnipseed, D. L. An Exploratory Study of the Hardy Personality at Work in the Health Care Industry, *Psychological Reports* 85(3, pt 2):1199–1217, 1999.

Wegscheider-Cruse, S. Codependency: The Therapeutic Void. In *Codependency: An Emerging Issue.* Health Communications, Pompano Beach, FL, 1984.

Whitfield, C. Co-Dependence Health Communications Inc. Deerfield Beach, FL, 1991.

Williams, R. B. et al. Type A Behavior Hostility and Coronary Atherosclerosis, *Psychosomatic Medicine* 42:539–549, 1980.

Zuckerman, M. Dimensions of Sensation Seeking, *Journal of Consulting and Clinical Psychology* 36:45–52, 1971.

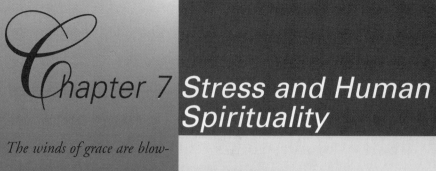

Chapter 7 Stress and Human Spirituality

The winds of grace are blow-

ing perpetually. We only need

raise our sails.

—Sri Ramakrishna

To write a book about stress without addressing the concept of human spirituality would be a gross injustice to both topics. In my quest for understanding and personal journey of enlightenment, I have met these two at the junction of many a crossroad. I know I am not alone. Human spirituality and stress seem to be as inseparable as the Taoist yin and yang, earth and sky, and, quite literally, mind and soul. I became aware of this relationship in my first year of teaching stress management in 1984. Many of the topics I taught, and several of the issues I was asked to address by students, had strong parallels with the cornerstones of several (if not all) religions: relationships, values, the meaning of life, and a sense of connectedness—the common denominator of these four being a level of human consciousness known as human spirituality. British author Aldous Huxley called this the *perennial philosophy,* or a transcendent reality beyond the limitations of cultures, religions, and egos.

The association between eustress (those moments of exhilaration and ecstasy) and spirituality, those cosmic moments Maslow called peak experiences, is so profound that it is often taken for granted or overlooked. The converse, distress, is quite another matter. I have learned that, in many cases, stress (specifically, unresolved anger and fear) can be a roadblock to spiritual well-being, and that a strong human spirit can be a vital asset to dismantling roadblocks, resolving stress, and promoting a greater sense of inner peace. In turn, the resolution of life's stressors can actually enhance the strength and health of the human spirit. Although stress and the human spirit appear, on the surface, to be at opposite poles, they are quite literally partners in the dance of life.

It is no coincidence that as the topic of stress grabs headlines across the nation, Americans seem to be on the verge of a new spiritual awareness. In fact in the past decade alone, the word *spirituality* has begun to take on a greater level of comfort in the vocabulary of the media and the population in general. This new awareness of human spirituality, promoted by a nucleus of individuals with grass-roots inspiration, goes by several names—the human potential movement, the consciousness movement, and the New Age movement, among others—all of which imply both spiritual bankruptcy and spiritual awakening in humankind, at least in the Western hemisphere. In his book, *As Above, So Below,* Ronald Miller describes a collective search for new forms of spirituality with which to make our lives more meaningful and relevant in today's world of global social upheaval. With an appetite greater than that which can be satisfied by their existing institutions, people have begun to look beyond their own backyards to answer questions about how they fit into the bigger picture. As indicated by the title of Miller's book (which is an axiom from ancient Egypt), there is a growing appreciation and understanding that no separation exists between the two worlds. Rather, the divine essence "above" resides within ourselves, making the two one.

The momentum of this movement has also been fueled by a rising interest in ecology and protection of the environment; a wake-up call of sorts. For example, the discovery of a second hole in the earth's ozone and the rapid depletion of our natural resources, including the tropical rain forests,—are fire alarms beckoning us to set aside our cultural and political differences and work together as one people. This was most clearly stated by then-Senator Al Gore in his best-selling book, *Earth in the Balance: Ecology and the Human Spirit,* in which he wrote, "The ecological perspective begins with a view of the whole, an understanding of how the various parts of nature interact in patterns that tend toward balance and persist over time. But this perspective cannot treat the earth as something separate from human civilization; we are a part of the whole too."

A Spiritual Hunger?

In times of crises, peoples of every generation and every culture have been known to seek help from a divine source. In the past, people took spiritual refuge in their religion traditions. However, today people seem a little disenchanted with their standard religious practices because they just don't seem to provide answers to the problems looming on the horizons of humanity. In an article titled "Choosing My Religion," Cimino and Lattin stated the following:

> In 1958, for example, only one in twenty-five Americans had left the religious denomination of

their upbringing. Today, more than one in three have left or switched. Most still believe in God, but now they are looking for a personal spiritual practice. According to a recent survey from the McArthur Foundation, seven out of ten Americans say they are religious and consider spirituality to be an important part of their lives. But about half attend religious services less than once a month or never.

In what is being referred to by some as the post-denominational age, many people do not feel a loyalty to one particular religious upbringing; rather people seek a host of sacred traditions, blending various practices to form their own spiritual path. There are Catholics who practice Buddhist meditation, Jews who participate in American Indian sweatlodges, and Methodists, Mormons, and Greek Orthodox who participate in Sufi dancing. Even hell has gotten a makeover, as the biblical conception of the most dreaded place in the universe moves from a literal to a figurative interpretation. Once described as eternal flames of death, the Vatican now describes hell as "a state of those who freely and definitively separate themselves from God". Many of those who claim to have already been to hell (on Earth, that is), as well as those who have come close are seeking a better understanding of God.

The expression used today is called "spiritual hunger," a term that describes a searching or longing for that which cannot be attained by traditional religious practices. Another term used in conjunction with spiritual hunger is "spiritual bankruptcy," a concept that suggests a sense of moral decay, perhaps due to an emptiness that cannot be filled with material possessions. Yet a strong element of human nature (the ego) encourages us to try anyway. One only need reflect on the 1999 shootings at Columbine High School in Colorado, or other similar events, to see that something is terribly amiss.

The Reverend Billy Graham, interviewed on the eve of the new millennium, stated, "I am afraid that people are losing their faith in God and replacing it with a faith in technology that will solve all our problems. They are being lead down the wrong path. There must be a change in the human heart." The change he referred to is what is typically called a spiritual awakening. A third phase commonly heard today is "spiritual dormancy." It refers to people who for one reason or another chose not to recognize the importance of the spiritual dimension of health and well-being at both an individual and societal level. The result of such inaction often leads to a state of dysfunction (a term many now call the "national adjective"). Like a person who hits the snooze button on the alarm clock, falling asleep on the spiritual path can have real consequences, because one is not only ill-equipped to deal with the problems at hand but with potential problems down the road as well.

A Turning Point in Consciousness

There are a number of factors that have come together to raise human consciousness to today's current level of awareness. They include but are not limited to:

- ✦ Vatican II, which in the 1960s changed the Catholic mass from Latin to various indigenous languages around the world, thereby opening the doors to a wealth of knowledge of Christianity (which had pretty much remained known only to a chosen few, since Latin is not a contemporary language).

- ✦ The invasion of Tibet by China in 1959, which not only forced thousands of Tibetans into exile around the world, but ultimately allowed for the sharing of their sacred knowledge, which had been largely in accessible for thousands of years.

- ✦ The Apollo Space Project, with its mission to land Americans on the moon in 1969, allowed us for the first time to see planet Earth as a whole, suspended in space, a planet without borders. This view altered many minds with regard to the future of the planet and her many inhabitants.

- ✦ The proliferation of self-help groups that use variations of the 12-Step program, as outlined by Alcoholics Anonymous, that provide for relinquishing control of addiction to a higher power. Self-help membership is non-denominational.

+ The American Indians, particularly the Lakota and Hopi, who for decades have been told by their elders *not* to share various aspects of their cultural heritage and spirituality due to lack of trust, have now been told this is the time to reveal their sacred knowledge, and they have done so. The Lakota Sioux prophecy foretold of the age of the white buffalo, when a shift in consciousness would appear. A white buffalo named Miracle was born in Janesville, Wisconsin, on August 20, 1994.

+ The Hebrew Kabalah, the sect of Jewish mysticism held on by a chosen few for the past several millennia, has recently been made available to anyone who has an interest in this topic.

+ Since the early 1970s, near death experiences (NDE) have been studied in earnest to learn more about the survivor's recollection. Research compiled *by U.S. News and World Report* in 1997 revealed that over 15 million documented NDE occurred in the previous twenty-five years alone, among people of every religious denomination. Those who recall their experience describe a new mission of compassion and inner peace. Children, many of whom have not been exposed to various spiritual matters, come back to consistently describe experiences of a divine mystical nature.

+ In the 1990s South American shamans have for the first time shared their wisdom of healing with "their younger brothers" in the northern hemisphere.

+ The Telecommunications Revolution opened the door of information to anyone with access to the Internet or World Wide Web. In doing so, knowledge from around the world in all its many sources suddenly became accessible without the censorship of intellectuals, religious leaders, or politicians, who for centuries have played a major role in keeping people in the dark about a great many issues and facts. Access to information has become a major stepping stone toward higher consciousness.

Unthinkable a decade ago, today it is not uncommon to see universities and corporate health-promotion programs including courses on spiritual well-being as well as more traditional programs on physical well-being. In addition, concepts of human spirituality served as the foundation of the twelve-step program, Alcoholics Anonymous, which has since become the model for nearly every self-help recovery organization for addictions. Today, for the first time ever, as the information age of the twentieth century unfolds, concepts from all cultures, religions, and corners of the globe are now accessible to us. As the pieces of this jigsaw puzzle called the human spirit are assembled, it becomes increasingly obvious that despite subtle nuances and obvious differences, there are several common denominators that tie and bind the integrity of the human spirit. First and foremost is a desire to learn, a personal quest of self-exploration. Be it instinctual or a learned trait, human behavior is often inspired by self-improvement, and herein lies the first step of the journey. In the words repeated by many Zen masters in the spirit of Chinese philosopher Lao Tzu, "There are many paths to enlightenment. The journey of each path begins with the first step."

The material in this chapter is a synthesis of several different perspectives on human spirituality. Some of these ideas may resonate with your way of thinking while others seem foreign, perhaps even intimidating, to your attitudes, beliefs, and values. The purpose of this chapter is not to intimidate you, but to show that despite our varied backgrounds and religious differences, there are elements common to all of us (Box 7.1). I ask you to focus on these common elements, not the differences, as you read. It would serve you best to respect and be receptive to all ideas different from your own because, as you will see, an open attitude will ultimately strengthen your own beliefs and the integrity of your spiritual well-being.

The Golden Rule

Box 7.1

A version of the Golden Rule—Do unto others as you would have them do unto you—is promulgated by each of the world's major religions, demonstrating the universal importance of proper conduct to the perennial philosophy. The following are excerpts:

Buddhism: A clansman should minister to his friends and familiars . . . by treating them as he treats himself.

Christianity: All things, therefore, whatsoever ye would that men should do unto you, even so do ye also unto them.

Confucianism: The Master replied: ". . . what you do not want done to yourself, do not do unto others."

Greek Philosophy: Do not do to others what you would not wish to suffer yourself. Treat your friends as you would want them to treat you.

Hinduism: Do naught to others which, if done to thee, would cause thee pain: this is the sum of the duty.

Judaism: Take heed to thyself, my child, in all thy works; and be discreet in all thy behavior. And what though thyself hatest, do to no man.

Taoism: To those who are good to me, I am good; and to those who are not good to me, I am also good. And thus all get to be good. To those who are sincere with me, I am sincere; and to those who are not sincere with me, I am also sincere. And thus all get to be sincere.

Adapted with permission from *The World's Living Religions* by Ernest Hume, Copyright © 1978. Reprinted by permission of Prentice-Hall, Inc., Upper Saddle River, NJ.

Definition of Spirituality

It would be fair to say that human spirituality has been the focus of countless conversations dating back to antiquity. Yet despite the millions of words and hundreds of philosophies exploring this concept, human spirituality is still a phenomenon for which no one definition seems adequate. Undoubtedly it includes the aspects of higher consciousness, transcendence, self-reliance, self-efficacy, self-actualization, love, faith, enlightenment, mysticism, self-assertiveness, community, and bonding, as well as a multitude of others. Yet no aspect alone is sufficient to describe the essence of human spirituality. In various sources, the human spirit has been described as a gift to accompany one through life, an inner drive housed in the soul, and even a living consciousness of a divinelike presence within us and around us. These descriptions are poetic and profound, but they don't bring us any closer to an understanding of what human spirituality really is. In many cultures, the word *spirit* means "first breath": that which enters our physical being with our first inhalation at birth. The Hebrews called this *ruah,* and even as the word is spoken, you can hear the rush of wind pass through your lips. Among some Eastern cultures, *pranayama,* or diaphragmatic breathing, is thought to have a spiritual essence that enhances physical calmness by uniting the body and mind as

one; by breathing the universal energy. The ancient Greeks used the words *pneuma* to connote spirit and *psyche* to describe the human soul, the latter of which is now commonly associated with the study of human behavior, psychology. More recently, the World Health Organization (WHO) defined human spirituality as "that which is in total harmony with the perceptual and nonperceptual environment."

Sometimes defining what a concept is *not* becomes a type of definition in itself. For instance, human spirituality is neither a religion nor the practice of a religion. Religion is based on a specific dogma: an active application of a specific set of organized rules based on an ideology of the human spirit. Being actively involved in a religion is considered enhancing of one's spirituality. This is one of religion's primary goals, and on the whole, religions are very effective in this. But recently it has been noted by several psychologists that, like too much of anything at one time, too much religion can impede the growth of the human spirit for some people, leading to what psychologists Anne Wilson Schaef and Leo Booth call an addiction to religion. By the same token, elements of spirituality pushed to the extreme are considered unhealthy too. Comedian Steven Wright jokingly states, "My girlfriend and I had conflicting attitudes. I wasn't into meditation and she wasn't into being alive." There is no doubt that religion can promote spiritual evolution; the two are very compatible. But individuals can be very spiritual, and not "religious" (in the sense of attending services), just as they can be very religious but have poor awareness of their spirituality. It is often said that where religion separates, spirituality unites. In the words of psychiatrist Viktor Frankl, "Spirituality does not have a religious connotation, but refers specifically to the human dimension." Spirituality, like water, and religions, like the various containers that attempt to hold it, are related yet separate concepts.

To define a term or concept is to separate and distinguish it enough from everything else to gain a clear focus and understanding of what it really is. All non-related aspects must be factored out to reach a clear and undiluted meaning. This is where the difficulty lies when one attempts to formulate an adequate definition of the word *spirituality*. It appears that human spirituality encompasses so many factors, possibly everything, that to separate anything out denies a full understanding of the phenomenon. On the other hand, perhaps at this time, we just don't possess the vocabulary to express it to our complete comprehension. Sometimes, in order to understand a concept, you just have to experience it, and experiences will certainly vary, as will their interpretation. Typically, people tend to describe their collective spiritual experiences as a journey or path. Most important, for a path to enhance the maturation or evolution of the soul, it must be creative, not destructive; progressive, not regressive. It must stimulate and enhance, not stifle, spiritual well-being. Given this premise, remember, too, that there are many paths to enlightenment. No one path is superior to the others, so it doesn't matter which path you take, but only that you keep moving forward (growing) on the path you have chosen. To quote Carlos Castaneda in *The Teachings of Don Juan*, "Look at every path closely and deliberately. Try it as many times as you think is necessary. Then ask yourself, and yourself alone, one question. Does this path have a heart? If it does, the path is good; if it doesn't, it is of no use."

Theories of Human Spirituality

Human spirituality has been studied by several academic disciplines, most notably philosophy, theology, sociology, and psychology. More recently, this topic has begun to be investigated in the fields of physics, nursing, and clinical medicine as well. Thus, human spirituality will be described below in terms of the various theories devised to provide a better understanding of this concept in several different disciplines.

In the scientific disciplines, theories give rise to operational (working) definitions. From these definitions come conceptual models. From models come tools to assess and measure, and from measurements comes a holistic picture of understanding. More often than not, the synthesis of a number of theories offers a mosaic that, up close, may look confusing, and even incomprehensible; but from a distant perspective, it closely approaches a representation of this mystical phenomenon. If human spirituality were compared to a huge mountain, then the individuals who created these theories are the ones who have bushwhacked a path to the top by articulating their own perspectives. Metaphorically speaking, what follows is an aerial view of this mountain, capturing but a few of the many paths reaching toward the summit. The paths described here are by individuals who have encountered and studied matters of the soul with various prophets, sages, and masters. Their personal perspectives, which arise from a range of disciplines and cultures, contribute pieces of the mosaic we call human spirituality. But they only begin to illustrate the nature of this unique human characteristic.

The Path of Jung

Typically, when individuals first consider the source of the human spirit, their search leads them to external things, like nature and the heavens above. It was the work of psychiatrist Carl Jung who, as a pioneer in psychology, turned the search inward to explore the depths of the mind, as a means to understand the spiritual nature of humanity. Jung was fascinated with the human psyche, especially the relationship between the conscious mind and the unconscious mind. He spent much time learning about intuition, clairvoyance (dreams foretelling events that later actually happened), seemingly bizarre coincidences, and supernatural occurrences. His fascination led him to explore the mystical side of the mind, and for this reason he was ridiculed by many of his contemporaries. Yet, with time, perceptions have changed. Although Jung is still considered ahead of his time by many, today his theories are recognized as the cornerstones of not only mental and emotional well-being, but spiritual well-being as well. And although Jung did not advocate any particular religion, his work is studied, taught, and cited by psychologists, theologians, and spiritual leaders around the world. Moreover, his work has given impetus to a new discipline of healing called **transpersonal psychology** or **psychospirituality,** the study of the relationship between the mind and the soul.

Unlike his mentor, Freud, an atheist who hypothesized that humans functioned at an instinctual level, Jung proposed that there was a spiritual element to human nature, a spiritual drive located in the realm of the unconscious mind, which manifests itself when it bubbles to the conscious level. As a man who studied the myths and belief systems of many cultures on virtually every continent, Jung observed similarities in the symbols in dreams and art by various races of people who had no possible way of communicating them to each other. From research conducted during his professional experiences as well as intensive self-reflection, Jung theorized that these similarities were often represented in symbolic forms he called **archetypes.** Archetypes are primordial images or concepts originating in the unconscious mind at a level so profound that they appear to be common elements, or elements of unity, among all humankind.

Remember that Jung proposed a dichotomy of levels constituting the unconscious mind (see Chapter 4): the personal unconscious and the collective unconscious (Fig. 7.1). The latter he described as universal consciousness: a unifying force within all individuals, or the collective soul. He believed that the collective unconscious was divine in its nature, the essence of God within all of us. According to Jung, this divine essence manifests in the conscious mind through several cognitive functions, including intuition, creativity, and the interpretation of dreams.

In his exploration of dreams, Jung discovered several people who dreamed of events they could have no possible knowledge of at a conscious level, only to discover that their dreams emerged as crystal-clear predictions of circumstances yet to come. In addition, sometimes during his counseling sessions, Jung would find himself in awe of coincidences that unfolded right in front of him. One example was listening to a client's dream about spotting a fox while the two were

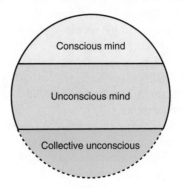

A symbolic representation of Jung's view of the mind with *Figure 7.1* the collective unconscious residing in the depths of the unconscious mind. This aspect of the mind surfaces to consciousness through intuition, creativity, and dreams.

walking along a dirt road, only to have a fox appear seconds after the animal was mentioned. Studying the phenomenon of coincidences more closely, Jung concluded that when two seemingly unrelated events happen at once, there is a reason and purpose for it, whether significant or banal, a purpose that cannot be explained rationally by cause and effect. He coined the term *synchronicity* to explain this phenomenon. He also hypothesized that in reality there is no such thing as coincidence; rather, everything is connected, and events unfold simultaneously for a reason. His study of Taoism and the *I Ching* led him to believe that there is a connectedness extending beyond the individual throughout the entire universe, a concept not well accepted in the West during his lifetime.

Jung was once quoted as saying that "every crisis a person experiences over the age of thirty is spiritual in nature." While some only credit Jung with addressing the midlife-crisis phenomenon, Jungian psychologists have maintained the importance of spirituality to the individual, especially at midlife. With regard to this spiritual crisis, Jung further believed that modern men's and women's inability to get in touch with their inner selves provided fertile ground for life's stressors. He added that sickness is a result of not being whole, that is, never connecting with the divine qualities of the unconscious mind to clarify values and gain sharp focus on one's life meaning.

Another of Jung's theories is that there are characteristics of the personality called the shadow that indi-

Figure 7.2 A symbolic representation of Peck's conception of human spirituality as a maturation process with four hierarchical stages.

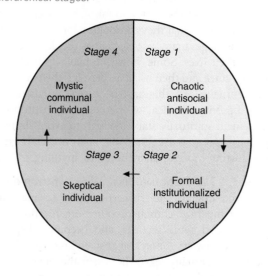

the gap between the conscious and unconscious mind. Jung believed that as technology and materialism increased, people would spend less and less time cultivating their inner selves. This observation, made in 1933, has come to pass at the end of the twentieth century. It is interesting to note that Jung advised one of his clients that psychoanalysis alone would not cure him of his chronic alcoholism. In a letter to this client, Jung suggested that his best chance for cure was a "spiritual conversion." After Roland H.'s recovery, which he attributed to spiritual enlightenment, he and a friend, Bill W., started the now well-known organization for problem drinkers called Alcoholics Anonymous. Although this program is not tied to any particular religion, it is based on a very strong sense of spirituality.

Shortly before his death in 1961, Jung was interviewed by John Freeman of the British Broadcasting Corporation. When asked if he believed in God, Jung replied, "No." Then he paused for a moment, and stated, "I Know."

The Path of Peck

In 1978, M. Scott Peck ushered in a new age of spiritual awareness in American culture with a book entitled *The Road Less Traveled.* As a psychiatrist who spent many years counseling clients with neurotic and psychotic disorders, Peck became aware of a commonality among virtually all of them: either an absence or immaturity of spiritual development. He also noted that not all people were at the same level of spirituality, which made it a challenge to treat his clients.

Upon intense reflection on his own spiritual beliefs, coupled with what he observed in his clients, Peck developed a framework he called the road to spiritual development. This framework consists of four systematic, hierarchical stages of spiritual growth and development (Fig. 7.2): chaotic antisocial, formal institutional, skeptical, and mystic-communal. (These stages are similar to James Fowler's stages of faith.) Admittedly, Peck states in his book, *The Different Drum*, that not everyone falls neatly into one of these four categories. Some people hover between stages, while others migrate back and forth from one stage to another. Despite its shortcomings, which Peck admits to, this model provides a basis from which we can

viduals keep hidden, even from themselves, but which they usually project onto other people. Confronting the shadow of the soul, or attaining profound self-awareness, allows individuals to come to terms with several issues that form the undercurrents for stress in their own lives so that they may become whole.

In a story recounted in his autobiography, *Memories, Dreams, Reflections,* Jung tells of a young boy who asked an old wise man why no one in this day and age ever sees the face or hears the voice of God. The wise old sage replied that man no longer lowers himself enough to God's level. Jung tells this story to reinforce the idea that people in "civilized" cultures have become distant from the wisdom and knowledge seated in the fathoms of the unconscious mind. Instead, they see God primarily as an external force or supreme being in the clouds. By contrast, Jung suggested that God is a unifying force that resides in all of us, in the depths of the unconscious mind. Like the ancient Asian mystics he studied, who practiced meditation to attain spiritual enlightenment, Jung advocated personal responsibility to examine the conscious and unconscious mind in order to find what he called psychic equilibrium. In *Modern Man in Search of a Soul,* he further warned that the advancement of technology and materialism, now accepted by many to be stressors, would further widen begin to understand the maturation of the human spirit. The stages are described as follows:

Stage 1: *The chaotic, antisocial individual.* The first stage of Peck's road to spiritual development is an undeveloped spirituality, or in some cases, a spiritual absence or bankruptcy. As a rule, young children fall into this category due to their immaturity, but among adults, the chaotic antisocial individual is someone whose life is in utter chaos. This chaos can be represented by various attitudes and behaviors, including drug or alcohol addiction, codependency, or a helpless-hopeless attitude. Chaotic antisocial individuals can be very manipulative and unprincipled, and they often find that controlling others is easier than taking responsibility for their own lives. Individuals at this stage have a poor self-relationship, completely avoid self-awareness, maintain poor relationships with family, friends, and co-workers, hold a weak value system with many unresolved conflicts, and show an absence of a meaningful purpose in their lives. Some people remain at this stage their whole lives. A life-threatening situation, however, can act as a catalyst to move to the next stage. In preparation to leave this stage, the chaotic antisocial individual looks for some kind of structure to make order out of their chaos, and to help slay some personal dragons masking themselves as chronic stressors.

Stage 2: *The formal institutional individual.* Institutions such as prisons, the military, and in many cases, the church, provide structure. They offer rules, structured guidelines, and dogma to help individuals leave personal chaos behind and rebuild their lives. People who make the transition to this stage from the chaotic antisocial stage desperately need rules, dogma, and guidance to survive. While many young people enter this stage through the influence of their families (e.g., going to religious services with their parents), Peck found that adults enter it by making an almost overnight conversion, a "born-again" transformation. In essence, they adopt the dogma of an institution as a means of personal survival. Peck observed that when an individual advances to this stage, it may be not only very sudden but also perhaps unconscious. A relationship with God parallels the parent-child relationship, where God is a loving but punitive God. In the words of Peck, "God becomes an 'Irish cop' in the sky." A supreme being is personified in human terms,

and perhaps most important, God is purely an external figure who rewards and punishes one's behavior. People who advance to this stage come looking for personal needs to be met, and for life's answers. Quite often they find what they are looking for. Comfortable with this stage, many people stay at this level for the rest of their lives. Some, however, may slip back into the first stage and then oscillate between the two. Others eventually leave this stage because of unmet needs. They become skeptical of (perhaps) all institutions, yet remain spiritually stable enough to avoid slipping back to stage one. At this point, such people begin a free-floating process, unanchored to anything.

Stage 3: *The skeptic individual.* When a person questions the dogma and rules necessary to maintain membership in a church or other organization that has provided some security, and becomes skeptical about the answers (or lack of answers) received, he or she may eventually leave the safety the organization once provided. Peck said that this is a crucial stage of spiritual development, when one begins to question the understanding the institution represents. This is also a very risky stage, because there are no guaranteed answers elsewhere. Tongue in cheek, Peck calls people in this stage born-again atheists. People become skeptical when they find that the institution they joined does not fulfill or answer all their needs or expectations. Frustration turns into distrust, and they often leave the institution they once joined for refuge, becoming very cynical about it and perhaps about life in general. The skeptical individual is looking for truth, and according to Peck, is more spiritually developed than many devoted churchgoers. Some college students, and even more college graduates, reach this stage after years of following their parents' religious lead, and then find that the beliefs on which they were raised no longer seem adequate for the situations in which they currently find themselves. The skeptical individual finds him- or herself in a very tenuous position, however, as everyone needs sure footing or an anchor eventually. Two outcomes are possible at this stage. Either one samples other church institutions and makes a half-hearted compromise along the way, or progresses to the next and final stage of spiritual development.

Stage 4: *The mystic-communal individual.* In the continual search for answers to life's questions, some people eventually come to the realization that there are questions that have no answers. Unlike the skeptical individual who fights this premise, the mystic-communal individual takes delight in life's paradoxes. These people find comfort in the unanswerable, yet like sleuths, they seek out the continuing challenge, ever hungry for clues and possible answers. People in this stage of spiritual development love a good mystery, and they love to explore. Mystic-communals begin to depersonify God and come to the realization that God is an internal source (the power of love, faith, and will) as much as an external source (an unexplained energy or consciousness). Mystic-communals begin to see an outline of the whole picture even though several pieces are missing. These people see spirituality as a living process, not merely an outcome or heaven-oriented goal. Perhaps as important, they see the need to build and maintain a sense of community by developing quality relationships built on acceptance, love, and respect. They see and feel the need to be connected. Upon arrival at this stage, individuals realize that it is only the beginning of a very long but fruitful journey.

Like Jung, Peck hints that the continued inability to deal with psychological crises often manifests itself as spiritual immaturity, or not progressing through these stages of spiritual growth. And, similar to Maslow's hierarchy of needs, Peck agrees that individuals regress when stressful situations cause them to lose their footing on this road. For example, a person in the mystic-communal stage who experiences the death of a loved one may feel anger or guilt if the death is perceived as a form of punishment (Why me?). Many stressful situations cause individuals to focus on the external side of "God" (or lack thereof), often causing them to slip back into stage two or three. While the road to spiritual development is an independent one, Peck suggests that we are not alone on this journey. Love and grace are the guides that lead the way, when we choose to listen.

The Path of Hildegard von Bingen

The word *spirit* often conjures up the expression *mystic* for many, and in the case of Hildegard von Bingen this adjective is most accurate. However, the word *mystic* alone is not enough to describe this unique woman who lived in Germany at the turn of the twelfth century (1098–1179). Visionary, poet, composer, healer, artist, and saint are also words used to describe her, yet even these seem inadequate to capture the essence of Hildegard von Bingen. Born of a noble family near the town of Mainz, Hildegard was eight years old when she first experienced a vision of light, followed by a period of intense illness. At first not familiar with the meaning of her experience, she soon understood that this vision was in some way a message from God. Not long after her first vision, she acquired a remarkable psychic ability, which left her family rather puzzled. As was the custom of her day, Hildegard, the tenth child in her family, was brought to a monastery to be looked after and raised in the hope that her work and accomplishments would please the church.

The first vision was actually one of many to occur throughout her life. Hildegard was encouraged by members of her order to write what she saw in these visions.

> What I write is what I see and hear in the vision. I compose no other words than those I hear, and I set them forth in unpolished Latin just as I hear them in the vision, for I am not taught in this vision to write as philosophers do. And the words of the vision are not like words uttered by the mouth of many but like a shimmering flame, or a cloud floating in a clear sky.

In what is considered to be her most impressive writing, *Scivias,* she describes a series of visions illustrating the story of creation, the dynamic tension between light and darkness, the work of the holy spirit, and several words of encouragement to ponder and savor as we each journey on the human path. Her writings didn't go unnoticed. Word soon traveled to Pope Eugenius III, who sent for copies of these writings. So impressed was he that he not only gave his blessings, but sent words of support to Hildegard to continue her writings, thus making her a celebrity.

In the time of the Dark Ages, the vision Hildegard saw wasn't just a ray of light in the shadows, it became a philosophy that breathed life into a people with a spiritual hunger. And in a time when women took a back seat to the dominance of male authority, Hildegard's presence and renown demonstrated a higher order of humanity.

Her message was simple: There is a holistic nature to the universe, just as there is a holistic nature to humanity. And just as man and woman are essential parts of the universe, so too is the universe an essential part to be found within each individual. In other words, this message is similar to the axiom, As above, so below, or, As the microcosm, so the macrocosm. As if extending an invitation into nature, she encouraged the "greening" of the soul, a process whereby one engages with the natural world as a part of it, instead of shutting oneself off from it. Hildegard also spoke to the principle of each soul. She routinely emphasized that our soul is not to be found in our body; rather, it is our body that resides in our soul. The body, she said, is the instrument of the soul, a means by which our divine essence can function in the material world. The soul, a unique aspect of our divine nature, is boundless and contains our dreams, hopes, wishes, and desires. Can all things be spiritual? This, indeed, was the message of Hildegard von Bingen. From her visions described in *Scivias* she learned that all things are sacred, "Every creature is a glittering, glistening mirror of divinity."

In times of spiritual hunger, people often look back to those in earlier times who were able to hold the light of divine essence and in turn share it. Perhaps this is why today, after nearly 1,000 years, the music composed by Hildegard von Bingen has been recorded in a popular CD entitled *Vision,* along with a similar best-selling recording of the Benedictine Monks entitled *Chant.*

The Path of Black Elk

American Indians in the United States number some several hundred tribes. Although cultural differences abound among them, from the Algonquins in the Northeast to the Navaho in the Southwest, their spirituality is fairly consistent regardless of tribe. One voice that ascended the heights of consciousness in American Indian culture was that of Black Elk, a medicine man of the Oglala Sioux (Lakota) nation. His mystical visions, recorded by John G. Neihardt in the book *Black Elk Speaks,* have galvanized the understanding and appreciation of American Indian spirituality, also referred to as Mother Earth spirituality. Despite the devastation of his culture by European traditions and values, Black Elk's vision was quite profound and elaborate with respect to the essence and integrity of the human spirit and the bonding rela-

tionship between the two-legged (man) and his natural environment.

Perhaps the features that most distinguish American Indian spirituality from that of other cultures are its set of values demonstrating respect for and connectedness to Mother Earth. Black Elk is not alone in voicing this philosophy; it has been expressed by a great many American Indians. In the words of Shoshone shaman Rolling Thunder, who describes the earth as a living organism, "Too many people don't know that when they harm the earth they harm themselves" (Boyd, 1974). In his book, *Mother Earth Spirituality,* Ed McGaa (Eagle Man) both expounds on Black Elk's vision and augments this knowledge with additional insights of the American Indian culture to provide a more profound understanding of Black Elk's enlightenment. The following is a brief synopsis of American Indian paths to spiritual healing.

First, despite the conviction of Christian missionaries that Indians were pagans, American Indians had established a very profound relationship with a divine essence. Unlike Europeans, who personified this higher power, American Indians accepted divine power as the Great Mystery, with no need to define or conceptualize God in human terms. In the words of Chief Seattle, transcribed for a letter to President Franklin Pierce in 1855, ". . . One thing we know, our God is the same God. You may think you own Him as you wish to own land, but you cannot. He is the God of man; and his compassion is equal for the red man and the white. The Earth is precious to Him, and to harm the earth is to heap contempt on its creator. Our God is the same God. This earth is precious to Him" (Gore, 1993). This preciousness was and continues to be represented in the bonding relationship between each American Indian and the Earth's creatures, the wind, the rain, and the mountains.

North American indigenous peoples see Mother Earth as a symbol of wholeness and represent it with a medicine wheel. Just as the seasons are divided into quarters, so too are many concepts of American Indian spirituality. Some for examples, are the four elements: earth, fire, water, and air; four earth colors: red, yellow, black, and white; four directions: east, west, north, and south; and four cardinal principles or values of the Red Way: to show respect for Wankan Tanka (the Great Mystery or Great Spirit); to demon-

*B*ox 7.2 | A Letter from Chief Seattle (1855)

The president in Washington sends word that he wishes to buy our land. But how can you buy or sell the sky? the land? The idea is strange to us. If we do not own the freshness of the air, and the spark of the water, how can you buy them? Every part of this earth is sacred to my people. Every shining pine needle, every sandy shore, every mist in the dark woods. All are holy in the memory and experience of my people. We know the sap that courses through the trees as we know the blood that courses through our veins. We are part of the earth and it is part of us. Perfumed flowers are our sisters. The bear, the deer, the great eagle; these are our brothers. The body heat of the pony and man belong to the same family. The shining water that moves through the streams and rivers is not just water, but the blood of our ancestors. If we sell you our land, you must remember it is sacred.

Each ghostly reflection in the clear water of the lakes tells of the event and the memory in the life of my people. The water's murmur is the voice of my father's father. The rivers are my brothers. They quench our thirst, they carry our canoes and feed our children. So you must give to the river the kindness that you would give any brother. If we sell you our land, remember that the air is precious to us. The air shares its spirit with all life which it supports. The wind that gave our grandfather his first breath also receives his last sigh. The wind also gives our children the spirit of life.

So if we sell you our land, you must keep it apart and sacred as a place where man can go to taste the wind that is sweetened by the meadow's flowers. Will you teach your children what we have taught our children; that the earth is our Mother? What befalls the earth, befalls all the sons of the earth. This we know: the earth does not belong to man, man belongs to the earth. All things connect, like the blood that unites us all. Man did not weave the web of life, he is merely a strand in it. Whatever he does to the web, he does to himself. One thing we know: our God is your God. The earth is precious to him and to harm the earth is to heap contempt on the creator.

Your destiny is a mystery to us. What will happen when the buffalo are all slaughtered, the wild horses tamed? What will happen when the secret corners of the forest are heavy with the scent of many men and the view of the ripe hills is blotted with talking wires? Where will the thicket be? Gone! Where will the eagle be? Gone! And what is it to say good-bye to the swift pony and the hunt—the end of living and the beginning of survival. When the last red man has vanished in his wilderness, and his memory is only the shadow of a cloud moving across the prairie, will these shores and forests still be here? Will there be any spirit of my people left? We love the earth as a newborn loves his mother's heartbeat. So if we sell you our land, love it as we love it. Care for it as we have cared for it. Hold in your mind the memory of the land as you received it. Preserve the land for all children, and love it as God loves us all. As we are part of the land, you too are part of the land. It is precious to us, it is also precious to you. One thing we know: there is only one God. No man, be he red man or white, can be apart. We are brothers after all.

From *The World of Joseph Campbell,* vol. 1, *The Power of Myth* (St. Paul, MN: High Bridge Productions, 1990). Adapted by Ted Perry, loosely based on Chief Seattle's 1854 oration, "The Great Ecology" as it appeared in the *Seattle Sunday Star,* Oct 29, 1887.

strate respect for Mother Earth; to show respect for each fellow man and woman; and to show respect for individual freedoms. The American Indian medicine wheel is a symbol of Mother Earth spirituality from which the lessons of nature are used to better understand oneself (Fig. 7.3). To people of these cultures, each quadrant of the wheel represents a specific aspect of spiritual growth and various lessons to learn. The eastern quarter represents the Path of the Sun, where respect is shown for ourselves, others, and the environment. The southern quarter is the Path of Peace and is characterized by the traits of youth, innocence, and wonder. The western quarter is referred to as the Path of Introspection, where time is allocated for the soul-searching process and striving for a balance between physical substance and spiritual essence within oneself. The northern quarter represents the Path of Quiet. The Path of Quiet symbolizes the importance of mental health, in which the intellect is stimulated by the lessons of nature.

While there are several ceremonies to celebrate American Indian spirituality—the most famous being a feast of Thanksgiving taught to European settlers nearly 400 years ago—one practice, called the vision quest, exemplifies the strong bond with Mother Earth especially well. The vision quest is recognized as a time of self-reflection, which helps one to understand one's purpose in life, to become grounded in the earth and centered with the Great Spirit, and to reach a clearer understanding of one's contribution to the community. During a vision quest, an individual isolates him-or herself in the wilderness, on a hilltop, a large meadow, or any area that provides privacy. The vision quest creates an opportunity for emptying the mind (meditation) and body (fasting). The emptying process allows the human spirit to be filled with energy from the Great Spirit, leading the individual toward a path of self-enlightenment and self-improvement. Typically performed as a rite of passage from adolescence into adulthood, a vision quest can also be taken any time there is a need for spiritual growth or guidance.

Nearly extinguished by Christian missionaries a century or more ago, many elements of American Indian spirituality are now beginning to be recognized and respected, particularly in light of concerns about the poor "health status" of the planet (the environment). Ironically, it is now the "white man" who is adopting this value from the American Indian.

The Path of Fox

Matthew Fox is a former Roman Catholic theologian who, much like American Indians in the centuries before, was silenced by the Vatican in 1988 for his "progressive" views on human spirituality and has since been excommunicated from the church. The premise of Fox's theory is that the Judeo-Christian concept of spirituality, formulated when it was believed that the earth was the center of the universe, has not kept pace with scientific discoveries of the earth as but a piece of the whole universe and by no means its center. Fox has attempted to unite many concepts of theology with the laws and theories of physics in what he terms "creation spirituality." Creation spirituality suggests that divinity can be found in any act of creation, from the atom to the far reaches of the cosmos, and every particle in between. The seed of

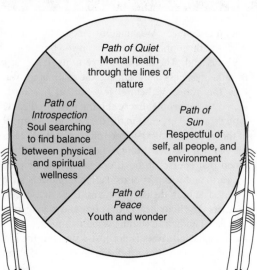

A symbolic representation of an American Indian medicine wheel described by Black Elk.

Figure 7.3

creativity is energy, an element that binds all things together. And, as stated in the First Law of Thermodynamics, energy is neither created nor destroyed.

Fox was inspired by the work of the thirteenth-century German theologian Meister Eckhart, many American Indians, Albert Einstein, and a divine presence he terms the cosmic Christ. Through these influences, he has developed four paths or attitudes of creation spirituality (Fig. 7.4), which in his opinion raise individual consciousness and thus the spiritual level of humankind as a whole. These paths are as follows:

Path 1:   *Via positiva.* A sense of awe and wonder at the design and creation of all that surrounds us. Like the wonder of a young child, via positiva is a continual awareness and appreciation of all things, from the simplicity of a blade of grass to the mechanical complexity of the space shuttle. All creation should be celebrated, not feared or shamed.

Path 2:   *Via negativa.* The process of emptying or letting go of thoughts, feelings, values, even possessions, that weigh down, enclose, and smother the soul, depriving it of nutrients for growth. Via negativa is a period of darkness, silence, even fasting of the soul,

Figure 7.4 A symbolic representation of Fox's creation spirituality.

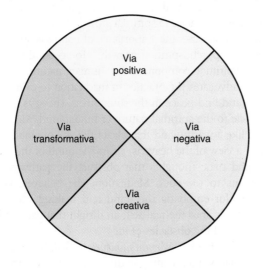

for only when emptiness occurs is there room for new growth. This process may be emotionally painful at times, yet it is necessary for the maturation of the human spirit.

Path 3: *Via creativa.* A breakthrough or explosion of enlightenment, which fills the space vacated through the cleansing process of via negativa. This enlightenment may come in the form of divine inspiration, intuitive thoughts, or imagination. Via creativa is human creativity, which increases the quantity and quality of awe in the universe.

Path 4: *Via transformativa.* Fox calls via transformativa the path of struggle, compassion, and celebration. With this path comes the responsibility to act on the enlightenment and inspiration from via creativa by channeling divine energy into personal acts of creation, and using this positive creative energy for the betterment of humankind.

Fox suggests that all people see themselves as acts of creation, deserving of awe and wonder. In turn, the ability to use one's imagination and creativity will add to the awe of the universe. These four paths align themselves in what Fox calls a sacred hoop, or a circle symbolizing wholeness, with each path nourishing the others to their full potential. The connection between each element of this hoop is compassion. Compassion, as

defined by Fox, is a continual celebration of life and includes the fulfillment of love, forgiveness, and a personal as well as public display of one's spirituality. Thus, human spirituality involves the integration of all four paths into one road, or what Fox refers to as a " **'personal cosmology'**—a relationship to the divine presence that dwells in us." When asked how to cultivate this divine relationship, Fox in turn asks these questions: What poets do you read? What music moves you? What acts of creation are you involved with? What social issues are your passion? What work do you most love doing? What pain is in your emptiness? When do you feel a connection to the universe? From Fox's perspective, the fulfillment of these answers nurtures the growth of the human spirit.

The Path of Borysenko

New to the emerging discipline of psychoneuroimmunology, Joan Borysenko hit the ground running as cofounder, therapist, and director of the Mind/Body Clinic affiliated with the Harvard Medical School in Boston, Massachusetts. Through working with her mentor, stress physiologist Dr. Herbert Benson, her patients, and her personal journey of self-enlightenment, Borysenko began to synthesize an understanding of the connections between the body, mind, and soul. One observation inspiring her journey was that some of her clients' personal faith seemed to be stronger than any clinical medicine; faith that caused cancerous tumors to go into spontaneous remission, healed several illnesses, or simply brought inner peace in the last moments of life.

But just as faith can heal, its absence can quicken the pace of physical illness and even death. Borysenko is among a growing number of clinical specialists who believe that the mechanistic approach to medicine (discussed earlier in the book) is very much outdated. As explained in *Guilt Is the Teacher, Love Is the Lesson,* the mind and spirit play a crucial role in the health and healing process of the body. For example, for a new medicine to be proven clinically effective, it must cure more than 35 percent of the people who use it. Below this point of demarcation, cures are considered the result of the placebo effect, or healing by faith alone. That is, sugar water and sugar pills have a healing rate of 35 percent (and in some cases up to 70 percent) among people who believe they will cure them of their disease. In addition, in a now-famous study cited by Borysenko, patients who had a view of nature outdoors from their rooms were released from the hospital sooner, indicating a significantly faster recovery rate, than those patients who had either no view or a view of adjacent brick buildings. These facts and several others indicated to Borysenko that a significant factor in the human equation has been ignored regarding the treatment of illness and disease—the factor of human spirituality.

In her campaign of health promotion, which has included several books, interviews, and national presentations, Borysenko advocates healing the human spirit as an integral part of physical healing and emphasizes the important role of spirituality in the self-healing process. Spirituality is defined by Borysenko (1990) as "a reconnection (remembrance) of our eternal connection with a lifeforce or power that we are a part of." Strongly influenced by the works of Jung, Larry Dossey, and others, Borysenko advocates the importance of building a relationship with the inner self and taking the time to get to know the real self. The distance that people keep from this self-center—distance created by shame, guilt, and the expectations of who we should be rather than who we really are—is fertile ground upon which to sow the seeds of stress. She also believes that through the ability to know the self we strengthen the bonds with higher consciousness as well as with the people within our community. In her original definition, influenced by Richard Lazarus, she believed stress to be the inability to cope, but she now proposes that stress is a lack of connectedness.

Borysenko (1990) describes two possible attitudes relating to the development of the human spirit: **spiritual optimism** and **spiritual pessimism.** She defines spiritual optimism as "an intuitive knowledge that love is the universal energy and the human condition is ripe for learning experiences in which love manifests." Conversely, spiritual pessimism she describes as an attitude that nurtures low self-esteem, guilt, and all that impedes the way of love. Borysenko adds that spiritual pessimism is directly tied to low self-esteem, which produces psychological helplessness. In her work, she has observed many emotional roadblocks that not only impede spiritual development, but also appear to wreak havoc on the physiological systems of the body, leading to the onset of disease and illness. These emotions are commonly seen in the stress response: fear, anger, worry, and guilt, with guilt (in her opinion) as one of the largest obstacles to spiritual growth. Like Fox, Borysenko emphasizes the importance of compassion: "the flower of psychospiritual growth." To access this and other spiritual components of human nature, Borysenko advocates the practice of meditation to calm the mind and find peace in the soul. Stress, she says, is an obstacle to the spiritual nature of humankind. Meditation, like a warm wind that clears the sky of clouds to allow a view of the heavens, clears the mind of the taxing and toxic thoughts that obstruct the pathway of nutrients to the soul. Meditation, she believes, is a process for emptying the mind and making way for new insight into the real self, an insight that can guide one around the obstacles of life.

In her book *A Woman's Journey to God,* Borysenko notes that women comprise the greatest percentage of Americans she labels as "religious drop-outs"—those women who leave the institution of their religious upbringing to wander, drift, and possibly reconnect to another affiliation with more acceptance. One reason for this apathy can be found in the language of several religions where male pronouns describing God exclude the female gender: a big issue to many women in an age of equal rights. She states that the white-male hierarchy has become a huge roadblock on the spiritual path to women of the baby-boomer generation and their children.

Borysenko describes each woman's quest for a relationship to the divine as a spiritual pilgrimage. While not outlining a systematic progression of steps on this pilgrimage, Borysenko shares her insights on how a woman might journey through various stages of the feminine quest. Borysenko suggests that each woman connect to the creative aspect of the divine and not see God entirely as a male entity. She cites menses and childbirth as examples of the creative process. Next she conveys the importance of resolving anger issues that develop (some as early as childhood) in what she terms as the first step to healing. Borysenko then speaks of the practice of rituals as a means to remember the divine connection. Rituals may include baby showers, candle ceremonies, retreats—anything to place one in the conscious recognition of God or Goddess. A final aspect of the feminine path Borysenko talks about is the connection to other women through support groups, prayer circles, or other venues where women can share their stories. For generations upon generations, stories have been the vehicle by which women have passed on spiritual truths to each other and their children.

In *A Women's Journey to God* Borysenko writes, "A quiet awakening is underway as women are coming together to worship, to tell stories, and find their place spiritually, if not always religiously, in the household of God. Women's spirituality groups are popping up everywhere . . . Women often report a deep sense of connection to God as part of friendship, or mothering. We see God in others." It is this aspect of the feminine path that Borysenko shares in the hopes of inclusiveness and healing of the human spirit.

The Path of Deepak Chopra

One might think that spirituality and medicine would go hand and hand since both honor the essence of life, but that is not how Deepak Chopra, M.D., nor any of his physician colleagues and peers were introduced to the science of medicine. An endocrinologist by training, Chopra came to the United States from India and landed a job in New Jersey in 1970. With his sights set on a bigger hospital, he soon ended up outside of Boston, working as chief of staff at New England Memorial Hospital. Frustrated at the limitations of Western medicine, Chopra returned to his Indian roots and began to explore Ayurvedic medicine, an ancient form of holistic health care which, when translated, means the science of life where mind, body, and spirit connect as one. On a path that led him from allopathic to holistic medicine, Chopra soon discovered that mind-body medicine or psychoneuroimmunology as it is referred to clinically, is really mind-body-spirit medicine, in which the human spirit plays an integral role in the healing process. His search into psychoneuroimmunology and the essence of spirituality led him to study with the founder of transcendental meditation (TM), Maharesi Yogi, where he began to understand the concepts of mind and consciousness. This exposure to consciousness began to galvanize his understanding of the intricacies of the human condition in states of disease and health and matters of the soul.

But Chopra didn't rest there. An avid reader, he, like a child with a crayon, began to connect the dots of wisdom from all corners of the earth, including the writings of Einstein, Blake, Rumi, the Bhagavad Gita, the Bible, the Koran, Lao Tzu, Tagore, and others to synthesize a comprehensive if not universal understanding of the nature of God and the laws that govern all creation.

The author of several books, including *Quantum Healing, Perfect Health,* and *Ageless Body, Timeless Mind,* Chopra has now focused his attention on the matters of the soul. In his book *The Seven Spiritual Laws of Success,* Chopra presents a simple guideline of seven principles for embracing the spirit of life in everyday living.

The Law of Pure Potentiality. Understanding that at the core of our essence is pure consciousness, the law of pure potentiality reminds us to enter in silence the core of our being and tap the universal wisdom in which to create and reach our potential. In the Western culture, it is common to seek validation through external objects. The law of pure potentiality reminds us that we only need look inside to find our divine essence. Once this source is accessed, we become co-creators and active participants, rather than passive victims on the human journey.

The Law of Giving. According to this law, the universe is a dynamic cornucopia. Nothing is static. Energy flows freely. In support of the axiom, as you give, so shall you receive, the law of giving reminds us to keep open the channels of our heart, for when the heart is closed, the energy becomes blocked and the stagnation of universal energy leads to an atrophy of the spirit. Chopra points out that the derivation of the words *affluence* and *currency* has nothing to do with money. Rather, it means to flow, a lesson the law of giving teaches. Nature abhors a vacuum; however, she is not fond of gluttony either. The law of giving reminds us to walk in balance.

The Law of Karma (or Cause and Effect). As if taken from a law of physics stating that every action has an equal and opposite reaction, the law of karma invites us to become more responsible for our thoughts and actions. The law of karma, similar to the Christian expression, "as you sow, so shall you reap," invites us to shed the habits that inhibit our growth, break the bonds of conditioned thoughts and become responsible (the ability to respond) for our every action.

The Law of Least Effort.   Nature teaches us that water finds its own level. The universe unfolds in its own time and place. If we try to rush it, we only tire ourselves. The law of least effort invites us to go with the flow, not resist what we cannot change or influence. Chopra writes that nature's intelligence functions effortlessly. To be in harmony with nature means to go with the flow. One aspect of least effort is to accept those things we cannot change. A second aspect of least effort is to initiate self-responsibility rather than cast blame on others. The law of least effort asks us to travel the human path lightly, discarding those opinions, beliefs, and attitudes that are defensive in nature, for when we carry these, the human journey becomes a struggle, rather than a delightful sojourn.

The Law of Intention and Desire.   We attract what we submit to the universal consciousness through intention. "Intention," writes Chopra, "grounded in the detached freedom of the present, serves as the catalyst for the right mix of matter, energy, and space-time events to create whatever it is that you desire." The Buddha once said that all suffering comes from desire. What is implied in the teachings of the Buddha is that the partner of desire is detachment or letting go. Attachment to our desires most likely will create suffering when our intentions are not fully realized. As you intend, so must you detach, and let the universe take care of the details.

The Law of Detachment.   The law of detachment is an invitation to let go of our desires, wishes, and dreams. It's not that we don't want the desired outcome, but detachment allows the desire to stand on its own two feet. This law serves as a reminder that we are co-creators in the universe of our lives, but not co-dependent on it. Detachment means to let go of the emotions that align with our desires—fear and anger, if our desires go unfulfilled. The law of detachment is one of the hardest laws to honor, because we often place our security in those things we keep near us. Implicit in the law of detachment is the concept of trust. When we let go of thoughts, wishes, and desires, we are trusting that whatever the outcome, it is in our best interest. So if we apply for a job (intention) and we don't get it, we must realize that at a higher level of consciousness, this was in our best interest. Those things in our best interest will come back to us as intended.

The Law of Dharma or Life Purpose.   Each of us has a unique gift and talent to share with the community of humanity. This law invites us to realize what our life purpose or mission is, and to act on it, so that we help raise consciousness for one and all. *Dharma* is the ancient Sanskrit word for purpose or mission. The acceptance of life on Earth requires that we not only realize our purpose, but act to fulfill it so that all may benefit from it.

In his most recent book, *How To Know God,* Chopra uses the template of the seven chakras to expand one's level of awareness to a higher level of consciousness. It is Chopra's thesis (and he is not alone in this thought) that each person must journey back to the divine source by cultivating a relationship through mind and heart. In doing so, we come to realize that we partner with God in the creation process of our own lives.

Chopra has become a bridge that unites not only spirituality and medicine, but many facets of humanity that have become divided through ego and fear. If asked, he and others like him will tell you that we, the human species, stand on the precipice of great change. For us to weather this change and become self-realized, we must work to evolve our soul growth, and this can be done by honoring and practicing the seven universal laws of spirituality.

The Path of Jesus

Over 2,000 years ago, a unique man appeared in the Middle East, and his presence has since left an indelible mark on humanity. His teachings were profound, his healings miraculous, and his death a mystery. Some people called him a prophet, others called him the Messiah, and still others called him a heretic. Little is known about Jesus of Nazareth other than that he was born in a barn, worked as a carpenter, shared his philosophies with others, and died a cruel death. He never wrote down any of his teachings; rather, he shared his simple yet profound wisdom with followers who yearned to understand his enlightenment, and they in turn created a community years later called Christianity. Decades after his death, in an effort to remember those teachings, his followers recorded his wisdom, stories, and healing practices in a collection of manuscripts now known as the New Testament of the Holy Bible. Scholars and theologians continue to

Figure 7.5 A symbolic representation of human spirituality from the perspective of Jesus of Nazareth.

study and interpret his words of wisdom today. It may be difficult, if not impossible, to separate the messenger from the message, but if we focus on the fundamental principle taught by Jesus, we find that his basic premise is the power of unconditional love (Fig. 7.5). What follows is a small sampling of insights and reflections on this theme.

When Jesus began teaching in the Middle East, there was much civil conflict and strife. The Hebrews in Jerusalem were oppressed by the Romans and in essence were treated as second-class citizens in their own country. Many were searching for a political leader to save them and return them to a life of undisturbed peace. In this time of ambivalence and hatred, Jesus preached and practiced the power of unconditional love. He was charismatic, his style uniquely humble, and he attracted many followers who in their hearts believed he possessed the qualities of a great political leader. But Jesus of Nazareth regarded himself as a spiritual leader only. By his example and teachings, he showed men and women how to restore and maintain inner peace through a loving relationship with God. Beyond all else, he believed that through love all things were possible.

Based on the inspirational words of Jesus and his followers, many people have since attempted to illus-trate the concept of love on the canvas of their own hearts. Scottish theologian Henry Drummond described love as a spectrum of several attributes, including patience, kindness, generosity, humility, unselfishness, and sincerity. Theologian Thomas Merton wrote in his book *The Ascent to Truth* that love is the source of one's merit, and as such, it is in love that God resides. Psychiatrist Gerald Jampolsky defines love as an experience absent from fear and the recognition of complete union with all life. To Jesus, the expression of love is like a passageway. For love to be effective as a channel of communication or healing energy, there must be no obstructions and no conflicting thoughts to pollute it. In other words, there must be no conditions or expectations placed on the expression of love. Like a child who acts spontaneously, the expression of love must be uninhibited, not filtered by conscious (ego) thought. As Jesus elaborated, people under oppression, whether by foreign rulers or the perceptions of their own minds, begin to close and harden their hearts. Their ability to feel and express love is overridden by critical, judgmental, and conditional thinking, thought processes often rooted in fear. But as described by Ken Carey in the book *Starseed,* these two concepts are mutually exclusive: you cannot experience love and fear at the same time. From the writings of Jesus' followers, we see that it is fear, expressed in terms of hatred, greed, and guilt, that is the greatest obstacle to love.

Love has an inherent healing power all its own, and it was this power that Jesus demonstrated in performing his miracles of giving sight to the blind and health to the infirm. Inspired by the book *A Course in Miracles,* Jampolsky cites love as a divine energy that knows no bounds. In his own book, *Teach Only Love,* Jampolsky explains that when love is undiluted it becomes the most powerful source of healing energy. When there is a conscious shift from the motivation of fear to the motivation of love, then nothing real is impossible.

Once while teaching, Jesus was asked about the greatest rule to live by. His reply was to love unconditionally; specifically, to love God and to extend this love to each human being as you would to yourself. Jesus further explained that God resides in each and every one of us: "The Kingdom of God is within you." These words, while not new, were novel in their meaning. Given the hatred and fear in the hearts of the Hebrews at the time, it seemed incongruous to love one's enemy as Jesus suggested. His message here was

Stress With a Human Face

IT STARTED AS A FEW WORDS OF INSPIRATION: "Practice random kindness and senseless acts of beauty." No sooner did these words leave the lips of Mill Valley writer Anne Herbert than they seemed to take on a life of their own. Within days, this saying had spread across the country like wildfire, appearing on billboards in Baltimore, barns in Iowa, bumperstickers in Florida, and napkins in San Francisco.

It was Herbert's intent to make the world a better place to live when she coined this phrase. Subtle words can have dynamic consequences, and intuitively she knew that peace on Earth begins when there is good will toward men and women everywhere. In her mind, there is no such thing as a small act of kindness, for every act of kindness is an act of immeasurable love.

These words of inspiration did more than cause doubletakes by those reading this passage on their way to work. The saying transformed itself from a thought to a behavior in many ways. Where the phrase was posted, people began to drive more courteously. Consumers took more time while shopping to smile and converse with store clerks and fellow shoppers. They spent a moment picking up a piece of trash on the street, or digging into their pockets to drop some change into the cup of a homeless person. These people confessed that by doing random and spontaneous acts of kindness and beauty, they received an uplift that made them tingle inside. The dividend of random kindness is immeasurable. ✦

that forgiveness is a crucial element of unconditional love. To elaborate on this theme, he shared the story of the prodigal son, a young man who wasted his inheritance on foolish pleasures and then came crawling back home destitute. Yet his father welcomed him back and forgave him completely. This was an example of the depth of God's unconditional love for all people.

Jesus also spoke about faith and its relationship to love. Faith, a confident belief and conviction in the power of God's love, is the intent or desire to express love. Jesus explained the concept of faith through metaphors and parables. In one such case, he compared faith to a tiny mustard seed, implying that a small seed of faith could expand to phenomenal proportions and overcome the trials of human experience. To paraphrase the words of theologian C. S. Lewis, faith is a necessary virtue to complete the will of God. And in the words of President John F. Kennedy, "God's work must truly be our own."

Paul, one of Jesus's earliest followers, in a letter to friends in the city of Corinth (which has since been recited at many weddings), described love this way:

Love is patient and kind, never jealous or envious, never boastful or proud, never haughty or selfish or rude. Love does not demand its own way. It is not irritable or touchy. It does not hold grudges and will hardly ever notice when others do it wrong. It is never glad about injustice, but rejoices whenever truth wins out. Above all there are three things that remain, faith, hope, and love. The greatest of these is love. Let love be your greatest aim.

The Path of Joseph Campbell

The word *myth* comes from an ancient Sanskrit word, meaning the source of truth. Today the word myth had become synonymous with the word fallacy, but it is fair to say that every myth is based on a source of truth, perhaps exaggerated to make a point, but truth nevertheless. Joseph Campbell is the most respected scholar in the study of mythology. For over sixty years, he studied myths, legends, and stories from all cultures: from the ancient Hindus to several American Indian tribes. Campbell left no stone unturned when it came to looking behind the message of each story. What he found was not only astonishing parallels (e.g., virgin births, resurrections, healings, etc.), but remarkable patterns, regardless of the story's origin, which speak to the nature of the human spirit. His own quest brought him to the front door of psychologist Carl Jung, mystic Jiddu Krishnamurti, poet Robert Bly and scores of luminaries over the world, all of whom added to his collective wisdom.

Campbell's work went largely unrecognized outside of academic circles during the twentieth century until PBS television host Bill Moyers aired a six-part special, titled "*The Power of Myth,*" with Joseph Campbell in the spring of 1987. Campbell died soon thereafter on October 30. Despite his death, his work grows increasingly popular as people discover the links between mythology and spirituality—a legacy for all to share.

In the first episode with Bill Moyers, Campbell explained the connection between mythology and human spirituality like this:

"Myths are clues to the spiritual potentialities of the human life. Our problem today is that we are not well acquainted with the literature of the spirit."

Having studied the myths and legends of every culture throughout the ages, from Zeus to Star Wars (George Lucas was a student of Campbell's), Campbell noticed an interesting trend. In each myth there is a hero, and although the face of the hero may change over time, the story line remains consistent. In his book *The Hero with a Thousand Faces,* Campbell highlights the progression of the hero's journey, which as it turns out, mirrors our own life sojourn. The stages include departure, initiation, and return. Let's take a closer look at each one.

+ **Departure:** The first step in any adventure is to leave your place of origin. Whether one travels like Ulysses on a ship or like Luke Skywalker on a spacecraft, every hero must leave home to go and find himself or herself. The departure stage is also referred to as severance or separation, where the reluctant hero is forced into a situation unwillingly. Campbell cites Adam and Eve as examples of reluctant departure. Stepping outside of the classic myth tale, departure may begin with the first year in college away from home, the death of a parent, or the end of a marriage. Departures can occur in a great many ways. With the first step out the door and across the threshold, the journey has begun.

+ **Initiation:** Traveling down the road far away from home, the hero is put to the test. Campbell calls this stage "the road of trials."

For some it may be dragons (the symbol of fear), for others it may be a symbolic river to cross (the River Styx). Yet still for others it may be an evil witch, a wicked stepmother, a rescue, or the betrayal of a close friend. In the legend of King Arthur, it was the apprenticeship with Merlin. In the life of a college student, initiation can manifest itself in thousands of ways, including the roommate from hell to the abusive alcoholic parent. In every mythological story, the hero must demonstrate strength, courage, patience, and will power. If he fails the first test, another will appear until he is strong enough to conquer it and move on.

+ **Return:** At some point in the journey, usually upon success with the initiation process, the hero must return home. Upon crossing the threshold of return, the hero shares the wealth of riches acquired on the road. Symbolically the return home is accompanied with a trophy of sorts: magical runes, the golden fleece, or Medusa's head. Campbell points out that there may be a reluctance to go home, caused either by feelings of shame or the lust for additional conquests. But return we must to complete the story. The stage of return is also called incorporation, where the returning hero is accepted by his family and peers as an equal, and everyone benefits from his wisdom as a master of two worlds: the one he conquered and the one he has returned home to. The return phase offers a promise that all ends well.

There was a time when the sharing of myths was passed down from parent to child, not merely for entertainment purposes but as wisdom to guide the child on his or her own life journey. Stories from the Bible, the *Bhagavad Gita,* and other sacred scriptures as well as scores of legends, fairy tales, and folklore all serve the same purpose. However, for the most part the tradition of finding wisdom from these stories has vanished in the American culture. In his discussion about *The Power of Myth,* Campbell drew a connection between the rising state of spiritual hunger and the absence of our connection to mythological stories. As he explained, when a society forgoes the power of myth, instead replacing it with information, technology, or perhaps nothing, the society becomes less civilized and more destructive.

Knowing the power of myth himself, Campbell had ever the optimistic outlook on the journey of humanity itself, for he knew the end of the story. "We are at this moment participating in one of the very greatest leaps of the human spirit—to a knowledge not only of outside nature, but also our own deep inward mystery—the greatest leap ever!"

The Path of Lao Tzu

Around 500 B.C., the writings of China's most famous philosopher, Lao Tzu, were first published under the title of *Tao Teh Ching.* Originally written primarily for the leaders of his country, this collection of 5,000 words soon became the doctrine of Chinese living, outlining the path to spiritual enlightenment through inner peace. Lao Tzu used the word *Tao* to describe the movement, path, or way of universal energy. The literal translation of the title of Lao's book is "the path that leads straight from the heart," and the Chinese character for this title symbolizes "walking wisdom." Lao's writings speak of building a peaceful world through inner peace. Only when peace is created within yourself can you move in tandem with the energies that circulate within and around you in order to establish world peace.

The concept of Taoism suggests that all things connect with a flow of energy called *chi.* To move along with the patterns of flow allows a peaceful coexistence with both oneself and the environment. Movement against the flow causes internal as well as external disturbances, often with far-reaching consequences. This movement of life energy goes in cycles, like the ebb and flow of the ocean tide. One of the many concepts the *Tao Teh Ching* teaches is balance between the opposing forces of yin and yang, which provides harmony, patience, and timing of the events of life. That is, to move with rather than against the flow promotes and maintains inner peace. Lao's *Tao* invites the individual to look inward, beyond the superficial facade of humanness, and sense the inner rhythms that move in harmony with the universal rhythms. By doing this, not only is inner peace achieved, but harmony with nature and all relationships. Lao also spoke of the importance of self-reliance: "Wise people seek solutions, the ignorant only cast blame." Although initially Taoism may seem like a foreign concept, it can be found in many Western writings as well. Perhaps the best example of it is the Taoist mannerisms and character of Winnie the Pooh, described by Benjamin Hoff in the renowned bestseller, *The Tao of Pooh.* In fact, with a closer look, Taoist principles can be found virtually everywhere.

In her book *The Tao of Inner Peace,* Diane Dreher explains that Lao outlined four "great disciplines" to help achieve inner peace through the way of the Tao: oneness, dynamic balance, cyclical growth, and harmonious action (Fig. 7.6).

The Principle of Oneness.   The principle of oneness suggests that we are part of the whole, connected to a dynamic network of universal energy. Oneness means to be one with, or a part of, nature, not above or apart from it. When we see ourselves as separate from the whole, we distance ourselves from other people and the natural elements. This distance weakens our spiritual strength. Just as there is strength in numbers, there is also strength in oneness.

The Principle of Dynamic Balance.   Taoist philosophy speaks of the composition of all creation as two complementary opposites: yin and yang. In simple terms, yin comprises the quiet, feminine, receptive elements of nature, while yang is seen as active, dynamic, and masculine. Alone, each side is overbearing. The union of yin and yang within the individual provides a perpetual movement that strives for balance and harmony. After rain comes sunshine. After disaster comes calm. To live in dynamic balance

A symbolic representation of the four principles of Taoism created by Lao Tzu.

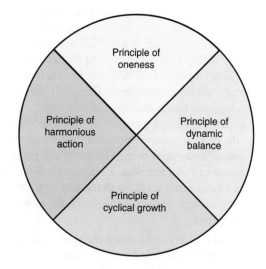

in the world, one must move with the flow through the mountains and valleys of life. To stay always static or always dynamic goes against the laws of nature of which both men and women are very much a part.

The Principle of Cyclical Growth.

The natural world consists of many cycles: day and night, birth and death, winter and summer. Each human life is also filled with cycles, from the life cycle of a red blood cell to the highs and lows of our emotions. The wisdom of the *Tao* advocates that these cycles be recognized and appreciated. Too often, impatience blinds human vision to the natural cycles of which we are a part. The universe is not still. The *Tao* encourages patience.

The Principle of Harmonious Action.

As a part of nature, we must work in cooperation with it and not try to dominate, monopolize, or destroy it. The wisdom of the *Tao* advises individuals to live in harmony with nature, respecting her many components, including the lives of others. To live in harmony means to live in moderation, not excess; to live with simplicity, not complexity; and to slow down, know oneself, and make wise choices. One concept of harmonious action is called the *wu wei,* which means knowing when to wait for the right moment, and knowing when to be spontaneous, moving with the rhythms of life.

There are many ways to reinforce the attitudes of Taoist philosophy behaviorally. The most commonly known techniques are yoga, meditation, and *T'ai Chi.* These are discussed in Part IV.

The characteristics of a *Tao* person are very similar to those of the self-actualized individuals described by Maslow, and those of the hardy personality described by Kobasa and Maddi. These characteristics include self-acceptance, humor, creativity, commitment, challenge, and self-control, and they serve as buffers against the perceptions of stress. *Tao* individuals have faith in themselves and what they do. They carry no illusions about who they are. They embrace life joyously. This is what it means to be "one with the *Tao.*"

The Path of Einstein

It may seem rather strange to include a physicist among the several people noted here who have speculated on the nature of human spirituality, yet at the same time it would be a gross oversight to omit this perspective. The fields of physics and theology, which were so bitterly divided over 300 years ago, are finding they have more commonalities than differences today. These commonalities were first brought to scientific light about 100 years ago by a physicist named Albert Einstein, who took it upon himself to challenge the accepted principles of natural physics developed by Isaac Newton. Like an earthquake, Einstein's concepts of the physical laws of nature rocked the foundations of the scientific community. But as can be seen today, the ramifications of this challenge actually parallel, and may eventually validate, the concept of a higher power, albeit somewhat differently from the way that many people currently perceive it. In 1999, *Time Magazine* named Einstein "Man of the Century," not solely for his scientific theories or Nobel Prize, but rather for changing the paradigm of thought of humanity in a nonthreatening way.

Curious about the nature of the universe and the laws that govern it, Einstein was convinced that all matter is comprised of energy, and that time and space are not locked into a continuum as previously thought, giving way to his famous theory of relativity: $E=MC^2$. Very simply put, this suggests that all matter is energy that is not confined to the "local" concept involving space and time. While the complexities of this theory are beyond the scope of this book, the premise of Einstein's theory, once rejected by his peers, is now completely accepted by the scientific community, as well as those mystically inclined individuals, who see Einstein's theory as a stepping stone toward higher consciousness. Moreover, the impact of Einstein's work has reached far beyond science to the fields of poetry, art, and even psychology. (It was Einstein's theory of relativity that gave Jung the idea for the collective unconscious.) With energy being the word that opened the door to understanding, theologians also gravitated toward Einstein's theories, making the concept of light a solid foundation from which to explore the divine nature of the universe. Compare, for example, the concept of universal energy with the following description (Dreher, 1991):

> We look at it and we do not see it;
> It's name is The Invisible.
> We Listen to it and we do not hear it;
> It's name is The Inaudible.
> We Touch it and don't find it;
> It's name is The Subtle.
>
> —Lao Tzu, *Tao Teh Ching,* 14

Stepping out of the scientific box that Newton had created centuries earlier, Einstein paved the way for others to follow. With the initial theoretical basis contructed, other physicists (Heisenberg and Chew) quickly added corollaries to Einstein's theory, leading the way to the field of quantum physics. Today pioneers in the field of energy medicine (see Chapter 3) credit Einstein with building a conceptual model from which to understand the human energy field and even human consciousness. Biophysicist Itzhak Bentov expounded on Einstein's concept that "energy equals matter" in his widely acclaimed book, *Stalking the Wild Pendulum*. From his added insight we begin to see that consciousness is actually a form of energy that surrounds, permeates, and connects all living objects. Like the atom's electrons, which vibrate to give off an energy field, so too does the human body produce an oscillation and energy field, which Bentov refers to as *subtle energy*. He hypothesized that this subtle energy is comprised of many layers or "frequencies," which he suggests constitute various layers of human consciousness (and the soul itself).

Since the introduction of the theory of relativity, physicists have discovered that subatomic particles called photons appear to travel at or greater than the speed of light. Renowned quantum physicist Dave Bohm has combined this knowledge with that of emotional thought and neuropeptide activity. He too postulates that thoughts are a form of energy: negative thoughts (e.g., fear and anger) are expressed by electrons, and positive thoughts (e.g., love and peace) are conveyed through the movement of photons. This idea has gained momentum among those who have taken a scientific look at the power of prayer and clairvoyant "coincidences." For instance, in a double-blind study designed by cardiologist Randolph Byrd (1986), over 300 hospital patients were randomly assigned to either a "prayed for" group or control group. Results demonstrated a statistically significant difference on various health parameters between those who received prayer and those who did not, suggesting that there may actually be a healing power in prayer. Even more significant, the people doing the praying lived hundreds if not thousands of miles away from the hospital where the patients were located. Additional studies of prayer have been conducted by the Spindrift Organization in Lansdale, Pennsylvania, using both direct and indirect prayer on the metabolic rate of plants. These studies have produced results similar to those found by Byrd.

A symbolic representation, from the perspective of Einstein, of the universe as one colossal source of energy.

Figure 7.7

An analysis of case studies by psychiatrist Jean Bolen in her book *The Tao of Psychology* indicated that distance (time and space) was not a factor among people who experienced a clairvoyant "coincidence," but that love (a positive emotion) was.

Dr. Larry Dossey, author of the books *Space, Time, and Medicine; Recovering the Soul;* and *Healing Words,* applauds Einstein for his "quantum leap" of new understanding regarding both the universe and its relevance to human consciousness. Dossey, a former internist at the Dallas Diagnostic Association, synthesized the theories of quantum physics and medicine in an attempt to validate that human spirituality is a vital element in the healing process. Borrowing a term from the field of physics, Dossey refers to the spiritual-healing nature of mankind as the nonlocal mind, meaning thoughts that are not bound by time or space. Dossey also explains that there is a connectedness to all things in the universe and that this connectedness has a spiritual quality to it. It is this same spiritual quality that Pelletier (Chapter 3) referred to as the "missing piece" of the stress and disease model, and why he suggested that the principles of quantum physics be included in the study of psychoneuroimmunology (Chapter 3). In the words of Dr. Richard Gerber, "With respect to his theory of relativity, Einstein was more right than even he imagined."

With a greater understanding of the theory of relativity, several physicists have noted connections between the world of physics and the spiritual nature of the universe. In his book *The Tao of Physics,* Fritjof Capra outlined many similarities and parallels between the disciplines of physics and the eastern mystical philosophies of Buddhism, Hinduism, and Taoism, suggesting that there is an incredible linkage between them and that whether it is called "energy," the "Tao," or the "Holy Spirit," its essence appears to be very similar. Capra writes, "Physicists and mystics deal with different aspects of reality. Physicists explore levels of matter, mystics levels of mind. What their explorations have in common is that these levels, in both cases, lie beyond ordinary sensory perception." Capra suggests that these two disciplines in effect, are looking at the same mountain, but from different vantage points and through different binoculars. To Capra, the paradigm shift which occurred in physics with Einstein's theory of relativity is currently rippling through other Western disciplines, including clinical medicine and psychology. In his autobiography *Memories, Dreams, Reflections,* Jung wrote, "There are indications that at least part of the psyche is not subject to the laws of space and time." The collective unconscious and subtle energy in which all things connect may, in fact, be the same component of human spirituality. As science continues to explore the realm of human energy and consciousness, the fields of physics and theology may not only connect, but someday become one and the same.

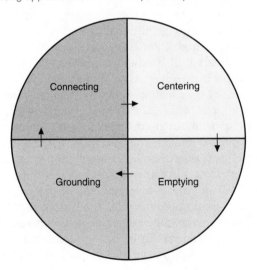

Figure 7.8 A symbolic representation of the common themes among approaches to human spirituality.

Those who knew him and studied his works say that Einstein was a spiritual man but not a religious one. Yet these same people note that he appeared to be driven by a spiritual quest to understand the nature of the universe. One of Einstein's most famous quotes speaks to this fact: "I want to know the thoughts of God, the rest are just details." And while some people infer from his theory of relativity that his view of the cosmos is impersonal at best (with the order of the universe simply calculated by mathematical equations), Einstein retorted, "God does not play dice with the universe." From his own writings it becomes very obvious that he was not only a scientific genius, but a world class philosopher as well. A person who spent much time in deep personal reflection, he once wrote,

> A human being is part of the whole, called by us "universe," a part limited in time and space. He experiences his thoughts and feelings as something separate from the rest, a kind of optical delusion of his consciousness. This delusion is a kind of prison for us, restricting us to our personal decisions and to affection for a few persons nearest us. Our task must be to free ourselves from this prison by widening our circle of compassion to embrace all living creatures and the whole of nature in its beauty.

Einstein spent the better part of his later years conceiving his unified field theory (a thesis to explain the relationship of gravity and electromagnetic energy), as well as playing a more subtle role as pacifist for world peace—a moral position in which he took great pride. Yet through it all, it was light, symbolically and literally, that fascinated Einstein.

"For the rest of my life, I want to reflect on what light is," he said.

Common Bonds of Human Spirituality

While no one path seems to offer complete insight into the mystery of the human spirit, some common themes run through the various paths. Specifically, these common themes are four processes which collectively nurture the growth of the human spirit: centering, emptying, grounding, and connecting (Fig. 7.8). These processes provide a nurturing enlightenment to our own spiritual growth. And some or all of these processes are found in virtually every form of relaxation and several coping techniques used to deal with stress.

Centering Process

The centering process involves deep reflection on one's real self: who we are and what our purpose in life is. Jung devoted much of his professional as well as personal life to understanding the centering process. He was deeply committed to the idea that centering our thoughts, or more specifically, accessing the powers of the unconscious mind, was imperative to mental, emotional, spiritual, and even physical well-being. The American Indian vision quest is also an exercise in centering. It is uninterrupted time devoted to addressing those questions that can only be answered by the soul in the midst of deep solitude. Likewise, Lao Tzu was an advocate of the centering process: "Be still, and discover your center of peace. Returning to the center is peace." Fox's creation spirituality theory also extolls the virtue of centering: the ability to appreciate the creative process within and to initiate the emptying process, which plants the seeds of personal transformation. Borysenko advocates centering to unite the body, mind, and soul as one. She suggests many ways this can be done, including journal writing, yoga, and meditation. As Borysenko points out, the purpose of virtually every relaxation technique is to create an opportunity for centering.

Emptying Process

It appears that for spiritual growth to continue there must be a continual process of emptying, or cleansing, of our consciousness. Some people refer to this as entering the void. Emptiness typically occurs as a result of sustained centering, where the individual discovers and makes peace with the real self by an act similar to spring cleaning: getting rid of old ways of thinking, toxic thoughts, and perceptions and feelings that inhibit spiritual growth. Jung referred to this process as confronting the shadow of our unconscious mind. Peck's Stage 3 is an emptying process, where one tosses out the old concept of an authoritarian God, the "Irish cop in the sky," and questions any divine existence at all. The American Indian vision quest is a time of fasting and removing oneself from the community to find a deep sense of self-awareness and self-purpose. Via negativa, as Fox stated, is also a period of emptiness, when one edits out of one's life the thoughts, feelings, and even possessions that obstruct the path of spiritual growth. Darkness symbolizes this emptiness. The wisdom of the Tao also advises emptying oneself. To quote Lao Tzu, "Close your mouth, shut your doors and live close to the Tao. Open your mouth, be busy all day and live in confusion." Borysenko, as well as many others, cites the practice of meditation (clearing the mind of thoughts) as a vehicle for the emptying process. Journal writing also serves this purpose.

This emptiness process can be painful. Peck compares it to a walk in the desert. Fasting will make one's stomach growl just as Jung's shadow and Fox's darkness will promote their respective growls. Chopra reminds us that detachment is the cornerstone of the emptying process. Regardless of how it is done, this emptying must be a conscious process. It is not a process you fall into by chance, but rather one that is intentionally created.

A Zen story illustrates the concept of emptiness. Years ago, an American professor toured Asia. One day he came upon a Buddhist monk and sat down to talk with him over a cup of tea. The professor graciously held out his cup while the Zen monk poured—and continued to pour, until the cup was overflowing. The professor, baffled, asked, "Why do you keep pouring?" The monk smiled kindly and replied, "Your mind is like this cup. It is so full of concepts that there is no room for new wisdom." The emptying process is a cleansing of the spirit. Just as the body needs exercise to rid itself of chemical waste, and the mind exhibits laughter and tears as emotional catharsis, so too the soul needs to empty and cleanse itself.

Grounding Process

The grounding process quickly follows the emptying process. In this stage, the soul or spirit is filled with new insight and knowledge made possible by the "space" made available during emptying. This insight may occur immediately, as an intuitive thought, or be synthesized over a short period of time and unfold right in front of you. If the emptying process is like plowing a field, the grounding process is planting and harvesting. During grounding comes the vision of the vision quest, answers to life's most difficult questions, and light to replace the darkness of the emptiness stage. It is a time of revelation and resolution with regard to life purpose and value conflicts, respectively. In Eastern cultures, the grounding process is referred to as enlightenment. To be grounded also means to feel secure with the insight received during this process. In a literal sense, groundedness means being connected to the earth and feeling a part of nature. In a figurative sense, grounding is the ability to feel comfortable in your surroundings, in your own environment. Grounding also means establishing clear paths of communication between the conscious and unconscious mind, thereby giving focus to one's life. From a Taoist perspective, to be grounded means to be in touch with the cycles of nature (phases of the moon, the seasons of the earth) and to move in rhythm with these cycles. In the vision quest, a new name (e.g., Walking Rainbow) is chosen to symbolize the vision, and is "worn" proudly upon return to the community.

Connecting Process

In the Taoist philosophy, all things connect; nothing is separate. This is the premise of the principle of oneness. Quantum physics, likewise, has reached this conclusion. Jung proposed that we are all connected by a universal soul he called the collective unconscious. Peck cites connectedness as a crucial element

in the development of both inner and world peace. In a process described as community building, he explains that bonding with others in one's environment builds a community of oneness and is the manifestation of the spiritual nature of humankind. This connecting process is what some people refer to as social well-being, and it is best manifested by participation in formal or informal support-group activities. Originally, a vision quest was completed only when the individual returned to the community, reunited with friends and family, and shared insight gained from his or her unique vision. But American Indians believe in connecting not only with other people, but with all creations on Mother Earth, from trees and lakes to animals, birds, and fish. Chief Seattle wrote, "What is man without beasts? If all the beasts were gone, men would die from great loneliness of spirit, for whatever happens to beasts, soon happens to man. All things are connected." Thus, connecting is based on respect for all creation. Borysenko also cites the importance of the connecting process as the foundation of support groups for individuals overcoming addictions. The strength of the connecting process is related to the power of centering, emptying, and grounding oneself. Finally, the work of Jesus of Nazareth was about building bonds of love between persons so that all may become one people.

Clearly, the order of the four steps is important to the effectiveness of the process as a whole. Each step alone confers strength, but the dynamics of the four steps in sequence is an unparalleled strategy to nurture inner strength and enhance spiritual well-being.

A Model of Spirituality for Stress Management

In my efforts to integrate spiritual well-being into the wellness paradigm of total well-being for corporate health promotion, I created an integrative theoretical model to emphasize the dynamic relationship between stress and human spirituality (Fig. 7.9). I synthesized this spiritual well-being model from the psychological theories of Jung, Maslow, Frankl, Peck, Fox, Selye, Schaef, and Borysenko, and several other influences from American Indian and Asian cultures. In this model, human spirituality is defined as the maturation process of our higher consciousness as developed through the integration of three facets: an insightful, nurturing relationship with oneself and others, the

Figure 7.9 *An integrative model of spiritual well-being. [From B. L. Seaward, Spiritual Wellbeing—A Health Education Model, Journal of Health Education 22 (1991): 166–189. (Journal of Health Education is a publication of the American Alliance for Health, Physical Education, Recreation, and Dance, 1900 Association Drive, Reston, VA 22091)]*

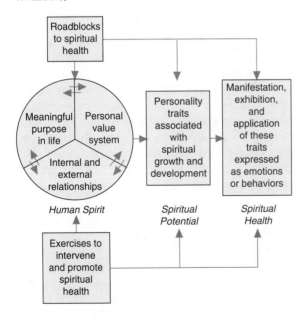

development of a strong personal value system, and a meaningful purpose in one's life. These facets, each tightly integrated with the other two, constitute a dynamic configuration which, when attended to and nurtured, will advance human consciousness to a higher level of understanding, that is, seeing oneself as a part of a larger whole.

Let us take a closer look at the three facets.

Internal and External Relationships

Internal and external relationships involve a twofold process whereby one explores, confronts, and resolves one's inner thoughts, feelings, and perceptions, as well as strengthens ties or connectedness with others in one's environment. In some ways, human spirituality can be thought of as a form of self-government. It consists of both a domestic policy, or a personal philosophy and behavioral guidelines for the relationship with oneself, or the self, and a foreign policy concerning relationships with all other people in one's environment. A weak domestic policy will carry over into a weak foreign policy. Human spirituality works the same way: a poor internal relationship carries over into weak relationships with family, friends, co-workers, and other people with whom you come in contact. For optimum spiritual well-being, there must be a healthy balance between internal and external relationships. In other words, love your neighbor as yourself.

An Insightful Internal Relationship. The internal relationship begins with the practice of centering, or discovering and nurturing your real Self. Some ancient mystics referred to the centering process as "entering the heart." According to Lao Tzu, "The way of inner peace begins with self-acceptance, to seek peace outside is to leave it behind." This process of centering involves dedicating quality alone-time to self-discovery, and separating who you are from what you do, as well as from your relationships with other people. Centering means coming to terms with the constituents of your identity and going beyond asking "What?" during the process of internal dialogue to ask "Why?" Similarly, in the process known as individuation, Jung emphasized the importance of self-reflection to bridge the gap between the conscious and the unconscious mind, thereby accessing the divine power within to help resolve spiritual crises. Jung was convinced that continual soul searching strengthened one's internal resources, including intuition, creativity,

willpower, faith, patience, optimism, and humbleness. A strong internal relationship is characterized by improving and maintaining honesty in your inner thoughts, feelings, and even dreams, through introspection and exploration of your conscious and unconscious mind. The quest for self-knowledge is a soul-searching effort that leads to awareness of inner wisdom from the unconscious mind. It is this quest that develops the strength of your human spirit. In both accepting your fixed personal limitations and expanding your conscious barriers, you are led to new heights of spiritual development and consciousness, or what Jung referred to as spiritual evolution. The result of increased self-awareness, and ultimately the most powerful of inner resources is the ability to accept and love yourself.

Divine Personifications. Consensus among leaders in the emerging field of psychospirituality suggests that as you develop your own internal relationship, you also strengthen the bond to a higher power residing both within and beyond your physical domain. This, in fact, is a necessary part of the internal relationship: to see yourself as whole, yet a part of a bigger whole. In the words of Fox, this bond is "a personal cosmology—a relationship to the divine presence that dwells in us." Thus, a strong internal relationship also includes a comfortable and nurturing relationship with a higher power, however you might perceive that to be. Perceptions, however, need to be refocused, perhaps even changed, as this relationship matures. At a young age, our first introduction to a higher power is often through personification. A higher power of consciousness is given a name (e.g., God, Yahweh, Allah, Supreme Being) and described with human features, which are easy for children to identify, understand, and find comfort in. More often than not, however, this image does not develop or keep pace with a person's physical, emotional, and intellectual maturation into adulthood. In fact, Fox notes that many adults still envision God as a wise old man in a white robe resting on a cloud.

A comparable example is the American personification of the spirit of Christmas, in which the concept of loving kindness is symbolized by the human figure of Santa Claus. For those children who were introduced to the jolly fat man in a red suit, a new reality seeps in somewhere between the ages of six and ten years. With the death of the personification, so wither away other elements of the essence of Christmas, and sometimes these elements are lost forever. Likewise, many adults experiencing a painful emptiness, choose not to find their "God," but rather elect to leave this relationship underdeveloped. In theology circles, the phrase "killing off the old gods" is used to describe the depersonification process at this stage of maturation, as individuals are counseled to strengthen their internal relationship. Sometimes even the word *God* can be too limiting to conceptualize this mystical phenomenon. In fact, for many people the word *God* carries with it a lot of baggage. Be that as it may, a strong and maturing relationship with a higher power is the anchor of the soul in the rough seas of crises. It provides a means of connectedness on a very personal and special level. Internal relationships are augmented by activities of solitude, meditation, reflection or prayer, and vision quests, where quality alone-time is allocated for the purpose of strengthening this relationship with the real self. Many relaxation techniques and coping skills are rooted in the premise of centering to nurture this relationship.

External Relationships. External relationships constitute a healthy bonding with anyone or anything outside the relationship with the inner self, including family, friends, acquaintances, and the creations of Mother Earth such as animals, trees, lakes, and the planet itself. External relationships are improved and maintained through your expression of acceptance, peace, compassion, communication, and respect for all individuals in your environment as well as your sense of connectedness with nature on the planet earth. More specifically, strong external relationships include open tolerance, acceptance, and respect for other people's opinions, beliefs, and values, even when they don't agree with your own. This aspect of spirituality includes a forgiving (accepting) attitude toward others when their behavior is different from or inconsistent with your own ideals. Remember the saying espoused by all major religions: Do unto others as you would have them do unto you.

To Peck, this element of human spirituality also involves building community. Community is defined as the bonding and belongingness of supportive individuals in your collective environments. Building community means reaching out to other people to raise the level of human consciousness and human potential, for in the face of stress there is strength in numbers. Some scholars have designated social well-being as a fifth and separate component of well-being.

However, a sound understanding of spirituality includes this social aspect in the framework of external relationships and community building. Finally, healthy external relationships necessitate the continual nurturing of the spiritual growth and love of other individuals in your environment through behaviors that will raise your human consciousness and human potential to new heights.

Both internal and external relationships require continuous work to further your spiritual evolution. Relationships are living organisms which, like plants and animals, need nutrients to survive. Neglect leads to starvation, atrophy, root rot, and eventual death of the human spirit. A loss of connectedness is detrimental to the health of the human spirit. Peck once remarked that true evil is masked as laziness and apathy. With regard to human spirituality, there is a consensus among his colleagues that he is right.

Personal Value System

The identification, clarification, and implementation of a personal value system is tantamount to spiritual well-being. Values, as described by Lewis (1990), are constructs of importance: personal beliefs based on the concepts of goodness, justice, and beauty that give meaning and depth to our thoughts, attitudes, and behaviors. Values, including love, honesty, self-esteem, independence, leisure, education, privacy, forgiveness, and respect for Mother Earth, to name a few, typically dictate our attitudes and behaviors. As suggested by the research of Milton Rokeach (1972), values—both basic or core, such as love and honesty, and supporting, or those that support the core values, including trust and creativity—constitute a collection of ideals, or hierarchy of values, specific to each person. Individuals adopt many values unconsciously throughout their lives. However, most values are acquired in early childhood. Values such as acceptance, love, respect, and trust are learned from our parents, teachers, and respected individuals when there is strong interaction and the development of emotional bonds with them. These and other values are adopted as a means of acquiring approval from role models, or figures of importance, whom one chooses to emulate in the development of one's own identity.

Values that are adopted consciously or unconsciously lay the developmental groundwork for personality traits and behaviors. In addition, they construct a framework for self-validation and development of moral judgment of right and wrong, good and bad, and pain and pleasure. Values are abstract in nature, yet are often symbolized by material objects or possessions that represent a specific thing. For example, a diploma is a symbol of the value of education, and a television set is a symbol of leisure. As we mature, our value system also changes, but it continues to account for the way we think and behave. Like earthquakes caused by movements of the earth's tectonic plates, our values shift in importance as we mature, causing our own earth to quake. These shifts are called value conflicts, and they can result in a great deal of stress. Jung referred to this type of stress as a spiritual crisis, as these conflicts rock the foundations of the soul. Examples of value conflicts abound, ranging from those on the personal level all the way up to the governmental level. The abortion controversy is an example of a values conflict at the governmental level. Another example is the preservation of national wetlands versus the push for housing and industrial development. Both of these issues have caused much stress in the national consciousness. On a more personal level, leisure versus work, sexual pleasure versus personal integrity, love (relationships) versus religion, and fame versus privacy are just a few examples of value conflicts causing stress at a spiritual level.

According to psychiatrist Viktor Frankl, "We are our values." Frankl observed that stress arises when values conflict with each other, leading to an arousal of inner tension, thus disturbing the homeostasis of the mind. But Frankl saw opportunity where others saw disaster, believing that resolution of value conflicts brings with it incredible strength of inner resources. The challenge is to assume responsibility for bringing these conflicts to resolution. Maslow (1976) considered the ultimate disease of our time to be "valuelessness," the condition wherein society's traditional value systems have proven ineffective and value conflicts at all levels go unresolved. He believed that a new valid, useable system of human values must be created, initially by the individual, and then adopted by society. This new value system, he argued, must be based on trust rather than on the false hopes and ignorance inspired by laziness, greed, and inability to know oneself. Conflicts in values can be helpful in our own maturation process if we work through the conflict to a full resolution. But this takes work, which many people would rather avoid. However, a strong personal value system is one in which the hierarchy of basic and supporting values is regularly assessed and

reorganized, allowing conflicts of values to be resolved in order to promote inner peace.

Meaningful Purpose in Life

A major facet of the spiritual-well-being model is represented by one's meaningful purpose in life. According to Frankl (1984), a life mission can be accomplished through the design and achievement of a series of life goals, and through the experience of a value conflict or emotional suffering. Frankl asserted that the health of the human spirit rapidly declines with the loss of meaning in one's life, while a continual search for and fulfillment of one's aim in life is essential to spiritual development. He was convinced that the search for meaning was a primary force, instinctual in nature, and not merely a rationalization by humans, for humans (Fig. 7.10).

In my work with Olympic athletes, I was introduced to the concept of the "Olympic blues," a period of time directly after the Olympic Games when nonmedal winners lost all sense of meaning in their lives. The rebound time could be months or even years. Sim-

(Courtesy of Stratton.)

Figure 7.10

"The meaning of life, and make it snappy -- we're double parked."

Figure 7.11 Dr. Martin Luther King, Mother Teresa, and the Dalai Lama are among the recipients of the Nobel Peace Prize, the highest possible honor for humanitarian achievement in the world.

ilarly, mothers suffer the empty-nest syndrome when their last child leaves home, creating a vacuum of life purpose. Men and women who retire after thirty to forty years of employment may also suffer from feelings of lack of purpose. Frankl suggested that there is no ordained life purpose for each person; rather, a series of progressive life goals culminates in a life mission. He believed that emotional suffering at the completion of a goal is an essential part of the process of moving to the next ambition and continuing with one's purposeful meaning. The premise behind his logotherapy was to help people move beyond the suffering and thereby find a new meaning on which to focus. Finding a new life purpose in the ashes of suffering is not impossible, but this, too, takes work. One must create new goals and ambitions to aim for and accomplish.

Hans Selye, renowned for his work in stress physiology, later turned his attention to matters of the spirit as well. In his book, *Stress without Distress,* he stated that one's health status is dependent on the ability to maintain a purpose in life that commands self-respect and pride. As a result of his research on the effects of perceived stress and the physiological manifestations of the stress response, Selye theorized that the most significant strategy for conquering stress is to pursue what he called the aim of life. This aim, or meaningful purpose, of one's life is the foundation of health, and is built on both short-term and long-term attainable goals. The process of pursuing and completing the aim of life is initiated by self-reflection; giving strength to the individual's internal relationship.

In this model of spiritual well-being, all components are so tightly integrated they are difficult to separate. Each facet—nurturing, insightful, and bonding relationships; a strong personal value system; and an assessment of progress in one's meaningful purpose in life—is mutually inclusive of the other two. Moments of solitude and self-reflection lend themselves to the assessment of personal values and steps toward conflict resolution, as well as toward refinement of one's purpose in life. Values influence the direction of life's meaningful purpose. For example, the expression of love, perhaps the strongest spiritual value, not only nurtures self-growth but also influences the strength of external relationships and inspires the direction of one's life mission. This integration of components is exemplified by the works of Nobel Peace Prize winners Martin Luther King, Mother Teresa, and the Dalai Lama, as well as thousands of lesser known but equally inspiring individuals (Fig. 7.11).

Spiritual Potential and Spiritual Health

This spiritual well-being model suggests that the configuration of the three components to promote higher consciousness yields a host of personality traits specific to the integrity of the human spirit. I call these traits or inner resources *spiritual potential,* and they can be either dormant or active parts of one's personality. Creativity, will, intuition, faith, patience, courage, love, humility, and optimism are examples of these human spiritual traits. The manifestation of spiritual potential, which I label *spiritual health,* is expressed as specific emotional responses and behaviors that often expand the limits of human potential as a whole. Employing faith or an optimistic attitude in the face of diversity exemplifies spiritual health. In addition, Maslow might have considered creative acts or peak experiences to be examples of spiritual health; Peck cites community building, while Schaef would describe it as a "living process." Spiritual *potential* is like a group of instruments (e.g., violin, cello, and piano), and spiritual health is the music created by the individual with the instrument in hand. With practice, we are all capable of making beautiful music.

Roadblocks and Interventions

In Eastern philosophies, the division between the conscious and unconscious mind is considered the major obstacle to spiritual enlightenment. In Western philosophies, the walls of the ego, serving to protect one's thoughts, feelings, and identity, can hinder one's spiritual growth and human potential. While the ego wall is an abstract concept, elements that constitute its bricks and mortar are more easily recognized. These obstacles, some specific and concrete, others quite general and abstract, might include the following: laziness, greed, despair, anger, fear, low self-esteem, unresolved loss, substance addictions, and codependency. Roadblocks, both specific characteristics and/or related behaviors, undermine the maturation process of human spirituality to the detriment of spiritual health and total well-being. Roadblocks actually perpetuate the stress response rather than minimize it. Like behavioral changes to influence physical well-being (e.g., aerobics, smoking cessation, balanced diet), intervention techniques can be utilized to enhance the development of inner resources and behaviors associated with spiritual health. The most common technique mentioned as an intervention is meditation. Meditation includes many styles of increasing self-awareness (see Chapter 18). In line with the idea that all things are connected, you will see that most, if not all, of the coping skills and relaxation techniques described in this book have some tie to the concepts discussed in this chapter. Art therapy, music therapy, humor therapy, communication skills, and several others include many aspects of spiritual well-being that integrate the concepts of centering, emptying, grounding, and connecting. They reinforce the importance of internal and external relationships, value systems, and the search for a meaningful purpose in life. In many Eastern cultures, relaxation techniques and coping skills were originally created as vehicles to enhance spiritual enlightenment and inner peace. Western cultures adopted several of these techniques and even created a few more, but lost in the translation were their true meaning and purpose. Slowly, this purpose is being rediscovered and recognized as an essential factor in these techniques, integrating the spiritual component with total well-being.

As we begin to understand the dynamics of human nature, it becomes increasingly obvious how important spiritual well-being is to total well-being. Spirituality involves many academic disciplines, including theology, psychology, and quantum physics. The theories presented here are only a handful of concepts describing personal insights on the elements associated with human spirituality and the soul. Because of the sensitive relationship between spirituality and religion, this area of health promotion, particularly as it applies to stress management, has often been neglected altogether, or not incorporated fully, as a significant aspect of the wellness paradigm. As researchers continue to explore and measure human consciousness, they may reveal that the mind and the soul play integral roles in both the understanding of human stress and the most effective ways to deal with it.

Summary

+ The term *spirituality* is becoming a more comfortable one in the Western world. While stress seems to be omnipresent in American lifestyles, there also appears to be a spiritual awakening taking place, from seeds planted by the human consciousness movements of the late 1960s. The World Health Organization cites spiritual well-being as critical to overall well-being.

+ Spirituality has proved elusive to define because its essence seems to permeate everything. Harmony with self, others, Earth, and a higher power is often considered a description of this concept. Spirituality and religion are related, but separate, concepts.

+ Several viewpoints of human spirituality by intellectuals from Eastern and Western cultures representing several disciplines, including psychology, theology, philosophy, physics, and medicine, were described.

+ Jung postulated that there is a profound, divine level of unconsciousness, the collective unconscious, which unites all people. Poor spiritual health results from the inability to access this source within us.

+ Peck outlined the road to spiritual development, a systematic path consisting of four stages: chaotic antisocial, formal institutional, skeptical, and mystic communal.

+ Hildegard von Bingen was a mystic who reminds us of the mystical side of human nature, and that every aspect of creation is spiritual and sacred in its own way.

+ American Indian spirituality, called Mother Earth spirituality, was described to Anglo-Americans by Black Elk. It includes four cardinal principles: respect for the Great Spirit, respect for Mother Earth, respect for fellow men and women, and respect for individual freedoms. The vision quest, a soul-searching retreat, is one of the most profound experiences of Mother Earth spirituality.

+ Fox synthesized several concepts of theology and physics into creation spirituality, which consists of four phases: via positiva, via negativa, via creativa, and via transformativa.

+ Borysenko outlines a categorical difference between spiritual optimism and spiritual pessimism: the former, an asset to total well-being; the latter, a significant contributing factor to the stress-and-disease relationship.

+ Deepak Chopra reminds us to continually explore our consciousness and live in harmony with the spiritual laws of the universe. These include the laws of pure potentiality, giving and receiving, karma, least effort, intention and desire, detachment, and Dharma or life purpose.

+ Jesus spoke of love as a divine source that resides in every one of us. It is this source that longs to bond with all others. His message was to love ourselves and then share this love with each member of humanity.

+ Campbell stated that the hero's journey involves three distinct phases: 1) departure, 2) initiation, and 3) return.

+ Lao described spirituality as the *Tao*. He outlined four principles of the *Tao* that help to clarify human interaction with the universe: oneness, dynamic balance, cyclical growth, and harmonious action. Many of the traits associated with these principles can be seen as parallels to Maslow's characteristics of self-actualization.

+ Einstein's theory of relativity brought new light to the concept of energy and mass and properties of the nonlocal mind. His theory bears a remarkable resemblance to Jung's theory of the collective unconscious.

+ Four common themes among theories of human spirituality constitute a systematic series of processes to strengthen the human spirit: centering, emptying, grounding, and connecting.

+ Human spirituality can be defined operationally as the maturation process of higher consciousness as developed through the integration of three facets: an insightful, nurturing relationship with oneself and others; the development of a strong personal value system; and a meaningful purpose in life.

+ There are many roadblocks to spiritual evolution, perhaps the most significant being the stress emotion, fear.

+ Many coping and relaxation techniques share characteristics that foster the spiritual process of centering, emptying, grounding, and connecting.

Concepts and Terms

Archetype
Centering process
Chaotic antisocial stage
Connecting process
Creation spirituality
Divine personification
Emptying process
Formal-institutional stage
Grounding process
Hero's journey
Internal and external
  relationships
Law of detachment
Law of giving
Law of intention and desire
Law of karma

Law of least effort
Law of pure potentiality
Mother Earth spirituality
Mystic-communal stage
Nonlocal mind
Perennial philosophy
Personal cosmology
Personal value system
Principle of cyclical growth
Principle of dynamic growth
Principle of harmonious action
Principle of oneness
Psychospirituality
Purposeful meaning in life
Skeptical stage
Spiritual bankruptcy

Spiritual dormancy
Spiritual health
Spiritual hunger
Spiritual optimism
Spiritual pessimism
Spiritual potential
Synchronicity
Transcendence
Transpersonal psychology
Unconditional love
Via creativa
Via negativa
Via positiva
Via transformativa
Vision quest

Self-Assessment

Roadblocks on the Human Path

1. If our experiences on the human path indeed constitute the evolution of our souls, then the metaphor of roadblocks can be used to describe a halt to this evolutionary process. Roadblocks on the human path are those aspects of our lives that separate us from the divine source and either stifle or inhibit the evolutionary process of soul growth.

    These roadblocks take many forms, including unresolved anger or fear, greed, apathy, laziness, judgment, and denial, to name just a few. Reflecting on the growth process of your soul and the journey of your human path, can you identify any obstacles or obstructions that have left you in the ranks of the spiritual couch-potato? If not roadblocks, distractions? Make a list of these, being as specific as possible.

    1. FACING INCEST AT A VERY YOUNG AGE
    2. CHANGING OF MY WRITING HAND FROM LEFT TO RIGHT IN 1ST GRADE
    3. ALCOHOLIC FATHER EXPERIENCING VIOLENCE AND THE NEED FOR SAFETY
    4. NOT FORGIVING MY MOTHER FOR NOT PROTECTING ME AS A CHILD
    5. LIVING YOUTH WITH NO JUNK FOOD OR RARELY WAS TABOO CAUSED ME TO DO
    6. WRONGFUL ACTS FOR CANDY OR SODA
    7. ANGRY THAT MY MOTHER NEVER BETTERED HERSELF OR STUCK UP FOR HERSELF

2. Like Alexander the Great, who cut through the unsolvable knot with his sword, we have at our disposal several resources with which to cut through, dissolve, climb over, or transcend the roadblocks on the human path. These resources include, but are not limited to, optimism, humor, courage, faith, willpower, curiosity, creativity, imagination, and compassion. These resources comprise part of the fabric of our souls. They are tools to aid us in the evolutionary process. These inner resources are not gifts for a chosen few; rather, they are everyone's birthright. Yet, without proper use, these resources, like atrophied muscles, can prove less than effective as aids on the journey of the human path. From a holistic viewpoint, we can see that we are both jeweler and jewel.

    Take a moment to reflect on the state of your inner resources. What are they? Make a list; then ask yourself which of these seem most effective and in what ways you can utilize them to your advantage. Which of these inner strengths have you let atrophy? Which now need cultivation to bring them to their fullest potential?

    A PASSION FOR COMPASSION

    1. COURAGE — MOST EFFECTIVE
    2. COMPASSION
    3. PASSION — MOST EFFECTIVE — KEEP ME ON THE PATH OF WHOLENESS OR WELLNESS
    4. SEARCH FOR TRUTH —
    5. FAITH — MOST EFFECTIVE — KNOW THAT ALL IS WELL AND WILL BE TAKEN CARE OF
    6. HUMOR — A WAY TO LIGHTEN THE LOAD — FREE FLOW
    7. CURIOSITY — ALWAYS WANTING TO KNOW WHAT IS STORED IN THE PAIN WHICH LEADS TO THE SEARCH FOR TRUTH

TRUST - ATROPHIED

References and Resources

Bellingham, R. et al. Connectedness: Some Skills for Spiritual Health, *American Journal of Health Promotion* 4:18–31, 1989.

Benedictine Monks. *Chant.* Angel Records, 1993.

Bentov, I. *Stalking the Wild Pendulum.* Destiny Books, Rochester, VT, 1988.

Bobko, J. *Vision: The Life and Music of Hildegard Von Bingen.* Penguin Studio Books, New York, 1995.

Bohm, D. Toward a New Theory of the Relationship of Mind and Matter, *Frontier Perspectives* 1(9), 1990.

Bolen, J. S. *The Tao of Psychology.* Harper & Row, New York, 1979.

Bonham, T. *Humor: God's Gift.* Broadman Press, Nashville, TN, 1988.

Booth, L. *When God Becomes a Drug.* Tarcher Press, Los Angeles, 1991.

Bopp, I. et al. *The Sacred Tree: Reflections on Native American Spirituality.* Four Worlds Development Press, Wilmot, WI, 1985.

Borysenko, J. *Fire in the Soul: A New Psychology of Spiritual Optimism.* Warner Books, New York, 1993.

Borysenko, J. *Guilt Is the Teacher, Love Is the Lesson.* Warner, New York, 1990.

Borysenko, J. *The Ways of the Mystic: Seven Paths to God.* HayHouse, Carlsbad, CA, 1997.

Borysenko, J. *A Woman's Journey to God.* Riverhead Books, New York, 1999.

Boyd, D. *Rolling Thunder.* Delta, New York, 1974.

Byrd, R. C. Cardiologist Studies Effect of Prayer on Patients, *Brain/Mind Bulletin,* March 7, 1986.

Byrd, R. C. Positive Therapeutic Effects of Intercessory Prayer in a Coronary Care Unit Population, *Southern Medical Journal* 81(7):826–829, 1988.

Campbell, J. *The Hero's Journey* (edited with Phil Cousineau). Element, Shaftsbury England, 1999.

Campbell, J. *The Hero with a Thousand Faces,* 2d ed. Princeton Bollinger, Princeton, NJ, 1968.

Campbell, J. *The Power of Myth* (with Bill Moyers). Doubleday Books, New York, 1988.

Campbell, J. Radio Interview on New Dimension Radio. San Francisco, CA, 1988.

Capra, F. *The Tao of Physics,* 3rd ed. Shambhala Publications, Berkeley, CA, 1991.

Carey, K. *Starseed: The Third Millennium.* Harper-Collins, San Francisco, 1991.

Carlson, R. and Shield, B., eds. *Handbook for the Soul.* Little, Brown, Boston, 1995.

Carlson, R. and Shield, B. *Healers on Healing.* Tarcher, Los Angeles, 1989.

Castaneda, C. *The Teachings of Don Juan: A Yaqui Way of Knowledge.* Pocket Books, New York, 1968.

Catford, L. and Ray, M. *The Path of the Everyday Hero: Strategies for Finding Your Creative Spirit.* Tarcher, Los Angeles, 1991.

Chapman, L. Developing a Useful Perspective on Spiritual Health: Wellbeing, Spiritual Potential, and the Search for Meaning, *American Journal of Health Promotion* 1:31–39, 1987.

Chapman, L. Spiritual Health: A Component Missing from Health Promotion, *American Journal of Health Promotion* 1(1):38–41, 1986.

Chopra, D. *The Higher Self.* Nightengale-Conant, Chicago, 1994.

Chopra, D. *How to Know God: The Soul's Journey into the Mystery of Mysteries.* Harmony Books, New York, 2000.

Chopra, D. Personal Conversations, October 14 & 15, 1995.

Chopra, D. *The Seven Spiritual Laws of Success.* New World Library, San Rafael, CA, 1995.

Cimino R. and Lattin, D. Choosing My Religion, *American Demographics.* April: 60–65, 1999.

Clark, R. W. *Einstein: The Life and Times.* Avon Books, New York, 1971.

Cochran, T. and Zalenski, J. *Transformations: Awakening to the Sacred in Ourselves.* Bell Tower, New York, 1995.

Course in Miracles. Foundation for Inner Peace, Farmingdale, NY, 1975.

Coutuier, L. Speaking in Silence, *New Women Magazine,* March:58–61, 1992.

Crow-Dog, M. and Erdoes, R. *Lakota Woman.* Harper Perennial Books, New York, 1990.

Dossey, L. *Healing Words.* Harper Collins. San Francisco, 1993.

Dossey, L. *Recovering the Soul: A Scientific and Spiritual Search.* Bantam New Age Books, New York, 1989.

Dossey, L. *Reinventing Medicine.* HarperSan Francisco, San Francisco, 1999.

Dossey, L. *Space, Time, and Medicine.* Bantam New Age Books, New York, 1982.

Dreher, D. *The Tao of Inner Peace.* Harper Perennial Books, New York, 1991.

Drummond, H. *Drummond's Address.* Henry Altemus Company, Philadelphia, 1891.

Einstein, A. *Ideas and Opinions.* Crown, New York, 1954.

Eley, G. and Seaward, B. L. *Health Enhancement of the Human Spirit.* National Center for Health and Fitness, Spiritual Well-being Symposium, Washington, DC, April 16–17, 1989.

Elliot, W. *Tying Rocks to Clouds.* Image Books–Doubleday, New York, 1996.

Fahlberg, L. and Fahlberg, L. Exploring Spirituality and Consciousness with an Expanded Science: Beyond the Ego with Empiricism, Phenomenology, and Contemplation, *American Journal of Health Promotion* 5:273–281, 1991.

Fields, R. et al. *Chop Wood, Carry Water: A Guide to Finding Spiritual Fulfillment in Everyday Life.* Tarcher Books, Los Angeles, 1984.

Foster, S., with Little, M. *Vision Quest: Personal Transformations in the Wilderness.* Prentice-Hall, New York, 1988.

Fowler, K. *Stages of Faith: The Psychology of Human Development and the Quest for Meaning.* HarperSan Francisco, 1981.

Fox, M. *Creation Spirituality.* Harper Books, San Francisco, 1991.

Fox, M. *Illuminations of Hildegard von Bingen.* Bear and Company, Santa Fe, NM, 1985.

Fox, M. *A Spirituality Named Compassion.* Winston Press, Minneapolis, MN, 1979.

Frankl, V. *Man's Search For Meaning.* Pocket Books, New York, 1984.

Freeman, J. *Interview with Carl Jung.* British Broadcasting Corporation, 1959. Film.

Gerber, R. Personal Communication, Nov. 25, 1991.

Gore, A. *Earth in the Balance: Ecology and the Human Spirit.* Plume Press, New York, 1993.

Grof, C. *The Thirst for Wholeness: Attachment, Addiction and the Spiritual Path.* HarperCollins, New York, 1993.

Hand, Floyd. *Learning Journey in the Red Road.* Learning Journey Communications. Toranto, Ca. 1998.

Hammerschlag, C. *The Theft of the Spirit: A Journey to Spiritual Healing.* Fireside Books, New York, 1994.

Hoff, B. *The Tao of Pooh.* Penguin Books, New York, 1982.

Hoyman, H. The Spiritual Dimension of Man's Health in Today's World, *Journal of School Health* February 1966.

Huxley, A. *The Perennial Philosophy.* Perennial Library, New York, 1945.

Jampolsky, G. *Teach Only Love.* Bantam Books, New York, 1983.

Jung, C. G. *Man and His Symbols.* Anchor Books, New York, 1964.

Jung, C. G. *Memories, Dreams, Reflections.* Vantage Press, New York, 1964.

Jung, C. G. *Modern Man in Search of a Soul.* Harvest/HBJ Books, San Diego, CA, 1933.

Jung, C. G. *The Undiscovered Self.* Mentor Books, New York, 1958.

Kennedy, J. F. Inaugural Address, January 20, 1961, *Department of State Bulletin* February 6, 1961.

Klivington, K. et al. Does Spirit Matter? Four Commentaries, *Advances* 8(1):31–48, 1992.

Krishnamurti, J. *On God.* HarperSan Francisco, New York, 1992.

Lao Tzu. *Tao Teh Ching,* trans. J. C. H. Wu. Shambhala, Boston, 1990.

Leichtman, R. *Einstein Returns.* Ariel Press, Columbus, OH, 1982.

Lesser, L. *The New American Spirituality.* Random House, New York, 1999.

Lewis, C. S. *Mere Christianity.* Collier Books, New York, 1960.

Lewis, H. *A Question of Values.* Harper & Row, San Francisco, 1990.

Living Bible. Tyndale, Wheaton, IL, 1971.

Maslow, A. H. *The Farther Reaches of Human Nature.* Penguin Books, New York, 1976.

Maslow, A. H. *Religion, Values, and Peak Experiences.* Penguin Books, 1964.

McFadden, S. *Profiles in Wisdom: Native Elders Speak about the Earth.* Bear and Co., Santa Fe, NM, 1991.

McGaa, E. (Eagle Man). *Mother Earth Spirituality: Native American Paths to Healing Ourselves and the World.* HarperCollins, San Francisco, 1990.

Merton, T. *The Ascent to Truth.* Harcourt Brace Jovanovitch, San Diego, CA, 1951.

Miller, R. S. *As Above, So Below.* Tarcher, Los Angeles, 1992.

Millman, D. *The Laws of Spirit.* H. J. Kramer, Tiburon, CA, 1995.

Moore, T. *Care of the Soul.* HarperCollins, New York, 1992.

Muller, W. *Sabbath: Restoring the Sacred Rhythm of Rest.* Bantam Books, New York, 1999.

Naranjo, C. and Ornstein, R. *On the Psychology of Meditation.* Esalen Books, New York, 1971.

Neihardt, J. G. *Black Elk Speaks.* University of Nebraska Press, Lincoln, 1972.

O'Murchu, D. *Reclaiming Spirituality.* Crossroad, New York, 1998.

O'Murchu, D. *Quantum Theology.* Crossroad, New York, 1997.

Peck, M. S. *The Different Drum: Community Making and Peace.* Simon & Schuster, New York, 1987.

Peck, M. S. *The Road Less Traveled.* Simon & Schuster, New York, 1978.

Pilch, J. Wellness Spirituality, *Health Values* 12(3):28–31, 1988.

Redwood, D. Rediscovering the Soul: A Scientific and Spiritual Search (interview with Larry Dossey), *Pathways,* Spring:19–29, 1992.

Remen, R. N. On Defining Spirit, *Noetic Sciences Review* 63:1988.

Remen, R. N. Spirit: Resource for Healing, *Noetic Sciences Review* 61–65, 1988.

Rokeach, M. *Beliefs, Attitudes, and Values.* Jossey Bass, San Francisco, 1972.

Roman, S. *Spiritual Growth: Being Your Higher Self.* H. J. Kramer, Tiburon, CA, 1989.

Schaef, A. W. *When Society Becomes an Addict.* Harper & Row, New York, 1987.

Seaward, B. L. From Corporate Fitness to Corporate Wellness, *Fitness in Business* 2:182–186, 1988.

Seaward, B. L. Giving Wellness a Spiritual Workout, *Health Progress* 70:50–52, 1989.

Seaward, B. L. Spiritual Wellbeing, A Health Education Model, *Journal of Health Education* 22(3):166–169, 1991.

Seaward, B. L. Reflections on Human Spirituality at the Worksite, *American Journal of Health Promotion,* 9(3):165–168, 1995.

Seaward, B. L. *Stand Like Mountain, Move Like Water.* Health Communications Inc., Deerfield Beach, FL, 1997.

Seaward, B. L., Meholick, B., and Campanelli, L. Introducing Spiritual Wellbeing in the Workplace: A Working Model for Corporations, Wellness in the Workplace National Conference, Baltimore, MD, March 21, 1990.

Seaward, B. L., Meholick, B., and Campanelli, L. A Program in Spiritual Wellbeing at the United States Postal Service, *Wellness Perspectives* 8(4):16–30, 1992.

Seaward, B. L. *Health of the Human Spirit,* Allyn & Bacon, Boston, 2001.

Selye, H. *Stress without Distress.* Signet Books, New York, 1974.

Shield, B. and Carlson, R., eds. *For the Love of God: New Writings by Spiritual and Psychological Leaders.* New World Library, San Rafael, CA, 1990.

Siegel, B. *Peace, Love, and Healing.* Walker, New York, 1990.

Spindrift Inc. Century Plaza Bldg., 100 W. Main St, Suite 408, Lansdale, PA 19446 (215) 361–8499.

Spirituality, Happiness, and Health, *Christopher News Notes,* New York, 1991.

Storr, A. *Solitude: A Return to the Self.* Ballantine Books, New York, 1988.

Sweeting, R. *A Values Approach to Health Behavior.* Human Kinetics, Champaign, IL, 1990.

Taylor, E. Desperately Seeking Spirituality, *Psychology Today,* Nov/Dec: 54+ 1994.

von Bingen, H. *Scivias,* Bruce Hozeski, trans. Bean & Co., Santa Fe, NM, 1986.

von Bingen, H. *Vision.* The music of Hildegard von Bingen. Angel Capitol Records, Los Angeles, CA, 1995.

Williams, R. Social Ties and Health, *Harvard Mental Health Letter,* April: 4–5, 1999.

World Health Organization, as quoted in "Spirituality, Happiness and Health." Christian News Notes. New York, 1991.

Young-Sowers, M. *Spiritual Crisis: What's Really Behind Loss, Disease, and Life's Major Hurts.* Stillpoint Publishing, Walpole, NH, 1993.

Part III

Coping Strategies

"There is no such thing as a problem without a gift for you in its hands. You seek problems because you need their gifts."

-Richard Bach

When we encounter a situation or event we perceive as a stressor, some part of us feels very vulnerable and threatened. To survive the threat, whether minimal or colossal, some type of coping strategy is created to deal with it. Each stressor necessitates its own coping strategy. Some coping strategies are second nature to most people when the stressor is minimal, and a course of action is taken with little or no conscious thought involved. But as the number and intensity of stressors increases and a critical mass of tension manifests, then routine coping strategies may fail to do an effective job. The result can be feelings of immobilization, mental paralysis, and emotional fatigue until a more effective coping technique, or combination of techniques, is employed. For the most part, the expression *coping responses,* unlike defense mechanisms, has a positive connotation, suggesting that a positive outcome is likely. However, this is not always the case, as some coping behaviors perpetuate stress rather than promote inner peace.

The word *coping,* as defined by stress scholar Richard Lazarus, is "the process of managing demands that are appraised as taxing or exceeding the individual's resources." He went on to add that coping consists of both cognitive and action-oriented (behavioral) efforts. According to Lazarus, this managing process involves several important criteria, including some or all of the following: an increased awareness process of oneself, the situation, and the environment; an emotional regulation process he referred to as palliative coping; and quite often, a series of behavioral changes, referred to as instrumental coping, which accompany this awareness and cognitive process. Lazarus also believed that coping isn't the employment of several techniques so much as it is a specific frame of mind. Part of this mind frame is a personality trait, self-efficacy, a term coined by psychologist Albert Bandura to describe an inner sense of faith culminating in a "can-do" attitude. Self-efficacy describes access to several inner resources including self-confidence, faith, willpower, and self-reliance. The possession and implementation of this trait tend to divide those who choose effective coping strategies from those who elect noneffective ones. In other words, your dominant coping style may be a function of your personality.

To date, the best and most comprehensive conceptual model to understand the coping process is that created by Lazarus and colleagues (Fig. III.1). According to Lazarus, every stressor undergoes primary appraisal to determine the extent of damage. It is then reprocessed in a secondary appraisal. At this point, a series of coping responses are lined up with the stressor to see which is the best course of action. These coping responses fall into one of two categories: action-oriented, such as time management or assertive behavior, or intrapsychic (acceptance). The responses used to cope with stress can be derived internally (from inner resources) and/or externally. Inner resources include, among other things, willpower, sense of humor, creativity, sense of reason, self-efficacy, faith, and optimism. External resources would include time, money, and social support from friends and family. Lazarus cites the purposes of coping skills as the following:

1. To reduce harmful environmental conditions
2. To tolerate or adjust to negative events or realities
3. To maintain a positive self-image
4. To maintain emotional equilibrium
5. To continue satisfying relationships with others

Coping responses can elicit three outcomes: (1) to regain emotional status quo, (2) to resume normal activities interrupted by the stressor, or (3) to feel psychologically overwhelmed.

Other researchers have noted a dichotomy of coping styles: avoidance versus confrontation (Holahan and Moos, 1987) and combative versus preventive (Matheny et al., 1986). From the first perspective, both have positive and negative aspects. When avoidance is used to minimize exposure to a stressor (e.g., staying clear of a bee's nest), this is considered effective. When avoidance perpetuates the stressor (e.g., not talking to your boss about his sexual advances), then this is considered ineffective. Likewise, to confront a stressor takes courage, but there is a world of difference between diplomacy and vigilantism. Again, coping styles seem to be closely tied to personality. Matheny's dichotomy highlights the positive aspects of each style. The combative style, like confrontation, is considered to be a physical reaction or response, whereas preventive coping, initially, is more cognitive in nature, with the intent to buffer oneself against the impending stress. Taylor (1990) notes that coping styles may be a direct result of the strength of available resources. For instance, a wealthy person with many social contacts may rely more on external resources, whereas a person without these is going to have to access inner resources to deal with his or problems, or suffer the consequences.

Successful coping strategies to deal with the cause of perceived stressors involve four basic components.

Figure III.I The coping model created by Lazarus. (From S. Taylor, *Health Psychology,* 2nd ed. [New York: McGraw-Hill, 1991].)

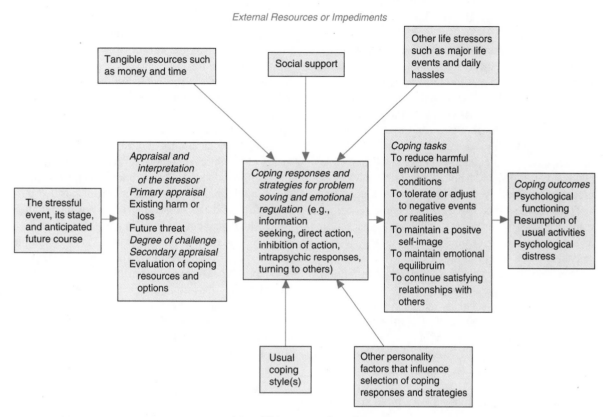

External Resources or Impediments

Internal Resources or Impediments

The first is an increased awareness of the problem: a clear focus and full perspective on the situation at hand. By their very nature, stressors tend to encourage a myopic view, distorting both focus and perspective. A good coping strategy will begin to remove the blinders to the true nature of the problem, and open your view to a host of possibilities. Second, effective coping strategies involve some aspect of information processing. The dynamics of information processing include adding, subtracting, changing, and manipulating sensory input to deactivate the perception of the stressor before physical damage occurs. Lazarus referred to this as secondary appraisal. Information processing also includes assessing all available resources that could be used in *peaceful confrontation.* Thirdly, The result of information processing will most likely include a new series of actions, or modified behaviors, which, combined with the new cognitive approach, ambush the stressor from all sides. The fourth and perhaps most important component is peaceful resolution. For a coping strategy to be effective, it must work toward a satisfactory resolution. If closure is not successfully brought to the stressor at hand, then the coping technique is less than effective. The following equation highlights the concepts of effective coping strategies:

Effective coping strategies =
Increased awareness
+ Information processing
+ Modified behavior
+ Peaceful resolution

While some coping strategies may seem appropriate for a particular situation, they might fail to achieve a peaceful resolution, in which case a new strategy should be chosen. Coping strategies can be either positive or negative. Positive coping techniques are those that prove effective in satisfactorily dealing with stress, based on the accomplishment of a peaceful resolution. This is the goal of all effective coping strategies: not merely to survive, but to thrive in the face of adversity.

Negative coping strategies, on the other hand, provide no enlightened resolution. Instead, they perpetuate perceptions of stress and further ineffective responses in a vicious circle that may never be broken or intercepted. Some examples of negative coping strategies are avoidance of the problem or inhibition of action, victimization, emotional immobility (worrying), hostile aggression, and self-destructive addictive behaviors, (e.g., drinking, drugs, and food binging).

Is there a relationship between the use of effective coping strategies and personality? Some researchers think so. People who exhibit Type A behaviors, codependent behaviors, and helpless-hopeless behaviors are more likely to employ a negative coping style and claim victimization by their stressors. People who exhibit components of a hardy personality, self-actualization, or sensation seeking (Type R) are more likely to take calculated risks, confront rather than avoid problems, and see their stressors through to peaceful resolution. More recently, as the secrets of split-brain functions have been revealed, scholars and practitioners in the field of stress management and psychotherapy are recognizing the importance of unifying the efforts of the right and left brains to effectively deal with stress. This means that some coping techniques that access different cognitive functions are most effective when employed together, such as creative problem solving combined with communication skills.

Researchers agree there are literally hundreds of coping strategies. Each coping strategy can be used alone, but quite often several are used together for a stronger defense against the effects of perceived stress. And there are a host of positive coping techniques from which to choose. Those strategies that emphasize increased awareness and information processing include journal writing, art therapy, cognitive restructuring, humor therapy, dream therapy, and creative problem solving. Coping skills emphasizing a course of action or behavior change include time management, assertiveness training, social engineering, and communication skills. Like learning to use a personal computer or improve your tennis game, coping techniques are skills, and their effectiveness increases with practice. It is important to remember that no coping technique will work as a defense against all perceived stress. This is why it is important to have as wide an assortment to choose from as possible; it will make the path of resolution easier to travel. You may notice that some coping techniques, as well as relaxation techniques, have the word *therapy* attached to them. This word may connote clinical treatment for a physical or emotional problem to you, but the term is used here as an encouragement, and a reminder that each person must take an active role in his or her own well-being.

It would be impossible to cover all of the positive coping techniques in this book. But the following chapters cover some of the more common and effective strategies offering assistance to the monumental stressors and daily hassles we encounter. The format of the chapters is the same throughout Part III. First, the elements of the specific coping technique are introduced and defined, followed by a brief historical account where applicable. Then a description of positive psychological (and physiological) effects are highlighted, and each chapter concludes with a list of steps on how to initiate the coping mechanism as a viable technique in your own strategy for stress reduction. (An exception is Chapter 13, Creative Problem Solving, which deviates a bit from this format in a creative style all its own.)

You may notice a crossover effect with some coping strategies; that is, some designed specifically to deal with the causes of stress also seem to promote the relaxation response. Conversely, some relaxation techniques can augment or even become coping mechanisms in their own right. This is no coincidence, as the mind and body can no longer be viewed as two separate entities. Humor therapy and laughter, once thought to be defense mechanisms, are now proven to produce a physiological homeostatic effect that strengthens the integrity of the immune system. In some people, habitual practice of endurance exercise triggers a switch to include right-brain cognitive functions, thus augmenting awareness and information-processing abilities. In fact, there can be many crossover effects. In the organization of this book, however, I designated each technique as either primarily a coping skill or primarily a relaxation technique, and placed it according to its greatest influence on either resolving the cause of stress or intercepting the stress response.

I recommend that you try all the following coping techniques when and where appropriate. Each technique has its particular strength. You may find many of these suitable to your own current management style. As time moves on and the effectiveness of some techniques diminishes, you may want to reread some of the chapters to reacquaint yourself with other coping techniques that may become more suitable later on in your journey through life.

Concepts and Terms

Avoidance vs. confrontation
coping style

Combative vs. preventive
coping style

Coping responses

Increased awareness

Information processing

Instrumental coping

Modified behaviors

Palliative coping

Peaceful resolution

Self-efficacy

References and Resources

Bach, R. *Illusions: The Adventures of a Reluctant Messiah.*
Dell, New York, 1981.

Holahan, C. J., and Moos, R. H. Personal and
Contextual Determinants of Coping Strategies,
Journal of Personality and Social Psychology
52:946–955, 1987.

Kaplan, A., ed. *Health Promotion and Chronic Illness.*
World Health Organization, Geneva, 1992.

Lazarus, R. S. The Stress and Coping Paradigm. In C.
Eisdorfer and A. Kleinman, eds., *Conceptual Models
for Psychopathology.* Spectrum, New York, 1981.

Lazarus, R. S. and Folkman, S. Coping and Adaptation.
In W. D. Gentry, ed., *Handbook of Behavioral
Medicine.* Guilford Press, New York, 1984.

Lazarus, R. S. and Folkman, S. *Stress, Appraisal, and
Coping.* Springer, New York, 1984.

Matheny, K. et al. Stress Coping: A Qualitative and
Quantitative Synthesis with Implications for
Treatment, *Counseling Psychologist* 14:499–549,
1986.

Rice, P. R. *Stress and Health,* 2nd ed. Brooks/Cole, Pacific
Grove, CA, 1992.

Taylor, S. *Health Psychology,* 4th ed. McGraw-Hill, New
York, 1998.

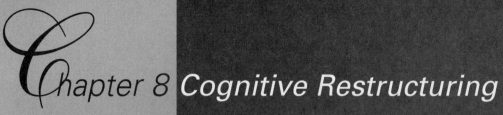

Chapter 8 Cognitive Restructuring

Everything can be taken away

from man but one thing—the

last human freedom, to choose

one's attitude in any given set

of circumstances.

—Viktor Frankl

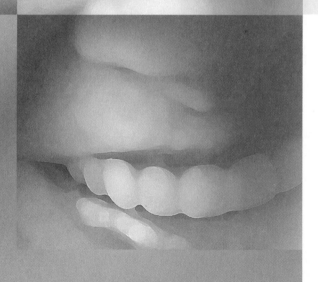

A bounced check. A flat tire. Alcoholic parents. Stressors come in all shapes, sizes, and degrees of intensity. Scholars concur that it is not the circumstance that is stressful, but the *perception* or interpretation of the circumstance. We now know that if the perception is negative, it can become both a mental and physical liability. Whatever the event, perceptions can become distorted and magnified entirely out of proportion to their seriousness. This is referred to as cognitive distortion, and it turns everyday problems into gigantic monsters. Attempts have been made to deal with the "stress monster" from all angles, including decreasing or manipulating sensory information and teaching people to control the stress response by employing various relaxation techniques. Perhaps the coping skill most advocated—which goes right to the heart of the matter but is initially very difficult to employ—is favorably altering the stressful perception of the circumstance that has precipitated feelings of anger and/or fear. This alteration in perception is made through changes in cognition. Cognition is the mental process that includes an assortment of thinking and reasoning skills. Across the country, this coping technique goes by several names: cognitive restructuring, cognitive reappraisal, cognitive relabeling, cognitive reframing, cognitive therapy, and attitude adjustment. Despite the variations, they all suggest the same approach: to favorably alter the current mind frame to a less threatening perception, from a negative, self-defeating attitude to a positive one, which may then allow the initiation of the steps toward a peaceful resolution.

The seeds of cognitive therapy took root in 1962 with the work of Albert Ellis in what he referred to as rational emotive therapy (RET). The premise of Ellis's work was that stress-related behaviors are initiated by *perceptions* and that these self-defeating perceptions can be changed. He explained that all stimuli sent to the brain go through a process of interpretation. When enough stimulation is interpreted as threatening, it becomes a critical mass of negative thought. Ellis was of the opinion that once a critical mass of perceived stress arises, it dims the ability to think rationally. As a result, a self-defeating attitude becomes reinforced day after day, year after year, through internal dialogue that is scripted by the tone of these irrational thought processes. Ellis became convinced that people could be educated and trained to favorably alter negative or stress-related perceptions (irrational thoughts) into positive attitudes, which in turn would decrease the intensity of perceived stress. Soon thereafter, the term **cognitive restructuring** was coined by Meichenbaum in 1975, to describe a coping technique for patients diagnosed with stress-related disorders. This coping style aimed to modify internal self-dialogue by tuning into the conversation within the mind. The practice of cognitive restructuring was an important step in what Meichenbaum referred to as stress inoculation, a process to build up positive thoughts when negatively perceived events are encountered. Work by Bandura in 1977 and Beck in 1976 also supported the concept of cognitive change of perceptions as a means to effectively deal with stress. To understand how stimuli are interpreted and interpreted thoughts are structured from stimuli, let us take a closer look at how the human thought process works.

A Thinking-Process Model

The human mind is an extremely complex phenomenon, and one that we are only beginning to comprehend. Scholars in the discipline of cognitive science have created a theory, the information-processing model, to attempt to explain exactly how the mind processes information (Fig. 8.1). This theory suggests that sensory input (e.g., a flashing blue light in your rearview mirror), sensory manipulation (e.g., danger, speeding violation, slow down, court hearing), and cognitive/behavioral output (e.g., foot on the brake, pull over to the side of the road, pray), as well as a

Figure 8.1 The information-processing model of human thought.

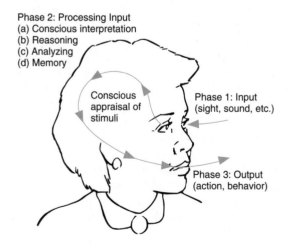

Phase 2: Processing Input
(a) Conscious interpretation
(b) Reasoning
(c) Analyzing
(d) Memory

Conscious appraisal of stimuli

Phase 1: Input (sight, sound, etc.)

Phase 3: Output (action, behavior)

feedback system to correct or refine this mechanism (e.g., several officers going to the scene of an accident, calm down), are synthesized to produce a linear progression of mental processes. Each cognitive deciphering process begins with an *interpretation* of the stimulus that comes into any of the five (possibly six) senses, in order to determine its threat potential. In simple terms, stimuli can be interpreted as either threats or nonthreats. Resulting attitudes can be labeled one of the three ways: (1) defensive (negative), (2) neutral (innocuous), or (3) offensive (positive). Fragments of information, as well as memories of previous similar experiences, are then manipulated in a process that results in the accessing and utilization of either left- (analytical) or right- (receptive) brain cognitive functions, or a combination of both. (For a more detailed explanation, see Chapter 18.) In the final outcome, perceptions and attitudes are by-products of the interpretation of all sensory information. It is both the manipulation of stimuli and the subsequent interpretation process that are targeted in cognitive restructuring to convert negative thoughts to neutral or positive ones.

The purpose of cognitive restructuring is to widen one's conscious perspective and thus allow room for a change in perception. The ability to expand perception is not merely a poetic expression. Research by optometrist Jacob Liberman (1991) shows that an individual's perceptual field of vision actually constricts under stress. Thus one literally sees less than the whole picture. Data analysis by Anderson and Williams (1989) corroborates this evidence, showing a casual relationship between perceived stress and loss of peripheral field of vision. As Liberman points out, stress forces one to see through a small hole rather than view the entire field of vision or whole picture.

Unconsciously, many people use a nonproductive coping technique called rationalization that they think is one and the same as cognitive restructuring. Cognitive restructuring should not be confused with this defense mechanism. Rationalization is making excuses, blaming, and shifting responsibility away from oneself toward someone or something else. Freud referred to this as denial of reality. Cognitive restructuring, on the other hand, involves assuming responsibility, facing the reality of a situation, and taking the offensive to resolve the issues causing stress. Creating and adopting a positive mind frame takes

some work. People often find it simpler to avoid this responsibility and be consumed by their own negative thinking styles, which produce a preponderance of toxic thoughts.

Toxic Thoughts

Negative perceptions are often the result of low self-esteem. They also perpetuate it by suppressing or obliterating feelings of self-worth and self-acceptance. It has been suggested (Canfield, 1988; John-Roger, 1989) that toxic thoughts originate from repeated exposure to feelings of shame and guilt in early childhood. Canfield cites a study conducted at the University of Iowa where parent-child interactions were observed over a period of several days. Results revealed that, on average, there were 400 negative comments for every positive one spoken to the child. It was concluded that negative thoughts are actually a conditioned (learned) response that is then carried into adulthood. Catastrophic thoughts are also reinforced in the messages we receive from the headlines: rarely does a human interest story beat a cataclysmic event on the six o'clock news. Disasters, world problems, and crimes permeate the news, which tends to condition our thinking toward the negative side of things. John-Roger even argues that negative thinking has an addictive quality to it.

The term *toxic thoughts* was coined in the early 1980s by several psychologists to educate their clients about the dangers of negative thinking. Pessimism, a personality trait heavily grounded in negativism, promotes toxic thoughts. To demonstrate just how destructive they could be, Dr. Leslie Kaymen conducted a study at the University of Pennsylvania in 1989 to determine the physiological responses to stress between individuals who identified themselves (through a psychological survey) as either optimists or pessimists. All subjects were exposed to minute doses of pathogens (tetanus, mumps, and yeast) which, when placed on the skin, would indicate their stress-tolerance levels. Subjects were then divided by attitude into two groups, and both groups were given an impossible task to complete in a brief time period. While the pessimists quickly gave up, the optimists continued until the last possible moment. Days later, the PNI response (skin rashes) of the pessimists was significantly greater than that of the optimists. These

Stress With a Human Face

VIOLENT CRIME MAY BE DOWN, BUT NOT long ago it was different in the Nation's capital. Washington, D.C., held the reputation of being the crime capital of the nation, with an average of one person shot and killed per day. Neighborhoods that were once peaceful urban hamlets became combat zones in the war on drugs. Like a thick fog, fear permeated the District after sunset, year round.

Lucy lives in one of these D.C. neighborhoods. Of course she would have liked to move out, but relocation was out of the question for her and her son. In Lucy's own words, "I not only realized that I could not afford to purchase the type of home that I had in mind, but I also realized that I could no longer be a prisoner in my own house." Lucy was left with only one choice: "I had to keep myself in a more positive mental state. In reading about cognitive restructuring, I learned that I have the capacity to choose what I think, and I have the power to turn negative

thoughts into positive ones." In this new mind frame, Lucy stopped seeing herself as a victim and took the initiative to change some habits that reinforced her negative attitude. Instead of watching the evening news, which was filled with stories about events outside her front door, she opted to listen to soft, relaxing music. She also restructured her daily responsibilities so that she used daylight hours for activities elsewhere and learned to enjoy the evening hours at home. "The changes I have chosen to make in my thinking are working very well at this point, and as I evaluate new situations, I will look for alternatives and keep remembering that I have a choice in reducing the arousal of fear and turn it into faith instead." ✦

results revealed that an optimistic attitude was associated with sound physical health, whereas a negative attitude perpetuated the mental and physical stress response. In short, negative thoughts can have a toxic effect on the body. Kaymen's data analysis confirms the hypothesis that negative thinking can suppress the immune system.

Attitude has also been observed to be a determining factor in the longevity of breast cancer patients. A study by Pettingale and colleagues in 1985 revealed that patients with a "fighting spirit" were more likely to survive five years than were those with a stoic nature or those who appeared to give in and give up. The work done by Dr. Bernie Siegel is also based on the supposition that positive thoughts can and do have a positive effect on the body. The organization of a cancer-support group called ECaP was developed for what Siegel called the "exceptional cancer patient," one who employs hope, love, faith, and even humor to deal with his or her illness. Siegel was quick to

point out that death is the final outcome for everyone, yet from his experience, he observed that a positive attitude made the transition much easier regardless of when death occurs.

Is it really possible to change the programming in our minds to break the habit of negative thinking? According to Richard Bandler and John Grinder (Andreas and Faulkren, 1994), the answer is a definitive yes! Years ago, Bandler, a psychologist, and Grinder, a linguist, combined their efforts to create and teach the theory and application of changing our mental language. They called it neurolinguistic programming (NLP). The premise of NLP is based on the concept of uncovering hidden grammar woven in the unconscious and conscious thoughts of our vernacular, systematically removing these expressions as we think or speak, and learning to develop a language of affirmative thoughts to positively change the direction of our lives. NLP is an empowering skill to reprogram the software of human linguistics so that our human energies can be focused in the direction of our highest human potential or human excellence. Part selective awareness, part self-hyponosis, the dynamics of NLP work to eliminate the self-defeating thoughts that inhibit our energies and keep us from reaching our goals. Over the years, the NLP program has proven quite successful and is used by athletes, actors, executives, business associates, lawyers, and professionals from all walks of life. By encouraging reprogramming and eliminating from daily vernacular words, phrases, and thoughts that reinforce stress-prone behaviors, NLP helps one to unlearn old thoughts and learn a new approach toward optimal excellence. NLP Comprehensive, based in Boulder, Colorado, offers seminars and workshops in the dynamics of NLP. Understanding that one cannot change behaviors quickly as a result of a one- or two-day workshop, the NLP training coaches participants through what they call a 21-day Achievement Program to help decondition and reprogram the human thought process.

Far more than creative and optimistic thinking styles, Western culture rewards and praises critical thinking, the ability to judge and analyze situations, breaking them down into smaller, more manageable parts. In theory, when problems are dismantled into smaller pieces, they are easier to understand. Under stress, an emotional side effect of critical thinking is that smaller pieces of stressful stimuli may be considered less threatening to the ego and thus help to minimize emotional pain. In practice, though, when critical thought processes are directed toward the self, judgmental and analytical thoughts often nurture a negative perspective about yourself, making you more vulnerable to the perceptions of stress. When threatened, critical thought can become a defensive weapon to protect the components of your identity. In addition to critical thinking, a common mental attitude seen in American culture is victimization. Victimization is a perceptual attitude wherein one feels specifically targeted by events or circumstances and has no choice but to suffer the consequences. Individuals who see themselves as victims often seek pity and sympathy from their friends as a means of coping with the stressors at hand. Through the sympathy of others, they validate their own perceptions of personal violation. People who express feelings of victimization apply what psychologists refer to as attribution theory, blaming other people or factors for perceived injustices (Taylor, 1998).

The concept of victimization is closely associated with Rotter's concept of locus of control, where people who feel violated by stressors are more greatly influenced by external sources than internal strength and inspiration. Here is a simple test to detect use of the victimization attitude: During the next casual conversation you encounter, listen objectively to what is said and notice how often people appear to fall victim to their bosses, spouses, roommates, kids, traffic, the weather, or any other circumstance in the vicinity. Next, listen objectively to how you present your perceptions to others when you describe your own levels of stress. Do you consciously or unconsciously label yourself as a victim? Many people take great comfort in being a victim because it fulfills an immediate need to feel needed, as well as the instant gratification of sympathy and pity. People who take on the role of one of life's victims (a characteristic of codependency) often see themselves as martyrs. This is a socially rewarding role, so they find it difficult to change their perceptions.

Can optimism be learned? According to Martin Seligman the answer is yes! In his much-acclaimed book, *Learned Optimism,* Seligman states that we are most likely to learn the traits of optimism or pessimism from our parents, but even if the environment in which we were raised was a negative one, we can cultivate the aspect of optimistic thinking and gravitate toward a positive approach to life. Seligman studied several nationally ranked swimmers prior to the 1988 Olympics and soon realized that optimism is not only an inherent trait, but one that can be augmented or learned. In a term he coined as *flexible optimism,* Seligman states that although the trait of optimism is not a panacea for the bumps in the road for life, we can harness the power of positive thinking to help us achieve our goals and promote a greater state of health and well-being (Fig. 8.2).

The dialogue mentioned earlier that seems to run nonstop in our minds is referred to as **self-talk,** and it has been observed that the preponderance of this is negative self-thoughts. Schafer (1992) has identified several types of negative self-talk thinking patterns that produce and/or perpetuate the toxic-thought process. He lists them in the following categories: pessimism, or looking at the worst of almost every situation; catastrophizing, making the worst of a situation; blaming, shifting the responsibility for circumstances

Figure 8.2 Stress is just a perception. A positive attitude can help disarm negative perceptions. Robert Mankoff © 1987 from the New Yorker Magazine, Inc. All rights reserved.

"Hey, is this great traffic, or what?"

to someone other than yourself; perfectionism, imposing above-human standards on yourself; polarized thinking, where everything is seen as an extreme (good vs. bad) and there is no middle ground; "should-ing," reprimanding yourself for things you should have done; and magnifying, blowing problems out of proportion. One technique to convert negative thoughts to neutral thoughts, similar to Ellis's RET, is called thought stopping. When you catch yourself thinking negatively, you interrupt the flow of consciousness and say to yourself, "Stop this thought." With practice, thought stopping can help to disarm your negative critic and give balance to your emotional thoughts.

As you can see, toxic thoughts are very real. Over time, these can have consequential effects on the body as well. But stimulation received by the brain is open to reinterpretation, and perceptions can change. Metaphorically speaking, some people appreciate the beauty of the rose petals, some people sense the pain of the thorns. Cognitive restructuring is a way to focus on the rose petals. During World War II, a song by Johnny Mercer and Harold Arlen hit the air waves and quickly became a national hit. It was called "Accentuate the Positive, Eliminate the Negative," and this song was one of many credited with helping the nation deal with the consequences of war.

The Choice to Choose Our Thoughts

In his book *Man's Search for Meaning,* Frankl credited his survival in Auschwitz to his ability to find meaning in his suffering, a meaning that strengthened his willpower and choice of attitude. Frankl noted that despite the fact that prisoners were stripped of all their material possessions and many essential human rights, the one thing concentration camp officials could not take away was the ability to choose their perceptions of their circumstances.

One concept which evolved from Frankl's theory of logotherapy is brief grief, which means acknowledging and mourning an unmet expectation but not prolonging the grieving process beyond a reasonable period of time. Death-education experts suggest there are three basic stages of grief: shock (denial), anger (depression), and understanding (acceptance). The time for each stage will vary depending on the person as well as the magnitude of loss. Feelings of loss, sadness, anger, pain, and fear are all natural, but not for prolonged periods of time. To deny these feelings is unhealthy, just as it is abnormal to prolong these feelings beyond their purpose. Brief grief is a strategy to allocate the correct amount of time to the grieving process (finding meaning in the suffering) and then move on to personal resolution and growth. When many people are introduced to the concept of cognitive restructuring, they incorrectly sense they must adopt a "Pollyanna" or cheerful attitude and that grief is not an appropriate sensation to acknowledge. As a result, they reject the entire idea of looking at the "brighter side" of a situation. Until feelings of suffering, no matter how big or small, are brought to awareness, it will be difficult to adopt a new frame of mind. Frankl wrote that even in suffering there can be tragic optimism; the discovery of light-hearted moments and personal meaning in the saddest of times. Even in the death-grip of the concentration camp, Frankl found it possible to laugh at many of life's absurdities. Moments like these helped him get through his ordeal.

In her book *Minding the Body, Mending the Mind,* Borysenko refers to the preponderance of negative thoughts as "awfulizing." The process of awfulizing consists of judgmental and analytical thoughts that greatly narrow one's perspective and put our mental processes into a shallow, one-track mode. The result is what Borysenko calls regressive coping, a nonproductive coping skill. Awfulizing creates worst-case scenarios for every situation, and while it is good to prepare for all possibilities, a worst-case scenario is only one in a wide spectrum of possibilities.

Psychologists use the term *self-fulfilling prophecy* to describe the link between perceptions/beliefs and their related behaviors. The self-fulfilling prophecy can work to one's advantage as well as one's disadvantage. Sports events are filled with stories of athletes who believed they were winners and proved that indeed they were. In highly competitive events like the Olympics, the difference between a gold medal and a silver or bronze is not only a superlative athletic body, but an accompanying winning attitude. Many an athlete has lost an event, and thus failed to meet an expectation, because a seed of self-doubt took root somewhere between the starting block and the finish line. Individuals who harbor negative thoughts about themselves or the situations they encounter promote behaviors generated by these perceptions. The result can be a negative cycle that sets the stage for recurring stressful perceptions and what appears to be a stagnant black cloud over one's head; this is the fulfillment of the self-fulfilling prophecy.

An example of this concept occurred in the 1990 hit movie *Pretty Woman,* when actress Julia Roberts, in the role of a Hollywood hooker, described to actor Richard Gere how she fell into her "career rut." She stated that while growing up she received a lot of negative feedback from her parents and peers, and that these were so much easier to believe, eroding her self-esteem. This "underdog" trait in Roberts's character was one many audience members could identify with and relate to, perhaps because this attitude is so prevalent in American society.

To break this self-defeating thought cycle, Borysenko suggests employing the concept of reframing. Reframing involves looking at the same situation from a new reference or vantage point and finding some good aspect in it. Quite often, stubbornness and the comfort of our own opinions become obstacles to the reframing process. Tools to initiate the process and dismantle the obstacles include the use of humor, positive affirmations, and creativity. Positive affirmations are designed to bolster self-esteem. Confidence building through self-praise in the form of positive feed-

back tends to counterbalance the voice of the inner critic constantly telling us we're not up to standards when we compare ourselves with others. For example, as a health promotion and stress management consultant, I gave many seminars during the restructuring and downsizing at AT&T. My interactions with employees have allowed me to experience firsthand the expression of the hardy personality that scholars Kobasa and Maddi described as a stress-resistant personality. Here is one story.

> Marge had worked for AT&T for fifteen years. She enjoyed her career there immensely and considered her fellow employees her second family. In an effort to become more competitive, however, her division was restructured in the spring of 1991 and she learned that her position was terminated. Like most employees in her situation, she had the option to relocate to another position in another part of the country, should one become available, or leave the company altogether. But unlike other employees, Marge harbored no resentment toward the company. She saw this as an opportunity for growth. Although her children were still in high school and she had a low-interest home mortgage on a house she adored, Marge looked at the silver lining of the cloud and perceived an opportunity for adventure. She fine-tuned her managerial and marketing skills, and within six months relocated to Denver, Colorado, to start a new career with a new company. "It wasn't easy," she remarked later. "It was a heck of a challenge, but I'm happy as a clam now." Marge reframed a negative situation into a positive one and became a victor rather than a victim.

One final thought about reframing (Fig. 8.3). Borysenko recounts the story of an Australian friend, Ian Gawlen, who was diagnosed with bone cancer and given two weeks to live. This man adopted the attitude that if he had two weeks to live he was going to make the best of it. So he proposed to his girlfriend, got married, and went off on a honeymoon to the South Pacific. Twenty years later, telling of his experiences to Borysenko, he explained why he was still alive. He discovered for himself that the unconscious mind does not respond to negative thoughts such as "cannot,"

Figure 8.3 According to some experts, the unconscious mind does not acknowledge negative thoughts. Thoughts such as "I won't get nervous," are interpreted as "I will get nervous," which then often results in nervous behavior. Thinking positively allows the conscious and unconscious minds to work together.

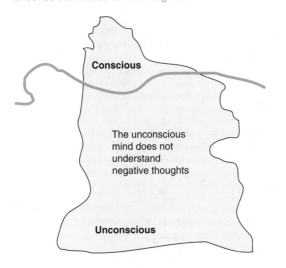

months to adopt and implement. Often, acceptance involves some aspect of forgiveness (see Chapter 16). The concept of acceptance is very similar to one described by Lao in the *Tao Teh Ching*. Tzu suggested that we move in rhythm with the universal energy, not against it. Denial and manipulation, like spinning car wheels in the dirt, prove fruitless because they go against the rhythm of natural energy. Swimming against the tide can prove exhausting, and sometimes fatal. As the saying goes, sometimes it takes more strength to let go than to hang on. Finally, the use of acceptance or forgiveness appears to be a greater tool in the face of anger than of fear.

There have been hundreds of empirical studies to determine the effectiveness of cognitive restructuring on health-related problems associated with stress. These studies have focused on both mismanaged anger (coping skills for men who battered their wives and children) as well as anxiety disturbances, most notably substance abuse and eating disorders. The results of these studies indicate that thought processes can be changed to produce a better state of health, although this is not effective in all cases.

Steps to Initiate Cognitive Restructuring

A simple, four-stage process introduced by the field of behavioral medicine by Roger Allen (1983) is a model for implementing changes in lifestyle behaviors through cognition to promote health. The following model explains how cognitive restructuring can be implemented as a coping technique to reduce stress. Initially, this process does not appear to take a lot of time. Thoughts last less than seconds, yet they may resurface often in the course of a day. And the feelings these perceptions generate can last for days and weeks. A closer look suggests that cognitive restructuring is a refinement of the continuous dialogue of the mind, and as a result is, for the most part, an ongoing process. The stages are as follows:

"won't," and "don't." Therefore, rather than telling himself, "I cannot die," which the unconscious mind would understand as "I can die," he fed himself a flood of positive thoughts like, "I will live," and he has.

Acceptance, an Alternative Choice

Many times we encounter situations we have no ability to control: a manipulative boss, an obnoxious roommate, or a significant personal loss. The reality of the situation is not pleasant in the best of moments. A common theme found among the theories of many psychologists in these cases is acceptance (see Chapter 4). The acceptance of situations we have no control over is thought to be paramount as a stress management strategy, yet it is perhaps the hardest frame of mind to adopt. There is a fine line between control and acceptance. This is the essence of Reinhold Niebuhr's Serenity Prayer for Alcoholics Anonymous: "Lord, grant me the serenity to accept the things I cannot change, the courage to change the things I can, and the wisdom to know the difference." Acceptance is not an "overnight sensation," but rather, an attitude that may take several days, weeks, or

1. *Awareness.* The awareness process has three steps. In the first, stressors are identified and acknowledged. This may include writing down what is on your mind, including all frustrations

Optimism and Pessimism

Box 8.1

Over the years I have asked various people for their definitions of optimists and pessimists. All cliches aside, here are some of their answers:

An optimist is someone who:

✦ sees the positive, even in a bad situation.
✦ is carefree and seems to enjoy life without reservation.
✦ doesn't let failure limit his growth as a human being.
✦ can find redeeming qualities in just about everyone.
✦ sees lots of clouds in the sky and describes the day as mostly sunny.
✦ takes personal setbacks as only a temporary inconvenience.
✦ counts blessings instead of misfortunes.
✦ loses a job and says there is a better one waiting.
✦ has the ability to reevaluate her expectations so as not to become depressed when she falls short.
✦ is a happy person who is nice to be around.
✦ takes things in stride, is able to enjoy himself and is able to adapt to the situation at hand.
✦ sees things clearly, and accepts what is or cannot be changed and doesn't spend time fighting it.
✦ describes a pessimist as a person with potential.
✦ continually explores new areas of life, can accept others who are different as unique.
✦ has enough faith in herself to see her through a crisis.
✦ on his deathbed, says, "I have no regrets."
✦ has a sparkle in her eyes and a song in her heart.

A pessimist is someone who:

✦ expects the worst possible outcome from a situation.
✦ lacks faith and confidence in himself.
✦ spends a lot of time worrying about the bad things that *may* happen.
✦ is a cynic, a person with a perpetual frown on her face.
✦ cannot accept opposing viewpoints or thoughts as valid.
✦ enjoys nothing more than finding out that his negative view is right.
✦ typically prejudges and pigeonholes others before getting to know them.
✦ delights in Murphy's Law that anything can and will go wrong, at the worst possible moment.
✦ constantly sees obstacles in her way, which are usually put there by herself.
✦ is a terminally unhappy person.
✦ gains energy by drawing toward a negative perspective.
✦ claims to be a realist, but he's not fooling anybody.
✦ sees no silver lining to the clouds, just rain and dampness, which is a reflection of her soul.
✦ screens his experience through a filter of negative perceptions that continually keep his expectations low so disappointment is tolerable.
✦ expects very little from other people and treats them accordingly.
✦ describes an optimist as being out of touch with reality.
✦ not only has a black cloud of negativity over her head, but created the thunderhead as well.
✦ faces a major change in life, gives up, and slowly dies inside.

and worries. The second step of the awareness process is to identify why these situations and events are stressors and, more specifically, what emotional attitudes are associated with each. In the last step, a primary appraisal is given to the main stressor and acknowledgement of the feelings associated with it. If the original perception appears to be defensive or negative, and inhibits you from resolving this issue, then the next stage is:

2. *Reappraisal of the situation.* A secondary appraisal, or reappraisal, is a "second opinion" you generate in your mind to offer a different (objective) viewpoint. A reappraisal is a new assembly or restructuring of the factors involved, and the openness to accept a new frame of mind. At this stage, a second or third opinion involves choosing a neutral, or preferably positive, stance to favorably deal with the issues at hand. Remember, a new

appraisal isn't a rationalization process, nor is it a suppression of emotions. Also, remember exactly what factors you can control and what you must accept as out of your control.

3. *Adoption and substitution.* The most difficult part of any attitudinal change is its implementation. Once a new frame of mind is created, it must then be adopted and implemented. Humans tend to be creatures of habit, finding comfort in known entities even if the "known" is less than desirable. Pessimism is a defense mechanism, and although it is not seen as enhancing human potential, there is comfort in the familiarity of old ways, and change does not come easily. There are risks involved in change. Substituting a positive attitude for a negative perception may make you feel vulnerable at first, but like other skills that improve with practice, a new comfort will emerge. With cognitive restructuring, the new mind frame must often be substituted when the stress is encountered, and repeated again and again.

4. *Evaluation.* The test of any new venture is to measure its effectiveness. Did this new attitude work? Initially, it may not. The first attempt to shoot a basket through the hoop may result in an embarrassing miss. Evaluate the new attitude and decide how beneficial it was. If it turns out that the new mind frame was a complete failure, return to stage 2 and create a new reappraisal. If the new mind frame worked, repeat this process with stressors that demand a change in attitude to resolve and bring closure.

Some Additional Tips for Cognitive Restructuring

1. *Initiate a relaxation technique to calm your mind.* When a relaxation technique is employed, the mind begins to unwind and consciousness shifts from an analytical mode to one of receptivity. In this unwinding process, unimportant thoughts begging the conscious mind for attention are dismissed, allowing greater receptivity to a wider perspective on the issue at hand. A wider perspective in turn fosters personal enlightenment and room for positive thoughts. (See Chapter 18, Meditation.)

2. *Take responsibility for your own thoughts.* In times of stress we may feel victimized. We may also feel that things are out of our control. A way to gain temporary control is to blame others for the personal injustice of the perceived stressor. Blame is associated with guilt and guilt can be a toxic thought. If you find yourself blaming others for events that make you feel victimized, ask yourself how you can turn this blame into personal responsibility for your own thoughts and feelings *without* feeling guilty.

3. *Fine-tune expectations.* It is believed to be easier to refine expectations prior to meeting a stressor than reframing an attitude after the fact. Many times we walk into situations with preconceived expectations. When these expectations are not met to our satisfaction, then negative feelings are generated. Fine-tuning expectations doesn't mean abandoning ideals or lowering self-esteem. Rather, it means running your perceptions through a reality check, questioning their validity, and allowing them to match the given situation.

4. *Give yourself positive affirmations.* The constant internal conversation going on within the conscious mind tends to be dominated by negative thoughts generated by the ego to defend itself. Although created with good intentions, a preponderance of negative self-feedback erodes self-esteem. Positive affirmations balance this internal conversation with good thoughts to enhance self-confidence and self-esteem. Repeat a phrase to yourself that boosts your self-esteem (e.g., "I am a loveable person," or "I am a winner").

5. *Accentuate the positive.* There is a difference between positive thinking and focusing on the positive. Positive thinking is an expression of hope concerning future events. It is often characterized by setting goals, wishful thinking, and dreaming. While positive thinking can be healthy, done to excess it can be a form of denial. Focusing on the positive is reframing the current situation. It is an appreciation of the present moment. Acknowledge the negative. Learn from it, but don't dwell on it. Focus on the positive aspects and build on them.

Summary

- All stimuli received by the brain are processed through interpretation and classified as negative, neutral, or positive; this process is called perception.
- When the interpretation is exaggerated, it is referred to as cognitive distortion.
- Cognitive restructuring means changing a perception from a negative interpretation to a neutral or positive one, making it less stressful. This process is also called reappraisal, relabeling, reframing, and attitude adjustment.
- The seeds of this coping technique were planted by Ellis in rational emotive therapy (RET); the term *cognitive restructuring* was coined by Meichenbaum in 1975.
- The information-processing model describing how stimuli are interpreted consists of four components: sensory input, sensory manipulation, cognitive/behavioral output, and a feedback system.
- Negative thoughts are often called toxic thoughts. Research has now substantiated the hypothesis that negative thoughts can suppress the immune system.
- Negative thoughts are a conditioned response, starting as early as childhood, to negative feedback given by parents, which are transformed into guilt and shame.
- Toxic thoughts come in various styles, including pessimism, catastrophizing, blaming, perfectionism, polarized thinking, should-ing, magnifying, and self-victimizing.
- Frankl brought to light the fact that we have the ability to choose our own thoughts, to alter our thinking process and adopt new perspectives.
- Borysenko calls creating negative thoughts awfulizing, and explains that the way to change these thoughts is through reframing, wherein the stressful event is reframed in a positive light.
- When there seems to be no positive light available, acceptance of the situation (not to be confused with giving in) is suggested. Acceptance, in terms of Taoism, means to go with, rather than against, the flow of universal energy.
- Allen introduced a four-point plan to reconstruct negative thoughts: (1) awareness, (2) reappraisal of the situation, (3) adoption of a new frame of mind, and (4) evaluation of the new mind frame.
- Additional hints for cognitive restructuring include meditation to clear your mind, taking responsibility for your own thoughts, fine-tuning expectations, giving yourself positive affirmations, and accentuating the positive aspects of any situation.

Concepts and Terms

Acceptance
Awfulizing
Blaming
Brief grief
Catastrophizing
Cognitive distortion
Cognitive restructuring
Flexible optimism

Information-processing model
Magnifying
NLP (Neuro-linguistic programming)
Perfectionism
Pessimism
Polarized thinking
Rational emotive therapy

Reframing
Serenity Prayer
Should-ing
Thought stopping
Toxic thoughts
Victimization

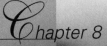

Self-Assessment

It's time to look at your list of stressors again. What's on your mind? Survey your thoughts and feelings and write them down, along with their corresponding problems, issues, concerns, or gripes. Then examine your list and write down at least one positive thing about each situation or circumstance. The purpose of this exercise is to get in the habit of putting a positive spin on a less-than-desirable situation, even if the only positive thing is that you learned from this experience how *not* to do something or how to do it better next time.

Current thoughts and perceptions	**Reframed thoughts (a positive focus)**
1. _____	1. _____
2. _____	2. _____
3. _____	3. _____
4. _____	4. _____
5. _____	5. _____
6. _____	6. _____
7. _____	7. _____
8. _____	8. _____
9. _____	9. _____
10. _____	10. _____

References and Resources

Allen, R. J. *Human Stress: Its Nature and Control.* Burgess Press, Minneapolis, MN, 1983.

Anderson, M. D. and Williams, J. M. Seeing Too Straight: Stress and Vision, *Longevity,* August, 1989.

Andreas, C., with Andreas T. *Core Transformation: Reaching the Wellspring Within.* Real People, Moab, UT, 1994.

Andreas, S. and Faulkven, C. (eds.). *NLP: The New Technology of Achievement.* Quill books, New York, 1994.

Bandura, A. *Social Learning Theory.* Prentice-Hall, Englewood Cliffs, NJ, 1977.

Beck, A. T. *Cognitive Therapy and the Emotional Disorders.* International University Press, New York, 1976.

Borysenko, J. *Minding the Body, Mending the Mind.* Bantam Books, New York, 1987.

Canfield, J. *Self-Esteem and Peak Performance.* Vantage Communications, Nyack, NY, 1988.

Charlesworth, E. and Nathan, R. *Stress Management: A Comprehensive Guide to Wellness.* Ballantine Books, New York, 1984.

Ellis, A. *Reason and Emotion in Psychotherapy.* Stuart Press, New York, 1962.

Frankl, V. *Man's Search for Meaning.* Pocket Books, New York, 1974.

Hay, L. L. *Heal Your Body.* Hay House, Santa Monica, CA, 1988.

Janis, I. L., *Stress, Attitudes, and Decisions.* Praeger, New York, 1982.

John-Roger, and McWilliams, P. *You Can't Afford the Luxury of a Negative Thought.* Prelude Press, Los Angeles, 1989.

Katz, S., and Liu A. *The Codependency Conspiracy.* Warner Books, New York, 1991.

Kaymen, L. P. Learned Helplessness, Cognitive Dissonance, and Cell-Mediated Immunity, Doctoral dissertation, University of Pennsylvania, 1989.

Kobassa, S., Maddi S., and Kahn, S. Hardiness and Health: A Prospective Study, *Journal of Personality and School Psychology* 42(1):168–177, 1982.

Liberman, J. *Light: Medicine of the Future.* Bear & Co., Santa Fe, NM, 1991.

Meichenbaum, D. H. *Cognitive-Behavior Modification.* Plenum Press, New York, 1977.

Meichenbaum, D. H. A Self-Instructional Approach to Stress Management: A Proposal for Stress Inoculation. In C. D. Spielberger and I. Sarsason, eds. *Stress and Anxiety* vol. 2. Wiley, New York, 1975.

Neisser, U. *Cognition and Reality: Principles and Implications of Cognitive Psychology.* Freedom Press, New York, 1976.

Ornstein, R. and Sobel, D. *Healthy Pleasures.* Addison Wesley, Reading, MA, 1989.

Peale, N. V. *The Power of Positive Thinking.* Prentice-Hall, New York, 1987.

Pettingale, K. W. et al. Mental Attitudes to Cancer: An Additional Prognostic Factor, *Lancet* March 30: 750, 1985.

Pretty Woman. Orion Pictures, Los Angeles, CA, 1991. Film.

Rasmussen, L. *Reinhold Niebuhr: Theologian of Public Life.* Augsberg Fortress Press, Minneapolis, MN, 1991.

Rice, P. *Stress and Health: Principles and Practices for Coping and Wellness,* 2nd ed. Brooks/Cole, Pacific Grove, CA 1992.

Schafer, W. *Stress Management for Wellness,* 2nd ed. Harcourt Brace Jovanovich, Dallas, TX, 1992.

Seigel, B. *Love, Medicine, and Miracles.* Perennial Press, New York, 1987.

Seligman, M. *Learned Optimism.* Knopf, New York, 1991.

Taylor, S. *Health Psychology,* 4th ed. McGraw-Hill, New York, 1998.

Wilde, S. *Affirmations.* White Dove International, Santa Fe, NM, 1987.

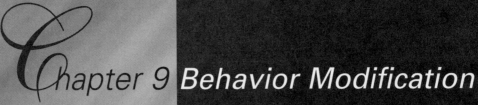

Chapter 9 Behavior Modification

How many psychiatrists does it take to change a light bulb? One, but the light bulb has really got to want to change.

—Anonymous

At one time or another, everyone has considered some plan of action for self-improvement. This is especially the case at particular times in our lives (e.g., when we turn thirty or forty) and specific times and seasons during the calendar year: Lent, the summer beach season, and most notably New Year's Eve, when the proverbial mental slate is swept clean by new resolutions. Implementing a change to advance one's human potential, however, is not always easy. It takes concentration, will power, and a strategy to stay on a new course. One look at the low success rates of those who initiate diets confirms the difficulty involved in self-improvement. The reason changes are difficult to institute and maintain is that there are so many variables to manipulate. These variables include, among other things, psychological, sociological, environmental, and biological elements, all of which can act as deterrents. Book stores are stacked with how-to self-improvement literature. To their credit, works of this nature tend to have the longest shelf life of any books, save literary classics. Bibliotherapy, or self-improvement through information seeking, has quickly become one of America's most frequently utilized coping mechanisms. Yet, while these books can help educate, influence, and even inspire, they cannot instill willpower or a desire to change. This inner resource can only be cultivated, not created, within the individual.

Behavior as a Component of Personality

One school of thought in psychology states that personality is made up of three factors: values, abstract constructs of importance; attitudes, perceptions derived from values; and behaviors, conscious and unconscious actions based on attitudes and perceptions. They are defined as follows:

Values are those aspects that give meaning to our lives. Values are abstract constructs we adopt early in life by emulating figures of authority, including our parents, grandparents, and older brothers and sisters, as well as school teachers and other influential people from whom we seek love and acceptance. They are intangible concepts such as love, honesty, freedom, joy, wealth, pleasure, education, privacy, and creativity, to name a few. They are often made tangible through objects that symbolize their value. For example, education is a value, and it is symbolized by

books and a diploma. Creativity may be symbolized by a musical instrument. Values may consist of morals and ethics, but they include more than these. Research by Milton Rokeach in 1972 suggests that each person has a hierarchy of approximately two dozen values. This hierarchy consists of two levels. The first tier he described as instrumental values, a handful of values that are "core" to the meaning of the individual. The second level he called terminal values, those important constructs that lend support to the core values. A personal value system is not static. Values can change in order of importance, moving up and down the continuum, to be replaced by or even exchanged for others. When values shift or are deleted, this may represent a conflict in values, and stress may ensue.

Attitudes are beliefs based on our values. While the number of values in our personal value system is limited, Rokeach states that each value may carry with it hundreds of attitudes. Attitudes are beliefs, perceptions, and feelings based on a specific value. Attitudes can be positive or negative in nature. Negative attitudes are associated with perceived stress.

Behaviors are considered to be any action, direct or indirect, that is based on a conscious or unconscious thought. Behaviors are thought to be physical manifestations of an attitude based on a specific value. For example, clapping your hands at the end of a concert is a behavior influenced by your perception that the music you heard sounded pleasant. The music, in turn, can symbolize a value of freedom, or creativity. In terms of well-being, behaviors can be considered either health promoting or health impeding. The behaviors deleterious to one's health are often targeted for change.

In Chapter 6, it was mentioned that personalities are deemed difficult, if not impossible, to change. Of the three components comprising personality, psychologists suggest that values are the most difficult to influence. Attempts to change attitudes have met with some success (e.g., through cognitive restructuring); however, attitudinal changes may not last without significant attention devoted to their associated responses. Behaviors, on the other hand, have been shown to be the most likely modified or favorably altered factor to improve health status. Millions of dollars and years of research have been spent in this century to understand the concepts involved in behavior, particularly with respect to those lifestyle diseases resulting in astronomical health care costs. Results from these studies indicate that changes are possible when several factors (biological, psychological, and sociological) are collectively taken into consideration. For example, in the treatment of alcoholism the factors taken into account include genetics, stress levels, and social contacts.

As complex as human behavior is, there is no shortage of theories as to why we behave the way we do. Whether our behaviors are learned or innate, we are creatures of habit. Here are some of the more well-recognized theories of human behavior as applied to the practice of behavior modification. Understanding the nature of these theories may help you to modify your behavior.

Classical Conditioning.   The concept of classical conditioning was first described by Russian physiologist Ivan Pavlov in the late 1920s. Pavlov's theory, based on his research with dogs, suggests that animals become conditioned to specific stimuli to act in a specific way. What Pavlov observed was that his dogs began to salivate when they heard a bell that they associated with food. People, like dogs, can also become conditioned to behave in a certain way. In this regard, when a stimulus is coupled with a physiological reflex, the result can be a behavior with some pretty deep roots, one that can take years to unlearn. I am reminded of a student of mine who, upon listening to a relaxation tape with the natural sound of a brook, felt the undeniable urge to go to the bathroom. Slightly embarrassed, she approached me after class and told me that she felt very uncomfortable with the tape. When she was a young child, she told me, her mother, who was often in a hurry to do shopping or errands, would run the water in the bathroom to get her to urinate quickly. Now whenever she hears running water, she gets the urge to go to the bathroom.

Operant Conditioning.   Unlike classical conditioning, in which the behavior is specific to physiological autonomic functions, operant conditioning speaks to the nature of voluntary behaviors—those that we make a conscious decision about. Although the concept of operant conditioning dates back to the late eighteenth century, this approach to human behavior became the primary focus of psychologist B. F. Skinner, whose significant work spanned from 1930 to 1970. In simple terms, operant conditioning is based on the concepts of rewards and punishments, in which good behavior is reinforced and bad behavior is disciplined. The logic to operant conditioning is that when behavior is positively reinforced, the behavior is likely to be repeated, whereas punishment is used to deter unbecoming behavior. Most likely your parents raised you under the influence of operant conditioning, as child rearing typically uses this style of behavior modification. But it doesn't stop in childhood; motivational techniques such as incentives are used with great frequency in the business world to boost profit margins and work productivity. Variations of operant conditioning are also used in a host of recovery programs as well.

Modeling.   Little children aren't parrots, but if you were to listen to how closely a child imitates his mom or dad, you would be amazed at the degree of accuracy in both language and body postures. Modeling is a name given to the concept of imitation, a behavior learned through imitation. Modeling differs from operant conditioning in that usually no direct reinforcement is involved. Out of sheer will, a person is motivated to copy one or several aspects of someone with whom they are closely bonded or to whom they find some degree of attraction. It may be parents, but in the age of multimedia exposure, it could be any public figure with whom the individual wishes to identify. As might be expected, negative as well as positive behavior can be imitated, and often is. More often than not, the expression "life imitates art" comes to mind when individuals are seen to model negative behavior seen on television or in the movies. Although children often model those they see as heroes, we never outgrow the capacity to model our behavior after someone we admire. During the aging process, the word *hero* changes to *role model,* or *mentor.* Modeling is typically used as a crucial component in the practice of building self-esteem (see Chapter 6).

There are several types of *behavior modification* programs currently conducted in the United States that focus on negative health habits. Most of these programs center on substance addictions (alcoholism, eating disorders, smoking cessation, and drug addictions) and behavioral addictions (workaholism, shopping, sexual habits, etc.). Additional programs target lifestyle improvement changes, including time management and assertiveness. Regardless of focus, the bottom line in all positive behavioral-change programs is building and maintaining self-esteem. The focus of this chapter will be assertiveness skills, which are considered paramount in the development and maintenance of self-esteem. But before we look at the skills highlighted in assertiveness training workshops, let's examine the dynamics involved in behavioral change.

The Behavior Modification Model

In learning about their stress-prone personalities, individuals often see themselves, or parts of themselves, that are less than flattering. Acknowledgement of these traits may in fact contribute to their stress. Whereas some individuals recognize these traits and behaviors and make corresponding changes to fine-tune their personalities, others have difficulty overcoming the obstacles to change. Thousands of investigations have been conducted to determine the effectiveness of changes in behaviors to promote health. The topics of these studies include everything from substance abuse and wife beating to eating disorders and insomnia. The majority show that it is far easier to *initiate* a new behavior than to *maintain* it over a prolonged period of time. Motivation, it appears, is strong at the start but fades fast (in about one to two weeks) when immediate effects are not observed. To first understand and then favorably alter factors associated with unhealthy behaviors, psychologists in the field of behavioral medicine have devised a model based on observational research. All successful programs contain this progression of steps to change behavior. When applied to lifestyle and behavior changes, these steps may lead toward improved health status and quality of life. This behavior modification model has one precursory phase (denial) and five distinct systematic stages.

Several behavioral psychologists and therapists agree that denial is actually the initial stage of or a precursor to a behavioral change. For example, in Chapter 4 we learned that Freud described denial as a defense mechanism employed to soften the blow of perceived threats to the ego. In the denial stage, people refuse to admit either that they practice an unhealthy behavior, or that a specific behavioral practice they engage in is unhealthy. A prime example is someone with a chronic drinking problem who refuses to admit he or she is unable to control his or her drinking. While not everyone starts with this stage, many people do. It is often this difficult stage therapists and counselors help their clients to work beyond, to get to what many people agree is the primary stage of behavior modification: awareness.

1. *Awareness.* In the awareness stage, you realize that you actually think or behave in a certain way that is unhealthy or less than ideal. In the context of this book, these behaviors are stress-producing habits. Awareness may come about as a result of some educational experience (e.g., a class, public service advertising, a newspaper article, journal writing, or the advice of a close friend) wherein your consciousness is raised about a certain behavior. Awareness can also occur when you simply admit that indeed one (or more) of your current behaviors is no longer desirable. Once you see this undesirable behavior in yourself (e.g., codependent tendencies such as ardent approval seeking and victimization, or Type A behaviors including hostile aggression) then the process of change can begin.

2. *Desire to change.* Many people recognize they practice a negative health behavior, yet they are not inspired to change it. Without the desire to alter behavior, even when it becomes obvious how damaging it might be, no change will occur. Many people are aware that consuming foods with cholesterol is related to heart disease or that cigarette smoking causes cancer, yet these behaviors remain intact because the will to change is less than the immediate desire to hang on to whatever benefits the behaviors provide. Desire to change usually comes about when the behavior no longer provides the ability to cope, and in fact places one square on the path to either disaster or death. The expression "hit bottom" is often used to describe the ultimate low point experienced by people, who then generate a desire and become quite motivated to make a behavioral change.

3. *Cognitive restructuring.* In this stage, you actually catch yourself in the act of the undesirable behavior and think of a new and suitable alternative. For example, rather than ask someone a closed-ended, approval-seeking question such as "Did you like my performance last night?" you ask an open-ended question like, "What did you think of the performance last night?" This gives the responder a chance to answer freely and

Figure 9.1 Changing behaviors is not always easy if they have been lifelong habits. Some behaviorists suggest that change will only take place when there is sufficient desire.

takes the focus off you. Cognitive restructuring is really self-dialogue recognizing both current and pending behavior, as well as the option to favorably change it (see Chapter 8).

4. *Behavioral substitution.* In the substitution stage, an undesirable behavior is consciously replaced with a healthy or stress-reducing behavior. Sometimes this substitution process is thought out or rehearsed in the form of mental imagery before it is acted out. In a case where you have become aware of the habit of

self-victimization (in the way that stressors are described to others), you change the description of this circumstance to friends or relatives, thus shifting the emphasis off yourself and onto the real problem. Not all changes are substitutions. Some modifications may be additions to the repertoire of your behaviors. For example, the initiation of one or more of the several coping skills and relaxation techniques described in this book may be an example of additions to your behavior. Usually, however, when a new behavior is adopted, due to time limitations, something else in one's daily schedule gets pushed out of the way. This is a reflection of one's priorities and values.

5. *Evaluation.* After a substitution has been made, you should figuratively "step back" to analyze whether the new behavior worked, ask yourself why or why not, and decide what can be done to fine-tune this process when the occasion arises again.

Note that when people desire to change or improve their lifestyles they are typically eager to change all their undesirable behaviors at once, almost to become new individuals altogether. This approach, while most admirable, is often doomed to failure. Behavioral psychologists suggest altering one undesirable behavior at a time as the best method.

Many behavior theories, including self-monitoring, classical conditioning, operant conditioning, and modeling, suggest that behaviors can indeed be changed. From the nature of these theories and the research that led to them, it can be seen there is no one best way to change behavior. The current school of thought is that the best approach to behavioral change is a multimodal approach (also called the biopsychosocial or holistic model) wherein many theories and their related techniques are combined in order to produce a lasting effect. One major focus of all these theories is self-esteem. It appears that low self-esteem is associated with virtually every stress-related behavior. Therefore, it has taken on major importance with regard to behavior modification, particularly as it relates to assertiveness and assertiveness skills.

Stress With a Human Face

IF YOU COULD SEE PATTY'S FACE TODAY, YOU would notice a glow about her. She radiates self-reliance and love. As brilliant as her smile is now, it wasn't always like this. In Patty's case, the road to inner peace began with a side trip to hell. At the age of sixteen, she looked to all the world like a normal teenager. But the allure of Fifth Avenue beauty in a weight-conscious society soon found Patty with an obsession to control her eating habits. Anorexic behaviors gave way to bingeing and purging, and the pattern remained an addictive ritual well into her twenty-third year.

Reflecting back on her earlier years, Patty confided, "I was a perfectionist. I was obsessed with my weight. Food became a way to escape from my own feelings. Until I was nineteen, I denied I really had a problem, then I tried several methods to stop. Nothing worked."

In the fall of 1992, Patty pulled out the white flag and checked into a hospital. As she put it, "I hit rock bottom. It was this or die." The recovery program she started, well grounded in the twelve-step approach, led Patty to become fully aware of her behaviors and then slowly allowed her to substitute positive thoughts and actions for existing negative ones.

"Oh, I still get the urge now and then," she admitted during a quick visit to my office one day. "But, I have never been happier in my life than I am now. I am at peace with myself and my higher power. I am very grateful," she sighed. The gratitude showed; the sparkle in her eyes said it all. ✦

Assertiveness

Assertiveness is described as the ability to be comfortably strong-willed about one's thoughts, feelings, and actions; and neither inhibited nor aggressive in actions for the betterment of oneself in the surrounding environment. Andrew Salter is credited with introducing the term *assertiveness,* in 1949, to mean an inner resource to deal peacefully with confrontations. The term was reintroduced by Arnold Lazarus, who defined it as "expressing personal rights and feelings." Since its introduction, it has become the major focus in changing stress-related behaviors.

Psychologist Dennis Jaffe (1984) developed a continuum of behavior styles employed by people in their relationships with others. Behavior styles at either end of the continuum are conducive to stress:

| Passive behavior | Assertive behavior | Aggressive behavior |

Stress often produces many needs. Specifically, it produces the need to express one's feelings; other needs are often an offshoot of these expressions. The need to be assertive exists when situations arise that involve contact with other people. The assertive style, rather than the passive or aggressive, is advocated to minimize feelings of anger or fear associated with stressful encounters, and to work toward a peaceful resolution. The following is a more detailed explanation of these three dominant personality styles:

1. *Passive behavior style.* The passive style is where one is too intimidated to express thoughts and feelings. As a result, the person usually forfeits his or her rights and freedoms. A person employing this style comes across as shy and gives in to other people's demands so he or she will be more easily accepted. A passive style avoids confrontations at any cost. Consequently, this style makes one feel used and taken advantage of. The passive style is thought to be anxiety-driven, yet the enactment of passive behavior results in feelings of resentment and victimization. The passive style is often employed by the codependent personality.

2. *Aggressive behavior style.* The aggressive style is where one acts to intimidate others and gain

control of their thoughts and actions. Aggressive behavior includes manipulation, intimidation, accusations, and perhaps fighting. There is little or no regard for other people's feelings. Aggressive behavior may result in personal gain, but also breeds loss of respect and trust in those who were walked over and bruised on the way. The aggressive style is thought to be anger-driven. It is often used by people who exhibit Type A behaviors.

3. *Assertive behavior style.* This is the preferable style, in which a person focuses on specific issues and problems, neither belittling him- or herself nor attacking others in the process of problem solving. An assertive person recognizes his or her individual rights and stands up to protect those rights. Assertiveness includes expressing your opinion and being able to defend your rights, but not at the expense of violating others' rights. The assertive style minimizes opportunities to be taken advantage of by others. Assertive individuals are open, tolerant, and considerate of other people's feelings. To be assertive means to be able to overcome feelings of fear and to confront issues that demand resolution as well as communicate feelings of anger diplomatically, without putting others on the defensive.

Assertiveness carries with it the recognition of legitimate personal rights. These have been described by several therapists, including Davis, Eshelmann, and McKay (1988), and involve the following:

1. To say no and not feel guilty
2. To change your mind about anything
3. To take your time to form a response to a comment or question
4. To ask for assistance with instructions or directions
5. To ask for what you want
6. To experience and express your feelings
7. To feel positive about yourself under any conditions
8. To make mistakes without feeling embarrassed or guilty
9. To own your own opinions and convictions
10. To protest unfair treatment or criticism
11. To be recognized for your significant achievements and contributions

Typically, there are some people toward whom we are less than assertive in our manner. Usually these are people of higher authority, such as bosses and parents. Being unassertive, however, can occur with anyone by whom we feel intimidated, including members of the opposite sex, people perceived to be more attractive than ourselves, and all strangers.

Assertiveness Skills

To change one's behavior, there must first be recognition that current behavior is undesirable and may in fact be stress promoting. Once awareness and the will to change occurs, then alternative behaviors can be devised and implemented. From workshops on assertiveness training come a host of skills that may be included in one's behavioral approach to potentially stressful encounters. The following are advocated to help improve assertiveness:

1. *Learn to say no.* We are often asked to assist friends, family, and co-workers with their responsibilities. There are in fact times when we cannot complete a task alone. An American ethic has evolved suggesting that we must work together and help each other in times of need. Over time, this ethic has become warped so that individuals put other people's needs before their own. Saying no is mistakenly equated with rudeness, and doing so results in feelings of rejection in the other person. But saying yes when it is inconvenient or impossible results in resentment and victimization in oneself. Assertiveness training teaches people to say no without feeling guilty about hurting someone else's feelings. People have the right to refuse a request without harboring feelings of guilt. Remember that other people's problems are no more or less important than your own, and that you are not required to solve all the world's problems. If you have personal obligations which conflict with requests by others, then diplomatically refuse to offer your support at that time. Do not let other people's comments generate feelings of guilt (Fig. 9.2).

2. *Learn to use "I" statements.* When one examines stress-prone personalities, it is evident that the inability to feel and express emotions is

common among the various types. Assertiveness training teaches people to feel comfortable expressing themselves by using "I" statements (e.g., "I feel angry about . . .", or "I perceive what you said to me as incorrect."). This skill also teaches people to be more spontaneous with their expressions, rather than suppressing their feelings. The use of "I" statements encourages a person to claim ownership of thoughts, feelings, opinions, perceptions, and beliefs. Assertiveness training programs teach that opinion statements may take time to formulate. Don't feel compelled to say the first thought that comes to mind. Rather, take a moment to consolidate your thoughts into a concise and direct response.

Nonassertive people often avoid describing their feelings for fear that others will disagree. Fearing rejection, they also tend to agree with other people's thoughts and take a middle-of-the-road position rather than risk expressing their own feelings. The use of "I" statements strengthens ego boundaries. Although strong ego boundaries might seem more indicative of an aggressive behavior style than an assertive one, the constituents of one's identity must first be recognized before they can be adjusted or exchanged in the ego development process.

3. *Use eye contact.* Body language is a very important communication skill. Nonverbal communication is more readily believed than the spoken word (see Chapter 14). Lack of eye contact during self-expression is perceived by others as either dishonesty or feeling insecure about what you are saying. Eye contact is often most difficult when you express your feelings toward someone else, for fear of rejection. Assertiveness training involves increasing eye contact while expressing various thoughts, feelings, and opinions. Learning this skill starts with a short time interval (one or two seconds) and progresses up to eight- to ten-second periods. When pauses in eye contact are taken, people are advised to direct their eyes neither down nor up, but in a lateral direction momentarily, and then return again to direct eye contact. Just as poor eye contact communicates lack of confidence, staring (prolonged eye

Figure 9.2 In the 1980s, First Lady Nancy Reagan started a campaign to stop drug use with the now-famous slogan "Just say no!" This same degree of assertiveness can be used in all types of situations, including taking on additional responsibilities you simply do not have time for.

Hey, Jackie! Can you help me move next Saturday?

Sorry, but I have to say no, John. I've made other plans.

contact) is perceived as a violation of personal space and should be avoided.

4. *Use assertive body language.* An assertive tone of voice with a wimpy posture sends a mixed message to the person with whom you are communicating. The message is interpreted as either insincere or unsure. Postures, the ways in which you carry your body, either reinforce your message or detract from it. In addition to eye contact and tone of voice, your spinal posture and head position reveal at an unconscious level how you really feel about the messages you are communicating. It is suggested that your posture be erect, with your body weight equally distributed between both legs and your center of gravity directly above your feet.

5. *Practice peaceful disagreement.* When opinions and facts are voiced peacefully, so that all perspectives can be viewed during a decision-making process, then disagreement is considered healthy. This assertiveness skill allows the individual to become comfortable

with peaceful confrontation. It is employed when you feel the need to express an opposing view and want it to be acknowledged.

6. *Avoid manipulation.* In the course of asserting yourself, you may find that others may consciously or unconsciously try to block your efforts to accomplish resolution. The following are some roadblocks of manipulation to be aware of, as well as some suggested strategies that may help to dismantle them:

    a. *Intimidation.* Asserting yourself may intimidate others who are in the habit of using manipulation and control to get their way. They in turn may raise their voices and display their tempers. When you recognize this behavior, you can defuse it by saying that you want to hold off further discussion of this issue until the other person calms down. For example, "I can see that you are quite angry; let's talk about this after lunch."

    b. *Content substitution.* Sometimes people will draw peripheral issues into a discussion in order to derail the issue at hand. If you become aware that the concern you brought up has become lost in tangential issues, quickly shift focus back to the original topic until your issue has been put to rest.

    c. *Personal attacks (character assassination).* You may find that in an attempt to resolve an issue, the person you are talking to comes back at you with a character flaw. One way to get back on track is to agree, in part, about the character flaw and ignore the rest. Davis calls this response clouding, the attempt to deflect an attack by concurring with some part of it. When employing this technique, rephrase the attack in your best interest, and get back to the issue at hand.

    d. *Avoidance.* Often people deny there is a problem by avoiding specific issues or their feelings about certain concerns. This roadblock can be confronted with a bold inquiry—a direct question—to unlock their perceptions. For example, "Is there something I did to make you angry?"

7. *Respond rather than react.* A reaction is a type of reflex, almost instinctual in nature, and a very natural part of human behavior. Here, a reaction deals with spontaneous emotional thoughts. Although spontaneity is an admirable trait where creativity is concerned, following through on emotional reactions can lead to some regrets. A response, on the other hand, is a thought-out plan for a situation. Many times our response is the same as our reaction, and this is when we are likely to wish we had thought before we spoke or acted. Responding to a situation means acknowledging your initial reaction, then thinking of a reasonable response to the situation at hand. Not every response will seem adequate, but as you practice this skill, you will find that it will help you deal with your perceptions of stress.

These are just a few of the recommended behaviors taught in assertiveness-training workshops. The purpose of all these skills is to build and maintain self-esteem. Box 9.1 contains exercises to increase your awareness of your own assertiveness skills. They are based on common circumstances that typically produce feelings of anger, fear, and/or victimization.

Steps to Initiate Behavior Modification

To begin to change an undesired behavior, like smoking, biting your fingernails, or worrying about issues you seem to have no control over, you must first become aware of what this behavior is. Using the behavior modification model, select a behavior that you wish to change or modify. The following is a systematic approach to behavior modification:

1. Select an undesirable behavior you are aware that you perform.

    _____

    _____

    _____

2. Ask yourself how motivated you are to change this behavior. (As with any change there will be sacrifice involved.) Ask yourself if the costs will outweigh the benefits.

    _____

    _____

    _____

Assertiveness Exercises

Box 9.1

Write your initial reaction to each of the situations described below, followed by a more assertive response, if necessary.

Situation 1: Job Performance Appraisal

A photocopy of your job performance evaluation is submitted to you and you are angry that (a) it was completed *without* your boss meeting with you, and (b) the poor rating is based on several inaccuracies.

Initial reaction:

Assertive response:

Situation 2: Strong Back Favors

Your best college buddy has to move out of his apartment at the end of the month and has found a new place to live a few miles away. He tells you that he really needs some help moving and that he also needs a truck like yours, and asks if you will be able to help. You have two term papers due about the same time.

Initial reaction:

Assertive response:

Situation 3: Noisy Neighbors

You check into a hotel room, throw your stuff on the nearest bed, and head back outside to sightsee. After a few hours of touring and getting a bite to eat, you head back to your room to get a good night's sleep. Once the lights are out, you are awakened by noise coming from the room directly above yours.

Initial reaction:

Assertive response:

3. Think about what changes in your perceptions and attitudes must accompany this behavioral change.

    _____

    _____

    _____

4. Specify what new behavior you wish to adopt. It is best not to think of stating that you want to stop the old behavior, a negative thought process (e.g., I don't want to bite my nails). The new behavior should be expressed as a positive goal (e.g., I would like to have long fingernails).

    _____

    _____

    _____

5. After trying the new behavior, ask yourself how you did. Was your first or second attempt successful? Why or why not? If not, what other approach can you take to accomplish your goal?

    _____

    _____

    _____

It is a good idea to regularly monitor the thoughts and actions that seem to surface during stressful episodes and issues that disrupt your sense of inner peace. Then, using the behavior modification model, take yourself through the remaining steps. Remember, it is important not to change all target behaviors at once. Try to modify one behavior at a time.

Summary

- People are constantly trying to change, improve, and manipulate their behaviors. Behaviors associated with poor health are those most often targeted for change.
- Personality is thought to be comprised primarily of values, those abstract qualities that give meaning to our lives; attitudes, perceptions derived from these values; and behaviors, any actions based on one or more attitudes. Of the three, behaviors are thought to be the most easily influenced.
- Many variables affect behaviors, including biopsychosocial influences. To positively affect behaviors, a multimodal approach is advocated, where biological, psychological, and social factors are all considered in order to provide a holistic approach to well-being.
- There are many ways to change behavior, all having a common format called the behavior modification model. This progression of stages includes denial that a behavior contributes to poor health, or that one practices an undesirable behavior; then (1) awareness of the undesirable behavior; (2) desire to change; (3) cognitive restructuring, a conscious attempt to change; (4) behavioral substitution; and (5) evaluation of the results.
- Although any conscious change in behavior can be referred to as behavior modification, in terms of stress management, behavior modification generally includes assertiveness training. The three styles of social behavior are passive, assertive, and aggressive; with assertive being the most effective.
- The purpose of every behavior modification program is to foster assertiveness. Such programs educate participants to practice several types of assertiveness skills, on the premise that assertiveness increases self-esteem.
- The best results occur when an individual tries to favorably alter one behavior at a time until it becomes part of his or her regular routine. If several behaviors are targeted at once, the person often feels overwhelmed and within a short time reverts back to old habits.

Concepts and Terms

Aggressive behavior style
Assertiveness
Assertive behavior style
Attitudes
Awareness

Behaviors
Behavior modification model
Behavior substitution
Classical conditioning
Denial

Evaluation
Modeling
Operant conditioning
Passive behavior style
Values

Self-Assessment

Go back to the self-assessment exercise in Chapter 6 and look at your answers to the questions regarding Type A behavior and codependent personality. Select three to five behaviors that you recognize as stress-producing. If you are not sure which behaviors are stress-producing, review the material in Chapter 6.

List these traits here:

1. _____
2. _____
3. _____
4. _____
5. _____

Ask yourself what feelings surface as a result of engaging in these behaviors. Not all feelings are bad. List your feelings.

1. _____
2. _____
3. _____
4. _____
5. _____

List five situtions or circumstances in which you feel these behaviors tend to surface.

1. _____
2. _____
3. _____
4. _____
5. _____

Now, select one of these behaviors and think of two ways that you can change your perceptions and behaviors in order to make a positive change.

1. _____
2. _____

References and Resources

Alberti, R. E. and Emmons, M. *Your Perfect Right,* rev. ed. Impact Press, San Luis Obispo, CA, 1974.

Bandura, A. *Principles of Behavior Modification.* Holt, Rinehart, & Winston, New York, 1969.

Beech, H. R., Burns, L. E., and Scheffeld, B. F. *A Behavioral Approach to the Management of Stress.* Wiley, Chichester, England, 1982.

Beighle, D., G. Dancing with Yesterday's Shadows. Gospel Films, Inc., Nashville, TN, 1998.

Bloom, L. Z., Coburn, K., and Pearlman, J. *The New Assertive Woman.* Dell, New York, 1975.

Bower, S. A. and Bower, G. H. *Asserting Your Self.* Addison-Wesley, Reading, MA, 1976.

Davis, M., Eshelman, E. R., and McKay, M. *The Relaxation and Stress Reduction Workbook,* 3rd ed. New Harbinger Press, Oakland, CA, 1988.

Dyer, W. *Pulling Your Own Strings.* Avon Books, New York, 1978.

Jaffe, D. T. and Scott, C. D. *Self-Renewal.* Fireside Books, New York, 1984.

Lazurus, A. *Behavioral Therapy and Beyond.* McGraw-Hill, New York, 1971.

Levert S. The Complete Idiot's Guide to Breaking Bad Habits. 1998.

Martin, G. Pear, J. Behavior Modification: What It Is and How to Do It. 1994.

McKay, M., Davis, M., and Fanning, P. *Messages: The Communication Skills Book.* New Harbinger Press, Oakland, CA, 1983.

Pavlov, I. *Conditioned Reflexes.* Dover, New York, 1927.

Peck, M. S. Journeys along the Road Less Traveled, Life Cycle Learning Workshops, Arlington, VA, Dec. 2, 1989.

Rokeach, M. *Beliefs, Attitudes, and Values.* Jossey Bass, San Francisco, 1972.

Salter, A. *Conditioned Reflex Therapy: The Direct Approach to Reconstruction of Personality.* Allen & Unwin, London, 1952.

Skinner, B. F. *The Behavior of Organisms.* Appleton, New York, 1938.

Smith, M. J. *When I Say No I Feel Guilty.* Dial, New York, 1975.

Taylor, S. E. *Health Psychology,* 4th ed. McGraw-Hill, Englewood, NJ, 1998.

Tubesing, D. A. *Kicking Your Stress Habits: Y's Way to Stress Management.* Whole Person Associates, Duluth, MN, 1981.

Chapter 10 Journal Writing

All sorrows can be borne, if

you put them in a story.

—Isak Dinesen

At the turn of the twentieth century, British East Africa, as Kenya was then known, was a land ripe with adventure, from Mount Kilimanjaro to the Serengeti Plain. It attracted many an expatriate from the shores of Europe, Asia, and the Americas. Among these new residents was Dane Karen Blixen, new wife of Baron von Blixen, who settled down to carve out a life at the foot of the Ngong Hills, just outside Nairobi. A life of high adventure is not without its stressful episodes. In her seventeen years on the African continent, Karen would contract syphilis from an unfaithful husband, sever her relationship with him, lose her farm to fire, and her land to bankruptcy. Perhaps worst of all was losing the one man she loved, Denys Finch Hatton, in the crash of his two-seater Gypsy Moth plane.

Throughout her life in Africa, Karen wrote. Writing and storytelling became a release, almost an escape, but in every case, a means to cope with the changes she encountered. Upon what she called "an ungraceful return" to her home in Denmark, Karen began to orga-

nize and compose the memories of her African adventures. The result: a wonderful collection of personal experiences intertwining the sad with the sublime (written under the pen name Isak Dinesen) that became the classic memoir *Out of Africa*. While not everyone is a novelist, we all have life adventures that merit, often necessitate, expression—expression that helps to ease the pain of the soul. In the words of Karen Blixen, "All sorrows can be borne, if you put them in a story."

To open up and disclose feelings, perceptions, opinions, and memories has always been found to be therapeutic. Confessions of the mind lighten the burden of the soul. Many religions have adapted this concept for spiritual healing. This is also the cornerstone on which modern psychology is based. Although conversation is the most common method of disclosure, writing down thoughts occupying the mind is extremely therapeutic as well, as was revealed by several people who were rescued after the Oklahoma City bombing in 1995. Therapeutic **journal writing** can be defined as a series of written passages that document the personal events, thoughts, feelings, memories, and perceptions in one's journey throughout life leading to wholeness. The practice of journal writing has proven a formidable coping technique to deal with stress. For years, it has been used by psychologists and health educators alike as a tool for self-exploration and the enhancement of personal development.

Historical Perspective

For centuries, people have felt the need to keep personal records or logs of important information, from celestial navigation to the rise and fall of the Nile River's water levels. Written records served as a basis of comparison for annual events, lunar eclipses, famines of epic proportion, and changes of world leaders. In Europe's Age of Exploration, when men were inspired to explore and travel the globe, written records were of paramount importance. To this very day, world leaders, including the President of the United States, keep a daily journal.

The word *journal* comes from the French word *journée,* meaning from sunrise to sunset. Journals originally started as a means of guidance on long trips, or as a record of orientation for a safe return passage. Long before there were newspapers, most news was written by people who were describing events contributing to their own life journeys. Even today, much of what we

Figure 10.1 Starting a journal may seem hard at first and perhaps even intimidating, when staring at a blank piece of paper. After a few attempts, it gets much easier. (THE FAR SIDE © 1985 FARWORKS, INC. Distributed by UNIVERSAL PRESS SYNDICATE. Reprinted with permission. All rights reserved.)

Tarzan contemplates another entry.

call world history is based on the journal writings of travelers and explorers, including Columbus, Lewis and Clark, Admiral Perry, and even today's astronauts. Journals were kept to record the passage of time as well as distance. Throughout history, many people have kept journals or diaries to record their everyday experiences. Many important historical perspectives have been gained from the written passages of Vermont farm wives, homesteaders on the Oregon Trail, schoolteachers in the Southeast, and panners in Alaska's Klondike gold rush. Originally, journal writing was something men did, as women were not educated to read or write. But when women adopted this idea as their own, the word *diary* became associated with women who kept journals. Today the words *diary* and *journal* are used synonymously, yet there still appears to be a feminine association with the word *diary*. The distinction appears to be that diary writing is a listing of personal events, while journal writing expands personal awareness and creativity, and offers seeds of resolution in personal struggles.

One of the first psychologists to study the use of journal writing was Dr. Ira Progoff in 1975. Trained in Jungian psychology, Progoff discovered that his own journal writing allowed direct access to a higher consciousness or spiritual awareness, which encouraged the search for meaning in his own life. The fruits of these efforts led him to share this coping technique with others who might benefit from it. Journal writing, Progoff suggested, allows for the synthesis of personal thoughts, feelings, perceptions, attitudes, and insights toward spiritual growth. In 1966, he established a seminar, called the Intensive Journal Workshop, in which he trained participants in the art of journal writing for self-improvement. Progoff's method of journal writing, with its use of a three-ringed notebook divided into twenty-one sections separating various components of one's thoughts, sought to open doors in the mind through various themes or springboards to self-exploration. His sections included Daily Log, Stepping Stones, Time Stretching, Dialogue Dimension, Imagery Extensions, A Personal Autobiography, and Dream Interpretation, as well as a series of personal dialogues on a host of topics, from body awareness to societal expectations. Collectively, these topics provided lessons in making order out of chaos from the glut of sensory information that is continually processed in the mind. Journal writing, Progoff said, allows the writer to initiate a positive confrontation with several issues that contribute to the understanding of one's personal existence.

In an experiment to examine the effects of journal writing on personal growth, 300 people were recruited from New York City's welfare and unemployment programs and introduced to the practice through Progoff's workshop, in conjunction with a job training program. Within a twelve-month period, over 90 percent of those enrolled in the workshop improved their job status and housing conditions. Credit for these improvements was given to the enhanced state of self-reliance attained through journal writing. As Progoff states in his book *At a Journal Workshop,* journal writing "plays an active role in reconstructing a life, but it does so without imposing any external categories or interpretations or theories of the individual's experience. It remains neutral and open-ended so as to maintain the integrity of each person's development, while drawing him further along the road of his own life process." He refers to journal writing as *transpsychological,* a word describing the therapeutic effects of self-discovery through active awareness, which allows the individual to access personal resources and promotes wholeness.

The Intensive Journal Workshop offered a very organized method to journal writing, yet some people felt it lacked the spontaneity and freedom that makes self-expression through journal writing unique. The current approach to journal writing, advocated by journal therapist Kathleen Adams, is called humanistic journal therapy, where journal writing is a vehicle for the development and maintenance of the transpersonal self or the bonding between oneself and one's enlightened self. In Jungian psychology, the transpersonal self would be described as a union of the conscious and unconscious minds through communication of words, symbols, and dreams to enhance human potential.

In the past twenty to thirty years, journal writing has often been combined with other coping techniques for personal growth. In the Outward Bound program, for example, which is loosely based on American Indian rite-of-passage custom, risk-taking skills are taught. At the culmination of this week-long experience, where survival skills are put to the test, participants are given journals to write down their feelings in order to enhance the soul-searching and soul-strengthening processes. In a similar type of program conducted in the Sierra Nevada, author Steven Foster writes in his book *Vision Quest* of journal writing as a supplemental tool for self-exploration in a three-day soul-searching rite of passage. Portions of

Figure 10.2 Journal writing is a means of self-exploration of thoughts and feelings.

his book are painfully revealing, with candid descriptions written by those who shared their experiences of inner growth and spiritual development.

Once a privilege of the upper class, reading and writing have now become birthrights of people in almost every nation. Yet, although journal writing was once a popular pastime, the evolution of the high technology age, which, in effect, has placed a barrier between humans and the natural environment, has also undermined the impetus for self-exploration. People just don't take time to sit and write anymore. Instead they watch television or surf the Internet. Sociologists today hypothesize that future generations will never quite understand citizens of the twentieth century as well as those of previous centuries because there will be less documentation of people's personal thoughts, feelings, and subjective perceptions to study. In previous generations, clergy filled the role of sounding boards to hear confessions of guilt, the sorrow of loneliness, depression, and emotional suffering. Today that role has been largely filled by psychologists, who act much the same way. While little scientific research has been conducted regarding journal writing, its value as a coping mechanism has not been dismissed. Rather, it is a practice strongly encouraged in the allied health professions. In the field of psychology, too, journal writing has surfaced as a viable tool in the journey to the self.

Journal Writing as a Coping Technique

Journal writing is perhaps the most effective coping skill available to provide profound internal vision and enhance the self-awareness process. Journal writing initiates the communication of self-reflection between the mind and the soul, the necessary first step in the resolution and closure of perceived stress. Journaling, in its own way, is a vehicle for meditation. As a technique to clear the mind of thoughts (by either focusing on one particular theme or jotting down random thoughts as they surface and circulate through the conscious mind), a calming effect takes place as thoughts and feelings are transferred from the mind to the written page.

Although few studies have investigated the effectiveness of expressive writing, there is consensus that when encouraged, this technique can prove meaningful on many fronts, from expressing guilt and worry, to planting and harvesting the seeds of creative problem solving. It is suggested by many scholars, however, that American academic philosophy may inhibit interest in writing, particularly of a self-reflective nature. In a study examining the uses of writing at the secondary-school level, Britton (1975) reviewed over 2,000 essays and written papers. He labeled over 85 percent of these as transitional—writing to instruct, inform, or persuade. Approximately 7 percent of academic writing was of a poetic or fictional nature, while the remaining 4 percent was categorized as expressive writing of an introspective type. But journal writing, as described by Fulwiler in his book *Teaching with Writing,* synthesizes the constructs of past and present knowledge as a guide to future understanding of oneself. Journal writing holds the potential to open a student's mind to a host of concepts and issues faced during the maturation process toward and during adulthood. It also stimulates imagination, in itself an important tool to deal with stress. Fulwiler, in the company of several others who employ this technique, of course believes that journal writing is only beneficial if it is perceived so by the writer.

Current research suggests that journal writing is not only good for the soul, as a mode of catharsis to express the full range of emotions, but it has proven to be good for the body as well. In a series of studies conducted by psychology professor James Pennebaker (1989, 1990), students at Southern Methodist University were asked to write about a traumatic experience for fifteen minutes on four consecutive days. While the immediate response to these journal entries was often tears, even unpleasant dreams, Pennebaker observed that the subjects subsequently frequented the campus health center for "illness visits" less often than the control subjects who wrote about superficial topics. When this experiment was repeated in collaboration with J. Kiecolt-Glaser, with blood samples taken before and after the writing episodes, it was noted that those people who searched their souls to uncover latent, unresolved feelings associated with personal traumas showed "heightened immune function" of T-lymphocyte cells, when compared to those who addressed superficial topics in their journals.

In 1986, I conducted a study at the University of Maryland to determine the effectiveness of relaxation techniques (progressive muscular relaxation, autogenic training, and mental imagery) when coupled with the coping technique of journal writing. While all sixty-nine subjects learned and practiced several relaxation techniques with proficiency, only thirty-two engaged in regular daily journal writing. Over twelve weeks, a periodic self-assessment was conducted to monitor physical manifestations of stress (e.g., headaches, skin rashes, gastrointestinal problems, etc.). Results revealed that a comprehensive approach to stress reduction, employing both coping and relaxation techniques, proved more effective (i.e., reduced the number of stress-related symptoms) than the practice of relaxation techniques alone.

Prose is not the only style that is thought therapeutic for journal entries. Poetry is strongly suggested as a proven means to foster emotional catharsis as well. Although not all poems employ rhyme, the use of rhyme in writing poetry allows the author to make "order out of chaos," thus giving a feeling or sense of control. In addition, poetic license to use metaphors and similes describing personal feelings allows a deeper sense of emotional expression. Emily Dickinson credited her poetry with the ability to gain a better perspective on the expression of her own feelings. The healing process of self-expression through poetry described by Morris Morrison in his book, *Poetry as Therapy,* incorporates imagination, intuition, and the development of personal insight—three characteristics essential in the healing process. The poems in turn augment the self-awareness process, as each poem is first written and then read in its entirety. As with other journal entries, poems can address a whole host of issues and emotions. For this reason, poem therapy is currently used as a therapeutic tool in the treatment of emotional disorders. Thus, this method of writing is encouraged as a complementary journal-writing style.

As a coping technique, journal writing seems to offer both immediate and long-term effects.

Immediate effects. For a host of varied reasons, people naturally tend to have an inability to fully express the entire range of human emotions. This conscious inhibition of emotional expression, coupled with the unconscious suppression of perceptions, attitudes, and feelings, may eventually result in neurotic (worrisome) behavior or the manifestation of physical symptoms. The results can be devastating, perhaps leading one to several visits to a psychologist. One of the primary goals of psychotherapy is to nurture self-awareness and honest self-expression.

In the short term, self-expression through journal writing may serve as an emotional catharsis by getting out on paper the toxic thoughts roaming through one's head. Journal writing allows the release of thoughts, feelings, and perceptions that liberates the mind and softens or expands the walls of the ego. Journal writing has often been called a writing meditation because as old thoughts are permitted to leave, the empty space they once occupied allows for expanded awareness of one's internal landscape as well as expanded depth of thought. This expanded awareness is analogous to a panoramic view from a mountain top compared to an obstructed view

*B*ox 10.1 **Reflections: A Journal Summary**

by Jason Alvine, University of Northern Colorado

Having never kept a journal or even thought of writing down my feelings, this was a new experiment for me. Although I wasn't fond of the idea in the beginning, I learned many things from these exercises. From thinking of myself as an optimist to thinking of what makes me angry, I enjoyed writing my thoughts and feelings in a journal. This activity definitely taught me a lot about myself, how I view others, and what makes me tick. The main thing this journal taught me was that I care about others' feelings more than I let on. I think that I have more of a sensitive side than most guys would admit to, but this is by no means a bad thing. I looked at my values, which is something that I hadn't done in a long while, and realized I needed to focus more on the values that I was raised with than the values of my friends. I also looked back and saw that I have a great distaste for violence against another human being. I strongly believe that violence is a way for people who don't know how to deal with their

stress properly to relieve themselves of this perceived negativity.

These exercises really made me examine myself and look at how I was, and how I want to strive to be. These entries made me look at my future and think about what I want to do with my life. I feel that the exercises reinforced that the best way to a successful future is to have success in the present. I do this by keeping up in my classes and trying to work as much as possible. Working gives me a sense of what I want to do with my life, and what I don't want to do. With my jobs in the past I have seen the effects of not having a college degree and where you can end up without it. The journal also made me think of continuing to write my thoughts down. Because it is a new technique, I learned to vent my frustrations and reveal my thoughts without telling anybody. This was a most beneficial activity and it made me think about finding new ways to let go of my stress.

---

from the base. Increased awareness opens the door for increased understanding of ourselves in our many environments. Writing down personal thoughts gives one permission to let them go, no longer thinking about them with the intensity that may have cluttered the mind and drained energy. Release of thoughts and feelings may also act as a personal confession, an honest confrontation of one's behaviors. And this is an initial step toward healing both one's internal relationship and personal relationships with others. In addition, unlike conversation or internal dialogue, use of writing as a channel of self-expression makes the writer accountable for, or allows the writer to take solid ownership of, feelings as abstract thoughts become tangible on paper. (See Box 10.1.)

Long-term effects.   Lewis and Clark made daily journal entries during their expedition to the Northwest coast, and they often referred back to them in order to orient themselves for a safe return to St. Louis. Similarly, on a day-to-day basis it may prove difficult to observe changes in personal perceptions and attitudes toward events and circumstances perceived to be stressful. But by periodically retracing one's steps, by rereading previous journal entries with a degree of objectivity,

an awareness of patterns begins to emerge regarding values, attitudes, and even behaviors that inoculate against, precipitate, or perpetuate the stress response. Clues from reading between the lines may shed light on the precursors to stress: elements of anger and fear, and levels of self-esteem that make oneself vulnerable to stressors. This new awareness becomes extremely valuable when efforts are made to change these factors. Perhaps the best phrase to sum up the long-term effects of journal writing is "personal resolution." When thoughts are transferred to paper, the writer can begin to detach him- or herself from the scribed contents and begin to look at these as an impartial outsider would.

As a component of stress-management courses I have taught, I ask my students to keep a stress-management journal. At the end of the course, each person is asked to reread all entries from the duration of the course (typically sixteen weeks) and write a summary. A journal summary is not a recapitulation of four months of stressors, but rather what the individual learned from him- or herself by rereading the entries and noticing trends or patterns in thoughts and behaviors, primarily trends that promote anger and/or anxiety, as well as conflicts in values and factors promoting or deflating self-esteem.

More Journal Summary Excerpts

Box 10.2

"For a long time now, I've known what stresses me the most. It has been a long time since I've been able to confide in or let anyone get really close to me. I've been so wrapped up in school for the past eight years of my life, and it's really getting lonely. As time goes on, it gets harder and harder to express myself. In a sense, I'm scared of situations because I don't know how I'll react. In this aspect, I don't know myself very well and I'm afraid to find out. This journal has really helped me get in touch with myself."

"This stress-reduction journal offered no cure-all for my problems, but it gave me valuable help. It helped me understand and see what I thought. By knowing what was going through my mind, I began to realize things about myself, some things I might have never known. A common phrase I saw in my journal was 'good enough.' The paper was 'good enough,' the letter I wrote home was 'good enough,' I was doing things so they would be 'good enough,' and in doing so, not achieving my potential. I was striving for mediocrity. I'm trying to break this bad habit and I think I have made a little headway. Creativity is now more clear and interesting to me than ever before. I found myself writing short stories in my journal or just creating ideas for work or pleasure.

"When I divorced my husband of seven years I cried on everyone's shoulder for months. That was a year ago. But people get tired of the same old complaints, even from best friends. So I took refuge in writing in my journal. It served as a great sounding board. It certainly help me heal some very deep wounds. I've learned that there are some thoughts that are best left between my mind and the pages of a journal notebook."

Sometimes, first-hand accounts of the benefits of journal writing are more influential than the theories on which they are based. In Box 10.2 are selected passages from summaries written to describe what some students learned from this coping-technique experience.

Steps to Initiate Journal Writing

Only three essential elements are needed for effective journal writing: (1) a notebook dedicated solely to the journal, (2) a pen or pencil, and, perhaps most important, (3) a quiet, uninterrupted environment to collect your thoughts and then put them down on paper. There appears to be no best time of day to write; it varies from person to person. The end of the day may seem ideal, but perhaps not convenient. Although the time of day to write may vary, the suggested frequency of entries is more established. It is recommended that a good goal to start with is a minimum of fifteen to twenty minutes for each entry, and three entries per week, to realize the benefits of this technique. Typically, people start out writing a couple of paragraphs mainly emphasizing events of the day rather than perceptions of these events. If continued, however, entries become longer, with more elements of the author's personality.

The current school of thought suggests that there really are no rules on keeping a journal. However, as an effective coping technique, there are some things to keep in mind. A journal should include descriptions of both stressful events *and* positive experiences. Life is comprised of highs and lows, and over the course of time, your journal should reflect both sides of the emotional teeter-totter. In addition, journal writing is not limited to thoughts and feelings expressed solely in words. Drawings serve as a wonderful expression of feelings, thoughts, and memories that words often cannot fully describe. Sketches also help augment recollections of images to complement the written text (see Chapter 11, Art Therapy). It is important for you to remember that you write for yourself and not for the pleasure or intent of others. In fact, the best journal entries are those that are completely confidential. The premise of journal writing is to strengthen the bond of honesty from your mind to your soul. The contents of a stress-reduction journal aren't for publication; thus they are and should remain confidential. Thoughts should be articulated, yet unedited. When this premise is acted on, thoughts and feelings become easier to articulate and the rewards of inner peace are more substantial.

Although there is no specific formula for successful journal writing, some criteria may aid the writer to use this coping strategy to deal more effectively with perceived stress. These include the following:

1. *Try to identify those concerns and problems that cause the most frustration, grief, and tension.* Identification and prioritization of stressors are essential in the

self-awareness process. For the first two to three weeks, this may be all you choose to include in each journal entry. Journal entries often can best be started by answering one or two questions, such as How was my day today? or What thoughts are occupying my mind right now?

2. *Ask yourself what emotions are elicited when these stressors are encountered.* The two major stress emotions are anger and fear; however, there are many shades of these emotions, including impatience, jealousy, frustration, sadness, grief, guilt, and worry. After identifying your current emotional state, the question Why? should be pondered to identify the origins of your emotions (e.g., Why do I feel frustrated? Why do I feel victimized?).

3. *Allow the writing process to augment your creative process to further resolution.* When you have begun to feel comfortable with identifying stressors and the respective emotions they produce, the next phase is to create a process of resolution for the concerns and problems. This includes searching for viable options and employing them to bring satisfying closure to the circumstances that promoted stress (see Chapter 13, Creative Problem Solving).

Perhaps in an effort to address the needs of people searching to use journaling as a coping technique, several books have appeared on the market in the past decade providing guidelines to the art of journal writing. The following is a compilation of tips, hints, and suggestions that appear to have the consensus of therapists who advocate this coping technique:

1. *Centering.* Before you begin to write, take a moment to relax. Close your eyes, take a few deep breaths, and try to unwind. Centering means to be well grounded or well connected to the here and now. Sometimes playing soft music or sipping hot tea can help foster the centering process.

2. *Label your journal entries.* Identify each entry with day, date, and year. On occasion you will want to review your past entries and it is much easier to recall the events surrounding the journal entry when this information is at the top of the page.

3. *Uncensorship.* Write whatever comes to mind without editing your thoughts before you put them on paper. Don't censor your thoughts as they travel from your mind to the tip of your pen. Let them flow naturally. Journaling is transcribing your conscious dialogue. Don't be inhibited about expressing how you really feel. Also, don't worry how your writing style appears. Neat or sloppy, it makes no difference as long as you can read it; that is all that matters.

4. *Spontaneity.* Let your thoughts be free-flowing. You don't have to write in sentences and paragraphs all the time. Often, in trying to phrase a thought just the right way, the essence of the thought becomes diluted or lost. Get whatever thoughts you have down on paper and then sort them out however you choose. If you get a mental block when in front of a blank piece of paper, draw lines and store your ideas in separate boxes, or make lists of your thoughts. It is good to have variety in your journal entries, or the routine of writing becomes a boring chore. If words fail you, make a sketch or perhaps try writing a poem.

5. *A private place.* In theory, journal entries can be written anywhere, but having a designated place of solitude lends depth to self-disclosure. Find a place you can call your own. Open spaces also provide the opportunity for mind expansion. If the weather is conducive to sitting outdoors for a while, find a tree, beach, mountaintop, or grassy knoll, and make this spot your own as well. Sometimes combining this technique with music therapy (Chapter 21) allows the mind to wander more freely and emotions to surface to a greater level of consciousness.

6. *A private journal.* Experts agree that your journal is for your eyes only. If you make it a habit to share entries frequently, then the vow of honesty with yourself is compromised. If you live with other people (i.e., roommates, girlfriend/boyfriend, spouse, parents), then it would be a good idea to keep your journal away from wandering eyes. A journal is like Pandora's box to anyone but the author. You may choose to make it known that you keep a journal and specifically ask that no one invade your privacy. If someone does, it is at his or her own risk.

7. *Overcoming writer's block.* One reason people find writing in a journal challenging is that there is the risk of pain from confronting one's innermost thoughts. People become scared of learning what is below the surface of immediate thoughts. Pain arises when the premise of our thoughts and perceptions doesn't match the ideals or expectations we set for ourselves. Fears surface with the realization of unmet expectations or a change in our current reality of ourselves. These conflicts can be painful to the ego. But with pain comes the opportunity for learning, and learning sows the seeds of personal growth and development. Remember that Frankl believed suffering to be an essential part of the personal-growth process.

At the novice stage of journal writing, a blank piece of paper, not to mention an empty notebook, can look mighty intimidating. Some people are reluctant to write due to the unrealistic expectation that something profound must be written on every page. A journal serves as a catalyst to begin and strengthen your relationship with yourself. Relationships begin with introductions, background information, and questions. Journal entries can begin the same way. Writer's block happens to everyone at some point. Many people go in cycles, where they write religiously for months at a time, get a block, and then abandon their journals for a stretch. Sometime later, they come back to this coping style after a hiatus of a few weeks to a month. Writer's block can be overcome by trying a new approach or theme to journal entries, including creative writing or entries in the form of letters. For example, the book *The Color Purple* was written as a series of letters by author Alice Walker to a fictitious sister in Africa. If you find yourself with writer's block, try a new format of writing.

In his book *Opening Up: The Healing Power of Confiding in Others,* author Jamie Pennebaker advocates journal writing as a means of self-expression. Just as there can be benefits to journal writing, however, it can also be used incorrectly, negating the potential personal gains to be made. The following are suggestions to keep in mind when using journal writing as a positive coping technique:

1. *Journal writing should not be used to replace a more viable coping technique.* Journals can be great sounding boards. The echos from these passages should be a strong personal invitation to find solutions to the problem at hand. Remember, for a coping technique to be effective, it must work toward a peaceful resolution. When journal writing is employed in place of more appropriate coping techniques, such as effective communication with other people (Chapter 14) or social engineering of factors for the betterment of your environment (Chapter 16), resolution is compromised, if not completely prevented, and full closure on stressors never comes.

2. *Journal writing should encourage, not discourage, honest feelings.* As a coping technique, journal writing invites the writer to soul-search and turn thoughts inward. While many writing themes, concepts, and philosophies can be used as vehicles to explore and augment the soul-searching process, these should not be the specific focus of one's writing. The primary theme is the writer. Ideally, journals should be kept confidential, though often people choose to share parts of journal entries, sometimes entire passages. However, if journal entries are written for an audience other than yourself, then the likelihood of honesty is greatly compromised.

3. *Paralysis by analysis.* Sometimes, when people get too absorbed in the expression of their thoughts and feelings, awareness gets fogged in and the effectiveness of self-expression and self-reflection is stifled. Cognitive paralysis sets in, which deters rather than augments the coping process. Be careful not to get caught in this trap. Journal writing is meant to give a wide perspective on yourself in your environment. Make sure you are able to see the forest as well as the trees.

Pennebaker reached some interesting conclusions about subjects he observed keeping journals. First, only a handful of people (3 percent) wrote every day in their journals; and while more women than men kept journals, the difference was not significant. Second, journal entries were centered less on emotions than on facts to describe specific events, a style that may not have been as beneficial an experience as perceived by the journal writer. Last, he found that journal writers seemed to fall into two distinct categories. The first group tended to write only during periods of mental frustration and monumental stress. The journal became a sounding board and tended to carry the burden of anxieties. The second group wrote nearly every day; however, when a major stressor arose (e.g., death of a spouse, career stress), a time when writing might be the most help, a safe distance was kept from the journal and no writing took place. Pennebaker noted a third group of people, though, who instead of keeping a journal, wrote letters. Although this may seem similar to journal entries, letters are often less than candid about internal feelings about oneself to oneself. In my work with clients, I have also noticed a fourth group: people who do not necessarily write frequently, perhaps once or twice a week, but whose journal entries tend to be balanced between positive and negative experiences. The positive experiences are more factual, and perhaps even integrated into a creative story. The narratives of negative experiences include inner feelings to describe the reasons for these emotions.

Journal Writing Styles, Themes, and Ideas

While journal entries can consist of a daily report on personal events, they can also be inspired by specific themes that surface and merit exploration to give the writer a new vantage point on him- or herself. Examples include dreams, rites of passage, values assessment and clarification, unwritten letters, self-esteem issues, relationships, things to do, wish lists, creative story writing, poems, or any topic the writer chooses to expound upon. Themes can also be conveyed in many styles of writing, including linear (left to right), circular (rotating the paper as you write), in boxes, and free-form. Three of these are as follows:

Figure 10.3 Buzan Diagram.

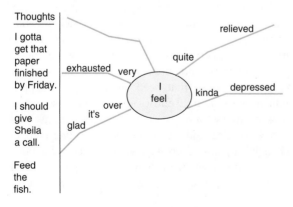

1. *The Buzan style.* One style for journal entries, developed by Tony Buzan (1983), involves words in a pictorial fashion that accesses both right- and left-brain cognitive functions. In this technique (Fig. 10.3), you draw a vertical line to the left of center on the page. Everything to the left of this line is reserved for thoughts or perceptions. Examples might include "I have to feed the dog tonight before I go out," or "My boss was a jerk today." In the center of the remaining two thirds, draw a circle, and in the middle write the words, "I feel." Every time you feel an emotion, draw a line from the circle out. On each line, describe how you feel in three words. (Buzan suggest the use of a different colored pen or pencil for each feeling.) Whatever comes into your mind, write down as either a thought or feeling; do this for about fifteen to twenty minutes. You may want to listen to some soft, relaxing instrumental music at the same time. This type of journal entry serves as an eraser to clean the blackboard of your mind. Once the thoughts are on paper, the mind becomes uncluttered and achieves a state of mental homeostasis.

2. *A dream journal.* Dreams make fascinating material for journal entries. Jung, remember, believed attempting to understand the symbolism of one's dreams would lead to psychic equilibrium, a balance of the conscious and unconscious minds promoting personal wholeness. Often the loose ends of perceptions and emotions associated with stress materialize in the dream state as the unconscious mind works on its own analysis and resolution process of thoughts and sensory information received in the conscious state. The unconscious mind is rich in color and symbols, yet poor in its ability to express these symbols as words. Thus, the collaboration of the conscious and unconscious mind is a dynamic one to deal with stressors. While we often do not remember all our dreams, everyone does dream. But many times, dreams seem to fade into thin air the second we wake up and enter the conscious world. Researchers who study dreams have come up with the following list of ways to help people remember their dreams:
   a. First, before you go to sleep, write a review of the day's events and your feelings about them.

b. As you drift off to sleep, remind yourself, silently or out loud, that you want to remember your dreams.

c. Reserve a few quiet moments, with your eyes closed, when you wake up to recall your dreams. Linger in a semi-dream state to observe dream thoughts.

d. Keep your journal and a pen/pencil handy by your bedside to record your dream thoughts or fragments when you wake up.

e. Dream thoughts can surface to the conscious state when triggered by some event in the course of your day. Write any dream fragments down.

Return to the passages describing your dream images and ponder what their symbolism can reveal to you. Jung believed that every dream was a source of information. Prompt recording of your dreams can help prevent distortions created by the conscious mind. Journal writing can also be a good outlet to draft a written closure or final scene of a recurring dream. Recurring dreams often represent serious unresolved issues that need to be addressed. While writing a final scene to a recurring dream may not fully resolve each stressful issue, it does initiate increased awareness which may aid in the resolution of the stressor that causes this type of dream.

3. *Unsent letters.* Another topic common to journal writers is called "unsent letters." One type of resolution people tend to avoid like the plague is rifts occurring in relationships of any kind. The hardest rift to resolve occurs when a friend or loved one dies without your getting the chance to say goodbye. Kathleen Adams (1990) states that unsent letters provide the opportunity for "the three C's": catharsis, clarity, and completion. As a cathartic tool, the drafting of an unsent letter allows release of suppressed emotions including grief, anger, or guilt. For this journal technique to prove effective, it is a given that the letter does *not* go in the mail, so that emotions can bubble up freely and surface without fear of self-censorship or reprisal. We all carry excess emotional baggage from unresolved relationships. The drafting of unsent letters allows us to lighten our emotional load. Clarity

becomes evident when the writer realizes there is no chance for rebuttal from the addressee. Under this circumstance, you can be as direct as you wish and state exactly how you feel and why you feel this way. While writing a letter to someone you need to communicate with does not resolve all issues, it does *begin* to bring the unresolved issues to closure. A variation on this journal technique is to write down thoughts of anger and hostility and then crumple up the paper and throw it away. The crumpling adds to the emotional catharsis.

Best Application of Journal Writing

Good quality journal writing has several purposes. The first is to act as a personal sounding board; to cleanse the mind overloaded with perceptions, emotions, and toxic thoughts. Journal writing is a great way to vent anger. In moments of rage, a verbal description helps pinpoint how and why these feelings are surfacing. Sometimes writing how you feel, and perhaps what you should have said or would like to say, becomes a draft script to resolve issues between you and the person(s) involved in your perceived stress. Writing down feelings of anxiety and apprehension is a good release of emotions that can drain your energy. Effective coping involves the ability to access and employ both internal and external resources.

The second purpose is to map out strategies for resolution. Depending on the situation, these two purposes can be used as an offensive tactic in the face of stress, or in strategic planning when in momentary retreat. As an offensive tactic, journal writing can be used to cope with an immediate problem. Just by pulling out a pad of paper and pen and writing down what is on your mind, thoughts become organized and order begins to emerge from chaos. In many stressful events, however, this option is not possible. Then journal writing can be used as a postponed coping response, perhaps at the end of the day, to collect your thoughts and process major events—those chronic stressors—that need attention. Last, a periodic review of journal entries serves to increase awareness of trends and patterns in your thoughts and behaviors. Recognition of trends is the first step in changing undesired or negative thoughts and actions in an effort to reach your highest human potential and enjoy inner peace. Although the primary resource

From a Distance

Sometimes when we distance ourselves from our problems we can get a different and perhaps more objective viewpoint on the perceptions we have. Looking at ourselves through someone else's eyes gives us a chance to detach ourselves from our emotions long enough to find a new way to deal with a problem. When people write journal entries, they almost exclusively write in the first person. This first-person viewpoint is what separates autobiographical truth from a third-person point of view, which is often incomplete because it lacks significant personal insight. But let us assume for a moment that an occasional journal entry could be written in the third person. Imagine what could be revealed: that unique insight only you could provide, along with the objectivity of a third person with no emotional attachment: the best of both worlds.

A journal entry of this nature would read like a story or screen play. It would have a plot (your stressor of the day), character development (your thoughts and feelings as described by this observer), and mystery (how to resolve the stressor). It might even have adventure and romance, but let's not get carried away.

Save this journal entry for when you have had a really bad day or your mind has been weighted down so heavily that you just cannot be objective in your thoughts. Then pull out a pen, and as you write about a particular concern, give it the slant of someone else looking at the situation. You'll be surprised just how therapeutic and revealing this type of entry can be.

The Child Within

To see a universe of life in a few blades of grass while lying face down on a lawn under the summer sun. To catch yourself laughing at the silliest idea, or crying with remorse without any inhibition. To believe in the power of magic and be suspended in time with curiosity. To see life as an adventure and be swept away in the colors of a rainbow to a faraway land. To love without conditions. These are the precious moments of childhood. Of course, childhood can be filled with many dark and lonely moments as well; battles of sibling rivalry, abusive parents, ridicule from peers, and unending hours of loneliness. At times, childhood can be filled with both glorious naiveté and painful abandonment. Some of these aspects of our youth fade too quickly as the seasons of our life spin faster and faster toward adulthood, while others linger on in unresolved feelings.

Despite maturation to adulthood, within each of us there still remains a child, one who continually needs to be nurtured, loved, and protected. Let's pretend for a moment that you could actually meet a younger version of yourself at about age four or five. Behind the ruffled hair, bright eyes, and missing tooth is a child longing to be loved, begging for acceptance. With years or decades of experience behind you now, what would you say to this child? What could you say to comfort, love, or nurture this child within you? Ponder for a moment some comforting words of advice, some thoughts of love you might have liked to have heard at that age to help you in the transition into adolescence and adulthood.

Any good conversation is a dialogue so listen closely to the child within, and discuss what he or she is begging to tell you. Perhaps your child will suggest that it's been too long since you lay face down on a summer lawn under the sun and explored blades of grass. Perhaps he or she will tell you it's okay to cry or laugh out loud again, or to explore your sense of creativity and curiosity. We have much to learn from the child within us. Share your thoughts with your younger self.

needed for journal writing is a single notebook, you might consider having two: one very private one to be used exclusively at home, and a second one, perhaps less structured, at work.

Personal computers have added a whole new dimension to journal writing that was inconceivable just a decade ago. Many people have found that using a word processor actually allows them to write as fast as they think, thereby enabling them to capture the essence of several thoughts simultaneously, rather than fighting to retrieve some. If you find it easier to type entries in a personal computer file than in a notebook, give it a try.

Box 10.3 shows two additional descriptive journal themes from the workbook accompanying this text. If so inspired, try these as possible entries in your journal.

Summary

- Journal writing has been used as a form of self-expression and soul searching for centuries. Psychologists and health educators have advocated journal writing for decades as a means to increase self-awareness on issues that need attention.
- Journal writing is said to promote emotional catharsis when thoughts, perceptions, attitudes, values, beliefs, and the tensions these create are allowed to work themselves out on paper.
- Use of soul searching is no coincidence as a stress-management technique, since this activity is the epitome of the emptying process.
- There are short-term and long-term effects of habitual journal writing. Short-term benefits include releasing pent-up feelings of anger and anxiety. When a series of journal entries are reread, long-term effects include seeing patterns and habits of thought, perceptions, and behaviors that are not detectable on an entry-to-entry basis. Putting thoughts down on paper also widens one's perspective to become more receptive to solutions and resolutions to stressors.
- An additional benefit, demonstrated by Pennebaker, is that writing about personal experiences in a journal increases the integrity of the immune system.
- Not all journal entries have to be written in prose form. Poetry therapy is likened to making order out of personal chaos. This coping style is used in many settings, including prisons, nursing homes, hospitals, and counseling centers.
- There is no wrong way to write a journal, save writing too infrequently. This chapter gave a number of guidelines for effective journal writing, including several themes (Buzan, dreams, and unsent letters) that can add variety to your repertoire of entry styles.

Concepts and Terms

Buzan writing style
Journal writing

Poetry therapy
Transpsychological

Writer's block

Self-Assessment

Here Comes the Judge

> The problem with judgmental thinking is that sometimes it
> channels our thinking in the wrong direction.
>
> —Roger von Oech

To judge or not to judge, that is the question! We have an amazing ability to perceive the world around us. By and large, we perceive through our sense of judgment; that's good, this is bad, this is nice, that sucks, and so on. From an early age, one of the first thinking skills we access is pattern recognition, a type of judgment skill. From here we are taught to judge by what is deemed good or bad.

Judgment is considered to be a left-brain thinking skill. When we combine judgment with other left-brain functions such as analysis, linear thinking, rational thinking, and logical thinking, we become left-brain dominant, focusing on problems. The eye of critical awareness can also be directed inward, making it hard to live up to our own expectations of perfection.

Judgment is not altogether bad. We need judgment skills to help us make decisions in times of stress, many of which may seem like life or death situations. But if we tend to overuse this thinking skill, we begin to force judgment on everything. As psychologist Abraham Maslow once said, "If your only tool is a hammer, you will see every problem as a nail."

1. Do you see yourself as a judgmental person? If so, why?

   YES AND NO, I SEEM TO BE MORE JUDGMENT WITH PEOPLE I LIVE WITH
   BUT ON THE OUTSIDE LESS APT TO JUDGE. FRUSTRATING FOR BOTH
   PARTIES

2. When do you think using your sense of judgment is stress relieving rather than stress producing?

   WHEN THE JUDGEMENT KEEPS ME FROM HARM - PHYSICAL EMOTIONAL
   OR MENTAL

3. As described, left-brain dominant people tend to be more critical, judgmental, rational, and logical. Right-brain dominant people tend to be more accepting, receptive, intuitive, and playful. Ideally, the best scenario is to have a balance of both right- and left-brain skills. If you were to choose between right- and left-brain dominance, which would you say best described you? Why?

   RIGHT BRAIN - BECAUSE I THINK I'M MORE OF A KID THAN AN ADULT
   YET KNOW HOW TO BALANCE. I ALSO THINK I'M PRETTY RECEPTIVE AND
   INTUITIVE ALTHOUGH I CAN BE OVER RATIONAL + LOGICAL

   If you are not sure to what extent your mind thinks critically, you may want to consider taking the Myers-Briggs inventory to see just how strong this aspect of your thinking skills is.

References and Resources

Abbott, H. P. *Diary Fiction: Writing as Action.* Cornell University Press, New York, 1984.

Abercrombie, B. *Keeping a Journal.* McKelderry Books, New York, 1987.

Adams, K. *Journal to the Self.* Warner Books, New York, 1990.

Baldwin, C. *One to One: Self-Understanding through Journal Writing.* Evans & Co., New York, 1977.

Britton, J. et al. *The Development of Writing Abilities.* Macmillan, London, 1975.

Brophy, B. Dear Diary: A History, *U.S. News and World Report,* October 23:89, 1995.

Buzan, T. *Use Both Sides of Your Brain.* E. P. Dutton, New York, 1983.

Cappachione, L. *The Creative Journal.* Swallow Press, Athens, GA, 1979.

DeVota, Bernard, ed. *The Journals of Lewis and Clark.* Houghton Mifflin, Boston, 1953.

Dickinson, E. *Selected Poems and Letters of Emily Dickinson.* Doubleday, New York, 1959.

Dinesen, I. *Out of Africa.* Random House, New York, 1983.

Foster, S., with Little, M. *Vision Quest: Personal Transformations in the Wilderness.* Prentice-Hall, New York, 1988.

Fulwiler, T., ed. *Journals across the Disciplines.* Northeast Regional Exchange, Chelmsford, MA, 1985.

Fulwiler, T. *Teaching with Writing* Boynton/Cook Pub., New York, 1987.

Goldberg, N. *Writing Down the Bones.* Shambhala, Boston, 1986.

Hagan, K. L. *Internal Affairs: A Journal-Keeping Workbook for Self-Intimacy.* Escapadia Press, Atlanta, GA, 1988.

Holly, M. L. *Writing to Grow: Keeping a Personal Profession Journal.* Heinemann Educational Books, Portsmouth, NH, 1989.

Kaiser, R. B. The Way of the Journal, *Psychology Today* 15:64–65, 1981.

Leedy, J. L. *Poetry Therapy: The Use of Poetry in the Treatment of Emotional Disorders.* Lippincott, Philadelphia, 1969.

Mallon, T. *A Book of One's Own: People and Their Diaries.* Tickner and Fields, New York, 1984.

Mayer, H., Lester, N., and Pradl, G. *Learning to Write, Writing to Learn.* Boynton/Cook, Portsmouth, NH, 1983.

Metzger, S. *Writing for Your Life: A Guide and Companion to Inner Worlds.* Harper, San Francisco, 1992.

Morrison, M. R. *Poetry as Therapy.* Human Sciences Press, New York, 1987.

Pennebaker, J. W. Confession, Inhibition, and Disease, *Advances in Experimental Social Psychology* 22:211–244, 1989.

Pennebaker, J. W. *Opening Up: The Healing Power of Confiding in Others.* William Morrow, New York, 1990.

Pennebaker, J. W., Colder, M., and Sharp, L. Accelerating the Coping Process, *Journal of Personality and Social Psychology* 58:528–537, 1990.

Pennebaker, J. W. and Francis, M. E. Putting Stress Into Words: The Impact of Writing on Physiological, Absentee, and Self-Reported Emotional Wellbeing Measures, *American Journal of Health Promotion* 6(4):280–287, 1992.

Plaut, T.F. Symptom Reduction After Writing about Stressful Experiences, *JAMA* 282(19):1811–1812, 1999.

Progoff, I. *At a Journal Workshop.* Dialogue House Library, New York, 1975.

Progoff, I. *The Practice of Process Meditation.* Dialogue House Library, New York, 1980.

Rainer, T. *The New Diary.* J. P. Tarcher, Los Angeles, CA, 1978.

Rico, G. L. *Writing the Natural Way.* J. P. Tarcher, Los Angeles, CA, 1983.

Seaward, B. L. Effects of a Comprehensive Stress-Management Program on Self-Reported Physiological Manifestations of the Stress Response, *Psychophysiological Monographs* 5(3):1–7, 1988.

Siegel, A. Dreams: The Mystery that Heals. In *The Holistic Health Handbook*, Edward Bauman, ed. And/Or Press, Berkeley, CA, 1972.

Simons, G. F. *Keeping Your Personal Journal.* Ballantine/Epiphany, New York, 1978.

Walker, A. *The Color Purple.* Harcourt Brace, New York, 1992.

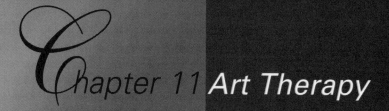

Chapter 11 Art Therapy

Draw me how you feel.

—Sharlene Gin

Art, as a mode of self-expression, dates back several thousands of years to the cave drawings in Lascaux, France, and perhaps much earlier. But just recently in the development of modern civilization has art become a recognized coping technique in the field of stress management. **Art therapy** is based on the premise that many thoughts, feelings, and insights are verbally inexpressible. Several abstract constructs of the human mind lack the necessary vocabulary to adequately describe the focus, intensity, and understanding of daily encounters that the mind tries to process and grasp. Self-expression through visual artistic media offers a balance to verbal expression in the search for wholeness through the understanding of our personal thoughts, feelings, and perceptions.

Art therapy has been described by the American Art Therapy Association as "the use of art in a creative process to provide the opportunity for a nonverbal expression and communication in which to reconcile and foster self-awareness and personal growth." Art therapy is centered on exploration of the individual's internal landscape, carved and shaped by one's collective experiences and delivered through a visual, artistic sense. Art therapy can strengthen the bonds of self-communication, thereby promoting greater self-awareness and self-comfort. Art therapy can also be described as a voyage of self-discovery, with process and product uniting to promote self-realization and self-healing. For this reason, art therapy is considered a coping technique in the strategic plan to deal with stress, as awareness of problems must occur before steps to resolve perceived stress can be taken.

Origins of Art Therapy

The seeds of this discipline took root as early as the field of professional psychology itself. At the turn of the twentieth century, Freud and Jung engaged several of their patients in drawing to better understand several psychological disorders through the visual expression of their emotions. But it was the work of Margaret Naumberg, an American art teacher and director of Walden Art School, who found the use of art a powerful form of therapeutic communication for several children she taught. Naumberg observed that self-expression through spontaneous art became a psychotherapeutic treatment in its own right. With the backing and assistance of her colleague, Dr. Nolan

Lewis, she conducted research involving children classified with problem or troublesome behaviors at the New York State Psychiatric Unit. Her first findings were published in 1947; however, it would take several more years for her theory to take root. Naumberg's theory dealt primarily with the unconscious expression of nonverbal thoughts as an important tool in psychoanalysis. She proposed that with the interpretive help of a therapist, the patients' art work would aid in their own treatment and recovery.

A second theory, developed by art teacher Edith Kramer in 1971, suggested that the process of drawing itself was therapeutic, and that more attention should be given to the creative, cathartic process than to the final product, the illustration. Since its inception as a discipline, many theories have been added to the study of art therapy, based on the foundation by Naumberg and Kramer. The role of the art therapist has also matured in this evolution. Originally seen as the primary vehicle for interpretation of the artist's work, the art therapist is now viewed as a blend of artist, therapist, and teacher. The art therapist serves as a catalyst to help the artist uncover his or her own meaningful interpretation and to use that interpretation as an awareness tool to further personal growth and development. According to art therapist Eleanor Ulman, the role of an art therapist is "to help people bring out from within themselves a source of motivation—the wish to organize the experience of their inner and outer worlds into a coherent form."

Not until the 1960s did art therapy emerge as its own discipline, with specialists becoming trained and certified in the theoretical basis and application of this type of therapy. In 1969, the American Art Therapy Association was established. Originally, in its most clinical form, art therapy was designed as a diagnostic tool used by art therapists and psychologists to understand personality development and self-expression of patients with clinical disorders. In the late 1970s and early 1980s, however, art therapy became recognized and accepted as a coping technique for all individuals to increase self-awareness, as well as act as an outlet for emotional expression. Currently, the benefits of visual expression through various art media are acknowledged for everyone. To date, research in the field of art therapy consists mostly of clinical case studies, that is, individuals, who, in their recovery process, have attained a breakthrough in self-discovery through creative art.

Conventional wisdom indicates that art therapy initiates a stronger partnership between the nonverbal, artistic, spatial right-brain functions and the analytical, logical, and verbal left-brain functions. With the evidence gathered from split-brain research, it has now become obvious that the optimal human potential involves balance and integration of the right and left cognitive functions of the brain. As the discipline of art therapy continues to expand beyond the clinical setting, a greater understanding of its benefits will be realized.

Today, art therapy is recognized for its many therapeutic effects on aspects of mental, physical, spiritual, and, most notably, emotional well-being. Art therapists agree that there are several goals associated with this technique to enhance the healing process and well-being. As described by art therapist Myra Levick (1983) these include:

1. *To provide a means for strengthening the ego:* to allow a better sense of identity through discovery of personal interests and growth issues

2. *To provide a cathartic experience:* to let emotions that have an immobilizing effect be released in the physical act of creating personal expression through art

3. *To provide a means to uncover anger:* to employ the use of colors and shapes to express and detect feelings of aggression

4. *To offer an avenue to reduce guilt:* by conveying inner thoughts of past feelings and behavior associated with the guilt process

5. *To facilitate impulse control:* to allow freedom of self-expression, rather than its repression, through a positive behavior

6. *To help patients/clients use art as a new outlet during incapacitating illness:* to use art as a tool to strengthen the mind-body connection by using various art media to augment the imagery aspect of self-healing

Clinical Use of Art Therapy

Art therapy, primarily drawing and illustration, has been employed in many settings, including drug rehabilitation centers, eating-disorder clinics, veterans' hospitals, clinics for the emotionally disturbed, prisons, and oncology (cancer) hospital wards. Often, the manifestations of physical and emotional problems inhibit people in the verbal expression of their feelings. Yet, without some type of communication or self-expression, the progress of healing is stifled. Art therapy serves to break through this barrier. The dichotomy of hemispheric cognitive functions, revealed through split-brain research, has validated the concept that verbal communication is only one way to express our innermost thoughts. Feelings of anger, depression, fear, grief, guilt, and worry, when expressed in graphic form, begin to release residual toxins of these thoughts from the depths of the unconscious mind. In guided art therapy, drawings are either directed—suggested themes or guidelines by the art therapist to follow—or spontaneous, with the freedom to draw whatever comes to mind, in order to help release suppressed or toxic feelings.

Every mark, every spot, and every line drawn, painted, or sketched is considered an extension of the individual's mind. Through repeated analysis and interpretation of the works created by a host of patients from every conceivable background and with every health-related problem, some recurring archetypal images appear to represent specific parts of one's personality. For example, trees (Fig. 11.1) are thought to represent energy levels or a perspective on one's life. A full, leafy tree with broad trunk is indicative of vibrant energy and strong-willed nature, while a barren, skinny tree suggests frailty, lack of hope, perhaps even death. Houses may represent either security or imprisonment, depending on the size of windows, doors, and the location of people in the setting. All images have importance, just as all aspects of each image convey a

A simple drawing of a tree can indicate a great many things about someone and his or her level of self-esteem.   *Figure 11.1*

special meaning to the person who drew the picture. The recognition of this importance reveals various aspects of one's psychic landscape. And, as much can be revealed by what is not drawn as by what is pictorially represented. For instance, in self-portraits, people who draw faces with no mouths or ears suggest an inability to express their feelings verbally. Long arms may express a desire to reach out for help or affection. Short arms may signify feelings of withdrawal. Short necks indicate stubbornness. Boxed shoulders hint of the inability to let matters roll off the back.

According to art therapist Evelyn Virshup (1978), the importance of art therapy is in the process, not necessarily the outcome. The expression of oneself through art far exceeds the aesthetic quality to the viewer: "Someone who is asked to draw how they feel, and is then measured by the yardstick of aesthetics will

Figure 11.2 A 12-year-old cancer patient personified her chemotherapy treatment as the hero "Chemo Girl" who set out to save the world "one treatment at a time." (From Richmond, *Chemo Girl* [© 1996 by Jones and Bartlett Publishers, 1-800-832-0034.] Reprinted with permission.)

feel betrayed, and will repress further feelings. Creativity of expression is stifled by judgmental evaluation." A crucial factor in the practice of art therapy is the collaborative verbal description of the picture once it has been drawn. The role of the art therapist is to guide the artist through his or her understanding of each work. This is done by asking open-ended questions such as, What does the picture mean? In many cases, the artist may not overtly recognize the emotional significance of the work (e.g., missing features, significant color selection, or unproportional figures), or may not be quite ready to accept verbally what has been depicted graphically. Art therapists suggest that, upon completion of the drawing, the artist try to explain what the figure represents, perhaps even to write it down on the corner of the drawing. This serves to balance the nonverbal with the verbal expression and further the communication process of the conscious and unconscious mind. This combination leads to better awareness and comprehension of the situation at hand and the emotions associated with it.

In 1971, a radiation oncologist named Carl Simonton formulated a concept for cancer patients involving, among other things, the integration of mental imagery and art therapy. In a pioneer program to teach cancer patients to take an active role in their own recovery, Simonton and his then-wife, Stephanie, designed a strategic approach to attack cancer from all sides—mentally, physically, emotionally, and spiritually—with a host of progressive coping and relaxation techniques. In perhaps the most significant plank to bridge the fields of alternative and modern medicine, mental imagery and art therapy were employed as complementary tools to fight cancer cells and help rejuvenate the body.

On the premise that people must take active responsibility for their own health, Simonton asked his patients to imagine a flood of white blood cells attacking and devastating the cancer cells in their bodies. In the creative minds of his patients, the white blood cells took on metaphorical images of armies of white knights in shining armor (Fig. 11.2), or schools of great white sharks in confrontation with their prey. Simonton had several patients draw pictures of these images to reinforce the power of visualization. Additional pictures were drawn at various stages of their illnesses. The progression of visual images gave striking evidence of the patients' attitudes toward their disease and their willingness to attempt to either augment the healing process through enhanced willpower and positive attitudes (with some cases of "terminal" cancer going into remission), or remain passive, even helpless, victims.

In her pioneering work, Kübler-Ross has also used art as a therapeutic tool with children who have cancer. Those with a limited vocabulary but total lack of inhibition about drawing were able to express a multitude of feelings surrounding the many progressions of the death process. Kübler-Ross found that the utilization of illustrations and sketches by terminally ill children served as a phenomenal coping technique toward the resolution of the emotional and spiritual stress associated with this traumatic experience. She believes that self-expression through art has the potential to become a vehicle to promote wholeness in the individual.

Using an approach similar to Simonton's and Kübler-Ross's, physician Bernie Siegel has also employed art therapy among his cancer patients. While most physicians have their patients first fill out medical-history questionnaires, Siegel hands out blank sheets of white paper and boxes of crayons and asks individuals to draw themselves in their current state of health or disease. According to Siegel, mental imagery in the form of art therapy is more useful than a battery of laboratory tests to assess a patient's disease state and prospects for recovery. He adds that the analysis of these illustrations is one of the most accurate tools in determining the prognosis of disease and, potentially, the development of other health-related problems.

As a general surgeon with a speciality in oncology, Siegel was struck by several factors hinting at which patients would succumb to their disease and which would defy the odds of terminal cancer. Those who seemed to grab the bull by the horns and took responsibility for their recovery, he referred to as exceptional cancer patients (ECaP). More specifically, critical factors included will-power, humor, hope, and love, all of which were represented in some aspect of the patients' illustrations. Not all of his patients had this exceptional ability, and their drawings often foreshadowed imminent death. In the spirit of Jung, Siegel soon came upon the realization that messages from the unconscious mind manifest in symbolic images and characteristics. These images accentuate the patient's fears, angers, levels of self-esteem, grief, guilt, and the intensity of the personal problems and conflicts that ultimately pave the path to disease. In one illustration, a patient drew herself at the extreme

right-hand, bottom corner of the page, leaving the rest of the paper blank. This was interpreted to suggest low self-esteem, which was later confirmed by the artist. In a similar episode, a young boy drew only the top half of his body over the entire page, leaving the physician curious and frightened. The young boy then turned the page over to reveal the bottom half, hinting that recovery was well on its way—and putting a huge smile on Siegel's face.

Although there are exceptions, Siegel discovered that color selection, as well as the objects drawn and space utilized, often paralleled emotional expressions regarding states of health. From his observations and explanations, he has made the following associations between colors and their meanings:

Black: grief and despair

Brown and natural colors: groundedness

White: cover-up, avoidance, fear

Red: passionate emotional peaks, from pleasure to pain (perhaps even anger)

Orange: change (either positive or negative)

Yellow: energy

Blue and green: happiness and joy (blue may even mean creativity)

Violet/purple: highly spiritual, love

Not all professionals agree on the association between color selection and its interpretation; art therapist Rebecca Crane offers a slightly different explanation. In her professional experience, yellow and orange signify pleasantness or happiness. Violet and red convey unhappiness. Specifically, violet represents grief or death, while red is used to express anger, frustration, and annoyance.

Although cancer patients have received the most publicity from their use of art therapy as a coping technique, art therapists have also used this tool in the awareness and recovery process of other stress-related problems, including migraine headaches, (Fig. 11.3), gastrointestinal problems, anorexia, and posttraumatic stress disorders of patients surviving the atrocities of war. The creation of sketches and sculptures has been a significant tool in the treatment of Vietnam veterans with posttraumatic stress disorder (PTSD) as described by J. Horgan in *Scientific American*. Horgan reported that many former soldiers were still held

Figure 11.3 An example of art therapy used to treat migraine headache.

Figure 11.4 Doodles may not seem like a form of therapy, but they, too, reveal what cannot be expressed verbally.

prisoner by the haunting memories of death and carnage, leaving them emotionally immobilized after returning home. But through the introduction of this type of therapy, veterans found a tremendous sense of relief through transferring their destructive images from the depths of their minds onto paper, canvas, or clay. While not particularly anxious to talk about their war experiences, the vets used their illustrations and sculptures as an outlet to help vanquish the emotions associated with their traumatic experiences and to initiate one facet of the healing and growth process.

The treatment of eating disorders, particularly anorexia nervosa, has also included art therapy as a part of the process. In this disease, the patient often feels helpless to control his or her existing environment and identity. Perceptions of stress are turned inward and manifested through a process of slow physical self-destruction. Inner conflicts regarding control issues are manifested through significant weight loss, which is paralleled by a distorted body image. In a study conducted at Goldsmiths College employing art therapy with anorexics (Levick, 1983), it was noted that the subjects rarely drew human figures. When they were drawn, however, they showed adolescent characteristics suggesting a denial of adult responsibilities and physical maturation. Paintings and sketches by patients often depicted images of isolation and loneliness; in one case, a subject drew herself as a cactus. Progress was noted when subjects began to represent their true physical conditions; that is, they drew themselves in human form. Art as a means of self-expression by anorexic patients was perceived to help increase self-awareness by opening the lines of communication within the individual, thus acknowledging strengths and weaknesses, and an increased comfort with both.

As recently as the Persian Gulf war in 1991, the children of those sent to Saudi Arabia from San Antonio, Texas, were often asked to draw their feelings regarding the war and their parents' involvement in it. School teachers employed this technique to allow the children a healthy emotional outlet for their feelings. The drawings often revealed fears of abandonment, detachment, sorrow, and loneliness.

Just as much can be revealed by a picture, much can also be revealed by casual doodles, the kind that accompany lecture notes, grocery lists, or are scribbled on paper napkins (Fig. 11.4). Psychologist

Robert Burns has researched the meanings of doodles only to find that they are another form of art therapy. Doodles are nonverbal messages that surface from the unconscious mind, each doodle or mark important in its own right. Often, doodles are symbols of thoughts, feelings, and perceptions in visual form. While the understanding of "doodling" is in its infancy, several observations have been made by Burns (Jaret, 1991). Aggression is often expressed in dark, heavy, jagged lines with arrows or points. Horizontal lines convey inner peace. Happiness is typically represented by soft, curvy lines. Burns discovered that men typically draw geometric shapes—squares, triangles, circles—while women tend to sketch faces. Like the conscious effort to draw a graphic representation of our feelings, unconscious doodling also conveys important messages about the internal landscape.

Steps to Initiate Art Therapy

The beauty of art therapy is that anyone can participate and its significant therapeutic effect benefits not only cancer patients but anyone experiencing the signs and symptoms of perceived stress. In this case, as with other coping and relaxation techniques, the word *therapy* does not reflect weakness or needing help. Rather, art therapy serves to augment understanding of the personal awareness and resolution process. Art therapy appears to trigger a progression of two responses. The first is a cathartic effect, whereby you can release pent-up emotions and thoughts from your mind onto paper (or clay). The second is a greater sense of personal awareness based on an objective look at or interpretation of the art work, that is, the message it suggests or implies. This interpretation or awareness is often a communication from the unconscious mind regarding less-than-obvious symbolic images. While an interpretation can be helpful in the self-awareness process, without some prior knowledge or assistance, meaning could also be overlooked, mistaken, or misconstrued. Thus there are several factors to consider to ensure the effectiveness of this technique, including artistic roadblocks, materials, illustrative themes, and interpretation.

Artistic Roadblocks

The most common reaction people have to art therapy is, "I can't draw!" The truth is, everyone can draw, in a way specific to their own talents and abilities. A case in point is Irishman Christie Brown. A paraplegic without use of his hands due to cerebral palsy, he painted with his left foot. Many people are hesitant to draw out of embarrassment. But in art therapy it doesn't matter what your abilities are. Whether your creative talents are best described as third-grade stick figures, or are undisputed recreations of Old Masters, it makes no difference. Abstract images, fine-detailed sketches, simple lines, colors, and shapes are all equally important. Art therapy is noncompetitive. There is no right or wrong. With this obstacle out of the way, you're ready to give it a try.

Materials

Opinions vary greatly on the choice of medium recommended for art therapy. The one factor agreed upon is that there should be a wide assortment of colors to allow full expression. Art therapists generally agree that the best medium is colored pastels, as they are the easiest to work with for both broad strokes and fine lines. Siegel, on the other hand, advocates crayons. Crayons not only come in all colors of the rainbow, says Siegel, but they bring out the child in the artist, a characteristic that promotes familiar receptivity to this medium. While pastels and crayons are preferred, colored pencils can also be used. Virshup advocates the availability of all media, including string dipped in paint and dragged across the paper. The purpose behind all these media is to have as wide a variety of colors as possible, so pen and pencil are not advocated, but in a pinch will suffice. Finger paints have been used with children, and modeling clay has also been shown to be effective for this technique. Paper selection is a less problematic decision. Art therapists highly recommend the economical blank newsprint (18 " × 24 "); Siegel suggests a white sheet of paper; however, any type of paper in most any size will suffice. Once you have these materials, all you need is an idea and some inspiration to put pastel or crayon in your hand and draw.

Illustrative Themes

When art therapy is used as a coping technique to deal with stress, there are a host of themes and concepts providing inspiration to choose from. One approach is just to start drawing (anything) until you achieve some level of comfort with this technique. Other themes are more specific to events, feelings, or situations that words seem inadequate to describe. I have tried (with much success) the following themes in my classes:

1. *Art therapy images.* Introductory art therapy sessions are typically initiated with two or three themes such as:
a. *Draw something that represents you.* This could be a symbol of yourself, a picture of something you identify yourself with, such as your profession, family, hobbies, home, or something that gives you inner strength.
b. *Draw two fantasy animals.* Whatever two animals come to mind, even creations of animals that do not exist on the planet. Then describe the animals you have drawn in a few words (approximately three adjectives) on the back of the paper (from Virshup's art therapy workshop).
c. *Close your eyes and draw a line on the paper.* Make the line any shape—straight, curved, jagged, fuzzy, or thin, whatever strikes your fancy, but keep your eyes closed while you draw. Next, open your eyes and take a look at what you see. You may want to rotate the paper around slowly until something strikes the fancy of your creative eye. Then, complete the drawing. Make something out of the line you drew. Give the line meaning. Do with it whatever comes to mind.
2. *Healing images.* Although art therapy has been used extensively with cancer patients, many other diseases and symptoms can be represented on paper. The following themes are ideas to enhance positive internal image, body awareness, and mental imagery.
a. *Draw yourself.* Sketch an image of yourself in a state of perfect health.
b. *Draw a picture of a part of your body you feel needs special attention.* Draw an area that you feel is perhaps a target organ of stress, one that shows signs of excessive wear and tear, or a part of your body that does not feel completely whole. For example, a headache, sore back, stomach cramps, clenched teeth. On another sheet of paper (or the back side), draw an image of this same body region fully healed.

Use your imagination to restore this image to health through metaphor (e.g., a sock completely darned to represent a healed stomach ulcer).

3. *Mental images.* Art therapy can be a vehicle for mental imagery also. The images drawn provoke the mind to wander. For example:
a. *Draw a peaceful image.* Draw an image that makes you feel relaxed just by thinking about it. It can be a place you have been to that you would like to return to, if only on paper. It can also be a place you have never been to but have always wanted to go.
b. *Draw how you feel right now.* What emotion(s) are you feeling now? Anger, fear, guilt, worry, love, joy, peace? What does your anger look like to you? How would you illustrate your feelings of love? Try to visualize your emotions on paper.
c. *Draw a dream image.* Try to include whatever fragments of a particular dream you can recall. Include the use of colors.

Interpretations

Interpretations are the hardest component of art therapy. They are difficult because there is wide latitude for impressions and understanding the figures, colors, shapes, and sizes that have made their way onto paper. Jung once said that the most important factor in dream analysis is the patient's impressions, since dreams are the creation of the dreamer. Drawings and sketches are no different when it comes to interpretation (Box 11.1). As a cathartic experience, interpretations of drawings are secondary to simply getting feelings down on paper. Art therapists, and even psychologists who now use art therapy in their practices, engage in a fair amount of training to understand the commonalities, expressions of colors, and a host of other components of drawings. When interpreting the colors you have chosen, be careful to keep in mind both the context of the illustration and mood you were in when you drew the picture. For example, black is often used to represent death or grief, but for an African American, the color may also symbolize pride.

Interpretation is the search for understanding as the unconscious mind communicates to the conscious mind thoughts and feelings best described through a visual medium. In all art therapy sessions, patients are

Illustration Themes and Interpretations

Box 11.1

The following were drawn by college students during art therapy sessions. Of the images suggesting a personal struggle, the drawing itself became a vehicle for resolution, as the artists, within a month's time, attained closure on the issues surfacing during the therapy experience.

The illustration below was drawn by a student who saw herself as having high self-esteem. The fish represents beauty and freedom. The color (orange) seems to indicate a major life change in the months ahead (the artist was a graduating senior).

This picture was drawn by a student who was grieving over the loss of her dear friend who was murdered. The tears down her cheek have formed a pool of blue and green water. Her black hair is a symbol of her grief, yet the sunshine is working it's way to warm her heart.

continued

Box 11.1   Illustration Themes and Interpretations (cont.)

Facing surgery and radiation for breast cancer, this student chose to imagine the radiation as light energy that would heal her body. "Unlike some women who are forever worrying about body image, I am very proud of my body," she explained. A year later she wrote to say that she is cancer free.

"This is how I feel when I am angry—I often feel full of rage, but feel like my mouth is a closed zipper, and I cannot express my feelings. The dress represents my family and friends expecting me to act feminine instead of showing my rage, the beer cans tell the rest of the story."

continued

Illustration Themes and Interpretations (cont.)

Box 11.1

"I drew a TV for my head because I feel like there are many things going on in my life, many things distracting my attention, the remote control in my hand offers some help, but not really much control at all."

encouraged to explain their drawings to members of their group. Members, in turn, ask questions that may aid the artist in understanding his or her drawing. If done alone, a written description of the work helps with this process. But caution should be used when trying to interpret the meaning of your own art work. First, go for the obvious. In the words of Freud, "Sometimes a cigar is just a cigar."

Best Application of Art Therapy

Art is an expression of one's thoughts and feelings—expression that is not only necessary but therapeutic as well. There are many circumstances, in times of both ecstasy and torment, in which words do not adequately describe the full extent of our emotions. These are the times to employ art therapy. Remember that emotional well-being is defined as the ability to feel and positively express the full range of human emotions. As crazy as it may sound, keeping a box of crayons or colored pencils in your desk drawer is as important as having an address book or weekly planner. If you don't have art suppliess, it might be a good idea to obtain them. And remember, pictures don't have to be masterpieces. They can start off as doodles.

Summary

- Art as a means of self-expression dates back to antiquity. Art therapy has its roots in Freudian and Jungian psychology, where illustrations were used to aid in understanding unconscious thoughts.
- In 1969, the American Art Therapy Association was established to educate and certify people in the skills of art therapy. Art therapy has since been introduced into a variety of settings, including counseling centers, hospitals, and addiction treatment centers, as well as nontraditional settings such as corporate wellness centers. It has proved an effective coping technique for all types of people to get in touch with their emotions in a nonverbal way.
- Art therapy is described as the creative use of art to provide for nonverbal expression and communication through which to foster self-awareness and personal growth.
- Every stroke, every color, every detail has some relevant meaning at the unconscious level.
- There are varying opinions on the use of materials for art therapy, meaning that there is no preferred method. Crayons, pastels, colored pencils, finger paint, and clay are all possibilities. Art therapists do suggest that a wide variety of colors be available. Colors provide specific meaning to thoughts and unconscious messages.
- Art therapists offer a series of themes to explore in this type of nonverbal communication, including a picture of yourself, a fantasy animal, and a house with trees.

Concepts and Terms

Art therapy

Artistic roadblocks

Nonverbal expression

Posttraumatic stress disorder

References and Resources

Adamson, E. *Art as Healing*. Coventure, London, 1990.

American Art Therapy Association, 1202 Allanson Road, Mundelein, IL, 60060. (708) 949–6064.

Asperheim, J. T. Art Cure: Colors, Shapes, and Images Can Say as Much as Words, *Health*, March:31–32, 1982.

Betensky, M. *Self-Discovery through Self-Expression*. Thomas, Springfield, IL, 1973.

Catacchione, L. *The Creative Journal: The Art of Finding Yourself*. Swallow Press, Athens, GA, 1979.

Cornell, J. *Mandala*. Quest Books, Wheaton, IL, 1994.

Crane, R. R. An Experiment Dealing with Color and Emotion. In *Art Therapy Viewpoints*, eds. Levy and Ulman. Shocken Books, New York, 1980.

Dalley, T., ed. *Art as Therapy*. Tavistock, New York, 1984.

Farrelly-Hansen, M. and Kingsley, J. *Spirituality and Art Therapy: Living the Connection*, Jessica Kingsley, London, 2001.

Fink, P. J. Art as a Language, *Journal of Albert Einstein Medical Center* 15:143–150, 1967.

Franklin, M. Becoming a Student of Oneself: Activating the Witness in Meditation, Art, and Super-vision, *American Journal of Art Therapy* 38(1):2–13, 1999.

Gin, S. Draw Me How You Feel, paper presented at the American University, Washington, DC, Nov. 20, 1992.

Harms, E. The Development of Modern Art Therapy, *Leonardo* 8:241–244, 1975.

Horgan, J. Rx: Art; Drawing or Sculpturing Can Help Traumatized Vietnam Veterans, *Scientific American* June:38, 1988.

Jaret, P. How Do You Doodle? *Health* 5(2):34–37, 1991.

Jung, C. G. *Man and His Symbols*. Anchor Press, New York, 1963.

Keyes, M. *The Inward Journey: Art as Therapy for You*. Celestial Arts, Berkeley, CA, 1974.

Kramer, E. S. *Art as Therapy with Children*. Schocken Books, New York, 1971.

Kramer, E. S. The History of Art Therapy in a Large Mental Hospital, *American Journal of Art Therapy* 21:75–84, 1982.

Kübler-Ross, E. Keynote address, American Holistic Medicine Association Conference, LaCrosse, WI, 1981.

Levick, M. *They Could Not Talk So They Drew*. Charles C. Thomas, Springfield, IL, 1983.

Levy, C. and Ulman, E., eds. *Art Therapy Viewpoints*. Shocken Books, New York, 1980.

McKim, R. *Experiences in Visual Thinking*. Brooks/Cole, Pacific Grove, CA, 1972.

Mills, J. C. and Crowley, R. J. *Therapeutic Metaphors for Children and the Children Within*. Brunner/Mazel, New York, 1986.

Naumberg, M. *Dynamically Oriented Art Therapy: Its Principles and Practice*. Grune and Stratton, New York, 1966.

Rhyne, J. *The Gestalt Art Experience*. Brooks/Cole, Monterey, CA, 1973.

Robbins, A., ed. *The Artist as Therapist*. Human Sciences Press, New York, 1987.

Rubin, J. *Child Art Therapy*. Van Nostrand Reinhold, New York, 1978.

Shovlin, K.J. "Discovering a Narrative Voice through Play and Art Therapy: A Case Study, *Guidance and Counseling* 14(4):7–11, 1999.

Siegel, B. *Love, Medicine, & Miracles*. Harper & Row, New York, 1986.

Simonton, O. C., Mathews-Simonton, S., and Creighton, J. *Getting Well Again*. Bantam Books, New York, 1978.

Sutherland, J.I. Art Therapy with A Woman Who Has Multiple Medical Conditions, *American Journal of Art Therapy* 37(3):84–98, 1999.

Swenson, A. Relationships, Art Education, Art Therapy, and Special Education, *Perceptual and Motor Skills* 72:40–42, 1991.

Taylor, P. Art as Psychotherapy, *American Journal of Psychotherapy*, February:599–605, 1950.

Ulman, E. Art Therapy: Problems of Definition, *Bulletin of Art Therapy* 1:10–12, 1961.

Virshup, E. *Right-Brain People in a Left-Brain World*. Guild of Tutors Press, Los Angeles, 1978.

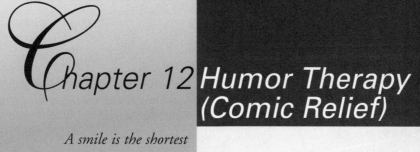

Chapter 12 Humor Therapy (Comic Relief)

A smile is the shortest

distance between two people.

—Victor Borge

In 1964, a man admitted himself to a hospital for severe pain throughout his entire body. After a series of tests, he was diagnosed with a rare rheumatoid disease called ankylosing spondylitis, a progressive deterioration of the body's connective tissue. Chances for recovery were predicted to be roughly one in five hundred; the disease was quite advanced. Like most people, Norman Cousins decided to learn all he could about the etiology of his disease. He soon discovered that there is a strong correlation between stress, particularly negative perceptions and emotions, and his specific disease. So the question occurred to him: if negative emotions like guilt, worry, and anxiety are thought to be related to, and perhaps even to promote, disease, is it possible for positive emotions to maintain health, or even restore one's health? He came to the conclusion that in order to increase his chances of recovery, he had to assume responsibility for his treatment. And that he did. He had nothing to lose.

With a defiant determination to recover and the support of his personal physician, Cousins checked out of the hospital and into a nearby hotel. As the story goes, he acquired copies of humorous movies and TV shows, including Laurel and Hardy and the Marx Brothers. One of his friends, Alan Funt, even sent some classic clips from his hit TV show *Candid Camera*. Cousins later wrote in his now-famous book, *Anatomy of an Illness,* that "ten minutes of laughter allowed two hours of pain-free sleep." After a time, he checked out of the hotel and went home; his disease had gone into remission. On the advice of his doctor, Cousins wrote up his story as a case history for the *New England Journal of Medicine.* While he attributed his successful healing process to several factors, including large doses of vitamin C, the interpretation by those who read the article was that Cousins literally laughed himself back to health.

Norman Cousins's story is now just one of many supporting the idea that positive emotions do indeed have healing effects on health. However, it was this single case study of comic relief, perhaps more than any other, that paved the road to a whole new field of study called psychoneuroimmunology (PNI), and Cousins will always be remembered for his generous contribution to it. What has been learned since his hospital discharge is that positive emotions play an incredible role in maintaining the health of the human body. Humor therapy, or comic relief, is the use of humor to promote well-being through positive thoughts, attitudes, and emotions by counterbalancing the deleterious effects of negative thoughts, perceptions, and emotions on one's health. Humor as a coping technique is not a panacea for all ills, but it does provide benefits in a bad situation, whether in a hospital bed, or outside a locked car, with your keys still in the ignition.

Historical Perspective

Humor is a human magnet: it attracts all ears and minds. And laughter is a universal language, breaking through cultural barriers when words cannot. Cousins certainly was not the first person to use humor as a coping technique. Comic relief has been pondered since men and women first tickled their funny bones. The ancient Greeks held humor as a virtue. The philosopher Plato, for instance, believed humor nurtured the soul, and he advocated its use as a healing practice. From the ancient Greeks came the formulas for theater, including comedy, still used today. And as far back as Old Testament times, people in the Middle East believed "A merry heart doeth good like a medicine, but a broken spirit drieth the bones" (Proverbs 17:22). In fact, humor as a "healing medicine" can be found at the root of virtually every culture on the globe, from the earliest practices of the native peoples of Africa to those of the Americas. It seems that humor and the viruses it helps to fight are equally contagious.

The word *humor* comes from a Latin word of the same spelling that means "fluid" or "moisture." According to the physiology of the medieval period in Europe (the age of alchemy and potions), there were four basic body fluids, with each "humor" associated with a specific mood or general disposition. Choler, the yellow bile produced by the gallbladder, allegedly made one melancholy and depressed. Similarly, black bile, produced by the kidneys or spleen, was responsible for anger and hostility. A happy, cheerful spirit was associated with blood; while phlegm, produced by the respiratory system, was the reason behind apathy and sluggishness. If any one humor was produced in excess, it was thought to change mood, which put the individual at risk of social ridicule; ergo, the first comedians. If all body fluids were balanced, however, a person was said to be "in good humor." Note, too, that the practice of blood letting, or draining the body of fluids to relieve symptoms and causes of these ailments, was a common practice in the United States as well as Europe until 1850. Sad to say, many a person died from melancholy, and a career as a physician was not looked upon with favor as it is today.

Intrigued with the use of humor as a healing agent, Dr. Raymond Moody surveyed several history books in 1978 to discover the following. In the year 1260, a progressive French physician, Henri de Moundeville, saw the important relationship between positive emotions and sound health, and made a practice of allowing family and friends to cheer and joke with their sick relatives. He wrote, "Let the surgeon take care to regulate the whole regimen of the patient's life for joy and happiness." European monarchs also saw the importance of laughter, and often employed court jesters (those guys with funny shoes) to add mirth to their castle courts. Perhaps the most renowned court jester was Richard Tarlton, who was credited with keeping British Queen Elizabeth I (1533–1603) in better health than did her team of physicians.

Figure 12.1 Because laughing and smiling were thought to be a sin, no one did so in front of a camera for fear of being blackmailed with the proof.

But laughter has not always been looked upon with favor. Europeans in the middle ages and Puritans on the eastern shores of North America, among others, perceived laughter to be the work of the devil. People caught laughing out loud were often denounced as witches or believed to be possessed by Satan. The expression of humor was considered a sin in many Christian denominations. Other comments from those days about laughter (Moody, 1978):

> Laughter on any occasion is immoral and indecent. Laughter obscures truth, hardens the heart, and stupefies understanding.
> A man of parts of fashion is therefore only seen to smile, but never heard to laugh.
> —Lord Chesterfield, 1748.

And if you look at the portraits of European nobility commissioned over a period of several hundred years, you are hard-pressed to find anyone smiling (except the Mona Lisa).

The words "say cheese" were not coined for use with the first camera in the nineteenth century, either; people were afraid of being caught sinning in public (Fig 12.1). In fact, according to Allen Klein (1989), it was not until the twentieth century that people would risk a smile in a photograph.

Social norms are often influenced by figures of authority, so humor scholars have turned to the American presidency, a high-stress job, to observe the use of humor in the Oval Office. Lincoln was reported to use humorous stories in his political speeches and even read jokes to his cabinet during the Civil War period. Jimmy Carter once said to reporters at a press-conference dinner, "I'm not going to say anything important, so you can put your crayons away." When Ronald Reagan, a politician known for his sense of humor, was brought to George Washington University Medical Center hospital after the assassination attempt on his life, he turned to the assembled medical team and said, "I hope you're all Republicans." And when Dan Quayle's father said that his son studied only "booze and broads" in college, presidential candidate George Bush was heard to reply, "Not many students had a double major." President Clinton's jokes we cannot print in this book. It appears that humor helps in the stressful role as president, too.

Times have changed since the days of Victorian prudery. With the help of the American and European entertainment industries, from vaudeville to Hollywood to television, the use of humor has gained wide acceptance throughout the world as a prominent factor in enhancing positive emotions. Slow to join this opinion until it had undisputable proof, the medical community now also accepts humor as a viable technique for health promotion and wellness. And it is Norman Cousins we have to thank for validating the use of humor as an authentic therapy in its own right.

Types and Senses of Humor

For all the philosophical studies on the topic of humor—and there have been many—there has yet to be consensus on what humor really is. It encompasses so many facets and seems so profoundly complex that it has proved quite difficult to define succinctly. Most experts agree that humor is not itself a positive emotion, but that it can elicit positive emotions, including happiness, joy, love, faith, hope, and willpower. Humor is not a behavior, although it can produce actions (laughter and smiling) that are specific to its nature. Humor is best described as a perception, for as we all know and have experienced, what one person finds funny someone else does not. The following are two definitions to illustrate this elusive perception (McGhee, 1979):

1. Humor is "the mental experience of discovering and appreciating ludicrous or absurd ideas, events, or situations that bring pleasure or enjoyment to the individual."
2. Humor is "the quality of being funny or appreciating funny thoughts or acts of behavior; the ability to perceive/enjoy what is funny or comical, a state of mind, feeling, or mood."

It appears from the definitions that humor has two fundamental aspects. Simply stated, these are give and take. First, humor can be absorbed like a sponge, or experienced by internalizing this perception cognitively. Second, humor can be expressed externally through an action in an effort to share it with others. It is accepted that everyone has a sense of humor, although from your personal experience, you may think you have proof to deny this statement. Among those who have studied humor, McGhee (1979) cites three factors that must be present for humor to exist:

1. Sources that act as potential stimuli (e.g., a pie thrown in someone's face)
2. A cognitive and intellectual activity involved with the perception and evaluation of these sources (perceiving a faceful of whipped cream to be amusing)
3. Behavioral responses that are the expressions of humor (i.e., smiling or laughing)

Types of Humor

Perhaps the reason humor has been so difficult to define is that there are so many shades of it that can be internalized or expressed. Furthermore, types of humor overlap and integrate with each other so that it is hard to separate them out sometimes. While there are several theories of how humor can be categorized, I list them here in a particular order—parody first and sarcasm last—according to their efficacy at coping with stress. Everything between parody and sarcasm is fairly equal, and powerful in its own way, as either a subtle means to dissolve anger and fear, or to distract attention away from stress long enough for the body to return to homeostasis.

1. *Parody.* Parody is a work of humor that closely imitates something, or someone, for comical effect. Parody is typically a verbal or physical expression of humor bringing imperfections to light. This type of humor is considered to be one of the best, if not the best, types of humor to deal with stress, as long as it doesn't sacrifice self-esteem. Exaggerating behaviors and personality traits are examples. Good-natured parody, however, should not be mistaken for self-criticism expressed as an appeal for sympathy. When individuals can begin to parody and laugh at their own shortcomings, in their own minds, it will have the wonderful effect of reducing perceptions of stress. Celebrity "roasts" are probably the best known parodies. The *Onion*, a national college paper, and the music of Weird Al Yankovic are prime examples of parody.

2. *Satire.* While satire and parody have many commonalities, satire is most often thought of as a written expression of personal and social flaws. In the use of satire, many personal, political, and cultural quirks are described and exaggerated for humorous effect. America's most celebrated humorists, Art Buchwald, Erma Bombeck, Tom Robbins, P. J. O'Rourke, Molly Ivans, and Dave Barry, are well known for their styles of satire.

3. *Slapstick comedy.* In the early days of American vaudeville, many actors used physical farce to generate laughs (Fig. 12.2). Slipping on a banana peel, getting a pie in the face, or reeling from a slap on the cheek was sure to get a rise out of the audience. While banana peels and cream pies were real, face slaps were faked. Behind the curtain stood a person making the sound effects. Originating in the French theater, the slap stick was a piece of leather nailed to a flat board. At the appropriate moment on stage, use of the slap stick would also produce laughs. The Marx Brothers, Laurel and Hardy, Abbott and Costello, the Three Stooges, and Lucille Ball all had their professional roots in American vaudeville. Scholars note that slapstick comedy is an aggression-based humor through which audience members can release latent anger in a cathartic way (laughing) by watching someone else give and receive physical, yet harmless, blows.

4. *Absurd/nonsense humor.* Absurd or nonsense humor is described as two or more concepts that unite to result in a stupid, ludicrous, or ridiculous perception. The best example of this

Figure 12.2 Many slapstick comedians from Hollywood's Golden Age got their start in vaudeville comedy: Lucille Ball (left) and Groucho Marx (right).

style of humor is cartoonist Gary Larson's cartoon strip *The Far Side* (Fig. 12.3). Cows driving cars, sharks wearing horned-rimmed glasses, and cheetahs using vending machines on the Serengeti plain are all absurd. Dan Piraro's *Bizarro* strip conveys the same humor (Fig. 12.4) Steven Wright is to stand-up comedy as Gary Larson and Piraro are to cartoons, with a brand of absurd humor that has to be heard to be believed. An example from Wright's first CD, *I Have a Pony*, goes like this: "I like my dental hygienist very much. In fact, while in the waiting room, I eat an entire box of Oreo cookies. (pause) Sometimes they have to cancel all their other appointments."* Absurd or nonsense humor is also thought to be a good brand of humor to reduce stress because it acts as a diversion from the inundation of daily stressors. Both styles put a gentle chaos back into the order of everyday thinking, making one realize that life shouldn't be taken too seriously.

5. *The double entendre.* The double entendre is a type of wordplay, where the expression has two meanings (usually of a sexual nature). James Bond movies are filled with these verbal gags. Bumper stickers are notorious for these wordplays as well. Even Disney cartoons are written at two levels—for both kids and parents—where each laughs, but for what appears to be different reasons. Double entendres abound in everything from cartoons to political commentaries on *Comedy Central*. For example, Chris Rock notes that in determining legislation about the legalization of marijuana, both houses of Congress went into a joint session. Here is another example, in honor of EARTH DAY 2000: Clean up the Earth, it's not Uranus!

6. *Black humor.* **Black humor** is not a type of ethnic humor as some people are led to believe. Black, or "gallows," humor is based on the fear of death. It is sometimes described as a "flirtatious brush with death." Death is a common fear among human beings, and one way the human mind has devised to deal with this fear is to poke fun at it, attempting to become more comfortable with the concept, if

*Reprinted courtesy of Mr. Wright

Figure 12.3

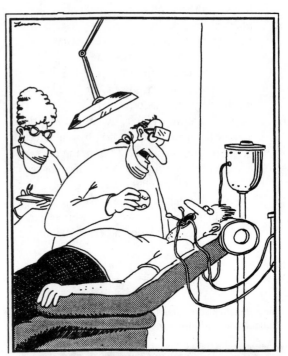

"Now open even wider, Mr. Stevens....Just out of curiosity, we're going to see if we can also cram in this tennis ball."

only momentarily. Typically, during national tragedies, black-humor jokes surface as a way to cope with the gruesome reality of death, as was the case when jokes circulated immediately after the Challenger Space Shuttle explosion in 1986. Some of the best examples of black humor can be found in films and videos like the infamous *Harold and Maude* and the more recent *Being John Malkovich* and *American Beauty*. Much of the comic wit used in the television series *M*A*S*H* expressed various shades of black humor. Cartoonists, including Gary Larson, also make light of this phenomenon in their illustrations.

The dead as well as the living seem to have the last laugh, as expressed in the last words of American humorist Dorothy Parker (etched on her tombstone), "Pardon my dust." In a survey of gravestone epitaphs, Louis Schafer (1990) discovered that cemeteries are

Figure 12.4 (© Creative Media Services, P. O. Box 5955, Berkeley, CA 94705.)

not devoid of tongue-in-cheek black humor either, as illustrated in the following examples:

John Strange
Here lies an honest lawyer.
This is Strange.

Here lieth the body of Martha Dias
Always noisy, not very pious,
Who lived to the age of three score and ten
And gave to worms what she refused to men.

Here lies John Bun, He was killed by a gun,
His name is not Bun, but Wood,
But Wood would not rhyme with gun, but Bun would.

William Reese
This is what I expected, but not so soon.

Here lies the body of Susan Louder,
who died while drinking a seltzer powder.
Now she's gone to her heavenly rest,
She should have waited till it effervesced.

7. *Irony.* Irony is described as two concepts or events, which when paired together, come to mean or expose the opposite of the expected outcome. Life is full of ironies: receiving a surprise check for one hundred dollars in the mail only to find a credit card bill for one hundred dollars the same day. Bumper stickers, such as "My other car is a broom" often use irony. Irony can also be seen in everyday occurrences such as buying four candy bars—and Diet Coke. Oxymorons (two opposite concepts) provide yet another type of irony. Examples are military intelligence, honest politicians, and jumbo shrimp. One of the best examples of irony I have ever heard, though, went like this (Klein, 1989): Charlie Chaplin once entered a Charlie Chaplin Lookalike Contest, and won third prize! Many stand-up comics, including Jay Leno, Robin Williams, Rodney Dangerfield, and Billy Crystal, use this type of humor in their acts, and playwright Neil Simon uses ironic twists in his films and Broadway plays.

8. *Dry humor and puns.* Dry humor can be described as clever, esoteric wit. It often involves double entendres, words with more than one meaning or connotation (e.g., a Jewish zydeco band called So How's Bayou), frequently with sexual innuendo. Mark Twain, Will Rogers, Groucho Marx, Winston Churchill, the cast of Britain's *Monty Python's Flying Circus* and more recently, Garrison Keillor of *Prairie Home Companion* are fine examples of creators of esoteric wit. Puns, or plays on words, also fall into this category. It has often been said that puns are the lowest form of humor because, unlike clever wit, they border on the silly or inane. Actually, puns have no malicious intent and therefore are not the lowest form of humor. You may find it takes effort to laugh at puns, however, whereas other types of humor provoke laughter more spontaneously. Here's one: You can pick your friends and you can pick your nose, but you cannot pick your friend's nose.

9. *Sarcasm.* The word *sarcasm* means "to tear flesh," and if you have ever borne the brunt of sarcasm, then you know all too well that this is

a figurative yet accurate description. While sarcasm may share elements with clever wit, it reveals latent anger (see Chapter 4). It is an attempt to get verbal revenge. Sarcasm is perceived by its users to be a socially acceptable way to express hostile feelings through words rather than physical aggression, but words can hurt as much, if not more, than physical abuse, and the memory of it far exceeds that of physical pain. A sarcastic remark is typically followed by the punch line, "I'm just kidding," to take the sharp edge off the potential pain inflicted. Sarcasm is the lowest form of humor. While sarcastic remarks may seem funny, they actually induce stress rather than relieve it in the person toward whom they are aimed. For this reason, sarcasm is not advocated as a vehicle for expressing humor. Almost everyone employs it to some extent, but its use should be minimized if not altogether abandoned.

Although types of humor have been compartmentalized into various categories here, for the most part, in practice they mix and blend together to form a score of permutations. Examples would be a sarcastic joke about death, or a parody of slapstick. It is equally difficult to neatly categorize senses of humor, or why individuals laugh at what they do.

Senses of Humor

Just as there is more than one type of humor, experts of humor research have identified several senses of humor. Senses of humor appear to be a function of one's upbringing and collective environments. Quite possibly, each individual has the makings for all the senses of humor, but one type tends to dominate in each personality. For this reason, it is complicated to give general advice on ways to improve one's sense of humor. In his book *Laugh after Laugh*, Dr. Raymond Moody identifies and describes four categories describing most people's senses of humor:

1. *Conventional.* In the conventional sense of humor, two or more people find common ground by sharing a similar humorous perception and laughing at the same thing. Laughter occurs with someone, not at someone. There is a mutual appreciation for things that appear universally funny. Johnny Carson's sidekick, Ed McMahon, who laughed at nearly everything, might be an example of the conventional sense of humor.

2. *Life of the party.* While some people soak up humorous episodes like a sponge, others have the ability to provide laughable moments for the amusement of everyone else. People with this sense of humor are the ones who wear the lamp shades at parties, recite numerous jokes and always remember the punch lines, and can tell any story and make it funny. These people love an audience and may have played the role of class clown in school in younger days. They are spontaneous, creative, and quick-witted. They have the ability to make everyone laugh, or at least smile. This is the kind of person you want to call up when you're feeling down and need to lift your spirits. Someone who pulls up alongside you at a red light, rolls down the window, and asks if you have any Grey Poupon mustard has this sense of humor.

3. *Creative.* This sense of humor is best observed in those whose professional career is joke writing. They are extremely quick-witted, very imaginative, and creative. These are people who can find humor in just about anything. People with the creative sense of humor frequently laugh to themselves, and if you ask them, "What's so funny?" they might tell you, or they might just say, "It was nothing." They are easily entertained. Although creative in their joke making, they often prefer to let someone else make the delivery. Anonymous graffitists also fall into this category.

4. *Good sport.* A good-sport sense of humor is demonstrated by those who can laugh at their own foibles and mistakes and enjoy being human. These people know how to employ self-parody and make good use of it. With this style, laughter is used to cope with personal imperfections rather than rationalize pitfalls. These people can take a practical joke without calling a lawyer afterward. In the sense of good sportsmanship, the walls of the ego are low if not completely dissolved after a practical joke.

Theories of Humor

For ages, perhaps longer, humankind has tried to understand just what it is that makes somebody laugh. As might be expected, no one answer appeared. To date, there are four major theories to explain the lighter side of human nature, as described by humor scholars Ziv (1984); Goldstein and McGhee (1972); and Bonham (1988). First, according to Steve Allen, Jr., "Humor is a physical release, one of four, actually. These include crying, yawning, orgasm, and laughter. You can do them in succession, just get the order right." Where appropriate, I have included a joke from Novak and Waldok's *Big Book of American Humor* to illustrate these theories.

Superiority Theory

Superiority theory, thought to be originated by Plato during the fourth century B.C., is the oldest one attempting to explain people's affinity for the ridiculous. When laughter occurs at the expense of someone else, as in mockery or ridicule, so that the end result is that the jokester feels better than the object of ridicule, then the reason for laughter illustrates superiority theory (Box 12.1). To laugh at someone else's misfortunes gives slight, and temporary, comfort to our own condition. Typically, the greater the dignity of the object—for example, President Clinton and his sexual escapades, Queen Elizabeth picking her nose in public, and Vice President Dan Quayle and his misspellings and verbal gaffes—the greater the laugh.

Superiority theory is also said to be the reason for negative and offensive humor. According to Goldstein and McGhee (1972), superiority theory explains aggression-based humor used to define and maintain ego boundaries. It is often used to boost or lower self-esteem, depending on which end of the joke you are on. At the extreme in this category are sarcasm, and ethnic, sexist, and racist jokes.

Incongruity (Surprise) Theory

On *Saturday Night Live,* parodies of commercials are part of the format and sometimes only seasoned veterans can distinguish the real ads from the fake ones. In one car commercial, to demonstrate how smoothly the car rode over roads filled with potholes from hell, in the back seat a circumcision was performed on a crying newborn. To the delight (and relief) of the parents, the operation was a success.

Incongruity theory concerns two unrelated thoughts joined for a surprisingly comic effect (Box 12.2). Humor

Box 12.1

You know what city I hate? Billings, Montana. Don't go. The 7-11 is called a 2-5. They had a fashion show at Sears & Roebuck. No models. They would open a catalog and point. And I would come on stage—you want to be good even though it's Billings, Montana—and I looked down and there was this woman nursing a child. Do you find that normal? The kid was fourteen years old. Turns out it wasn't hers, thank God!

—Joan Rivers

Box 12.2

A cabbie picks up a nun. She gets into the cab, and the cab driver won't stop staring at her. She asks him why is he staring and he replies, "I have a question to ask you but I don't want to offend you." She answers, "My dear son, you cannot offend me. When you're as old as I am and have been a nun as long as I have, you get a chance to see and hear just about everything. I'm sure that there's nothing you could say or ask that I would find offensive."

"Well, I've always had a fantasy to have a nun kiss me." She responds, "Well, let's see what we can do about that: but first, you have to be single and second, you must be Catholic." The cab driver is very excited and says, "Yes, I am single and I'm Catholic too!" The nun says "Ok, pull into the next alley." He does and the nun fulfills his fantasy. But when they get back on the road, the cab driver starts crying. "My dear child," said the nun, "why are you crying?" "Forgive me sister, but I have sinned. I lied, I must confess, I'm married and I'm Jewish." The nun says, "That's OK. My name is Tom and I'm on my way to a Halloween party."

arises because the mind just doesn't expect the outcome. As eighteenth-century philosopher Immanuel Kant once said, "Laughter is the affliction arising from the sudden transformation of a strained expectation into nothing."

Ziv (1984) maintains that a surprise in the processing of information can best be described as incongruous; the juxtaposition of two strikingly different concepts (e.g., a Chinese mariachi player). Oxymorons fall into this category. Humor and creativity are lifetime partners in incongruity theory. Koestler (1964) described this creative thought process as bisociation, the catalyst of humor, especially incongruous humor.

There are said to be two types of incongruity: ascending, or "ah ha," which produces wonder and awe, and descending, or "ha ha," which produces humor.

Thus, the incongruity theory is a cognitive-based theory necessitating the intellectual processing of information. The formation of thoughts that do not fit the mold of pattern recognition trigger either a light-bulb effect, or a smile.

Split-brain research on subjects who suffered cerebral strokes indicates that humor is most likely a right-brain function. In a study reported by Vera Robinson (1991), stroke patients with right-brain damage showed no sign of amusement at the punch lines of a series of hundreds of jokes. Incongruity theory suggests that the left brain tries to analyze the joke's contents. When the punch line is revealed, the left brain is stumped and the right brain picks up the meaning, resulting in a laugh. But as Confucius said, "He who laughs last didn't get the joke."

Release/Relief Theory

Release/relief theory suggest that people laugh because they need to release nervous energy built up from repressed thoughts. This theory is credited to Freud. In his study of the psychology of humor, which included works by Mark Twain, Freud asserted that the act of laughter is a physical release or expression of sexual and hostile impulses suppressed by the conscious mind. He believed that the greater the suppression of these thoughts, the greater the laughter in response (Box 12.3). Thus, humor, Freud postulated, is a reflection of underlying anxieties. Release/relief theory is applied to taboo humor, those subjects that are not socially acceptable in mixed company or professional settings. Freud's theory attempted to explain the popularity of these jokes. Taboo subjects that include sexual references are "dirty jokes," but jokes can come from other social taboos such as illegal drugs and questionable behavior, as shown on the bumper sticker "Cocaine addiction is God's way of saying you make too much money." Freud believed that humor was a "rare and precious gift," and he called it the most advanced defense mechanism. (By the way, Twain was not impressed with this or many other of Freud's theories.)

Divinity Theory

Although recognized intuitively for quite some time, the newest theory of the humor phenomenon is that it strengthens the spiritual nature of humanity. The divinity theory suggests that humor is a gift from God.

Box 12.3

One day a man came home and, as he walked into the kitchen, his wife smacked him over the head with a frying pan. As he got up off the floor and shook himself off, he said to her, "What did you do that for?" She replied, "Because you're a rotten lover." The man politely grabbed the frying pan out of his wife's hand and proceeded to smack her on the head with it. After she got up off the floor and shook herself off, she said to him, "Why did you do that?" Her husband replied, "That's for knowing the difference."

A very rich couple lived a comfortable life in a very affluent suburb. But soon times got tough and money was becoming an issue. One day, after going over his finances for the third time, the husband turned to his wife, and said, "We have to makes some changes in our lifestyle. We cannot afford to live this life of luxury. If you could learn to make breakfast, lunch, and dinner, we could fire the cook. His wife replied, "And if you could learn to make love, we could fire the butler and chauffeur."

In his book *Humor: God's Gift,* author Tal Bonham supports his theory with a host of anecdotes, from stories in the Bible to well-researched case studies. The same theory is espoused by Cal Samra in his book *The Joyful Christ.* Humor, they believe, makes order out of chaos by dissolving threats (both anger and anxieties) to the ego (Fig. 12.5). Humor can also reveal the naked truth about topics people are often unable to address any other way; in the words of Chaucer, "Many a truth be told in jest." Perhaps most importantly, humor has an adhesive quality that connects and bonds people together, if only for the duration of a joke, and connectedness is a component of spiritual well-being. This theory is also shared by the Dalai Lama, who advocates laughing and smiling as means to cleanse the spirit.

Humor, as Bonham explains, is God's way of telling us we're not perfect. Laughter and giggling are natural responses by children as they explore life. It is ironic that in a child's first year, parents are elated when the baby smiles and giggles; in fact, these behaviors are strongly encouraged. But as children mature, they are told to wipe the smile off their faces, act their age, and stop laughing. A strong message may be received that the expression of humor isn't appropriate or appreciated, to the detriment of their spiritual development.

There is also a connection between clowns and a divine presence in many cultures spanning the globe. Medicine men and shamans have dressed in funny outfits and acted in outrageous ways, which has been, and continues to be, regarded as clownlike in their respective cultures. A similar concept was adopted in Europe with the introduction of clowns in circuses as a form of entertainment. With an androgynous face mask or makeup that was neither male nor female, these people held the mystical power to heal. To this day, clowns still have this appeal and are used in hospital wards, especially in children's hospitals throughout the United States. There is even a story that, years ago, in Sunday services held for employees of the Barnum and Bailey Circus, the altar boys were always the circus clowns. Does God have a sense of humor? Most theologians think (and hope) so.

It is quite possible for some of these theories to blend or combine together to explain the laughter response. For example, if the Queen of England were to tell a Polish joke (which she hasn't done), it could be interpreted as an argument for superiority theory. However, laughter could also arise from the incongruity of this sense of humor among royalty, or even the release of anxiety from the perception of ethnic jokes as taboo. Despite the different theories as to why we laugh, one idea is agreed upon: humor helps us cope with the stress of everyday life.

Humor Therapy as a Coping Technique

In simplest terms, the use of humor is a defense mechanism. Yet, unlike other conscious or unconscious defense strategies to protect the ego, such as rationalization and projection, humor seems to dissolve the walls of the ego rather than intensify them.

Figure 12.5 The divinity theory of humor becomes evident in cartoons like *Non-Sequitur. (NON-SEQUITUR © Wiley Miller. Dist. By UNIVERSAL PRESS SYNDICATE. Reprinted with permission. All rights reserved.)*

Humor is the one defense mechanism that can increase pleasure and reduce pain at the same moment; two effects for the price of one. Theorists agree that humor is an adaptive coping mechanism liberating the ego. A 1978 article in *Psychology Today* asserted that the average person laughs about fifteen times per day (with approximately the same frequency of anger episodes). Humor's greatest asset is to balance the emotional scale between positive and negative perceptions. While the study of psychology has maintained a particular bent toward the darker side of the human psyche, even this is beginning to change, in both the focus of research and the application of psychotherapy. Many psychologists argue that the expression of laughter and smiling is nothing less than a catharsis of emotions, a physical release tied to emotional thoughts. Overall, a well-intended catharsis can be quite healthy to the mind and body. But the complexity of humor hints of something more than just catharsis. In any event, mirth serves as a catalyst to unite mind, body, and spirit for total well-being.

Humor can be used to diffuse both anger and anxiety, and it can be quite powerful at reducing both emotions. Frank Prerost (1987), of Western Illinois University, conducted a study on the use of humor as catharsis for aggression. Subjects (144 women) were first measured with a Health Locus of Control survey. Then they were asked to rate the funniness of twelve jokes. Results indicated that aggression-based humor was the most effective in allowing a catharsis of anger in women with an internal locus of control. Research by Leftcourt and Martin (1986) and Porterfield (1987) also indicates that humor acts as a "stress buffer," or moderator, to decrease the impact of stressful experiences, particularly the anxiety of major life-event changes and everyday annoyances.

Frankl, the survivor of Auschwitz discussed in earlier chapters, noted in his book *Man's Search for Meaning* that humor was a saving grace among fellow prisoners in the shadows of death. Frankl wrote, "Humor was another of the soul's weapons in the fight for self-preservation." Fear of death even has its own brand of mirth: black humor. People often joke about death and dying in an effort to ease their tension and perhaps better understand their own mortal plight. Hollywood often uses comic relief in horror movies (e.g., *Jaws* and *The Silence of the Lambs*) so that the audience isn't so emotionally spent that they miss the film's climactic scene. It is virtually impossible to be both angry and happy at the same time. Thus, if you can separate yourself from your aggression for a moment and see how silly and out of character prolonged anger really is, feelings of hostility dissipate, succumbing to a crescendo of mirth. For this reason, self-parody is thought to be the type of humor best suited to dispel anger.

In the book *The Healing Power of Humor,* Klein states that the use of humor gives a sense of power in the midst of chaos. Being able to make light of a stressful circumstance allows people to feel they have control over a situation. Humor becomes a weapon to disarm the cause of the stress response. While some consider humor as a catalyst to tap the power of intelligence and emotional fortitude, others see it as a diversion tactic. In this case, humor allows for an intermission in the cognitive war against stressors and a "cease fire" of the stress response. The use of **humor therapy** in several hospital settings, as noted by Norman Cousins in his book *Head First,* helps to alleviate the sterile atmosphere these institutions are known for by allowing cancer patients to momentarily forget intravenous tubes, chemotherapy, radiation treatments, and bedpans.

In an attempt to better understand humor appreciation, *Psychology Today* conducted a survey of its readers in 1978. Thirty jokes were printed along with a questionnaire to gauge readers' opinions of their quality and laughability. Over 14,000 questionnaires were returned, and responses varied as much as the styles of jokes printed. Humor, like beauty, is a relative concept. The study concluded that sexual humor was the most popular topic of jest, with ethnic humor running a close second. Humor scholar Avner Ziv (1984) offers two reasons why sexual humor remains so popular. First, the craving for sexual humor compensates for the continuous desire to physically satisfy this basic human drive. Second, sexual humor may compensate for the disappointment of unmet sexual expectations.

Comic relief is currently used as a mode of therapy in many rehabilitation programs, including the treatment of physical trauma, alcoholism, and drug addiction. Psychologists who recognize the effectiveness of humor and utilize comic relief with their patients identify it as both an assessment tool, to indicate values, inner feelings, and meaning in life, and a therapeutic tool, to encourage a cathartic release of emotions. In psychotherapy, it is the patient's own use of humor that is nurtured and encouraged; it is not initiated by the therapist. When patients begin to joke about their conditions or predicaments, it is acknowledged as a breakthrough in the emotional self-healing process. Once manifested, the practice of comic relief is encouraged during laughable moments. Humor has been found to be very effective in aiding patients through the transitions of the many stages of recovery.

Just like other coping techniques that can prove ineffective for resolution, the power of humor can be abused. Negative and offensive humor such as racial, ethnic, and sexist humor, as well as sarcasm in both its delivery and reception, do not lend themselves to satisfaction as coping mechanisms. Negative humor may inflate self-esteem, but it is a false inflation with no lasting value. Humor can also be used as a means of seeking approval, by controlling other people's attitudes and making them feel good. Used in this manner, humor takes on an addictive quality, where each laugh becomes a "fix" leading to the next laugh. Thus, humor employed to win the approval of others takes on the quality of codependent behavior. In a study by Fisher (1983) investigating the personalities of comedians, it was observed that many professional comedians and humorists were raised in less-than-enviable environments, including homes with alcoholic parents (Carol Burnett), orphanages (Charlie Chaplin, Art Buchwald), or broken families. In these cases, the use of humor often brought recognition, approval, and a feeling of self-validation. In her book *It's Always Something,* comedian Gilda Radner described her use of comedy as an occasionally negative behavior: "Comedy is very controlling—you are making people laugh. You feel completely in control when you hear a wave of laughter coming back that you have caused. Probably that's why people in comedy can be so neurotic and have so many problems. Sometimes we talk about it as a need to be loved, but I think that with me it was also a need to control."

As a coping technique, humor therapy has the immediate effect of increasing awareness of the cause of stress, which may then lead to the path of resolution. The greater the quantity of laughs and the quality of humor, the greater the sensation of pleasure. The long-term effects of comic relief as a coping mechanism at best remain a mystery, particularly because

these have not been investigated to any great degree. In a study conducted at the headquarters of the United States Postal Service, a humor course was offered to a select group of employees. Meeting once a week during the noon hour for a month, participants were exposed to both theories of humor therapy and several comedy videos and cassette tapes. Participants were then measured, by means of questionnaires, to evaluate self-esteem prior to and after the completion of the course, as well as perceived stress before and after each session. Results revealed that exposure to humorous material seemed to have the immediate effect of decreasing perceived stress levels, but apparently had no significant prolonged effect on self-esteem, indicating that humor therapy is most effective in dealing with current perceptions and their related emotions.

The Physiology of Humor

Norman Cousins was right: Positive emotions augment the mind/body relationship. Laughter indeed influences the body's physiology, resulting in restoration and possibly healing. In his own clinical tests, Cousins noted that several hours of laughter produced a small but significant decrease in the sedimentation rate of his blood, a predictor of inflammation or infection. In *Anatomy of an Illness,* Cousins wrote, "The drop itself (five points) was not substantial, but it was cumulative." Once thought of as only a coping technique, humor therapy now qualifies as a relaxation technique as well because of its physiological effects. Since this discovery, scientists have investigated the mysteries of the immune system and its relationship to the experience and expression of various emotions.

Dr. William Fry has devoted his life to the investigation of this mind-body relationship, and his work has yielded some fascinating results. Laughter appears to have both short-term and long-term effects on the body's major physiological systems. In the short term, a bout of laughter appears to initiate the stress response, with a slight increase in heart rate, blood pressure, muscle tension, and ventilations. But this is quickly followed by a rebound effect, where these parameters decrease to below previous resting levels. The overall effect is a profound level of homeostasis, much like that seen when progressive muscular relaxation is practiced. In the short term, laughter is credited with stabilizing blood pressure, "massaging" vital

Stress With a Human Face

IT WAS A HOT SUMMER DAY, AND THE POOL looked so inviting. Andrew was a bright, good-looking, athletic kid about to enter high school. That day, he and his younger brother were making the most of their summer freedom. The odds of what was about to happen were about as great as winning $20 million in the lottery, except Andrew wasn't that lucky. For some reason no one seems able to explain, the angle at which he entered the deep water was just enough to snap his second vertebra and paralyze him from the neck down. Within the blink of an eye, freedom became a word he would cry over. And cry he did. In his therapy, he withdrew into his own world of darkness.

But one of his nurses had a natural funny bone that reverberated in its enthusiasm, and in time it became infectious. Soon Andrew asked to have some cartoon books brought in to him, as well as some comedy videos. His bouts of depression became fewer and fewer. It seemed that with his change in attitude came a desire to leave the hospital and get back to as normal a life as could be expected.

If you could see Andrew today, you would be drawn immediately toward his smile, an attribute he cherishes. Oh, he still has his down times like

the rest of us, but he will be the first to tell you of the healing power of humor and how it enabled him to cope with a stressor he would have never imagined facing that fine summer day. Currently, he is a self-proclaimed ambassador of humor therapy for the disabled, traveling around the country to share his stories of comic relief. The new joy in his life is his wife, Lauren, and their newborn baby girl, Alexis. ✦

organs, stimulating circulation, facilitating digestion, and increasing oxygenated blood throughout the body. Fry (1986) stated that, "Laughter is clearly related to the reduction of stress and the physical symptoms related to stress."

Fry also conducted a series of studies on the composition of tears, those shed from pain and laughter as well as those artificially induced (e.g., from cutting onions). His research revealed that the constituents of emotional teardrops include a greater percentage of proteins and toxins than those produced artificially. Fry concluded that tears due to emotional responses serve to rid the body of stress-related toxins. Once again, this suggests that physical expressions—both laughter and crying—are natural and healthy to the

well-being of the individual. As author Kurt Vonnegut once quipped (Klein, 1989), "Laughter and tears are both responses to frustration and exhaustion. I myself prefer to laugh, since there is less cleaning up to do afterward."

Perhaps more impressive than the short-term effects of laughter are its long-term effects. Through the new multidiscipline of PNI, researchers are now finding that the immune system plays an ever-increasing role in the mind-body relationship. In the words of Bernie Siegel, "Thoughts are chemicals; they can either kill or cure." It appears that thoughts and perceptions are quickly transformed in the brain into chemical reactions that have impact throughout the body. Negative thoughts actually trigger the neural release of the stress hormones, and suppress the immune system. Positive thoughts strengthen the integrity of the immune system by inducing the release of special neuropeptides from the pituitary gland and other tissues located throughout the body. Neuropeptides—endorphins, interleukins, and interferon, to name a few—act as messenger molecules to various organs throughout the body.

Recent research has revealed that neuropeptides are also manufactured and released by the lymph nodes and other components of the immune systems (see Chapter 3). While only sixty neuropeptides have been discovered to date, scientists believe there may be several more acting in the interest of the body's immune system. In effect, laughter causes the body to produce its own pain killers. A study by David McClellen (1989) measured changes in secretory immunoglobin A (S-IgA), a salivary immune-defense agent, as a result of three emotional responses (humor, cynicism, and trust) elicited by three types of movies. Films of W. C. Fields and Mother Teresa produced a significant rise in S-IgA, while a Nazi propaganda film corresponded with a decrease. The long-term effects of humor and the positive emotions it produces may serve as one of the most beneficial health practices currently known to humanity. It would be unwise to suggest that humor-induced laughter can cure all ailments; this simply isn't true. But humor can "lighten the load," making the pain of some diseases more bearable. In some remarkable incidences, such as that reported by Norman Cousins, there may also be a true healing effect. As discussed in Chapter 3, there are currently too many missing pieces to complete the mind-body model to our full comprehension. But in the short time that humor therapy has been employed as a therapeutic agent in cancer wards, many patients have been given the opportunity to die with a smile instead of a lonely frown. And their loved ones have that fond memory to look back on.

Steps to Initiate Humor Therapy

In 1991, I designed and taught an experimental course entitled Humor and Health. At least once a week, I was asked by students how they could improve their sense of humor. From the volumes of resources I read in preparation for this course, I gleaned a number of ways to incorporate humor therapy into your arsenal of stress-management coping techniques. The best suggestions are as follows.

1. *Learn not to take life too seriously.* Chris Flanagan, R.N., is the head nurse on the oncology unit at Shady Grove Adventist Hospital in Rockville, Maryland. Chris was awarded a grant from the Hyatt Foundation to start a Humor Cart on her cancer ward. Describing her work, Chris said, "We have a policy on my floor: Take your work seriously, but take yourself lightly." Most oncology wards have high turnover rates among nursing staff, but this philosophy has kept the nursing staff at Shady Grove intact for several years now. In a nutshell, this attitude means seeing yourself as more than your work. Many times we place all our eggs in the career basket, and if we have a bad day at work, then our self-esteem withers away. See yourself as a whole person, with many aspects and talents, not just as a student, spouse, or professional. People who are able to laugh at their mistakes are considered more emotionally sound than those who fret at the slightest hint of imperfections. We start out in life as a square block. Through a multitude of life's experiences, we polish the rough edges, and by the end, finish up a gem.

2. *Find one humorous thing a day.* Humorous events and concepts are around us all the time. Life is full of ironies, incongruencies, and just plain funny stuff. One's frame of mind is either receptive to these, or simply dismisses them. If humor is a perception, as is currently believed, then the way to adopt comic relief as a coping mechanism is to adopt this humorous frame of mind and make it your own (cognitive restructuring). It is commonly understood that if you make yourself consciously aware of and receptive to an idea, you will attract things to reinforce this perception many times over. Take planning a holiday, for example. You decide that this summer you want to go on a safari in Kenya. Once you commit yourself to the trip, you discover all kinds of people who have gone on safari with the same touring company, you start noticing ads in magazines and TV

American Graffiti

Box 12.4

I thought drugs were fun, til I started studying pharmacology.

Contraception should be used at every conceivable moment.

Linguistics is the exact opposite of screaming.

Talk is cheap, until you hire a lawyer.

If corn oil comes from corn, and coconut oil comes from coconuts, where does baby oil come from?

All I ask for is the chance to show that money cannot buy happiness.

If pro is the opposite of con, what is the opposite of progress?

No man is an island, but when you piss, urination!

If I told you you had a beautiful body, would you hold it against me?

There is no gravity, the earth sucks!

If a sheep is a ram, and a donkey is an ass, how come a ram in the ass is a goose?

There once was a monk from Algeria
Who's knowledge was somewhat inferior.
One night of good fun
With a comely young nun,
And now, she's mother superior.

---

specials, and your mind becomes a magnet for news and ideas about Africa. The same can be done with humor, if you make yourself receptive to the lighter side of life. Tell yourself that you want to find one funny thing each day. You will find that instead of just one little tickle, you will discover a wealth of humorous experiences each and every day. In addition, allocate some fun time for each day, whether this means watching your favorite sitcom on television, reading comics, or going to your nearest comedy club.

It is important to remember, however, that there are times when it is inappropriate to laugh. People can interpret laughter as rude during serious moments; so use caution and judgment. On the other hand, life is full of *laughable moments,* when it is quite acceptable to laugh and smile. When these times arise, capitalize on them and give yourself permission to let go and enjoy.

3. *Work to improve your imagination and creativity.* Creativity and humor are virtually inseparable. One has only to read headlines in supermarket tabloids to be reminded of this: "Termite Baby Eats Newlyweds' House," "Bigfoot Seen Boarding a UFO," "Ski Mask Found on Surface of Mars," "Teenager Swallows Seed, Grows Palm Tree in Stomach." Lately, the creative

"muscle" of many an American has atrophied as the adrenal gland has hypertrophied. Remember, the funny bone is just as susceptible to the general adaptation syndrome as is your adrenal gland. Start placing more emphasis on this target organ. It is commonly thought (and currently under study) that the use of one right-brain cognitive function enhances other functions of the same hemisphere. Imagination is a right-brain function. So is humor. They tend to feed off each other. So how does one augment imagination skills? Here are a few suggestions:

a. Read more books (fiction and nonfiction) and watch less television.

b. Write a story, fable, or poem every now and then.

c. Play with children. Kids have wonderful imaginations. Maybe some of theirs will transfer to you by osmosis. Get closer to the earth. Observe the world from the eye level of a young child.

d. Go exploring. Do something completely new and outrageous. Spend an afternoon in a hardware store, a museum of fine art, or a greenhouse. Get out of the comfortable rut you take refuge in and discover the world all over again.

e. Create something. Pull out a cookbook and play "Chef Tel." Make your own holiday presents this year. Invent something. Plant a garden. Bonsai a tree. Plan a trip around the world. Start a new hobby. Make your world a better place to live in.

4. *Start a joke/cartoon-of-the-week swap with a friend.* Use either the U.S. mail, fax, or e-mail so that you have something to look forward to, as well as making someone else's day with a chuckle.

5. *Learn to hyperexaggerate when describing a situation or story.* A comedian begins his monologue, "I knew a guy so ugly . . ." and a call comes back from the audience, "How ugly was he?" The comedian continues, "He was so ugly that if you were to look up the word *ugly* in the dictionary, you'd find his picture beside the definition." Exaggeration is a staple in virtually all comedians' joke repertoires. Comparisons are hilarious when they are exaggerated, and they can lighten up the description of the most stressful event. Ways to employ exaggeration include substitution of familiar words with others (e.g., since your last communiqué . . .) and use of figurative versus literal meanings (e.g., Why do we drive on a parkway, and park on a driveway?). Creative use of metaphor is also a component of exaggeration for a good laugh, as in "My final in economics was worse than the Spanish Inquisition."

6. *Build a humor library.* One of the essentials of coping is the use of available resources, which can include anything and everything. For humor therapy, resources involve the collection and use of books, tapes, and videos, and even hand buzzers and water guns. Designate a small corner of your home for a humor library and start to fill the shelves with a collection of every conceivable resource. Record and video stores have designated comedy sections; book stores have humor sections. No matter how often you have heard favorite tapes or read favorite books, they will still trigger a laugh. Don't let these resources collect dust, either. Make a habit of using them frequently.

Here is another idea: start a *tickler notebook.* Buy a notebook and fill it with anything that puts a smile on your face. It can include,

among other things, cartoons, favorite jokes, letters, funny photographs with your captions attached, favorite newspaper columns, love poems, and a host of personal items (birthday cards, postcards, photographs, etc.) that make you feel good inside. When I assigned the tickler notebook to my Humor and Health students, I gave these instructions: "Imagine that one day you are diagnosed with a major illness (e.g., cancer). What humor time capsule can you assemble that upon review is bound to jack up your white blood cell count and put you on the road to recovery?" We all have down moments; this is perfectly natural. But an extended period of negative emotions is neither natural nor healthy. A tickler notebook is your personal prescription. And it is a growing organism; keep feeding and looking after it. Treat it well and it will repay you a hundred times over.

7. *Find a host of varied humor venues.* Telling jokes is only a pebble of the mountain we call humor, yet it is often the first thing we think of when we hear the word. But humor can be found in a multitude of venues, and the greater the access to a wide variety of humor media, the more advantageous this coping skill will be to deal with stress. Humor venues include (but are not limited to) movies, theater, books, music, television, and live stand-up comedy. Humor and entertainment are also very compatible, if not always the same. The human mind likes to be entertained. Be on the lookout for ways to incorporate a wide variety of humor venues into your lifestyle.

8. *Access your humor network.* Every now and then, there are bound to be times when you find yourself on the bottom rung of the emotional ladder. These moments should be recognized, and perhaps for a short time, even appreciated. But if, after an allocated period of "emotional down time," you need some help getting up again, don't be afraid to call for help. We all know someone who can make us smile at the mere thought of his or her name. Call this person up and ask for a "humor lift." It's the next best thing to being there. Conversely, it would be a good habit to

Patch Adams, M.D., has dedicated his career in the healing profession to the use of humor rather than drugs as his primary tool of trade. Sharing humor seems to multiply the effect of laughter on well-being.

Figure 12.6

minimize time spent with people who seem to live with black clouds over their heads; their pessimism is not conducive to enhancing your positive emotions. You don't have to go down with their ship.

9. *Improve your self-esteem.* It is hard to laugh when your self-esteem is deflated. At times, we all think we are fat, ugly, or stupid, and these characteristics constitute the punch line of many a joke. Low self-esteem derives from negative feedback we create in our own minds and come to believe. Remember Einstein's theory: everything is relative. Separate fact from fiction. Give yourself positive affirmations every day, accentuate your good qualities, and learn to accept and love yourself and all your human potential.

Best Application of Comic Relief

Humor therapy integrates a little cognitive reappraisal, a little behavior modification, and a lot of fun. Employing comic relief as a coping style involves a conscious effort to live life on the lighter side. Humor therapy does not try to eclipse the emotions associated with anger, fear, or sadness; it only attempts to neutralize them so that there is balance to your emotional responses. To best apply the use of humor in your life, take note of what sense of humor you best identify with and see if you can sharpen this edge a little. Also note which type of humor you find most gratifying and make a habit of employing more of it in the course of each day. In addition, monitor your high and low moods and their durations. If you find that the majority of your thoughts are negative, jaded, or laced with pessimism, try to balance these out with a greater number of positive, even humorous, thoughts. No one who advocates humor therapy suggests that everybody should always be smiling. This is neither realistic nor healthy. Emotional well-being is the ability to feel and express the *full* range of human emotions, both positive and negative. The danger lies in the imbalance of positive and negative emotions, as a preponderance of the latter will ultimately inflict bodily damage. Cousins highlighted humor as a symbol of all the positive emotions that can lend themselves to emotional well-being. Use humor therapy to find and maintain that balance of human emotions in your life.

Summary

- Cousins legitimized the use of humor therapy when he treated himself with hours of funny films, which contributed to the remission of his fatal disease. The premise of the therapy was that if negative thoughts can result in illness and disease, positive thoughts should enhance health. He also believed that for his health to return he had to take personal responsibility for it.

- Greeks advocated humor therapy over 2,000 years ago, as did ancient Africans, American Indians, and medieval European kings and queens. However, laughter was declared by the Puritans to be the work of the devil, and to laugh or smile was considered a sin.

- Humor is *not* a positive emotion, but it can elicit several positive emotions. Humor, like stress, is a perception.

- Humor is a very complex phenomenon. There are many types of humor, including parody, satire, slapstick, absurd/nonsense, black, irony, dry, and sarcasm. Self-parody is thought to be the best type of humor to reduce stress, whereas sarcasm is the worst.

- Just as there are different types of personalities, there are also several senses of humor, including conventional, life of the party, creative, and good-sport.

- There is no one accepted reason why we laugh. Four theories attempt to explain the nature of the funny bone: superiority theory, incongruity (surprise) theory, release/relief theory, and the divinity theory.

- Research investigating the psychoneuroimmunological effects of laughter have found that there is a strong relationship between good health and good humor. In essence, laughter helps restore physiological homeostasis.

- Studies also show that humor promotes mental, emotional, physical, and spiritual well-being.

- There are many ways to tickle your funny bone and augment your sense of humor, but like anything that is worth having, you have to work at it.

Concepts and Terms

Absurd/nonsense humor

Black humor

Bisociation

Conventional sense of humor

Creative sense of humor

Divinity theory

Double entendre

Dry humor/puns

Good-sport sense of humor

Humor

Incongruity theory

Life of the party sense of humor

Parody

Release/relief theory

Sarcasm

Satire

Senses of humor

Slapstick

Superiority theory

Tickler notebook

Self-Assessment

1. How would you rate your sense of humor? Excellent   Good   Fair   Poor

   Why? _____

   _____

   _____

   _____

2. Into which of the four classifications of sense of humor (conventional, life of the party, creative, good sport) does your sense of humor fall?

   _____

3. Are you a person who uses sarcasm often?   Yes   No

   If so, why? _____

   _____

   _____

   _____

4. List the ways in which you use humor to cope with stress. If your list is short, add to it by thinking up ways in which you could introduce more humor therapy into your life.

   1. _____

   2. _____

   3. _____

   4. _____

   5. _____

   6. _____

   7. _____

   8. _____

   9. _____

   10. _____

References and Resources

Allen, S., Jr. Humor and Creativity Conference, Saratoga, NY, Apr. 21, 1990.

Anthony, J. and Hurley, J. Humor Therapy: To Heal Is to Make Happy, *Nursing Clinical Currents.* Shady Grove Adventist Hospital, Rockville, MD 2(1):1–4, 1989.

Apte, M. *Humor and Laughter.* Cornell University Press, Ithaca, New York, 1985.

Black, D. Laughter, *Journal of American Medical Association* 252:2995–2998, 1984.

Blalock, J. The Immune System as a Sensory Organ, *Journal of Immunology* 132:1067–1069, 1984.

Blumenfeld, E. and Alpern L. *The Smile Connection: How to Use Humor in Dealing with People.* Prentice-Hall, New York, 1986.

Bombeck, E. *I Want to Grow Hair, I Want to Grow Up, I Want to Go to Boise.* Harper & Row, New York, 1989.

Bonham, T. *Humor: God's Gift.* Broadman Press, Nashville, TN, 1988.

Borge, V. International Humor Treasure, *Humor Matters* 7:127–139, 1991.

Boston, R. *An Anatomy of Laughter.* Collins Press, London, 1974.

Chapman, A. and Foot, H. *Humor and Laughter.* Wiley, New York, 1976.

Cousins, N. *Anatomy of an Illness.* Norton, New York, 1976.

Cousins, N. Anatomy of the Illness (as Perceived by the Patient), *New England Journal of Medicine* 295(26):1458–1463, 1978.

Cousins, N. Beware of Those Who Can't Stand Good News, *Christian Science Monitor,* December 27, 1988.

Cousins, N. *Head First.* Penguin Books, New York, 1989.

Dossey, L. Now You Are Fit to Live: Humor and Health, *Alternative Therapies in Health and Medicine* 2(5):8–13, 98, 1996.

Ed, F. *God Grant Me the Laughter: A Treasury of Twelve-Step Humor.* CompCare Publishers, Minneapolis, MN, 1989.

Fisher, S. and Fisher, R. Personality and Psychopathology in the Comic. In *Handbook of Human Research.* ed. P. McGhee and J. Goldstein, Springer-Verlag, New York, 1983.

Frankl, V. *Man's Search for Meaning.* Pocket Books, New York, 1956.

Freud, S. *Jokes and Their Relation to the Unconscious.* Norton, New York, 1960.

Fry, W. and Rader, C. The Respiratory Component of Mirthful Laughter, *Journal of Biological Psychology* 24:38–50, 1977.

Fry, W. and Salameh, W., eds. *Handbook of Humor and Psychotherapy.* Professional Resource Exchange, Sarasota, FL, 1986.

Goldstein, J. and McGhee, P. *The Psychology of Humor.* Academic Press, New York, 1972.

Graham, B. The Healing Power of Humor, *Mind-Body Health Digest* 4(2):1–6, 1990.

Hageseth, C. *Positive Humor 101.* Berwick, Fort Collins, CO, 1989.

Hassett, J. and Houlihan, J. Different Jokes for Different Folks, *Psychology Today* 12:64–71, 1979.

Hassett, J., and Houlihan, J. What's So Funny? *Psychology Today* 12:101–113, 1978.

Hillard, N. *Laughing: A Psychology of Humor.* Cornell University Press, Ithaca, New York, 1982.

Kant, I. *Critique of Pure Reason,* ed. K. Norman. St. Martin's, New York, 1969.

Keller, D. *Humor as Therapy.* Pine Mountain Press, Wauwatosa, WI, 1984.

Klein, A. *The Healing Power of Humor.* Tarcher Press, Los Angeles, 1989.

Koestler, A. *The Act of Creation.* Hutchinson, London, 1964.

Koller, M. *Humor and Society: Expectations in the Sociology of Humor.* Cap and Gown Press, Houston, TX, 1988.

Krieger, D. Brain Peptides: What, Where, and Why, *Science* 222:975–984, 1983.

Kuhlman, T. *Humor and Psychology.* Dow Jones-Irwin, Homewood, IL, 1984.

Leftcourt, H. and Martin, R. *Humor and Life Stress.* Springer-Verlag, New York, 1986.

Lynn, K. S. *The Comic Tradition in America.* Norton, New York, 1958.

Long, P. Laugh and Be Well, *Psychology Today* 21:28–29, 1987.

Martin, R. and Leftcourt, H. Sense of Humor as a Moderator of the Relations between Stress and Moods, *Journal of Personality and Social Psychology* 45:1313–1324, 1983.

McClelland, D. C. and Kirshnit, C. The Effect of Motivation Arousal through Films on Salivary Immunoglobin A, *Psychology and Health* 2:31–52, 1989.

McGhee, P. *Humor: Origins, and Development.* Freeman, San Francisco, 1979.

McGhee, P. and Goldstein, J. *Handbook of Humor Research, Applied Studies,* vols. I & II. Springer-Verlag, New York, 1983.

Minders, H. *Laughter and Liberation: Developing Your Sense of Humor.* Nash Publications, New York, 1971.

Moody, R. *Laugh after Laugh: The Healing Power of Humor.* Headwaters Press, Jacksonville, FL, 1978.

Morreal, J. *The Philosophy of Laughter and Humor.* SUNY Press, Albany, New York, 1987.

Morreal, J. *Taking Laughter Seriously.* SUNY Press, Albany, New York, 1983.

Nahemow, L. *Humor and Aging.* Academic Press, Orlando, FL, 1986.

Novak, W. and Waldoks, M., eds. *Big Book of American Humor.* Harper, New York, 1990.

Peters, L. and Dana, B. *The Laughter Prescription.* Ballantine Books, New York, 1982.

Polivka, J. Cartoon Humor as an Aid in Therapy, *Clinical Gerontology,* Fall:63–67, 1987.

Porterfield, A. Does Sense of Humor Moderate the Impact of Life Stress on Psychological and Physiological Wellbeing? *Journal of Research and Personality* 21:306–317, 1987.

Prerost, F. Health Locus of Control, Humor, and Reduction in Aggression, *Psychological Reports* 61:887–896, 1987.

Provine, R. *Laughter: A Scientific Investigation.* Viking, New York, 2000.

Radner, G. *It's Always Something.* Simon & Schuster, New York, 1989.

Rickler, M. *The Best of Modern Humor.* Knopf, New York, 1983.

Robinson, V. *Humor and the Health Professions.* C. S. Slack, Thorofare, New Jersey, 2nd edition 1991.

Samra, C. *The Joyful Christ: The Healing Power of Humor.* HarperCollins, New York, 1986.

Sanfranek, R. and Schill, T. Coping with Stress: Does Humor Help? *Psychological Reports* 51:222, 1982.

Schafer, L. S. *The Best of Gravestone Humor.* Sterling, New York, 1990.

Schill, T. and O'Laughlin, S. Humor Preference and Coping with Stress, *Psychological Reports* 55:309–310, 1984.

Seaward, B. L. Good Vibrations: The Healing Power of Humor, *Bridges. ISSSEEM Magazine* 6(3):5–7, 16, 1995.

Seaward, B. L. Humor as a Coping Technique in the Corporate Setting, unpublished manuscript, The American University, Washington, D.C., 1992.

Seaward, B. L. Humor's Healing Potential, *Health Progress* April: 66–70, 1992.

Shaeffer, N. *The Art of Laughter.* Columbia University Press, Baltimore, 1981.

Siegel, B. *Love, Medicine and Miracles.* Perennial Books. New York, 1986.

Silberman, I. Humor and Health: An Epidemiological Study, *American Behavioral Scientist* 30:100–112, 1987.

Weisenberg, M., Tepper, I. and Schwarzwald, J. Humor as a Cognitive Technique for Increasing Pain Tolerance, *Pain* 63(2):207–212, 1995.

Wooten, P. Humor: An Antidote for Stress, *Holistic Nurses Practice* 10(2):49–56, 1996.

Wright, S. *I Have A Pony.* Warner Brothers Records, Los Angeles, 1985.

Yoshino, S. et al. Effects of Mirthful Laughter on Neuroendocrine and Immune Systems in Patients with Rheumatoid Arthritis, *Journal of Rheumatology* 23(4):793–794, 1996.

Ziv, A. *Personality and Sense of Humor.* Springer, New York, 1984.

Chapter 13 Creative Problem Solving

*Make it a practice to keep on
the lookout for novel and
interesting ideas that others
have used successfully. Your
idea only has to be original
in its adaptation to the problem you are working on.*

—Thomas Alva Edison

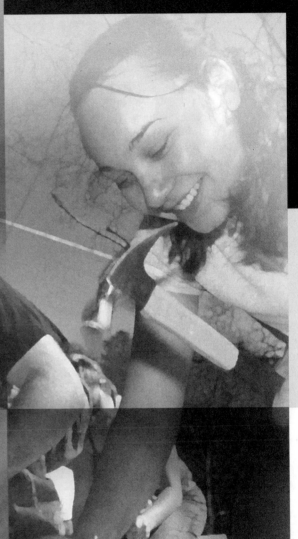

ightbulb. Bicycle. Printing press. Airplane. Cotton gin. Telephone. Each one has become an item of necessity. Necessity, it is said, is the mother of invention, and the human mind has risen to the occasion to create some fantastic inventions. There is no better time for necessity to bear the fruits of creativity than during times of frustration when one needs to get from point A to point B.

At one time, the United States took pride in its American ingenuity. Young in age and pregnant with possibilities, early generations of Americans made more improvements to the proverbial mouse trap than there are stars in the sky. Before the turn of the twentieth century, the United States was a productive society, the vast majority of its citizens making over 70 percent of their household items themselves. As the country became a consumer society, however, more and more items were bought rather than made at home. The availability of several new inventions, like the washer and dryer, provided more leisure time. But with some of these inventions, lifestyles became very comfortable, and our collective creative skills became dull. With the advent of television, it is said, the creative American mind began showing signs of atrophy. People now take a passive role in the creative process, letting other people do the important, creative thinking. Experts agree that a happy mind is a creative mind. The inability to deal with many problems is directly related to the inability to tap into and utilize creativity. It would be unfair to point the finger of blame solely at television. Many critics believe that the American educational system continues to play a role

in the decline of creative skills as well, by stifling the limits of imagination with conformity and critical-thinking skills. The dominant style of thinking in the Western hemisphere is considered left-brained: linear, logical and rational, analytical, and judgmental. Left-brain modes of thinking are those most rewarded in both school and work environments. And this style of thinking has devalued recreational and play time.

Music. Poetry. Architecture. Fiction. Art. Pottery. Photography. If necessity is the mother of invention, then play can be said to assume the paternal role in this relationship. Creativity definitely has a playful, relaxed side to it. Playing is as much a part of human nature as is work, although playful behavior often atrophies as individuals make the transition from childhood to adulthood. But play, like the creativity it stimulates, can be nurtured. It has been said that more good ideas have arisen from play in garage and basement workshops than anywhere else, including the genesis of Xerox Corporation, Hewlett Packard, and Apple Computers. Why is creativity so important? Why do corporate executives currently pay big bucks to bring in creative consultants to conduct workshops for their employees? The answer can be summed up in one word: change.

Change is inevitable. There is comfort in familiar routines, even if they are boring or stressful. Change meets resistance. Someone once said that the only person who likes change is a wet baby. But we live on a planet that travels at a rate of 66,000 miles per hour in its ellipse around the sun, with a population of over 6 billion people. Given these dynamics alone, change

Figure 13.1

is inevitable. In 1970, Alvin Toffler wrote a book, *Future Shock,* describing the rapid changes the human race would encounter in the age of high technology by the end of the twentieth century and beyond. The book might have been titled *Future Stress* because, as Toffler indicated, the shock from rapid change can be very difficult to handle, and even more difficult to adapt to. Resistance to change seems to be a basic part of human nature. Change is often equated with chaos, and chaos spells stress. This is where the importance of creativity comes in.

Creativity can help make order out of chaos. It has the ability to make change palatable, even enjoyable. But to be creative takes the right attitude and a workable strategy. The ability to be creative resides within each and every one of us. Creativity is not a gift, it is a human birthright. But like muscles that atrophy with disuse, creativity must be exercised to be effective. For those of you who have let your creative abilities slip into hibernation, here is a refresher course in the basics.

Julia Cameron is convinced that creativity is truly a birthright for each individual. In her book *The Artist's Way,* Cameron states that due to a series of factors found in American society, we have, in essence, not only dulled the edge of our creative abilities, we have even buried them. But what is lost can certainly be recovered, if not discovered, by reacquainting ourselves with the creative juices that course through our human veins. Cameron insists that the creative process is a spiritual one, and that to engage in the creative process invites us to participate as co-creators with that aspect of the divine self. Connecting with what she calls "spiritual electricity," Cameron invites people to step outside the left-brain way of thinking and unite both hemispheres of thought when calling upon the creative forces to solve problems, or to enjoy life in its fullness. Quoting sources from Johannes Brahms and Louis Armstrong to Louis Pasteur and Carl Jung (who all give credit to a divine co-partnership in innovativeness), Cameron illustrates a tapestry of creative skills that is available to everyone.

The Creative Process

The creative process is not complex, but it is wonderfully profound; profound, because there are so many possible ways to get from point A to point B. During the 1980s, intense interest in the human creative process developed. And like the goose that was cut open to find out how she laid the golden egg, the creative process has since been examined from every side, angle, and perspective, and has been dissected and inspected. Unlike the goose, though, the process wasn't killed; instead, it has become well understood, so that the creative muscle could flex with strength, power, and agility for the whim and benefit of those anxious to use it.

Figure 13.2 Creativity isn't a gift for the chosen few, it is standard equipment in the human intellect: Whoopi Goldberg (left) and Walt Disney (right).

The creative process has two parts, which by no coincidence match the functions of the right and left hemispheres of the human brain. Remember that Maslow (1987) observed a number of characteristics contributing to total well-being, or as he called it, self-actualization. Creativity was among these characteristics. In his later work on self-actualization, Maslow concluded that the creative process and the path to self-actualization were one and the same. He called the creative process the "art of being happily lost in the present moment." He divided the creative process into *primary* and *secondary* parts. Primary creativity is the origin of ideas; the playground of the mind where ideas are generated and hatched. Secondary creativity describes the strategic plan to bring to fruition the ideas brought forth in primary creativity. Secondary creativity is like the mind's workshop: a place to saw, chisel, glue, hammer, and polish ideas.

Players on the Creativity Team

Creative consultant Roger von Oech took Maslow's idea one step further, dividing primary and secondary creativity each into two phases. In his book *A Kick in the Seat of the Pants,* von Oech's model of creative thinking includes a team of four players—the explorer, artist, judge, and warrior. The explorer and artist comprise primary creativity, and the judge and warrior secondary creativity. The explorer and artist team together for what von Oech calls the germination phase of creativity. In this phase, inspiration and imagination are used to their fullest potential. The germination phase involves soft, pliable, right-brain thinking. Examples of this thinking style include irrationality, nonlinear perceptions, synthesis, metaphor, dreams, humor, and global awareness. The judge and warrior join forces in the harvesting of the creative crops sowed in the depths of imagination. The harvest phase of creativity involves hard, critical, left-brain thinking. Examples include logic, rationality, linear analysis, and factual thinking. Each type of thinking style has an equal responsibility in the creative process. The key is to let each player do its job without interference from the other three. The overall goal of creative thought is to sharpen the skills of all four team players, so that one or two aspects don't overpower the others, cause them to atrophy, and stifle the entire process. Let us take a more detailed look at the members of the creative team.

If you think you're not creative, you'll prove yourself right. You may not be a Disney, but everyone has the makings of a creative person.

Figure 13.3

The Explorer. While some ideas may actually bubble to the surface of consciousness, the human mind generally needs to be stimulated. If the mind is like a field, it needs frequent fertilization for robust growth of ideas. In the words of Nobel Prize winner Linus Pauling, "The best way to get a good idea is to get a lot of ideas," and to get a lot of ideas you need to look around. Whether abstract or concrete, the construction of almost everything requires raw materials. The explorer searches for raw materials with which to create ideas. People tend to get into cognitive ruts. We become prisoners of familiarity, unwilling to leave our turf, and the consequence is boredom and burnout. The walls of security can become the bars of imprisonment. As a result, our ability to create becomes obstructed. Where should you explore? Anywhere and everywhere; the possibilities are limitless. Bookstores, national parks, museums, magazines, rock concerts, libraries. Leave your territory and go explore a new environment. Make an adventure out of it. In the spirit of *Star Trek,* "Go where no one has ever gone before."

Pop/folk musician Dan Fogelberg, during a radio interview, was once asked if he ever got into a creative rut. He answered that it happened "a few times," but that on one occasion he came across Tchaikovsky's *1812 Overture* and used the melody as a springboard to a new piece of music. Fogelberg soon had a new hit song, "Same Old Lang Syne." (If you listen carefully, you can hear this melody in his song.) Examples like this abound in the arts and humanities. The most important equipment the explorer needs, then, is an open mind: a container in which to put the raw materials. If you explore with a closed mind, there will be no room to transport the makings of ideas to your mental workshop. Negative thoughts, too, close a mind watertight. An open mind employs several attitudes to act as fertilizer; among these are curiosity, optimism, and enthusiasm. Curiosity is permission to get lost. In fact, many explorers do get lost. And when they emerge from the "woods," often they have discovered something far different, and more important, than what they had set out to find. Columbus was looking for spices in the Far East and "discovered" a whole new hemisphere. Roger Sperry was looking for a cure for epilepsy and discovered how the left and right hemispheres of the brain process information. Alexander Graham Bell set out to create a hearing aid and invented the telephone instead. Exploration should be fun. Fun is generated from optimism, a positive outlook, and enthusiasm, the application of optimism. When doubt or fear are introduced, fun disappears and the mind closes up like a steel trap. Another important piece of equipment for the explorer is a notebook or pad of paper. Good ideas are like butterflies: they may land, but they soon take off again. Write them down!

The Artist. Poet William Blake once said that every individual is "an artist, a child, a poet, and an animal." While you may not consider yourself the likes of Picasso or Rembrandt, every individual has what it takes to be an artist. In the role of the artist, you cultivate, manipulate, and sometimes incubate the raw materials gathered for ideas until they are molded into functional use. The role of the artist is perhaps the most challenging. It also takes some dedication and persistance. If the explorer asks Where? then the artist asks How? and What? How can I adapt other ideas for my own use? What can I do to make this idea my own?

A creativity course was introduced into the College of Business at Stanford University in 1981 in response to the criticism that American business lacked creativity. In their 1986 best-selling book *Creativity in Business,* Michael Ray and Rochelle Myers highlight this aspect of the creative process by including a chapter entitled "Ask Dumb Questions." To the artist, questions are the paintbrush and canvas; to the architect, questions are the pencil and tape measure.

Questions probe for the seeds of solution. Questions can also be entertaining, introducing humor as well. On the early *Saturday Night Live* TV shows (with the original cast of John Belushi, Gilda Radner, Chevy Chase, Dan Ackroyd, and the rest of the Not Ready for Prime Time Players), there was a parody of a talk show called What If? In these skits, ludicrous hypothetical questions were posed to world experts and then analyzed. Two examples: What if Eleanor Roosevelt could fly? (Answer: We could have used her as a bomber in World War II.); and What if Superman was a Nazi? (Answer: We would all be speaking German now.) "Dumb" questions shift the train of thought from the left (analytical) to the right (receptive) hemisphere of the brain, and receptivity is needed to play with the raw materials of thought. What if? questions are as valuable a tool to the artist as the compass and map are to the explorer. Asking What if? questions gives permission to manipulate and tailor ideas. Sometimes being an artist means being ridiculous, turning thoughts upside down or inside out. To an artist, paint, clay, plaster, and bronze are some of the media with which to create. In the creative process, there are many cognitive media as well. Thinking styles to manipulate ideas include reversing the perspective on concepts (e.g., throwing a barbecue for Christmas), connecting ideas together (a squirt gun and toothpaste), or comparisons ("Life is a cabaret, old chum"). And here is some food for thought: Picasso once said that "every act of creation first involves an act of destruction." Ideas that worked well in one situation may not be applicable to other circumstances; however, they can be adapted to the situation at hand.

The Judge. When the role of the judge comes into play, a shift from soft to hard thinking takes place. The crops are ready to be harvested. The judge decides thumbs up or thumbs down for each idea, with the good ideas becoming reality. The role of judge is crucial, for it can just as easily destroy good ideas as bring good ones to fruition. In American culture, the judge is usually the strongest player on the creative team. More often than not, in fact, the strength of the judge overwhelms and destroys the team. Rational thought and over-analysis used at the wrong time are a waste of both time and resources. To kill or use an idea before it has been manipulated by the artist's hands is like walking out of the middle of the best movie you ever saw. You wouldn't do that. Nor would you make a habit of eating unripe fruit. As a rule, Americans are "top-heavy" in judgment to the detriment of the other necessary aspects of the creative process. In the Stanford creativity course mentioned previously, one of the first concepts students were taught was to "unlearn" judgment skills. Judgment in the germination stage of creativity is unhealthy. Later on, in the secondary phase of creativity, judgment skills are reassembled and strengthened. The skill of intuition is also emphasized. While intuition is regarded as a right-brain function, it serves as a bridge to left-brain thinking. Intuition is the quarterback in the football game of creativity.

The role of judge involves taking risks. As inventor Grace Hopper once said, "A ship in a port is safe, but that's not what ships are built for." To that we can add this advice from business executive Harry Gray: "No one ever achieved greatness by playing it safe" (von Oech, 1986). Risk taking can seem like a dangerous proposition because there is always the possibility of failure. Failure, of course, can prove painful, a sensation the ego would rather avoid. With failure is the chance of rejection, and rejection tends to lower self-esteem. This may sound incongruous, but failure is the first step to success. Edison tried 1,800 different types of filaments before he found one that worked in the lightbulb. Author Mario Puzo approached nineteen different publishers before he found one that would accept his manuscript entitled *The Godfather.* Contrary to popular opinion, failure isn't lack of achievement, it is lack of effort. In the words of comedian and film producer/director Woody Allen, "If you're not failing every now and again, it's a sign that you're not trying anything innovative."

Risks can be classified as either good or bad. With a little bit of intelligence, a calculation can be made regarding the strength of an idea. A good judge weighs the positive aspects against the negative ones. A good judge isn't biased by assumptions that preclude future possibilities. In the event of a calculated risk that sours, failure can still be a great teacher. Use your intuition and go with the good risks.

The Warrior. Giving the green light to go ahead with a good idea doesn't signify the end of the creative process. As von Oech explains, the role of the warrior is to campaign for the idea. It tries the idea out and markets it. The warrior is the anchor leg of the creative

relay team, and it doesn't take any coaching experience to figure out that the anchor leg has got to be strong. Many good ideas sit around collecting dust because the warrior never finished the race. The role of the warrior, in tandem with the judge, is to take creative ideas to completion. The warrior devises a strategy, a winning game plan. On Wall Street, the importance of strategy and campaigning is summed up as: To know and not to do is not to know. Warrior skills include good organization and administration abilities. The warrior also takes risks, but good risks. To be a good warrior, you need strength and endurance; strength to carry the idea to reality, and endurance to carry it far, if need be. A good warrior is an optimist. A good warrior has confidence. And a good warrior is persistent.

A quick review of books on creativity reveals that although women are just as creative as men, they rarely receive any acknowledgements. Madame Curie, Fanny Mendelssohn and Georgia O'Keefe not withstanding, women receive little if any credit for their creative efforts. In her book *The 12 Secrets of Highly Creative Women,* author Gail McMeekin not only highlights scores of creative women and their achievements over the past few centuries, but notes the trends that got them to success. Like von Oech, McMeekin sees the creative process in distinct stages. Some of the twelve secrets include: acknowledging your creative self, following your fascinations, conquering your saboteurs, and selecting empowering alliances.

Obstacles to the Creative Process

The act of creation can be most pleasant. Roger von Oech called it "mental sex." Maslow (1987) called the feelings associated with it "peak experiences," describing exhilaration or euphoria. If creativity is so much fun, why do so many people shy away from it? Lately, researchers have directed much attention to the reasons people shun the creative process as a whole, as well as its constituents.

Contrary to what you might think, creativity is not solely a right-brain function. Rather, it is a partnership between the right brain, the house of the imagination, and the left brain, the source of organization. There are many reasons why the creative process becomes stifled. Most of these have to do with

Figure 13.4 Slice a pie into eight pieces using only three cuts. There is more than one right answer.

Figure 13.5 The creative word game.
In the following line of letters, cross out letters so that the remaining six letters, without altering their sequence, will spell a familiar English word.

BSAINXLEATNTEARS

the inability to access the functional powers of the right brain, the overbearing powers of the left brain, or a combination of the two. What is needed is a balance of right- and left-brain cognitive skills. Lack of balance is induced by attitudes and other obstacles that block the creative process. These attitudes are called mental blocks, or in von Oech's terms, mental locks. Von Oech describes ten mental blocks in his book *A Whack on the Side of the Head,* each an attitude debilitating to the creative *process.* Four of the most common pertaining to stress management are The Right Answer (explorer), I'm Not Creative (artist), Don't Be Foolish (judge), and To Err is Wrong (warrior). According to von Oech, "We all need a whack on the side of the head to shake us out of routines and force us to rethink our problems." With each "lock" described below is an exercise to "whack" the side of your head so that you become more creative.

The Right Answer

Is it possible there is more than one right answer to any problem? More than likely, yes! (Fig. 13.4.) But people generally look for just one answer, call it right, and then stop looking. Years ago, singer/songwriter Harry Chapin wrote a song called "Flowers Are Red." The song was inspired by a note sent home with his preschool-aged daughter that said that she had not colored the flower assignment correctly. "Flowers are red, not black," the note said. "My flower died," his daughter explained. Chapin's daughter symbolizes just one of many millions of such experiences. From day one we seemed to be educated that there is a "right" way and a "wrong" way to everything. In the germination phase of the creative process, there are many possibilities. If you are in search of one right answer, you will surely stop once you have found it. Nothing could be more dangerous.

I'm Not Creative

In one of my courses, I assign students a creativity project on the first night, to be completed by the end of the semester. The moans can be heard from one coast to the other: "I'm not creative." But in the words of author Richard Bach (*Illusions*), "Argue for your limitations, and sure enough, they're yours." Creativity isn't a perception, it is a process. When it is thought of as a perception, it can be very stifling. Everyone is creative—it just takes work. What separates Picasso, Frank Lloyd Wright, Georgia O'Keeffe, and Paul McCartney from those who say they are not creative is belief in their own creativity. The inspiration from this belief is phenomenal. At the end of each semester, I am told repeatedly by students that the creativity exercise was the best thing they ever did, because it taught them they really could be creative.

Don't Be Foolish

Have you ever dropped your tray in the cafeteria, walked around all day with your fly open, made a presentation with food stuck in your teeth, or locked your keys in the car? The embarrassment resulting from such episodes is painful to the ego. Being foolish is thought of as being stupid, and stupidity earns no points in the game of life. We are so cautious about making mistakes for fear of how we will look in public that we constantly keep our guard up. But guarded behavior promotes conformity, and conformity breeds staleness. In the creative process, this mentality can lead to a concept called groupthink, where everyone conforms, goes along with the crowd. Groupthink is dangerous; it stifles creativity. Sometimes it is necessary to be foolish. A giddy outlook gives a new perspective on a situation. Playing the fool can augment the role of the judge to determine the worth of ideas. Being foolish can also mean having a sense of humor, and humor and creativity make wonderful partners (see Chapter 12).

To Err Is Wrong

There are times when making a mistake is not a good idea. It may cost you your job, marriage, or life. Then again, there are times when making a mistake may result in the most appropriate course of action. Mistakes offer invaluable learning experiences. In the creative process, mistakes are necessary. Each mistake bushwhacks a clearer path to a more viable answer. Errors are steppingstones to the next workable possibility. Fear of failure can immobilize the creative process. To the mind of Thomas J. Watson, founder of IBM, "The way to success is to double your rate of failure."

From a different vantage point, Arthur VanGundy discusses several types of obstacles or roadblocks to the creative process in his book *Training Your Creative Mind.* They include the following:

1. *Perceptual roadblocks.* Perceptual obstacles involve the inability to separate yourself from the problem. Ego attachment blurs creative vision. Perceptual problems occur when left-brain cognitive skills overrule the primary creative processes. Analysis, judgment, and negative perceptions place plaster casts around the creative muscle and cause it to atrophy. There is a time to open up, and a time to narrow your vision. Creativity is like humor: timing is everything.

2. *Emotional roadblocks.* The primary emotion acting as an obstacle to creativity is fear—fear of making a mistake, fear of the unknown, and fear of rejection, once others find out about past mistakes. When people say they are not creative, many times what they are saying is, "I am afraid of failure." Fear of failure can paralyze the creative thought process. Fears are natural, but with a little work they can be alleviated or resolved to

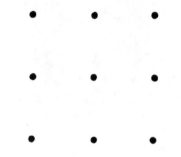

Connect all nine dots with four straight lines. Go through each dot only once. Do not lift your pencil from the paper. (And don't be afraid to make a mistake or two.)   *Figure 13.6*

enhance creativity. Conversely, sometimes we fall so deeply "in love" with an idea we have given birth to that we become blind to its true value or contribution. In these cases it is often best to "sit on" the ideas, and give them time to hatch and prove their merit. But don't sit on an idea too long, or someone else might come along with the same idea and leave you bobbing in the wake of their creativity.

3. *Intellectual/expressive roadblocks.* Humans rely very heavily on vision and hearing, sometimes to the exclusion of other senses. The consequence can be poor receptivity to additional information that could be employed in the gathering and processing of creative ideas. Language can also be a real barrier. Words have specific but different connotations to the people who hear them. For example, a doorway to one person is a passageway to someone else. Each word represents a different image and a different result. Don't let language become a barrier to your creative thoughts.

4. *Cultural roadblocks.* We become socialized to certain thinking patterns. Western culture is now widely recognized as encouraging left-brain-dominant thinkers. That is, the critical styles of thinking associated with the left brain are praised, while the cognitive thinking styles

of the right brain are ridiculed or ignored. The net result is asymmetrical thinking. How can this barrier be dismantled? One way is to access your right-brain thinking styles through meditation, yoga, or recreation. Sidney Parnes, a creative consultant to the Disney Corporation, advocates listening to instrumental music to set the imagination free and get creative juices flowing (see Chapter 21).

5. *Environmental roadblocks.* Environmental factors include personal constraints such as time, noncreative influences (i.e., your friends, spouse, or boss), and resources such as a support network of other people. Have you ever had what you thought was a really good idea and then received feedback that was less than favorable? Negative feedback invariably has a toxic effect on creativity. Be on the lookout for toxic influences and learn to avoid them.

Roadblocks are seldom dead ends. They are merely influences impeding the fruits of creative labor. Several of these roadblocks are self-defeating attitudes, but attitudes can change. If you want to move beyond a roadblock, surrender the attitude. Other roadblocks may involve people, places, or things. In these cases, a roadblock just means that you have to travel a longer distance to get to your final destination. The removal or diversion of roadblocks takes a little time. Sometimes you have to be creative even in the dismantling of obstacles. But in the end, much strength will result from the effort.

From Creativity to Creative Problem Solving

Creativity is perhaps one of the most valuable coping techniques to use in your personal battle against stress. If the mechanics involved in creative problem solving—awareness, new ideas, new courses of action, and evaluation—seem familiar, it is because they are the cornerstones of many other coping techniques as well. In addition, several coping techniques can be included in the creative strategic plan (e.g., cognitive restructuring, social engineering, and communication skills). At first glance, creative problem solving might appear to be a linear sequential process. Linear thinking, however, is a left-brain skill. Without a trip through the corpus callosum for a visit to the right side of the brain, your chances of bringing troublesome situations to closure are about as good as an ice cube's in hell. It makes sense, then, that use of creative skills in the problem solving process may be circuitous rather than straight-line. Creativity may be used to make order out of chaos, but no one ever said that orderly is synonymous with linear. This is all right, because many problems are nonlinear too. Some are like amoebas, amorphously stretching about.

To illustrate nonlinear thinking (Fig. 13.7), let us say that you start out gathering ideas to solve a problem, which is the most logical way to begin. So you put on your pith helmet and go exploring to collect ideas. When you have a lot of raw materials, you pull out your artbox, toolbox, or whatever toys you need to play

Figure 13.7 Creative problem solving is rarely a linear process.

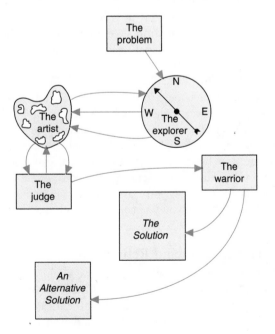

with, and hammer away. But in the course of playing, you find you need a few more ideas. So you change hats and explore some more, and then return to hammering away again. Soon the hammer becomes a gavel as the judge steps in to review the progress so far. The judge approves. "Hmm, not bad," says the warrior, "Let's take this baby out and see if it flies." In flight, the artist says, "Wait! Let's add this to make it stronger." So there are a few more trips back to the workshop before the product is finished. As you can see, the process, in practice, is anything but a straight line.

Steps to Initiate Creative Problem Solving

Just as there are many paths to enlightenment, there are many solutions to each problem. Granted, some may be more viable than others, but rarely, if ever, is there only one way out. This is perhaps the most important concept in **creative problem solving.** Among the several theories of creative problem solving, some common concepts do emerge (Fig. 13.8), yet the paths to and from these concepts vary significantly depending on the person using them. The first step in creative problem solving is to write everything down on paper. This will make the other steps easier.

Description of the Problem

Before you can attack a problem successfully, you have to understand it. This means looking at the problem from all sides. Objectively state the problem. Define it. Give it some history. Give it someone else's perspective. Project its future influence. Then subjectively state how you feel about it, the depth of your involvement, and the impact or influence it has had on you. Next, analyze the problem. Dissect it. Look at its components. What are its strengths and weaknesses? What is its face value and what is the bottom line? Once you have a handle on the nature of the problem, then you can move on. Remember, though, that throughout the creative process, you will want to revisit this description because over time you will gather more information about it. Any subsequent changes to it may in turn

The map of creative problem solving.   *Figure 13.8*

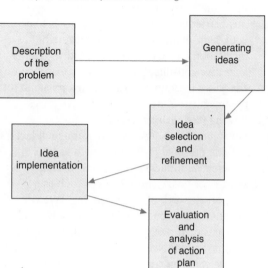

alter the final approach you select to handle the problem.

Generating Ideas

Generating ideas is fun; it is also challenging. So where do ideas come from? Memory is a good place to start—previous experience is always a good teacher. But memory alone isn't enough. Ideas should come from any available resource, both internal and external, from books, to people, movies, museums, and you name it. This is where the explorer role comes in. The more ideas you can come up with, the better your chances of solving the problem effectively. When searching for ideas, leave mental censorship behind. Take in every conceivable idea, even if it seems ridiculous. If you start to censor ideas before you gather them, you will come up empty-handed.

Idea Selection and Refinement

Not all of your ideas will be good or useable. But you won't know that until you spread them all out and look at them collectively. Play with the ideas. Order them. Circle them. Line them up like an army of troops. Once your ideas are out on the table, one or two are likely to jump out at you. You might also want to rank-order (judge) your ideas by degree of feasibility (plan A, plan B, plan C, etc.) because not every idea will work, and the idea that looks best now might flop the hardest. Now bring in the artist again and manipulate your idea of choice. Manipulation means adapting the idea to "best fit" the problem. You may need to streamline the idea, or to otherwise change it a little to suit your specific needs. Once you have selected your first choice, play it out in your mind. Visualize the idea. What are the pros and cons? Explore hypotheticals and look for potential weaknesses that could be corrected to avoid major pitfalls. Expect the unexpected. Now remember plan B and plan C. A person without options is a person in trouble, so you will want to have some backups. Give some thought to your second and third choices because there is a good chance you will some day use them. Once you have narrowed your ideas down to one choice, it is a good idea to do a quick inventory to see what resources it may require. Not all ideas require additional resources, but many do. Remember that resources may include people as well as material goods, and don't overlook those intangible resources, the hidden talents within each individual.

Idea Implementation

Implementation takes bravery—perhaps not much, but in the face of stress, maybe a lot. Implementation involves a game plan, a strategy. This means thinking about how the idea can be put into effect and end in resolution. It means trying the idea out. In addition to bravery, implementation requires faith.

Evaluation and Analysis of Action

A good inventor observes his or her invention to see how well it works. When the tests are through, either a bottle of champagne is opened or there is a trip back to the proverbial drawing board. Problem solving works the same way. The final lesson a problem has to offer is if and how well it has been resolved. This takes a bit of analysis, so once again call the judge back in to declare a verdict. But there is no verdict of guilty or not guilty. There is either a hard pat on the back or a soft kick in the seat of the pants. In life's journey, you will do well to have an equal number of each, as all of our rough edges need to be polished.

Box 13.1 contains some hypothetical problems (based on real-life experiences) that call for creative problem solving. They are only exercises, but they can provide good practice for the time when you will need to apply these skills to real problems in the future. Follow the steps in the problem-solving format and see what you come up with. Try to generate at least four ideas for each hypothetical problem.

Best Application of Creative Problem Solving

We all have the skills to be creative; the issue is whether or not we choose to use them. With this coping technique, there really is no choice if you want to deal effectively with stress. How good are your exploring skills? Do you have a curious nature? When is the last time you ventured someplace you have never been to before to shop around for ideas? How good are your artistic talents? When is the last time you played in the garage or basement? For that matter, when is the last time you just plain played? Is your artist's hammer a judge's gavel in disguise, ready to smash an idea before it is ripe? These are some questions to ask yourself in order to find out your strengths and weaknesses in the creative process. Once you identify these areas, you are ready to sharpen these skills.

Psychologist Abraham Maslow said that creativity is a necessary skill to deal with the stress of change. As the understanding of right- and left-brain cognitive skills continues to unfold, it is becoming increasingly obvious that the mind is capable of much more intelligence than was thought before. Creative problem-solving skills are life skills; skills to not only survive but also thrive through the potential chaos of change. Once refined, these skills can and should be used repeatedly as the foundation of every strategy used to confront and resolve stress.

Creative Problem-Solving Exercises

Problem 1: Roommate/Spouse Problems
Situation: After six weeks of living with your roommate (or two years with your spouse) you have lost your tolerance for this person and want out.

1. Describe the problem:

2. Generate ideas:

3. Select and refine idea:

4. Implement idea:

5. Evaluate and analyze action:

Problem 2: Looking for a Job
Situation: You are about to graduate from college and seek a job (or perhaps you can't stand the job you currently hold).

1. Describe the problem:

2. Generate ideas:

3. Select and refine idea:

(continued)

Creative Problem-Solving Exercises (cont.)

4. Implement idea:

2. Generate ideas:

3. Select and refine idea:

5. Evaluate and analyze action:

4. Implement idea:

Problem 3: Zero or Negative Cash Flow
Situation: It's the same old economic story—supply doesn't meet demand.

1. Describe the problem:

5. Evaluate and analyze action:

Summary

- Necessity is the mother of invention. When problems arise, solutions come from creative thinking. However, in American culture, critical rather than creative thinking is rewarded.
- Maslow found two stages to the creative process: primary creativity, where ideas are generated in a playful mode; and secondary creativity, where these ideas are refined and implemented.
- von Oech outlined four phases of creative thinking: the explorer, the artist, the judge, and the warrior. The first two roles are responsible for searching out and generating ideas, whereas the second two refine and implement the selected idea.
- Roadblocks to the creative process can occur at any stage; however, most occur at the explorer

and artist phases. Four roadblocks were described in this chapter: The Right Answer, I'm Not Creative, Don't Be Foolish, and To Err Is Wrong.
- VanGundy categorizes obstacles to creativity as roadblocks—emotional, intellectual/expressive, cultural, and environmental.
- The creative problem-solving strategy has five phases: describing the problem, generating ideas, idea selection and refinement, idea implementation, and evaluation and analysis of action.
- Creativity is a large component of mental well-being. The right and left hemispheres of the brain work together as a team to overcome problems resulting in acute or chronic stress.

Concepts and Terms

Artist
Creative obstacles
Creative problem solving
Cultural roadblocks
Emotional roadblocks

Environmental roadblocks
Explorer
Intellectual roadblocks
Judge
Perceptual roadblocks

Primary creativity
Secondary creativity
Warrior

Appendix: Answers to Creative Problems

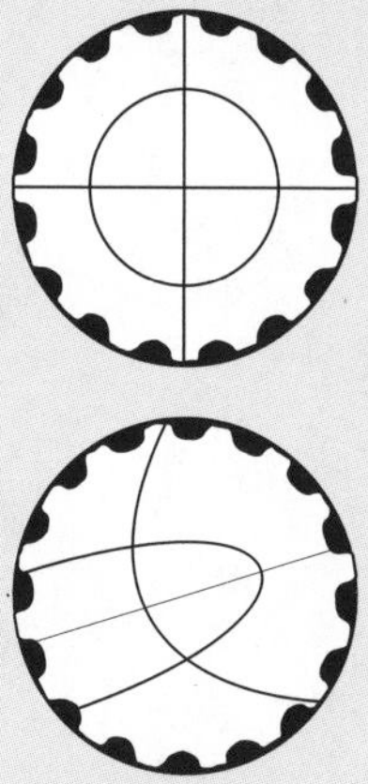

Figure 13.4

BANANA and/or LETTER

Figure 13.5

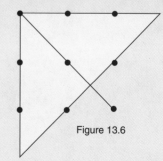

Figure 13.6

References and Resources

Allen, W. *The Complete Prose of Woody Allen*. Outlet Books, Avenal, NJ, 1991.

Bach, R. *Illusions: The Adventures of a Reluctant Messiah*. Dell, New York, 1977.

Bartlett, J. *Familiar Quotations,* 6th ed., J. Kaplin, ed. Little Brown, Boston, 1992.

Brightman, H. J. *Problem Solving: A Logical and Creative Approach*. College of Business Administration, Georgia State University, Atlanta, 1980.

Buzan, T. *Use Both Sides of Your Brain,* 2nd ed. Dutton, New York, 1983.

Cameron, J. *The Artist's Way*. Jeremy Tarcher/Putnam Books, Los Angeles, CA, 1992.

Crandall, R., ed. *Break-Out Creativity: Bringing Creativity to the Workplace*. Select Press, Corte Madera, CA, 1998.

Dossey, L. Creativity: On Intelligence, Insight, and the Cosmic Soup. *Alternative Therapies in Health and Medicine* 6(1):12–17, 1999.

Elijah, A. M. *Thinking Unlimited*. Institute of Creative Development, Pune, Delhi, India, 1980.

Gardner, H. *Creative Minds*. Basic Books, New York, 1993.

Gawain, S. *Creative Visualization*. New World Library, San Rafael, CA, 1978.

Gorman, C. K. *Creativity in Business: A Practical Guide for Creative Thinking*. Crisp Publications, Los Altos, CA, 1989.

Harman, W. and Rheingold, H. *Higher Creativity*. Tarcher Press, Los Angeles, 1984.

Kelly, T. et al. *The Art of Innovation: Lessons in Creativity from IDEO*. Doubleday, New York, 2001.

Maslow, A. *The Farther Reaches of Human Nature*. Esalen/Penguin Books, New York, 1971.

Maslow, A. H. *Motivation and Personality,* 3rd ed. Harper & Row, New York, 1987.

McMeekin, G. *The 12 Secrets of Highly Creative Women*. Conari Press, Berkeley, CA, 2000.

Moyers, B. *A World of Ideas*. Doubleday, New York, 1989.

Olson, R. W. *The Art of Creative Thinking*. Harper-Collins, New York, 1986.

Parnes, S. J. *Visionizing*. D. O. K. Publishers, East Aurora, NY, 1988.

Ray, M. and Myers, R. *Creativity in Business*. Doubleday, New York, 1986.

Shallcross, D. J. *Teaching Creative Behavior*. Bearly Limited, Buffalo, NY, 1985.

Stok, G. *The Book of Questions*. Workman Press, New York, 1987.

Toffler, A. *Future Shock*. Bantam Books, New York, 1970.

VanGundy, A. B. *Techniques of Structured Problem Solving*. Van Nostrand Reinhold, New York, 1981.

VanGundy, A. B. *Training Your Creative Mind*. Prentice-Hall, Englewood Cliffs, NJ, 1982.

von Oech, R. *A Kick in the Seat of the Pants*. Harper & Row, New York, 1986.

von Oech, R. *A Whack on the Side of the Head* (revised edition). Warner Books, New York, 1998.

Chapter 14 Communication Skills

The three most important words for a successful relationship are: communication, communication, and communication.

—Anonymous

If you were to make a list of your top ten stressors, you would probably find that at least half of these involve relationships with family, friends, and co-workers. Strong relationships necessitate good communication skills. To paraphrase poet John Donne, "No man is an island entire of itself. Each is a piece of the continent, a part of the main," and as such, our lives are filled with much interaction. Like molecules ricocheting around a glass jar, we are bound to come in contact with a number of people over the course of any day. These "contacts" often prove stressful due to the nature of our communicative interactions. Experts indicate that the average person spends approximately three quarters of his or her waking day communicating with others. Included under the rubric of communication are phone calls, lectures, staff meetings, dinner conversations, listening to radio and television, and simply talking with friends and acquaintances. The degree of perception and interpretation required for communication, and the many layers of meaning in even common words, leaves much room for misunderstanding—and hence stress. This is why the practice of good communication skills is so important, to help minimize and resolve misunderstandings. Good communication skills are *essential* as a coping technique.

To be a good communicator, one must not only express thoughts and feelings in understandable words, but listen, clarify, and process information as it is intended. Communication skills are so important in the business world that workshops and seminars are given regularly on this topic; poor communication skills are simply not cost effective. As you will see in this chapter, almost every theory and accompanying skill is based on common sense. Yet common sense is often bound and gagged when the ego is threatened. When people are defensive, their ability to gather, process, and even exchange information becomes greatly impaired. The result is miscommunication and the stress that miscommunication produces.

Conversational Styles

Each person has his or her own distinct style of communication. According to linguistics expert Dr. Deborah Tannen of George Washington University (1986), not only do the interpretations of words cause misunderstandings in relationships, but so do the styles in which people speak. Both, she notes, are a major rea-

son for marital problems and, in some cases, divorce. Moreover, Tannen indicates that people from different regions of the country have specific communication styles (e.g., New York City versus Texas). And, perhaps to no surprise, men typically display a different communication style than women. Communication styles include, among others, dominant, interruptive, manipulative, polite, creative, sarcastic, and passive means. It is friction caused by differing conversational styles that causes or adds to conflict. In our attempts to communicate under stress, styles become exaggerated, which Tannen terms schismogenesis, thus further widening the gap of misunderstanding.

A particular conversational style is a type of behavior, which in some situations may need to be refined, adapted, or changed to resolve issues between two people. Take, for example, the case of a woman from Texas who moved to Washington D.C. as an assistant director of human resources management for a large company. Within weeks her communication style and demeanor were perceived as unassertive, whereas in Texas she had been praised for being appropriately polite.

In her much-acclaimed book *That's Not What I Meant,* Tannen also describes the serious problem of misinterpretation of the spoken message. Tannen calls the underlying intent of communications metamessages, or the meanings of the messages that are clear to the speaker but masked by a particular vernacular and style construed as polite or nonoffensive. Misunderstanding is compounded by the interpretation of the listener as well. For instance, upon learning that his sister Sheila is pregnant, Mark may ask, "Did you quit smoking yet?" The metamessage expresses concern for the health of the baby. But Sheila's interpretation may be that Mark is passing judgment on her health habits, making her quite angry. From Tannen's research, she has come to the conclusion that people—or Americans, at least—tend to be indirect rather than direct in the messages they communicate (Box 14.1), whether out of politeness, fear, or manipulation. This indirectness is a precursor to perceived stress, and greatly compromises the effectiveness of communication, leading to further misunderstanding and potential conflict. Verbal communication is one way to get a message across, but by no means the only way. Metamessages also are stated indirectly through postures, clothes, and facial expressions. Thus, communication is basically categorized as verbal and nonverbal.

What the Professor Really Means

Box 14.1

What He or She Said	What It Really Means
You'll be using one of the leading textbooks in the field.	I used it as a grad student.
The answer to your question is beyond the scope of this course.	I don't know.
You'll have to see me during my office hours for a thorough answer to your question.	I don't know.
In answer to your question, you must recognize that there are several disparate points of view.	I really don't know!
Today we'll let a member of the class lead the discussion. It will be a good educational experience.	I stayed out late last night and didn't have time to prepare a lecture.
The test will be 60 questions, multiple choice.	The test will be a 60-question multiple guess, plus three short-answer questions (1,000 words or more), and no one will score above 75 percent.
The test scores were generally good.	Some of you managed a B.
The test scores were a little below my expectations.	Where was the party last night?
Some of you could have done better.	Everyone flunked.
Are there any questions?	I'm ready to let you go.

Reprinted by permission of J. Timothy Petersik.

Verbal Communication

Verbal language is a series of expressive thoughts and perceptions described through word symbols. Linguistic experts divide verbal communication into two components: encoding and decoding (Fig. 14.1). Encoding is the process wherein a speaker attempts to frame thoughts and perceptions into words (e.g., someone saying to the person next to her, "Boy, it's stuffy in here"). Decoding is the process wherein the message is translated, dissected, analyzed, and interpreted by the listener (e.g., the person hearing this thinks, "Yeah, the room does smell rather gamey"). Misunderstanding, confusion, and stress can arise anywhere in this process.

While it may seem that two people who speak English would have a common understanding of all English words, in fact variations in the meanings given to words can lead to much confusion as well. Anyone who has traveled to Great Britain, Australia, or New Zealand has discovered that even in English-speaking countries, language barriers exist. For example, a jumper is a dress in the States, whereas it is a sweater Down Under. Moreover, you don't have to leave America to experience this phenomenon; vernacular differences can be found all across the country. For example, the words *tonic, soda,* and *pop* are all used colloquially to describe soft drinks. But in the Boston area a tonic is considered a cola, whereas in Denver it denotes seltzer. Additionally, cultural vernacular gives rise to new meanings for words, often representing the opposites of their dictionary definitions. For example, the word *bad* may have negative connotations to you, but currently many people employ this adjective to describe something emphatically good, as in "That's a bad hat." Quite often, the meanings of words are arbitrary. And possessing both literal and figurative meanings, words and expressions can also be ambiguous. FBI chief J. Edgar Hoover once corrected a memo his secretary typed with a note to "watch the borders" (margins). Misunderstanding,

she added his comment to the memo and sent it out nationwide. Immediately all FBI agents on the Canadian and Mexican borders were placed on alert. Verbal and written communication is more complex than meets the ear or eye.

The key to interpersonal communication can be summed up as: Say what you mean, and mean what you say. In others words, be direct. Implementing this rule in our conversational style, however, is extremely difficult. One reason confusion arises is that there are many concepts, ideas, and particularly feelings that are difficult to articulate within the limits of vocabulary. Thoughts, like color photographs, can often be described only in black and white terms, leaving many details to assumption, interpretation, and imagination. Some thoughts cannot be expressed in words at all, and the words we choose to describe the contents of our conscious minds can limit our own understanding of what we wish to express as well.

The Sapir-Whorf hypothesis, created to explain the use of words, suggests that our perception of reality is largely based on the depth of the vocabulary in which we express ourselves. In others words, our vocabulary limits our understanding of our current reality. For example, Aleuts have over fifty words to describe snow. In the Lower 48, there are just a handful of words in English. So, someone with a limited vocabulary will have a more difficult time expressing him- or herself, as is easily illustrated when learning a new language. Even when vocabulary does appear to describe thoughts adequately, words are often used to camouflage true feelings in an attempt to avoid hurting others or even ourselves. The inability to express how we really feel can also promote unacknowledged anxiety.

Communicating Ideas and Feelings

Sharing personal ideas and feelings is referred to as self-disclosure, opening up and revealing a part of you that is not obvious from external appearances. Self-disclosure is based on mutual trust. It is believed by those who study communication skills that all verbal communication involves some element of self-disclosure. It can be a double-edged sword, for there is risk in divulging personal insights and feelings. When individuals sense that sharing feelings will promote a closer relationship or bonding, then the risk is assessed as minimal and opening up is worth it. If rejection or alienation may ensue, however, then the degree of openness will be greatly limited. Likewise, when trust has been violated in the past, the ability to self-disclose is greatly compromised. One might think that the closer two people are, the greater the depth of self-disclosure there is, and initially this may be true. But in many cases, once the parameters of a relationship are established, laziness sets in and styles are taken for granted, thus leaving many perceptions to assumptions that may or may not represent true feelings.

Describing feelings differs from expressing feelings, in that description involves the use of words, whereas expression may include physical responses such as crying, laughing, touching, or some other physical action. Although there are many ways to express emotions, verbal communication is deemed essential when they involve other people. When feelings are not put into words, assumptions occur in the minds of those with whom you interact, and assumptions can be dangerous. These guessing games often lead to confusion about intentions and thoughts of everyone involved. Again, the result is frustration and emotional pain.

Stress With a Human Face

SWIMMING WAS JOHNNY'S PASSION, AND YOU could tell just by listening to him talk about it. He was a freestyle sprinter, and proud of it. Training and competition are not without their stressful moments, nor is the transition from high school to college swimming an easy one. In a visit to my office one day, Johnny confided that he was having some problems, specifically communication and attitude problems, with the coach. "I'm a sprinter, not a distance swimmer," he exclaimed. "And I thrive on positive reinforcement. All I seem to get is negative talk. I can tell he really doesn't like me."

"Johnny, have you made it a point to sit down and talk with the coach?" I asked. "Does he even know you feel this way?" The answer was No! "I know this guy," I continued, "and he's a lousy psychic. He can't read your mind. You've got to talk to him. Make an appointment to see him, tell him how you feel, and give it to him straight. Tell him exactly what you've told me."

It didn't take much for Johnny to agree this was the only reasonable course of action.

Although I saw him at several home swim meets after that, the subject never came up and I never thought to ask about it. But about six months later, when I was at a basketball game talking with the swimming coach and he mentioned Johnny's name, I inquired about the rapport between the two.

"Oh, we get along great," the coach replied. "Less than a month into the season, he came to see me and presented his perception of our relationship, his need for lots of positive feedback, negotiating some sprinting events with distance events, and a few other aspects of training." I just nodded and smiled. I know someday Johnny will be not only a fine swimmer but a wonderful coach himself. ✦

Nonverbal Communication

Nonverbal communication is described as any communication that does not involve words. It may include postures, facial expressions, touch, and even style of clothing. Nonverbal communication differs from verbal communication in that it is multichanneled—addressing all senses—not merely stimuli received through the sense of hearing. Nonverbal communication is not only indirect, but often unconscious. Conversely, verbal communication is typically dominated by conscious thought. Ideally, nonverbal messages support verbal communication, reinforcing words with gestures to promote a clearer understanding of the intended message. However, a spoken message can also be contradicted by nonverbal gestures. The result is a series of mixed messages and the feelings these incongruencies generate.

Research shows that when a contradiction occurs between verbal and nonverbal messages, people are more inclined to believe nonverbal cues ("the body doesn't lie"). Several factors have been identified as elements of nonverbal communication, any of which can either reinforce or contradict spoken messages. These are categorized as either physical or nonphysical elements.

Physical Elements

Research shows that there are many styles of nonverbal communication, involving a number of physical movements:

1. *Touch.* Touch is thought to be a universal form of communication. Handshakes, pats on the

back, and hugs are the most common forms of touch. As a rule, Americans tend to be noncontact-oriented, although comfort levels vary greatly from one person to another. Depending on the style of touch, the individual, and the circumstances, this nonverbal form of communication can be perceived as either threatening or reassuring.

2. *Emblems and Illustrators.* Emblems are defined as physical gestures that replace words, such as the "ok" symbol and the thumbs-up sign. Many emblems have been incorporated into American Sign Language, used by the hearing-impaired. Illustrators, on the other hand, are movements that augment verbal communication, such as waving your hand by your face to show how hot you are. Emblems are often used when speech is prohibited (in a church or lecture hall), while illustrators typically accompany a verbal narrative.

3. *Affect displays.* Facial expressions are often used to express a point also made through the spoken word. Banging your thumb with a hammer hurts, and the facial contortion usually following afterward suggests the intensity of the pain.

4. *Regulators.* Regulators are nonverbal messages used to regulate or manipulate a conversation. Eye movements, slight head movements, and shifting weight from foot to foot can send a message for the speaker to speed up, slow down, repeat, or hurry up and finish a sentence. While regulators are sometimes important to communication, they can also be construed as rude, depending on their nature.

5. *Adaptors.* Adaptors are often called body language, and they are important (Fig. 14.2). Adaptors are believed to be among the most difficult physical elements to decode in nonverbal communication. Folding your arms across your chest or crossing your legs away from the speaker may, or may not, indicate boredom, defensiveness, or aggression.

6. *Paralanguage.* Paralanguage consists of the elements of speaking that color the use of words. Pitch, volume, and rate all convey inferences that influence the listener.

Nonphysical Elements

Many additional factors sensed by speakers and listeners communicate a host of impressions, from values to feelings:

1. *Territorial space.* Each individual maintains an area of comfortable personal space or territory around him- or herself. When personal space is invaded, it causes feelings of discomfort. Too great a distance between people may also cause uneasiness, or feelings of rejection.

2. *Clothing.* Styles of clothing send very strong messages about personal values, attitudes, and behaviors, and either meet the expectations of other individuals in one's environments or not. Professional settings, for example, call for a particular style of clothing. That which deviates from the expected or normal dress code can communicate anything from ignorance, to disrespect, to a rebellious attitude.

Figure 14.2 Body language can be more revealing than the spoken word. Studies show that people trust body language more than verbal communication.

Knowing that communication involves both verbal and nonverbal messages, it is important to recognize and utilize elements of both to make your style of communication as effective as possible. Recognition and utilization of effective verbal and nonverbal skills requires, specifically, listening, attending, and responding skills.

Listening, Attending, and Responding Skills

The process of communication is like the two sides of a coin. The first side represents self-expression; the second, listening. You have probably heard someone say, "He heard me, but he didn't listen to what I said!" Hearing is the *reception* of auditory sensations, whereas listening is the *understanding* of these auditory sensations. Research shows that in a typical day over 50 percent of communication involves listening. Under closer observation, however, individuals show a general complacency about listening and attending skills; they may hear, but they do not listen very well. In the words of Tannen (1986), "Communication is a system. Everything that is said is simultaneously an instigation and reaction, a reaction and an instigation. Most of us tend to focus on the first part of that process while ignoring or downplaying the second." Typically, in conversation, when people finish expressing a thought or feeling, they almost immediately begin to prepare their next statement, listening only to the first couple of words of response. The most common example occurs during introductions, when a new person states his or her name while you prepare to say yours. Seconds later, you cannot remember what the person's name is. As a rule, the concentration required for listening is very tiring.

The key elements involved in effective listening, attending, and responding are the following:

1. *Assume the role of listener.* Listening requires that all attention be paid to what the speaker is saying. Your mind should be clear of all thoughts that direct attention away from the speaker. Attention to your own thoughts, rather than the message directed to you, is the primary reason for poor listening habits. Although the role of speaker and listener shifts back and forth several times in the course of a conversation, don't prepare comments or rebuttals while you are in the role of listener.

2. *Maintain eye contact.* Good eye contact is considered essential to effective listening. Wandering eyes suggest wandering thoughts. Lack of eye contact can also convey disinterest in the subject or the person. Good eye contact does not mean continual staring, as this can be construed as an invasion of personal space. Good eye contact conveys respect for the person to whom you are listening.

3. *Avoid word prejudice.* Some words elicit obvious emotional responses, which then lead to disinterest or surprise. Words such as *feminist, gay, Jew,* or *liberal* can press buttons and set emotional wheels spinning, resulting in raised eyebrows, frowns, and side glances. Recognition of these types of words and the responses they elicit will enable the listener to prepare to be objective. The listener's objectivity is believed to enhance the communication process.

4. *Use "minimal encouragers" to indicate that you are on the same wavelength as the person speaking to you.* Minimal encouragers include short word questions such as "oh?" and "uh-huh?" and repeating key words to encourage the speaker to give you more detailed information. These should be used genuinely, not mechanically.

5. *Paraphrase what was said to ensure understanding.* Paraphrasing is a more elaborate style of minimal encouragement. In addition to repeating key words, paraphrasing also includes the use of personal observations to ensure understanding of the content of the message intended.

6. *Ask questions to improve clarity of statements.* When you are at a loss to understand facts,

concepts, or feelings expressed to you, questions become imperative. But beware. Questions can sometimes put the speaker on the defensive. Use questions to clarify your understanding, not to confuse the person you are listening to.

7. *Use empathy to reflect and share feelings.* Empathy is thought to be an important attending skill that galvanizes the listening experience. Empathy refers to attention to the speaker's feelings as well as thoughts. This does not imply that you must adopt these feelings as your own. Rather, you should recognize the feelings in the individual with whom you are conversing.

8. *Provide feedback.* Responding to the speaker often requires feedback from the listener. Before you offer feedback, however, inquire whether it is desired. Sometimes people speak as a means to increase self-awareness using you, the listener, as a sounding board. The speaker may not want feedback. If your viewpoint is wanted, offer comments and criticism in a constructive way. Feedback should be specific, combining feelings and reasons for or details of your opinions. If and when criticism is elicited, balance positive and negative perceptions, and be specific. To be effective, criticism should offer insights.

9. *Summarize the content of what was said.* Summarization is similar to paraphrasing thoughts, but it requires more concentration on and synthesis of the speaker's thoughts and feelings into an integrated understanding.

These are just a few elements that can be used to enhance your listening skills. They can also increase the effectiveness of delivery and interpretation of your thoughts and perceptions. Regardless of how effective you think your communication skills are, under the best circumstances, there is still room for misunderstanding and conflict as, for example, in the interpretation of a mixed message.

Conflict Resolution

Conflicts often arise due to misunderstanding both verbal and nonverbal messages that are sent and received. While conflicts can occur within yourself as well as between you and other individuals, it is the latter type of conflict this section will address. Typically, conflicts between individuals involve emotions associated with anger and fear. Left unresolved, they can generate many toxic thoughts, including resentment and hostility. Ideally, conflicts should be resolved right away; however, not every situation allows for this. A roommate who goes away for the weekend leaving the apartment a shambles, or a boss who faxes a memo at 4 P.M. asking you to hand in a report by 5 P.M. are two instances that necessitate a postponement of conflict resolution. People often need some time to organize their thoughts for conflict resolution. In any case, the sooner a plan of resolution is implemented, the better. While conflicts tend to be multidimensional, scholars divide them into three categories:

1. *Content conflict.* Content conflicts arise from the misunderstanding of factual information, definition of terms or concepts, goals, or elements of strategies used in a cooperative effort. Disagreement occurs over the perception of information available. In this type of conflict, the problem is not in dispute; rather, it is the solution to the problem that generates conflict. Examples include how to finance a house, where the best place to go on vacation is, or what time the movie starts at the cineplex.

2. *Values conflict.* When a person has conflicting values within his or her own value system, value clarification is needed. But when values between people collide, resolution is much harder. Value conflicts can often be seen on the political scene, as when forces lobbying for the environment (spotted owl) oppose economic forces (lumber industry). The result is often a compromise, neither side obtaining a complete (or satisfactory) victory.

3. *Ego conflict.* Ego conflict is based on a win-lose mentality. Conflicts of this nature are based on manipulation and control to support one's identity, and to prove one is right. Ego conflicts are based on power, competency, identity, and emotional attachment. They are thought to be the hardest type to resolve (Fig 14.3).

Conflict-Management Styles

There are several management styles that deal with conflict. Not all styles are beneficial, and in fact, some may actually perpetuate conflict. The following offers descriptions of both negative and positive conflict-management styles:

1. *Withdrawal.* When a conflict seems overwhelming, the first reaction is usually avoidance. Withdrawal can be defined as either a physical or psychological removal from the problem. Walking out of a room, taking a circuitous route to your office or dorm room, or merely remaining silent are examples of avoidance. Many people fear confrontation due to previous conflict experiences that left deep emotional scars. Withdrawal is seen as a coping style, albeit regressive, when conflicts involve figures of authority, such as bosses or parents, or when a person feels outnumbered by colleagues or peers. On the positive side, withdrawal can be beneficial when it is used as a time out to cool off, as long as a "time in" follows shortly thereafter. Withdrawal is typically regarded as immature behavior, and thus a negative conflict-management style, because physical or verbal absence prevents resolution.

2. *Surrender.* To habitually give in to a situation or problem is also construed as a negative conflict-management style. Like withdrawal, surrender is a type of avoidance people use to appease fellow workers, family, peers, and especially close friends and spouses for fear of rejection and damaging relationships. But surrendering to the will of others deflates self-esteem. What might look like a noble act actually inhibits complete resolution. Resolution of conflicts involves decisions by all parties involved. When one person holds back,

Communication skills are paramount in resolving conflicts, but each person must have a chance to share thoughts and feelings to make this skill effective in reducing stress. *Figure 14.3*

"Just hear me out, then tell me I'm wrong."

merely expressing dissatisfied agreement, the merits of a solution are unbalanced. This style of conflict management generates feelings of victimization.

3. *Hostile aggression.* The words *conflict* and *confrontation* often bring to mind visions of yelling, fists pounding, and objects flying across the room. Indeed, this is how some conflicts are handled. Aggression is often used as a form of intimidation, to manipulate others into submissive agreement. Verbal aggression is more common than physical aggression, with the use of harsh words and increased speaking volume to win points. Rarely does aggressive behavior result in the resolution of any conflict, and in fact, it often perpetuates resentment. Unbroken, this cycle can repeat itself forever.

Figure 14.4 Communication skills have been paramount in the efforts to find a breakthrough in the Arab-Israel peace settlement.

4. *Persuasion.* Persuasion is defined as an attempt to alter another person's attitude or behavior. It is believed by some scholars that all verbal expression is rooted in persuasion. When persuasion is used to win a conflict at the expense of others, it is viewed as negative. But persuasion can be a positive style as well. In the initial stage of the conflict-resolution process, all voices need to be heard. Persuasion may include the use of reason, emotional awareness, or motivation to get a point across. When used tactfully, persuasion opens new lines of thinking, which can then be tools to resolve issues and promote mutual agreement.

5. *Dialogue.* Dialogue is a verbal exchange of opinions, attitudes, facts, and perceptions that opens the doors to greater understanding of the nature of the problem. During the dialogue process, discussions center around the costs and benefits of solving a problem. Dialogue involves the same steps as those employed for creative problem solving (see Chapter 13). In dialogue, negotiations are a means to a solution to which all parties feel they have made a contribution. Compromise plays an important role in the dialogue process as the intent is to reach a decision that is agreeable to everyone.

Steps to Enhance Communication Skills

The following are additional suggestions to strengthen your communication skills and help promote conflict resolution. They may look like common sense, but they bear listing because under stress the walls of the ego are thick. The more we remind ourselves of these skills, the more likely we will be to use them.

1. *Speak with precision and directness.* To express yourself clearly, select words that accurately describe your thoughts and feelings. Be direct about your thoughts and perceptions by verbalizing the intent of your message as clearly as possible.

2. *Enhance your vocabulary.* Vocabulary affects the effectiveness of verbal communication. A small vocabulary decreases the ability to express yourself, whereas a greater number of words to choose from provides you with greater flexibility to say what you want to say.

3. *Use language appropriate for your listening audience.* The manner in which you speak to a child probably differs from that which you use with an adult. Assess which words, expressions, and gestures are most conducive to getting your point across.

Pillow Talk

Box 14.2

A chapter on communication skills would be incomplete without some mention of the dialogue that takes place between sexual partners. In light of the facts that over a million people in the United States are now infected with AIDS or HIV and that the incidence of date rape is so high, this aspect of human behavior can no longer be left to assumptions. Tannen was right that men and women have different styles of communication, and nowhere is this more evident than in sexual relations. Because of American social mores, the issues surrounding sexual relations are still considered taboo in normal conversation. Ironically, it may be these very mores that have nurtured an environment of hostility and anxiety with regard to sexual issues. At a time when trust is paramount, sexual desire and arousal seem to short-circuit the self-disclosure so vital to one's health.

There are many issues involving sexual intercourse that are stressors behind closed doors. These include contraception, birth control, the risk of pregnancy, infertility, sexually transmitted diseases, vaginismus, molestation, celibacy, guilt, rape, self-respect, abortion, impotency, premature ejaculation, intimacy, the ability to reach orgasm, homosexuality, and sexual satisfaction. As you can see, this (incomplete) list is quite long, and each topic weighs heavily as a stressor for those who experience it. Problems of a sexual nature do not go away once a couple has initiated sexual relations, either. To the contrary, if communications are poor at the start of a relationship, they only tend to get worse as the relationship continues. Sex counselors advise that *before, during, and after* every act of sexual intimacy there should be a thorough conversation airing problematic sexual issues. As any AIDS patient or woman with an unwanted pregnancy can tell you, the short-term pleasures of sex are surely not worth the risks involved. And days, months, or years of agony may ensue when other sexual matters go unresolved. Make a point to include a healthy conversation as part of your sexual habits.

4. *Attack issues, not people.* When trying to resolve conflicts with others, focus on the problem, not the people involved. In other words, avoid character assassination. Attacking people clouds the issue and makes it harder, if not impossible, to resolve issues.

5. *Avoid putting others on the defensive.* When initiating self-disclosure or a dialogue to resolve conflicts, begin your statements with, "I perceive . . ." Placing the responsibility of understanding on yourself rather than blaming others minimizes defensiveness.

6. *Avoid asking someone else to pass on your thoughts and feelings to a third party.* The most effective communication involves talking with someone face to face. Involving a third party (e.g., "Please tell my roommate to call John") not only increases the chances of miscommunication but not making personal contact also sends one or more nonverbal messages.

7. *Avoid information overload.* Attention span is limited, as is the amount of information that can be received and processed. The greater amount of information given, the greater the chances some of it will get lost. Be careful to pace your conversation, allowing ample time to process the messages that have been expressed.

8. *Validate your assumptions.* Confirm what you think to be true with those who have given you this impression.

9. *Resolve problems when they arise.* If you feel there is a misunderstanding, there probably is. Avoiding it, or giving it too much time to fester, allows the conscious mind to validate feelings of victimization, anger, or fear. Try to deal with issues as they surface by talking them out with those involved. In the short term, this may seem confrontational and threatening, but in the long term, it relieves the pressure of undue stress and promotes inner peace.

Summary

- Three-quarters of our waking day is spent in some form of communication. Typically, stressors involving other people are due to miscommunication.
- There are many conversation styles. Miscommunication may result when two or more styles are incompatible.
- Schismogenesis refers to the process wherein people become more deeply entrenched in their own communication style, widening the gap of misunderstanding.
- Tannen believes that one reason for misunderstandings between people is that they tend to speak in metamessages, or indirect expressions of thoughts. Indirectness can result from many different intentions.
- Communication is divided into verbal and nonverbal forms. Verbal communication involves both encoding our thoughts into words, and decoding other peoples' words through the sifter of our perceptions. During the encoding and decoding process, some thoughts can get lost in translation.
- Verbal communication involves some level of self-disclosure. The degree of disclosure depends on the level of trust among those involved.
- Nonverbal communication involves a host of gestures and postures, as well intonation. Handshakes, hugs, finger gestures, clothing, and territorial space are examples of how we communicate nonverbally.
- Communication also involves listening and attending skills: the ability to receive and interpret information as it is intended.
- Miscommunication can lead to conflicts, which are broken down into three types: content conflicts, value conflicts, and ego conflicts. The last is the hardest to resolve.
- There are effective and noneffective conflict styles. To withdraw, surrender, or act aggressively is not effective. Persuasion and dialogue are advocated as effective ways to negotiate, compromise, and come to peaceful resolution.
- Sexual intimacy without dialogue is an open invitation to acute and chronic stress. Sex counselors advocate a healthy dialogue before and after every act of sexual intimacy.
- Several suggestions, based on common sense, were listed to improve your communications skills. For these skills to be effective, they must be practiced regularly.

Concepts and Terms

- Adaptors
- Affect displays
- Conflict-management styles
- Conflict resolution
- Decoding
- Emblems
- Encoding
- Illustrators
- Metamessages
- Nonverbal communication
- Paralanguage
- Regulators
- Sapir-Whorf hypothesis
- Schismogenesis
- Self-disclosure

Self-Assessment

Based on the information in this chapter, what would you say is one area of communication in which you have the greatest need of change? Why?

_____

_____

_____

_____

_____

_____

Thinking of the people in your life with whom you are actively engaged in relationships (e.g., parents, siblings, girlfriend, boyfriend, roommate, children, in-laws, friends), who are you currently having problems with in terms of communication?

1. _____

2. _____

3. _____

4. _____

5. _____

Select one of these people and develop a strategy with specific steps you can take to improve your communication skills to resolve whatever issues are currently unresolved.

_____

_____

_____

_____

_____

_____

_____

_____

References and Resources

Barker, L. L. and Collins, N. Nonverbal and Kinesic Research. In P. Emmert and W. D. Brooks, eds., *Methods of Research in Communication*. Houghton Mifflin, Boston, 1970.

Burley-Allen, M. Listening: *The Forgotten Skill*. John Wiley & Sons, New York, 1995.

Fanning, P. *Messages: The Communications Skills Book*. New Harbinger Pub., Oakland, 1995.

Gordon, L. *Passage to Intimacy*. Fireside Books, New York, 1993.

Gray, J. *Men Are from Mars, Women Are from Venus: A Practical Guide for Improving Communication and Getting What You Want in Your Relationships*. Harper Collins, New York, 1992.

Ivey, A. and Gluckstern, N. *Basic Attending Skills*. Microtraining Associates, North Amherst, MA, 1982.

McKay, M., Davis, M., and Fanning, P. *Messages: The Communication Skills Book*. New Harbinger Press, Oakland, CA, 1983.

Satir, V. *Making Contact*. Celestial Arts, Berkeley, CA, 1976.

Scott, G. G. *Resolving Conflict with Others and within Yourself*. New Harbinger Press, Oakland, CA, 1990.

Snelling, A., Meholick, B., and Seaward, B. L. Communication Skills, *Fitness Management* 6:40–41, 1990.

Tannen, D. *Talking From 9–5*. Avon Publishing, New York, 1995.

Tannen, D. *That's Not What I Meant: How Conversational Style Makes or Breaks Relationships*. Ballantine Books, New York, 1986.

Tannen, D. *You Just Don't Understand: Women and Men in Conversation*. Ballantine Books, New York, 1990.

Verderber, R., and Verderber, K. *Inter-Act: Using Interpersonal Communication Skills*, 3rd ed. Wadsworth, Belmont, CA, 1983.

Williams, F. *Executive Communication Power*. Prentice-Hall, Englewood Cliffs, NJ, 1983.

Wilmot, W. W. *Dyadic Communication*, 3rd ed. McGraw-Hill, New York, 1987.

$\mathcal{C}$hapter 15 Time Management

"Oh dear! Oh dear! I shall

be too late!"

—*The Rabbit in*

Lewis Carroll's

Alice in Wonderland

The constructs of seconds, hours, days, months, and years are creations of the human mind. It is believed that the concept of time was originally created to master the natural environment, particularly the position of the sun over the earth and the change of seasons. The Babylonians are credited with the first 360-day calendar, comprised of twelve lunar months each with thirty days. In due time, five days were added to the year by the Egyptians to compensate for rotational differences between the earth and moon. Additional changes were made by the early Romans, and again by Pope Gregory XIII in 1582, who devised the contemporary, or Gregorian, calendar. On a smaller but no less important scale, the first mechanical clock is credited to an eleventh-century Chinese man, Su Song. Two more centuries would pass before a similar machine would appear in the Western world, a clock constructed of iron gears and weights built for an English monastery. The pendulum clock arrived 300 years later, through the creativity of a Dutch scientist, Christian Huygens. Pocket watches were in vogue at the turn of the twentieth century until the invention of the wrist watch. With the advent of high technology, time is now measured in nanoseconds through the use of quartz crystals and digital displays.

As civilizations developed and technology was shared among cultures, awareness and utilization of time contributed to the organization and advancement of the human race, and hence became accepted ways to make order out of chaos. Time became a tool used by various societies to unite and synchronize the efforts of individuals in their communities. American time zones (Eastern, Central, Mountain, and Pacific), for example, were created by railroad companies to synchronize their schedules over various parts of the country, and were eventually adopted by the United States government in 1883. Global time zones followed suit in 1884.

Once conceived, time has been manipulated constantly. The international dateline, daylight savings time, and leap year are three examples of attempts to refine and manipulate the basic constructs of time. The eight-hour workday is another. In an attempt to harness time and manipulate it for gain and pleasure, however, citizens of the industrialized world have often found themselves to be slaves to the concept rather than masters of it. The result: time, or the lack thereof, is now considered to be a premier stressor in the lives of many people. And while time is not considered a precursor to disease and illness in itself, a rushed lifestyle, or as psychologist Robert Levine calls it, "clockwork blues," which constantly disrupts the body's biological clock, is now associated with the incidence of coronary heart disease, ulcers, and other stress-related illnesses. Perhaps not surprisingly, more people have heart attacks on Monday mornings than on any other day of the week.

Looking busy might be considered a status symbol to some people, but not to Stephan Rechtschaffen, M.D. In his highly acclaimed book *Time Shifting,* Rechtschaffen explains that being overproductive is an index of stress, a fast-paced rhythm that leads to dysfunction. Rechtschaffen says that the rhythm of society itself is increasing, and many people are unaware they are caught up in it. People are entrained by the rhythm of their working environment in what he calls *hyperproductivity.* The short-term gains may seem impressive. The long-term results are devastating to one's health. Rechtschaffen, who founded the Omega Institute for Holistic Studies in Rhinebeck, New York, suggests that we need to learn to time shift—that is, to decelerate from the fast-paced lifestyle by consciously changing the rhythm of our activity to live in the present moment.

Current research into leisure habits suggests that the two limiting factors (stressors) on recreation and leisure are time and money. Many people who have come to the conclusion that time equals money compound the effects of this stressor. With advances in technology and perceived increases in responsibility, time, or the mismanagement of it, has often become an enemy—and a major stressor unto itself. In light of time as a stressor in today's culture, this chapter will place special emphasis on changing negative perceptions of this construct as well as manipulating it to allow individuals to make order out of their personal chaos.

Time management is actually a part of a larger coping skill referred to as **social engineering.** Social engineering is a cognitive strategy employed to help minimize stressors without avoiding them. This technique is a reorganization process where you manipulate factors and elements (not people) in your environment to your best advantage in order to travel the path of least resistance. Social engineering involves analyzing a problem, creating a series of viable options, and then choosing the best option to clear stress-prone obstacles out of the way (see Chapter 17). To manipulate time in a well-organized fashion so that it can bear the fruit of productivity is the essence of time management.

According to time management expert Robert Roesch, despite the fact that the pace of life is speeding up with the rush of technological advancements, from cell phones to palm computers, the age-tested means to manage time remain the same. However, with the impending invasion of technology in our personal lives, maintaining proper boundaries is paramount to one's sanity and overall health. To paraphrase Roesch, unless you are a physician on call, you do not need to be accessible twenty-four hours a day through cell phones. Finally, technology is marketed to be time-saving, all in the name of increased productivity. As we all know, this is not always the case. Use technology to simplify, not complicate, your life.

In attempting to be more efficient, the human mind tends to break down and compartmentalize entities, such as time, into smaller parts to better comprehend and manipulate them. Neurophysiologists who have studied right- and left-brain cognitive functions have observed that the right hemisphere has no concept of time, and they therefore agree that time awareness is clearly a left-brain function. Yet imagination and spatial awareness have been found to be crucial factors in the effective utilization of time. So it would be wise to assume that the effective management of time involves the cognitive functions of both cerebral hemispheres.

Time management can be defined as the ability to prioritize, schedule, and execute personal responsibilities to personal satisfaction. Time management is a relatively new concept in both personal and professional development. Corporations who desire greater productivity invest their own time and money in creative consultants to train and educate their employees to manage time more efficiently. The following are some of the lessons they teach.

Roadblocks to Effective Time Management

Before one can begin to employ strategies for the more efficient use of time, several roadblocks must be overcome. With a greater awareness of pertinent attitudes, issues, and concerns, the ability to employ time-management skills, without becoming stressed in the process, will become a strong coping strategy when needed. There are many reasons for mismanaged time, including attitudes about oneself and one's working environment or organization, personality styles, values, and lack of knowledge about time-management skills.

The most prevalent of these are attitudes and their associated behaviors. In her book *How to Put More Time in Your Life,* Dru Scott addresses some of these attitudes. Scott refers to these as "secret pleasures," because the human ego can actually derive pleasure from them; they ultimately act as defense mechanisms. Some of these simple pleasures include attention or recognition for being late (e.g., for meetings and appointments); manipulation or control; avoidance—walking or running away from the task at hand; and "hex-insurance" or rationalization—an attitude that too much organization will result in something bad down the road. As a defense mechanism, mismanagement of time is actually considered a good quality.

Scott also cites several myths people harbor with respect to the feasibility of effective time-management skills. One myth is the illusion that time is an adjustable, rather than fixed, variable and that there are more than twenty-four hours in a day. This perception suggests that there will always be "more time" to get a job done. A second myth, perhaps based on one's prior experience, is that time-management techniques just don't work. This perception arises when specific time-management skills are used individually instead of collectively and then fail to meet expectations. Another common perception is that a methodical strategy to organize oneself is unexciting and even boring, compared to the stimulation of a crisis orientation. In other words, some people (e.g., codependents) thrive on crisis management.

Personality Styles and Behaviors

To try to understand the attitudes that become obstacles to efficient time management, scholars have also targeted behaviors that influence one's personality as a whole. Six distinct personality behaviors have become evident. These are Type As, workaholics, time jugglers, procrastinators, perfectionists, and those who fall into lifestyle traps. These behaviors are labeled "time robbers," or time wasters, because they steal valuable time rather than promote effective time usage. While these behaviors are listed separately, it should be noted that the personalities of some people include many of these behaviors, making effective time management even more elusive.

1. *Type A Personality.* Type A personality is thought to be comprised of several dominating behaviors: time urgency (a rush to meet deadlines), anger/hostility (explosive aggression), lack of planning (poor organization skills), and polyphasia (preoccupation with many thoughts at one time). While time urgency might seem to be the target behavior for efficient time management, the combination of all four factors contributes to inefficient use of time. People who exhibit traits of Type A behavior may *appear* to be organized and productive, but studies indicate that Type A individuals are less organized and complete no more work than their Type B counterparts, and their work is often of lower quality.

2. *Workaholism.* Workaholics spend grossly excessive amounts of time working (Fig. 15.1).

Workaholism is considered a process addiction wherein self-validation is received from prolonged working hours to maintain a sense of importance or self-esteem. While the average person may spend eight hours a day at work, the workaholic spends ten to fourteen hours. Workaholics spend time doing many little tasks between 9 and 5, then feel the need to stay longer to get the big projects completed. They tend to shy away from time-saving techniques and productivity measures because these threaten the security of their self-confidence-building strategy. Workaholics may complain about the excessive time they spend on work, but the simple truth is, long hours give them great pleasure.

3. *Time juggler.* A time juggler is someone who tries to do more than one thing at a time. An example might be someone who shaves or puts on make-up with one hand while making a call on the car phone with the other hand, leaving the knees to handle the steering wheel. Time

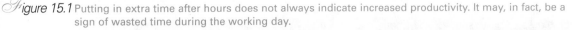

Figure 15.1 Putting in extra time after hours does not always indicate increased productivity. It may, in fact, be a sign of wasted time during the working day.

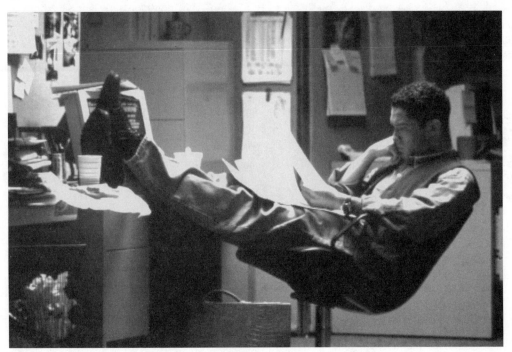

Stress With a Human Face

THERE IS AN OLD JOKE IN THE BUSINESS world that goes like this: "Talk is cheap, until you hire a lawyer." Bonnie would know about lawyer fees. She manages the Washington office of the fifteenth largest law firm in the country, and as manager she is in charge of many aspects, including all finances. Actually, her responsibilities include everything from coordinating plans to relocate the firm to a new building to running the firm's wellness program to overseeing all aspects of human resources. It is a very demanding job, but one she does with great skill and much grace. On top of all this she is a single mother of two children and is actively involved in the Parent–Teachers Association.

How does she do it? Excellent time-management skills! Before she leaves for home each night, Bonnie lays out what she needs to do the next day. From experience, she has learned to establish boundaries, so that when her office door is closed, colleagues know not to bother her. When she is involved with a project that requires large blocks of time, she lets the phone system record her voice mail, and when she walks into a meeting, of which there are several, she is well prepared. And her troubleshooting skills are superb.

Physical exercise is an essential part of Bonnie's stress-management program, and she has a passion for running. Blocking out time to exercise every day is one of her first priorities, and although she may have to schedule workouts around various professional responsibilities, she always manages to get it done. On weekends, she is an avid hiker, which has become a great way to separate from the work environment. She confides that there is an occasional time when she brings work home, but she doesn't make this a habit because when she is home with her children, that is her time to be with them.

Bonnie will admit that sometimes things get a little hectic, like the day she had to leave work to go to the hospital because her son hit his head in school, or the day when the security system failed and disrupted an important partners meeting. But when days don't go as planned, she smiles confidently to herself that all will work out well. "It always has," she says. ✦

jugglers also schedule themselves to be at more than one place at a time, and make cameo appearances at both or skip one altogether with an award-winning excuse. Time jugglers overbook and doublebook appointments in hopes that something might be canceled. In any case, a time juggler is someone who bargains for time, and quite often loses: many responsibilities get dropped in the juggling process.

4. *Procrastinator.* Procrastination is a diversion tactic. Procrastinators avoid responsibilities and put off until tomorrow what should have been done today. There are three factors associated with procrastination: laziness or apathy, fear of failure, and need for instant gratification. Scholars of time management classify procrastinators as follows:

   a. *Straightforward procrastinator.* Someone who knowingly does something other than the job at hand, like going to a ball game or movie rather than studying for an exam.

   b. *Deceptive procrastinator.* Someone who takes a stab at a task (e.g., filing taxes or creating a resumé), but finds excuses to drift away from completion of it until the last minute. On the surface, it looks like progress is being made, but it is a deception.

   c. *Time-trap procrastinator.* Doing the less difficult tasks rather than required ones (e.g., cleaning, washing the car, or walking the dog before completing homework or term papers). The result here is that there is not enough time for a quality job, and these procrastinators then feel like they are painted into a corner with the clock ticking. In addition, other responsibilities are neglected while completing the required task at the last minute.

5. *Perfectionist.* A perfectionist is someone who is obsessed with carrying out every task and responsibility to perfection. While aiming for quality is an admirable attribute, the perfectionist gets too caught up in the details and never sees the whole picture. Thus, projects (or other aspects of life) are compromised. Evidence shows that about 20 percent of all human acts are mistakes. Total perfection is an illusion; it does not exist. But the perfectionist deceives him- or herself by thinking it is possible.

6. *Lifestyle behavior trap.* People who fall into this category are individuals who have a hard or impossible time saying no. These individuals, who show many codependent traits, are extremely nice people. They receive validation of their self-worth by helping other people, often at the expense of their own needs. These people take on inappropriate responsibilities (e.g., house sitting, feeding the neighbor's cat, driving someone to the airport, etc.), often for approval or acceptance to build self-esteem. They may even volunteer for responsibilities they have not been asked to do. But feelings of victimization may result after the task is completed, when just a thank-you is not enough and self-esteem is not enhanced.

Steps to Initiate Time-Management Techniques

Effective time management can be broken down into three skills: prioritization, scheduling, and execution.

1. *Prioritization.* Prioritization means ranking responsibilities and tasks in their order of importance. Before this can be done, however, a list of all current responsibilities must be made (Box 15.1). List making is an invaluable skill in one's time-management strategy. The following two methods are advocated:

a. *The ABC rank-order method* involves assigning the letters A, B, or C to various responsibilities, A for the highest priority activities (must do immediately), B for second-priority activities (anything that is not A or C but should do soon), and C for low-priority tasks or things you would like to do (can wait to do). In this method of prioritization, once a list of responsibilities has been made and a letter assigned to each item, then rewrite the list in this new order and complete the tasks in the same order.

b. *The Pareto principle* states that 20 percent of the tasks we do give 80 percent of the rewards or satisfaction. Also referred to as the 80/20 Rule, this principle suggests that individuals should focus on one or two significant tasks that are worth the time invested in them. According to this principle, out of every ten responsibilities listed, only two will produce recognizable gains. These tasks should be given attention and time. (These two tasks will most likely fall in the A category, suggesting that completion of C, and even B, items may prove unfruitful in the long run.)

c. *Important-versus-urgent method.* Sometimes it is difficult to differentiate among responsibilities, all of which seem important. To use this method, divide your responsibilities for the week into the four boxes. Note that people tend to direct their energies toward box IV because these responsibilities look quick and easy. But attention and efforts should go toward items listed in box I because they are high in both importance and urgency. Next your efforts should go toward box II because these responsibilities are important but not quite so urgent, followed by those items listed in box III, and finally those in box IV.

2. *Scheduling* (Box 15.2). Scheduling is time allocation for prioritized responsibilities, or the skill of matching a specific task or responsibility with a designated time period in which to accomplish it. Time-management experts use the three-Cs method and the three-Ps method for

Time-Management Skills Worksheet

*B*ox 15.1

Prioritizing

To Do List

Date:_____

Write down all the things you need to get done today, with no regard for order.

1.
2.
3.
4.
5.
6.
7.
8.
9.
10.

ABC Rank-Order Method

Direction: In column A, list all the things that *must* get done as soon as possible. In column C, list all the things you would like to do but that are not essential. In column B, put everything else.

A	B	C
_____	_____	_____
_____	_____	_____
_____	_____	_____
_____	_____	_____
_____	_____	_____

Now try organizing your list of things to do in the important-versus-urgent matrix:

	Importance	
	Low Importance	*High Importance*
High Urgency	III. A. B. C.	I. A. B. C.
Low Urgency	IV. A. B. C.	II. A. B. C.

Urgency

Then begin to work on these tasks in the following order:

I. A. _____
  B. _____
  C. _____
II. A. _____
  B. _____
  C. _____

III. A. _____
   B. _____
   C. _____
IV. A. _____
   B. _____
   C. _____

Box 15.2 | **Time-Management Skills Worksheet**

Scheduling

Once you have a solid idea of what needs to get done, there are several choices you can make about scheduling your responsibilities. If you have a few major projects to do, try the boxing method.

Boxing

Divide your day into five parts: morning, noon hour, afternoon, dinner hour, and evening. Then write down the significant tasks and assign them a block of time that is most suited to your schedule.

8–12 noon _____

12–1 _____ Lunch _____ (perhaps do some small errands) _____

1–6 _____

6–7 _____ Dinner _____ (exercise)

_____

7–10 _____

Remember: To be effective you will want to take small breaks during these large blocks of time.

If you have a zillion little things to do, try the time mapping schedule.

Time Mapping

8:00 _____
8:30 _____
9:00 _____
9:30 _____
10:00 _____
10:30 _____
11:00 _____
11:30 _____
12:00 noon _____
12:30 _____
1:00 _____
1:30 _____
2:00 _____
2:30 _____
3:00 _____
3:30 _____
4:00 _____
4:30 _____
5:00 _____

scheduling. The three-Cs method consists of clocks, the designation of time periods for short-term time management; calendars, for weekly, monthly, and even yearly forecasts of goals and responsibilities; and completion times/dates of designated goals and responsibilities. The three-Ps method is planning, implementing a schedule of tasks; priorities, doing a regular check on the relative importance of tasks; and perhaps most important, pacing, or the rate at which each task is performed. The following scheduling techniques are advocated. Remember, though, that flexibility in scheduling is essential, or these time-management techniques will cause stress rather than reduce it.

a. *Boxing.* The concept of boxing involves breaking down your daily waking hours into three- to five-hour chunks or boxes of time such as morning, afternoon, and evening. In each time box, you designate a specific responsibility. Boxing is primarily geared toward big projects that necessitate large blocks

of time (e.g., yard work, term papers, and other major projects). Example:

8–9 A.M. ⎫
9–10 A.M. ⎪ Term
10–11 A.M. ⎬ paper research
11–12 noon ⎭ at library
12–1 P.M.   Lunch/exercise
1–2 P.M. ⎫ Word
2–3 P.M. ⎬ process
3–4 P.M. ⎭ paper

b. *Time mapping.* Time mapping is similar to boxing, but with this strategy, the day is broken down into very small blocks of time, usually about quarter- to half-hour segments. Specific tasks (e.g., drafting a letter, making a phone call, running a quick errand) are designated for specific times:

9 A.M.—Meet with boss, pass in budget report
9:15 A.M.—Mail letters
9:30 A.M.—Phone Atlanta
9:45 A.M.—Pick up book at library
10:00 A.M.—Pick up resumes at printer

c. *Clustering.* Clustering is a scheduling technique for the completion of errands outside the house or office. Responsibilities are listed and then clustered or mapped out by location. Clustering is a time-saving device allowing the individual to complete errands in close proximity to one another rather than ricochet around town.

   As you can see, prioritization and scheduling are partners. At the end of each day, look at your list to see what tasks weren't finished and then reprioritize your responsibilities for the next day.

3. *Execution* (Box 15.3). The execution of responsibilities is a systematic progression of steps taken toward the satisfactory completion of each task. More specifically, execution can be described as the implementation of an established schedule. A prioritized schedule is like a blueprint or military strategy. The most effective method of execution is the establishment of goals. Here are some tips to improve execution:

a. Assign a deadline (goal) for each task or project.

b. Break large projects down into smaller tasks, and assign a deadline for each task.

c. Work on one section or task at a time. Work on it until it is complete. Experts indicate that it is better to have one or two completed tasks than a handful of unfinished ones.

d. Reward your accomplishments with small pleasures to motivate yourself to accomplish designated goals. Avoid immediate gratification, though. In other words, reward yourself after satisfactory completion of each job, not before.

Additional Time-Management Ideas

The following are some additional ideas that don't fall into any specific category but are nevertheless helpful in managing your time effectively:

1. *Delegation.* The old adage, "If you want something done right, you have to do it yourself" can lend itself to stress if you feel you have to do *everything* yourself. Many people dislike delegating responsibilities; it is equated

---

Time-Management Skills Worksheet   *Box 15.3*

Execution

Sometimes to motivate yourself to get things done you need to outline some objectives. You may also want to reward yourself when the task is completed.

   Take a moment to write down some of your objectives for the day, week, or even month to get a bigger picture of what your personal strategy is. Objectives are usually large in scope and context; goals are steps to help you accomplish your objectives. Next to each objective, think of a reward you can give to yourself upon completion of this task. Remember: The bigger the job, the bigger the reward.

Objective

1. To _____
2. To _____
3. To _____
4. To _____
5. To _____
6. To _____
7. To _____
8. To _____
9. To _____
10. To _____

Reward

with loss of control and personal identity. Delegation involves trusting yourself to relinquish control, as well as trusting the individuals to whom you delegate the responsibilities. In many cases, items marked as B or C on your To Do list can be delegated to or shared with other people. When you delegate responsibilities, explain instructions clearly and assign a completion time or date to each task. Avoid delegating responsibilities for which the time to explain the task exceeds the time to complete it. Follow-up is a crucial component of delegation to prevent reverse delegation, wherein the task comes back to you unfinished.

Figure 15.2 Good time management requires you to balance your life between work and leisure. Remember that balance is essential for optimal well-being.

2. *Schedule interruptions.* One time-management technique advocated by experts is to be flexible with your work schedule. Office visits, phone calls, meetings, and two-hour "power lunches" can become distractions and interrupt your work when they are not expected. Resulting feelings of frustration, impatience, and anger can contribute to the pressures of task completion. If you allow for a small number of interruptions of your day, however (Fig. 15.2), anger and hurriedness can be minimized. Experts suggest that interruptions should actually be scheduled into your daily activities, allotting seven to ten minutes per hour. Conversely, interruptions should also be prevented during crucial time periods when continuity of work flow is paramount. Taking the phone off the hook, closing the office door, or leaving the worksite where distractions are unavoidable may be necessary.

3. *Schedule personal time in each day.* Experts agree that a day filled to the brim with career and family responsibilities, leaving no time for oneself, results in burnout and possibly disease and illness. Your health should be a high priority. Time allocated for a walk, jog, or meditation alone is crucial to the effectiveness of carrying out personal responsibilities. But health is often taken for granted until illness occurs. So keep your health a top priority. As Ben Franklin once said, "An ounce of prevention is worth a pound of cure."

4. *An idea book.* An idea book, like a journal, is a place to record various ideas that surface to the conscious mind. Often important thoughts flash into the conscious mind at the most inopportune moments. The mind has limited awareness, with many thoughts competing for attention. An idea book, like a second brain, can become a receptacle for a multitude of important thoughts. Once written down, you can refer back to them at any time. An idea book can include To Do lists, dream lists, names and phone numbers, or any other idea you don't want to forget.

5. *Edit your life.* This journalistic phrase is used here as a personal house-cleaning technique. (It is also known as the emptying process of

spiritual well-being.) Despite the fact that civilization has progressed light years since the days when people lived in caves, we have not lost the Neanderthal trait of hunting and gathering possessions. Whether material in nature or not, we tend to carry around a lot of excess baggage. In the editing process, a regular assessment of physical, mental, emotional, and spiritual needs is conducted. This includes an objective evaluation of relationships, values, and personal needs. Once you have listed your various needs, decide which factors in your life are essential or core to your life, and which factors are peripheral ones draining your energy. Then let go of the ones you feel are draining off valuable time and energy. The editing process, then, is a technique by which you reduce your life to its simplest terms. In the book *The Dove,* a true story of a teenager who sailed around the world by himself, author Robin Lee Graham said, "It's not how much I need to survive, it's how little I need to survive."

6. *Networking skills.* Tracking down resources to accomplish tasks can be a time waster if the time it takes to access the resource exceeds its importance. In many cases, people are resources. There is a saying in the business world: "It's not what you know but who you know." In reality, time management requires a combination of the two, as all the connections in the world will not help without a brain to use them. Connections are important, and networking is the establishment of solid connections. Learn who can help you accomplish the satisfactory completion of tasks that cannot be done alone. Learn who you can rely on for help, whether you need an important phone number, to borrow a truck, or a helping hand to move to a new apartment.

7. *Organizational skills.* While some people think that organizational skills are innate, the truth is that, with practice, anybody can learn strong organizational skills to increase personal productivity. The following tips will help to sharpen your organizational skills:

a. A place for everything, and everything in its place. Much time is wasted looking for items that seem to have fallen into a black hole. Precious time can be saved by designating a place for bills, assignments, budget sheets, and so forth, and keeping these items where they belong.

b. Learn what resources are available to help you complete what you need to get done.

c. Learn where these resources are, and when you can use them.

d. Make a list of deadlines, or responsibilities with a time limit attached to them. Update the list regularly.

e. Buy a master calendar or daily planner and write down all your deadlines to get a comprehensive picture of the events in your life. Learn to look at the entire week, and then the entire month to get a wider perspective. Then zoom in and focus on immediate as well as long-term needs.

f. Learn to make outlines of projects, papers, lectures, and proposals—introduction, development, conclusions.

g. Correspondence. Keep files of letters (both incoming and outgoing) to refer to when you need to get in touch with someone. Also, regardless of what letter or paper crosses your desk, *handle it once.* Studies show that when mail is opened and stacked to be responded to, the more times that it is looked at, the longer it takes to get done. Handle it once and be done with it.

h. Phone calling. Learn when people you need to contact are available. Learn/remember to tell others where you are or when you can be reached.

i. Learn/recognize your physical/mental limitations. Learn *how* to say no to people who plead for time you don't have (e.g., I'm sorry, but I simply don't have time). Be gentle but firm! Learn *when* to say no to people who plead for time you don't have.

j. E-mails. Some people receive up to 100 e-mail messages a day. Reading and responding to these can become a full-time job. Here is a tip: If emails are a stressor in your life, delete all the forwarded emails to save time for those that are really important.

k. Cell phones. Once used in cars for emergencies, portable cell phones can now be found attached to anyone's ear practically anywhere rather than just for emergencies. Make it a habit to limit cell phone use to practical hours and turn it off while at the movies, restaurants, classrooms, and other inappropriate places.

l. The Internet. A lot of time can be wasted waiting for web pages to download off the Internet (this might actually be a great time to practice diaphragmatic breathing). Addiction to the Internet is no laughing matter. Monitor your computer usage time and if it exceeds two to three hours a day (outside of work), consider limiting it to a respectable amount.

8. *Balance.* All work and no play means poor work quality. Balance your life between work and play. Don't place all your self-esteem eggs in one basket.

True to the puritan ethic that worth equals work, Americans, by and large, spend an inordinate amount of time at their jobs. In fact, according to the U.S. Department of Labor statistics, since 1980 the average American spends five to ten more hours per week at his or her job. Because of corporate downsizing and restructuring, people are more inclined not to use their entire vacation time, for fear that if they take time off from their job, they might be next in line to leave permanently. Time-management expert Jeff Davidson notes that not only do more people spend more time at work, but also they tend to sleep fewer hours, resulting in feelings of fatigue and irritability while on the job. Davidson also notes that as we continue to indulge in the throes of the information age, we tend to become suffocated in information, from junk mail to the Internet. The following are some additional tips from Davidson on managing your time more effectively:

1. *Watch less television.* Television is definitely a time robber. People say they watch TV to relax, but what is really happening is that they are substituting one form of sensory stimulus for another. And due to the addictive nature of television watching, even though you may only plan to watch one half-hour show, you end up sitting in front of the television for the entire evening, wasting the night away.

2. *Clean your office, room, desk, or work space once a week.* Things tend to accumulate rather

quickly in the course of a week. Mail, books, papers, and odds and ends all take up space. Not only do these things take up space, they also compete for your attention. Using what Davidson calls the "urge to purge," don't be afraid to throw away those things you know no longer serve you. By making a habit of clearing off your desk and work space, you not only spend less time searching for things throughout the week, but at the same time, you start the cleansing process in your mind to focus on your work as well.

3. *Get a good night's sleep every night.* The average recommended time for sleep is between six and eight hours a night. When we get pressed for time, the allocation of time for sleeping is often the first thing cut. In the short term, what may seem like a clever idea to cram for an exam, write a paper, or finish a project, is in the long run an invitation to disaster. Although scientists who study sleep do not agree why adequate sleep is necessary, they all agree that sleep is essential to our health and well-being. Denying ourselves adequate sleep not only affects the quality of the work we do the next day, but ultimately affects the quality of our health as well.

4. *Create personal boundaries, and honor them.* Boundaries are those invisible lines we draw around ourselves to keep our identity and give structure to our lives. Just as it is important to be flexible and go with the flow when working with the element of time, it is equally important to honor personal boundaries, both yours and those of other people in your life. Honoring boundaries includes knowing when to leave the library, office, worksite, or friend's house and call it a day. By honoring your boundaries, you maintain a sense of personal integrity. When boundaries are not honored, feelings of victimization surface, and these too can have a negative impact on the quality and quantity of the work you do.

5. *Do one activity at a time.* In this day and age, it is easy to get caught up doing many things at once, like sending a fax while talking on the phone, or writing a term paper while watching

the football playoffs. Dividing your attention between two or more activities results in less quality in the work done. It wastes time as well. Learn to focus yourself by doing one task at a time.

6. *Learn and practice the art of decision making.* We are constantly faced with choices in both our personal and professional lives—where to eat, what movie to see, what topic to present, or what job to take. Decision making requires a good sense of judgment, coupled with a sense of compassion. Some decisions can be made rather quickly, while those with long-term implications need more time to survey and process. When we have big decisions to make we tend to drag our feet and, in the information age, it is not hard to become overwhelmed with tidbits of facts and figures. In the words of Davidson, more choices mean more decisions. He suggests that we avoid being overwhelmed by learning to limit our choices and, hence, the decisions that come from so many choices.

Best Application of Time-Management Skills

Time-management skills can appear overwhelming and stress producing if they are seen as dogmatic and rigid. Use of time-management skills should be proportional to the number of responsibilities one assumes. In all likelihood, you are already fairly adept at these time-management techniques and may even use some of them in your normal working schedule. It is during periods when responsibilities accumulate beyond normal that these techniques may assist in your overall coping strategy. Before you begin to apply these techniques, first inventory your attitudes and behavior styles for the roadblocks listed earlier in the chapter. See if you can relate to any factors that sabotage efforts to get tasks accomplished on time. Then experiment with the techniques to find out which work best for you. After employing these techniques, evaluate their effectiveness. It is fair to say that virtually all other stress-management skills hinge on time management, for without adequate time allocated to rethink strategies to deal with stress or practice relaxation techniques, learning them serves no lasting purpose.

Summary

- Time is a man-made concept. Calendars and time zones were created to bring organization to cultures and civilizations that needed to coordinate activities.
- Although the concept of time was created to help organize, people often find themselves becoming slaves to the clock, and hence become stressed by it.
- Time management is defined as the ability to prioritize, schedule, and execute responsibilities to personal satisfaction. Time-management skills are now taught to people to help them gain a sense of control over personal responsibilities.
- There are several roadblocks to effective time management, which impede productivity and, in essence, rob us of valuable time. They include Type A personality, workaholism, time juggling, procrastination, and lifestyle behavior trapping.
- Three methods of prioritization are the ABC rank-order method, the Pareto principle, and the important-versus-urgent method.
- Recommended scheduling techniques are boxing, time mapping, and clustering.
- The execution of personal responsibilities is the last step of time management. Setting goals and providing rewards can be powerful incentives to finishing the task at hand.
- Additional tips to help manage time better are delegation of responsibilities, scheduling interruptions and personal time each day, using an idea book, editing your life to the bare essentials, and using networking and strong organizational skills.

Concepts and Terms

ABC rank-order method

Boxing

Clustering

Delegation

Important-versus-urgent method

Lifestyle behavior trap

Networking skills

Pareto principle

Perfectionist

Scheduling

Straightforward procrastinator

Time juggler

Time management

Time mapping

Time-trap procrastinator

Type A personality

Workaholism

Self-Assessment

1. What would you say are your greatest time robbers?

   a. _____
   b. _____
   c. _____
   d. _____
   e. _____

2. Take a serious look at your time-management skills. Do unresolved feelings of anger toward somebody or something (perhaps even yourself) impede you from getting things done? If so, explain.

   _____
   _____
   _____
   _____
   _____
   _____

3. What big projects do you have going on right now?

   a. _____
   b. _____
   c. _____
   d. _____
   e. _____

   Break the first two projects on your list down into parts that are easier to finish:

   A_____   B_____

   Parts or phases of this project: Parts or phases of this project:

   1. _____   1. _____
   2. _____   2. _____
   3. _____   3. _____
   4. _____   4. _____
   5. _____   5. _____

4. We all have moments of lethargy and laziness. What can you do to break the cycle of inertia so that you can accomplish your responsibilities?

   a. _____
   b. _____
   c. _____
   d. _____
   e. _____
   f. _____

References and Resources

Allen, D. *Getting Things Done: The Art of Stress Free Productivity.* Viking Press, New York, 2001.

Beech, H. R., Burns, L. E., and Sheffield, B. F. *A Behavioral Approach to the Management of Stress.* Wiley, Chichester, Eng., 1982.

Bliss, E. *Getting Things Done: The ABCs of Time Management.* Scribner's, New York, 1976.

Boslough, J. The Enigma of Time, *National Geographic* 177(3):109–132, 1990.

Charlesworth, E. A. and Nathan R. G. *Stress Management: A Comprehensive Guide to Wellness.* Ballantine Books, New York, 1984.

Covey, S. *First Things First.* Fireside Books, New York, 1996.

Davidson, J. *The Complete Idiot's Guide to Managing Your Time.* Alpha Books, New York, 1995.

Girdano, D., Everly, G., and Dusek, D. *Controlling Stress and Tension: A Holistic Approach.* Prentice-Hall, Englewood Cliffs, NJ, 1990.

Graham, R. L. *The Dove.* Bantam Books, New York, 1972.

Hout, T. M. and Stalk, G. *Competing against Time.* Free Press, New York, 1990.

Lee, M. D. *Management of Work and Personal Life.* Praeger, New York, 1984.

Levine, R. The Pace of Life, *Psychology Today* 20:42–46, 1989.

Mackenzie, A. *The Time Trap.* AMACOM, New York, 1990.

Mayer, J. *Time Management for Dummies.* IDG Books, Indianapolis, IN, 1995.

Morgenstern, J. *Time Management from the Inside Out.* Henry Holt, New York, 2000.

Oldenburg, D. Fast Forward: Living in Artificial Time, *Health* 20:52–56, 80–81, 1988.

Peterson, K. *The Tomorrow Trap.* Health Communications, Inc., Deerfield Beach, FL, 1996.

Quirk, T. J. The Art of Time Management, *Training* 26(1):59–61, 1989.

Rechtschaffen, S. *Time Shifting.* Doubleday, New York, 1996.

Roesch, R. *Time Management for Busy People.* McGraw-Hill, New York, 1998.

Rutherford, R. D. *Just in Time: Immediate Help for the Time-Pressured.* Wiley, New York, 1981.

Scott, D. *How to Put More Time in Your Life.* Rawson, Wade, New York, 1980.

Tucker, M. *It's Your Time—Use It or Lose It.* Exposition Press, New York, 1980.

Yates, B. *Applications in Self-Management.* Wadsworth, Belmont, CA, 1986.

Yates, B. *Self-Management.* Wadsworth, Belmont, CA, 1985.

Chapter 16 Additional Coping Techniques

*One cannot collect all the
beautiful shells on the beach,
one can collect only a few.*
—Anne Morrow Lindbergh

According to several psychologists, just as there are many shells on the beach, there are hundreds of coping techniques. Some fall nicely into well-defined categories; others do not but are every bit as important in their function and outcome. Much like acquiring a personal collection of seashells, chances are you will choose a handful of coping strategies for your own stress-management program and leave the rest behind. And just as a return to the beach may inspire you to pick up a new shell, which at another time seemed unattractive or banal, a new encounter with stress may entice you to select a new method of coping. This chapter will outline some additional coping techniques that are often used to deal with stress effectively. While they may not serve as your first line of defense in every case, at some point in your life you may find them very helpful.

Information Seeking

Fear of the unknown accompanies many formidable stressors, from job interviews to cancer diagnoses. Several circumstances we encounter are perceived as threats because of our lack of information about the event. Lack of information allows the mind to fill in missing pieces with hypothetical facts or worst-case scenarios, which often perpetuates the stress response.

Figure 16.1 (ZIGGY © 1986 ZIGGY AND FRIENDS, INC. Reprinted with permission of UNIVERSAL PRESS SYNDICATE. All rights reserved.)

To conquer fear of the unknown, gathering information about a specific circumstance becomes one of the best defenses against stressors. Information seeking involves collecting and processing facts about a stressful event or situation, which can then be used to help solve the problem and regain emotional stability. As suggested by psychologist Shelly Taylor (1990), the gathering and processing of information also allows mastery of control, as knowledge can become a powerful tool with which to confront and dismantle a stressor.

Information seeking has been found to be an essential skill following diagnosis of terminal illness, in the recovery process of alcoholics and drug abusers, during pregnancy, and for any other stressor that makes an unpredictable change in your life, however big or small. When encountering stress, people pose many questions in an attempt to gain a handle on the unknown. When an individual contracts a disease such as cancer, multiple sclerosis, or atherosclerosis, all attention becomes focused on gathering answers to a host of questions. What is the nature of this disease? How did I contract it? What is the best method to manage it? Similarly, when your car breaks down, a set of questions runs through your mind. What's wrong with the engine or transmission? How long will it take to fix? How much will it cost? Can I afford this? Like a large jigsaw puzzle, small pieces of information become crucial to the ability to cope with the cause of the stress so as to assemble a wider perspective on the whole problem as well as potential solutions.

In times of distress, questions necessitate answers, and there are many resources that are typically accessed to provide answers. The three most common references are people, books and the internet. An individual becomes a source of reference when he or she appears to be "in the know" about a certain situation, either because of personal experience or the acquisition of knowledge pertaining to your situation. Usually when information is disseminated through people, however, facts are intertwined with emotional perceptions. As a result, the objectivity of this information must be assessed very carefully. Books, journals, magazines, the internet and newspapers are also valuable sources of information on virtually every topic known, often offering several viewpoints (Fig. 16.1). The use of these references to cope with stress even has its own name: bibliotherapy.

Like other coping techniques, though, information seeking can be a liability as well as an asset. Too much information can be as detrimental as too little, because it can feed the imagination to create worse-case scenarios, which are then adopted as reality. Nevertheless, when you are confronted with a stressor that promotes fear of the unknown, information seeking can be your best strategy to begin to cope with this problem.

Social Engineering

Perhaps the most common response to events or circumstances that elicit the stress response is avoidance. While avoidance of life-threatening events such as fire is wise, avoidance of mental, emotional, and spiritual threats is not a viable option. Avoidance is a defense mechanism deeply rooted in the ancient flight response. It is popularly believed that if we avoid situations that cause fear or frustration, our lives will become simple and stress-free. But what may seem like a quick fix offers no permanent resolution, only further problems down the road. Avoidance is a negative coping style, especially when the stressors involve relationships and human confrontation.

Can you make educated choices about how to minimize stressful situations? Yes! The answer is **social engi-**

Stress With a Human Face

CURIOSITY IS ONE OF HUMANITY'S NOBLEST traits. And for every dangerous situation that may result from too much inquisitiveness there are ten times the number of stories that result in personal victories. None, however, is as compelling as that of Augusto and Michaela Odone, which has to be the epitome of information seeking as a coping strategy.

The story began in 1984, when their son, Lorenzo, then six years old, was sent home from school for displaying hyperactive behavior. As days turned into months, additional symptoms appeared, and eventually Lorenzo was diagnosed with the newly named and little understood adrenoleukodystrophy (ALD), a lethal genetic disease of dysfunctional nerve tissue, resulting from an extremely high number of very long fatty-acid chains in the blood. Lorenzo was given a maximum of two years to live.

But his parents did not accept Lorenzo's death sentence. Upon learning of the prognosis for their son, Augusto and Michaela took turns going to the National Library of Medicine to research ALD and staying home to care for Lorenzo.

With persistence, willpower, luck, and what Augusto calls a "whole lot of love," their search for clues not only enlightened the medical community about the dynamics involved in the etiology of the disease, but led to the creation of a medication, Lorenzo's Oil, which arrested the progression of the disease. Lorenzo's Oil is now used to treat this disease in children all over the world.

A lawyer for the World Bank, Augusto has earned an honorary doctorate in medicine for his achievement. And although Lorenzo still waits for a cure to repair his damaged myelinated nerve tissue, hundreds of children are living normal lives thanks to the inquisitive nature of Augusto and Michaela Odone. But in the words of Augusto, "I wouldn't like it that people think our efforts were out of intellectual curiosity. This is a story of love." ✦

neering. Social engineering is a positive coping style designed to help minimize stress by following a path of least resistance, but not avoidance. Social engineering involves analyzing a problem, creating a series of viable options, and then choosing the best option to resolve feelings and perceptions of stress. Social engineering is also described as a reorganization process wherein individuals manipulate factors and elements (not people) in their environment to their best advantage.

There are two approaches to the social-engineering process. The first is to change factors in your environment that can cause stress. If this is not a viable option, your health status is at risk, and attempts at cognitive reappraisal prove fruitless, then the second approach is to change your environment. Changing factors in your environment might include driving a different route to work or blocking out time periods during the day during which you do not answer the phone so as to get a major task completed. In situations where you change specific factors, you attempt to manipulate or control your environment so that your encounters with potential stressors are minimal. To change your environment means relocating from unhealthy or intolerable living conditions to a new setting that is conducive to better health status. Because changing one's environment is both costly and time consuming, this approach is often used as a last resort. Keep in mind that if you choose to change your environment to avoid people or run away, then this coping technique is being used improperly and no resolution is guaranteed. Also remember from Chapter 1 that Homes and Rahe found that relocating to a new environment is a stressful experience in itself.

On a larger scale, social engineering can be seen in many political grassroots efforts; lobbying Congress to pass legislation favoring particular issues and concerns, for example. In fact, social engineering is the coping skill of choice at both local and national governmental levels for issues such as landfills and recycling. On a smaller scale, social engineering is a strategy we employ regularly with personal chores and responsibilities, but it is an effective one in the management of major life stressors.

A prime example of social engineering where factors in the environment were changed is the October 17, 1989, earthquake that hit the city of San Francisco and surrounding areas. After an initial assessment of the damage and loss of life, attempts were made to put the Bay Area quickly back on its feet again, though projections indicated that more than twelve months would elapse before a return to complete normalcy. One of the biggest problems to solve was the devastation of several bridges, leaving commuters unable to travel back and forth from Oakland to San Francisco. Crisis-management teams were consulted and several factors were manipulated around the Bay Area to ensure continuity of employment and ease the stressful aftermath of the quake. These included opening temporary branch offices in Oakland for people who could not get across the Bay, employees buying modems for personal computers so they could work at home, and augmenting transportation across the Bay by bringing in several new ferries. Although the earthquake caused major inconveniences, people adapted quickly to the changes made through social engineering.

In another example, in 1978 people in a small community began to document evidence of disproportionate serious illness in their area. In 1981 Love Canal, New York, was deemed by the Environmental Protection Agency to be a major health hazard to its residents due to incredible amounts of pollutants and carcinogens that had leaked into the water supply from a nearby chemical-treatment plant. Shortly thereafter, the federal government offered to relocate those families most directly affected by the toxins. Even though some people elected to stay, most people relocated to a healthier environment. Similar circumstances arose in 1978, when radioactive leakage was reported at the nuclear power plant at Three Mile Island, Pennsylvania.

While social engineering is often the coping skill of choice for large-scale issues like earthquakes and man-made disasters, the ability to change factors in the environment can be done at a personal level as well. Many coping skills are used at the same time to deal with a stressor; there is strength in numbers. Thus, social engineering may incorporate the use of other coping skills including assertiveness, cognitive restructuring, creative problem solving, and time management. Cognitive restructuring is essential to create a new frame of mind in which to manipulate factors in the environment. The following is a step-by-step process for social engineering adapted from a model created by Allen and Hyde (1983):

1. *Define your stressors.* Write down what is bothering you by trying to describe what this

stressor really is (e.g., an obnoxious roommate, a bad marriage, car repair problems, etc.).

2. *Identify your initial response.* Do you feel angry, frustrated, afraid, impatient, or resentful? Does this stressor cause you to worry or feel guilty? What emotions are running through your mind? Write these down. Next, describe what your first reaction or course of action to this stressor is (or was). Do you feel the urge to avoid a certain person? Do the words *retaliation* or *avoidance* come to mind? How would you describe your first course of action?

3. *Generate alternatives.* This is the creative stage, where you write down any and all possible solutions. Let us say, for example, that the route you drive to work is under construction and now it takes you an extra twenty-five minutes to get there. You find yourself feeling pretty irritated with the traffic and the fact that you are wasting so much time. What are some viable alternatives? Perhaps carpooling, taking a bus or subway, leaving for work twenty minutes early, finding a new route to work, working at home on a computer with modem hook-up, and walking.

4. *Choose the best alternative.* Once you have a handful of ideas that are plausible, pick the one that seems most suited to your circumstances. Regarding the example above, let us assume that the walk is too far, and that there is no mass transit or potential carpool members readily available. Working at home with a modem hook-up sounds attractive, and you decide to go with this plan of action. To your surprise, your plan is approved by your boss for three out of five work days until the road construction is done. So you work at home, while miles away road construction takes place.

5. *Evaluate the outcome of your choice.* In this last step, you take a moment to analyze the option you have chosen to measure its effectiveness. If the option is a good one, you keep it. If not, you pick a new option and give it a try. In the case of the road-construction problem, it turns out that working at home seems to require much more discipline than you realized. It

actually takes more time to get your work done because of distractions by the refrigerator and the television. After evaluating this option, you decide to return to your office, leaving thirty minutes earlier than before, and this second option works fine.

The key to social engineering is to provide yourself with many viable options from which to choose. Options are like cushions that soften the blow when a stressor disrupts your center of gravity, causing you to fall. People with only one option—or worse, no options—begin to feel that a stressor is beyond control and that they are victims of their environment. By creating and choosing one of several options, you strengthen your internal locus of control and get an early start on resolving the issues at hand.

Social-Support Groups

There is an old proverb suggesting that misery loves company. This does not mean that we wish our troubles on others, nor does it mean that we are happy to see others encounter the same problems we faced ourselves. Rather, it means that when two or more people experience a problem of daunting magnitude, the emotional burden seems to be shared, is more bearable, and is consequently not as heavy a load as a solo attempt at working against the odds. This is the premise that has given rise to the recommendation of regular social contact, and the plethora of support groups across America.

The first support group to gain a foothold of respect in the American culture was Alcoholics Anonymous. Since its inception over fifty years ago, this group has helped millions of people cope with the problems of alcohol addiction through the care and love shared by its members. Because of its tremendous success, the philosophy, format, traditions, and twelve-step recovery process have been borrowed by virtually every support group for all substance and process addictions.

Research has also shown that feelings of connectedness, belongingness, and bonding arising from social contact contribute to one's health (Fig. 16.2). This is the social well-being aspect of spiritual well-being. The desire to belong is considered a basic human need, as was first suggested by Maslow in 1943. There are several theories as to why **social support** is considered an aid in the coping process. The Buffer theory, proposed

Figure 16.2 More and more, evidence points to the idea that strong social support from friends may act to buffer against the ill effects of stress, and add to both the quality and quantity of life.

by Cassel and colleagues (1976), suggests that social support acts as a buffer against stress, in that social ties tend to filter out the deleterious effects of both ordinary hassles and devastating life events. This theory is shared by several researchers in the field of health psychology, but the exact dynamics of this buffering action are still uncertain. Connell and D'Augelli (1990) hypothesized that when individuals express fondness for others and make themselves available to both receive help (succor) as well as give help (nurturance), perceptions of stress are significantly decreased. In the compensation theory, social support is thought to act as a compensation for those who are at an emotional loss due to life's stressors. The direct-effect theory, hypothesized by Andrews and Tennant (1982), indicates that social contact only provides positive exposure to the individual and that these positive stimuli are pleasing to the ego. Finally, the cognitive-dissonance theory states that when individuals are engaged in social contact where values and attitudes are similar, the collective energy far exceeds negative feelings experienced by any one person individually.

Pilisuk and Parks (1986) found evidence supporting the hypothesis that social support not only acts as a buffer against stress, but that it may in fact contribute to health and longevity by enhancing the integrity of the immune system. Results from both the Alameda County Study (Berkman and Syme, 1979) and the Tecumseh Community Health Study (House, Robbins,

and Metzner, 1982) revealed that social support was a significant factor in both the health status and longevity of those subjects studied. These investigations, as well as those conducted by Kaplan and colleagues (1988) and Berkman (1986), indicated that men seem to benefit more than women with regard to the effects of social support on the progression of cardiovascular disease. Raphael (1977) and Lowenthal and Harven (1968) reported that social withdrawal was a significant factor in coronary mortality in bereaved spouses, most notably men. From these and other studies, it seems that companionship is truly a basic human need. When this need is filled through the demonstration of caring, love, and moral support, the intensity of stress is alleviated, suggesting a greater tolerance for frustration and worry. In their reviews of the merits of social support as a coping technique, Brannon and Feist (1992) and Pelletier and Herzing (1988) concluded that it is a significant factor contributing to health and longevity. Thus, its use as a coping strategy is strongly encouraged.

Hobbies

Is there such a thing as a therapeutic escape? Perhaps. While psychologists and stress-management counselors caution against the hazards of avoidance, the practice of diversions has often been advocated as a bona fide coping strategy. Healthy diversions are any activities that offer a temporary escape from the sensory overload that can produce or perpetuate the stress response. Diversions offer the conscious mind a "change of venue" to promote clear thinking. Taking your mind off a problem, or removing an issue from conscious attention for a designated period of time, and diverting attention to an unrelated subject focuses the mind and enables it to deal better with these issues upon return. As with most strategies, diversions offer either positive or negative repercussions. Positive diversions are those in which the individual takes an *active role* in the escape process. (An example of a passive escape is watching television or sleeping.) Active escapes are those that contribute to one's identity, character, and self-esteem. With this in mind, the best temporary active escape is said to be a hobby (Fig. 16.3), the pursuit of a leisure interest that provides pleasure (Kaplin, 1960). Most hobbies, such as needlepoint, photography, and many others, involve some degree of creativity as well as the ability to make order out of chaos on a very small and manageable

Figure 16.3

Involvement in hobbies allows people to make order out of chaos on a small scale, which often transfers to larger-scale problems. Any activity that boosts self-esteem is thought to be worthwhile.

scale. The latter factor tends to give a person a sense of control over life, which in turn augments self-esteem. And high self-esteem transfers from outside interests to areas of one's life where factors contribute to personal stress. Moreover, the ability to bring order to a small-scale operation, like haute cuisine cooking or bonsai gardening, also has a carry-over effect in dealing with larger problems. In fact, many people find that their time spent in the pursuit of hobbies transfers to solutions for major life problems.

However, not all experts agree that hobbies are stress relieving. Relaxation therapist Edmond Jacobson in his book, *You Must Relax,* warned of drawbacks of hobbies, indicating that they produce tension and frustration when expectations are not met. Jacobson believed that for relaxation to be most effective, the individual must be doing absolutely nothing. In his opinion, leisure activities, hobbies in particular, actually compound the accumulation of stress. His point is valid when people focus on perfectionism rather than leisure. When pleasure is absent from leisure activities, it is definitely time to stop and do something else.

One reason why hobbies are advocated as self-esteem builders is that they allow you to invest your-self in several areas. If you have a bad day at the office or school, hobbies can neutralize the negative feelings and bolster self-esteem. In essence, self-esteem remains intact when not all eggs are placed in one basket.

Forgiveness

Every stressor generated by anger that results in feelings of victimization is a prime candidate for forgiveness. Forgiveness is a cognitive process, and while it might seem to fall in the domain of cognitive restructuring, its significance as a process merits separate recognition. In their book *Forgiveness,* authors Sidney and Suzanne Simon describe acts of pardon as an essential step in the resolution of major life stressors. When many people hear the word *forgiveness,* they associate the process with condonement, absolution, and self-sacrifice, which, in the opinion of some, perpetuates feelings of victimization. Consequently, because of the emotional pain involved, forgiveness is not initially looked upon as a viable option to reduce personal stress. Strange as it may seem, holding a grudge or feelings of resentment appear to be a form of control over the person or circumstance involved.

But these feelings are an illusion of control. The toxicity of these thoughts sours one's outlook on life and eventually seeps into other aspects of one's personality, causing defensiveness and even more vulnerability to stressors, perpetuating the cycle of self-victimization.

Simon and Simon paint a different picture of forgiveness as a coping style. They describe it as an internal healing process where self-esteem is restored through devictimization, where toxic thoughts and emotions are diluted and released, and where one can begin to move on with one's life, not by just forgetting the past, but by coming to terms with stressful issues to find peace. As directors of several workshops for adults who were sexually abused, adult children of alcoholics, and the divorced, Simon and Simon teach that forgiveness is not an easy process. Based on their research, they propose six emotional steps to work through in the process from victim to survivor. These steps are very similar to those outlined in the grieving process by Kübler-Ross (Chapter 4): the denial stage, or refusal to admit you have been wronged or taken advantage of; self-blame stage, or directing hurt inwards and accepting other people's responsibility as your own; victimization stage, or realization that you have indeed been violated; indignation stage, or anger toward those you feel have violated your personal rights; survivor stage, or reassessing your self-worth and beginning to feel whole again; and finally, the integration stage, or forgiving and getting on with your life. Simon and Simon agree that the major hurdle to jump in order to get to the last stage is the ability to demonstrate unconditional love toward yourself and others.

Dream Therapy

Since ancient times, dreams have been espoused as a vehicle of divine communication. They have also been valued as a tool to unravel the complexities of life in waking state. Although for centuries dreams have been regarded as an intriguing aspect of human nature, their importance to mental and emotional stability has been neglected for quite some time. It was not until the work of Freud that these nocturnal images produced by the unconscious mind were considered worthy of scientific investigation. Like Hippocrates in ancient Greece, Freud discovered that dreams were closely related to the physical symptoms many of his patients demonstrated. It was this insight that led Freud into the study of dreams and dream analysis.

Calling dreams "the royal road to the unconscious," Freud became convinced that they act to disguise sexual desires and thought. It was his exploration in the field of dreams that paved the way to a greater scientific understanding of the unconscious mind. But, whereas Freud viewed dreams as a means to *conceal* conscious thoughts, his protégé, Jung, regarded dreams as means to *reveal* a whole new language to understand human consciousness and restore psychic balance. The work of these two men gave birth to the modern practice of dream therapy. Today, this work continues with dream researchers Gayle Delaney (1988), Patrick Garfield (1995), and Robert Van de Castle (1995).

The popularity of dream interpretation with the American public has waxed and waned throughout the twentieth century in tandem with that expressed in clinical research. But from research in this area, it has become clear that dream analysis and the therapeutic effects of dreams are considered powerful means to increase awareness of personal issues as well as viable tools to help resolve them (Fig. 16.4). The

Figure 16.4 Dream therapy experts believe that the more we try to remember our dreams, the better we are able to deal with problems in our waking state.

following is a collection of observations reported by several experts in the field about the dream process:

+ Everyone dreams, though not everyone remembers their dreams.

+ For the average person, the dreams that stand out are those that are perceived as utterly bizarre, terrifying, or triggered by something in the course of a day.

+ The majority of dreams are comprised of information received in the waking state during the previous day or two.

+ Recurring dreams represent significant unresolved issues.

+ Dreams were once thought to occur only during rapid-eye-movement (REM) periods, but are now thought to occur during several other times in the course of a night's sleep.

+ Opinions vary on the issue of categorical dream symbols (e.g., water signifying the spirit of life), but virtually all experts agree that interpretation ultimately resides with the person who created the dream.

Dream therapy is a cognitive process that includes dream interpretation, dream incubation, and lucid dreaming. The purpose of dream therapy, which can be done either with the assistance of a therapist who specializes in dream therapy or by yourself, is to access a greater share of consciousness through dream images and symbols to clarify and resolve personal issues.

Dream interpretation involves three phases. After writing down the actual dream images, the first step is to find any possible associations between these images and those that take place during the waking state. The best method is to write down brief descriptions of a dream and then list as many associations with the symbolic images that come to mind. For example, viewing a plane crash from a farmer's field could be associated with one's career, a relationship, driving a car, or a new diet. The more associations that can be made, the greater the chance for a solid connection. Dream therapist Robert Johnson, in his book *Inner Work*, states that the second phase is to draw parallels with these associations by asking yourself a series of questions. For example, What do I have in common with that image? Have I seen this image in my waking state? What behavior(s) do I have that is like that por-

trayed in this image? What emotional response does this dream image elicit, and what circumstances in everyday life elicit this same emotional response? The third phase of the interpretation process is to select the interpretation that seems to be most relevant to your life at that moment. The best choice can also be made by asking questions such as the following: What is the central message of the dream? Did the dream have any advice or moral to it? When choosing a dream interpretation, consider each possibility a viable one, because the ego-controlled conscious mind tends to protect itself from that which is unflattering or potentially harmful to itself. Dream expert Ann Faraday advises looking at the dream from someone else's perspective to allow a greater expansion of possibilities to choose from. Then make a selection with your heart, not solely with your analytical mind.

Dream interpretation is still an art form, not a science, and the true interpretation rests solely with the dreamer. However, Johnson's advice to get the best results is, first, to consider as an interpretation something you don't already know; second, to avoid interpretations that inflate the ego; and third, to disregard dream interpretations that pass blame from you to someone or something else. Fourth, be careful to consider only the obvious, as dream symbols look different from various perspectives. Finally, Johnson says, dream interpretation is useless if it is not acted upon. Each dream, no matter how obvious its relevance, is a message. And messages that are ignored may prolong the stress associated with them. It is up to the dreamer to grasp the message and resolve the issue that inspired it.

Just as dreams reveal messages to the conscious mind, they can also be used as drills to tap the wealth of knowledge hidden beneath consciousness for advice when dealing with problems, a practice dating back to ancient Greece. This process is called dream incubation, and has been explored by researcher Gayle Delaney. To incubate a dream, a person ponders a specific concern or issue by asking a question and perhaps even writing it down before going to sleep. Upon awaking, he or she writes down whatever images come to mind and then follows the process of dream analysis to determine what information the unconscious mind has suggested. From her research, Delaney has found this technique to be very effective in the resolution of stressful issues. It can be combined with journal writing to augment the awareness process.

Lucid dreaming is the ability to enter the dream state while still conscious. As in the practice of Jung's active imagination or creative visualization, in lucid dreaming you consciously choose to add aspects of your dream while in the waking state. In essence, you direct the script of your dream. Lucid dreaming is often practiced to finish dream fragments or to provide an ending to a recurring dream.

When utilized effectively, dreams offer a wealth of knowledge that begs to be addressed during the hours of conscious thought. To ignore the advice, to waste this resource, to leave inaccessible the knowledge of the unconscious mind only perpetuates the perceptions, emotions, and behaviors associated with stress. The importance of dreams cannot be overstated; they have proved many times over to provide a means of mental stability. Or, as Jung stated in his book *Man and His Symbols,* "One cannot afford to be naive about dreams."

Prayer and Faith

Prayer is one of the oldest and most commonly used coping mechanisms known to humankind. In its simplest form, prayer is thought: a desire of the heart, and often a call for help in what can best be described as a plea for divine intervention. Although prayer is not synonymous with meditation, these two processes share many similarities in that they both initiate a process of centering, increased concentration, and connectedness. They differ in that as a coping technique, prayer specifically elicits the element of divine intervention. It is a request, whereas meditation can encompass many modes of thinking and is not specifically limited to divine thought (see Chapter 19). Studies by Manfredi and Pickett (1987) and Koenig (1988) report that prayer is the most common coping style used by the elderly, especially when dealing with issues related to death. Schafer (1992) writes that prayer can lower anxiety, increase optimism, and instill hope in the individual. Yet when abused, prayer can promote dependency, escape, and even doubt.

Although there are many definitions of stress, one that comes to mind with regard to spiritual well-being is this: "Stress is a 'perceived' disconnection or separation from our divine source." The operative word is *perceived,* for in the words of sages and wisdom keepers the world over, we are never disconnected from our divine source. It is unresolved fear and anger that creates the illusion of separation. The premise of prayer as a coping technique is faith: the belief that each person is connected to a divine source (however this is named or described). Faith in a higher power, the ultimate source, can certainly be tested in times of stress.

Types of Prayer

When it comes to prayer, the styles are countless. Perhaps most common to many people is a recited prayer (much like a poem) that draws our attention from the self to the higher self. American Indians dance their prayers so as to reinforce their connection to the earth. South Africans have an expression: When you sing, you pray twice. There are prayers of gratitude and prayers of forgiveness. Prayers come in many forms. The type of prayer most commonly associated with stress is called *intercessory prayer.* Basically, this is a call for help, in which one seeks divine guidance or, more likely, divine intervention. Intercessory prayer is most common in two situations. The first is when you need help yourself; the second is when you offer a prayer for the assistance of others. Those who study the nuances of prayer describe it as a form of energetic consciousness. In simple truth, all thoughts are prayers.

Of Prayer and Meditation

There is a joke by comedian Lily Tomlin that goes like this: How come when we talk to God, it's called praying, but when God talks to us, it's called schizophrenia? To some, prayer and meditation may be the same activity, but in the strictest sense, they are not. As you will see in Chapter 18, meditation is a clearing of the mind to gain insight and wisdom. Praying, specifically intercessory prayer, is more of a soliloquy. As the expression goes, praying is when we talk to God, meditation is when God talks to us. Indeed, there are times when prayer and meditation may seem the same, and this is all right. However, to those who study the art of meditation, there are significant differences.

Research on Prayer and Faith

With regard to scientific inquiry, there is no lack of studies on the healing power of prayer, particularly in the past decade. As mentioned in Chapter 7 with regard to Einstein's view of spirituality, the most famous study on prayer was conducted by Randolph Byrd involving prayers for cardiac patients. Shying away from the word *pray,* researchers have coined the more scientific term "intercessory distant healing." To date, Byrd's study has been replicated several times (Sicher and Targ, 1998; Harris, 1999), showing statistical significance beyond pure chance. Some scientists remark that if divine intervention is scientifically valid some of the time, why not all of the time? Perhaps the answer is found in the standard joke: When you pray to God and your prayer isn't answered, it isn't that God didn't hear you. It's just that the answer was "No!"

Are people who pray more healthy? Well, as usual with research studies, there is proof that lines up on either side of the argument. In a study conducted at Duke University it was found that people who attended church services were more likely to be healthy than those who did not. A study by Pressman and colleagues found similar results. Keeping in mind that science and religion have been at odds for several hundred years, these findings came under much scrutiny. In his book *The Faith Factor,* Matthews cites habitual attendance to church or synagogue as a factor that promotes health. While the conclusions of these findings suggest that a strong relationship with the divine is certainly healthy, skeptics argue that religious behavior (attendance) itself and not belief per se, as well as the support of friends in church and marital status, are the true health factors. As was also men-tioned in Chapter 7, religious practices are easy to measure but spirituality is not. There are those who are spiritual but not religious, and there are those who are religious, but not spiritual.

Prayers for Non-believers

Are people who are less than sure about a higher power, or who perhaps don't believe in a divine source, divinely disadvantaged in times of stress? Perhaps not (Fig. 16.5). There is no research that suggests that agnostics (those who don't know) and atheists (those who don't believe in a higher source) fall dead at an earlier age or are prone to lifelong chronic illnesses. More than likely the conversation in their heads resembles a style of non-scripted prayer that might be heard in the heads and hearts of believers in a higher power. Just as no religion has a monopoly on THE style of prayer that gets the best results, people of strong faith are not necessarily at an advantage. Remember that coping with stress involves changing perceptions that are threatening. Prayer (in whatever form, whether it be a Hail Mary, or a positive affirmation) is a way in which to allay the fear involved. Similarly, faith for believers is trust in the unknown, whereas faith for non-believers may be viewed as an internal locus of control. Like prayer, faith is subjective, meaning that it comes from a personal experience, not something learned in a book. Intention is paramount.

Figure 16.5

B.C.

Ways to Pray

Is there a right way to pray? You may ponder this very question should you feel at times that your prayers have not be answered. Author Sophie Burnham (*A Book of Angels*) states that the style of communication is very important in the process of prayer. Burnham hypothesizes that people are rarely taught to pray correctly, and she offers the following criteria to practice this coping skill most effectively so that these thoughts may be received as intended.

1. *Clear transmission* of prayer thoughts is crucial to delivery of the message. A mind cluttered with several thoughts is analogous to a radio tuned to static. Clearing your mind of all thoughts save that which necessitates attention is imperative to the prayer process. There is no sacred place to pray. It may help to find a quiet spot, but temples, churches, and mosques are no better a conduit for this form of communication than your bedroom, shower, or car.

2. Prayers, Burnham explains, must be expressed in the *present tense*. With divine energy, as expressed by Jung as the collective unconscious, by Einstein as the cosmos, or by whatever term you wish to use, time does not exist. It is a man-made concept, a fabrication of the human mind. Therefore, past tense and future tense are not understood. Prayers as thought forms must be expressed in the present moment.

3. Next, Burnham writes that prayers must be phrased in a *positive context* and not a negative one. The universe, she states, does not understand the words *not, can't,* and *don't*. When a prayer such as, "Don't let me do badly on this exam" is expressed negative terms it is interpreted as "let me do badly on this exam." Similarly, the unconscious mind does not recognize negative words. Stress therapist Joan Borysenko tells a story of an Australian friend who lost a leg to bone cancer and was subsequently given a few months to live. Twenty years later this gentleman is enjoying life to the fullest. She explained that his coping mechanism focused on positive rather than on negative thoughts; instead of thinking, "I can't die," he thought, "I must live." Like Burnham, Borysenko insists that the unconscious mind does not recognize negative verbs.

Burnham adds to this list that special attention be made to notice the response. She says that in many cases people ignore or deny the response because the prayer or the timing of it was not answered to one's liking. One's style of prayer may be a function of one's personality type. Research by the Spindrift Organization in Salem, Oregon, suggests that introverts and extroverts tend to organize their prayer thoughts in different ways. The prayer style of extroverts tends to be more goal-oriented, while introverts are noted as being more general (e.g., Thy will be done, or go with the flow), with both styles showing effectiveness.

If the word *prayer* doesn't feel comfortable, how about the word *wish*? Author and psychoneuroimmunologist Paul Pearsall writes about the power of wishing in his book *Wishing Well*. Synthesizing the information from scores of research studies regarding distant healing, intentionality, and the non-local mind with his native Hawaiian tradition of the huna healers, Pearsall outlines a guideline for prayer in the form of heartfelt wishes. Using the premise of intentions from the heart (rather than thoughts from the head), Pearsall suggests four steps: 1) a clear mind and a patient heart; 2) a clear intention, which he calls "an image"; 3) sensitivity: may the intention be for the highest good of all concerned; and 4) an open heart—engaging the compassion of the heart rather than the greed of the ego to bring peace back to your personal existence.

Pearsall notes that framing your wish within these perceptions helps make the wish come true: patience, harmonious connection, humbleness, and compassion. And as a reminder of what many sages say about prayer, your wish comes true if it's in your best interest to happen.

There are those who hesitate to include prayer as a viable coping strategy because they believe that it nurtures false (negative) hope and perhaps even encourages an external locus of control, both of which are thought to negate the premise of positive coping techniques. However, it is held by those who do believe in prayer as a viable coping strategy that it can draw upon those inner resources that contribute to dealing with stress successfully. In the words of Jackson H. Brown, "Do not pray for things, but rather pray for wisdom and courage." When prayer is used as a means to strengthen faith and provide hope, it can be an effective coping mechanism; in the words of John F. Kennedy, *"God's work must truly be our own."*

Summary

- No one strategy works for all people in all situations to cope effectively with the causes of stress. In many cases, several coping techniques should be used together.
- For a coping technique to be effective, it must do one or all of the following: increase awareness of the cause of stress, help process information about the stressor, and adjust attitude and possibly behavior to work toward a peaceful resolution.
- Information seeking is a coping technique that helps to increase awareness of facts regarding the problem at hand.
- Social engineering is called the path of least resistance. The purpose of this technique is to favorably alter specific factors in your environment to minimize stress, or change environments completely if current conditions are deleterious to your health.
- When people bond together in times of trouble, they are better able to cope with the problems at hand. There is mental, emotional, physical, and spiritual strength in numbers. Social-support groups provide coping that individuals cannot generate themselves.
- Avoidance is considered a negative coping technique; however, to step outside your problems for a short while to gain a better perspective on them is thought to be quite healthy. Hobbies can be used as positive diversion tactics that allow for a healthy release from daily stressors. When approached in this way, hobbies can contribute to self-esteem, which then transfers to other areas of one's life.
- Stress can induce a sense of personal violation. Harboring feelings of resentment and anger is a means of maintaining control over someone we feel has unjustly attacked us. But when feelings of anger are not released correctly, they become toxic. Forgiveness allows these feelings to be released so that a peaceful resolution is the final outcome.
- Dream therapy—the practice of dream seeding and dream interpretation to find answers to problems and decode the meaning of dream symbols and images, respectively—is a cognitive technique that has been employed since ancient times. The use of dreams to resolve problems with the help of the unconscious mind continues to be used and explored in the field of psychology as a means to deal with stress.
- Prayer, the original chat room, is one of the oldest coping techniques known to humankind.
- Although there are many different ways to pray, intercessory prayer is the most common type in times of crisis.
- Prayer and meditation are not the same thing.
- Several research studies on the topic of prayer reveal a statistical significance with intention, particularly relative to aspects of health and healing.
- Although there is no one way to pray, suggestions for intercessory prayer are similar if not identical to mental imagery (Chapter 20).
- The relationship between stress and spirituality is gaining more and more attention in the allied health fields. Prayer is defined as a thought form directed toward divine consciousness. In more subtle terms, prayer is a request to nurture our self-reliance.

Concepts and Terms

Agnostic
Atheist
Buffer theory
Cognitive-dissonance theory
Compensation theory
Direct-effect theory

Dream incubation
Dream therapy
Faith
Forgiveness
Hobbies
Information seeking

Intercessory Prayer
Social engineering
Social-support groups
Wish

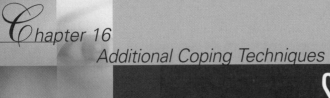

1. As this chapter described, there are many different ways to cope with stress. Do you use any additional coping techniques that were not described in this chapter?

    1. _____
    2. _____
    3. _____
    4. _____
    5. _____

2. One coping technique that merits more attention is hobbies. What hobbies or interests do you actively (currently) engage in?

    1. _____
    2. _____
    3. _____

3. Assuming that your school and work responsibilities are extremely time consuming so that there doesn't appear to be time for the luxury of a hobby, what would you do if you did have the time? List five activities or areas of interest that you would like to engage in if you had the time.

    1. _____
    2. _____
    3. _____
    4. _____
    5. _____

4. Social support groups are also an important means of coping with stress. Who would you say constitutes your support group? Divide this list into two groups: the people you seek out regularly (perhaps a roommate or best friend) and the people (such as family members) with whom you may not always be in constant touch, but who are still there for support.

    Core support group members:

    1. _____
    2. _____
    3. _____
    4. _____
    5. _____

    Peripheral support group members:

    1. _____
    2. _____
    3. _____
    4. _____
    5. _____

References and Resources

Ai, A. L. et. al. The Role of Private Prayer in Psychological Recovery among Midlife and Aged Patients Following Cardiac Surgery, *The Gerontologist* 38(5):591–601, 1998.

Allen, R. J. *Human Stress: Its Nature and Control.* Burgess, Minneapolis, MN, 1983.

Allen, R. J. and Hyde, D. H. *Investigations in Stress Control.* Burgess, Minneapolis, MN, 1983.

Anderson, N. *Work and Leisure.* Free Press, New York, 1961.

Andrews, G. and Tennant, C. Life-Event Stress, Social-Support Coping Style, and the Risk of Psychological Impairment, *Journal of Nervous and Mental Disorders* 166(7):605–612, 1982.

Ashby, J. S. and Lenhard, R. S., Prayer as a Coping Strategy for Chronic Pain Patients, *Rehabilitation Psychology* 39(3):205–209, 1994.

Begley, S. The Stuff That Dreams are Made of, *Newsweek,* August 14:41–44, 1989.

Benson, H. "Spirituality and Healing in Medicine" Conference. Denver, CO, March 19–21, 2000.

Berkman, L. F. Social Networks, Support, and Health: Taking the Next Step Forward, *American Journal of Epidemiology* 123:559–562, 1986.

Berkman, L. F. and Syme, S. L. Social Networks, Host Resistance, and Mortality: A Nine-Year Follow-up Study of Alameda County Residents, *American Journal of Epidemiology* 109:186–204, 1979.

Borysenko, J. Personal conversation, Oct. 25, 1991.

Bower, B. Dreams May Be Gone But Not Forgotten, *Science News,* September 15:173, 1984.

Brannon, L. and Feist, J. *Health Psychology: An Introduction to Behavior and Health,* 2nd ed. Wadsworth, Belmont, CA, 1992.

Brown, J. H. *Life's Little Instruction Booklet.* Rutledge Hill Press, Nashville, TN, 1991.

Burnham, S. *A Book of Angels.* Ballantine Books, New York, 1990.

Butler, M.H. et. al. Not Just Time-Out: Change Dynamics of Prayer for Religious Couples in Conflict Situations, *Family Process* 37(4):451–474, 1998.

Capel, I. and Gurnsey, J. *Managing Stress.* Constable, London, 1987.

Cartwright, R. D. Happy Endings for Our Dreams, *Psychology Today,* December:66–76, 1978.

Cassel, J. The Contribution of the Social Environment to Host Resistance, *American Journal of Epidemiology* 104:107–123, 1976.

Chollar, S. Dreamchasers, *Psychology Today,* April:60–61, 1989.

Clift, J. and Cliff, W. *Symbols of Transformation in Dreams.* Crossroad, New York, 1986.

Connell, C. M. and D'Augelli, A. R. The Contribution of Personality Characteristics to the Relationship between Social Support and Perceived Physical Health, *Health Psychology* 9:192–207, 1990.

Craig, K. T. *The Fabric of Dreams.* Dutton, New York, 1918.

Delaney, G. *Living Your Dreams.* HarperCollins, New York, 1988.

Dossey., L. *Prayer Is Good Medicine.* HarperCollins, San Francisco, 1996.

Dossey, L. *Be Careful What You Pray For: You Might Just Get It.* Harper SanFrancisco, SanFrancisco, 1997.

Dossey, L. *Reinventing Medicine.* Harper SanFrancisco, San Francisco, 1999.

Duke Study, *Journal of Gerontology and Biology Medical Science* 54(M370–376), 1999.

Evans, C. *Landscapes of the Night.* Viking, New York, 1984.

Faraday, A. *Dream Power.* Berkley, New York, 1972.

Foulkes, D. *Dreaming: A Cognitive-Psychological Analysis.* Erlbaum, Hillsdale, NJ, 1985.

Freud, S. *The Interpretation of Dreams.* Modern Library, New York, 1950.

Gachenbach, J. and Bosveld, J. Take Control of Your Dreams, *Psychology Today* October:27–32, 1989.

Garfield, P. L. *Creative Dreaming: Plan and Control Your Dreams to Overcome Fears, Solve Problems and Create a Better Self,* Fireside, New York, 1995.

Gundersen, L. Faith and Healing, *Annals of Internal Medicine,* January, 2000.

Hadfield, J. A. *Dreams and Nightmares.* Pelican Books, New York, 1973.

Hall, J. A. *Clinical Use of Dreams.* Grune and Stratton, New York, 1977.

Harris, W. S. et al. A randomized controlled trial of the effects of remote, intercessory prayer on outcomes in patients admitted to the coronary care unit. *Archives of Internal Medicine* 159:2273–2278, 1999.

Hawley, G. and Irurita, V. Seeking Comfort through Prayer, *International Journal of Nursing Practices* 4:9–18, 1998.

House, J. S., Robbins, C. and Metzner, H. L. The Association of Social Relationships and Activities with Mortality: Prospective Evidence from the Tecumseh Community Health Study, *American Journal of Epidemiology* 116:123–140, 1982.

Jackson, H. *Life's Little Instruction Book.* Rutledge Hill Press, Nashville, TN, 1991.

Jacobson, E. *You Must Relax.* McGraw-Hill, New York, 1987.

Johnson, R. A. *Inner Work: Using Dreams and Active Imagination for Personal Growth.* Harper & Row, San Francisco, 1986.

Jung, C. G. *Man and His Symbols.* Anchor Press, New York, 1964.

Jung, C. G. *Memories, Dreams, Reflections.* Vintage Press, New York, 1964.

Jung, C. G. *The Wisdom of a Dream,* vols. 1–3 (videos). RM Associates, 1989.

Kaplan, G. A. et al. Social Connections and Mortality from All Causes and from Cardiovascular Disease: Prospective Evidence from Eastern Finland, *American Journal of Epidemiology* 128:370–380, 1988.

Kaplin, M. *Leisure in America: A Social Inquiry.* Wiley, New York, 1960.

Katra, J. and Targ, R. *The Heart of the Mind.* New World Library, Novatno, CA, 1999.

Kelsey, M. *Dreams: A Way to Listen to God.* Paulist Press, New York, 1978.

Koenig, H. Religious Behaviors and Death Anxiety in Later Life, *Hospice Journal* 4:3–24, 1988.

Laberge, S. *Lucid Dreaming.* Tarcher, Los Angeles, 1979.

Langs, R. *Decoding Your Dreams.* Ballantine Books, New York, 1988.

Levine, A. *Love Canal: Science, Politics, and People.* Lexington Books, Lexington, MA, 1982.

Lindbergh, A. M. *Gift from the Sea.* Pantheon Books, New York, 1975.

Lowenthal, M. F. and Harven, C. Interaction and Adaptation: Intimacy as a Critical Variable. In B. Neugarten, ed., *Middle Age and Aging.* University of Chicago Press, 390–400, 1968.

Mahoney, M. *The Meaning of Dreams and Dreaming.* Citadel Press, New York, 1970.

Manfredi, C. and Pickett, M. Perceived Stressful Situations and Coping Strategies Utilized by the Elderly, *Journal of Community Health Nurses* 4(2):99–110, 1987.

Maslow, A. Dynamics of Personality Organization, *Psychological Review* 50:514–518, 1943.

Matthews, D. A. *The Faith Factor.* Penguin Books, New York, 1998.

Oman, M. *Prayers for Healing.* Conari Press, Berkeley, CA, 1997.

Pearsall, P. *Wishing Well.* Hyperion, New York, 2000.

Pelletier, K. and Herzing, D. Psychoneuroimmunology: Toward a Mindbody Model, *Advances* 5(1):27–56, 1988.

Pilisuk, M. and Parks, S. H. *The Healing Web: Social Networks and Human Survival.* University Press of New England, Hanover, NH, 1986.

Pressman, P. et al. Religious Belief, depression and ambulation status in elderly women with broken hips, *Am J. Psychiatry* 147: 758–760, 1990.

Raphael, B. Preventive Intervention with the Recently Bereaved, *Archives of General Psychiatry* 34:1450–1457, 1977.

Rathbone, J. *Teach Yourself to Relax.* Prentice-Hall, Englewood Cliffs, NJ, 1957.

Roth, R. *The Healing Path of Prayer.* Harmony Books, New York, 1997.

Rycroft, C. *The Innocence of Dreams.* Pantheon Books, New York, 1913.

Savary, L. M., Berne, P. H., and Williams, S. K. *Dreams and Spiritual Growth: A Christian Approach to Dreamwork.* Paulist Press, New York, 1984.

Schafer, W. *Stress Management for Wellness.* Harcourt Brace Jovanovich, Fort Worth, TX, 1992.

Schlitz, M. and Braud, W. Distant Intentionality and Healing: Accessing the Evidence, *Alternative Therapies in Health and Medicine* 3(6):62–73, 1997.

Sicher, F. and Targ., E. A Randomized Double-Blind Study of the Effect of Distant Healing in a Population with

Advanced AIDS: Report of a Small-Scale Study, *Western Journal of Medicine* 169 (6):356–363, 1998.

Siegel, A. Dreams: The Mystery That Heals. In Bauman, Brint, Piper, and Wright, eds., *The Holistic Health Handbook*. And/Or Press, Berkeley, CA, 1978.

Simon, S. B. and Simon, S. *Forgiveness: How to Make Peace with Your Past and Get on with Your Life*. Warner Books, New York, 1990.

Stauth, C. Adventures in Dreamland, *New Age Journal:* 79–83, 145–149, 1995.

Stewart, W. A. and Freeman, L. *The Secret of Dreams*. Macmillan, New York, 1972.

Targ, E. Evaluating Distant Healing: A Research Review, *Alternative Therapies in Health and Medicine* 3(6):74–78, 1997.

Targ, R. and Katra, J. *Miracles of Mind*. New World Library, Novatno, CA, 1998.

Taylor, S. *Health Psychology*, 2nd ed. McGraw-Hill, New York, 1990.

Ullman, M. and Limmer, C. The *Variety of Dream Experience*. Continuum, New York, 1987.

Van de Castle, R. *Our Dreaming Mind*, Ballantine Books, New York, 1995

Weiss, L. *Dream Analysis in Psychotherapy*. Pergamon Press, New York, 1986.

Part IV

Relaxation Techniques

"That the birds fly overhead,
this you cannot stop. That they
build a nest in your hair,
this you can prevent."

-Ancient Chinese Proverb

We process information from the five senses: vision, hearing, smell, taste, and touch. Stimuli picked up through one or more of these senses are then delivered to the cerebral cortex and deciphered, and then processed by the subcortex of the brain. Each piece of information tracked by the senses is labeled with a perception, which is interpreted as either a threat or a nonthreat. If a stimulus is perceived to be a threat, then an alarm is sounded and the body is activated as a means of survival.

To relax the body from a heightened state of physical arousal to homeostasis, action must be taken to alter both the quality and quantity of stimuli taken in by the five senses. In other words, the five senses must be deactivated or reprogrammed, temporarily, to allow the body to calm down. The purpose of relaxation techniques is to do just that: to deactivate the body's sensory system, decrease stimuli and their associated perceptions, and replace these with nonthreatening sensations that promote the relaxation response. In effect, the primary purpose of relaxation techniques is to *intercept* the stress response, specifically at the neurological and hormonal levels, and return the body to physiological homeostasis.

Of the five senses, two are paramount in the acquisition of sensory information for processing: vision and hearing. By no coincidence, these same two senses are targeted for deactivation during relaxation, through various relaxation techniques such as mental imagery and music therapy, to name two. In addition, because muscle tension is considered the most common symptom of stress, touch is also targeted through techniques such as progressive muscular relaxation, massage, and physical exercise.

When the field of stress management unfolded in the early 1970s, the emphasis of attention and instruction was placed solely on relaxation techniques due to the apparently strong association between stress-related symptoms and ensuing diseases. As mentioned in Chapter 1, this is still the common medical approach to the treatment of disease and illness: to first treat the symptoms of the problems. Originally, relaxation techniques were used in both prevention of and intervention for stress-related health problems. What was discovered through this approach, however, was that relaxation techniques alone offered only temporary solutions to long-term problems or chronic stressors. Moreover, if the relaxation techniques were practiced irregularly or discontinued, then stress-related symptoms returned. Thus, by themselves, relaxation techniques are only half the solution. To effectively deal with stress in a preventive or interventive manner, techniques for relaxation must be integrated with positive coping techniques.

Unfortunately, relaxation techniques are not magic. What may provide a calming effect for one person may offer nothing but added frustration for others. The ability to relax (even heal) is largely dependent on the individual. So experts in the field of stress management suggest that you become acquainted with several different techniques and add these to your arsenal of stress defense. As you might expect, some techniques and their intended reactions are less suited to certain situations than others. For example, you cannot easily plug yourself into a biofeedback machine during a traffic pile-up on the highway, but you can try some mental imagery and diaphragmatic breathing. Ultimately, the choice is up to you and your experience as to how you should employ relaxation techniques. In addition, relaxation techniques, like playing the piano or shooting hoops, are skills; and skills require regular practice to achieve proficiency. Experts agree that regardless of which technique is chosen (and many may be used in combination), you must practice some form of relaxation every day, usually for twenty minutes. Done effectively, these skills will serve your goal to achieve inner peace.

Because the mind-body connection is so strong, relaxation techniques promote not only physical calming but rebound to calm mental processes, creating mental homeostasis. This allows for greater self-awareness. For this reason, several relaxation techniques provide fertile ground for the seeds of several coping strategies. When Jim Fixx wrote the bestseller *The Complete Book of Running,* he thought he would address the physiological relationship between cardiovascular fitness and coronary heart disease. However, with virtually every runner interviewed by Fixx, the first topic mentioned was not the physiological effects of running, but the mental and emotional effects—the runner's high. At first, researchers dismissed runner's high as an extraneous effect. Now, a more serious approach has been adopted to understand the mysteries of this profound connection between mind and body. As you will see, there is a strong crossover between the two, and we have only scratched the surface of the wealth of knowledge to be learned about this unique relationship.

The origins of relaxation techniques span many continents and cultures over many centuries. In Part IV,

East meets West as techniques from the Orient dating back thousands of years are paired with contemporary techniques from the New World. Over the past twenty years, some components of the older techniques have begun to merge with the newer techniques, lending to them depth and strength. Some methods are best suited as intervention techniques, to be done right on the spot in the face of stress. Others are more appropriate when postponed to later in the day. Yet all the techniques are preventive in nature. So read through these techniques and try them. See what you think. Chances are, there are some you will take an immediate liking to, while others won't do much for you. Once you have tried them all, select one or two that seem very effective and begin to incorporate these into your daily routine. With regular practice, you will be amazed at how your body responds, not only in terms of immediate effects but over time as well. Should there come a time that your favorite relaxation technique seems to lose its ability to bring calmness, then select an alternative technique. There are many to choose from.

Like Part III, most chapters in this section include a historical introduction to each relaxation technique, as well as a full description of the technique, specific physiological (and psychological) effects induced by the technique, and best steps to take to incorporate the technique into your personal strategy for stress management.

Exercise Relaxation through the Five Senses

Please list ten ideas for relaxation for each of the five senses. Describe each in a few words or a sentence. Be creative!

The Sense of Sight
1.
2.
3.
4.
5.
6.
7.
8.
9.
10.

The Sense of Taste
1.
2.
3.
4.
5.
6.
7.
8.
9.
10.

The Sense of Sound
1.
2.
3.
4.
5.
6.
7.
8.
9.
10.

The Sense of Touch
1.
2.
3.
4.
5.
6.
7.
8.
9.
10.

The Sense of Smell
1.
2.
3.
4.
5.
6.
7.
8.
9.
10.

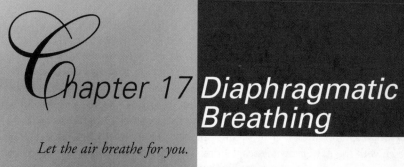

Chapter 17 Diaphragmatic Breathing

Let the air breathe for you.

—*Emmett Miller, M.D.*

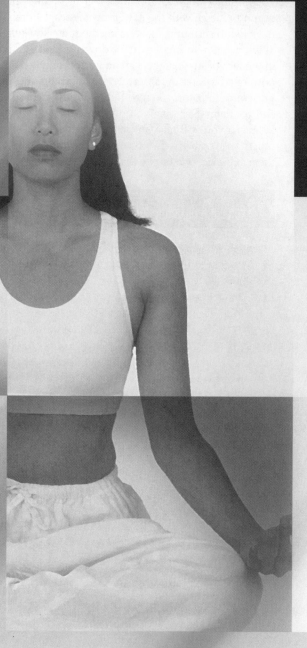

Diaphragmatic breathing is unequivocally the easiest method of relaxation to practice. It is easy because breathing is an action that we do normally without thought or hesitation. In its simplest form, **diaphragmatic breathing** is controlled deep breathing. It is symbolic of a deep sigh, or a big breath taken when one is about to regroup one's thoughts, gain composure, or direct one's energies for a challenging task. What makes normal breathing different from diaphragmatic breathing is its emphasis on expansion of the chest. Diaphragmatic breathing involves the movement of the lower abdomen. In the practice of yoga, this technique is called the *pranayama,* or the restoration of one's energy or life force, the breath behind the breath.

Most Americans breathe emphasizing upper chest and thoracic cavity while deemphasizing abdominal movement. This is thought to be a learned behavior influenced by cultural preferences for a large chest and small waist. As children mature, they shift from abdominal to thoracic breathing. When fast asleep, however, without the influence of the conscious mind, all individuals revert back to breathing by distending the stomach as the diaphragm is allowed to expand and contract without inhibition.

Over the past two decades, the use of diaphragmatic breathing has become well accepted in childbirth (Nakahata, 1993). A major tenet of the Lamaze childbirth method is controlled belly breathing. In Lamaze classes, expectant mothers (and fathers) are taught to place the emphasis of their breathing on the lower stomach. Then, during the several hours of labor and delivery, this breathing skill is employed to ease pain. And what is taught and practiced for the stressful event of childbirth is now taught and practiced for several other stressful situations as well.

The Mystery of Breathing

Under normal resting conditions, the average person breathes approximately fourteen to sixteen times per minute. In a state of arousal, breathing is fast-paced and shallow, with pronounced muscular contractions of the chest cavity. During heavy exercise, ventilations per minute can increase to as many as sixty as the body tries to meet the increased demand for oxygen. In a relaxed state, the body's metabolism is significantly decreased, allowing for a slower and deeper breathing cycle. Physiologically speaking, when pressure due to the expansion of the chest wall and muscular contraction is taken off the thoracic cavity, sympathetic drive decreases. Parasympathetic drive overrides the sympathetic system, and homeostasis results. Itzhak Bentov (1988) offers a second explanation for the pacifying effect of diaphragmatic breathing, which he relates to vibrations emitted from the heart. The force of contractions of the left ventricle and the blood that it ejects sends a vibration through the aorta, which then reverberates throughout the body. A pause in the breathing cycle causes the reverberation to cease. Breathing from the diaphragm, which accents long pauses, decreases this resonance, creating a calming effect. Some Himalayan yogis, in a state of complete relaxation, are reported to take in as few as one or two breaths per minute. As you can imagine, this requires much concentration and practice. Typically, when people learn to modify their breathing from thoracic to diaphragmatic breathing, they can comfortably reduce the number of breaths to between four and six per minute.

Diaphragmatic breathing is as old as the ancient exercises of yoga and T'ai chi, and it is a fundamental component of these practices. The therapeutic power of breathing is often associated with higher consciousness or spirituality. In fact, the word *spirit* in many cultures is described as "the first breath." Currently, diaphragmatic breathing is itself a form of relaxation, but because of its simplicity and compatibility, it is often incorporated into other techniques, including progressive muscular relaxation, autogenic training, and mental imagery, for a combined relaxation effect. Many people consider diaphragmatic breathing to be the first recognized mantra; a singular repetitive thought or motion to cleanse the mind. Among those who practice yoga and T'ai chi, diaphragmatic breathing is thought to be more effective when inhalation and exhalation occur through the nasal passages as there is a greater ability to regulate air flow that way. Respiratory and sinus problems, however, invite use of both mouth and nose for this style of breathing. In any case, diaphragmatic breathing promotes concentration on one body sensation to the exclusion of all other sensory stimuli: feeling air slowly pass through the nose or mouth, down into the lungs, and then return via the same pathway.

Stress With a Human Face

"You know, I really thought all this breathing stuff was a crock," said Tom, a lieutenant in the Navy. "Yup! You could say I have a stressful life right about now." Tom was about to graduate from college, start flight school in Florida, and become a father.

All three events converged about two weeks later. Whatever mental toughness Tom had attained in boot camp melted away when the first labor pain arrived. What otherwise seemed like a short drive to the hospital became a comedy of errors as Tom faced traffic of biblical proportions on the Capital Beltway. And it only got worse when the right front tire was punctured by some glass by the side of the road. "I just kept telling Kathy, Take a deep breath, keep breathing, it will be all right:" I was breathing right along with her. I'm not sure who it helped more, me or her. You know, you always hear about babies being born in the back seat of a car, but I never thought mine would be one of those." ✦

Scientists have observed that over the course of a single day, barring colds or sinus problems, one nostril dominates the breathing cycle for several hours before allowing the other nostril to take over. Several studies now suggest that these changes in breathing patterns can actually enhance brain lateralization and their respective modes of thinking (Neimark, 1985). The right side of the brain controls and is influenced by actions of the left side of the body. Scientists suggest that allowing air to enter and exit through your left nostril will access right-brain functions more readily. Thus when right-brain thinking is preferred, as in the use of imagination, this style of breathing is advocated.

Steps to Initiate Diaphragmatic Breathing

1. Assume a Comfortable Position

The beauty of this technique is its simplicity. It can be done anywhere, at any time. To benefit most, first learn and then practice diaphragmatic breathing in a comfortable position, either sitting or, preferably, lying down on your back with your eyes closed (Fig. 17.1). To enhance this position, loosen constrictive clothing around the neck and waist. When first learning this technique, it is suggested that you place your hands over your stomach and feel the rise and fall of your abdomen with each breath. Once the technique is practiced with proficiency, it can be performed just about anywhere, under any circumstances, including while driving in heavy traffic, waiting in line at the post office, giving a public speech, and taking a final exam.

Figure 17.1

Lie on a carpeted floor with arms by your sides, back straight, and eyes closed.

2. Concentration

As with all relaxation techniques that offer respite to the body, diaphragmatic breathing requires focused concentration. Concentration can easily be interrupted by both external noises and internal thoughts. Whenever possible, take steps to minimize external interruptions by finding a nice quiet place to practice this technique. When first learning this and other techniques that require total concentration, you will notice that on occasion your mind begins to wander. This is common. When you notice competing thoughts, allow them to dissipate and refocus your attention on your breathing. One suggestion is to allow these interrupting thoughts to metaphorically escape your body as you exhale.

Normal breathing is for the most part an involuntary, unconscious act. It is regulated by the medulla oblongata of the brain, allowing the conscious mind to focus on other aspects of functional survival. Diaphragmatic breathing, though, necessitates a conscious decision to redirect your attention to this basic physiological function and turn off the autonomic influence that normally controls it. One approach to deeper awareness is to mentally follow the flow of air

Figure 17.2 Breathing Clouds exercise.

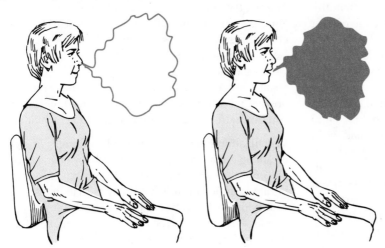

as it enters the body and travels to its destination in the lower lobes of the lungs and back out again. Sometimes a mental suggestion can help: "Feel the air come into your nose (or mouth), down into your lungs, and feel your stomach rise and then descend as you exhale the air, feeling it leave your lungs, throat, and nasal cavity." Repeat this with each breath.

Concentration can be augmented further by focusing on the components of each breath. Each ventilation is said to be comprised of four distinct phases:

Phase I: Inspiration, or taking the air into your lungs through the nose or mouth

Phase II: A very slight pause before exhaling

Phase III: Exhalation, or releasing the air from your lungs through the passage it entered

Phase IV: Another very slight pause after exhalation before the next inhalation is initiated.

These phases can be experienced to a greater extent by exaggerating the breathing cycle, taking a very slow and comfortable deep breath. When trying this technique, try to isolate and recognize the four phases as they occur. Remember not to hold your breath at any time during each phase. Rather, learn to regulate your breathing by controlling the pace of each phase in the breathing cycle. Diaphragmatic breathing is not the same as hyperventilation; this style of breathing is slow, relaxed, and as deep as feels comfortable. It is commonly agreed that the most relaxing phase of diaphragmatic breathing is the third phase, exhalation. At this phase, the chest and abdom-

inal areas relax, sending the relaxing effect throughout the whole body. It requires no effort whatsoever. So when focusing on your breathing, feel how relaxed your whole body becomes during this phase, especially your chest, shoulders, and abdominal region.

In addition to acknowledging the four phases of each breath, become aware of your capacity to breathe. In the tradition of yoga, there are said to be three regions of the lungs: the upper, middle, and lower lobes. During normal breathing, we typically use only the upper lobes. During the initial stages of relaxed breathing, both the upper and middle lobes are filled with air. But in deep breathing, all three lobes of the lungs are used. As you monitor your breathing, become conscious of filling each layer or region of your lungs.

3. Visualization

Breathing and imagery are dynamic partners in the art of relaxation. There are many images that can be combined with this breathing technique. The following are two common ones accompanied by suggestions often used in Asian relaxation practices.

Visualization Exercise 1: Breathing Clouds.   This technique can be traced back to the origins of yoga in Asia and Zen meditation in Japan. It was introduced as a cleansing process for the mind and body. To begin (Fig. 17.2), close your eyes and focus all your attention on your breathing. Visualize the air that you take into your lungs as being clean, fresh air; pure and energized air; clean air with the power to cleanse and heal your body. As you breathe in this clean, fresh air, visualize and feel air enter your nose (or mouth), travel up through the sinus cavities to the top of your head, and down your spinal column to circulate throughout your body. Now, as you exhale, visualize that the air leaving your body is dirty air—dark cloudy smoke that symbolizes all the stressors, frustrations, and toxins throughout your mind and body. With each breath you take, allow the clean, fresh air to enter, circulate, and rejuvenate your body, and expel the dirty air to help rid your body of its stress and tension. Repeat this breathing cycle for five to ten minutes. As you repeat the breathing clouds exercise, you may notice that, as the body becomes more relaxed through the release of stress and tension, the color of the exhaled air begins to change from grey to an off-white, symbolic of complete relaxation and cleansing.

Visualization Exercise 2: Alternate Nostril Breathing. This technique dates back to the origins of yoga and is also called *nadi shadhanam*. It may seem very difficult if not impossible at first, but with repeated practice it will enhance the relaxation response. To begin, close your eyes and focus all your attention on your breathing. Feel the air enter your mouth or nose and travel down into your lungs. Feel your stomach rise as the air enters, then slowly descend as you exhale. After becoming relaxed from the sensations of your breathing, take a slow, deep breath. Exhale, allowing the air to leave exclusively through your left nostril (Fig. 17.3). When your lungs feel completely empty, begin your next breath by inhaling air exclusively through your right nostril. Repeat this cycle for the next fifteen to twenty breaths by continuing to exhale air through your left nostril and draw air in through your right nostril.

When you feel completely comfortable with this air flow, take a very slow but comfortably deep breath through the right nostril again, but change the direction of the air flow, exhale through the right nostril and inhale through the left. Repeat this cycle for the next fifteen to twenty breaths. Throughout the whole process, try to visualize the flow of air as you breathe. You may want to hold a finger to your nose to feel the effectiveness of this visualization. Even if you don't feel a difference, keep trying. Although it may take a while, the nasal passages will begin to open up as a result of these suggestions. Although normally the two nostrils take turns dominating the breathing cycle, you can learn to control this as a relaxation technique.

Visualization Exercise 3: Energy Breathing. Energy breathing is a way to vitalize your body, by taking in air not only through your nose or mouth but, in effect, breathing through your whole body as well. In essence, your body becomes one big lung, taking in air and circulating it throughout. You can do this technique either sitting or lying down. There are three phases to this exercise. First, get comfortable and allow your shoulders to relax. If you choose to sit, try to keep your legs straight. Now, imagine that there is a circular hole at the top (crown) of your head. As you breathe in, visualize energy in the form of a beam of light entering the top of your head (Fig. 17.4). Bring the energy down from the

Alternate nostril breathing exercise. *Figure 17.3*

Energy breathing exercise. *Figure 17.4*

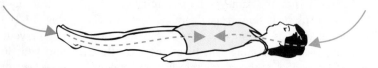

crown of your head to your abdomen as you inhale. As you exhale, allow the energy to leave through the top of your head. Repeat this five to ten times, coordinating your breathing with the visual flow of energy. As you continue to bring the energy down to your stomach, allow the light to reach all the inner parts of your upper body.

When you feel comfortable with this first phase, you are ready to move on to the second phase. Now, imagine that there is a circular hole in the center of each foot. Again think of energy as a beam of light. Concentrate only on your lower extremities, and allow the flow of energy to move up from your feet into your abdomen as you inhale with your diaphragm. Repeat this five to ten times, coordinating your breathing with the flow of energy. As you continue to bring the energy up into your stomach area, allow the light to reach all the inner parts of your lower body.

Once you feel you are coordinating your breathing and the visual flow of energy to your lower extremities, combine the movement of energy from both the top of your head and your feet, and bring it to the center of your body as you inhale with your diaphragm. Then, as you exhale, allow the flow of energy to reverse direction, leaving the way it came. Repeat this ten to twenty times. Each time you move the energy through your body, feel each body region,

each muscle and organ, and each cell become energized. At first it may be difficult to visually coordinate the movement of energy coming from opposite ends of your body, but with practice this will come more easily.

Summary

- Diaphragmatic breathing is thought to be the easiest method of relaxation. When the emphasis of breathing is centered in the lower abdomen rather than the thoracic cavity, a less sympathetic neural activity is generated, causing a greater relaxation effect.
- Diaphragmatic breathing, or belly breathing, is the basic relaxation technique taught in childbirth classes.
- In a normal state of consciousness, the average number of breaths is twelve to sixteen per minute. In a relaxed state, this number can be reduced to as few as three to four breaths very comfortably.
- Breathing is thought to be paramount to relaxation in nearly every culture, especially the Far East, where breath (*prana* or *chi*) is thought to give the body energy. Diaphragmatic breathing is incorporated into nearly every relaxation technique.
- Diaphragmatic breathing takes little more than a comfortable position, focused concentration, and a little mental imagery.
- Diaphragmatic breathing can be done anywhere, under any condition where stress arises. For this reason alone, diaphragmatic breathing is said to be the most accessible (and perhaps effective) technique to initiate the relaxation response.

Concepts and Terms

Diaphragmatic breathing   *Pranayama*

References and Resources

Bentov, I. *Stalking the Wild Pendulum: On the Mechanics of Consciousness.* Destiny Books, Rochester, VT, 1988.

Birkel, D. *Hatha Yoga: Developing the Body, Mind, and Inner Self.* Eddie Bowers, Dubuque, IA, 1991.

Borysenko, J. *Minding the Body, Mending the Mind.* Bantam Books, New York, 1987.

Caponigro, A. Healing with the Breath of Life, *Body Mind Spirit* 15(1):6–11, 1996.

Davis, M., McKay, M., and Eshelman, R. *The Relaxation and Stress-Reduction Workbook,* 3rd ed. New Harbinger Press, Oakland, CA, 1988.

Engle, B. T. and Chism, R. A. Effects of Increases and Decreases in Breathing Rate on Heart Rate and Finger-Pulse Volume, *Psychophysiology* 4:83–89, 1967.

Farhi, D. *The Breathing Book: Good Health and Vitality through Essential Breathwork.* Owl Books, New York, 1996.

Fixx, J. *The Complete Book of Running.* Random House, New York, 1977.

Funderburk, J. *Science Studies Yoga: A Review of Physiological Data.* Himalayan International Institute of Yoga Science and Philosophy, Honesdale, PA, 1977.

Hendricks, G. *Conscious Breathing.* Bantam Books, New York, 1995.

Iyengar, B.K. *Light on Pranayama: The Yogic Art of Breathing.* Cross Roads/Herder & Herder, New York, 1995.

Kabat-Zinn, J. *Full Catastrophe Living.* Delta Books, New York, 1990.

Miller, R. Working with Breathing, *Yoga Journal* Sept./Oct.:67–75, 1989.

Nakahata, A. K. Mastering Lamaze Skills: Discover Breathing and Relaxation Skills to Help You through Labor and the Years to Follow, *Lamaze Parents Magazine* 12:36–37, 1993.

Neimark, J. Brain Rhythms: What the Nose Knows, *American Health* May, 1985.

Rama, S., Ballentine, R., and Hymes, A. *The Science of Breath.* Himalayan Institute Press, Honesdale, PA, 1998.

Shannohoff-Khalsa, D. Breathing for the Brain, *American Health,* 5:16–18, 1986.

Spreads, C. *Breathing: The ABCs.* Harper & Row, New York, 1978.

Stern, R. M. and Anschel, C. Deep Inspirations as Stimuli for Responses of the Autonomic Nervous System, *Psychophysiology* 5:132–141, 1968.

Swami Rama, et al. *Science of Breath.* Himalayan International Institute of Yoga Science and Philosophy, Honesdale, PA, 1979.

Swayzee, N. *Breathworks: Strengthening Your Back from the Inside out.* Aron Books, New York, 1998.

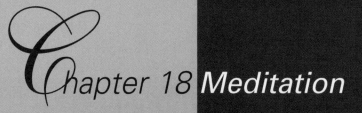

Chapter 18 Meditation

When the pupil is ready, the

teacher will come.

—Ancient Chinese Proverb

In case no one has officially said this to you yet, "Welcome to the information age." Today more than ever before, the human mind is barraged with data every waking hour, practically nonstop. The once humorous cries of "too much information" are not quite so funny anymore as we become deluged in information, with nonstop access to the Internet, cell phones, palm devices, and information technology that is being invented as I write this, but that will be commonplace by the time you read this. While the ability to access information is wonderful, the inundation of information is deafening to the mind. The term is sensory overload.

In every age of humanity, the mind has always needed a respite from thoughts, worries, and external stimuli. Meditation is the quintessential respite to calm the mind from sensory overload (Fig. 18.2). Today meditation is rapidly gaining recognition in the West as a powerfully effective relaxation technique. By all confirmed reports, meditation is not a religion. Rather, it is a solitary practice of reflection on internal rather than external stimuli. Technically speaking, meditation is an increased concentration and awareness; a process of living in the present moment to produce and enjoy a tranquil state of mind. The practice of meditation is the oldest recognized relaxation technique known. So accepted are several components of meditation that

Figure 18.1 We are guided by our inner wisdom only when we take the time to stop and listen.

they have become tightly integrated into virtually every relaxation technique known and practiced today.

Shakespeare once said, "The eyes are the windows of the soul." By closing the eyes now and again, the soul is given a chance to cleanse. Indeed, all the body's senses are ports of entry bringing in stimuli from outside for the mind to interpret and censor. Human beings are visually-oriented animals; we take in over two-thirds of our sensory information through vision alone. Stimulation from any sensory organ bombards the conscious mind, and under the influence of stress, the mind juggles many thoughts produced both externally and internally, as they compete for attention. Quite often, the result of this abundance of sensory stimulation is sensory overload. You have probably experienced this at the end of a long day of classes or work, or perhaps during a visit to an art museum, where after two hours every painting looks about the same. Sensory overload is like a blackboard filled to capacity with notes and scribbles that are quite difficult to organize and assimilate into use. When our minds are overloaded with information, concentration is compromised. The term *polyphasia* is used to describe an abundance of simultaneous thoughts cluttering the mind, and there is a strong association between a cluttered mind and a stressful mind.

To continue the simile, meditation is like an eraser that cleans the mind's blackboard. In fact, some would say, meditation gets rid of the blackboard as well. Meditation is a tool to unclutter the mind and bring about mental homeostasis. In the language of information technology (IT) meditation increases the bandwidth of human consciousness. When the mind is clear of thought, it is more receptive to new information, new perspectives, and new ways of dealing with unresolved problems. In the acclaimed book *The Prophet,* Kahlil Gibran writes, "No man can reveal to you aught but that which lies half asleep in the dawning of your knowledge." In other words, the student is also the teacher. But before lessons can be taught, the proper learning environment must be created. This is the primary purpose of meditation: concentration promoting self-awareness. Thus, as expressed in the ancient Chinese proverb, when the student is ready, the teacher will come.

Historical Perspective

Although it is likely that the practice existed much earlier, the roots of meditation can be traced back to

Asia in the sixth century B.C., when several individuals traveling separate paths to enlightenment took refuge and solace in contemplative and reflective thought. The fruits of this thought became the cornerstones of several philosophies, which gathered many followers eager to learn and share them. These followers in turn established rules and guidelines to live by, which evolved into several prominent religious philosophies: namely, Hinduism, Buddhism, Taoism, and Confucianism. Meditation, or self-reflective thought, was integrated into the practices of these religions as a means to cleanse and purify the soul. From this perspective, we can see that although meditation has been adopted by nearly every religion, it is not a religion in itself.

Self-reflection is considered essential to the maturation process. Every culture and every religious sect has some element of meditation or self-reflective practice, including Judaism, Catholicism, Protestantism, Islam, and the worship of several American Indian groups. There are subtle but significant differences between Eastern and Western cultures in their approach to meditation. Western views promote a search for inner peace through external means, whereas Eastern philosophies direct thoughts inward for harmony and atonement. This dichotomy of approaches has resulted in a high degree of perceived mysticism, and perhaps misunderstanding, in the West. In simple terms, like the mind it affects, meditation appears to have several layers. Initially, meditation has a calming effect on the mind's basic thought processes. Once this layer is peeled away, a deeper series of layers is unveiled to reveal insights of the soul, intuition, or enlightenment.

Eastern cultures have accepted the essence of meditation and all its many principles. Western cultures, more skeptical by nature, have only recently begun to appreciate meditation as a means to calm the mind and all its thought processes to achieve inner peace. Meditation became popular in the United States during the 1960s by way of the Beatles, whose music and lifestyles included meditation, thus influencing many people. Meditation gained additional momentum from the counter-culture movements of the 1960s, specifically the human potential movement, which sought to elevate all humanity to a higher level of consciousness. The materialism of the mid-1970s and '80s, however, nearly derailed this movement. With the advent of the twenty-first century, a

COSMIC BREADCRUMBS

After several attempts, Jason finally gets the hang of meditation.

Figure 18.2

revival of interest in the advancement of human potential and a quest for spiritual growth and development have emerged. Meditation has again become a major component of this movement, particularly in various self-help workshops, motivational retreats, and corporate seminars. One researcher, José Silva, has taken the concept of meditation one step further, integrating it into a technique to enhance what he calls personal mind control. In the Silva Method, meditation is used to access great thinking power and memory function. The premise of meditation has also been adapted to a concept called alpha thinking, named for the state of mind physiologically represented by alpha waves, in which specific meditation concepts are integrated with other relaxation techniques, including breathing, biofeedback, and mental imagery, to promote deep relaxation and improved memory.

The medical profession has now adopted meditation as its own behavior-modification technique to combat rising morbidity and mortality from stress-related heart disease. Originally doubtful of claims that meditation promotes physical calmness as well as inner peace, the American Heart Association now advocates it as a preventive health measure in conjunction with proper diet and aerobic exercise to reduce modifiable risk factors for coronary heart disease. In fact, Dr. Dean Ornish (1992) has proven that coronary heart disease is reversible, in some cases, in people who combine meditation with changes in diet and exercise. The National Institute of Health advocates meditation for the relief of cancer. Slowly, as Eastern and Western cultures become more closely integrated, the basic concepts of meditation will become even more readily accepted as a relaxation technique for both mental and physical homeostasis.

Meditation is typically thought of as a technique for personal enlightenment. More recently, though, an expanded concept has been introduced, based on Lyle Watson's "100th monkey theory" wherein a critical mass of conscious thought is suggested to influence the direction of human evolution. On this premise, it is believed that when a critical mass of people engage in meditation for world peace and ecological harmony, more and more people will eventually resonate with this mind frame to the point of significant positive influence. The end result will be higher consciousness among all people to act as one. In 1988, Edward Winchester, a financial analyst at the Pentagon, organized the Pentagon Meditation Club, in which members meditate to link as "human peace shields" for the moral protection of humanity. Though they have not claimed responsibility for the demise of communism, the fall of the Berlin wall, the breakup of the Soviet Union, or the current reduction in nuclear armaments, they do feel that their efforts were partially influential in these events.

Types of Meditation

From the seeds of Eastern philosophy grew two distinct branches of meditation: exclusive or **restrictive meditation,** and inclusive or **opening-up meditation.** While the two vary in style and format, the processes of concentration and awareness are paramount to the benefits of both of them. The end result is the same: a cleansing of the mind that leads to inner peace.

Exclusive Meditation

Consider this metaphor: The mind is a sky full of clouds, with several layers superimposed on one another above the earth. Each cloud layer represents a multitude of thoughts that compete for conscious attention. Exclusive meditation (also known as concentration meditation) involves the restriction of consciousness to focus on a single thought. This single thought becomes a device to wipe all other thoughts from the conscious slate. A single thought is like a gentle wind that blows the clouds away, leaving a clear blue sky. The power of this single thought is repetition, which continually breaks the surface of attention to the exclusion of all other thoughts. Restrictive meditation advocates a closed awareness to the external senses and all outside stimulation, and directs the focus of one's thoughts inward. In most cases, exclusive meditation is practiced with the eyes closed to prevent visual distractions. There are five actions used to refine one's attention on a single focused thought: mental repetition, visual concentration, repeated sounds, physical repetition, and tactile repetition.

1. *Mental repetition.* Mental repetition means a thought is produced over and over again. Mental repetition is most commonly done by use of a *mantra,* which is a one syllable word (e.g., *Om, one, peace,* or *love*) and should be done in conjunction with exhaling. A *mantra* can also be a short positive phrase (e.g., I feel good, I am worthy of love, or My body is calm and relaxed) to reinforce positive self-esteem. In some cases, prayers are also considered a type of mantra. In cultures where yoga meditation is practiced, it is believed that certain sounds (audible energy) have the power to heal. Thus, chanting in a soft whisper or silently repeating the word *Om* is believed to access the highest level of concentration, that which represents the essence of truth, love, and peace. This and other yoga mantras are created of special sounds that are thought to help release "blocked energy" impeding mental homeostasis. Chanting the word *Om* is thought to produce a vibration that draws the body's rhythm into synchrony with the earth's magnetic field, thus evoking a feeling of oneness with nature. Western philosophy suggests that the vibrations from any one word can have a calming effect. Regardless of philosophical bent, it is commonly accepted that when practiced regularly, the repetition of a one-word *mantra* will clear all other thoughts from the conscious mind.

2. *Visual concentration.* Visual concentration involves visually focusing on or staring at an object or image. In yoga meditation, this is called steady gazing or *tratak.* Visual concentration is like a visual *mantra.* The practice of *tratak* involves staring at an object about three to five feet away, without blinking, until it is etched on the mind's blackboard to the exclusion of all other thoughts. The suggested duration is about sixty seconds. Then close your eyes and visualize the object. If the mental image fades or vanishes, open your eyes and repeat this again. Common visual *mantras* include a candle flame, flower, sea shell, beautiful scene, or *mandala* (Fig. 18.3)—a circular object that is intricately designed, intense in color, and often divided into four quarters.

3. *Repeated sounds.* In some forms of meditation, a sound is repeated continually to help focus the mind's attention. The term for this is *nadam.* Examples of sounds are a beating drum, chimes, Tibetan bells, or Gregorian chants. Natural sounds such as the rush of a waterfall, ocean waves on the shore of a beach, or rolling thunder are also examples of *nadams.* In Western culture, some types of repetitive New Age music may be considered *nadams.*

4. *Physical repetition.* This is repetitive motion such as the sensation of breathing, or some forms of rhythmic aerobic exercise (e.g., running, swimming, or walking) that are believed by many to produce a meditative state (runner's high), either from the sound of breathing or rhythmic motions of feet and arms. Physical repetition is thought to shift the mind to an altered state of consciousness or relaxed thinking mode. Several people say their most creative thoughts come during this type of exercise. In Sufi religious practice, the whirling dervish dance is said to induce a trancelike state through the repetitive circular motion. Pranayama or diaphragmatic breathing is also used extensively as a physical repetitive mantra in virtually every relaxation course. This approach, where there is repetitive motion, is also called active meditation.

5. *Tactile repetition.* Holding a small object, such as a tumble stone or seashell, also brings focus to the mind. Hindu yogis use a strand of beads called a *mala* (108 small beads and one large *meru* bead), holding it in their right hand, and rolling the beads one by one between the thumb and third finger as they meditate. In Western culture, rosary beads offer a similar focus of concentration.

Meditation Position.   In all forms of meditation, but particularly in restrictive meditation, correct body position is essential. Perhaps the most recognized posture is the lotus position (Fig. 18.4). In the lotus position, an individual sits with his or her legs crossed and folded, each foot resting on the alternate thigh. A more comfortable position for beginners is the half-lotus position, with the legs simply crossed in a comfortable manner. In this passive position, one sits with the back (spinal column) completely aligned from the crown of the head to the tail bone. This alignment minimizes neural firing to the muscles and thus allows for increased (active) concentration on the mental focus. The hands can be placed on the thighs either with the palms down (to center oneself with the earth's energy) or face up with thumb and index finger joined (to receive energy). Breathing is regulated by placing emphasis on the expansion of the stomach area, rather than the chest, during inhalation (see Chapter 17). The position should be comfortable

A mandala is a circular object symbolizing wholeness which can be used as a visual mantra. (This is the famous stained glass window design of Notre Dame Cathedral in Paris, France.)

Figure 18.4 A meditation posture based on the lotus position.

Figure 18.4 A meditation posture based on the lotus position.

enough to maintain for approximately thirty minutes or more without interfering with your ability to concentrate. You may notice some pain in the muscles and joints of your hips and knees. If this occurs, stretch your legs to find a more comfortable position. Pain is not conducive to meditation.

There are several types of restrictive meditation. Transcendental meditation and the Relaxation Response are two examples.

Transcendental Meditation

Transcendental Meditation (TM) is a classic example of exclusive meditation. TM was developed by the Hindu Maharishi Mahesh Yogi. The story of the development of TM reads like an ancient fable. A young Hindu gentleman named Mahest Prasod Varma yearned to become a scientist, and in 1942 he received a degree in physics. But the winds of change soon brought him to study with the famed religious leader Swami Brahmanada Saraswati, with whom he spent the next thirteen years in divine worship. In this calling, he accepted the challenge to create a simple version of Hindu meditation, one that "anyone" could learn and practice. His life mission became to sow the seeds of world peace through the trained, tranquil soul of each individual. Off he went to the Himalaya Mountains, taking refuge in an abandoned cave. After a two-year retreat, he returned to India with the new technique we know today as TM. This technique, a simplified version of yoga meditation stripped of its spiritual dogma, was introduced into the United States in the late 1960s as a secular practice, and gained instant popularity. It was the favorite alternative for those whose recreational drug habits produced nasty side effects, as well as those who were seeking inner peace during the tumultuous and rocky decade of the Vietnam War. In the practice of TM, individuals are given a "special *mantra*" and taught to focus their thoughts on that one word. The *mantra,* the Maharishi and his teachers instructed, must remain secret to be effective, a statement later proved unfounded.

Within ten years' time, over a million Americans had learned this technique. People reported that it indeed brought inner peace and harmony to their lives when practiced with regularity. TM became the object of scientific curiosity, and inner peace soon became measured by significant decreases in resting blood pressure as well as the absence of many disease symptoms associated with stress. Intrigued by the possibility that TM could be a new relaxation technique, a team of medical researchers headed by Robert Keith Wallace and Herbert Benson (1972) investigated the effects of TM. To their surprise, they found that it proved quite effective as a mediating factor for chronic stress. In a Harvard laboratory, Wallace asked thirty-six subjects well trained in TM to practice this technique for three twenty- to thirty-minute sessions. Before, during, and after meditation sessions, oxygen consumption (VO_2), blood lactate, electrical skin conduction (sweating), and alpha brain waves were measured. Results revealed that TM did in fact induce a profound state of physiological homeostasis. Perplexed at the incongruity between its simplicity and the expensive price tag to learn TM (currently priced at $1,000), Benson Americanized the technique and called it the relaxation response.

The Relaxation Response

In his book *The Relaxation Response,* Benson describes four basic steps to follow to promote physiological homeostasis. These same four components can be found in virtually every relaxation technique, from mental imagery to progressive muscular relaxation. These simple components are as follows:

1. *A quiet environment.* A quiet environment can be any room with minimal distractions. It should be a room or area in which you feel completely comfortable. The premise of meditation is to reduce all sensory stimuli, including external stimuli such as ringing phones and doorbells, blaring televisions or radios, and outside street noise. A quiet environment also is interpreted to mean a reduction of internal stimuli, such as tense muscles and physical discomfort. Researchers have found that learning is enhanced when there are minimal distractions. Yet even nature itself is never completely silent, so you may need to balance your environment with "white noise," perhaps some soft instrumental music.

2. *A mental device.* A mental device is any object or tool used to replace all other thoughts. It is a focal point to direct all attention. A mental device can include repetition of a *mantra,* concentrated breathing, or a *tratak* or *nadam.* Benson suggested the word *one* for a *mantra.* He also suggested that if your mind wanders, use the word *no* to discontinue the free association. At first, repeating a selected word can seem rather monotonous. With time, he advised, it will become the perfect vehicle to clear your mind of mental chatter. Sometimes the combination of a **mantra** and diaphragmatic breathing makes this component easier.

3. *A passive attitude.* A passive attitude is a receptive attitude. A passive attitude is a frame of mind in which you are open to thoughts rather than blocking them out. At first this may sound contradictory to the exclusive nature of restriction meditation. But without this frame of mind, the walls of the ego censor any effort to relax completely. A passive attitude has also been interpreted as a state of physical calmness, for if the body is extremely tense throughout the process, then the meditation will be compromised. According to Benson, "A passive attitude allows the meditative process to begin."

4. *A comfortable position.* The earliest meditation advocates stated that to relax the mind, one must first relax the body. So you must first find a comfortable position. Benson advocates a sitting position with most of the body weight supported. The body should be relaxed, with no sign of muscular tension. Positions conducive to sleep should be avoided.

Inclusive Meditation

The second type of meditation is called **inclusive meditation.** It is also referred to as access meditation, insightful meditation, and **mindfulness.** Inclusive meditation appears to be very similar to free association, where the mind wanders aimlessly. In the practice of inclusive meditation, the mind is free to accept all thoughts; no attempt is made to control the mind's content. The conscious mind simply accepts spontaneous thoughts that make themselves available from the unconscious mind. There is one condition to this receptivity, however: All thoughts that enter the conscious mind must do so objectively and without judgment or emotional directive. This process is called *detached observation.* No emotional reaction can be connected with these thoughts. In effect, the mind becomes a movie screen with thoughts projected as images, and the individual observes without judgment or analysis. By detaching yourself from your emotions, the process of inclusive meditation allows barriers of the ego to dissolve. In this type of meditation the eyes are usually open, but you may find that this style can best be learned with the eyes closed.

Zen Meditation

Zen (Zazen) meditation, or some aspects of it, can be considered inclusive meditation. Zen meditation comes from Zen Buddhism. Around 590 B.C., a young man named Prince Gautama Siddhartha left his family, wealth, and life of foolish pleasures to become a monk, or "wanderer," living a simple life on the Ganges Plain. He became known as Sakyamuni (Prince of the Sakyas) and later on in life, the Buddha (the Awakened One). Sakyamuni began a journey of profound soul searching, pondering the meaning of life and death, leading to his own enlightenment. He soon became a recognized and respected teacher with a great many followers. What separates Zen from other similar

Stress With a Human Face

WHEN ADAM GRADUATED WITH HIS DEGREE in childhood education, he was ready to change the world, and he had every intention of doing so. An excellent student with excellent student-teaching evaluations from his supervisors, Adam believed he had everything he needed to start his teaching career. Like most college graduates, Adam believed he would take the summer off, go to Europe with a friend, then start work in the fall. As things happened, his plans changed when he ended up graduating in January. Adam found himself looking for a teaching job immediately. His prayers were answered when he landed a job in the Southeast section of the District of Columbia—or so he thought.

"You can learn all the theory you want in school, and you can do your practicum in the nicest schools around, but when it comes to working in a city school, I had to learn everything all over again. These kids need a lot of discipline and a lot more love, before they are ready to learn," he said in frustration.

As one of my former students in a stress-management class, Adam took an immediate liking to meditation, and from the second semester of his sophomore year, he practiced meditation regularly every morning. He mentioned to me several times that, as a varsity soccer player (now semi-professional), meditation was what kept him grounded before, during, and after his games. He reminded me regularly how valuable meditation had become in his life. Now entering the real world, meditation took on a whole new meaning.

"I come home from work exhausted, more so than after any soccer practice. Every day, those kids zap all my energy until I am completely drained. Do you realize how attentive you have to

be with kids like these?" he said one day over lunch. "And let me tell you something else," he added, "If I didn't meditate every morning before I go to work, I wouldn't have lasted the first week in that school. I can't tell you how important meditation is in my life. It's essential."

Adam proceeded to explain his daily meditation routine: a half hour of breathing exercises followed by some mental imagery. "Sometimes I even do it on the subway ride to school. In college, I used to do it for the mystical experience, which was pretty powerful in its own right, and to increase my concentration skills for soccer. I still do it for those reasons, but now more than ever, I do it to clear my mind." Meditation. It's not what you think! ✦

philosophies is the abandonment of the concept of dualities (good vs. bad, right vs. wrong, male vs. female), which are thought to separate rather than unite one with the universe. Thoughts expressed in either-or terms tend to be of an analytical or judgmental nature. Pure Zen thought is devoid of judgment,

thus connecting rather than separating one from the world. When the word *Zen* is heard, it is often associated with deep, pensive, intellectual thought. The purpose of Zen meditation is to reach the highest level of consciousness for the purpose of divine enlightenment. It is believed in Eastern cultures that truth and

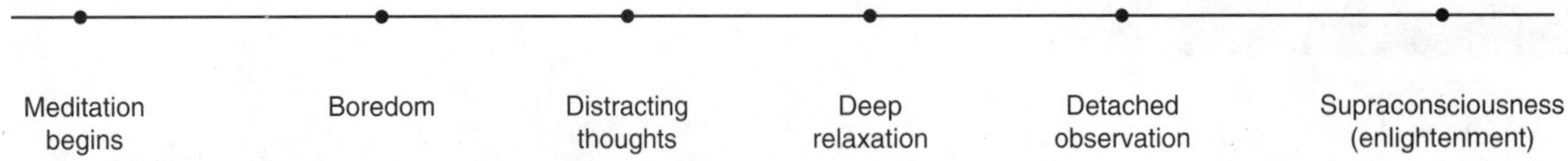

Figure 18.5

Everly and Rosenfeld's meditation continuum illustrates the cognitive stages that occur during restrictive or inclusive meditation. (From G. Everly and R. Rosenfeld. *The Nature and Treatment of the Stress Response: A Practical Guide for Clinicians* [New York: Plenum, 1981].)

| Meditation begins | Boredom | Distracting thoughts | Deep relaxation | Detached observation | Supraconsciousness (enlightenment) |

knowledge come from within and are housed in the soul. One must be patient to receive this gift of enlightenment, however, for it will not come if one is hurried in thought or strong in emotional attachment.

Zen meditation has many styles. Some have a restrictive nature to them (e.g., counting your breaths from ten down to one), while others lend themselves to opening the mind. Zen meditation is a very difficult and disciplined practice, often requiring several hours of motionless contemplative thought in one sitting. Moreover, Zen meditation includes the mind asking an unanswerable question, or *koan,* such as What is the sound of one hand clapping? Or, What did your face look like before you were conceived? Or this riddle: An egg is placed through the narrow opening of a glass bottle. In less than one day the egg hatches, yet the chick is too big to escape through the opening. How do you remove the chick from the glass bottle without harming the chick or destroying the bottle? Each *koan* invites profound contemplation. Because there are no answers, the mind acquiesces to the riddle. This submission through mental frustration is said to open the mind's door to new thought or sudden insight leading to greater awareness. The ultimate purpose of *koans* is to lead one up the path of enlightenment by learning, questioning, and accepting one's purpose in life. In Zen, meditation is only one step in the preparation for enlightenment.

Inclusive meditation is very difficult to practice at first. It is extremely challenging to try to divorce your emotions from your thoughts. But it is the walls of the ego that are believed to separate the mind from the soul, It is the ego, (the keeper of our identity) that is vulnerable to the perceptions of stress. Initially, opening up to uncensored thoughts can be a very difficult strategy to deal with stress. Perhaps for this reason, restrictive meditation is preferred over inclusive meditation and it is the former that is most commonly thought of when meditation is mentioned.

Everly and Rosenfeld created a meditation continuum highlighting the entire range of mental consciousness during the meditative process (Fig. 18.5). When one begins a meditation session, the first minute is devoted to preparation: getting comfortable, closing the eyes, perhaps even taking a few deep breaths, followed by more focused concentration. After this time, boredom may set in as the conscious mind fights the mental directive to block out all thoughts and their emotional attachments. (In many cases, people stop here in their first few encounters.) The conscious mind may then become distracted by any thoughts that will relieve the boredom. But once distracting thoughts are removed, the mind begins to enter a state of deep relaxation. In this state, a shift in dominance is said to occur from the left to the right hemisphere of the brain. This shift can be measured by a decrease in beta waves coupled with an increase in alpha waves on an electroencephalogram (EEG). With continued deep relaxation, any thoughts that appear on the mind's screen are observed objectively rather than given any emotional meaning. No judgment or analysis is associated with any thoughts. As the mind continues to observe, a state of supraconsciousness in which there is increased awareness of one's inner self begins to manifest itself. At this stage of meditation, the individual may feel almost euphoric, with sensations of enlightenment and connectedness with incorporeal surroundings; in essence, feeling one with the universe.

Split-Brain Theory

The idea that there is a distinct dichotomy of human thought processes (e.g., sequential vs. nonlinear) is not new; it has in fact been suggested for centuries. Anatomical studies even seem to support this idea when it was discovered that the human brain is an organ comprised of two hemispheres. But these theories became reality when an attempt was made to find a cure for epilepsy. In the mid 1950s, researcher Roger Sperry and his colleagues conducted a series of experiments designed to alleviate the intensity of grand mal epileptic seizures in monkeys. It was hypothesized that the intensity could be halved if a seizure could be contained to only one hemisphere of the brain. To their surprise, they found that by severing the corpus callosum, the neural isthmus uniting the right and left hemispheres, seizures significantly decreased in both frequency and severity. Curious to see if similar results would occur in humans, a new series of studies was conducted on four patients who volunteered to undergo this surgical procedure. Remarkably, this operation revealed neither damaging side effects nor noticeable changes in the patient's personality or intelligence. Some minor changes in cognitive thought processes were noticed, however, and it was these subtle differences in cognition and everyday behavior that soon gave rise to a new paradigm of human consciousness.

Under close observation after surgery, first it was noticed that the patient's right side of the body was controlled by the left hemisphere. Conversely, the left side was influenced by the right brain. Later these patients were asked to identify an object that was hidden from sight, placed alternately in each hand. In one study, when a pencil was placed in the right hand it was correctly described as a pencil (Fig. 18.6). When the pencil was placed in the left hand, however, no description could be given at all, suggesting the absence of verbal capacity in the right hemisphere. Additional experiments were then designed to combine visual and tactile objects. In one test, a picture of a spoon was shown to the left field of vision (right hemisphere), and subjects were asked to feel around with their left hand for an object resembling the picture. Patients had no difficulty identifying the spoon but again could not describe the item they retrieved. Thus, it was concluded that the right brain seemed to have poor verbal acuity but was extremely proficient in spatial perception.

From these and several other studies, it was concluded that each hemisphere appears to be responsible for specific types of thinking processes. Moreover, each hemisphere can function independently as a whole brain. Additional research with stroke victims seemed to confirm these findings. As a result, we now understand that each hemisphere is responsible for different information gathering and processing functions and yet they work together as one unit at the same time. It should be noted that most, if not all, of the research regarding left- and right-brain lateralization has involved epilepsy and stroke patients. Whether the brain works the same way among healthy people is still left to speculation. The work of Sperry and his colleagues has prompted many other studies on the dichotomy of cognitive functions. Table 18.1 provides a partial list of these distinct hemispheric functions.

Sperry's colleague and fellow researcher Robert Ornstein explains in his book *The Psychology of Consciousness* that right-brain cognitive functions are a foundation of intelligence yet to be explored. Intelligence is currently measured verbally; there is no standard method to evaluate nonverbal intelligence. This single approach to the duality of cognitive processes has limited the potential for human consciousness. Perhaps it has even contributed to perceptions of stress. In the words of Ornstein, "The problem is not that our technology is leading us to a path of destruction, but that our technical innovations have outstripped our perspective and judgment. We live in a world that is often difficult for us to understand." Ornstein supports the idea that the two modes of thinking are complementary, not competitive, and that they must be integrated and balanced for the health of the mind.

Figure 18.6 To test the split-brain cognitive functions of a subject, a word or object is projected onto a translucent screen. The subject is asked to retrieve the object, which is hidden from view and identifiable only by touch.

Cognitive Functions of the Left and Right Hemispheres of the Brain		*Table 18.1*
Left-Brain Functions	**Right-Brain Functions**	
Analytical skills	Synthesis skills	
Judgmental skills	Accepting, receptive nature	
Time consciousness	Non-time consciousness	
Verbal acuity	Symbolic imagery	
Linear thought progression	Nonlinear thought progression	
Rational thought process	Irrational thought process	
Math acuity	Intuition	
	Imagination	
	Music appreciation	
	Humor	
	Spatial orientation	

Since the initial discoveries, many inferences have been drawn from split-brain research. For example, comparisons have been made between the functions of the left and right brains and dominant thinking processes of Western and Eastern cultures, respectively. Western culture is considered by many to be left-hemisphere dominant (strong in analytical and judgmental skills, weak in intuitive abilities), while Eastern cultures are right-hemisphere dominant. It is also hypothesized by several sources (Schaef, 1986; Borysenko, 1987) that there is a strong association between left-brain thinking patterns and the frame of mind observed during the stress response. Although generalizations may cloud the understanding of both cultural differences and human cognition, comparisons of this kind may explain why meditation has been less readily accepted by industrialized nations in the Western hemisphere. It may also explain the role meditation plays in accessing right-brain functions to obtain a balance of hemispheric cognition.

Altered State of Consciousness

When the results of these and other studies by Sperry and his colleagues were made public, researchers saw strong similarities between the cognitive functions of the right hemisphere and those traits associated with the altered state of consciousness produced by meditation. Studies have since shown that the act of meditation produces a different type of brain wave than that observed in either nonmeditative waking states or sleep (Fig. 18.7). In a "normal" state of consciousness, the predominant brain waves emitted are rapid and jagged beta waves (15–20 cycles/second). They appear to signify rapid neural conductivity. Thought processes in our typical waking state are those characteristically observed when the left hemisphere of the brain is performing its specific cognitive functions. In other words, during a normal state of consciousness, the mind leans toward censorship, analysis, judgment, and rationality. Critics theorize that this normal state of consciousness is rewarded in academic, cultural, and social practices, and that as a result, alternative ways of thinking and processing information are frowned upon. The normal state of consciousness can be quite taxing to the brain: every now and then, for brief periods, we may catch ourselves in an altered pattern of consciousness, most likely daydreaming.

Meditation, on the other hand, tends to produce what is now called an altered state of consciousness. Although not advocated, alcohol and/or drugs are known to produce a similar response. An altered state of mind occurs where there is a shift in the thinking style of cognitive processes. Physiologically speaking, in an altered state the brain produces slow (7–10 cycles/second) and almost rhythmical oscillations called alpha waves, which represent a significant decrease in sensory input or a desensitization effect.

Figure 18.7 Neural patterns of brain activity are shown to be variable during different states of consciousness. Alpha waves are thought to suggest a relaxed yet fully alert consciousness.

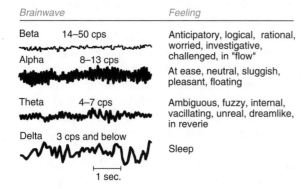

Brainwave		Feeling
Beta	14–50 cps	Anticipatory, logical, rational, worried, investigative, challenged, in "flow"
Alpha	8–13 cps	At ease, neutral, sluggish, pleasant, floating
Theta	4–7 cps	Ambiguous, fuzzy, internal, vacillating, unreal, dreamlike, in reverie
Delta	3 cps and below	Sleep

1 sec.

(Sleep produces delta and some theta waves, with beta waves during rapid-eye-movement periods.) In many ways, an altered state of consciousness closely parallels the functions characteristically observed in the right hemisphere of the brain: the mind is open to suggestion, receptive to new ideas, and able to observe without judgment.

During meditation, some characteristics that also indicate the occurrence of an altered state of consciousness have been noted (Allen, 1983). When these sensations are experienced, then the meditative processes are believed to have induced the desired switch from left- to right-brain dominance. They are as follows:

1. *Time distortion.* Time consciousness is a left-brain function. During meditation, a distortion of time perception may result as dominant thinking shifts from the left to the right hemisphere. The usual response is a sense of time loss in which a twenty-minute session appears to have been only a few minutes. The right hemisphere does not recognize the element of time; therefore, it can neither express nor judge the passage of time in the terms the left brain perceives in a normal state of consciousness. In addition, in an altered state there may be an inability to remember situations or circumstances directly prior to its onset, as they appear to have no relevance to the act of meditation.

2. *Ineffability.* Have you ever had an experience that was literally indescribable? One where you just could not find words to adequately describe the experience? Then you've experienced ineffability. The mind's verbal skills are housed in the left hemisphere. The right hemisphere "speaks" in symbols, images, and vivid colors. Many times an experience will occur during meditation that you simply will not be able to put into words. It can be appreciated in sensory (visual) form.

3. *Present-centeredness.* In a normal state of consciousness, the mind is darting at lightning speed among the past, present, and future. The past tends to be the repository for feelings of guilt, while the future harbors a wealth of worries about things that may or may not ever happen. The goal of meditation is to exist in the present moment; to be present and centered in the here and now. Rarely do we spend time in the present. In a normal state of consciousness, the present moment seems unproductive, and thus unappealing or uncomfortable. Yet in an altered state, the mind is pleasantly entertained in the here and now.

4. *Perception distortion.* If you have ever felt like your arms and legs have sunk into the floor or disappeared altogether while relaxing, then you have experienced perception distortion. It is not that the mind cannot process information during an altered state of consciousness; it is just that information is processed differently by the right hemisphere of the brain. Spatial orientation is a right-brain function. When the right brain is dominant during thinking, perceptions of space appear distorted when transferred to the left brain. Perception distortions during meditation also include what is called *synesthesia*, or sensory crossover. In synesthesia, sensory stimuli are processed by neurons usually designated for other cognitive functions, thus leading to quite different interpretations. For example, you might be able to *hear* colors and *see* sounds, which is impossible to fully explain in words.

5. *Enhanced receptivity.* In a meditative state, the walls of the ego are temporarily lowered, perhaps even dissolved altogether. When this

happens, thoughts from the unconscious mind enter the conscious mind freely. As consciousness expands, the mind becomes more receptive to ideas and thoughts from the unconscious mind that it might not access in a normal state of consciousness. Thus, enlightenment is self-generated. This characteristic of an altered state is similar to hypnotic or subliminal suggestion; however, in meditation, the suggestions come from the inner self.

6. *Self-transcendence.* Meditation really does appear to have a mystical, spiritual quality to it. It is spiritual in the sense that it evokes the ability to experience expanded consciousness or enlightenment that is not manifested in normal consciousness. This is the original premise of meditation as taught thousands of years ago to those seeking enlightenment: when the pupil is ready, the teacher will come. Self-transcendence also consists of the essence of positive thought, inner peace. Inner peace results from the realization of unity or oneness with the universe after censorship and all other barriers are removed. When a state of supraconsciousness is achieved, the lack of ego boundaries is experienced as a connectedness to virtually all things.

Physiological and Psychological Effects of Meditation

In reviewing the clinical studies regarding the physiological aspects of meditation, one also crosses the paths of yoga, biofeedback, and autogenic training. They all appear to be related. The first account of clinical research to measure mind control of the body occurred in 1935, when a French woman traveled to India with a portable electrocardiogram. Her findings revealed that the yogi masters who were her subjects possessed the incredible ability to decelerate their heart rates. One yogi was observed to have virtually stopped his heart from beating altogether. Therese Brosse's pioneer research went unremarked for about two decades, perhaps because her findings contradicted all previous thought about autonomic nervous system regulation. In 1957, attempts were made to replicate Brosse's original findings with better equipment. While no yogi meditators were observed to stop their hearts from beating, Bagchi and Wenger did

observe amazing control of the autonomic nervous system in their subjects. The Swami Ramma's cooperation as a subject in several clinical case studies at the Menniger Institute by Elmer and Alyce Green in the early 1970s gave much credence to the earlier studies by Brosse, and Bagchi and Wenger. Once again, mind control was exhibited to decrease heart rate and ventilations, and alter the distribution of blood flow.

With the introduction of TM in the United States, several great claims were made regarding its effectiveness as a technique for mental calmness and relaxation. Among these were the ability to control heart rate, ventilation, and blood flow. When these claims were put under the "scientific microscope" through a battery of investigations designed by Wallace and Benson (1970, 1972), they held up. More recent studies on Benson's relaxation response (Benson, 1989) revealed that meditation acts to reduce the release and responsivity of norepinephrine throughout the central nervous system. From original observations by Wallace and Benson and by Treichel et al. (1973), as well as more recent research by Michael Delmonte (1984, 1985), it now appears that the practice of meditation promotes an immediate decrease in both some physical responses and learned responses. The following physiological changes have been known to occur with regular meditation practice:

1. Decreased oxygen consumption
2. Decreased blood lactate levels
3. Increased skin resistance
4. Decreased heart rate
5. Decreased blood pressure
6. Decreased muscle tension
7. Increased alpha waves

With claims that meditation creates mental calmness, psychological effects were also investigated with great zeal. To no surprise, results proved it quite effective in reducing many factors related to perceived stress and improved mental health (Dillbeck, 1977). When subjects who meditated were compared with controls who never attempted this technique, the subjects showed less anxiety, as well as decreased smoking, alcohol, and recreational drug use (Marcus, 1974). Subjects who practiced meditation were also found to demonstrate greater degrees of self-actualization and increased internal locus of control, and were able to sleep more soundly (Rohsenow et al., 1985).

Meditation has proven effective as a tool for various types of rehabilitation as well. In one study conducted in 1987 by Bleick and Abrams, TM was taught to over 250 prison inmates in the California Department of Corrections. Conclusions were that the use of meditation had a more favorable effect on parole outcomes and recidivism compared to that of prisoners who did not learn meditation. Moreover, meditation seemed to produce more favorable results on recidivism than did prison education, vocational training, and psychotherapy. Similarly, meditation among patients who were addicted to alcohol and drugs was shown to be effective in significantly reducing anxiety and promoting greater internal locus of control. In general, these tests revealed that habitual meditation promoted greater psychological stability and allowed individuals to stop feeling like passive victims in their own environment, two major goals of psychotherapy. In a comprehensive review of the studies investigating the psychological effects of meditation, Delmonte concluded that, above all else, its practice did promote a greater sense of general well-being or inner peace. As a result of these and similar findings, the technique of meditation has been integrated into the practice of psychotherapy as a major tool to promote psychological well-being.

In the most extensive review on the physical and psychological effects of meditation, Michael Murphy and Steven Donovan conclude that meditation, in all its many methods, unequivocally produces beneficial changes to both mind and body.

Steps to Initiate Meditation

As pointed out by Benson, the elements of meditation are quite simple. All you need is a quiet space, a comfortable position, a receptive attitude, and a mental device or "meditative broom" to sweep clean the corners of your mind. One component that Benson neglected to emphasize, however, was practice on a regular basis. Meditation is a state of mind, but to be effective it requires the habitual practice of employing concentration. Concentration, like so many other behaviors, is a skill. The more you practice this skill, the better it will serve you.

The following are three meditation practices I use when teaching this technique. The first is an example of exclusive meditation, which was passed on to me by a yogi master. The second and third are exercises based on the concept of inclusive meditation. Read each exercise first to familiarize yourself with the technique. Then give it a try. Start with a short duration of time (five minutes), and with each session, add a few minutes until you build up to about thirty minutes. (It may take a few weeks to feel comfortable with this length of time.)

The Body Flame

The body flame is an example of restrictive meditation combined with mental imagery. It is a technique that seems quite effective for people who have ulcers and excess energy. It seems to work best lying down, at least at first. Once you are proficient, it can be done in any position at any time. Start by trying this technique for about five minutes. Continually add more time as your comfort level increases.

1. Lie comfortably on your back, keeping your spine aligned from your head to your hips.
2. Observe your breathing, making it comfortably deep and relaxed.
3. Close your eyes and try to locate the center of your body; your center of gravity. If you are like most people, it is about an inch or two below your belly button.
4. Imagine a flame hovering over that point on your body (Fig. 18.8). This flame is a symbol of your state of relaxation. It feeds off your body's energy. When the body has an abundance of energy—nervous or negative energy—this flame will be quite tall, perhaps even like a blow torch. When you are completely relaxed, your flame will be quite small—a "maintenance flame," like a pilot light on a gas stove.
5. Imagine the size of your flame. See its size relative to your body's level of energy. Look at its color. It may be an intense, brilliant yellow/white color. Now look at its shape. At the

Figure 18.8 The body flame.

bottom, it is round or oval shaped. The top comes to a jagged point. Your flame may even dance around a bit. As you look at this flame, feel it feed off the energy in your body. Let your flame burn off any excess energy you feel detracts from your ability to relax. If your thoughts start to wander away from the image of the flame, try to send these up through the flame and redirect your thoughts back to this image.

6. As you continue to watch the flame, feel your body slowly become calm and relaxed. As this happens, notice the flame decrease in height. Soon you will notice that your flame is only about one quarter to one half inch tall. Continue to notice the color, shape, and size; and feel your body relax as your attention is fixed on this image.

7. When you feel completely relaxed, with a very small, very still flame, allow this image to fade from your mind but retain the feeling of relaxation. Repeat this each day, or as often as you like.

Grand Perspective Mental Video

The grand perspective mental video is an example of inclusive meditation. In this exercise, you invite any and all thoughts to freely enter your conscious mind. During this exercise, try not to attach any emotional responses to the images that appear on your mind's screen. See the images, but detach yourself emotionally from them. Should you find that you sense some emotional attachment, simply allow that thought to fade and invite a new thought in. This exercise is often compared to free association, and you may find your mind wandering down a trail of thoughts that all seem connected; this is fine. Try this exercise for a three to five minute period. Each time you return to this exercise, add a few more minutes on. If one issue keeps appearing on the mind's screen and you find yourself unable to be objective about it, this may be an advisory to deal with it as soon as possible. You may elect to do this exercise with some soft instrumental background music; sometimes it can help.

1. Sit or lie comfortably, keeping your back completely straight. Take a deep breath and relax.

2. Close your eyes. Imagine that your mind's eye sees all the mind's thoughts projected onto the mind's screen. The movies that play on your mind's silver screen are produced and directed by you. But now your primary role is that of an observer or audience member.

3. Separate yourself from directing your thoughts. Just let them roll, unedited and uncensored. Take a back seat in the mind's theater to get a grand perspective on these images. To do this effectively, look at whatever thoughts come onto your mind's screen objectively, without emotional attachment, ownership, or analysis. This may seem rather hard to do at first, but with time it will become easy. Just sit back in the audience and enjoy the show.

Mindfulness

Meditation does not have to be done in the confinement of your room. The underlying premise of meditation is to enjoy the present moment. And to paraphrase Buddhist Thich Nat Hanh, meditation can be done anywhere. Mindfulness meditation means to be conscious of the present moment in all that you do; to fill your body's senses with what you are experiencing at the present moment. For example, mindfulness can be done while walking, by feeling your body's weight shift as you place each foot in front of you, and feeling each other movement of your body. Mindfulness can be done while washing dishes; becoming aware of the feeling of the water and soap on your hands. This exercise asks that you try to increase your awareness and concentration by eating an apple.

1. Pick an apple and hold it in your hand.

2. Sit comfortably, with your back straight. (You may choose to sit against a wall for support.)

3. Feel the weight of the apple in your hand. Feel the texture of the apple's skin. Feel the curves. Feel the stem (if there is one). Notice all the nuances of the apple with your fingers.

4. Look at the apple. What color is it? Look at it carefully. Study it. Know this apple so well that if it were put back into a barrel of apples, you could find it.

5. Now smell the apple. Close your eyes and focus your sense of smell on the apple. What does it smell like?

6. Bite into the apple. Savor its taste, both flavor and texture. Feel your tongue and jaws move as you chew. Feel your breathing pause as you swallow. Make each bite of the apple seem like the first.

7. Take note of any other observations about this experience.

Best Application of Meditation

It has been said that in the contemporary age, seldom if ever are we in the presence of silence for any length of time. Between the noises made by televisions, dishwashers, radios, refrigerators, and personal computers—not to mention air and street traffic—there is hardly an uninterrupted moment of mental calmness. As a result, the human mind becomes supersaturated with sensory stimulation. To keep one's sanity, one's mind has to unload these thoughts or it will suffer the consequences. The typical consequence for many people is heightened physical arousal, which leads to deciphering these sensory stimulations as potential threats. The mind craves homeostasis just as the body does.

Back in the days when yoga meditation was first taught, it was practiced in the early morning, between 4 and 6 A.M., as this was the time best suited to expanded awareness. Three thousand years later, early morning is still advocated as the best time to meditate. But time of day is not as important as length of time, which should be about twenty to thirty minutes per day. In any case, meditation necessitates a designated time period in your schedule; whatever fits into your daily routine. It is also helpful to specify a special place to meditate, any corner that you want to designate for this purpose.

However and whenever you do it, the bottom line is that we all need times of solitude to cleanse the cluttered mess from the mind. Unequivocally, meditation can be classified as a technique to help prevent the heightened, sustained arousal of stress. Rare would be the opportunity, however, to employ quality meditative skills in the face of stress, particularly during spontaneous moments of anger. It might be best used as a technique to quell the fires of fear. With practice, you will find that meditation has many layers and can create many profound effects of relaxation.

Summary

+ Meditation is thought to be the oldest form of relaxation. In simple terms, it is a mind-cleansing or emptying process. At a deeper level, meditation is focused concentration and increased awareness of one's being. When the mind has been emptied of conscious thought, unconscious thoughts can enter the conscious realm to bring enlightenment to our lives.

+ Basically, there are two methods of mind cleansing to exclude all thoughts from the mind save the one that is used to clear the rest out; and to include all thoughts but detach oneself emotionally from these images. Transcendental meditation and Zen meditation are examples of exclusive and inclusive meditation, respectively.

+ Benson Americanized transcendental meditation, calling it the relaxation response. He found that all one needs to relax are the following four components: a quiet environment, a mental device for concentration, a passive attitude, and a comfortable position in which to meditate.

+ The practice of meditation can lead to an altered state of consciousness, where sensory perceptions are different from those in a normal waking state of consciousness. Perceptual changes include time distortion, ineffability, present-centeredness, perception distortion, enhanced receptivity, and self-transcendence.

+ These changes in perception and information processing mirror those observed by Sperry, who found that when surgically separated, the left and right hemispheres of the brain demonstrate unique and separate cognitive functions, similar to those cited under normal and altered states of consciousness, respectively.

+ Research also shows that habitual meditation has extensive physiological effects on the body, among which are decreased resting heart rate, decreased resting blood pressure, and decreased resting ventilation, suggesting that there is a connection between mind and body that can profoundly influence homeostasis.

+ Meditation is now recommended by the American Heart Association as a means to reduce stress levels, which are thought to be a risk factor for heart disease.

+ Every relaxation technique involves some aspect of meditation.

Concepts and Terms

Active meditation
Altered state of consciousness
Detached observation
Enhanced receptivity
Exclusive meditation
Inclusive meditation
Ineffability
Koan

Mandala
Mantra
Meditation
Mindfulness
Nadam
Perception distortion
Present-centeredness
Relaxation response

Self-transcendence
Sensory overload
Split-brain theory
Synesthesia
Time distortion
Transcendental meditation
Tratak
Zen meditation

Self-Assessment

1. How often do you meditate? _____

2. What is your typical meditation routine?

   _____

   _____

   _____

   _____

   _____

   _____

   _____

3. Do your parents or friends meditate?   Yes   No

4. How do you feel after you meditate? Assuming you meditate regularly, do you ever notice a difference in your being if you happen to miss a day or two of meditating?

   _____

   _____

   _____

   _____

   _____

   _____

   _____

   _____

   _____

   _____

   _____

   _____

   _____

   _____

   _____

   _____

   _____

   _____

References and Resources

Alexander, C. et al. Transcendental Meditation, Mindfulness, and Longevity: An Experimental Study with the Elderly, *Journal of Personality and Social Psychology* 57(6):950–964, 1989.

Allen, R. J. *Human Stress: Its Nature and Control.* Burgess, Minneapolis, MN, 1983.

Allison, J. Respiratory Changes during Transcendental Meditation, *Lancet* 7651:833–834, 1970.

Anand, B. K., China, G. S., and Singh, B. Some Aspects of Electroencephalographic Studies in Yogis, *Electroencephalographology and Clinical Neurophysiology* 13:452–456, 1961.

Atwood, J. D. and Maltin, L. Putting Eastern Philosophies into Western Psychotherapies, *American Journal of Psychotherapy* 45(3):368–382, 1991.

Bagchi, B. K. and Wenger, M. A. Electrophysiological Correlates of Some Yoga Exercises, *Electroencephalography, Clinical Neurophysiology, and Epilepsy* 3:International Congress of Neurological Sciences, 1959.

Benson, H. The Relaxation Response, *Psychiatry* 37:37–46, 1974.

Benson, H. *The Relaxation Response.* Morrow Press, New York, 1975.

Benson, H. The Relaxation Response and Norepinephrine: A New Study Illuminates Mechanisms, *Australian Journal of Clinical Hypnotherapy and Hypnosis* 10(2):91–96, 1989.

Benson, H. *Timeless Healing.* Morrow Press, New York, 1996.

Bleick, C. and Abrams, A. The Transcendental Meditation Program and Criminal Recidivism in California, *Journal of Criminal Justice* 15(3):211–230, 1987.

Borysenko, J. *Minding the Body, Mending the Mind.* Bantam Books, New York, 1987.

Brosse, T. A. Psychophysiological Study of Yoga, *Main Currents in Modern Thought* 4:77–84, 1946.

Castillo, R. J. Depersonalization and Meditation, *Psychiatry* 53(2):158–168, 1990.

Cauthen, N. R. and Prymak, C. A. Meditation versus Relaxation: An Examination of the Physiological Effects of Transcendental Meditation, *Journal of Consulting and Clinical Psychology* 45:496–497, 1977.

Delmonte, M. An Overview of the Therapeutic Effects of Meditation, *Psychologia: An International Journal of Psychology in the Orient* 28(4):189–202, 1985.

Delmonte, M. Physiological Responses during Meditation and Rest, *Biofeedback and Self-Regulation* 9(2):181–200, 1984.

Dillbeck, M. C. The Effect of the Transcendental Meditation Technique on Anxiety Levels, *Journal of Clinical Psychology* 33:1076–1078, 1977.

Dumoulin, H. *Zen Enlightenment.* Weatherhill, New York, 1981.

Elson, B. D., Hauri, P., and Cunis, D. Physiological Changes in Yogi Meditation, *Psychophysiology* 14:52–57, 1977.

Everly, G. S. and Rosenfeld, R. *The Nature and Treatment of the Stress Response: A Practical Guide for Clinicians.* Plenum Press, New York, 1981.

Ferguson, P. and Gowan, J. TM—Some Preliminary Findings, *Journal of Humanistic Psychology* 16:51–60, 1977.

Fosshage, J. *Healing Implications for Psychotherapy.* Human Sciences Press, New York, 1978.

Gazzaniga, M. S. The Split Brain in Man, *Scientific American* 508:24–29, 1967.

Gibran, K. *The Prophet.* Knopf, New York, 1981.

Goldberg, B. Slowing Down the Aging Process through the Use of Altered States of Consciousness: A Review of the Medical Literature, *Psychology, a Journal of Human Behavior* 32(2) 19–21, 1995.

Goleman, D. J. and Schwartz, G. E. Meditation as an Intervention in Stress Reactivity, *Journal of Consulting and Clinical Psychology* 44:456–466, 1976.

Green, E. and Green, Alyce. *Beyond Biofeedback.* Knoll Pub. Inc., Topeka, KS, 1977.

Johnston, W. *Silent Music: The Science of Meditation.* Harper & Row, New York, 1974.

Jaret, P. "You Don't Have to Sweat to Reduce Your Stress," *Health,* Nov./Dec.:82–88, 1995.

Kabot-Zinn, J. *Full Catastrophe Living.* Delta Books, New York, 1990.

Kabot-Zinn, J. *Wherever You Go, There You Are: Mindfullness Living in Everyday Life.* Hyperion Books, New York, 1994.

Kapleau, P., ed. *The Three Pillars of Zen.* Doubleday, New York, 1980.

Kasamatsu, A. and Hirai, T. Studies of EEGs of Expert Zen Meditators, *Folia, Psychiatrica Neurologica Japonica* 28:315, 1966.

Keys, K. *The Hundredth Monkey.* Visih Books, Coos Bay, OR, 1987.

Kornfield, J. *Buddhist Meditation and Consciousness Research.* Institute of Noetic Sciences, Sausalito, CA, 1990.

Kuna, D. J. Meditation and Work, *Vocational Guidance Quarterly* 23:342–346, 1975.

Larkin, M. Meditation May Reduce Heart Attack and Stroke Risk. *Lancet* 355:206, 812, 2000.

Levey, J. and Levey, M. *The Fine Arts of Relaxation, Concentration, and Meditation.* Wisdom Books, Boston, MA, 1991.

Levey, J. and Levey, M. *Simple Meditation & Relaxation.* Conari Press, Berkeley, CA, 1999.

Marcus, J. B. Transcendental Meditation: A New Method of Reducing Drug Abuse, *Drug Forum* 3:113–136, 1974.

Merzel, G. *The Eye Never Sleeps.* Shambhala, London, 1991.

Motoyama, H. *Toward a Superconsciousness: Meditation Theory and Practice.* Asian Humanities Press, Berkeley, CA, 1990.

Murphy, M. and Donovan, S. *The Physical and Psychological Effects on Meditation: A Review of Contemporary Research with a Comprehensive Bibliography.* Institute of Noetic Sciences, Sausalito, CA. 1997.

Naranjo, C. and Ornstein, R. E. *On the Psychology of Meditation.* Esalen Books, New York, 1971.

Ornish, D. *Dr. Dean Ornish's Program for Reversing Coronary Heart Disease without Drugs or Surgery.* Ballantine Books, New York, 1992.

Ornstein, R. *The Psychology of Consciousness.* Penguin Books, New York, 1972.

Pagano, R. R. et al. Sleep during Transcendental Meditation, *Science* 191:308–309, 1976.

Pritz, A. *Pocket Guide to Meditation.* Crossing Press, Freedom, CA, 1997.

Rohsenow, D. J., Smith, R. E., and Johnson, S. Stress-Management Training as a Prevention Program for Heavy Social Drinkers: Cognitions, Affect Drinking, and Individual Differences, *Addictive Behaviors* 10(1):45–54, 1985.

Schaef, A. W. *Codependence: Misunderstood, Mistreated.* Harper, New York, 1986.

Shaffi, M. Adaptive and Therapeutic Aspects of Meditation, *International Journal of Psychoanalytic Psychotherapy* 2:364–382, 1973.

Shapiro, D. H. *Meditation: Classic and Contemporary Perspectives.* Aldine, New York, 1984.

Shapiro, D. H. and Zifferblatt, S. M. Zen Meditation and Behavioral Self-Control: Similarities, Differences, and Clinical Applications, *American Psychologist* 31:519–532, 1976.

Silva, J. and Miele, P. *The Silva Mind-Control Method.* Pocket Books, New York, 1975.

Sperry, R. The Great Cerebral Commissure, *Scientific American* 174:44–52, 1964.

Stek, R. J. and Bass, B. A. Personal Adjustment and Perceived Locus of Control among Students Interested in Meditation, *Psychological Reports* 32:1019–1022, 1973.

Sudsuang, R. et al. Effect of Buddhist Meditation on Serum Cortisol and Total Protein Levels, Blood Pressure, Pulse Rate, Lung Volume, and Reaction Time, *Physiology and Behavior* 50(3):543–548, 1991.

Treichel, M., Clinch, N., and Cran, M. The Metabolic Effects of Transcendental Meditation, *Physiologist* 16:472, 1973.

Wallace, R. K. and Benson, H. The Physiology of Meditation, *Scientific American* 226:85–90, 1972.

Wallace, R. K. Physiological Effects of Transcendental Meditation, *Science* 167:1751–1754, 1970.

Zaichkowsky, L. D. and Kamen, R. Biofeedback and Meditation: Effects on Muscle Tension and Locus of Control, *Perceptual and Motor Skills* 46:955–958, 1978.

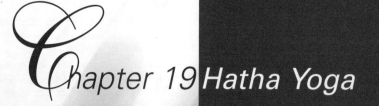

Chapter 19 Hatha Yoga

The main teaching of yoga is

that man's nature is divine.

—Swami Rama

The lotus position. Incense. Deep breathing. These and other thoughts come to mind when the word *yoga* is spoken. *Human pretzel* is another phrase, although this is a tongue-in-cheek description of several classic yoga positions. The word *yoga* comes from ancient Sanskrit. It is translated to mean "union"; specifically, the ultimate union of the mind, body, and soul. The development and practice of yoga are deeply rooted in the philosophy of spiritual enlightenment. As the practice of this technique migrated to the western hemisphere, particularly the United States, many traditional yoga positions were assimilated into American culture. They were adopted as flexibility exercises and used both prior to and following the completion of physical activity. Currently, the *shavasana,* or Corpse Pose, is employed in many relaxation techniques, including progressive muscular relaxation and autogenic training (see Chapters 24 and 25). But many other aspects of yoga, including breathing, and the symbolism and philosophy associated with the classic positions, were abandoned. Lately, however, as Americans have acquired a thirst for additional relaxation techniques, the original concepts of yoga have slowly reemerged. They form a simple yet profound technique to promote relaxation; and to unify mind, body, and spirit.

There are many yoga styles, and the practice of yoga can create many levels of inner peace. The **hatha yoga** style places special emphasis on physical postures, which are integrated with *pranayama,* or breathing control. The word *hatha* comes from two Sanskrit words, *ha* meaning "sun" and *tha* meaning "moon." The symbolic meaning of these words is the balance of universal life forces. The more concrete meaning is the balance of mind, body, and spirit through action, emotion, and intelligence. The following is a brief introduction to several hatha yoga concepts and postures. To learn hatha yoga, you must experience it. This chapter serves only as an invitation to pursue this technique under qualified instruction.

Historical Perspective

Scholars have traced the roots of yoga as far back as the sixth century B.C., to the teachings of the Hindu philosopher Kapila. These, along with teachings attributed to the Hindu deity Krishna, laid the foundation of several concepts to promote the enhancement of life through the union of mind, body, and spirit. While ancient scriptures cite Lord Shiva, or Supreme Consciousness, as the founder of yoga, credit for its earliest postures (*raja* yoga) is given to Patanjali, who codified these *asanas* (physical postures) in a written collection called the *Yoga Sutras*. Originally, *asanas* were created to cleanse the body, unlock energy paths, and raise level of consciousness. Through the ages, many variations or paths have emerged, each with its own interpretation of the path to enlightenment. The yogi master Swami Rama cites five yoga paths: *karma* yoga, the path of action; *bhakti* yoga, the path of devotion; *jnana* yoga, the path of knowledge; *kundalini* yoga, the path of spiritual awakening, an advanced form of meditation; and perhaps the most common style practiced in the United States, hatha yoga, the path of physical balance. Several yoga styles include a strong component of meditation to enhance the union of mind, body, and soul, and it is not uncommon for many people to use the terms *yoga* and *meditation* synonymously.

The premise of this mind-body-spirit union, as suggested by its earliest proponents, is that humanity's most salient nature is of a divine quality. The abyss that separates the corporeal and incorporeal is the wall of conscious intellect, or ego censorship. As described in the earliest teachings, divine enlightenment is made possible when this wall is dissolved through the realization of the self, transcending the limitations of consciousness. The remnants of the dissolved wall are then constructed as a bridge to greater understanding or enlightenment.

Yoga was first formally introduced into the United States when Swami Vivekananda made a presentation to the World Parliament of Religions in Chicago in 1893. His visit to America lasted well over two years as he traveled to several cities around the country. By the turn of the century, two *ashrams* (yoga centers) were established in California, with many more to follow throughout the nation. In 1970, Swami Rama, a yogi master from the Himalayan Institute, was invited to the Menninger Foundation in Topeka, Kansas. There, he collaborated in several clinical investigations into yoga and physiological adaptations to meditation as measured with various biofeedback modalities. It was observed that Swami Rama demonstrated nearly incredible control over several autonomic functions (e.g., respiration, heart rate, and blood flow), indicating to clinical researchers that many of the bodily functions previously thought involuntary could in fact be controlled, in a relaxed state, by conscious thought. In what can best be described as a grassroots movement, yoga has slowly become accepted in America as a proven means to relax.

It is raja yoga, or the "royal path," that most closely resembles the practice of restrictive meditation, wherein the body must be relaxed to open the mind. Hatha yoga, by contrast, integrates components of muscular strength, endurance, flexibility, and muscle relaxation, as well as serving as a catalyst for meditation.

Physiological and Psychological Benefits

Despite the fact that hatha yoga has been practiced in the United States for nearly a century, there is a dearth of clinical research to substantiate claims that following a habitual yoga routine improves overall health status. Proponents assert that the repeated daily series of selected *asanas* promotes longevity and cures several illnesses. To date, many of these claims appear subjective or anecdotal. Still, there is some research that has supported hatha yoga as part of a multimodal approach to stress management. Studies by Austin (1982) and Agne and Paolucci (1982) indicated that hatha yoga combined with other relaxation techniques, including diaphragmatic breathing, biofeedback, aerobic exercise, and recreational pursuits, were effective in the treatment of chemical dependency and alcoholism. In the majority of studies investigating yoga, emphasis has been on the relationship of the physiological homeostasis and its meditative qualities, rather than its physical postures and flexibility. The one physiological aspect of hatha yoga that has been scientifically investigated is the changes that take place during diaphragmatic breathing. As is recommended in hatha yoga, diaphragmatic breathing (more so than thoracic breathing), tends to elicit a greater parasympathetic response due to decreased thoracic pressure and baroceptor reflex response, thus promoting a pronounced physiological homeostatic effect (Stern and Anschel, 1968).

Without a doubt, hatha yoga improves flexibility. The more difficult *asanas* require muscle endurance and even strength, as these postures involve lifting the body off the ground. The practice of yoga is also thought to reduce blood pressure through the relaxation effect of these postures. But perhaps the best benefit provided by yoga is a greater sense of body awareness. It is no secret that the comforts of high-technology society and their consequent sedentary lifestyles often result in poor posture, muscle tone, flexibility, strength, balance, agility, and endurance. The progression of yoga *asanas* allows for greater awareness of all these components.

Many, if not all, yoga practitioners acknowledge a sense of mental enjoyment from habitual practice of *asanas,* but there is little empirical (scientific) evidence to support the idea that yoga contributes to emotional wellbeing. One study by Birkel (1991), however, compared a ten-week hatha yoga class with an interpersonal-relationship-development psychology course. Subjects were measured for self-concept and self-perception. Those enrolled in the yoga course showed a significant positive change in self-image, while no substantial change was found in the other subjects. This improvement in self-perception indicated decreased levels of perceived stress. In a more recent study by Birkel (2000) it was observed that the repeated practice of hatha yoga improved the breathing (vital) capacity, considered to be a significant factor for health. Further empirical study of yoga in all its forms can only help to contribute to our understanding of the various paths of the mind-body connection.

Steps to Initiate Hatha Yoga

Chances are, you have already done some of the yoga positions before, perhaps without even knowing they were yoga postures. If you are at all familiar with hatha yoga, this will be a brief review. If you are new to these exercises, the selection of yoga *asanas* below will introduce you to the concepts and applications of hatha yoga as a relaxation technique. In the original *Yoga Sutras* text, *asanas* are described as "comfortable and steady." They are to be done slowly, and gracefully. They are designed to awaken your sense of body awareness.

There are three stages of each *asana:* (1) moving into the pose, (2) maintaining the pose, and (3) coming out of the pose. Always remember to come out of a pose as slowly as you enter it. At first, perhaps all you will be aware of is the physical experience of each *asana.* With time, though, you may begin to notice an internal (mental) calmness to equal the physical tranquility (muscular relaxation). As in any new learning experience, there are a couple of things to remember.

First, pain and yoga *asanas* are incompatible. You should *not* push yourself to the point of pain. Some postures may seem quite easy, while others seem impossible. Move to the limit of your own physical ability. With practice, the more difficult *asanas* will become easier. Second, there are three concepts to remember when practicing yoga: breathing, conscious stretching, and counterpositions or balance.

The Art of Breathing

In the practice of hatha yoga, breathing plays a crucial role in the attempt to unite mind, body, and spirit. Breathing, or *pranayama*, influenced by the diaphragm, is the current that draws the flow of universal energy throughout the body. The word *prana* means "breath," and the word *yama* means "pause." As discussed in Chapter 17, diaphragmatic breathing is the most natu-

ral style of breathing. It differs from thoracic breathing in the expansion of the stomach area as air enters the lungs (Fig. 19.1). The emphasis of breathing from the abdomen allows for increased relaxation throughout the body. Unlike thoracic breathing, the *pranayama* invites conscious effort of the entire pulmonary system, including the nose, throat, lungs, intercostal muscles, and diaphragm.

With each yoga posture is a contraction phase and a release phase; muscles are slowly stretched and relaxed. Pranayama is integrated into each posture. Breaths are comfortably slow and deep, and correspond with the contraction and relaxation phases of each movement. As muscles are stretched, air is drawn into the lungs by the diaphragm. Then when the muscles relax, air is exhaled. Inhalations are usually taken when the head is lifted up and the body is going into a position or expanding. Air is exhaled when the head is down and the body is coming out of a position. Usually a breath is held for approximately ten seconds. When first learning these positions, you may find breathing sequences difficult to coordinate with movements. Over time, coordination will become easier.

The Art of Conscious Stretching

Have you ever noticed a cat or dog stretch after taking a nap? Animals do this to prepare the body for motion. Stretching is a natural reflex. In a sleeping or fetal position, the body coils up, and several muscles, specifically those on the back of the body, contract and shorten. To move efficiently upon awakening, these muscles must be stretched and elongated (Fig. 19.2). But the fetal position is not the only posture that allows muscles to constrict in this manner. Desk work, computer work, prolonged driving, even walking in high-heeled shoes cause muscles, tendons, and ligaments to shorten. Eventually, the body adapts to these positions and muscles remain contracted. The result is a significant loss in flexibility and restricted movements of certain joints. With time, loss of flexibility may result in muscular stiffness and joint pain as body alignment is slightly distorted.

Exercise physiologists have long known that chronically tight muscles are less capable of a full range of motion. Decreases in flexibility are also related to decreases in strength. Extremely tight muscles during a resting state may actually clamp off or occlude the blood supply at the microcapillary level,

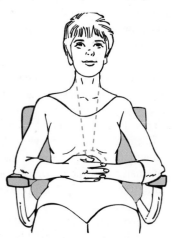

Figure 19.1 The art of breathing means becoming conscious of your breathing and allowing your abdominal area to expand as you inhale.

Figure 19.2 The art of conscious stretching means becoming aware of the flexibility of your muscles as you move a specific joint through a range of motion.

producing a vicious cycle of tension. Furthermore, as we mature physically (particularly after the age of thirty), the body gradually loses its ability to produce elastin, a protein that gives muscle fibers stretching capabilities. Thus, the need to maintain flexibility becomes more important throughout the aging process. For these—and perhaps some cultural—reasons, the yoga postures may seem difficult at first. However, with continued practice, the body will adapt and they will become easier.

It is important to remember that in all yoga postures, one should not go to the point of pain; this may result in tears to muscle, tendon, and ligament fibers. Body awareness is a kinesthetic skill; being fully conscious of each body movement and what each body part is experiencing; specifically, the contraction and relaxation of each set of muscles. Don't push yourself. Hatha yoga is meant to be enjoyable.

The Art of Balance

The art of balance refers to counterpositions. Yoga philosophy asserts that balance is the key to life. To find harmony in life, there must be balance. Thus, the practice of *asanas* is a reminder to seek balance in all thoughts and actions, and the progression of *asanas* is a subtle lesson in its meaning. As you try the *asanas,* you will soon notice that there is a progressive pattern to the series of positions. For example, a position that stretches the lower back muscles should be followed by a posture that relaxes muscles in that same area (Fig. 19.3). When the body can maintain a balanced position, as well as balance the tension and relaxation of muscles through a series of postures, then greater unity will be experienced between body, mind, and soul. Regardless of the philosophical underpinnings involved, the concept of balance demonstrated in the *asanas* will provide a better range of motion and potentially reduce the risk of injury with advanced postures.

The following is a series of simple yoga *asanas*. As you try these, slowly integrate the concepts of breathing, body awareness, and balance.

Salute to the Sun (Surya Namaskar)

The Salute to the Sun is a very symbolic series of *asanas*. It is traditionally performed at the beginning and end of each yoga session. *Surya Namaskar* began

The art of balance means following the natural laws of balance as the body moves into each position. Once one muscle group has been stretched, the body is balanced by performing the same posture on the opposite side.

Figure 19.3

as a form of meditation worship wherein one would start the day by facing east and performing the series of movements in order to maintain harmony throughout the day. Today it is recognized as an excellent exercise to stretch and limber muscles throughout the entire body, but particularly the spine and legs. Runners and joggers may recognize a few of these stretches, as they are excellent flexibility exercises for hamstrings and calf muscles. The Salute to the Sun should be performed slowly, and every effort should be made to maintain balance through each posture. Once the movements become more natural, the exercise can be done more rapidly. Each posture is counterbalanced in the next *asana*. A complete Salute to the Sun consists of two sequences. In the first cycle, lead with the right foot in positions 4 and 9, and in the second, lead with the left. It makes no difference what direction you face when doing this exercise; however, facing east marks symbolic awareness of the beginning of the life of each new day.

Pre-Position: Stand with your feet shoulder-width apart, spine completely aligned, and weight evenly distributed on both feet. Hold hands straight above head, palms facing out, with arms fully extended.

Position 1 (Figs. 19.4 and 19.5): Raise your arms in a wide circular motion over the head and then slowly

Figure 19.5

Figure 19.4

Figure 19.6

Figure 19.7

Figure 19.8

down in front of the face to the midpoint of the chest. Hold palms together and exhale.

Position 2 (Fig. 19.6): Raise your arms directly over your head, pushing from the waist, keeping legs straight and back slightly arched. As you do this, slowly inhale and look up to the sky.

Position 3 (Fig. 19.7): Leading with your hands, reach to your toes, exhaling as you lower your head to your knees. Keep your back comfortably straight and knees slightly bent. (Tight hamstrings will decrease the length of your reach. Reach only as far as is comfortably possible.)

Position 4 (Fig. 19.8): Place your palms on the floor, then bring your right foot between your hands. Extend the left leg behind you, and lower your knee

to the floor. Inhale as you extend the leg, arch your back, and look up to the sky.

Position 5 (Fig. 19.9): Bring the right foot back to meet the left, and exhale. Raise your hips and buttocks high, keeping your head down and eyes directed toward your feet. Arms should be fully extended.

Position 6 (Fig. 19.10): Lower your knees to the floor, followed by your chest and then your forehead. Hips should be slightly bent and raised off the floor. Breath is slowly exhaled throughout.

Position 7 (Fig. 19.11): Bring your hips to the floor, fully extending your legs behind you. Then inhale while placing your hands directly beneath your shoulders and raising your chest. Look up to the sky, and arch the head and back slightly.

Position 8 (Fig. 19.12): Raise hips and buttocks high off the floor, keeping your palms and feet flat on the floor. As you do so, exhale. Keep your head down, eyes directed toward your feet, and your arms fully extended.

Position 9 (Fig. 19.13): Place your left foot between your hands, extend your right leg back, and place the

Figure 19.9

Figure 19.10

Figure 19.11

Figure 19.12

Figure 19.13

Figure 19.14

Figure 19.15

Figure 19.16

knee on the floor as you inhale. Arch your back and head slightly, looking up to the sky.

Position 10 (Fig. 19.14): Bring your feet together, shoulder-width apart, with arms extended and hands reaching toward feet. Keep your back straight, and knees slightly bent. As you bring your head to your knees, exhale.

Position 11 (Fig. 19.15): Reach with your hands overhead, and slowly inhale. Extend your head back to look up to the sky, arching the back slightly.

Position 12 (Fig. 19.16): Lower your arms to midchest height, palms facing together, and exhale.

Now repeat the entire exercise, this time leading with the right foot in positions 5 and 10. Upon completion, turn your attention inward to observe physical sensations.

Hatha Yoga Asanas

The following asanas are arranged in order from standing, to sitting, to lying down. It is important to remember, however, that every posture should be counterbalanced with one that works the opposite muscle groups. Positions should be done slowly and held for about ten seconds. These thirteen *asanas* are but a few (the simplest) of the many hatha yoga postures. Even in hatha yoga, nuances in each position vary from instructor to instructor, so you may notice slight differences between these *asanas* and previous or future experiences. A sample workout of exercises is listed after the descriptions of the *asanas*. Remember that your yoga workout should end with the Corpse Position for a few minutes of quiet time. This time period can also include body awareness, with specific attention to relaxing all body parts (and self-reflection).

1. *Mountain Pose (Tadasana)* (Fig. 19.17): Stand with your feet about shoulder-width apart, spine completely straight, and eyes straight ahead. Raise your arms completely over your head, palms facing inward, and inhale. Hold comfortably for ten seconds, and exhale as you return your arms slowly to your sides.

2. *Head of Cow (Gomukhasana)* (Fig. 19.18): Stand with feet shoulder-width apart and spine straight. Reach under and behind your back with your left arm as if to scratch between the shoulder blades. Reach over and behind with your right arm. Try to touch hands behind your shoulders, and hold for ten seconds. (If hands cannot touch, you may use a handkerchief.) Relax. Then reverse arm positions and try to touch hands; hold for ten seconds. Breathe normally throughout this exercise.

3. *Fist over Head (Araha Chakrasana)* (Fig. 19.19): Begin with the Mountain Pose. Place arms behind the waist, grasping hands (fist) together. Lean forward while slowly raising hands over head. Hold for ten seconds, then slowly release hands, letting hang toward floor. Slowly straighten spine to fully erect position. Exhale as you raise fist over head, and inhale as you release and return to the Mountain Pose.

4. *Human Triangle (Trikonasana)* (Fig. 19.20): Beginning in the Mountain Pose, slowly move

Figure 19.18

Figure 19.19

Figure 19.20

Figure 19.17

legs to three feet apart. Raise right arm and hand straight above head. Rotate head to look at right hand. Bend slightly at the waist and extend left arm and hand down to left ankle, palm open and facing in. As you reach down, rotate left foot out to protect knee joint. Hold for ten seconds. Inhale as your right hand reaches up, then exhale. Inhale as you return to the Mountain Pose. Exhale upon completion.

5. *Thigh Stretch (Bandha Konasana)* (Fig. 19.21): Sit in a comfortable position with knees bent and soles of the feet facing each other. Gently press knees toward the floor until tension is felt, for ten seconds. Allow thighs to relax, and repeat. Breathe normally throughout.

6. *One Knee to Chest (Pawan Muktasana)* (Fig. 19.22): Lying on your back and keeping the back flat, bring the right knee to the chest by holding the back of the right leg at the knee

joint. Hold for ten seconds. Relax by extending the right leg back onto the floor. Then bring the left leg to the chest and hold for ten seconds. Exhale as each leg is brought to the chest; inhale as the leg is returned to full extension.

7. *Two Knees to Chest (Apanasama)* (Fig. 19.23): Lying on your back and keeping the back flat, bring both legs to the chest by holding the legs with your hands behind the knees. Hug the knees to the chest for ten seconds. Breathe normally throughout.

8. *Cobra (Bhujanghasana)* (Fig. 19.24): Lie on your stomach with legs fully extended and feet curled. Placing your hands directly under your shoulders, slowly raise your chest and head off the floor by contracting the lower back muscles. Try not to push with your hands. Hold for ten seconds, then slowly return chest to the floor. Inhale as the chest rises off the

Figure 19.21

Figure 19.22

Figure 19.23

Figure 19.24

Figure 19.25

Figure 19.26

floor, and exhale as you return to starting position.

9. *Sit and Reach (Paschimottasana)* (Fig. 19.25): In a sitting position, extend legs straight in front of the hips, keeping spine straight. Lean chest comfortably toward the knees, ankles, or feet, reaching forward also with the hands. Keep back straight; hold for ten seconds. Then relax by slightly bending the knees and sitting upright. Exhale as you lean toward the feet, and inhale as you relax. Repeat three more times. If having both legs extended is uncomfortable, try one leg at a time.

10. *Spinal Twist (Ardha Matsyendrasana)* (Fig. 19.26): In a sitting position, with spine erect, place left leg over right knee and position the foot flat on the floor. Extend right arm and place hand on left ankle. Extend left arm behind waist and place the palm on floor for balance. Turn head and trunk to the left side, keeping the chin up. Hold for ten seconds. Breathe normally throughout.

11. *The Fish (Matsyasana)* (Fig. 19.27): Lying on your back with legs fully extended, place hands palm down beneath lower back. Raise

chest by arching lower back and neck. Hold for ten seconds. Relax and then repeat three times. Breathe normally throughout.

12. *Back Arch (Dhanurasana)* (Fig. 19.28): Lying on stomach, grab either left or right foot with the opposite hand. Slowly arch back by pulling feet over buttocks. Hold for ten seconds. Relax with hands on floor by shoulders and legs fully extended. Repeat with each leg three times. Inhale as back is arched; exhale as body comes to full extension. (**Note:** This exercise should be avoided if you have lower-back problems.)

13. *Corpse Pose (Shavasana)* (Fig. 19.29): Lie on your back, shifting your legs back and forth to find a comfortable position. Rotate your arms from the shoulders and rest comfortably, palms facing up. Next, rotate your spine, turning your head side to side. Then return spine to resting alignment. Breathe from the diaphragm.

If you wish, you can start your workout with the corpse pose and return to this position intermittently or after each *asana*. A yoga session should always conclude with this position.

Figure 19.27

Figure 19.28

Figure 19.29

Sample Workout

1. Salute to the Sun
2. Mountain Pose
3. Head of Cow
4. Fist over Head
5. Human Triangle
6. Cobra
7. Two Knees to Chest
8. Mountain Pose
9. Salute to the Sun
10. Corpse (relaxation) Position

Additional Thoughts on Hatha Yoga

The following guidelines may add to the enjoyment of yoga:

1. It is best not to perform *asanas* on a full stomach. Allow one to two hours between eating and yoga practice.

2. Wear loose-fitting clothing and avoid heavy jewelry. Bare feet are recommended to make better floor contact.

3. Find a quiet place to practice; a well-lit and well-ventilated room is ideal. A thin rug is also suggested to perform the positions in greater comfort.

4. Early morning is the preferred practice time for conscious awareness. But evening is the time when the body is more limber, and yoga postures tend to have a greater relaxation effect after a busy day. Find a time that is best suited to your own schedule.

5. Concentrate on the postures, sensing each move and your body's response to it.

6. There are no nutritional guidelines accompanying this relaxation technique, but if you pursue yoga further, you will find that a healthy, well-balanced diet is considered an important part of the art-of-balance concept. (See Chapter 27.)

Stress With a Human Face

TO LOOK AT SUZIE YOU WOULD THINK THAT she is ten to fifteen years younger than the age stated on her birth certificate. But a few years ago, stress began to pile on Suzie when her marriage showed signs of coming apart at the seams. It wasn't long before the fairy tale cracked. A former high-school physical education teacher, Suzie tried many things to cope with the changes she was facing—exercise, transcendental meditation, and a host of other strategies. But what really changed her life was a yoga course she enrolled in. What started as a venture out of curiosity resulted in a whole new way of life. In fact, she was so affected by her experience that she became certified as a yoga instructor through the Kripalu Center in Lenox, Massachusetts, and now makes her living as a practitioner of yoga and yoga therapy. "I have to tell you, my life was a mess and I tried everything. Everyone has to find what works for them; for me it was yoga. Oh, I still exercise and meditate," she adds, "but

yoga is what really grounds me." In 1993 Suzie opened her own yoga center in Washington, D.C.

7. The ultimate goal of all aspects of yoga is to lower the walls of the conscious mind—the ego. If you approach it with a competitive attitude, there is no chance for the union of mind, body, and spirit to occur. Beginning yoga students often push themselves to match the postures of the instructor or fellow classmates. This can result in physical pain as well as a deeper abyss to enlightenment. In the words of yogi master Swami Rama, "This is absolutely not the way to practice yoga."

8. Meditation is not a requirement of hatha yoga, but it is a nice complement to it. After you finish your selection of *asanas* ending with the Corpse Pose (*shavasana*) is the perfect time to collect your thoughts and perhaps do some internal awareness or soul searching.

Because hatha yoga has become increasingly popular in the United States since the mid 1970s, finding quality yoga instructors is quite easy. It would be a good idea to sit in on a class to observe the instructor and see if his or her teaching style and health philosophy are compatible with your own. Most instructors will agree to an introductory class where you can either participate or observe. Classes are often offered at community recreation centers and YMCAs and YWCAs, as well as through private instruction. Check your Yellow Pages directory. One book on yoga stands far above the rest in its detailed explanations and wonderful photographs: *The Sivananda Companion to Yoga,* by Lidell et al. I recommend it for further reading on this special relaxation technique.

Best Application of Hatha Yoga

As previously mentioned, hatha yoga can be practiced at the start of each day or at the conclusion of each day. As a relaxation technique, it is best employed to unleash the stress and frustration that for whatever reason has to be postponed. The use of individual *asanas* to stretch various muscle groups during waking hours might be the best course of action when you feel muscles begin to tense. Although research has not investigated whether hatha yoga better addresses anger or fear, it is quite possible that it is equally effective for both emotional states. Those who teach hatha yoga recognize that the union of mind, body, and spirit is solidified by self-acceptance, self-love, and the absence of anger and fear in one's life. The inner peace derived from practicing yoga is credited with keeping people emotionally well balanced during unexpected encounters of the stressful kind.

Summary

+ *Yoga* is a Sanskrit word meaning "union," which is accomplished through meditation. More specifically, it refers to the union of mind, body, and spirit. Hatha yoga is one of five types of meditation and it emphasizes physical balance. *Hatha* actually translates to (a balance of) the sun (*ha*) and moon (*tha*). Hatha yoga is the most commonly practiced form of yoga meditation in the United States.

+ Hatha yoga is built on the premise of three concepts: the art of breathing, the art of conscious stretching, and the art of balance.

+ In most cases, a hatha yoga session will begin with the *namaskar* (Salute to the Sun), which is a series of movements or postures initiating integration of the mind, body, and spirit. It also serves as a warm-up for the other postures, or *asanas*.

+ There are literally hundreds of *asanas*. This chapter highlighted some of the more popular ones that can easily be incorporated into a yoga session.

+ Although not meant solely as a series of flexibility exercises, hatha yoga increases flexibility. It has also been shown to improve muscle tone and create inner calmness, which yoga instructors attribute to improved self-esteem.

Concepts and Terms

Art of balance

Art of breathing

Art of conscious stretching

Back Arch (Dhanurasana)

Bhakti yoga

Cobra (Bhujanghasana)

Corpse Pose (Shavasana)

Fish (Matsyasana)

Fist over Head (Araha Chakrasana)

Hatha yoga

Head of Cow (Gomukhasana)

Human Triangle (Trionasana)

Jnana yoga

Karma yoga

Kundalini yoga

Mountain Pose (Tadasana)

One Knee to Chest (Pawan Muktasana)

Pranayama

Salute to the Sun

Sit and Reach (Paschimottasana)

Spinal Twist (Ardha Matsyendrasana)

Thigh Stretch (Bhadrasana)

Two Knees to Chest (Apanasana)

Yoga

Yoga sutras

References and Resources

Agne, C. and Paolucci, K. A Holistic Approach to an Alcoholic Treatment Program, *Journal of Drug Education* 12(2):137–144, 1982.

Allen, R. J. *Human Stress: Its Nature and Control.* Burgess Press, Minneapolis, MN, 1983.

Austin, T. K. Stress Management, *Journal of Orthomolecular Psychiatry* 11(3):193–197, 1982.

Ballantyne, J. *Sankhya Aphorisms of Kapila.* Chowkhamba Sanskrit Series, Varanasi, India, 1963.

Birkel, D. *Hatha Yoga.* Eddie Bowers, Dubuque, IA, 1991.

Birkel, D. A. and Edgren, L. Hatha Yoga: Improved Vital Capacity of College Students, *Alternative Therapies* 6(6) 55–63, 2000.

Chaudhuri, H. Yoga Psychology. In *Transpersonal Psychologies,* C. T. Tart, ed. Harper & Row, New York, 1975.

Desai, Yogi Amrit. *Kripalu Yoga: Meditation in Motion.* Kripalu Publications, Lenox, MA, 1985.

Folan, L. *Lilias, Yoga, & Your Life.* Macmillan, New York, 1981.

Haich, E. and Yesudian, S. *Self-Healing, Yoga, and Destiny.* Aurora Press, New York, 1966.

Krishna, G. *The Kundalini: The Evolutionary in Man.* Shambhala, Berkeley, CA, 1971.

Lasater, J. Down in the Back: Poses for Lower Back Pain, *Alternative Therapies for Health and Medicine* 1(5):72–82, 1995

Lidell, L. with Rabinovitch, N. and Rabinovitch, G. *The Sivananda Companion to Yoga.* Simon and Schuster, New York, 1983.

Mishra, R. *Fundamentals of Yoga.* Julian Press, New York, 1959.

Ruiz, F. What Science Can Teach Us about Flexibility, *Yoga Journal,* March/April:92–101, 2000.

Sivananda, S. *Raja Yoga.* Yoga Vendanta Forest University, Rishikesh, India, 1950.

Smith, B. *Yoga for a New Age: A Modern Approach to Hatha Yoga.* Prentice-Hall, Englewood Cliffs, NJ, 1982.

Stern, R. M. and Anschel, C. Deep Inspirations as Stimuli for Responses of the Autonomic Nervous System, *Psychophysiology* 5:132–141, 1968.

Swami Karmananda. Relaxation through Yoga. In J. White and J. Fadiman, *Relax.* Dell, New York, 1976.

Swami Rama. *Lectures on Yoga.* Himalayan International Institute of Yoga Science and Philosophy, Honesdale, PA, 1979.

Swami Satyananda Saraswati. *Asana, Pranayama, Mudra, Bandha.* Bihar School of Yoga, Monghyr, Bihar, India, 1973.

Chapter 20 Mental Imagery and Visualization

Imagination is more

powerful than knowledge.

—Albert Einstein

Close your eyes for a moment and listen to the gentle, rolling waves of the ocean. See the clear, aqua-blue water break as it approaches the shore. Feel the white sand between your toes, the warm sun on your hair, and the soft wind as it caresses your face and continues on to sway the branches of a Royal palm tree behind you. The salt air fills your senses, and as you exhale, you feel completely relaxed.

Imagination is a powerful gift. It is one of the characteristics that makes humans unique creatures on Earth. As a cognitive skill, imagination is the first step of the creative process. Yet imagination is a skill we do not use to our full advantage or potential. When Einstein said that imagination was more powerful than knowledge, he meant that our wealth of knowledge is based on the framework of the depths of human imagination. Knowledge without imagination is like a car without fuel: It is not functional; it won't go anywhere. Now, it would be inaccurate to say that imagination isn't used in times of stress. It is. More often than not, though, it is used in the wrong way. Our imagination creates worst-case scenarios from our frustrations and fears. We imagine the most drastic consequences of stressful situations by making mountains out of molehills. Why do we do this? Have we been socialized to think this way? Is it a defense mechanism? One can only guess the real reason. It is fair to say, however, that when imagination is used in this negative way, it feeds behaviors that somehow reward the ego, or humanity would have discontinued this mode of thinking generations ago. Stress-management therapists have concluded that in the face of stress, imagination can be an asset as well as a liability. And as the saying goes, "If it was your mind that got you into this mess, then use your mind to get you out of it." Employed in a positive way, imagination can be a very valuable asset as a tool to conquer stress. The rewards produced through positive imagery range from slain metaphorical dragons, to attained goals and answered dreams, to an improved overall state of health.

The technique of **mental imagery** goes by several names, sometimes signifying variations in the purpose and use of this technique. The word **visualization** is often used synonymously with mental imagery, but it can also mean additional aspects of mental imagery not directly related to the relaxation effect. Psychophysiologist and biofeedback specialist Patricia Norris describes visualization as "a conscious choice with intentional instructions," whereas, "imagery is a spontaneous flow of thoughts originating from the unconscious mind." Mental training and mental rehearsal are also part of the mental imagery process. These terms are used primarily in sports psychology and behavioral medicine to express a more elaborate type of imagery for behavioral change. The purpose in these two disciplines is to promote positive behavioral changes as, for example, the refinement of motor skills for improved athletic performance, or positive changes in health behaviors such as smoking cessation. In cases where suggestions are given by an instructor, therapist, or counselor to enhance imagination, this technique is referred to as guided mental imagery. In his book *Visualization for Change,* Patrick Fanning defined visualization as, "the conscious, volitional creation of mental sense impressions for the purpose of changing yourself." The skill of visualization involves the creation of images, scenes, or impressions by engaging one's imagination of the body's physical senses of sight, sound, feel, smell, and even taste, for an overall pleasurable desired effect.

Mental imagery and visualization, when used to promote physical calmness, involve several components of meditation; specifically, increased concentration and expanded awareness of consciousness of the scene created in the mind's eye. Perhaps the greatest strength lies in the ability to turn down the volume and intensity of information received by the five senses, and in many cases to replace threatening stimuli with pleasurable ones from the depths of the imagination. The net result is an overall calming effect and, in some cases, even a healing effect.

Historical Perspective

The use of mental imagery as a healing technique can be traced back to the origins of virtually every culture on nearly every continent. In one form or another, mental imagery and visualization have been used by Australian aborigines, American Indian shamans, Hindu yogis, and the ancient Greeks as a supplemental tool to fight disease and promote health. For example, in the book *Black Elk Speaks,* a semi-autobiographical account of a Sioux medicine man, Black Elk describes the use of "visions" in his treatment of several sick people. Other cultures have their stories as well. Too sophisticated for cures of the mystical type, Western culture abandoned such practices centuries ago. During the European Renaissance, the Cartesian principle separated the study of the mind (philosophy) and body (medicine), and weakened the authority of mental imagery as a healing practice. Although visualization in its many forms was still practiced by various cultures throughout the world, it failed to gain approval of the influential medical community in the West until the turn of the twentieth century. As the field of modern psychology began to unfold, however, the concepts of mental imagery and visualization reemerged as viable means to connect mental and physical aspects of well-being.

In the early works of Joseph Breuer, Sigmund Freud, and Carl Jung, the elements of imagination were introduced into psychoanalysis. Each therapist documented cases in which patients' ability to tap into their imagination helped cure them of specific ailments. Whereas Freud theorized that imagination was insight into basic human drives, Jung believed that it was the wealth of knowledge in the unconscious mind surfacing as images to consciousness. Jung formulated a hypothesis that many images have an "archetypal nature," a term he used to describe symbols common to all people of all races. These include trees, circular objects (*mandalas*), and winged creatures. As early as 1940, Jung encouraged his patients to use **active imagination,** a creative exercise to complete the final scenes of recurring dreams, in an effort to find a peaceful resolution. In many cases, it helped to cure them of their physical ailments.

From Jung's lead, several other psychologists, including Robert Assaglioli, Erik Peper, and Paul Eckman, demonstrated the power of imagination to influence cognitive processing as well as physiological changes produced by creative thoughts. With time, mental imagery became well accepted in the practice of clinical psychology, with the Rorschach ink-blot test becoming one of the most renowned applications of this technique. Joseph Wolpe suggested the use of imagination when he advised that systematic desensitization be employed as a coping technique when known stressors will be encountered. Systematic desensitization is a process of progressive tolerance to stress through the replacement of stressful stimuli with more comfortable images created in the mind. (This will be described later in more detail.) In the 1970s, O. Carl Simonton and his wife, Stephanie, resurrected the use of active imagination, applying this technique to help fight cancer in patients who were terminally ill. It is largely their inspiring work that has prompted much research on the use of mental imagery in clinical settings.

Neurophysiologists now understand that of the hundreds of billions of cells in the human brain, only a fraction (approximately 2 billion or 10 percent) are used for conscious thought. The remaining cells may actually constitute the tangible network associated with unconscious mind. Work inspired by Sperry to gain a greater understanding of the cognitive functions of the right and left hemispheres of the brain has deduced that imagination, like intuition, music appreciation, and spatial awareness, is a right-brain function. And the ability to access and employ right-brain functions is considered an asset in dealing with perceived stress.

Mental Imagery Research

The practices of mental imagery and visualization as healing modalities are relatively new to Western medicine, and to this day, they are not universally accepted among health care professionals. Be that as it may, there are two scientific journals devoted to research in this topic: *The Journal of Mental Imagery* (Marquette University) and *Imagination, Cognition, and Personality* (Yale University). Studies can be found in several other journals (in sports psychology and behavioral medicine) as well. One focus of these journal articles involves the use of visualization as a complementary tool for improved health status in the treatment of cancer, elevated blood pressure, chronic pain, asthma, obesity, bone fractures and headaches, to name just a few. The promising results of these studies has given added sustenance to the emerging field of psychoneuroimmunology. Other studies involve positive changes in various behaviors through the use of mental imagery, including sports performance and recovery from chemical dependencies. The following are a sample of the type of research that has been conducted in this field.

To examine the effects of mental imagery as a relaxation technique on various biochemical reactions, Jasnoski and Kugler (1987) measured the response of salivary immunoglobin A (SIgA), cortisol, and mood states when under the influence of mental images specific to enhancement of the immune system. Results supported the hypothesis that when cognition is directed toward these biochemical factors, there is a subsequent change in neuroimmunomodulation. Ievleva and Orlick (1991), at Florida State University, studied the effects of mental imagery, positive self-talk, and goal setting on subjects diagnosed with knee and ankle injuries, compared to subjects with the same types of injuries who had no such treatment. Those subjects who practiced these relaxation techniques demonstrated more rapid healing of their injuries than the control subjects. Sokel et al. (1991) found that when children incapacitated by severe abdominal pain of unknown origin employed the skills of guided mental imagery, they were able to resume normal activities within three weeks, shorter period than that experienced by control subjects.

The stories emerging regarding the use of mental imagery for cancer are mostly anecdotal, but Epstein (1989) believes they must be regarded with as much validity as controlled studies. Jeanne Achterberg (1978, 1984, and 1985), renowned for her use of mental imagery in the treatment of cancer, is also of the opinion that this type of treatment is as essential as radiation and chemotherapy and must not be thought of as "a last alternative." She believes that mental imagery plays both a reactive and causative role in the biochemical healing process. Currently, researchers are combining mental imagery with hypnosis to deal with cancer and other terminal illnesses (Araoz, 1983; Wilkinson, 1990). Of course, physicians do not have definitive proof that mental imagery is a direct cause of healing when it occurs, the reason being that mental imagery is never the sole treatment used. In the prestigious *Saybrook Review,* Stanley Krippner, who pulled together a sizable number of research articles regarding the role of imagery in the healing process, writes that future research must somehow untangle this mystery.

Despite claims of remission of cancerous tumors, it should be noted that mental imagery has never been touted as a panacea for all ailments and diseases. Furthermore, not all studies of mental imagery show promising results. Barrie Cassileth (1990) at the University of Pennsylvania School of Medicine, for example, found no relationship between psychosocial factors (mental imagery and sheer will) and physiological effects in 359 cancer patients. These results confirmed

her hypothesis that mental imagery falls in the realm of "fraudulent quackery." A caveat to findings such as these is explained by health psychologist Shelly Taylor (1990) who, in an attempt to explain the placebo effect, indicates that the *attitude* of the physician is sometimes more important than the medicine he or she administers. Citing several clinical studies, Taylor notes that health care practitioners who show confidence in the treatment they administer, as well as professional bonding with the patient, always observe a stronger effect than those who are skeptical of the treatment. This occurs whether the medication is "real" (Feldman, 1956) or a placebo (Miller, 1989). Thus, Taylor considers the placebo effect neither a "medical trick" nor a purely psychological side effect, but a very real aspect of the healing process.

As director of biofeedback research at the Menninger Clinic in Topeka, Kansas, Dr. Patricia Norris documented several case studies in which mental imagery and visualization where used successfully to complement traditional medical treatment. She lists eight characteristics that help to make mental imagery effective as a healing tool, especially with regard to cancer. They are the following:

1. *Visualization needs to be idiosyncratic,* that is, it must be self-generated. Images that are created by the practitioner and not the patient appear to be ineffective in the healing process.

2. *Imagery must be egosyntonic.* This means that it must fit with the values and ideals of the person. If, for example, the individual has a pacifistic nature, then combative or warlike imagery will undermine the effectiveness of this type of treatment. Norris notes that typically there is emotional involvement with the imagery. Many patients actually protected their cancer in their imagery, even during disposal (e.g., in packing it out in garbage bags, or viewing cancer cells longing to be released, "they suck up the chemotherapy, they turn toward the light").

3. *There must be a positive connotation to the imagery.* Imagery that is negative reinforces negative thoughts, which are not conducive to healing. As an example, Norris notes that sharks, as a healing image, are not a good idea. Imagery must be what she calls "restorative and preparative."

4. *Imagery must be kinesthetic and somatic.* Rather than watch the imagery on a movie screen, you must feel the sensations of your images "in the first person." You must have a sense that what you are seeing is happening inside your body, not "out there somewhere."

5. *Imagery must be anatomically correct and accurate.* Knowing exactly what body region and physiological system is diseased and what the nature of the disease truly is should dictate the type of imagery used. In other words, you need to know whether to access the central nervous system or the immune system. As discussed in Chapter 3, certain diseases and illnesses fall under specific categories. Norris suggests accessing your body wisdom as well as clinical data and test results. She also states that more than one image can be used in the healing process. In her work with children, she noted that kids used both a symbolic (figurative) image as well as a literal (representational) one.

6. *Constancy and dialogue.* Constancy means regularity in your imagery. Norris suggests three fifteen-minute sessions per day, with brief intermittent thought messages at other times. When you feel pain in your body, your body is communicating to you. In fact, she refers to pain as a metaphorical friend. Through a dialogue of self-talk, she suggests thanking the pain for making you aware of a problem so that you may be able to fix it. Finally, she suggests destroying a tumor with its permission. Respond with love. Think of your afflicted part as a child you want to protect and nurture. Make peace with your body.

7. *Blueprint aspect.* A blueprint is a strategy. Norris suggests that you always see your imagery as a mission accomplished. A blueprint visualization is like a time-lapse photograph where a flower (symbolizing a tumor) is shown to bloom within seconds and then close back up and fade away. Visualize a formula and see it through to completion. An example would be to see the construction of a building, from the hole in the ground to opening day when you are cutting the ribbon at the entrance.

8. *You must include the treatment in the imagery.* Norris has found that patients who use mental imagery incorporating chemotherapy treatment and radiation do better than those who "fight" these medical procedures. She notes that it helps to have benevolent feelings (versus ambivalent feelings) toward the treatment. She suggests to mentally "welcome the treatment into the body." Consider the treatment a guest in your house. From her patients, she offers these examples:

   a. *Chemotherapy*—a gold-colored fluid that healthy cells, acting as a bucket brigade, pass along to cancer cells, who drink it up.

   b. *Radiation treatment*—a stream of silver energy aimed at the cancerous tumor(s). Ask the white blood cells to move out of the way—or shield themselves—and act like mirrors to reflect the radiation toward the cancer cells; then watch the cancer cells go belly-up.

Norris, like other researchers, admits that just how visualization promotes healing is still a mystery and that the answers to this mystery can be learned as we further explore human consciousness and the human energy field. Similar to the theory described by Pert in Chapter 3, Achterberg (1984) hypothesizes that the function of imagination, housed in the right brain, converts thoughts to biochemical messages and intentionally directs them toward target body regions. Although mental imagery and visualization have been hailed as wonderful adjuncts to clinical medicine, their benefits can be obtained by anyone in any state of health, especially to promote and enjoy a deep sense of relaxation.

Mental Imagery as a Relaxation Technique

Daydreaming may be the most common type of mental imagery used to relax. Researchers have come to understand that the conscious mind needs to break away periodically and "download" sensory information for "reprocessing." (Computer software screensavers are loosely based on this concept.) Many people are aware that they daydream, yet when asked to recall the images they are hard-pressed to give an answer. Mental imagery as a form of relaxation has taken the concept of daydreaming and organized it to give it a sense of legitimacy. People rarely daydream spontaneously during a bout of stress. Instead, as mentioned previously, the mind conjures up worst-case scenarios that seem more real than the actual event. So, to alter this mind frame, the daydreaming concept has been adapted to intercept the stress response and give the body a chance to unwind. It does this by replacing negative thoughts and perceptions with peaceful scenes. Just as real or imaginary thoughts can trigger the stress response, relaxing thoughts can promote the relaxation response. This is the primary goal and purpose of mental imagery. When imagination is used to promote relaxation, the body's five senses are in effect deactivated or desensitized to stressful stimuli. The body is allowed to recharge so that upon return to your physical environment, you can deal with perceptions of stress more effectively.

In many ways, the creation of mental imagery is like making a motion picture in which characters wear a number of hats. In this case, you take on all the roles: producer (selecting the sets and scenery), director (organizing the sensory cues), actor, and audience (experiencing the effects of the production). All the roles are equally significant to making the images as powerful as possible. With practice, the use of this technique will enhance your skills in all these roles and great satisfaction will be derived from participation in your own creation.

Over time, as the concept of mental imagery developed, it was divided into three distinct categories. As more and more people began to share this technique, many variations and combinations of these emerged. It is the original three that are discussed here.

Tranquil Natural Scenes

The use of guided mental imagery, as mentioned previously, gained popularity and clinical approval in the late 1960s and early 1970s when therapists and psychologists began to explore variations on meditative thought. In this type of visualization, patients are instructed to close their eyes and follow a series of suggested scenes during which they access and utilize the cognitive skills of imagination. In essence, through the creative process, individuals mentally place themselves in the peaceful and relaxing scenes. Natural set-

A beach scene such as this, reminiscent of some vacation areas, is often used by people to promote relaxation.

Figure 20.1

tings are selected because they simulate locations where people typically vacation to escape the stress of home or office environments. Images such as a tropical island beach, a mountain vista, or a path through an evergreen forest are often used.

Once introduced to this technique, participants who repeatedly engage in the practice of visualization find that, like actually being at a vacation site, the re-creation of these settings provides an equal if not more profound sense of relaxation. These natural scenes, full of vivid color, fresh air, natural sounds, and other elements of nature allow participants to put their thoughts in perspective. Natural scenes, like the real ones they imitate, have the ability to place perceptions and the people who harbor them in proportion to the rest of the natural world, turning distorted perceptions back into manageable thoughts. Moreover, with repeated practice of visualization, physical changes indicating a return to homeostasis begin to occur. Consequently, to gaze at a wide ocean horizon at sun-

Box 20.1   Peaceful Scenes to Promote Relaxation

As a class assignment, I ask my students to create five mental images that promote a sense of deep relaxation specifically for them. Some are long, some short, but each conveys an image that promotes calmness in the person who created it. I never cease to be amazed at what they come up with. The following is a "best-of" collection of mental imagery scenes as seen through the creative eyes of my students. Close your eyes for a moment after reading each one and decide whether it brings you a sense of tranquility.

1. Stretched between two trees is a hammock, and I am lying in that hammock swinging slowly in the breeze. There are a few trees around, and in front of me is a large meadow. The grass is lush green and spotted with hundreds of multicolored flowers that seem to stretch forever. The sky is blue and clear, with only a few small white clouds moving slowly across the sky. The breeze caresses my face in syncopation with the hammock's motion.

2. I am in the wilderness, staring into a clear, star-filled sky. There is a camp fire nearby, which is slowly losing its zest, but is still throwing off intense amounts of heat. I'm lying on my sleeping bag, my face is looking straight up. The fire occasionally crackles and a spark is seen shooting in the air. As I examine the sky, a shooting star lights up the darkness and throws a brilliant white light for what appears to be miles. My body snuggles into the sleeping bag as I dream of the wish I just made.

3. With my legs I can feel the sides of my horse expand as he breathes. We have stopped in the middle of a clearing. We have been riding through a woods blanketed with snow. The snow is no longer falling, and the air is cool and crisp. The horse's breath can be seen as mist rising from his nose. We remain still for a moment, listening to the sounds of the other animals in the woods. I give my horse a nudge and he responds, moving forward through this winter wonderland.

4. The water is turquoise, even at a depth of 30 feet, with perfect visibility. I am weightless. The rays of the sun pierce through the water, but seem to soften as they reach to touch the sand below. The coral varies in shape and color; I can't begin to describe its beauty. Schools of small fish surround my body and then disappear in the blink of an eye. With each kick, my body is caressed by the warmth of the water; the bubbles tickle as they pass my face headed for the surface.

5. I am soaring through the crisp blue air. I am flying as if I have wings. I do; I am hang gliding. The sky is a deep blue with white puffy clouds. As I float through one, it is silent. I am completely alone. I see Earth below me. It is far away. I feel weightless. I hear the soft hush of the breeze. My hands make waves in the air. I can see the sun. I can almost touch it as I glide effortlessly through the air.

rise or sunset, to stare at a deep blue sky filled with stars close enough to touch, or to reflect before a backdrop of jagged mountain peaks covered with snow tends to momentarily dwarf any problem, no matter how big or stressful. Although the visualization of these scenes will not make personal problems go away, it appears to help shrink them down to tolerable size, which then makes them manageable to deal with and resolve. And the acknowledgment of stressors in the presence of any one of these scenes makes the concern less threatening, if not insignificant altogether.

Of all the natural settings used to promote relaxation, the most common include water, such as ocean beaches, mountain lakes, or waterfalls and streams. It is commonly believed that scenes of water are reminiscent of the earliest sensations experienced in the womb. Any scene perceived to be relaxing, however, can have the same effect. The power of this type of imagery lies in using not just visual imagination sense but other senses as well. Seeing the image, hearing the sounds, smelling the fragrances or freshness of the air, sensing the air temperature, and feeling the wind and the sun on your skin all coalesce into a very powerful scene. By accessing the imagination of these sensations, you go from being a passive observer to an active participant in your own image. Furthermore, by acknowledging all sensations, you experience the calming effects of this technique first hand rather than observing them from a vicarious or "third-person" viewpoint.

There is no dearth of images that can help produce the relaxation response, nor is there one image that will have the same effect on everyone. Perhaps the greatest positive influence on the visualization of natural scenes is the perception that it indeed promotes tranquility. A disturbing association with a natural image may actually promote stress rather than decrease it. For instance, an image of a mountain vista may not be considered relaxing to someone with a fear of heights. When introducing guided mental imagery, a good instructor will suggest that participants take the liberty to augment or change the suggestions, so that the tailored image promotes a personal sense of relaxation. For example, because of my Colorado roots, I often use a mountain lake as a peaceful image when I teach mental imagery (See CD included with this book). But once I had a student who had never experienced a view of a mountain lake. As a former lifeguard, he instead took the concept of a body of water and envisioned looking at reflections from an undisturbed indoor pool. It was a scene he could relate to; it worked for him.

Some guided mental imagery invites individuals to compare the visualized image with their own state of physical relaxation. Such comparison tends to promote a deeper sense of calmness throughout the body. Box 20.2 is an image I created and share with my students and clients when I teach guided mental imagery. It uses the common image of a body of water to instill a sense of deep relaxation. Please feel free to use your own imagination to enhance or change this image to make it relaxing for you.

Behavioral Changes

For years many psychologists have held strongly to the belief that the key to addressing negative health habits is to change behavior. This, more than values and attitudes, is the part of personality that is easiest to change. Ingestive habits such as smoking, drinking, various eating behaviors, and substance addictions are the most common health concerns targeted for behavioral changes. Process-addiction behaviors (workaholism, shopaholism, and the like) fall into this category as well. Mental imagery combined with power of suggestion was taken up as the premise of behavioral medicine to help people change negative health behaviors into positive ones (see Chapter 9). Although

this technique alone will not produce changes, when used in conjunction with other behavior modification tactics and coping strategies, it has proved effective for some people. What mental imagery does is reinforce a new desired behavior. Repeated use of images reinforces the desired behavior more strongly over time.

Mental imagery used to influence behavioral changes is a specific style of cognitive restructuring. As mentioned earlier, in his work to help people overcome their fears, Wolpe created a process of mental imagery called **systematic desensitization.** In this process a person uses his or her imagination to help overcome anxiety related to a specific situation by building up a tolerance to the stressor through progressive exposures to it. The first step is for the subject to create the exposures in his or her own mind while in a relaxed state. For example, let's say that you have a fear of public speaking and you are slated to give a presentation to 300 people next month. In the process of systematic desensitization, you would create a scene in your mind where you are standing at a podium in an empty auditorium giving a flawless speech. Along with this image you might also practice some diaphragmatic breathing and mental imagery of tranquil natural scenes to calm down before you start talking. After repeating this image several times, you then imagine one or two people (very close friends) in the audience who applaud vigorously when you are done. After repeating this image enough to feel comfortable, you then imagine that you give your successful speech to half an audience, followed by the same great speech to a full house, both to thunderous applause. With practice, the strength of this calm image overrides the intensity of the stressor so that your stress response is minimal, if triggered at all. The second phase of systematic desensitization would be to actually rehearse your speech at a podium while recalling the images (either relaxing scenes or your image of success) to help recreate the feeling of calmness you attained earlier. Again the stress response is minimal, and disappears seconds after the speech starts.

Another example of someone who made behavioral changes through mental imagery is Allison, who tried numerous times to quit smoking. She cut down from two packs to six cigarettes per day, but still felt the need to smoke when she was driving to and from work. Attempting to quit smoking altogether, Allison practiced mental imagery wherein she visualized her-

Box 20.2 ## Solitude of a Mountain Lake

Imagine yourself walking alone in the early morning along a path in a primeval forest through a gauntlet of towering pine trees. Each step you take is softly cushioned by a bed of golden-brown needles. Quietness consumes these surroundings and then is broken by the melody of a songbird. As you stroll along at a leisurely pace, you focus on the sweet, clean scent of the evergreens, the coolness of the air, the warmth of the sun as it peeks through the trees, and the gentle breeze as it passes through the boughs of the pines and whispers past your ears.

Off in the distance, you hear the rush of water cascading over weathered rocks, babbling as it moves along. Yards ahead, a chipmunk perches on an old decaying birch stump along the side of the path, frozen momentarily to determine its next direction. Then in the blink of an eye, it disappears under the ground cover, and all is silent again.

As you continue to walk along this path, you see a clearing up ahead, and you notice your pace pick up just a little to see what is there. First boulders appear, then behind them, a deep blue mountain lake emerges from behind the rocks. You climb up on a boulder to secure a better view and find a comfortable spot carved out of the weathered stone to sit and quietly observe all the elements around you.

The shore of the lake is surrounded by a carpet of tall green grass and guarded by a host of trees: spruce, pine, aspen, and birch. On top of one of the spruce trees, an eagle leaves his perch, spreads his wings to catch the remains of a thermal current, and gracefully glides over the lake. On the far side of the lake, off in the distance, dwarfing the tree line, is a rugged stone-faced mountain. The first snows of autumn have dusted the fissures and crevasses, adding contrast to the rock's features. The color of the snow matches the

one or two puffy white clouds and early-morning crescent moon that interrupts an otherwise cloudless day. A slight warm breeze begins to caress your cheeks and the backs of your hands.

The slight breeze sends tiny ripples across the surface of the lake. As you look at the water's surface, you realize that this body of water, this mountain lake, is just like your body, somewhat calm, yet yearning to be completely relaxed, completely calm. Focus your attention on the surface of the water. The ripples you observe represent or symbolize any tensions, frustrations, or wandering thoughts that keep you from being completely relaxed. As you look at the surface of this mountain lake, slowly allow the ripples to dissipate, fade away, disappear. To enhance this process, take a very slow deep breath and feel the relaxation it brings to your body as you exhale. And as you exhale, slowly allow the ripples to fade away, giving way to a calm surface of water. As you continue to focus on this image, you see the surface of the lake becoming more and more calm, in fact very placid, reflecting all that surrounds it. As you focus on this image, realize that this body of water is like your body. Sense how relaxed you feel as you see the surface of the lake remain perfectly still, reflecting all that is around it. The water's surface reflects the images of the green grass, the trees, the mountain face, even the clouds and crescent moon. Your body is as relaxed as this body of water, this mountain lake. Try to lock in this feeling of calmness and etch this feeling on your memory so that you can call it up to your conscious mind when you get stressed or frustrated. Remember this image so that you can recall the serenity you have created to promote a deep sense of relaxation, and feel your body relax just by thinking of the solitude of this mountain lake.

self in her car driving to work. She imagined that she opened the window a little and played soft music on the radio. At traffic lights—a point of frustration and impatience—she looked for birds till the light changed. After having found a parking space, she got out of her car and imagined herself walking into the office without feeling the need for a cigarette. By taking herself through the drive to work in her imagination, Allison was able to envision herself accomplish-

ing the goal she set. The repeated use of her image laid the groundwork—the reinforcement of the desired behavioral change—enabling her to accomplish her task when she encountered the problematic situation directly.

At about the same time that mental imagery and visualization started being used in the clinical setting to promote positive behavioral health changes, the discipline of sports psychology took root and was also introduced into the world of athletics. The sport that first received publicity from the use of mental imagery was tennis. In the book *The Inner Game of Tennis*, Timothy Gallwey described his theory that by rehearsing the game in one's mind, one could improve one's game on the court. Studies employing this technique began to show support for the theory, concluding that when the mind rehearses a motor skill, the neural tract through which impulses are sent from the brain to the muscles is better defined (Harris and Robinson, 1986). An example is imagining practicing the serve into the service box. When repeated over and over again, the result is improved coordination during actual play. Thus, the technique of mental training became very popular in amateur and professional sports when athletes were sidelined with injuries, and it was soon incorporated into rehabilitation programs. In addition, athletes began to use visualization (Fig. 20.2) in their mental training programs to decrease competitive anxiety and to improve motivation and self-esteem through the use of positive affirmations.

Integrated into the technique of mental imagery to influence behavioral change is the use of verbal messages (positive affirmations) to reinforce the strength of the image. Positive affirmations are positive thoughts that the conscious mind sends to itself as well as to the unconscious mind to build confidence, assertiveness, and self-esteem. These positive thoughts, expressed in words, phrases, or sentences, are repeated to yourself through your inner voice while you are in a relaxed state. (Box 20.3 is a passage of guided mental imagery, inspired by the work of Bernie Siegel, that I share in my classes and workshops to enhance self-esteem.) Often they are used in conjunction with diaphragmatic breathing, and are repeated silently during the exhalation phase, when the body is most relaxed. The mind is most receptive to the message it hears in a relaxed state. For example, the famous coffee mug slogan "Damn, I'm Good" is a wonderful positive affirmation that can be combined with an image of personal success to reinforce its message. Members of Alcoholics Anonymous also use a number of these statements as mental reminders or mantras in their recovery program, the most common being "One day at a time."

The rationale behind positive-affirmation statements goes something like this. Either through learned behaviors or an innate characteristic common

Many athletes use mental imagery (mental training) to complement their physical training. To amateur and professional alike, the mental skills of competition are important.

Figure 20.2

to all humans, we tend to feed our minds a preponderance of negative thoughts. The cumulative effect of these thoughts is to erode the foundations of self-esteem. And low self-esteem makes us vulnerable to stress. The advertising industry employs this concept through ads that target our insecurities. They repeatedly suggest that we buy the products to improve our self-image. The underlying message is that we are not good enough unless we do. Research reveals that we are bombarded with an average of 1,500 media messages per day. While not all advertisers exploit our insecurities, so many slant their messages in a negative direction that they reinforce our tendency toward negative self-feedback, making the cycle even harder to break. We become our own worse critic. The voice inside our head, the sentry guard of the ego, constantly tells us that we are doing something wrong or that we fail to meet our own expectations. By contrast, the use of positive affirmations helps to balance the emotional scales, disarm the internal critic, and reinforce the foundations of positive self-esteem. Any positive thought or phrase will do. Take a moment to think of a phrase you can say to yourself to make you feel good inside. Once you have one, repeat it to yourself when you practice your relaxation techniques. When you are feeling low or stressed out, close your eyes for a moment and try to recall the phrase. Repeat it to yourself along with a supporting mental image and feel the strength it gives you. It may take a few tries, but this technique has proved effective for a

The Loving Hug

Imagine that you are walking alone down a long gravel road on an overcast day. As you look ahead, you see a tunnel, an old abandoned train tunnel. It's not a long tunnel; you can see light at the other end. Go ahead and enter the tunnel. As you walk along, you feel a drop in temperature and a cool dampness in the air. You can smell the earth as your feet pass over sand and pebbles. The moisture seems to enhance the smell. You can hear the dripping of water ahead. As you continue to walk, the light at the end of the tunnel grows brighter. Soon you approach the end of the tunnel, and as you proceed outside, sunshine illuminates your face and you see a world full of color: a deep blue sky; lush green grass under your feet; wildflowers of bright reds, pinks, whites, purples, and blues.

As you continue to walk on this path you notice a grove of trees to your left and a small playground to your right. You drift over to the empty playground, walk over to one of the empty swings, and take a seat. It's been a long time since you've been at a playground like this. As you sway back and forth with your feet anchoring you to the ground, you notice a small child playing in the sandbox to your left. The child is three or four years old and seems very content. The child looks up and smiles at you and you smile back and wave. There is something very familiar about the child's face, and suddenly you recognize your own youthful face looking back at you through your eyes. As you

look at this younger version of yourself, the child begins to walk over to you. He or she smiles and stands about two feet from you and says, "Hello." You smile back and invite the child to sit on your lap. Eagerly the child complies.

You hold the child around the waist and look into his or her eyes. You long to embrace this child, and immediately after that thought the child places his or her arms around your neck and holds on tightly. You do the same, feeling the fabric of the clothes, smelling the cleanness of his or her hair, feeling the softness of the skin, and hearing the small, shallow breaths. You take a slow, deep breath to relax. As you hug your younger self, you feel a wonderful positive feeling inside—a feeling of acceptance, love, and happiness. You whisper in an ear, "I love you," and you hear in reply an echo of your very words in the voice of your younger self.

After a long, long moment, the hug begins to loosen and foreheads touch. Then your heads slowly draw apart, your eyes connect, and you look with amazement and smile. Your younger self smiles instantly, giggles, and then, as young children do, climbs down off your lap, says "Bye-bye," and waves as he or she runs back to the sandbox. You close your eyes for a moment, feeling yourself begin to sway back and forth with your feet barely touching the ground, while you recapture the sensations of this loving hug and the wonderful feelings of love and acceptance inside you.

great many athletes in their games—and in the game of life. It can work for you too!

For example, I once worked with an Olympic athlete who years previously had defected from the (then) Soviet Union. Although he enjoyed his newfound freedom, at times he felt that he had lost his "European" competitive edge. He never took hold of the idea of positive affirmations, perhaps because he didn't believe this internal feedback would work. At the 1987 World Championships in Lake Placid, he once again found himself competing face to face against his former Soviet teammates. During the final competition, in a sudden burst of energy, he pulled ahead to win. After his victory, he told me about his new positive-affirmation statement. With an undeniable accent coming through a smile, he said, "I still got the goods."

Remember, not only can positive-affirmation statements combined with mental images augment a message during a relaxed state, but this same technique can be used during stressful encounters such as traffic jams, public speeches, or staff meetings. Many times negative behaviors or stress-prone behaviors are manifestations of low self-esteem, feelings of failure or rejection we place on ourselves. Positive visualization can often be used to boost and maintain high self-esteem.

Internal Body Images

The third type of mental imagery involves direct changes in physiological functions by using imagination to see a particular body region in a healthy state. Signs and symptoms of the stress response manifested throughout the body are by far the greatest concern to people. The major question posed by health practitioners is this: If stress-related thoughts produce physical ailments, can the mind repair the body with healing thoughts? This type of mental imagery was springboarded into the realm of progressive medicine in 1971 when Simonton and Simonton taught a group of cancer patients several relaxation techniques, including the use of mental imagery. Specifically, patients were invited to imagine the white blood cells of their immune systems fighting the cancerous tumor cells. Through employing their sense of imagination and assuming responsibility for their treatment and recovery, many patients saw their tumors go into remission. The Simontons' book *Getting Well Again,* which described the protocol used to develop this landmark program, served as a catalyst for similar programs across the United States.

In the past ten years, there have been many documented cases of people using mental imagery to rejuvenate and restore their bodies to health, from spontaneous remissions of cancerous tumors and dysfunctional organs, to mended bones and connective tissue. These cases have predominantly involved cancer patients, but other illnesses have been targeted as well, including hypertension, migraines, and lower-back pain. As mentioned previously, these cases are anecdotal in nature, in that control subjects were not observed. Moreover, mental imagery was not the sole intervention, but rather one of many therapies used. However, as described in previous chapters, these case studies imply that there is indeed potential benefit when mental imagery and other related therapies are used in conjunction with conventional medicine. The key is that the patient must begin to assume responsibility for his or her own health status.

As mentioned earlier, the healing mechanism of mental imagery is not fully understood scientifically. Achterberg (1984) hypothesized that the images produced in the mind, specifically the right brain, appear to send, or are converted to, biochemical messages, most likely through neuropeptides, and affix themselves to receptor sites on lymphocytes and perhaps other targeted cells to promote the healing process. This process somehow initiates a path of cancer-cell destruction or organ-cell reconstruction. Quite possibly this healing process employs the integration of several body systems, including the inhibition or sup-

pression of the nervous and endocrine systems from secreting stress hormones. Keep in mind that mental imagery is not meant to be a replacement for standard medical practices. But the use of this technique as a complement to medical treatment appears, for some people, to be more effective than pharmacological medicine alone. The stories of those who survive their ordeals with cancer are remarkable testimonials. It would be inaccurate and misleading, however, to imply that every case of mental imagery ended in successful spontaneous remission of cancerous tumors, or healed organic tissue.

Among the group of characteristics that affect the success of mental imagery, several factors seemed crucial to Achterberg, Simonton, Norris, and Siegel. These include willpower, or the desire to take responsibility for health status; and faith, the belief that self-generated thoughts will bear fruit and are not an exercise in futility. In addition, it has been shown that when individuals have a detailed understanding of their body's physiological functions, the nature and location of the disease, and the specific physiological mechanisms involved, suggestive imagery is more effective.

In an autobiographical case study reported in the book *Why Me?* by Garrett Porter and Dr. Patricia Norris, a young boy describes his fatal diagnosis of a malignant inoperable brain tumor and his fight to live. Through the use of mental imagery biofeedback, and art therapy, Garrett was able to "think" or visualize the cancerous tumor away by imagining the tumor being destroyed and eaten away by friendly yet hungry white blood cells (Fig. 20.3). Having an incredible sense of imagination and body awareness, and knowing exactly where the tumor was located, he visualized shrinkage of the tumor successfully. Within several months a CT scan revealed that the cancerous tumor had indeed vanished.

In her book *It's Always Something,* comedienne Gilda Radner also describes her use of mental imagery with her ovarian cancer, which eventually claimed her life. She created the image that her body was like a big, fluffy pink towel. Washing and drying the towel was symbolic of the chemotherapy. In her mind, Gilda saw the cancer cells as pieces of lint on the towel when it was pulled from the dryer. To rid her body of the unwanted cancer cells, she imagined that she would pull the lint off the towel and make it completely clean.

Figure 20.3 A sketch made by Garrett Porter to help him visualize the healing process in his body. The small "Pacman" creatures (white blood cells) are destroying and eating the tumor, which he named "planet meatball." (From Garrett Porter and Patricia Norris, *Why Me?* [Walpole, NH: Stillpoint, 1985]. Reprinted with permission.)

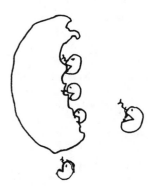

Healing images can be as specific as one ailment or illness (e.g., cancer or thyroid dysfunction) or general in scope, depending on the desired effect. It appears that images, whether direct or indirect (symbolic), can have the same effect on the healing process. Ulcers have been "healed" through images of darning the heels of socks as well as repairing spider webs. Elevated blood pressure has been decreased through images of the release of bottle-neck traffic jams as well as dilating blood vessels to reduce pressure and resistance. Box 20.4 shows two examples of a more general approach to imagery as an aid in the physical healing process. They can be adapted to a host of specific physical manifestations.

Color Therapy

Exposure to colored light and color imagery is another technique to promote relaxation. In a series of landmark studies to determine emotional and physiological responses to color stimulation, Faber Birren (1961, 1978) learned of differences between the colors red and blue. Red was associated with the heightened emotional responses of love, fear, and anger. Corresponding neural activity of the autonomic nervous system included increased heart rate, blood pressure, respiration, muscle tension, and perspiration. When subjects were in a state of emotional arousal, exposure to red light was perceived to be more "disturbing." Blue showed the opposite effect, a return to physiological homeostasis. Blue light was described as a calming color. In situations where babies are exposed to blue light, they tend to show a calm response, whereas the colors yellow and green give a neutral response. If you feel tense or frustrated, close your eyes and feel yourself surrounded by the color blue—aqua-blue, sky blue, indigo, any shade of blue you can imagine. Perhaps even imagine yourself floating in aqua-blue water. Then take a deep breath and feel your body relax all over.

Since Birren's initial work in color therapy, the ability to heal with colors has attracted new interest, particularly in the concept of "vibrational medicine." Light, as expressed in colors, it seems, is energy made visible. Colors are actually vibrations of energy particle waves at different rates. In his book *Light: Medicine of the Future,* Dr. Jacob Lieberman points out some interesting facts about light and light therapy. Artificial indoor lighting (incandescent and fluorescent) is not full-spectrum lighting; it is missing some wave particles, including the color blue. People denied exposure to full-spectrum lighting (which Lieberman calls malillumination) are more prone to bouts of stress and depression, more prone to dental decay, and likely to have higher levels of serum cholesterol. Studies conducted on plants grown under full-spectrum and different colors of light reveal that the health of the plant is dependent on full-spectrum lighting. According to Lieberman, the same may be true for people. He suggests that when proper lighting is not available, use your imagination to see your body as a prism that captures and splinters light into the colors of the rainbow (red, orange, yellow, green, blue, indigo, and violet). Colors that are pale or hard to imagine require more attention to bring them into detail. Furthermore, some specialists (Gardner, 1990) hypothesize that light therapy and color therapy may add yet another dimension to the healing process. According to Gardner, this theory, in conjunction with the vibrations of human chakras, is now being studied at MIT and UCLA.

Body Colors and the Healing Light

Box 20.4

Body Colors

Imagine yourself lying in a shallow pool of warm water. Visualize your internal body reflecting one color, white. As you look all throughout your body, you see the outline and the contents within as the color white. Now take a moment to examine all parts of your body from your head down to your toes. As you do this, search for any specific locations which feel tense or active. These can include muscles, joints, organs, or any part of your body that seems a little less calm than the rest. These might even include your mind, if thoughts are racing through and competing for attention. Try to locate those areas which, under stress and strain, have not been allowed to relax to the same extent as the rest of your body. These "active" areas are referred to as hot spots. When you find the area or areas of tension, envision that these are the color red. Red symbolizes a higher metabolic level of arousal or energy state. The color red is in contrast to the color white that the rest of your body reflects. As you envision your body represented by these two colors, a mass of white with one, two, or several red areas pulsating, focus now on the hot spots. Allow these areas to become as calm as the rest of your body. Imagine these hot spots slowly changing their color from an intense, bright red to orange. As you look at and feel the orange areas of your body, feel a sense of calm beginning to take over. The color orange is often symbolic of change. See the orange change from a bright orange to the color yellow. As you look at this color, you detect that the area(s) you are focusing on is becoming much more relaxed and much more calm, and begins to match the feelings of calmness you sense in the rest of your body. And as you look at this image, you notice that the yellow areas are now blending in with the white color that the rest of your internal body reflects. And as you continue to look at this image, you now see that your entire internal body is one color, a brilliant whiteness radiating light all around it. This color is a symbol of your complete relaxation and health.

The Healing Light

Once again feel your body lying comfortably in a shallow pool of warm water. Directly overhead, about four feet above you, is a pitcher suspended in the air. The pitcher contains white light, an unending supply of white light. This white light is a healing light, a healing energy that when poured over your body, has the ability to augment the healing process you initiated through the color-transformations imagery. Position the pitcher over that part of your body you feel needs reinforcement of the healing touch. Now allow the pitcher to tip its contents onto your body, onto that specific area. Feel the light softly penetrate your body. Feel the warmth of this healing light as it pours into your body. Feel the warmth of that location, and now feel the healing light pour all over your body. See the image of white light within you and around you. You feel relaxed, you feel calm, and you feel energized all at the same time. Take a moment to sense this complete mental and physical relaxation.

Steps to Initiate Mental Imagery

1. *Assume a comfortable position.* Mental imagery, like diaphragmatic breathing, can be done anywhere you can close your eyes momentarily to your current surroundings and allow your imagination to replace it with a setting more conducive to relaxation. When starting out, either sit or lie comfortably with your eyes closed and loosen any constrictive clothing around your neck and waist. You may even want to kick your shoes off. Sometimes it helps if you dedicate a special place to the practice of mental imagery.

2. *Concentration and attitude.* As with other relaxation techniques, mental imagery requires sound concentration. It is important to find a quiet place and try to reduce interrupting noises that may compete with the sensory images you create. Concentration, like imagination, is a skill, and the two are very compatible in their development. A mental image can last anywhere from seconds to minutes. Initial exposure to this technique may be short while, allowing powers of concentration to build. When employing

mental imagery, tap into the imaginative powers of all your senses to place yourself at the scene you have created. Focus your attention on the vividness of colors, shapes, textures, sounds, noises, silence, smells, and the entire feel of the environment you have created. At first it is common to visualize a third-person image of yourself in a scene. But the real power of imagery is delivered when you experience the image in the first person, as you normally do in life. If your mind begins to wander to other thoughts while you initiate an image, try to steer your attention back to the details of the image and allow it to hold you captive.

A positive attitude is crucial to the effectiveness of mental imagery. The cornerstone of a positive attitude is the faith that your imagination can deliver the goods. In the experience of Siegel, Borysenko, and Simonton, *belief* in the power of the image was as important as the image itself. Whether it is called hope, faith, or confidence, this is the element that dreams, and more importantly images, are made of.

3. *Visual themes.* Choice of mental images is unlimited. Begin by deciding the purpose of your visualization. Is it a momentary escape to clear your thoughts? Will it help promote a healthier lifestyle through adaptations of current health behaviors? Is it a healing image to restore and rejuvenate your body? Once you have decided, build on your purpose and tailor a vision to answer it. There are several images in this chapter to start with, but eventually you may want to use these to create your own special image. The use of imagination and creativity is a skill: the more it is employed, the stronger it becomes, and the better it is as a stress-

management resource. Sometimes on journeys travel guides are used to lead the way. In her therapy, Norris uses questions to help guide her patients through their mental-imagery experience. For instance, with an image of a house or castle, she may ask, What does your castle look like? What is it made of? What colors are the materials? Walk up to the entrance. What does the door look like? What do the doorknob and knocker look like? Push the door open and walk inside. What do you see? Norris states that by asking questions such as these, individuals are encouraged to create images from the depths of their own unconscious minds, the place where healing takes place.

Best Application of Mental Imagery

Mental imagery is very portable. Although it is best to learn mental imagery in a quiet environment, once you are proficient, the technique can be used right in the middle of a stress situation. It can be employed minutes before a public speech, at the start of an exam, waiting in line at the post office, sitting in the dentist's chair, during a boring staff meeting, or in any circumstances where you can close your eyes for a moment to regain composure. With practice, some people can even recall an image with their eyes open. Unlike other techniques, which need a minimum amount of time to be effective, mental imagery can be effective even when used for a short period. Thus, this is the optimal intervention technique to use in the face of stress. As a preventive technique, the art of visualization can be a powerful meditation practice for training the body to lower stress. Mental imagery is effective in both dispelling the thunderheads of fear as well as defusing the powder kegs of anger.

Summary

- Mental imagery describes the ability of the unconscious mind to generate images that have a calming, healing effect on the body. Visualization is one aspect of mental imagery, wherein there is conscious direction of self-generated images. Guided mental imagery is a variation wherein images are suggested by another person (either live or on tape).
- Mental imagery in some form has been used for thousands of years as a means to access the power of the mind to heal the body, mind, and soul.
- Freud and Jung reintroduced mental imagery in the twentieth century. Jung coined the term *active imagination* to mean the powers of the unconscious mind to help resolve issues associated with recurring dreams.
- Several studies have been conducted using mental imagery and visualization as a complementary healing tool, specifically with cancer patients. Norris outlined several criteria necessary for mental imagery to prove effective.
- Mental imagery can be divided into three types: peaceful natural scenes, or images that place one in a natural environment; behavioral changes, or images that allow one to see and feel oneself performing a different, more health-conscious behavior; and internal body images, or images of trips inside the body to observe damaged, diseased, or dysfunctional tissue being healed or repaired.
- Systematic desensitization is a technique that breaks down a stressor into small parts and allows one to slowly gain control of feelings and perceptions about a stressor through progressive exposures to it. Mental imagery is used to augment this process.
- Color therapy and light therapy, which are loosely associated with mental imagery, are also shown to have a healing quality to them. Colors of light have specific vibrations that may augment the healing abilities of the mind. Red is said to generate feelings of arousal, whereas blue is believed to have a calming quality to it.
- Certain criteria contribute to profound experiences with mental imagery: a quiet environment, a comfortable position, and a passive attitude.

Concepts and Terms

Active imagination
Behavioral changes
Blueprint aspect
Color therapy
Egosyntonic

Guided mental imagery
Idiosyncratic
Internal body images
Kinesthetic
Light therapy

Mental imagery
Systematic desensitization
Tranquil natural scenes
Visualization

References and Resources

Achterberg, J. *Imagery and Cancer.* Institute for Personality and Ability Testing, Champaign, IL, 1978.

Achterberg, J. Imagery and Medicine: Psychophysiological Speculations, *Journal of Mental Imagery* 8(4):1–14, 1984.

Achterberg, J. *Imagery in Healing: Shamanism and Modern Medicine.* Shambhala Publications, Boston, 1985.

Araoz, D. L. Use of Hypnotic Technique with Oncology Patients, *Journal of Psychosocial Oncology* 1(4):47–54, 1983.

Arnheim, R. *Visual Thinking.* University of California Press, Berkeley, 1972.

Becker, W. *Cross Currents.* Tarcher Press, Los Angeles, 1990.

Birren, F. *Color Psychology and Color Therapy.* Citadel Press, Secaucus, NJ, 1961.

Birren, F. *Light, Color, and Environment.* Van Nostrand Reinhold, New York, 1969.

Birren, F. *Color and Human Response.* Van Nostrand Reinhold, New York, 1978.

Bry, A. *Visualization: Directing the Movies of Your Mind.* Harper, New York, 1979.

Bryant, L., and Harvy, A.G. Visual Imagery in Post-traumatic Stress Disorder, *Journal of Traumatic Stress* 9(3):613–619, 1996.

Cassileth, B. R. Mental-Health Quackery in Cancer Treatment, *International Journal of Mental Health* 19(3): 81–84, 1990.

Clark, L. *The Ancient Art of Color Therapy.* Devon-Adair, Old Greenwich, CT, 1974.

Coue, E. *Self-Mastery through Conscious Auto-Suggestion.* Allen & Unwin, London, 1922.

Einstein, A. *Living Philosophies.* AMS Press, New York, 1979.

Epstein, G. *Healing Visualizations: Creating Health through Imagery.* Bantam Books, New York, 1989.

Fanning, P. *Visualization for Change.* New Harbinger Publications, Oakland, CA, 1988.

Feldman, P. E. The Personal Element in Psychiatric Research, *American Journal of Psychiatry* 113:52–54, 1956.

Fisher, S. *Body Experience in Fantasy and Behavior.* Appleton-Century-Crofts, New York, 1970.

Gallwey, W. T. *The Inner Game of Tennis.* Random House, New York, 1974.

Gardner, K. *Sounding the Inner Landscape.* Caduceus Publications, Stonington, ME, 1990.

Garfield, P. *Creative Daydreaming.* Simon and Schuster, 1975.

Gawain, S. *Creative Visualization.* New World Library, San Rafael, CA, 1978.

Gawain, S., with Grimshaw, D. *Reflections in the Light: Daily Thoughts and Affirmations.* Whatever Publishing, Mill Valley, CA, 1978.

Gebhardt, P. Helping Veterans Overcome Their Fears, *The Washington Post,* January 11, 2000.

George, L. Mental Imagery—Enhancement Training in Behavior Therapy: Current Status and Future Prospects, *Psychotherapy* 23:81–92, 1986.

Giusto, E. and Bond, N. Imagery and the Autonomic Nervous System: Some Methodological Issues, *Perceptual and Motor Skills* 48:427–438, 1979.

Harris, D. V. and Robinson, W. J. The Effects of Skill Level on EMG Activity during Internal and External Imagery, *Journal of Sport Psychology* 8(2):105–111, 1986.

Holt, R. Imagery, The Return of the Ostracized, *American Psychologist* 19:254–264, 1964.

Hope, A., and Walch, M. *The Color Compendenium.* Van Nostrand Reinhold, New York, 1990.

Ievleva, L. and Orlick, T. Mental Links to Enhanced Healing: An Exploratory Study, *Sport Psychologist* 5(1):25–40, 1991.

Jasnoski, M. and Kugler, J. Relaxation, Imagery, and Neuroimmunomodulation, *Annals of the New York Academy of Sciences* 496:722–730, 1987.

Jung, C. *Man and His Symbols.* Anchor Press, New York, 1964.

Katra, J. and Tang, R. *The Heart of Mind.* New World Library, Novatno, CA, 1999.

Klisch, M. The Simonton Method of Visualization: Nursing Implications and a Patient's Perspective, *Cancer Nursing* 33:295–300, 1980.

Krippner, S. The Role of Imagery in Health and Healing: A Review, *Saybrook Review* 5(1):32–41, 1985.

Lang, P. J. Imagery and Therapy: An Information-Processing Analysis of Fear, *Behavior Therapy* 8:862–886, 1977.

Leland, N. *Exploring Color.* North Light, Cincinnati, OH, 1985.

Lieberman, J. *Light: Medicine of the Future.* Bear & Co., Santa Fe, NM, 1991.

Maperstek, B. *Staying Well with Guided Imagery,* Warner Books, New York, 1995.

McKim, R. *Experiences in Visual Thinking.* Brooks/Cole, Monterey, CA, 1972.

Miller, N. E. Placebo Factors in Types of Treatment: View of a Psychologist. In M. Shepherd and N. Sartorious, eds., *Nonspecific Aspects of Treatment.* Hans, Hubur, Lewiston, NY, 1989.

Murphy, S. Models of Imagery in Sport Psychology: A Review, *Journal of Mental Imagery* 14:153–172, 1990.

Murphy, S. and Jowdy, M. Imagery and Mental Rehearsal. In T. Horn, ed., *Advances in Sport Psychology.* Human Kinetics, Champaign, IL, 1991.

Neihardt, J. G. *Black Elk Speaks.* University of Nebraska Press, Lincoln, 1988.

Norris, P. Psychoneuroimmunology: Visualization and Imagery, paper presented to the Association for Applied Psychophysiology and Biofeedback, Colorado Springs, CO, March 19, 1992.

Ornstein, R., and Sobel, D. *The Healing Brain: Breakthrough Discoveries about How the Brain Keeps Us Healthy.* Simon and Schuster, New York, 1987.

Parnes, S. *Visionizing.* D. O. K. Publishers, East Aurora, NY, 1988.

Peale, N. *The Power of Positive Thinking.* Prentice-Hall, Englewood Cliffs, NJ, 1956.

Pelletier, K. *Mind as Healer, Mind as Slayer.* Dell, New York, 1977.

Porter, G., and Norris, P. *Why Me? Harnessing the Healing Power of the Human Spirit,* Stillpoint, Walpole, NH, 1985.

Radner, G. *It's Always Something.* Simon and Schuster, New York, 1989.

Richardson, A. *Mental Imagery.* Springer, New York, 1969.

Richardson, M. et al. Coping, Life Attitudes and Immune Response to Imagery and Group Support after Breast Cancer Treatment, *Alternative Therapies* 3(5):62–70, 1997.

Samuels, M. *Seeing with the Mind's Eye.* Random House, New York, 1975.

Scarf, M. Images that Heal: A Doubtful Idea Whose Time Has Come, *Psychology Today* 14:33–46, 1980.

Simonton, O. C., Matthews-Simonton, S. and Creighton, J. L. *Getting Well Again.* Bantam Books, New York, 1980.

Singer, J. *Daydreaming.* Random House, New York, 1966.

Singer, J. *Imagery and Daydream Methods in Psychotherapy and Behavior Modification.* Academic Press, New York, 1974.

Singer, J. and Pope, K. *The Power of Human Imagination.* Plenum Press, New York, 1978.

Sokel, B., Devane, S., and Bentovim, A. Getting Better with Honor: Individualized Relaxation/Self-Hypnosis Techniques for Control of Recalcitrant Abdominal Pain in Children, *Family Systems Medicine* 9(1):83–91, 1991.

Taylor, S. *Health Psychology,* 2nd ed., McGraw-Hill, Englewood, NJ, 1990.

Wilkinson, J. B. Use of Hypnotherapy in Anxiety Management in the Terminally Ill, *British Journal of Experimental and Clinical Hypnosis* 7(1):34–36, 1990.

Winger, W. *Voyages of Discovery.* Psychogenics Press, Gaithersburg, MD, 1977.

Wolpe, J. *The Practice of Behavioral Therapy.* Pergamon Press, New York, 1969.

Chapter 21 Music Therapy

Music acts like a magic key,
to which the most tightly
closed heart opens.
—Maria Von Trapp

Perhaps since the first melodic birdsong was recognized by the human ear for its beautiful sound, music has been perceived to hold a special property of subtle mystical influence. Close your eyes for a moment and think of your current favorite song. Let the music linger in your mind, consciously savor it, and then sense how your body responds to the tones and rhythm of the melody. Without a doubt, the auditory stimulation called music can strongly influence our physical and emotional states. Music has the ability to motivate: For centuries it was utilized in the call to war with fife and drum. More recently, it has been used for a similar purpose during sports events with pep bands. But music can equally pacify or sedate: One need only think of a lullaby to help send a crying baby off to sleep.

For this reason, music in all its many styles can be considered a way to profoundly affect the human condition and, for the purposes of this book, a positive influence on relaxation. Although this seems to have been known intuitively for ages, music is now finally being recognized scientifically as possessing a strong therapeutic quality. There are two schools of thought regarding **music therapy.** The first advocates music making through singing and/or instrumentation for a therapeutic effect. This school of thought, clinically based on and shaped by specialists in the field, defines music therapy as the systematic application of music by the music therapist to bring about helpful changes in the emotional or physical health of the client. The second approach to music therapy seeks to achieve relaxation by listening to music. In this sense music therapy can be defined as the ability to experience an altered state of physical arousal and mood through processing a progression of musical notes of varying tone, rhythm, and instrumentation of pleasing effect. It is this approach to music therapy that receives the greater focus in this chapter.

Music therapy is a very popular relaxation technique. In a national study called the *Mitchum Report on Stress in the '90s,* over 75 percent of those questioned indicated that listening to music was their most common way to reduce stress. While music therapy is considered, for the most part, a treatment to promote relaxation, it has characteristics of a coping technique as well, the main one being to increase conscious awareness of the inner self. Listening to certain types of music is believed by several musicologists to enhance the mind's receptivity to new ideas by accessing the less dominant right-brain thought processes. More specifically, music is thought to enhance creativity through spontaneous mental imagery. In many ways, music soothes the "savage breast" of us all. Although investigations of this type of relaxation technique are quite young, and the human mechanisms affected are not fully understood, the benefits of music therapy are unequivocal. To best understand how music is currently used as a therapy, it is helpful to see how this tool has been used through the ages.

Historical Perspective

The earliest humans about which we have any knowledge believed that music could exorcise evil spirits and heal wounds. Ancient Greeks, including Aristotle, Plato, and Pythagoras, possessed an intuitive understanding of the healing power of music, suggesting that daily exposure could contribute to health. Aristotle held the notion that flute music offered a cathartic release of emotions. Plato indicated that music restored the harmony and contentment in one's soul as well as the moral welfare of the nation at large. "Music is the moral law," he wrote. "It is the essence of order and leads to all that is good, just, and beautiful, passionate and eternal form." Pythagoras credited the rhythm of music with special healing qualities. "All things are constructed of harmonic patterns. It is only when we are out of step with the natural harmonic that disharmony arises," he wrote (Merritt, 1990).

Medieval monarchs employed court minstrels, as well as jesters, to bring the comfort of peaceful melodies to their castles to relieve their melancholy, depression, and fevers. Later many classical musicians, including Bach, Pachelbel, and Mozart, were commissioned by royalty and nobility to compose pieces of music for this very reason. But the power of music was enjoyed not only by the upper classes: for centuries, long before radios, videos, and CD players, family members of all social classes gathered together regularly for words and melody. It was not uncommon for both parents and children to learn to play instruments for the purpose of soothing entertainment. The ability to play together harmoniously was a metaphor for attempts to live together in peace.

American Indian medicine men or shamans often used music in their healing rituals as a powerful medicine for the sick and dying, as well as for peace and prosperity. The musical incantations and accompanying drum beats served as a vehicle of divine communication to heal or strengthen the will of the human spirit. Likewise, across the ocean, Africans have been known for centuries to employ percussion rhythms as healing tools to lower heart rates and fever in the sick.

With the invention of the phonograph in 1877, music became more easily accessible to people in all corners of the globe. In the late nineteenth and early twentieth centuries, it became a respected therapeutic practice in Europe for the treatment of mental disorders. Not until 1926, however, was music recognized by the established medical community as a form of therapy for the treatment of several clinical disorders, most notably depression. And although music in its many forms and styles, and in nearly every culture around the world, has been accepted by the masses as a tool to promote relaxation and healing, it was not until 1946 that it was formally acknowledged in the United States as a bona fide therapy and legitimate discipline worthy of investigation. The introduction of music in several Veterans Administration hospitals serving World War II veterans with battle fatigue (now called posttraumatic stress disorder, or PTSD) demonstrated that this type of stimulation could boost morale and improve patients' mental state by decreasing symptoms associated with depression. The National Association for Music Therapy (NAMT) was founded in 1950. Through the work of several pioneer researchers, music therapy became advocated by the 1970s and '80s as a viable tool to deal with the clinical symptoms of stress.

Norman Cousins is most well known for introducing and legitimizing the healing power of humor and laughter, but in his acclaimed book *Anatomy of an Illness,* he dedicated a whole chapter to the healing properties of music. Recounting stories of when he met cello virtuoso Pablo Casals and famed physician Albert Schweitzer, Cousins described how both men took creative refuge in playing the piano. Cousins once observed Casals, at the age of ninety, get painfully out of bed, then become youthfully transformed when he sat down at the piano to play the Brahms B-flat Quartet. Similarly, Schweitzer, in his eighth decade of life, would balance his work in medicine with a nightly rendition of Bach's Toccata in D minor. Cousins saw in both men a regeneration and restoration in their savoring of music, hinting that it may have contributed to their health and longevity.

In the late 1970s and early '80s, about the same time that stress entered the consciousness of the American public and became a household word, there began to emerge a new type of relaxing composition now commonly referred to as New Age music. Markedly different from rock, pop, blues, classical, and jazz, New Age music consists of a slow-tempoed instrumental, often synthesized, and occasionally acoustic collaboration of melodies and chord progressions to alter moods and increase levels of conscious awareness. Musicologists Andrew Watson and Nevill Drury trace the beginnings of New Age music to the "psychedelic" counterculture period of the 1960s, when elements of rock, jazz, folk, Indian *ragas,* and meditative music were integrated to create repeated cycles of gentle "undulating sounds" for a relaxing effect. The band Pink Floyd is given credit for making this style of music popular with their "Meddle" album in which the entire second side, "Echos," is a single instrumental composition played on a synthesizer. The lineage of New Age musicians unfolded from Pink Floyd's inspirational work to include a collaborative effort by King Crimson's Robert Fripp and Roxy Music's Brian Eno entitled "Evening Star." Eno went on to record several albums, including "Music for Airports" and "Ambient Two," becoming a dominant force in the New Age genre. This style of music has now spread to all continents, giving rise to many other New Age and environmental musicians, including Kitaro (Japan), Andreas Vollenweider (Germany), Jean-Michel Jarre (France), Vangelis (Greece), Enya (Ireland), and Paul Horn, Philip Glass, Steven Halpern, David Lanz, and William Ackerman (North America), to name a few. Currently, sales of New Age CDs and radio programming of New Age selections suggest a growing interest in this style of music. But New Age music is just one of many styles that can promote relaxation. Classical, jazz, and acoustic folk are thought to be equally successful in effecting or enhancing the relaxation response. Today, music of all styles is used in many different clinical and professional settings as a therapeutic tool.

From Sound to Noise to Music

Sound is energy made audible. It is created through random or periodic vibrations that are represented as waves. Sounds can be perceived as either pleasant or unpleasant, the latter commonly referred to as "noise." Sound waves or oscillations are measured in Hertz (Hz)—cycles or vibrations per second. These oscillations are perceived as pitch by the human ear (Fig. 21.1). The audible frequency or sonic range detectable to the human ear is 20 to 20,000Hz, depending on the health and training of the auditory nerve tissue. Sound waves can also be detected, by means of different neural pathways, through the conduction of skin and bone tissue.

While vibrations are measured in Hertz, or frequencies representing a number of oscillations per second, sounds are recorded in units of measurement called decibels (dB), in honor of inventor Alexander Graham Bell. Decibels signify the air pressure specific sounds produce as detected by the human ear. One decibel is said to be the softest sound that can be detected by humans. In the days of horse-drawn carriages, calls for help could be yelled from windows and heard across town. With the advancement of modern technology, however, average ambient noise levels in metropolitan cities are currently measured at 122 dB, two decibels above the demarcation inducing pain. Today, a yell would not be heard over the cacophony of sounds two city blocks away. Repeated exposure to high-decibel noise can not only trigger the body's stress response, but also cause damage to the human ear. Noise-induced hearing impairment or loss is both cumulative and permanent. Tinnitus is the clinical name given to constant buzzing, hissing, or ringing in the ear that can arise from repeated exposure to loud noise. A concern exists today among the nation's audiologists that the onset of hearing impairment from ambient noise levels, combined with use of portable headphones, occurs at an increasingly young age. It has been speculated that not only can noise be perceived as stressful, but hearing dysfunction may become a low-intensity chronic stressor. Like hypertension, the early stages of hearing loss go undetected without a diagnostic test. Table 21.1 is a list of outdoor locations and various noise producers and their respective decibel levels.

Perhaps in reaction to noise pollution, sound stimulation, called white noise, has been used to mask, balance, or neutralize stressful, noisy environ-

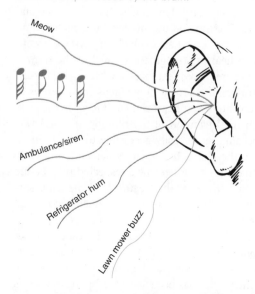

Sound waves enter the ear and pass through the ear drum to be processed by the brain.

Figure 21.1

Loudness of Some Everyday Sounds		*Table 21.1*
Sound	**Loudness(dB)**	
Rustling leaves	10	
Normal conversation	50	
Suburban neighborhood noise	52	
Vacuum cleaner	70	
City noise; busy traffic	80	
Inside a passenger jet (takeoff)	78–83	
Heavy trucks at 50 feet	76–88	
Home shop tools	65–110	
Subway noise	80–114	
Nearby jet airplane	150	
Shooting a gun	150–170	

Source: Alters, S. and Schiff, W. *Essential Concepts for Healthy Living*, 2nd edition. Jones and Bartlett Publishers, Sudbury, MA, 419, 2001.

ments. Technically speaking, white noise is comprised of broadband sounds that include all frequencies of the audible spectrum. While some music can serve as white noise, its greatest potential is in enhancing tranquility.

The Distinctive Qualities of Music

Music consists of many qualities that combine for an esthetic auditory experience:

Tone: an initial sound or vibration.

Pitch: the frequency of oscillations or vibrations. The higher the pitch, the more rapid the vibrations. A high pitch is thought to produce sympathetic nervous arousal, while a low pitch is thought to be conducive to relaxation.

Intensity: relative loudness or amplitude of vibrations. High intensity has the effects of emotional domination and coerciveness, while low intensity is considered more tranquil and serene.

Timbre: "tone color." Timbre is what makes the same notes played on different instruments sound very different.

Harmony: the ratio and relationship between tones (sounds) and their rhythmic patterns.

Interval: the units of the musical scale and the vertical distance between notes, giving rise to the structure of melodies and harmonies.

Rhythm: the most dynamic of musical qualities. Rhythm is described as the time pattern (horizontal distance) of music that seems to elicit such strong emotional responses. The bass frequencies most influence the rhythm of music.

Perceptual quality: the intellectual processing of sounds with the attachment of subjective attitudes to each sound.

Adapted from A. Watson and N. Drury, *Healing Music: The Harmonic Path to Wholeness* (Dorset, Eng.: Prism Press, 1987).

Music in its entirety is greater than the sum of its parts. In the words of music scholar Randall McClellan (1988) "Music is a dynamic multilayered matrix of constantly shifting tonal relationships unfolding within time." It is this dynamic matrix that induces a profound sense of relaxation.

Music as a Relaxation Technique

There are several schools of thought regarding the relationship between music and relaxation, developed by both the hard and soft sciences. Each can make a contribution to the understanding of music's role in the relaxation response. Regardless of the theory invoked, the frequencies transmitted as the sounds of music and received by the body significantly affect human physiology. But exactly how these frequencies are received is still in the speculation stage. Maybe the answer is a combination of two or more theories.

Biochemical Theory

Music appears to affect human physiology directly, through the cerebral cortex and autonomic nervous system. Through the ear's complicated structure, sound stimuli are received by the brain via special nervous tissue of the ear (organ of Corti, or hair cells), where vibrations are converted to electrical nerve

impulses. (It is interesting to note that these hair cells are only a membrane away from lymph fluid of the inner ear, suggesting a link to the immune system. In addition, the eardrum appears to have a liaison with the parasympathetic nervous system via the vagus nerve.) In a very complex network of neurons, these impulses are thought to be first decoded by the cerebral cortex, then deciphered by the subcortex, and subsequently directed from the limbic system through the autonomic nervous system, potentially throughout the entire body. Elements involved with these auditory sensations include pitch, rhythm, tone, tempo, volume, and perhaps most importantly, perceptual quality, or the emotional effects of deciphered sounds. Depending on interpretation (like or dislike), either the sympathetic or parasympathetic nervous system may be activated.

One theory proposed by neuropsychologist and composer Dr. Manfred Clynes (1982) suggests that humans have a dominant rhythm style (DRS), a pulse indirectly controlled by the heart, directed by neural and hormonal chemical processes. This DRS, like a thermostat, has a set-point specific to these internal influences. The body's rhythm, however, can be additionally influenced by external rhythms, from the repetitive pulsations of a jackhammer to the symphonic rhythm of Mozart's Piano Concerto in C Minor. The body's DRS is thought to be subject to the influences of musical resonance or sympathetic vibrations. Clynes hypothesizes that the nervous system contains several codes capable of influencing the body's responses to musical rhythm, melody, and tone. Clynes's theory implies that these codes are comprised of "essentic forms" that influence neuropeptide activity and thus the metabolic functions of body organs, most notably the heart muscle.

Although many organs are involved in producing the DRS, the most obvious window to the body's rhythm is heart rate. While there are variations from person to person, the average human heart rate has a rhythm of between sixty and eighty beats per minute. By no coincidence, music therapists have found, most Western music is paced at this same tempo, and some believe that music with this rhythm has the greatest influence on physiological homeostasis. Several studies have investigated the effects of music on electrical stimulation of the heart, with inconclusive results. Although some suggest that slow-paced music lowers heart rate, others find no significant effect. This may be related to the perceptual quality of the music, as other studies indicate the relaxation response is most pronounced when subjects select their own music.

A neurological study involving subjects connected to an electroencephalograph (EEG device) while listening to slow-tempoed music revealed that the musical rhythm quickly synchronized brain rhythms to its beat, an effect also seen with strobe lights, which promote a "photic driving" response on EEG tracings.

Other physiological effects of musical stimulation, including muscle tension and corticosteroids levels, have also been researched. In these cases, music was used in conjunction with other relaxation techniques such as guided mental imagery and biofeedback. In one study conducted by Mark Rider and his colleagues at Eastern Montana College in 1985, subjects listened to audio tapes of two orchestral pieces for a three-week period. Progressive relaxation techniques were dubbed over the music track. Results revealed decreases in cortisol levels much more pronounced than listening to relaxation techniques without a music track. Similarly, when music was integrated with biofeedback, the combined effect was even greater in reducing muscle tension than biofeedback alone. The use of relaxing music as a sedative has also been shown to be effective in reducing stress and muscular tension associated with the process of childbirth, especially when subjects

Figure 21.2

Headphones can provide a sense of solitude when listening to music. Repeated exposure to high volume with headsets, however, can impair hearing and result in early-onset deafness.

have had numerous positive exposures to a piece of music prior to delivery.

If a slow musical rhythm is conducive to relaxation, is there a rhythm or beat that is unhealthy? A theory called switching, postulated by Dr. John Diamond, hints of the validity of this notion. Measuring electrical conduction and strength in muscle fibers, Diamond found that the "stop anapestic beat" common in rock music (i. e., short, short, long, pause, or da-da-DAA-pause) decreased the force of muscle contractions. Diamond hypothesized that this "weak" beat distorts or switches the communication of neural messages from the right and left hemispheres of the brain. Diamond also believes this beat decreases several cognitive functions, including judgment and perception. In addition, Diamond suggests that music with this beat has an addictive quality and that repeated exposure may in fact be harmful. That is, music of this kind may be associated with the inability to return to a homeostatic baseline, as measured by higher resting-heart-rate and blood-pressure values.

Music appreciation is thought to be a right-brain function; it is the right hemisphere of the brain that recognizes and processes auditory stimulation in the form of musical note and chord progressions. This appears especially true when music is instrumental, or without lyrics. The left cerebral hemisphere, proficient in verbal acuity, is thought to intercept auditory stimulation of music *with* lyrics, if analysis of musical composition and instrumentation is initiated. For this reason, instrumentals are thought to promote a greater sense of relaxation than music combined with lyrics. In addition, music that consists of a series of repetitive notes or beats may act much like a mantra, inducing a meditative state of relaxation. Although yet unproven, it has been speculated by some that music may release endorphins (neuropeptides and chemical opiates) from the brain and other body tissues, which create a sensation of euphoria or inspirational high. Another neurotransmitter, melanin, has been researched to determine its effects as an electrical semiconductor. According to Dr. Frank Barr, melanin is capable of converting light energy to sound energy through neurochemical messages. Further research on these and other functions of special neurotransmitters may support biochemical theory (Barr, 1983).

Figure 21.3 The concept of entrainment was first observed in the motion of two pendulum clocks. It has since been observed in both animate and inanimate objects throughout the natural world.

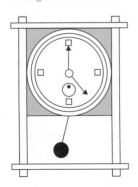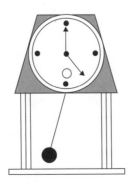

Entrainment Theory

Scientists are in agreement that cell metabolism operates on chemical energy—the breakdown of carbohydrates, fats, and proteins for energy metabolism at the biochemical level. There is also agreement that the human body is a channel for electrical energy that can be measured through various types of biofeedback including EKGs, EEGs, and EMGs, which record the electrical impulses given off by various organ tissues. You have probably experienced this type of energy when getting a shock from walking across a carpeted floor to turn on the stereo. A new theory, which parallels and possibly integrates with biochemical theory, suggests that sounds are received through a "sixth sense," the human energy field.

From physics we learn that virtually all objects produce oscillations, including living organisms. Any object that produces vibrations creates its own field of energy; and the movement of subatomic particles is typically called an electromagnetic field. In terms of human beings, this may be referred to as an energy field or aura. In quantum physics, research has shown that the smallest subatomic particles create vibrations. The human body contains many organs that produce biorhythmic oscillations (e.g., brain waves, heart rate, and those produced through muscle tension). But the body as a whole, comprised of jillions of atoms, also produces oscillations. As suggested by Itzhak Bentov in *Stalking the Wild Pendulum*, in a natural, relaxed state, the body itself produces a single unified series of oscillations at 7.8 Hz; this is the "frequency of human homeostasis." Schumann's resonance is a term used to describe the earth's own vibration, which is a function of its circumference and electromagnetic radiation calculated at a frequency of approximately 7.8 cycles per second. Remarkably, this frequency is identical to both the frequency of alpha waves produced by the human brain at rest and the sounds produced by dolphins. In the words of music therapist Steve Halpern (1985), "Being in harmony with oneself and the universe is more than a poetic concept."

In 1665 a Dutch physicist named Christian Huygens discovered that when he placed two clocks side by side, eventually their pendulums would swing together in a unified rhythm (Fig. 21.3). This matched rhythm is called **entrainment,** and is defined as the "mutual phase-locking oscillations of like frequencies in the same environment." When two or more objects produce oscillations in close proximity, the dominant frequency will prevail. Eventually, they will "entrain" together in a

Stress With a Human Face

THE SOUND OF APPLAUSE IS NOT USUALLY considered to be a symphony of sorts, but it is music to the ears of singer/songwriter Naomi Judd who, with her daughter Wynonna, became one of the nation's most renowned country music acts, the Judds. Stricken with a potentially fatal case of hepatitis C, Naomi's singing career was nearly cut short in the summer of 1990. Told she could only have a few years to live, her team of physicians gave a typical forecast for a person in Naomi's condition and then sent her home. A woman of great faith, Naomi decided to listen to the voice in her heart more than the voice of her physicians, and determined that she would not be a passive victim to her condition. Instead, she would become an active participant in her healing journey.

A longtime advocate of the mind-body-spirit connection, Naomi began to apply what she knew in her heart to be true. Setting her focus on healing, she planned a strategy for her recovery. One day, after calling her husband Larry, daughters Wynonna and Ashley, and her family to her bedside, she informed them of her game plan. In her heart Naomi knew that if she were to disconnect from her profession, her colleagues, and her music, she would die in record time. She decided to fight back.

She announced to those around her that she would go back on tour—a farewell tour. But this would be no ordinary tour. Not only would she give the gift of music, this time she would receive it as well—from the audience. Knowing how powerful the energy of love was, after performing each song, she would soak up the applause, the whistles, the cheers, and direct this energy throughout her body—asking the vibrations to stimulate her immune system to heal the cells of her liver and send the virus into remission. She said, "I would turn each standing ovation, this applause into prayerful support." And it worked! A decade later, she is doing well having tested "negative" three years in a row, and sharing the message of faith, hope, and love as essential components of the mind-body-spirit equation.

Music has always held a soft spot in Naomi's heart and that spot continues to grow as she shares her message of the healing journey that we all must take part in to nurture our souls and become whole. ✦

unified frequency. The entrainment of oscillation is thought to be nature's own attempt to conserve energy.

Like a tuning fork that begins to resonate when another tuning fork producing sound waves is brought in close proximity, entrainment theory suggests that if one organ—the heart, say—increases its oscillations as a result of heightened metabolic activity, adjacent organs will entrain to that frequency. If several body organs are influenced to entrain at a higher frequency, over time the result is a decreased ability to return to homeostatic condition. The same phenomenon occurs in response to external oscillations. Like a radio receiver, the body is a transformer; it receives (absorbs) as well as emits oscillations. If external rhythms are more dominant (i.e., greater than 7.8Hz), then they force the body to go "out of tune" with itself by entraining to a higher

vibration. The most common example of human entrainment is the female menstrual cycle. It has long been recognized, but until recently poorly understood, that when two or more women live or work together for prolonged periods of time, their menstrual cycles entrain—their menses occur on or about the same day. The same phenomenon has been observed in the blinking patterns of fireflies that land on the same bush, as well as the movement patterns of schools of fish and flocks of birds.

The entrainment theory gained support from a series of studies conducted in the early 1970s on the effects of music on the growth of plants, organisms with no known nervous system. Dr. Dorothy Retallack (1973), for example, conducted a study examining leaf growth and water absorption when corn, squash, petunias, zinnias, and marigolds were exposed to music. She found that some types of music induced a "fertilizing effect," promoting plant growth. Interestingly, she discovered that when in the presence of classical music (Bach) and Indian sitar music (Ravi Shankar), plants grew in the direction of the speakers (sometimes even around the speakers), showing a preference for these styles of music. When subjected to loud rock and roll or acid rock, though, they grew away from the speakers. In fact, many of these plants became dehydrated; some even died. Other comparable studies investigating the effects of music on animals have revealed that chickens lay more eggs and some cows produce more milk when music is piped into their living quarters. While obviously more complex than either plants or chickens, humans are thought to be influenced in much the same way.

Bill Monroe, former director of the Mutual Broadcasting Network and founder/director of the Monroe Institute, experimented with various frequencies and their effects on brain waves. His findings led him to conclude that specific frequencies (.5 to 20Hz), not musical rhythms, were what allowed the brain to entrain to an alpha rhythm, or what he called a frequency following response. Experimenting further with various frequencies directed toward the right and left ear, he found that he could actually entrain both cerebral hemispheres—which Monroe call "hemi-Sync"—producing a most profound state of relaxation and altered state of consciousness.

Thus, the entrainment theory concludes that relaxing music can have a calming effect because elevated body rhythms entrain with a slower, more natural homeostatic rhythm produced by a musical composition. Quite literally, relaxation occurs when the body is in harmony with itself and the natural world. Proponents of this theory indicate that many people who listen to up-beat music to relax may in effect throw off their natural body rhythm. This could explain why various parameters measured by biofeedback instruments have not shown a musically induced state of relaxation with all types of music. Currently, musicians are experimenting with incorporating the 7.8Hz frequency into music, including dolphin "songs" and whale "music."

Metaphysical Theory

The least scientific but perhaps the most intuitively true theory suggests that music has a divine quality. Music is a gift from God, or so Orpheus thought. Greek legend has it that Orpheus was given a lyre by Apollo (the god of music) to offer songs of praise. Although Apollo bequeathed this gift, it was the muses who taught Orpheus to play, hence the word *music*. While neurophysiologists have looked for "substance" in the calming effects of music, students of higher consciousness have searched for "essence." They theorize that music is a holy (i.e., making whole or healing) gift communicating through the soul or human spirit. Virtually every culture employs music as a vehicle for meditation, from European Gregorian chants, to American Indian "sings," to African-American gospels. Even classical composers such as Bach, Beethoven, and Mozart were often said to compose through divine inspiration. Bach was once quoted as saying that "The aim and final reason of all music should be nothing else but the glory of God and the refreshment of the spirit." Beethoven once said, "Music is the one incorporeal entrance into the higher world" (Merritt, 1990).

Proponents of this theory, including French psychologist and audiologist Alfred Tomatis, hypothesize that music and song have a transcending quality that provides a direct communications link to a higher power. This theory also gives credence to the idea that music is a universal language. Musicologist and composer Dr. Steven Halpern advocates a musical meditation that pairs musical notes with the body's seven metaphysical energy sources, or chakras. In an exercise he titles the spectrum meditation (Table 21.2), musical notes are paired with visualization of specific colors, body regions, and meditative thoughts in a particular sequence for a twenty-minute period. In research conducted by Halpern (1978) to measure the relaxing effects of musical composition, it was observed that both classical and New Age—specifically Halpern's spectrum meditation—produced a significant decrease in the stress response as measured by biofeedback (galvanic skin response).

Music therapist Stephanie Merritt (1990) suggests that music has the divine ability to unite or connect the human spirit of all individuals. Citing many examples of the powerful effects of classical music in her book *Mind, Music, and Imagery,* Merritt writes, "Music brings us back to the consciousness of our oneness and shows us, on a deep level, how much our progress as a human race depends on a mutual love and assistance." Integrating concepts of Jung's theory of individuation and intuition with elements of creativity and right-brain thinking,

Spectrum Meditation

Table 21.2

Note	Body Region (Chakra)	Color	Meditative Thought
C	Base of spine	Red	Energy to transmit life, groundedness
D	Below navel	Orange	Positive self-affirmation, centeredness
E	Solar plexus	Yellow	Self-forgiveness, receiving love
F	Heart	Green	Giving unconditional love
G	Throat	Blue	Strong willpower, life mission
A	Center of forehead	Indigo	Grace, wisdom, balance
B	Crown of head	Violet	Divine consciousness, connectedness

ADAPTATION OF chart from pp. 184–185 of *Sound Health: The Music and Sounds That Make Us Whole* by Steven Halpern. Copyright © 1985 by Steven Halpern and Louis Savery. Reprinted by permission of HarperCollins Publishers, Inc.

Merritt hypothesizes that music influences more than just neurons in the body. While not every type of music can raise one's spirits, the influence of music to provide inspiration of all kinds cannot be argued.

Psychological Effects of Music

Perhaps equal to the profound physiological effects produced by music are its apparent effects on attitudes and moods, including fear and depression. Typically the first thing people say when they hear music they like is how good it makes them feel inside. This was the desired effect when musical recordings were played for several World War II-veteran patients. Exposure to selections of music appeared to decrease symptoms of despondency and in some cases altered mood into modest expressions of joy and pleasure.

The limbic system, particularly the hypothalamus (known as "the seat of the emotions"), is believed to house the neurons that, when stimulated through auditory sensations, can alter mood or emotion. While individuals often recognize at the conscious level the influence music has on mood, auditory stimuli can also penetrate the unconscious mind and promote their own changes in perception and mood. In a study to determine the effects of background music on grocery shoppers, it was observed that consumers spent more time in aisles where slow-tempoed instrumental music was played, resulting in more purchases. Slow-tempoed music has also been introduced into settings of anxiety such as dentists' and

physicians' offices. The premise of this type of music is "stimulus progression," instrumental music that is easily digested by auditory channels. It is the basis for contemporary background music produced by the Muzak Corporation.

Music in all its complexity of arrangement can produce as well as reduce stressful emotions. In the days of silent movies, theaters would hire piano players to compose on-site "sound tracks" to enhance the emotions of viewers during both dramatic and romantic scenes. With the advent of "talkies," Hollywood incorporated musical sound tracks into its films to highlight emotionally charged scenes and fuel the emotional roller coaster from fear to love, a practice still employed in both movies and television commercials.

While music in elevators and grocery stores may appear normal these days, music in operating rooms may seem a rather novel approach to speeding the healing process. In an experiment to determine the effects of classical music on anxious hospital patients, music therapist Dr. Helen Bonny (1973) created a series of tapes to be played primarily in the intensive care units at Jefferson General Hospital in Port Townsend, Washington, and St. Agnes Hospital in Baltimore, Maryland. Results revealed significant reductions in both physiological parameters, including blood pressure, heart rate, ventilations, and muscle tension, and increased ability to sleep; as well as reductions in psychological factors including anxiety and depression. Nurses even noticed increased ease in changing intravenous needles.

Music can reach and extend our deepest thoughts and feelings in a way that verbal language cannot. Music has the ability to break down strong emotional defenses and allow for the expression of feelings. Thus, controlled music-therapy sessions have been conducted for hundreds of patients as an exercise for the cathartic release of latent or suppressed emotions. Loud, rapid-tempoed music has been used by music therapists to assist in the release of latent anger. Uplifting, slow, rhythmic music has been played to both sedate and rejuvenate the body's organ tissues.

There is no doubt that music does indeed have a profound effect on emotions at both the conscious and unconscious levels. Music heard for the first time often forms associations with the listener's state of mind at that time; hence, emotional attachments are often made to particular pieces of music. Thus, different types of music can be strongly correlated with physical arousal as well as relaxation. In a study to assess the relationship between type of music, musical selection, and enjoyment, and self-reported states of relaxation, Valerie Stratton and Anthony Zalanowski (1984) found no single type of music effective in enhancing relaxation for all subjects. Rather, the critical factor was the degree to which the subject *liked* the music selection. A similar study by McCraty (1998) found similar results. In another investigation, William Davis and Michael Thaut (1989) attempted to determine which types of music people considered relaxing. The music selected by subjects ranging in age from eighteen to forty-three included U2, Liz Story, Dan Fogelberg, Santana, Mozart, George Thorogood, Wynton Marsalis, Vangelis, William Ackerman, and Beethoven. As might be expected, it was observed that physiological homeostasis (as indicated by heart rate, muscle tension, and finger-skin temperature) was not attained through all musical selections. Subjects indicated, however, that *their* music selection was relaxing to them.

Other musicologists have attempted to study the relationship between performing—singing (the first instrument) or playing an instrument—and well-being. In his book *The Roar of Silence,* Don Campbell suggests that singing is, in itself, a relaxation technique as it positively alters body rhythms through its changes in ventilations, heart rate, blood pressure, and brain waves. Tone rather than rhythm, however, is believed responsible for these changes. Campbell relates the story of a policy change at a Benedictine monastery in southern France suspending the practice of Gregorian chants. As a result of being denied the opportunity to sing, the Christian monks manifested several symptoms of stress, including repeated bouts of fatigue and illness. When chanting was reinstituted, the health condition of the monks improved significantly. Interestingly, music performed in the form of chants differs markedly from both other lyrical melodies and talking. Halpern notes that singing (specifically Gregorian and Zen chanting) consists of clean vowel sounds, soft in nature, which trail off into a slight hum, creating a tranquil resonance throughout the body. Talking and pop vocals, on the other hand, emphasize consonants, which lend a less tranquil resonance.

Is it true that listening to classical music can make you smarter? According to one study, students who sang or played an instrument scored up to fifty-one points higher on their SATs than the national average. Classical music was proven to be as effective as Valium for some coronary care patients. These and other findings has led music therapist Don Campbell to call this "the Mozart effect." He explains this as music's lifelong effect on health, learning, and behavior. In his book of the same name, Campbell cites various studies supporting the premise that indeed, music not only calms the nerves but provides other benefits as well.

Visualization and Auditory Imagery

Music and imagination are wonderful partners. Perhaps the best example of this is the film *Fantasia,* in which Walt Disney and conductor Leopold Stokowski united cartoon images and several great classical music pieces in a truly inspiring achievement. Another example is the musical masterpiece by Prokofiev, *Peter and the Wolf,* a musical fable that pairs the sounds of particular musical instruments with its animal and human characters (Fig. 21.4). Both music and imagination are right-brain capabilities, which may explain the bond between the two. Dr. Sidney Parnes (1988), a creative consultant employed by Disney in the design of Florida's Epcot Center, advocates using music to generate ideas and enhance the imagination and creative processes. In his creative workshop training sessions Parnes often plays instrumental pieces to inspire imagination during creative exercises. Music's ability to augment imagination supports the idea that it can be a coping technique as well as a relaxation technique; imagination and creativity are essential tools in the resolution of stress. Often during

Russian composer Sergei Prokofiev combined music and imagination in his masterpiece, *Peter and the Wolf,* wherein each character is represented by a melody on a different instrument.   *Figure 21.4*

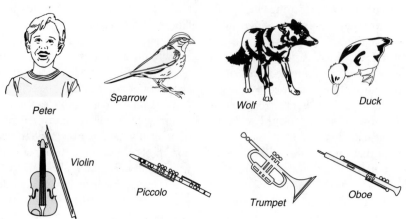

relaxation-training sessions, the sounds of natural environments are used to augment participants' imagination, including thunderstorms, ocean waves, mountain streams, and bird sanctuaries.

Merritt also advocates the use of music (classical) to unleash the creative powers of the mind. In workshops conducted for all age groups across the North American continent, she plays a series of classical selections and asks participants to answer the following questions: Did the music calm you? Did it energize you? Did it put you in a dreamlike state? Did it stir up your emotions? Did it focus your mind? Merritt contends that different music styles open up a universe of thoughts and images that lead listeners on a journey of creative expression.

Just as mental imagery can be performed anywhere you have a chance to close your eyes and visualize, the familiar sounds of music can be recreated in your mind without benefit of a tape recording. This practice is called audio imagery, or associative recall, and means that a song can be called up and played on the mind's own internal tape deck. An example might include thinking of the first couple of notes of Beethoven's fifth symphony, which then triggers the mind to "play" a portion of the melody or the entire melody. With repeated exposure to and practice of audio imagery, a desired song that promotes relaxation in an individual can be recalled and played any time, particularly when one feels the need to relax in the midst of stress.

Steps to Initiate Music Therapy

Because of the vast array of musical compositions, it should be recognized that individuals' tastes vary greatly with regard to this relaxation technique. Despite personal differences, however, certain factors are associated with effective music therapy as a relaxation technique (and possible coping strategy). The following suggestions will enhance its effects as a relaxation technique:

1. *Musical selection.* The type of music most conducive to relaxation and return to homeostasis involves two criteria:

a. *The music should be an instrumental or acoustic selection with a slow tempo.* This can include classical, improvisational jazz, New Age, or any music that falls in this domain. There are several types of classical music of varying tempo and rhythm, just as there are many types of jazz, from improvisation to fusion. Not all types of classical or improvisational jazz are slow or relaxing. Typically, classical composers wrote three movements of varying tempos in symphonies and concertos, the andante and adagio movements considered by most to be calming in nature. Research conducted by Dr. Charles Schmid at the Lind Institute found that classical music sequenced in a particular composition of pitch, tempo, and instrumentation proved most conducive to relaxation. The Baroque period was renowned for its calming musical pieces. And now New Age music has begun to integrate synthesized music and sounds of nature including ocean waves, babbling brooks, dolphins, and songbirds. Particular groups of instruments are credited with contributing to different components of wellness. According to musicologist H. A. Lingerman, brass and percussion instruments parallel the strengths of physical well-being; woodwinds and strings (violins) strengthen emotional well-being; strings (cello and piano) augment mental well-being; and synthesizers and harps nurture the soul.

b. *The selection should be enjoyable rather than disturbing.* No one piece of music will relax everyone equally. Experimentation with and an open mind to new musical compositions will lead you to a type of music that is right for you. A range of relaxation music can be found in special sections in record stores, special radio programs, and friends' music libraries. Music that is grating or agitating to listen to will promote stress rather than reduce it. Find something you like and build on this style.

2. *Listening environment.* To fully enjoy the effects of music therapy, all interruptions should be minimized or eliminated so that full attention can be directed toward this special auditory stimulation, and for a sufficient length of time. In his book *Sound Health,* author/composer Steven Halpern states that listening environment is second in importance only to selection of music. He believes that music therapy is best practiced at home in a peaceful environment. Once comfortable with this skill, you can then transfer it to the office or other stress-producing environments.

3. *Postures and cognition.* There are two suggested postures for music therapy. The first and most effective one is similar to a meditative posture, where the individual either sits or reclines in a comfortable position with eyes closed to minimize distractions. In this posture, a right-hemisphere cognitive style is adopted; that is, you accept the music without analysis of composition or instrumentation. Simply surround yourself with the music and let unedited thoughts appear on the mind's screen without subjectivity or emotional attachment. The second posture is an active one where the music serves as background sound to balance other auditory stimulation in your environment, whether you are involved with housework, homework, or office work. This approach also calls for a right-hemisphere cognitive style; that is, you assume an attitude of acceptance and harmony with your environment, seeing yourself as part of the whole, not the whole.

4. *Making your own music.* A more active style of music therapy is making your own music. This can mean singing, humming or whistling a song, or playing an instrument. It can also include programming your own cassette tapes with selections you want to play when you need or want to relax. As was illustrated by the monks who sang Gregorian chants, singing a song you like can be an uplifting experience. Try it sometime when you are down in the dumps. Before the advent of radios and VCRs, most homes had a piano or guitar. Playing an instrument also can be very rewarding, even if there is no audience but yourself. And at times when you can neither sing nor play an instrument, you can always carry a song in your heart.

Best Application of Music Therapy

Thanks to advances in technology, music today is very portable. It can be played in a host of environments, such as while driving a car, sitting in an office, or walking on a sidewalk, to create a more tranquil setting. In these cases, music is often used as background sound, an almost unconscious attempt to promote physiological calmness, while one's attention is directed elsewhere. Although this can certainly be effective, the ideal setting for getting the most out of music therapy is the home environment, with quality time dedicated *solely* to the enjoyment of each note. Audio imagery, like mental imagery, can be done anywhere. Music can affect any mood. Your favorite melody can dissolve anger in milliseconds. And if you have ever heard anyone whistling in the face of fear, remember that this, too, is effective at calming the body.

Summary

+ Music therapy is defined as "the systematic application of music by the music therapist to bring about helpful changes in the emotional or physical health of the client," and the "ability to experience an altered state of physical arousal and subsequent mood by processing a progression of musical notes of varying tone, rhythm, and instrumentation for a pleasing effect."

+ Music therapy includes both listening to and creating music for a soothing effect.

+ Music as therapy has been used for hundreds of generations. Music is also the most popular way to relax for Americans.

+ Music is energy made audible through sound waves. These waves are measured in vibrations (oscillations) per second and measured in terms of decibels. A sound above 120 decibels is known to cause damage to neural tissue in the ear. Tinnitus is the clinical name for buzzing and ringing in the ear caused by repeated exposure to high-decibel noises.

+ There are three explanations for how music promotes the relaxation effect. Biochemical theory states that music is a sensory stimulus that is processed through the sense of hearing. Sound vibrations are chemically changed into nervous impulses that activate either the sympathetic or parasympathetic nervous system. Entrainment theory suggests that oscillations produced by music are received by the human energy field and various physiological systems entrain with or match the hertz (oscillation) of the music. Metaphysical theory suggests that music is divine in nature.

+ Various clinical studies demonstrate that, under certain conditions, music can alter physiological parameters as well as mood; however, the exact means for these effects are still not completely understood.

+ For music therapy to be fully effective as a relaxation technique, it is best that the music be instrumental (without lyrics). Type of music selected, listening environment, posture, and attitude also affect the quality of the relaxation response.

Concepts and Terms

Auditory imagery
Biochemical theory
Decibel
Entrainment theory
Essentic forms
Hertz

Metaphysical theory
Mozart Effect
Music therapy
Perceptual quality
Pitch

Rhythm
Shumann resonanace
Tone
Timbre
Tinnitus

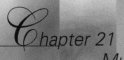

Self-Assessment

1. Do you use music therapy to promote relaxation?   Yes   No

2. What types of music do you like to listen to? Place a checkmark by all that apply.

   Classical _____   Rock & roll _____

   Jazz _____   Blues _____

   Acoustic _____   Reggae _____

   Environmental _____ Rap _____

   New Age _____   Other _____

3. Out of those categories, distinguish between types of music you find energizing (rock) and those you find calming (environmental).

   Energizing   **Calming**

   1._____   1._____
   2._____   2._____
   3._____   3._____
   4._____   4._____

4. Who are your favorite artists of calming music?

   1._____   6._____
   2._____   7._____
   3._____   8._____
   4._____   9._____
   5._____   10._____

5. Do you play a musical instrument?   Yes   No

   If so, which one(s)?

6. Singing is also an important part of music therapy. Do you ever find yourself singing in the shower, or while driving the car, walking, or sitting at home, work, or school?   Yes   No

References and Resources

Alvin, J. *Music Therapy.* Basic Books, New York, 1975.

American Music Therapy Association. 8455 Colesville Road, Suite 100. Silver Spring, MD 20910. www.amta.com.

Barr, F. Melanin, *Medical Hypothesis* 11:1–140, 1983.

Becker, R. *Cross Currents.* Tarcher Press, Los Angeles, 1990.

Bentov, I. *Stalking the Wild Pendulum: On the Mechanics of Consciousness.* Destiny Books, Rochester, VT, 1988.

Bonny, H. and Savary, L. *Music and Your Mind: Listening with a New Consciousness.* Harper & Row, New York, 1973.

Bonny, H.L. The State of the Art of Music Therapy, *The Arts in Psychotherapy* 24(1):65–73, 1997.

Borling, J. and Scartelli, J. The Effects of Sequenced versus Simultaneous EMG Biofeedback and Sedative Music on Frontalis Relaxation Training, *Journal of Music Therapy* 23:157–165, 1986.

Bryant, D. R. A Cognitive Approach to Therapy through Music, *Journal of Music Therapy* 24:27–34, 1987.

Campbell, D. *Introduction to the Musical Brain.* Magnamusic-Baton, St. Louis, MO, 1984.

Campbell, D. *Music: Physician for Times to Come.* Quest Books, Wheaton IL, 1991.

Campbell, D. *The Mozart Effect.* Avon Books, New York, 1997.

Campbell, D. *The Roar of Silence.* Theosophical Society, Wheaton, IL, 1990.

Capurso, A. *Music and Your Emotions.* Liveright, New York, 1952.

Chance, P. Music Hath Charms to Sooth a Throbbing Head, *Psychology Today* 21(2):14, 1984.

Clynes, M., ed. *Music, Mind, and Brain: The Neuropsychology of Music.* Plenum Press, New York, 1982.

Cousins, N. *Anatomy of an Illness as Perceived by the Patient.* Bantam Books, New York, 1979.

Crussi-Gonzalez, F. Hearing Pleasures, *Health* 21(3):65–71, 1989.

Davis, W. and Thaut, M. The Influence of Preferred Relaxing Music on Measures of State Anxiety, Relaxation, and Physiological Responses, *Journal of Music Therapy* 26:168–187, 1989.

Diamond, J. *The Life Energy in Music,* vol. I & II. Archaeus Press, New York, 1983.

Floyd, J., Kirkpatrick, J., and Rider, M. The Effect of Music, Imagery, and Relaxation on Adrenal Corticosteroids and the Re-entrainment of Circadian Rhythms, *Journal of Music Therapy* 22:46–58, 1985.

Gardner, K. *Sounding the Inner Landscape: Music as Medicine.* Caduceus Publications, Stonington, ME, 1990.

Goldman, J. Sound as Subtle Energy, Sound Colloquium, Loveland, CO, August 1998.

Golin, M. New Age Prescription for Sound Health, *Prevention* 40:66, 1988.

Gutheil, E. *Music and Your Emotions.* Liveright, New York, 1952.

Halpern, S. *Tuning the Human Instrument.* Spectrum Research Institute, Belmont, CA, 1978.

Halpern, S., with Savary, L. *Sound Health: The Music and Sounds that Make Us Whole.* Harper & Row, San Francisco, 1985.

Hanser, S.B. *The New Music Therapist's Handbook.* Berklee Pr Publisher, Milwaukee, 2000.

Hanser, S. Music Therapy and Stress-Reduction Research, *Journal of Music Therapy* 22:193–206, 1985.

Hanser, S. B., Larson, S. C. and O'Connell, A. The Effects of Music on Relaxation of Expectant Mothers during Labor, *Journal of Music Therapy* 20:50–58, 1983.

Heline, C. *Healing and Regeneration through Music.* New Age Press, Santa Barbara, CA, 1969.

Hodges, D. *Handbook of Music Psychology.* National Association of Music Therapy, Lawrence, KS, 1980.

Hoffman, N. *Hear the Music! A New Approach to Mental Health.* Star, Boynton Beach, FL, 1974.

Kenny, C. B. Music, A Whole Systems Approach, *Music Therapy* 5:3–11, 1985.

Kumar, A. et al. Music Therapy Increases Serum Melatonin Levels in Patients with Alzheimer's Disease, *Alternative Therapies in Health and Medicine* 5(6):49–57, 1999.

Larkin, M. Musical Healing, *Health* 17:12, 1985.

Leblanc, A. An Interactive Therapy of Music Preference, *Journal of Music Therapy* 19:28–42, 1982.

Lehmann, A.C. Affective Responses to Everyday Life Events and Music Listening, *Psychology of Music* 25:84–90, 1997.

Leonard, G., *The Silent Pulse*. Bantam New Age Books, New York, 1981.

Licht, S. *Music in Medicine*. New England Conservatory of Music, Boston, 1946.

Lingerman, H., *The Healing Energies of Music*. Theophysical Society, Wheaton, IL, 1983.

Llaurado, J. G. and Sances, A. *Biological and Clinical Effects of Low-Frequency Magnetic and Radiational Fields*. Charles Thomas, Springfield, IL, 1974.

Logan, T. and Roberts, A. The Effects of Different Types of Relaxation Music on Tension Levels, *Journal of Music Therapy* 21:177–183, 1984.

Marwick, C. Music Therapists Chime in with Data on Medical Results. *JAMA* 283:731–734, 2000.

McClellan, R. *The Healing Forces of Music*. New House Publications, Amity, NY, 1988.

McCraty, R. The Effects of Different Types of Music on Mood, Tension and Mental Clarity, *Alternative Therapies in Health and Medicine* 4(1):75–84, 1998.

McKinney, C.H. et al. Effects of Guided Imagery and Music (GIM) Therapy on Mood and Cortisol in Healthy Adults, *Health Psychology* 16(4):390–400, 1997.

Merritt, S. *Mind, Music, and Imagery*. Plume Books, New York, 1990.

Michael, D. E. *Music Therapy*. Thomas Books, New York, 1985.

Mitchum Report On Stress. Research & Forecast Inc. New York, NY, 1990.

Monroe, R. *Journeys out of the Body*. Bantam Books, New York, 1993.

Nelson, N. and Weatherbs, R. Necessary Angels: Music and Healing in Psychotherapy. *The Journal of Humanistic Psychology* 38:101–108, 1998.

Parnes, S. J. *Visionizing*. D. O. K. Publishers, East Aurora, NY, 1988.

Priestly, M. *Music Therapy in Action*. St. Martin's, New York, 1975.

Retallack, D. *The Sound of Music and Plants*. DeVorss, Santa Monica, CA, 1973.

Rider, M. S., Floyd, J. W., and Kirkpatrick, J. The Effect of Music, Imagery, and Relaxation on Adrenal Corticosteroids and the Re-entrainment of Circadian Rhythms, *Journal of Music Therapy* 22(1):46–58, 1985.

Rosenfeld, A. Music: The Beautiful Disturber, *Psychology Today* 19:48–57, 1985.

Scartletti, J. The Effect of EMG Feedback and Sedative Music, EMG Biofeedback Only, and Sedative Music Only on Frontalis Muscle Relation Ability, *Journal of Music Therapy* 21:67–78, 1984.

Scartelli, J. The Effect of Sedative Music on Electromyographic Biofeedback-Assisted Relaxation Training of Spastic Cerebral Palsied Adults, *Journal of Music Therapy* 14:210–218, 1982.

Schmid, C. *Relax with the Classics*. Lind Institute, San Francisco, CA, 1987.

Schrader, C. Modern Alchemy: Holistic High Tech, *Harper's Bazaar* 3316 (April):161, 1988.

Scofield, M. and Teich, M. Mind-Bending Music, *Health* 19:69–76, 1987.

Solomon, A., and Heller, G. Historical Research in Music Therapy, *Journal of Music Therapy* 19:161–177, 1982.

Stratton, V. and Zalanowski, A. The Relationship between Music, Degree of Liking, and Self-Reported Relaxation, *Journal of Music Therapy* 21:184–192, 1984.

Summer, L. Imagery and Music, *Journal of Mental Imagery* 9:83–90, 1985.

Thayer, G. *Music in Therapy*. Macmillan, New York, 1968.

Tomatis, A. *La Nuit Uterine*. Editions Stock, Paris, 1981.

Trapp, M. A. *The Trapp Family Singers*. Doubleday, New York, 1949.

Waldrop, M. Why Do We Like Music? *Science* 227:36, 1985.

Watson, A., and Drury, N. *Healing Music: The Harmonic Path to Wholeness*. Prism Press, Dorset, England, 1987.

Westle, M. Music Is Good Medicine, *Newsweek* Sept. 21:103, 1998.

Chapter 22 Massage Therapy

Oh, that the water softens

the rocks with time, may thy

hands craft my body soft like

the weathered rocks.

—Anonymous

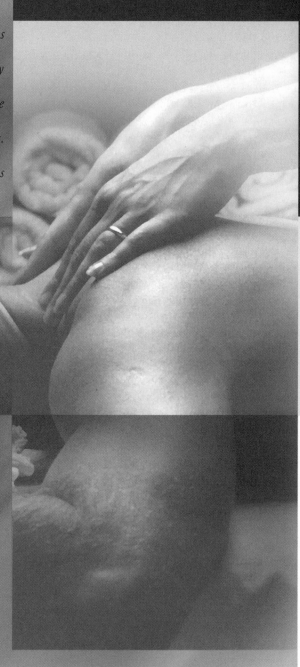

Of all the relaxation techniques available for reducing symptoms of stress, one requires special assistance: the muscle massage. While you can certainly rub and knead your own muscles to relieve soreness in some reachable body regions, an extra set of hands is a virtual necessity to get the full relaxation effect. Muscle tension is the premier symptom of the stress response, and massage therapy is the best technique to diminish it. Professional muscle massage is defined as the manipulation of skin, muscles, ligaments, and connective tissue for the purposes of decreasing muscle tension and increasing physical comfort of musculature and its surrounding joints. But massage therapy has a more profound effect than manipulation of tissue. In a very "touch-conscious" society, professional physical contact can nurture a sense of connectedness otherwise missing in our lives. In its own way, muscle massage creates harmony among the body, mind, and spirit.

In the past decade, as the world has grown smaller through increased accessibility of information and travel, a greater appreciation of muscle massage has spread throughout the global village, particularly the United States. According to articles in *U.S. News, Time,* and *Newsweek,* **massage therapy** has now hit the mainstream as an acceptable healing modality. This technique gained acceptance in the Western cultures as a result of the health and fitness boom of the 1980s, especially in health clubs and corporate settings in addition to the routine practices in professional- and amateur-sport locker rooms.

Massage therapy is now a bona fide practice certified through the American Massage Therapy Association (AMTA). Certification requires a six-month program of over 500 hours of classroom instruction in an approved school and three years of professional experience. Since the inception of the AMTA in 1943, the popularity of this practice has grown: as of 2001, there were 250 approved massage schools and over 47,000 certified members.

To be sure, an extra set of hands doesn't come cheap. Rates range from $30 to $80 per massage, depending on length of time and location involved (home visits are usually more). In some cases, corporations and insurance companies now cover the cost as a medical benefit for employees. Despite the expense, which is usually regarded as a luxury by some, anyone who has had a professional muscle massage will testify that the benefits are well worth it. The new focus of massage therapy is the use of warm stones (stone therapy) to heat muscle tissue to relieve soreness, stiffness, and pain. Regardless of the approach, the use of touch relieves stress.

Historical Perspective

Massage therapy has been in use for over 3,000 years, the earliest references to it being in Chinese treatises on medicine. It was believed that touch not only relieved muscle soreness, but also contributed a profound healing quality to one's life force or spiritual energy. Greek philosopher and physician Hippocrates, the "father of modern medicine," advocated a mind-body approach to physicians' care. In one of his writings he stated, "The physician must be experienced in many things, but most assuredly in rubbing." Muscle massage was apparently practiced in several other ancient cultures as well; records of the Persians, Hindus, and Egyptians all refer to it. The practice of healing touch is not even specific to the human species: many other members of the animal kingdom are known to use elements of therapeutic touch as well.

While there are several types of massage therapy, they all seem to fall into two categories: those originating in the East, particularly China and India; and those deriving from Scandinavian forms. Through the influences of these cultures, massage has long flourished as a viable relaxation technique in Asia and northern Europe. By contrast, Victorian cultural influences on the United States of a century ago made this therapeutic method less than socially acceptable. Even today, physical contact (of any kind) is not a dominant trait in America. Nevertheless, human beings in every culture need some regular form of healthy touch for their well-being.

The Need for Human Touch

In 1999 John Naisbitt, author of *Megatrends 2000,* said, "The more high technology around us, the greater the need for human touch." As he mentions in his book, high technology has been repeatedly cited as a reason for increased stress. Naisbitt's comment reveals the insight that as we move closer and closer to a full technology society, we distance ourselves further and further from the basic elements that used to provide physical, emotional, and spiritual sustenance. Even before the high-tech age, though, American culture was known for its habits and customs minimizing physical contact. In Naisbitt's opinion, technological advancement has only exaggerated this cultural idiosyncracy. Naisbitt is not alone in his thinking. Several health practitioners recognize what they call a "famine of touch," or touch deprivation, in the United States. But human touch is as much a necessity as air, food, and water. Clinical reports assert that babies deprived of touch can actually die. Tongue in cheek, but very serious about their message, health practitioners Bob Czimbal and Maggie Zadikov explain that people need vitamin T (touch) for their well-being (see Table 22.1) just like the other vitamins. So as the mind-body-spirit relationship continues to be acknowledged in the United States, active interest in the effects of massage therapy has developed, leading also to several research studies on this topic.

Massage Therapy Research

Research in the area of massage therapy has involved several demographic populations, including premature babies, cocaine-addicted babies, college students, recovering alcoholics, and the elderly, to name just a few. Overall, the findings of these studies indicates that massage (primarily Swedish massage) is a very viable technique to promote physical relaxation as well as other health-related benefits. Dr. Tiffany Field, who heads the Touch Research Institute at the University of Miami School of Medicine, has conducted several studies on the effect of massage on infant health. In a reliability study with Scafidi and associates (1990) (designed to validate previous findings) it was revealed that three fifteen-minute periods of massage therapy for three consecutive

Vitamin T (Touch)

Table 22.1

Type	Level	Examples
Public touch	T7	Introductions with handshakes
Professional touch	T6	Touch dispensed by professionals
Social touch	T5	Greetings, talk touch, social dance
Friendly touch	T4	Hugging, playful touch, comforting
Family touch	T3	Cuddling, hugging, kissing
Special touch	T2	Holding, sleeping, hugging, dancing
Personal touch	T1	Massage, bathing, time in nature
Sexual touch	TS	Passionate pleasure involving consenting adults

Vitamin T Terminology

Leveling—Achieving harmony between two people with differing comfort levels regarding touch, usually by expressing the less intimate level (e. g., T7 or T6)

Intimacy—Level of friendship, familiarity, or closeness with another person, reflected by the frequency, intensity, and duration of contact

Primary deficiency—An inadequate supply of Vitamin T

Space invaders—People who invade your personal space, physically or verbally

Ouch—A painful touch experience (Touch minus T = Ouch)

Stop—Refusal skills for dealing with space invaders or ouches

FROM B. Czimbal and M. Zadikov, *Vitamin T: A Guide to Healthy Touch* (Portland, OR: Open Book, 1991).

hours over a ten-day period stimulates growth in premature babies (Fig. 22.1). In twenty babies who received "tactile kinesthetic stimulation," a 21 percent average increase in weight gain per day was observed. Perhaps more impressive, these babies left the hospital an average of five days earlier than control subjects. Thus, Field is of the opinion that touch therapy is crucial in the development of the infant into childhood. Her theory is that those infants who are "touch deprived" (receive less than adequate physical nurturing) manifest several mind-body problems throughout life.

Massage was also studied by McKechnie and colleagues (1983). They found that connective-tissue massage aided in reducing resting heart rate, skin resistance, and muscle tension (as recorded by EEG), thus indicating that this mode of relaxation was beneficial in reducing the symptoms associated with anxiety. The combined effects of exercise and muscle massage on mood in college students were examined by Weinberg et al. (1988), who discovered that when combined, these two variables produced mood enhancement exceeding that by exercise alone. Subjects maintained high levels of "vigor," while at the same time they reported noticeably decreased levels of muscle tension, fatigue, anxiety, depression, and anger. In a similar study, Channon (1986) compared massage therapy with progressive muscular relaxation (see Chapter 24).

Figure 22.1 Research now indicates that touch (infant massage) is critical to babies' emotional development.

She found that as a relaxation technique, massage was far more effective in reducing muscle tension than Jacobson's relaxation technique. Using biofeedback technology, Naliboff and colleagues (1991) looked at the effect of muscle massage on skin conductance, skin temperature, and electromyographical activity in subjects receiving a thirty-minute "dermapoint massage" to forearm and trapezius muscles. This treatment resulted in a significant decrease in muscle activity and an increase in skin temperature of the forearm.

In the then Soviet Union, Kolpakov and Rumyantseva (1987) conducted a study to determine what effect regular eye massage would have on vision and eye fatigue in factory employees. They found that this treatment was effective in decreasing visual strain, and recommended massage as a viable form of medical treatment. In Japanese subjects, a daily twenty-minute facial massage, as reported by Jodo and colleagues (1988), seems to produce greater physiological homeostasis, including a greater sense of perceived relaxation, compared to controls. There have been many claims that massage influences biochemical reactions (hormones and enzymes) within the body as well as changes to peripheral body tissues. In an attempt to investigate these claims, one study by Green and Green (1987) measured the effect of massage therapy on biochemical constituents in saliva (SIgA) and cortisol. They found that a twenty-minute massage significantly increased salivary immunoglobin, suggesting that massage may actually enhance immune function. Likewise, Day and associates (1987) found that massage therapy had a significant effect on serum levels of beta endorphins and B-lipoproteins.

With regard to chemical dependency, a study conducted by Adcock (1987) noted that when patients combined drug or alcohol treatment with massage therapy, the detoxification period was shorter, and subjects reported a greater sense of physical relaxation and self-acceptance and self-esteem. Gauthier (1990) studied the use of massage therapy in children diagnosed as emotionally deprived as an effective part of a multimodal-therapy approach. From these and other studies, it can be concluded unequivocally that massage therapy is a viable technique to promote relaxation and several other health-related benefits.

Stress With a Human Face

CAROLYN NELKA DIDN'T START OFF AS A massage therapist. Actually, her career began as a nurse, but that was years ago. As a young widow with two children, Carolyn transitioned from the field of nursing to special education and then again to fundraising for a small private college in Baltimore, Maryland. The seven years at the College of Notre Dame, as the Director of Planned Giving, eventually took its toll on her. A pinched nerve became her Achilles heel and it was a message she couldn't avoid any longer.

"Here I was, my kids out of college, and my life is supposed to begin, right?" she said. "And there I was flat on my back—all because of stress. There was so much stress in my life, I couldn't deal with it. So I quit my job," she sighed in remembrance.

Reflecting on that time in her life, she said, "I am convinced that our bodies speak to us. Mine began yelling at me until the pain got so bad that I was forced to listen." Massage became one of the modalities of healing that Carolyn incorporated into her life. Although she admits it wasn't the sole treatment that healed her, frequent sessions of massage therapy taught her

how to recognize the accumulation of stress in the form of muscle tensions, and what to do about it.

An introductory course in massage at the Baltimore School of Massage enticed Carolyn to enroll for the entire accredited program. During her second year, she was exposed to the concepts of bioenergy medicine and Reiki. Becoming trained in Reiki as well, she integrated this technique with what she learned in the massage program and soon developed a thriving practice in bodywork.

But Carolyn's interest didn't stop there. She went on to help teach the infant massage program at Carroll Community College, based on a program designed by the School of Nursing at the University of Denver, and has since been asked to instruct workshops at the Baltimore School of Massage as well. ✦

Types of Massage

Massage can take many forms. Typically, licensed massage therapists are trained in most, if not all, of these techniques and then go on to specialize in one particular style. Some integrate various types in a synthesis all their own. There are five major types of massage this chapter will focus on—shiatsu, Swedish, rolfing, Myofascial Release, and sports massage—each with its own nuances. Additional methods worth mentioning, all classified as bodywork, include: Traeger, zero balancing, postural integration, cranial-sacral therapy, Reiki, Feldenkries, reflexology, and trigger-point therapy.

Although the primary benefit of massage is muscle relaxation, several therapists claim additional health effects, including increased blood and lymph flow

(making one less susceptible to illnesses), and a general sense of well-being. Many people add emotional well-being, which also contributes to the overall health of the individual. Knowing that emotional well-being is so closely tied to physical health, these claims are not unfounded. The healing power of touch has long been accepted in many cultures, and is now gaining recognition in the United States. While the techniques of massage are clearly directed toward physical constituents, primarily muscle, connective tissue, and bone and nerve endings, the neural, hormonal, and immune systems may unite for a healing effect yet to be clinically understood. Above all else, it is important to remember that the mind and body are one, not two separate entities; and relaxing the body through massage may certainly have a cross-over effect on other aspects of well-being. For this reason, massage therapy is now being fully integrated into medical practices, in nursing, physical therapy, and other aspects of clinical medicine. The five styles presented here are among the most popular styles of muscle-massage therapy.

Shiatsu

Shiatsu, also known as acupressure, is based on the concept of freeing blocked energy currents within the body. The term *shiatsu* translates as "finger pressure" (*shi* = finger, *atsu* = pressure). It is a distant cousin of acupuncture, and applies force through finger pressure as well as forearm, elbow, knee, and palm pressure instead of needles to unblock energy congestion (Fig. 22.2). In this ancient Japanese practice, based on the concept of *chi* or life force, pressure is applied to specific body locations that house the crossroads or meridians of energy. These energy paths in the body seem to parallel yet are unrelated to the nervous system. The manual application of gentle pressure relieves blockage, thus allowing free-flowing energy essential to health and longevity. On the surface, shiatsu appears only to relax muscle tension. Upon closer examination, it is believed to have a healing quality through the subtle anatomy as well (see Chapter 3). The philosophy of shiatsu, derived from the concepts of yin and yang, is that interruptions in the flow of energy create an imbalance in the life force that may manifest in a host of physical ailments. Restoration of

energy through energy channels is thought to relieve ailments specific to the site of blockage, which in many cases is distant from the region of discomfort.

There are fourteen segments or major meridians in the body. Points along these meridians, where pressure is applied, are called *tsubos*. The application and release of pressure to *tsubos* is thought to remove an energy block caused by muscle tension or toxins in the muscle tissue that can cause cramps. Once a specific *tsubo* is located, about twenty pounds of pressure are applied in a brisk, circular motion for fifteen to twenty seconds. This is then repeated on the equivalent pressure point on the opposite side of the body. Shiatsu uses primarily the thumbs to single out pressure points on the body with both a soft approach (the first interphalangeal joint) or a hard approach (the tip of the distal phalanx).

Although shiatsu is used specifically to reduce muscle tension, it has also been practiced to relieve sinus aches and tension headaches. Research investigating *tsubos* has found they are indeed in close proximity to neural plexuses and stretch receptors, validating the premise of this pressure-relief technique. While the effects of acupressure can be felt immediately, practitioners agree that daily applications for seven to ten days bring full restoration and energy balance. Shiatsu is often preferred over other types of massage for its simplicity; individuals can remain fully clothed while being treated. This type of massage is often used by individuals in the performing arts such as ballet. Other advantages of shiatsu include that: (1) it has no adverse side effects, (2) it can be practiced on individuals of any age, and (3) it allows for relaxation of the entire body.

Swedish Massage

Known to Americans as the total body massage, the Swedish or Western massage, created by Swedish fencing master and gymnast Peter Heinrik Ling, emphasizes decreased muscle tension and increased circulation. It is currently the most commonly practiced massage style in the United States and Europe. In Swedish massage, the individual disrobes and lies face down on the table with a towel over the buttocks. Massage oils or lotions are used on the regions of application to nourish the skin and avoid irritating friction by the massage therapist's hands. Relaxing music is often played in the background.

Figure 22.2 The practice of shiatsu is based on the premise that pressure applied to specific points on the body can release energy congested in the meridians of the body's subtle anatomy. Not all pressure points directly correspond to the area of the body that is sore or distressed.

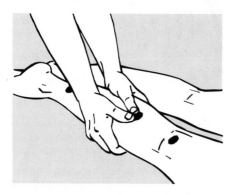

There are five progressive steps in Swedish massage. The first movement, called *effleurage* (Fig. 22.3), is a light stroking or long rhythmic striations along the length of the muscle fibers, typically done with the thumbs and generally in the direction of the heart. A motion to begin to limber muscles and prepare the body for the next phase, it may also include light strokes along the spine up to the base of the head. The second movement, *petrissage* (Fig. 22.4), is a series of rolls, rings, and squeezes made with either the finger tips or the palm of the hand. *Petrissage* motions include a little more pressure than is involved in the first stage. The third phase of Swedish massage is referred to as *friction* (Fig. 22.5) and involves a deep kneading action of muscle tissue between the fingers and thumbs. Friction can also include deep, small circular motions with the thumb, knuckles, or finger points to extend the penetration of friction beyond the surface of the skin. The fourth movement, *tapotement* (Fig. 22.6), similar in appearance to the percussive strokes of karate chops, is performed in specific regions to activate or revive nerve cells within extremely hard muscle tissue. The last phase, *vibration* (Fig. 22.7), is described as a "trembling shaking gesture" to increase circulation throughout a desired body region.

The area targeted by Swedish massage is the posterior side of the body—calves, hamstrings, lower back, neck, and shoulders. These muscle groups are most prone to tension from sleeping, walking, standing, and sitting postures because in these positions, muscles are shortened (contracted) for an extended period of time. Sleeping in a fetal position, for example, leaves the hamstrings and calf muscles contracted for six to eight hours. These lifestyle postures can create imbalance and disalignment in both anterior and posterior muscles.

Rolfing

If styles of massage were classified, as are the martial arts, from softest to hardest, rolfing would be designated as the hardest of all the massage techniques. In fact, there are those who would describe rolfing as physical torture due to the deep tissue work. Rolf therapists deny that rolfing is a type of massage at all, although like massage, they define it as "a manipulation of muscle and soft connective tissue" (Fig. 22.8). The technique of rolfing was developed by Ida Rolf

Effleurage.

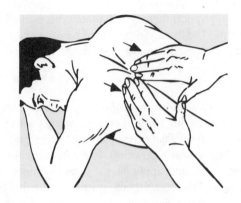

Figure 22.3

Petrissage.

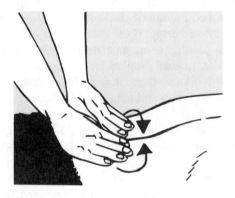

Figure 22.4

Friction.

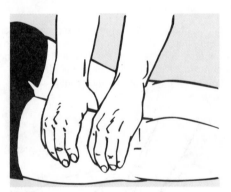

Figure 22.5

over a fifty-year period starting in 1925. Rolf, a researcher for the Rockefeller Foundation specializing in the study of collagen and connective tissue, hypothesized that human musculature begins to lose alignment from repeated movement established in

Figure 22.6 Tapotement.

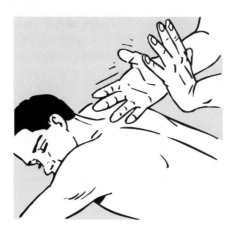

Figure 22.7 Vibration.

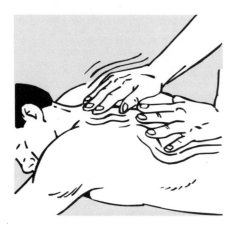

Figure 22.8 Rolfing is a very deep, penetrating massage used to realign muscles that have become shortened due to poor posture or maladaptive body positions such as sitting at computers or desks.

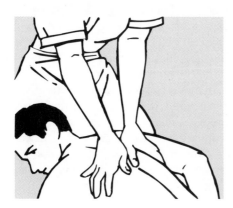

childhood and carried through to adulthood. These imbalances result from a shortening and thickening of the myofascia surrounding muscle fibers. Rolf's theory suggests that since the human skeletal structure is held in place by soft tissue (muscles, tendons, and ligaments), a muscle contracted for prolonged periods of time will pull the skeletal frame out of its natural alignment. Rolfing borrows the concept that the physical whole is greater than the sum of its muscular parts. The premise of rolfing is that deep muscular penetration can correct imbalances through slight but repeated alterations of body structure. If body segments become realigned, then the body as a whole can function more efficiently.

While other massage techniques apply gentle to moderate pressure, rolfing involves deep "digging" into soft tissue, often separating layers of muscles and stretching and lengthening them with the hands, elbows, and sometimes the entire body weight of the massage therapist. This technique is not advocated for everyone. Rather, it is suggested for highly muscular individuals or those suffering from intense stress-related problems that manifest in extreme muscular tightness such as lower back pain due to poor hip alignment and neck and shoulder pain. Rolfing therapists assert that changes in "pressure stretches" and muscle-fascia alignment over ten sessions can be maintained for improved health. While the initial manipulation is considered painful, individuals who experience this technique indicate that overall the effects are quite satisfying.

Myofascial Release

Not all forms of physical therapy are created equal, especially when one considers the holistic focus of Myofascial Release. Frustrated with the mechanistic approach to health care, specifically as it applied to physical manipulation, John Barnes, a physical therapist, searched for a greater understanding of the mind-body connection as it applied to the more clinical applications of bodywork. What led John on this search early in his career was the frustration he felt when, after restoring a sense of alignment and pain-free comfort in his patients, he would notice that their symptoms would reappear soon after they left his office. His search led him to all corners of the globe, to courses in acupuncture, joint mobilization, muscle energy, and bioenergy techniques. The synthesis of his experiences, well grounded in the fundamentals of physical therapy, soon became known as Myofascial Release. In the words of John Barnes, "Myofascial Release is the three-dimensional application of sustained pressure and movement into the fascial system in order to eliminate fascial restrictions and facilitate the emergence of emotional patterns and belief systems that are no longer relevant or are impeding progress."

Rather than placing the emphasis on muscular manipulation, as so many bodyworkers do, Barnes focuses on the fascial (connective) tissue itself, which in truth holds the muscles in place. When fascial strains occur throughout the body, as they will from vigorous movements, trauma, surgery, or the subtleties of the aging process, tightness occurs, resulting in a loss of flexibility and spontaneity of movement. Eventually, fascial tension can distort one's posture through the three-dimensional alignment of the vertebral column. Barnes notes that current estimates suggest that over 90 percent of patients treated in physical therapy have some level of myofascial dysfunction. Unlike various forms of bodywork that are often symptom-specific (massaging the lower back for lower-back pain), the technique of Myofascial Release is holistic in that connections among muscles through the fascia may require distant musculature to be worked in order to release the tension formed through the strands of connective tissue.

How does Myofascial Release differ from a Swedish or sports massage? First, an assessment is made by visually analyzing the human frame, searching for symptoms of distortion and imbalance. Next, by palpating the tissue texture of the various fascial layers, the therapist evaluates symmetry, rate, quality, and intensity of craniosacral rhythm, and possible energy disturbances in the gross or subtle anatomy. Upon locating an area of fascial tension, gentle pressure is applied in the direction of the restriction. With a gentle, sustained pressure, rather than a forced manipulation, the restriction is released. As the collagenous barrier is released, the tissue length is increased. And that's not all. Barnes notes that, because of the dynamic connection between mind and body, a release of fascial tension is often accompanied by an emotional release as well. In Barnes's words, "The tissue seems to hold a consciousness all its own. As releases occurred, patients reported memories or emotions emerging that were connected to past events or traumas. As their fascial systems changed, and the memories or emotions surfaced, patients improved, even though they previously were unresponsive to all forms of traditional care." The goal of Myofascial Release is to eliminate fascial tension, reduce pain and headaches, restore motion, and restore the body's equilibrium. When the body reaches a state of balance or equilibrium, full health is restored, and this, says Barnes, is what life is all about: finding balance.

Sports Massage

In the pursuit of athletic excellence, individuals now train three times as long per day as their colleagues did less than a decade ago. Since the creation of ultra-endurance sports including the triathlon (swimming, cycling, and running), Ride Across America (RAAM), and ultramarathons (50+ miles), athletes are pushing their bodies beyond where they have ever been before. The last thing any competitive athlete wants to encounter is damage to muscle tissue, which may result in prolonged injury. In the world of competitive athletics, any method or device to gain a competitive edge over one's opponent has merit. This edge is often found in the sports massage, which has quickly gained acceptance throughout the athletic community. Since the 1984 Los Angeles Olympics, where sports massage was made available to all athletes at no cost, the demand for such therapists has increased dramatically for all athletic purposes, from high school and college competitions to all levels of amateur and professional sports. It is now considered one of the responsibilities of professional physical trainers.

Sports massage appears to be a hybrid of shiatsu and Swedish massage in its emphasis on both compressive and rhythmic-pumping movements to remove the build-up of lactic acid in the muscles because of repeated contractions. Metabolic by-products of physical exercise, of which the most common is lactic acid, have fatiguing effects on muscle tissue. It is due to the repeated pumping motion to circulate metabolites for removal that has made sports massage so popular. In addition, however, repetitive movement often promotes micro-tears, most commonly at sites where connective tissue attaches to bone. So another purpose of sports massage is the restoration of cell tissue by increasing circulation to stimulate new cell growth.

Spectators at athletic events can watch sports massages being given to athletes during pre-event warmups, as a means to prepare muscles for activity; for postevent restoration; and occasionally during competition, between stages of coupled events. Most commonly, though, they are performed during training seasons to improve the rate of tissue regeneration after each workout. Although to date there is no scientific proof that lactic acid is removed in this manner—lactic acid clears the muscles within two hours (Fox, Bowers, and Foss, 1989)—sports massage enjoys the greatest degree of medical acceptance for healing muscle tissue.

Other Touch Therapies

Other techniques are closely associated with the concepts and practice of muscle massage so they have been placed in this chapter. These types of touch, while not new, have not been studied extensively, and therefore their dynamics for apparently causing relaxation effects are not completely understood. Be that as it may, they make for interesting additions to the category of therapeutic touch.

Aromatherapy.   Aromatherapy is a technique where perfumed scents are used to promote feelings of calmness. The practice of rubbing natural essences on the body to create tranquility dates back to the age of Egyptian pharaohs, when it was commonly believed that the fragrance of flowers and herbs forged a unique bond between body and soul. The technique was revived in the New World in the late 1920s by Dr. Edward Bach, a homeopathic physician, and again in 1990 in Japan, where various fragrances (e.g., peppermint) were introduced into the workplace as a means to stimulate productivity. There appear to be two theories to explain the effectiveness of aromatherapy. The first is that it replaces threatening sensations with pleasurable ones. More specifically, aromatherapy works to desensitize conscious thought, or sensory overload of all five senses, through fragrances perceived to be appealing to the olfactory sense. Many fragrances also elicit powerful thoughts and memories.

Many research studies have been conducted on the efficacy of aromatherapy, mostly in Europe and Asia. The National Association for Holistic Aromatherapy now publishes *Aromatherapy Journal* with a mission to revive the knowledge of medicinal use of aromatic plants and essential oils to its fullest extent. Essential oils have been used in the healing process of cancer patients. One study revealed that cancer patients became more relaxed with Roman chamomile essential oils (Wilkinson et al, 1999). And it is well known that the Sloan Kettering Cancer Hospital used vanilla extract as a means to relax patients who appear anxious to enter the CAT scan apparatus, just as many maternity wards use lavender to relax women ready to give birth.

It is recognized that the brain center processing olfactory sensations is in close proximity to the hypothalamus, which may explain why specific fragrances can elicit memories and their related emotions quite quickly. Furthermore, emotions are part of the right-brain domain, and it is accepted that when one part of the cerebral hemisphere is activated, in this case by positive emotions, then other hemispheric functions are enhanced. The second theoretical approach to aromatherapy involves the application of fragrance-laced oils to the skin during massage. The pores of the skin are believed to soak up the oils and circulate these essences through the body via the circulatory and lymphatic systems, cleansing the body internally and instilling a sense of physiological calmness.

The topic of aromatherapy has gained much interest in the past few years, in both esthetic and clinical practices. Clinical aromatherapy, as defined by Peter Holmes (1995), is a unique healing process achieved through aroma or scent by three means—physiologically, topically, and psychologically. According to Holmes, the main function of clinical aromatherapy is to affect "the specific actions for the purpose of altering human physiology (decreased stress hormone secretion), nurture the skin (through essential oils), and affect the psyche by promoting a sense of mental and emotional relaxation." Most frequently combined with massage therapy, acupuncture, and some nursing practices, clinical aromatherapy is thought to provide a unique dynamic to the integrity of the mind-body-spirit connection in terms of relaxation.

The following are some popular aromatherapy essences and their biomedical applications for stress reduction:

Lavender: Lavender is known primarily as a neurocardiac sedative, triggering the nervous system to decrease neural firing, thus allowing a decrease in resting heart rate and blood pressure. Used in a state of tension, this fragrance is said to calm, uplift, and relax the mind and body.

Juniper: Best known for its muscle-relaxant qualities, juniper is recommended for muscle spasms, fibromyalgia, intestinal and uterine cramps, and peptic ulcers.

Chamomile/Moroccan Blue: A fragrance that calms, nurtures, and regenerates, chamomile is also known as a nervous sedative/relaxant with the ability to help promote decreased blood pressure, act as a bronchodilator, and an anti-allergenic. It is used primarily for situations resulting in suppressed anger, irritability, and resentment.

Vetiver: Vetiver is known as a immunoregulator in that it is said to help boost the integrity of the immune system. It is used for immunodeficiency and autoimmune disorders. This fragrance is noted for its ability to make a person feel more grounded and centered.

Palmarosa: The palmarosa essence is used as an anti-infective agent for cases involving bacteria, virus, or fungus, as well as sinus infections, candidiasis, and Chlamydia. The healing vibration of palmarosa is thought to help boost the constituents of the immune system and bring the body back to a sense of homeostasis.

Hydrotherapy. Baths, hot tubs, and the new flotation tanks, which collectively make up the category of hydrotherapy, are distant relatives to muscle massage. The use of hot baths can be traced back to several ancient cultures, from the Romans and Japanese to the Maori of New Zealand. When the body is immersed in hot water, peripheral blood vessels (those nearest the skin and muscles) dilate. Blood is then shunted from the body's core to the periphery to dissipate heat. This influx of blood to the muscles reduces tension by decreasing neural firing at the site of the motor end plate, and the muscles soon become pliable and incredibly relaxed. The addition of water jets to the hot bath by Candido Jacuzzi in the early 1950s increased the effects of hot tubs, and this relaxation technique remains quite popular today.

In 1980, the movie *Altered States* introduced flotation tanks to the American public. While the movie was science fiction, flotation tanks are very real. The first such tank was created by Dr. John C. Lilly in 1954 at the National Institutes of Health. It was designed to eliminate all external stimuli, including gravity. The subject disrobed and was suspended vertically in water. All senses were basically "turned off." Earlier changes in tank design included the addition of Epsom salts, which allowed the body to float horizontally, and controlled water temperature. Today commercial flotation tanks are similar in concept, but with the use of computer technology they feature lighting, ultraviolet water purification, underwater stereos, and even optional video screens to cater to the preference of clients who can afford the $50 to $100 per flotation hour. Without a doubt, the cessation of sensations has a profound effect on both mind and body, sometimes lasting four to five days after immersion. Research conducted at the National Institutes of Health revealed that flotation-tank therapy decreases the following: depression, insomnia, muscle tension, plasma stress hormones (cortisol and ACTH), resting heart rate, resting blood pressure, anxiety, and physical (musculoskeletal) pain (Hutchinson, 1984). As a result, overall well-being is dramatically increased. Flotation tanks, in fact, are said to provide the ultimate relaxation experience (Harby, 1988).

Pet Therapy. With the recent discovery of a special neuropeptide called beta-endorphin, a natural morphinelike substance secreted by the brain, lymphocytes, and perhaps other cells, new theories quickly developed about its relationship to positive mood change as well as factors that may release it in the body. About the same time, a therapeutic practice was started in several nursing homes, clinical care settings, prisons, and some schools: pet therapy (Fig. 22.9). It was noticed that physical and psychological responses altered favorably when people came in contact with pet animals, suggesting a link between the two discoveries. Pet therapy involves the integration of animals into clinically directed therapeutic activities, particularly through holding and petting small domestic animals, such as cats and dogs, and in some rare cases, swimming with dolphins. In the past few years, pet therapy has moved from cats and dogs making the rounds in nursing homes to riding horses in Virginia and swimming with dolphins in Florida and Hawaii. The new name given to pet therapy is pet-assisted

Figure 22.9 Pet therapy has become quite popular with nursing home patients, widows, and children diagnosed as autistic. Researchers can only speculate what it is about holding and petting an animal that brings about a relaxing response.

therapy. Several years ago, a "pet partners" program was developed for burn victims through Hope Therapy Program of the University of Texas in Houston, in conjunction with the Moody Gardens in Galveston, Texas. Pet Partners, a national pet therapy program, is now located in forty-five states and four countries.

The results of pet therapy are quite remarkable: the tactile contact, combined with new companionship, seems to have a special healing quality. While changes in muscle tension were not investigated, significant changes in resting heart rate, blood pressure, and mood have been observed with interest (Cusack and Smith, 1984; Holden, 1984; Burke, 1992). In the company of pets, resting heart rate and blood pressure showed significant decreases while perceived mood improved. In addition, pet owners felt physically better when they touched and petted their animals. Professor Erika Friedman, at Brooklyn College, notes that survival rates for coronary patients are higher among pet owners than non–pet owners, and that elderly

people who own pets make fewer visits to their physicians (Burke, 1992). The conclusion from these and other findings suggests that physical contact with friendly animals promotes relaxation similar to that associated with meditation and biofeedback. Although the specific physiological factors associated with improved mood remain a mystery in the field of psychoneuroimmunology, current conventional wisdom suggests a strong link between the release of beta-endorphin and other neuropeptides and touch, which can indeed have a healing or restorative effect on the body. Researchers may one day find that the relaxing effect is related to entrainment of the animals' energy field with that of humans (see Chapter 3).

Therapeutic Touch.   Clinical medicine, which for centuries shunned the metaphysical aspects of healing through touch, is slowly beginning to acknowledge the possibility that this type of healing can augment standard medical treatment (see Chapter 3). Therapeutic touch (TT) was made popular by Dolores Krieger, RN, and has been taught to thousands of nurses worldwide. In her book *Hands of Light,* healer Barbara Ann Brennen discusses her collaborative efforts with prominent physicians, particularly in the field of oncology. Like shiatsu, therapeutic touch and bioenergy healing involves the manipulation of blocked energy centers, thus clearing the pathways (chakras) of the human energy field. Rather than applying pressure with the thumbs or palms, however, healing occurs through the laying on of the hands, which "conducts" positive or healing energy through the body's energy field. Similarly, the ancient Japanese Reiki method integrates physical manipulation of muscle and connective tissue with universal energy (*ki*). As the disciplines of physics and clinical medicine expand and the gap of understanding narrows regarding the dynamics of human matter, a greater collaboration of all aspects of healing may unfold.

Physiological and Psychological Benefits

Perhaps the most notable effect of massage therapy is the state of complete physical relaxation one experiences during and immediately after the experience. The application of touch at the site of tense muscles first increases neural reflex receptor activity, causing a dilation of blood vessels and increased circulation. This increase in blood supply apparently decreases neural drive through the afferent neural mechanism. In effect, this desensitizes the nerve endings receiving messages from the brain, thus decreasing muscle tension. Repeated claims have been made that massage cleans the muscles of metabolic waste products through gentle pumping of the circulatory and lymphatic systems; however, no scientific evidence supports this theory. A more likely theory, yet to be proven, is that touch triggers the release of neuropeptides, including betaendorphins, which may neutralize or diminish the effects of metabolic by-products. Despite the fact that many claims are yet unproven scientifically, it is commonly accepted that the effects of massage therapy to the musculoskeletal and neuromuscular systems, including increased flexibility and decreased muscle tension, are unrefuted. In fact, physicians are increasingly referring their patients with lower-back pain, bone fractures, multiple sclerosis, structural bone disease, and arthritis to massage therapists for treatment complementary to their own prescribed medical therapy for these ailments.

The physical effects of massage are only superseded by the emotional experience of relaxation. It appears the mind also benefits from the powers of touch, as described earlier. When the mind is cleared of thought, stress is minimized. The nursing community reports that massages also provide a sense of serenity and security to patients. In a study reported by Cohen (1987), where massage therapy was administered to cancer patients, questionnaires measuring mood and symptoms of distress revealed that massage promoted a greater sense of tranquility and vitality with less lethargy, compared to just "relaxing" in a prone position.

The reduction of tension headaches and other stress-related ailments suggests that there is a significant relationship between mind and body, and that both benefit from this relaxation technique. Massage therapists often comment on the ease with which their clients express themselves verbally while being massaged, suggesting the loosening of mental and emotional blocks as well as muscular knots. Note that there are times when massage is not recommended, for example, when people have skin rashes, severe bruises, and muscle strains; contraindications with which massage therapists are well acquainted.

Massage therapy can be a wonderful supplement to your collection of relaxation techniques. It is suggested, however, that you check the qualifications of the massage therapist, as there are many practitioners who have no certified training. In addition to certification, many states now require that massage therapists become licensed. (The state of New York requires competence in anatomy, physiology, kinesiology, neurology, pathology, hygiene, first aid and CPR, in addition to massage techniques.) For more information, see American Massage Therapy Association in References and Resources.

Summary

+ Muscle massage is the manipulation of skin, muscles, ligaments, and connective tissue for the purpose of decreasing muscle tension and increasing physical comfort in musculature and surrounding joints. This is the one relaxation technique that requires the assistance of someone else to achieve the full relaxation effect.

+ Massage therapy is now a bona fide practice, with over 22,000 practitioners certified through the American Massage Therapy Association. Massage therapists must go through formal education (500 hours of classroom instruction) as well as three years of practice before becoming certified.

+ Massage therapy not only aids in the reduction of muscle tension but provides an essential human need, touch. Research indicates that human touch is vital for well-being, and that as people become more involved with technology there is less human contact, resulting in what some call touch deprivation.

+ Landmark studies by Field showed that infants require human touch to thrive; speculation is that people of all ages need it as well. Other research shows that massage therapy is as effective in promoting the relaxation response as are other forms of relaxation.

+ There are several different types of massage, or bodywork. Swedish massage is the most widely recognized style in the West, but shiatsu, rolfing, Myofascial Release, and sports massage, well known in other parts of the world, are gaining in popularity as well.

+ Aromatherapy, hydrotherapy, pet therapy, and therapeutic touch are other related touch therapies.

+ Studies involving various massage therapies indicate that there is not only a physical relaxation effect, but in many cases an emotional benefit as well.

+ Since the advent of the fitness boom in the late 1970s and early '80s, massage has become a significant aspect of health maintenance. Today several corporations offer muscle massage as part of wellness programs for employees who spend workdays in front of a computer terminal.

Concepts and Terms

American Massage Therapy
  Association
Aromatherapy
Baths
Effleurage
Flotation tanks
Kneading

Massage therapy
Myofascial Release
Pet therapy
Petrissage
Rolfing
Shiatsu
Sports massage

Swedish massage
Tapotement
Therapeutic touch
Tsubos
Vibration

Self-Assessment

Massage therapy has become quite popular in the past five years, yet many people have never received a therapeutic massage.

1. **Have you ever had a session of massage therapy?**   Yes   No

2. **If so, what type of massage therapy did you have?**

   _____

3. **Have you ever had a session of energy work?**   Yes   No

   Reiki   _____

   Polarity therapy   _____

   Reflexology   _____

   Myofascial Release   _____

   Bioenergy healing   _____

   Other   _____

   Can you describe what it felt like?

   _____

   _____

   _____

   _____

   _____

4. **If you have not had a session of massage therapy, what is the reason (money, time, feelings of discomfort about the technique, not sure who to try)?**

   1. _____

   2. _____

   3. _____

References and Resources

Adcock, C. L. Massage Therapy in Alcohol/Drug Treatment, *Alcoholism Treatment Quarterly* 4(3):87–101, 1987.

American Massage Therapy Association, 820 Davis Street, Suite 1W, Evanston, IL 60201–4444. (847) 864-0123.

American Massage Therapy Association, *A Guide to Massage Therapy in America.* Chicago, 1989.

American Massage Therapy Association, *Sport Massage.* Chicago, 1986.

Ashton, J. Holistic Health Six: In Your Hands, *Nursing Times* 80(19): 54, 1984.

Auckett, A. *Baby Massage: Parent–Child Bonding through Touching.* Newmarket Press, New York, 1981.

Bach, E. A. Clinical Comparison between the Action of Vaccines and Homeopathic Remedies, *British Homeopathic Journal* 9:21–24, 1921.

Barber, B. *Sensual Water, A Celebration of Bathing.* Contemporary Books, Chicago, 1978.

Barker S. B. and Dawson, K. S. The Effects of Animal-Assisted Therapy on Anxiety Ratings of Hospitalized Psychiatric Patients, *Psychiatric Services* 49(6):797–801, 1998.

Barnes, J. Myofascial Release: The Search for Excellence. RSI-T-A, Myofascial Treatment Centers, Paoli, PA, 1990.

Barnes, J. Personal Conversation. Sedona, Arizona, August 5, 1995.

Box, D. Putting on the Pressure, *Nursing Mirror* 160:22, 1985.

Brennen, B. A. *Hands of Light.* Bantam Books, New York, 1987.

Burke, S. In the Presence of Animals, *U. S. News and World Report,* February 24: 64–65, 1992.

Caddy, S. H. and Jones, G. Massage Therapy as a Workplace Intervention for Reduction of Stress, *Perceptual & Motor Skills* 84(1):157–158, 1997.

Channon, L. D. Relaxation Techniques: Alternatives to Progressive Relaxation, *Australian Journal of Clinical and Experimental Hypnosis* 14(2):133–137, 1986.

Cohen, N. Massage Is the Message, *Nursing Times* 83(19):19–20, 1987.

Cusack, O. and Smith E. Pets and the Elderly: The Therapeutic Bond, *Activities, Adaptations, and Aging* 4(2–3):33–49, 1984.

Czimbal, B. and Zadikov, M. *Vitamin T: A Guide to Healthy Touch.* Open Book, Portland, OR, 1991.

Day, J. A., Mason, R. R., and Chesrown, S. E. Effect of Massage on Serum Level of B-Endorphin and B-Lipoprotein in Healthy Adults, *Physical Therapy* 67:926–930, 1987.

Downing, G. *The Massage Book.* Random House, New York, 1972.

D'urso, M. A. Massage for the Masses, *Health* 19:63–67, 1987.

Edmunds, A. and Tudor, H. *Some Unrecognized Factors in Medicine.* The Theosophical Society, London, 1976.

Feitis, R. *Ida Rolf Talks about Rolfing and Physical Reality.* Harper & Row, New York, 1978.

Feltman, J., ed. *Hands-on Healing.* Rodale Press, Emmaus, PA, 1989.

Field, T. Massage Therapy Effects, *American Psychologist,* December:1270–1281, 1998.

Field, T. Stressors during Pregnancy and the Postnatal Period, *New Directions for Child Development* 45:19–31, 1989.

Field, T. et al. Massage Therapy for Infants of Depressed Mothers. *Infant Behavior and Development* 19(1):107, 1996.

Fisher-Rizzi, S. *The Complete Aromatherapy Handbook.* Sterling Publishing Co., New York, 1990.

Fox, E., Bowers, R., and Foss, M. *The Physiological Basis of Physical Education and Athletics.* Dubuque, IA, 1989.

Gauthier, P. Development of a New Approach to Emotionally Deprived Children and Youth, *Child and Youth Services* 13(1):71–81, 1990.

Goleman, D. and Bennett, T. *The Relaxed Body Book.* Doubleday, Garden City, New York, 1986.

Green, R. and Green, M. Relaxation Increases Salivary Immunoglobin A, *Psychological Reports* 61(2):623–629, 1987.

Gurudas, H. *Flower Essences and Vibrational Healing.* Cassandra Press, San Rafael, CA, 1983.

Harby, K. Troubles Float Away, *Psychology* 22(2):20, 1988.

Harrison, A. Therapeutic Massage: Getting the Massage, *Nursing Times* 82(48):34–35, 1986.

Havemann, J. S. Rubbing out Workday Pain: Massage Rooms Win Departmental Support, *The Washington Post,* Feb. 6, 1989.

Hirsh, J. S. Doesn't Everyone Need to Be Kneaded Once in a While? *Wall Street Journal,* October 17, 1989.

Holden, C. Human–Animal Relationship under Scrutiny, *Science* 214(23):418–458, 1984.

Holmes, P. Aromatherapy: Applications for Clinical Practice, *Alternative & Complementary Therapies* 1(3):117–182, 1995.

Howdyshell, C. Complementary Therapy: Aromatherapy with Massage for Geriatric and Hospice Care-a-Call for a Holistic Approach, *The Hospice Journal* 13:69–75, 1998.

Hutchinson, M. *The Book of Floating: Exploring the Private Sea.* Quill Books, New York, 1984.

Jacobs, M. Massage for the Relief of Pain: Anatomical and Physical Considerations, *Physical Therapy Review* 40:93–98, 1960.

Jodo, E. R. et al. Effects of Facial Massage on the Spontaneous EEG, *Tohoku-Psycholigica Folia* 47(1–4):8–15, 1988.

Jorgenson, J. Therapeutic Use of Companion Animals in Health Care, *Image: Journal of Nursing Scholarship* 29(3):249–254, 1997.

Katcher, A. H. Physiological and Behavioral Responses to Companion Animals, *Veterinary Clinics of North America: Small Animal Practices* 15:403–410, 1985.

Kolpakov S and Rumyantseva, S. Use of a Combined Method of Correcting the Human Psychophysiological State during Work and Constant Vision Strain, *Human Physiology* 13(1):36–42, 1987.

Lacroix, N. *Massage for Total Stress Relief.* Random House, New York, 1990.

Lippin, R. Alternative Medicine in the Workplace, *Alternative Therapies* 2(1):47–51, 1996.

Maxwell-Hudson, C. *The Complete Book of Massages.* Random House, New York, 1988.

McKechnie, A. et al. Anxiety States: A Preliminary Report on the Value of Connective-Tissue Massage, *Journal of Psychosomatic Research* 27(2):1245–1249, 1983.

Muhammad, L. Animal Therapy Spurs Human Touch, *USA Today,* May 3:10D, 1999.

Muschel, I. J. Pet Therapy with Terminally Ill Cancer Patients, *Social Casework* 65(8):451–458, 1984.

Naisbitt, J. *Megatrends 2000.* Avon, New York, 1999.

Naliboff, B. D. and Tachiki, K. H. Autonomic and Skeletal Muscle Response to Nonelectrical Cutaneous Stimulation, *Perceptual and Motor Skills* 72(2):575–584, 1991.

Namikoshi, R. *The Complete Book of Shiatsu Therapy.* Japan Publications, New York, 1981.

National Association for Holistic Aromatherapy: www.naha.org.

Nixon T. Make Money with Massage, *Fitness Management,* September:40–42, 1989.

Pecher, K. Pet Therapy for Heart and Soul, *Prevention* August:80–84, 1985.

Pelletier, K. R. and Herzing, D. L. Psychoneuroimmunology: Toward a Mind-Body Model, *Advances* 5(1):27–56, 1988.

Pitcairn, R. H. Why Pets Are Good For Us, *Prevention* February:49–51, 1985.

Price, S. *Aromatherapy Workbook.* HarperCollins, San Fransico, 1993.

Proulx, D. Animal-Assisted Therapy, *Critical Care Nurse* 18(2):80–85, 1998.

Rimmer, L. "The Clinical Use of Aromatherapy in the Reduction of Stress, *Home Healthcare Nurse* 16:123–126, 1998.

Samples, P. Does Sports Massage Have a Role in Sports Medicine? *The Physician and Sports Medicine* March:177–187, 1989.

Scafidi, F. et al. Massage Stimulates Growth in Preterm Infants: A Replication, *Infant Behavior and Development* 13(2):167–188, 1990.

Sims, S. Slow-Stroke Back Massage for Cancer Patients, *Infant Behavior and Development* 13(2):167–188, 1990.

Smith, M. et al. Benefits of Massage Therapy for Hospital Patients: A Descriptive and Qualitative Evaluation, *Alternative Therapies in Health and Medicine* 5(4):64–71, 1999.

Steiner, R. *The Etherisation of the Blood.* Steiner, London, 1971.

Toufexis, A. Massage Comes out of the Parlor, *Time,* March:17–20, 1987.

Weaver, M. R. Acupressure: An Overview of Therapy and Application, *Nurse Practitioner* 10:38–42, 1985.

Weinberg, R., Jackson, A., and Kolodny, K. The Relationship of Massage and Exercise to Mood Enhancement, *Sport Psychologist* 2(3):202–211, 1988.

Wilkinson, S. et. al. An Evaluation of Aromatherapy Massage in Palliative Care, *Palliative Medicine* 13(5):409–417, 1999.

Willis, D. A. Animal Therapy, *Rehabilitation Nursing* 22(2):78–81, 1997.

Woody, R. H. *The Use of Massage in Facilitating Holistic Health.* Thomas, Springfield, CA, 1980.

Yacenda, J. Sport Strokes, *Fitness Management* 5(9):38–39, 1989.

Ylinen, J. and Cash, M. *Sports Massage.* St. Paul, MN, 1988.

Zimmer, J. The Pleasure of Giving a Great Massage, *Health,* April:52–53, 1985.

Chapter 23 T'ai Chi Ch'uan

Tension is who you think you

should be. Relaxation

is who you are.

—*T'ai Chi Saying*

There is a life force or subtle energy that surrounds and permeates us all, which the Chinese call *Chi*. To harmonize with the universe, to move in unison with this energy, to move as freely as running water is to be at peace or one with the universe. This harmony of energy promotes tranquility and inner peace. This is the essence of **T'ai Chi ch'uan**: a harmony and balance with the vital life force of the natural world itself. The words *T'ai* and *Chi* can be translated several ways. One is the "supreme ultimate," a meaning symbolic of balance, power, and enlightenment. T'ai Chi, the softest of the martial arts, is also called a "moving meditation." Similar to yoga, it is an exercise that demonstrates unification or harmony of mind and body, and with the *Chi* of the universe.

To understand *Chi*, it is helpful to view the concept in the cultural context where it originated. The Chinese concept of health is quite different from that of the Western hemisphere. Westerners view health as the absence of disease and illness produced by bacteria and viruses, while the Chinese see it as an unrestricted current of subtle energy throughout the body. When *Chi*, or subtle energy, which flows through the body in a network of meridians, or "energy gates," is restricted or congested, the body is susceptible to physiological dysfunction. In Chinese medicine, it is not necessarily bacteria or viruses that cause physical dysfunction or disease, as these are thought to be present everywhere. Rather, poor health is thought to be the result of low resistance, caused by nonharmonious (blocked) energy, to both internal and external factors that ultimately do one in. Stated another way, these "pathogens" are constantly present; it is low resistance to them that makes one vulnerable to disease. Just as acupuncture is used as a preventive intervention technique to unblock congested meridians to cure ailments, T'ai Chi ch'uan is a type of preventive exercise to maintain the peaceful flow of energy throughout the body and thus maintain good health. From a Chinese perspective, unrestricted flow of energy helps to maintain one's resistance to various influences, be they biological, psychological, or sociological in nature.

It may seem that the practice of self-defense is incongruent with relaxation. Upon closer examination, however, T'ai Chi reveals a profound expression of tranquility. It teaches one to remain calm and centered against the greatest opposition (stressors), to harmonize with aggression and fear, rather than fight

it. As a physical exercise, it teaches how to conserve and concentrate energy rather than to dissipate it randomly. The integration of this life force into this moving meditation of self-defense suggests that T'ai Chi is not a violent exercise. Rather, it is an exercise to maintain balance in one's life. For this reason alone, the practice of T'ai Chi is a wonderful metaphor for conscious relaxation and the ability to move in balance and harmony with our environments. If you were to walk the streets of Beijing or Shanghai in the early morning hours, you would see thousands of people exercising together, practicing T'ai Chi as a mode of physical exercise, much as you would see people in the States running or doing aerobics.

Historical Perspective

The practice of T'ai Chi dates back thousands of years. Its origins blend the essence of Chinese philosophy with the substance of physical survival. Legend has it that thousands of years ago a man observed a fight between a crane and a serpent. With repeated jabs of his beak, the crane tried to defeat his opponent. But the snake, in a series of calculated maneuvers, shifted its body weight at the right moments and was able to remain free of harm until the crane became tired, gave up, and moved on. Stories have also been handed down through the ages that T'ai Chi developed as a unique style of boxing that emphasized internal strength mixed with flexibility and agility rather than the exhibition of brute force. As the art developed, subtle philosophical concepts were integrated with the movements as a way to teach and emphasize proficiency in mechanical skills, thus lending support to its understanding and mastery.

Philosophy of T'ai Chi Ch'uan

What makes T'ai Chi different from all other forms of self-defense, and perhaps unique unto itself, is its basis in philosophy. The practice of its physical movements is a wonderful metaphor for the essential mental attitude to successfully deal with life's daily stressors. The physical movements are fluid: they move *with* force, not against it. Many times, when we are confronted with situations we perceive to be threatening, our first instinct is to force a change or try to manipulate something we have no control over. T'ai Chi suggests quite literally going with the flow, swimming with the tide, not against it. The philosophy of T'ai Chi involves the manipulation of force by controlling oneself and yielding to become part of it.

As T'ai Chi developed, it quickly assimilated many philosophical concepts from Taoism, and to a lesser extent, Confucianism. Even the symbol used to represent T'ai Chi—a circular mandala of white and black halves with each half carrying a smaller circle of the other inside—represents the balance of opposites (Fig. 23.1). These opposites, yin and yang, symbolize (among other things) the positive and negative aspects in nature. Together, they represent wholeness and essential balance. T'ai Chi strives to attain the harmony of these forces through avoidance of extremes. The philosophical concepts of Taoism are embroidered with metaphorical imagery—light with darkness, good with evil, life with death—all of which express the concept of stillness in motion. While not every concept can be categorized as "either-or," the theme of yin and yang, or wholeness, is to find peace by acknowledging the duality of these characteristics within yourself.

There are four basic philosophical concepts taught in T'ai Chi: fasting the heart, returning to nature, *Wu-wei*, and winning by losing. Fasting the heart is a concept to explain the flow of life's energy, a moving essence. Fasting means silence, the language of the soul. Fasting the heart also means to find comfort in solitude. The return to nature is another way of describing a regression to the joys of childhood, embracing innocence, joy, laughter, and play. These are traits that, as adults, we lose the ability to utilize and appreciate within ourselves. *Wu-wei* is described as the philosophy of nothing-doing, nothing-knowing. It means to act without forcing; to move in accordance with the flow of nature's course. In the words of the great Chinese philosopher, Lao Tzu, "Although water is soft and weak, it invariably overcomes the rigid and strong." Often *Wu-wei* is expressed in the comparison of opposites. For example, to shrink, first you must stretch; to enervate, first you must energize; to take, first you must give. Another example is that of a ping pong ball in water. No matter how many times you push it under, it always comes back up, and does so with little or no effort. The fourth component, winning by losing, advocates the success of failure. When failure is acknowledged, it becomes the first step to success. Winning by losing is an expression of unconditional acceptance. An additional concept of T'ai Chi is the realization that true understanding comes from emptying the mind (lowering the walls of the ego). This emptiness allows a liberation of the human spirit to unite with the universal life energy. Although this energy may seem elusive to those who have never practiced T'ai Chi, its effects cascade down through the body to influence the physiological systems as well.

Physiological and Psychological Benefits

Individuals who have practiced T'ai Chi, as well as those who instruct this traditional Chinese exercise, make several claims about the wonderful physical and mental benefits it has to offer. To date, there have been very few empirical studies to prove these claims, but the studies in existence are influential. One study by Jin-Putai (1988) investigated both physiological and psychological effects of T'ai Chi and found effects very similar to those produced by other types of aerobic exercise. In this study, heart rate, norepinephrine, cortisol, and mood were observed in both beginners and ardent followers (age range fifteen to seventy-five years). These variables were measured three times daily for a period of several weeks. Data analysis showed a marked decrease in postexercise resting heart rate as well as stress hormones over the course of a day. As a result of this technique, subjects reported less physical tension and fatigue, less anger and anxiety, and less mood disturbance. From these observations it was concluded that T'ai Chi does promote a relaxing effect. As reported by Koh (1981), a study by Munyi in 1963 indicated that habitual practice of T'ai Chi produced increased measures of muscular strength and flexibility

Figure 23.1 The Taoist symbol of yin-yang is a circle with two equal and opposite halves.

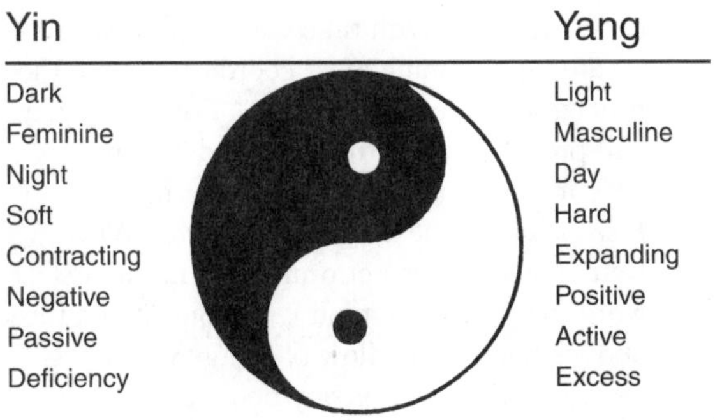

Yin	Yang
Dark	Light
Feminine	Masculine
Night	Day
Soft	Hard
Contracting	Expanding
Negative	Positive
Passive	Active
Deficiency	Excess

compared to sedentary control subjects. Furthermore, in a study concluded in 1981 by Plummer to compare the effects of T'ai Chi to acupuncture, it was observed that both techniques promoted physical (postural) homeostasis and psychological homeostasis, which together enhanced emotional control and tranquility. T'ai Chi has been recommended as an ideal activity for the mobile aged population, and is said to be as effective an exercise as cross-country skiing, swimming, and bicycling (Meusel, 1986). Claims from the Far East include that T'ai Chi can cure hypertension, asthma, and insomnia, as well as prevent atherosclerosis and spinal deformity. To date, these claims have not been clinically proven or medically substantiated because they just have not been studied. While these claims are yet unproven, it is believed by regular practitioners that T'ai Chi may play an important role in the prevention of disorders commonly associated with stress.

Although few studies have researched the effects of T'ai Chi on various health parameters, in the past decade numerous studies designed in China and Japan have measured the effects of Qigong. Like T'ai Chi, Qigong (pronounced chee gong) is an energy-based exercise; however, Qigong places no focus or attention on the aspects of self-defense. Rather, the movement of Chi throughout the body is the sole emphasis of this practice. In simple terms, energy is moved through the body by meditation and breathing, which in turn are combined with a host of physical movements, similar to those observed in T'ai Chi. When practiced regularly, these movements create a sense of balance in the meridian system by opening blocks and clearing congestion in the meridian gates. With regular practice of Qigong, the energy system throughout the entire body operates at its optimal level.

In an exhaustive literature review on the medical applications of Qigong, Kenneth Sancier highlights several ways in which Qigong has been used in the clinical setting to improve various aspects of health and wellness. Sancier notes that Qigong has proven to bring about remarkable and significant results with hypertension, stroke, cardiovascular efficiency, bone density, sex hormone levels, cancer, and even the early stages of senility. Although the majority of these studies have been conducted in China, the statistics indicate that Qigong can be a significant factor in promoting health. Currently, similar studies in the United States are underway with funding for one study supported by the National Institutes of Health's Office of Alternative Medicine.

T'ai Chi Ch'uan as a Relaxation Technique

There are over 100 positions or movements in T'ai Chi, with several similarities among some of them. Most people who learn T'ai Chi begin with formal lessons, either in a group or with private instruction. The purpose of this chapter is to provide exposure to some of its concepts and movements, and acquaint you with this exercise as an alternative relaxation technique. Keep in mind that initially T'ai Chi can be difficult to learn from reading and studying the movements in a book. It is my hope that this exposure may inspire you to take one or more lessons to further your appreciation of this exercise.

Before T'ai Chi can be practiced effectively, there are some important concepts to understand to make this exercise more enjoyable, which are taken from the *T'ai Chi Handbook* by Herman Kauz. As with yoga *asanas,* T'ai Chi movements may seem difficult at first. With time and practice, however, they will become so natural they will seem almost effortless. First and foremost, T'ai Chi is an egoless activity. That is, do not compare the precision of your movements with those of others who take part in this exercise for relaxation. And when you try the positions, go for the general movements first and then try to pick up the finer details later. There is no right or wrong, there only is.

1. *Breathe effortlessly.* Breathing should be natural. Some teachers instruct students to hold their tongue to the roof of the mouth, breathe through the nose, and allow the abdominal area to expand rather than the chest. When beginning, breathe in whatever fashion is easiest for you. With time you will find your breathing becoming more coordinated with the progression of each movement. Eventually you will probably adopt the suggested breathing style in coordination with the movements.

2. *Free the body of all unnecessary tension.* When watching someone perform T'ai Chi, the first word that comes to mind is *graceful.* When the body is relaxed, the flow of energy will move more freely. Tension in any body region

inhibits energy movement. Use only the minimal amount of muscle tension to complete the movement.

3. *Maintain a stance perpendicular to the floor.* With a perpendicular stance, the balance of each position, as well as transition to the next position, is more easily attained. It is important to keep the spinal column completely aligned (perpendicular to the floor). A common metaphor used in teaching T'ai Chi is to move as if you were a marionette suspended by a string from the top of your head. Many instructors teach the 70/30 stance, where in transition from one movement to the next, the forward foot maintains approximately 70 percent of the body weight with the back foot maintaining 30 percent.

4. *Keep your center of gravity low.* Your center of gravity is approximately an inch to two below your belly button. Stand up, close your eyes, and sense your body's center of gravity. A lower center of gravity means a more stable base to move and position yourself. When performing these movements, bend the knees slightly, especially when shifting your weight from one leg to the other.

5. *Maintain even speed.* The graceful movements of T'ai Chi are a result of a continuous flow of movement like the gentle flow of water. The progression of these movements should be even, not sudden or jerky. Try to feel the surrounding space with your hands, as if you are swimming in air. Move arms and hands in unison with the body.

6. *Integrate the mind and body as one.* When performing T'ai Chi, the mind should move with the body. Concentration should be sharp. Try not to let your mind wander off to distant thoughts. If this should happen, quickly bring it back to your body movements.

T'ai Chi Ch'uan Movements

The following movements are the first eight positions in this moving meditation as illustrated in Kauz's *T'ai Chi Handbook*. Points of orientation will be north, south, east, and west. For simplicity, the starting position will begin facing north, wherever you decide that to be located. Most people learn T'ai Chi barefoot or in socks, as this helps with initial foot placement. The feet also become more relaxed when less confined.

Position 1: *Starting posture* (Fig. 23.2). Stand erect with feet shoulder-width apart, arms by your side, palms facing back, chin up, and eyes looking directly ahead.

Position 2: *Beginning position* (Fig. 23.3). Raise your arms directly in front to about shoulder level, leading with the wrists. Elbows should be slightly bent, shoulders relaxed. Then slowly allow arms and hands to return to the starting position below waist level, leading with the elbows.

Position 3: *Left-hand ward-off* (Fig. 23.4). Shift weight first to the left foot, allowing the left knee to bend slightly. Next, pivot onto the right foot, slowly

Figure 23.2

Figure 23.3

Figure 23.4

Figure 23.5

Figure 23.6

rotating the body clockwise about 90 degrees. As you turn east, slowly raise the right hand to mid-chest level, palm facing down, while at the same time raising the left hand to waist level, palm facing up, as if carrying a beach ball in both hands. With completion of the pivot, the majority of your weight now rests on the right foot, and the left heel leaves the ground. Then rotate the body back (counterclockwise) and return weight to the left foot. (The right foot remains pointed eastward.) Return the right arm to your side, while slowly raising the left arm to mid-chest level, palm facing in. Hips should remain directly under the shoulders.

Position 4: *Right-hand ward-off* (Fig. 23.5). With the majority of weight on your left foot, raise your right heel off the ground and turn your body clockwise, to the east. Raise the left hand to mid-chest level, palm facing down, while turning the right palm upward just below the waist. Again, hold the imaginary beach ball between your palms. With your weight on your left foot, raise the heel of your right foot and direct it to the place where the right toe was previously, facing east. As you rotate your body east, shift 70 percent of your body weight from the left foot to the right, keeping knees slightly bent, hips directly parallel to shoulders, and pivoting the left foot east. At the same time, raise the right hand to shoulder level, palm facing toward the chest. Move the left hand with your body at mid-chest level.

Position 5: *Grasp the bird's tail (rollback and press)* (Fig. 23.6). Now shift your body weight from the right to the left foot (70–30 percent). With this shift,

begin to turn slightly north. Swing the left hand, palm facing in, slowly down past the waist and circle back, up, and over the left shoulder. Move the right hand, palm facing in, toward the chest. As the left hand comes back to mid-chest level, continue to rotate the body east again and transfer your body weight again to the right foot. Brush the left palm lightly against the right wrist at the same time.

Position 6: *Grasp the bird's tail (push)* (Fig. 23.7). Facing east, begin to separate the hands and lower them slowly to upper abdominal level, palms facing out. Shift your weight from the right foot to the left, as if you were slowly backing up. Then reverse weight back to the right foot and extend your hands out slowly as if you were pushing an object away from your face. As you push, be conscious of directing energy in that direction.

Position 7: *The single whip* (Fig. 23.8). Shift your body weight from the right foot to the left, and rotate your body counterclockwise to the north-northwest. Swing arms and hands slowly in the same direction, keeping hands directly in front at mid-chest level. Place right heel where the right toe was, now pointing north. Then shift weight to the right foot, rotating slightly to the northeast. Swing the left hand slowly to waist level by the right hip, palm facing up. Draw back the right arm to the right hip, leading with the elbow, and close the fingers as if dropping a coin into the palm of the left hand. Next, slowly rotate your body west, shifting weight from the right foot to the left by taking a step with the left foot. At the same time, raise the right hand to about shoulder

Figure 23.7   *Figure 23.8*   *Figure 23.9*

level, and sweep the left hand slowly in an upward arc from right to left, twisting the wrist to allow the palm to face out as the hand comes to about shoulder level.

Position 8: *Lift hands* (Fig. 23.9). Slowly lift your right heel off the floor and place it once again where the right toe was pointing north. As the heel makes contact, begin to shift your weight from the left foot to the right, coming back to face north. Starting with hands loosely extended out to the sides, draw palms close together facing inward, and position the left hand near the right elbow.

Additional Comments on T'ai Chi Ch'uan

T'ai Chi is unique unto itself. To feel your body move in a guided motion generates a sense of inner peace that seems unparalleled among relaxation techniques. But to be effective, T'ai Chi takes continual practice, a half hour or so per day. Some advocate early morning practice as a fresh start to the day, while others like to end the day with this exercise. There really is no time that is best; choose whatever time fits into your regular schedule. This technique can certainly be done alone, but group sessions add a whole new element of grace and relaxation. Several YMCA, YWCA, and community programs offer morning sessions open to people of all abilities. Remember not to compare your technique with others: make it an egoless activity. The practice also may necessitate additional lessons from a qualified instructor. Even the best instructors strive to improve their technique. When looking for a T'ai Chi instructor, be sure that his or her philosophy matches yours. Some instructors see T'ai Chi merely as a form of self-defense and teach it as such. Others teach it as a type of meditation, providing an atmosphere to enhance spiritual well-being as well as physical well-being. Sample several instructors before making a commitment to the advancement of your technique. Trust in the instructor is paramount in learning. Finally, this advice from my instructor, Steve Pearlman: "T'ai Chi classes should be lighthearted and fun. If you can have fun and be relaxed in a self-defense situation—in a situation of immediate physical harm—and you can learn to go with the flow, you can be relaxed anywhere. T'ai Chi teaches you how to be relaxed in all aspects of your life and how to stay relaxed in the face of stress."

Best Application of T'ai Chi Ch'uan

If you should find yourself getting bored with aerobic exercise or meditation and crave variety, try a session of T'ai Chi. Once you get beyond the idea that you may feel silly, this exercise can be dynamic in its ability to promote relaxation. Some people make T'ai Chi their only method of relaxation, whereas others use it to supplement their repertoire of techniques. When you first try it, remember that the nature of T'ai Chi is calm, not rushed. This moving meditation acts to defuse the emotions that disconnect us from the source of life's energy. To move with the force, not

Stress With a Human Face

BETTY STEWART HAD HEARD OF T'AI CHI over twenty years ago, but it wasn't until September of 1994 that she began to practice it in earnest. In the early 1970s she was intrigued to try this form of relaxation, and even bought a video so she could teach herself, but she said that just didn't work. Then one day she noticed that a class in T'ai Chi was to be offered at the Prestige Club, a unique hospital-based health promotion program for seniors with a special focus on bridging standard and complementary forms of healing. Betty wasted no time in signing up.

What makes Betty's story so remarkable are the changes she saw soon after she began taking the class, as well as those that occurred after the first year. Prior to beginning the course, Betty, at the age of 79, was all of 55 inches tall. To the amazement of her physician, Betty has since added over an inch to her height. And unlike most people her age who lose inches to bone demineralization, Betty's bone density remained unchanged in the two years of doing T'ai Chi. Recently she told me, "There was a chance to be involved in a bone demineralization study, but I didn't have time in my life to see if after four years of clinical trials, all I got was the placebo. I wanted the real thing, that's why I started T'ai Chi."

Aside from the benefits of bone integrity, Betty says there have been other benefits. "I have a much better sense of balance. Why, one day I tripped on an uneven sidewalk. Because I learned how to shift my weight, all that happened was a little bang, but no fracture. My coordination and concentration skills have also improved, as

has my level of energy. You know, you cannot do T'ai Chi if your mind wanders. You lose track of where you are in the progression of movements."

Aside from the physical movements, Betty is attracted to the philosophy of this moving meditation. There is a real poetic quality to T'ai Chi, she says with a smile in her voice. "I can tell you about stress too! Let's just say that both my husband and I have had our fair share of it these past few years. T'ai Chi has really kept me balanced. I think T'ai Chi is phenomenal and I recommend it to all your students." ✦

against it, is to abandon emotional attachment to the causes of stress. As a type of physical exercise, T'ai Chi requires its own time and space. Initially, implementation of this technique is not suitable for the overt confrontation of stress. But with practice and understanding, when balance is found, the physical arousal of stress is minimal when faced with a perceived threat.

To practice T'ai Chi, you need some room to move about, approximately five feet by five feet, although it can be done in less. Once the movements are committed to memory, they are easy to practice. But like any other skill, the benefits of this technique necessitate regular practice.

Summary

- *Chi* is a Chinese term representing the universal life energy that surrounds and permeates everyone, the life force. T'ai Chi ch'uan is a form of exercise that is thought to help regulate this flow of universal energy.
- The Chinese believe that poor health is a result of blockages and congestion in the flow of internal energy, which in turn lowers one's physical resistance and makes one vulnerable to various pathogens.
- T'ai Chi, considered by many to be the softest of the martial arts, is called moving meditation, or a series of movements that act to help unify the life force energy with that of the person.
- T'ai Chi is deeply rooted in philosophy, primarily Taoism, but to a lesser extent, Confucianism.
- The premise of this exercise is to move with, rather than against, the flow of universal energy. The positions (over 100 in all) reinforce the concept of consciously moving with, rather than against, perceived stressors in everyday life.
- There are four principles in T'ai Chi: fasting the heart, returning to nature, *Wu-wei,* and winning by losing.
- Studies investigating the physiological effects of T'ai Chi show that this technique is as effective as others in promoting relaxation.
- When practicing T'ai Chi, breathe effortlessly, hold no excess muscular tension, maintain a perpendicular stance, keep center of gravity low, move at a continuous speed, and integrate the mind and body as one.

Concepts and Terms

Beginning T'ai Chi position	Lift hands	T'ai Chi ch'uan
Chi	Return to nature	Winning by losing
Fasting the heart	Right-hand ward-off	*Wu-wei*
Grasp the bird's tail	Single whip	Yang
Left-hand ward-off	Starting posture	Yin

References and Resources

Alder, S. S. Seeking Stillness in Motion: An Introduction to T'ai Chi for Seniors, *Activities, Adaptations, and Aging* 3:1–14, 1983.

Bolen, J. S. *The Tao of Psychology.* Harper & Row, New York, 1979.

Capra, F. *The Tao of Physics,* 3rd ed. Shambhala Publications, Boston, 1991.

Channer, K. S., et al. Changes in Hemodynamic Parameters Following T'ai Chi Chuan and Aerobic Exercise in Patients Recovering from Acute Myocardial Infarction, *Postgraduate Medical Journal* 72(848):349–351, 1996.

Delza, S. *The T'ai Chi Experience: Reflections and Perceptions on Body-Mind Harmony,* State University of New York Press, New York, 1996.

Dreher, D. *The Tao of Inner Peace.* Harper & Row, New York, 1991.

Dunn, T. The Practice and Spirit of T'ai Chi Ch'uan, *Yoga Journal,* Nov./Dec., 1987.

Husted, C. et al. Improving Quality of Life for People with Chronic Conditions: The Example of T'ai Chi and Multiple Sclerosis, *Alternative Therapies in Health and Medicine* 5(5):70–74, 1999.

I Ching (Book of Changes). R. Wilhelm and C. Baynes, trans. Princeton University Press, Princeton, NJ, 1950.

Jacobson, B.H. et al. The Effect of T'ai Chi Chuan Training on Balance, Kinesthetic Sense and Strength, *Perceptual and Motor Skills* 8:27–33, 1997.

Jin-Putai, Changes in Heart Rate, Noradrenaline, Cortisol, and Mood during T'ai Chi, *Journal of Psychosomatic Research* 33:197–206, 1988.

Jou, T. H. *The Tao of T'ai Chi Ch'uan.* T'ai Chi Foundation, New York, 1988.

Kauz, H. *T'ai Chi Handbook.* Dolphin Books, New York, 1974.

Koh, T. C. T'ai Chi Ch'uan, *American Journal of Chinese Medicine* 8:15–22, 1981.

Lao Tzu. *Tao Te Ching One.* Gia-Fu Feng and Jane English, trans. Random House, New York, 1972.

Lo, B. *The Essence of T'ai Chi Ch'uan.* North Atlantic Books, Berkeley, CA. 1979.

Meusel, H. Zur Enignung von Sportarten und Ubungsfornan fur Altere (Sport and Exercise Training Suitable for Older People), *Zeitschruift fur Gerontologie* 19:376–386, 1986.

Miller, D. and Miller, J. An Ancient Art Can Change Your Running, *Runner's World,* March:58–61, 1982.

Perry, P. Grasp the Bird's Tail, *American Health* 5:58–63, 1986.

Plummer, J. P. Acupuncture and Homeostasis: Physiological, Physical (Postural), and Psychological, *American Journal of Chinese Medicine* 9:1–14, 1981.

Sancier, K. Medical Applications of QiGong, *Alternative Therapies* 2(1):40–46, 1996.

Sancier, K. Personal Conversation, January 24, 1996.

Suler, J. R. The T'ai Chi Images: A Taoist Model of Psychotherapeutic Change, *Psychologia—An International Journal of Psychology in the Orient* 34(1):18–27, 1991.

Wolf, S.L. et al., Exploring the Basis of T'ai Chi Chuan as a Therapeutic Exercise Approach, *Archives of Physical Medicine Rehabilitation* 78:886–892, 1997.

$\mathscr{C}$hapter 24 Progressive Muscular Relaxation

Relaxation is the direct

negative of nervous

excitement. It is the absence

of nerve-muscle impulse.

—Edmund Jacobson, M.D.

The body's muscles respond to thoughts of perceived threats with tension or contraction. Muscular tension is believed to be the most common symptom of stress, and although it may not send people to hospital emergency rooms like other stress-related disorders, its cumulative effects can be stiffness, pain, and discomfort. In extreme cases, it can distort and disalign posture and joint stability. The building blocks involved in muscular contraction are a motor end unit, a motor nerve fiber (neuron), a skeletal muscle fiber, and a stimulus from the nerve fiber to the muscle fiber called an action potential. Chemicals released from these neurons are referred to as neurotrophic substances, which flow from the nerve axon to the muscle fibers. Neurotransmitters secrete epinephrine, norepinephrine, and ACh to regulate and control muscle contraction.

The word *contraction* is often synonymous with shortening, but this is not always the case. Muscle fibers can, in fact, shorten like the barrel of a telescope, which is called concentric contraction. But some actually lengthen, in what is called eccentric contraction. Furthermore, muscles can contract without any noticeable motion; this type of contraction is called isometric contraction. The degree of intensity may vary considerably in isometric contraction, but tension at some level is exerted. Over time, this can result in stiffness and poor mobility of the joint to which the muscles are attached. It is primarily isometric contraction that is most commonly associated with the painful muscle tension produced by stress. With repeated excitatory neural stimulation, muscle tension can manifest in various ways, including tension headaches, stiff necks, lower-back pain, stomach cramps, and some forms of temporomandibular joint dysfunction (TMJ). Often, muscle tension produced by thoughts in the unconscious mind occurs while we sleep, and it has been known to cause joint stiffness and even damaged connective tissue in the jaw, neck, shoulders, and lower back. Progressive muscular relaxation (PMR) is a technique specifically designed to help reduce muscle tension.

Historical Perspective

Early in the twentieth century, an American physician named Edmund Jacobson noticed that his patients suffered from a host of physical ailments, but they all seemed to share one symptom: muscle tension. The thought occurred to Jacobson that if muscle tension was reduced or eliminated, these somatic diseases might decrease or perhaps disappear altogether. In questioning his patients, he discovered that they were completely unaware of the levels of muscle tension in their bodies. Moreover, when patients were invited to relax, the suggestion produced only a partial state of relaxation. A slight degree of muscle tension, called residual tension, could still be detected.

Jacobson understood that the body cannot be tensed and relaxed at the same time. In an effort to teach his patients how to relax, he created a simple technique to increase physical neuromuscular awareness called **progressive muscular relaxation.** In this exercise, patients were led through a series of steps in which they systematically contracted and relaxed each muscle group. Jacobson believed that if a comparison between tension and complete relaxation of muscle fibers could be recognized by the individual, the awareness would promote a deepened sense of relaxation, not only in the muscle itself but throughout the entire body. This technique, he advocated, could help restore the body's state of physical health; and this turned out to be the case in his patients who began to practice progressive muscular relaxation.

Jacobson presented his technique to the American public in his book *You Must Relax,* one of the first clinical attempts at preventive medicine. He stated that neither the word *stress* nor *relaxation* was heard in American vocabulary prior to World War II. It was Jacobson's work in this field that made *relaxation* a household word. Because of Jacobson's professional background, the medical community unequivocally embraced this technique as its own. For several decades, this was the sole prescribed relaxation technique practiced in the United States, long before the introduction of yoga, Zen meditation, visualization, meditation, and other international techniques now recognized and accepted as bona fide modes of relaxation. In fact, when relaxation courses were first introduced in colleges and universities across the country, progressive muscular relaxation was often the sole technique taught. The Jacobson technique proved very easy to learn and teach; virtually anyone could and did teach it. Consequently, today there are many variations on this theme. Regardless of the variation, the basic process of progressive muscular relaxation remains the same: a progressive series of systematic phases combining isometric muscle contractions with periods of complete muscle relaxation. This technique, perhaps more than any other, illustrates the interception of the stress response by direct, conscious inhibition of the excitatory neural drive to the muscle fibers.

The original steps of Jacobson's progressive muscular relaxation included the following:

1. The progression of muscle groups should start with the lower extremities and move up to the head.
2. Muscle groups should be isolated during the contraction phase, leaving all remaining muscles relaxed.
3. The same muscle groups on both sides of the body should be contracted simultaneously.
4. The contraction should be held for five to ten seconds, with a corresponding relaxation phase of about forty-five seconds.
5. The individual should focus attention on the intensity of the contraction, sensing the tension level produced.
6. During the relaxation phase of each muscle group, special awareness of the feeling of relaxation should be focused on, comparing it to how the muscle felt when it was contracted.

Physiological Benefits

Research employing PMR has found that this technique is indeed beneficial in decreasing levels of muscle tension, as well as increasing overall awareness of muscle tension. This concept has been the premise of investigations measuring electromyographical (EMG) activity, the electrical conductance of muscle tissue. Biofeedback studies (Belar and Cohen, 1979; Hayes, 1975) in which electrodes were attached to various muscle sites including the forehead, jaw, neck, shoulder, and lower back to determine neuromuscular tension revealed that tension levels significantly

decreased when this technique was practiced. Through biofeedback, individuals proficient in PMR learned to control the extent of neuromuscular electrical conduction, and to reach a "zero firing threshold" indicative of complete muscle relaxation. With regular daily practice, there was neuromuscular awareness. People became more attuned to muscular tension as it developed and were better able to release it.

Psychologists also suggest that this technique is effective in controlling muscle tension associated with anger, and some studies suggest cigarette smokers find this technique (without diaphragmatic breathing) more effective than meditation or mental imagery to "kick the habit" (Allen, 1983). Jacobson was of the opinion that once the body achieved a state of neuromuscular homeostasis, the mind would follow suit, allowing for a complete state of relaxation and rejuvenation. Currently, PMR is used to effectively intervene in physical disorders such as insomnia, hypertension, headaches, lower-back pain, and TMJ.

Steps to Initiate Progressive Muscular Relaxation

The purpose of Jacobson's technique is to promote a profound sense of relaxation by comparing the contraction and relaxation phases of each selected muscle group. What makes this technique different from Eastern-based relaxation techniques is strong body awareness in the absence of internal self-talk or positive thoughts. There is no attempt to expand consciousness with this technique.

Position: (Fig. 24.1). Jacobson's relaxation technique can be performed in a comfortable sitting position; however, the best position to learn and practice PMR is lying comfortably on a carpeted floor. Your arms should rest comfortably by each side, with your palms facing upward. Constricting clothing should be loosened around your neck and waist. It is also suggested that you remove jewelry, watches, and glasses.

Breathing: The breathing technique with PMR is quite simple. Inhale as you contract the muscles, then exhale as you release the tension. The release of tension corresponding to relaxation of the diaphragm allows for a deeper sense of relaxation throughout the body.

Figure 24.1 Starting position.

Concentration and ambiance: Although concentration is important, interruptions during this technique seem less bothersome than during other meditation-based techniques, when unbroken concentration is more difficult to recapture. Nevertheless, you may wish to minimize distractions by designating a specific time and place to practice. Attention should be given to room temperature, as a cool environment may produce muscle tension (shivering). Once proficient in the technique, you can do it anywhere: while sitting in traffic, standing in line, or lying in bed trying to fall asleep. Benefits may appear soon after the completion of each session, with more profound physiological adaptations evident after prolonged practice (approximately four to six weeks). Jacobson believed the best prescription for this technique was three five-minute daily sessions on a regular basis.

Alterations of several aspects of this technique have been introduced since its debut in 1929. Variations include: (1) starting with the head and working down to the feet instead of vice versa, (2) changing the intensity of the contraction phase, (3) diaphragmatic breathing after each muscle group, and (4) sitting instead of lying down. The original premise and process have not changed.

Remember that only the selected muscle group should be contracted, leaving the remainder of the body relaxed. It may seem hard at first not to involve surrounding muscles, but with practice it will come. When finished with the progression, lie still on the floor for a few minutes and internalize all somatic sensations. Enjoy the full sense of relaxation. Then begin to focus your thoughts on your current surroundings.

The following is a slight variation of Jacobson's original technique, which divides the contraction into three intensities—100, 50, and 5 percent—of five seconds each, followed by the relaxation phase after each. I have found this to be the most effective pattern. By sensing the differences between muscle contractions, you become more aware of your muscle-tension levels over the course of a day. The instructions below were written to be read yourself before you perform the technique, or to be read by a third party. Before you begin, find a comfortable position (preferably on your back on a carpeted floor),

loosen any constrictive clothing, kick off your shoes, and begin to unwind.

1. *Face.* Tense the muscles of the forehead and eyes, as if you were pulling all your facial muscles to the center of your nose (Fig. 24.2). Pull really tight, as tight as you can, and hold it. Feel the tension you create in these muscles, especially the forehead and eyes. Now relax and exhale. Feel the absence of tension in these muscles, how loose and calm they feel. Try to compare this feeling of relaxation with the tension just produced. Now, contract the same muscles, but this time at 50 percent the intensity, and hold it. Then relax and exhale. Feel how relaxed those muscles are. Compare this feeling to that during the last contraction. This comparison should make the muscles even more relaxed. Finally, contract the same facial muscles slightly, at only 5 percent intensity. This is like feeling a slight warm breeze on your forehead and cheeks. Hold it. And relax. Take a comfortably slow and deep breath and, as you exhale, feel how relaxed the muscles are.

2. *Jaws.* Take a moment to feel the muscles of your jaws. Notice any tension, even the slightest amount. (The jaw muscles can harbor a lot of undetected muscle tension.) Now consciously tense the muscles of your jaws really tight, as tight as you can, and hold it.

Facial stretch.

Figure 24.

Now relax these muscles, exhale, and sense the tension disappear completely. (You may even feel your mouth begin to open a little.) Feel the difference between how the muscles feel now compared to what you just experienced at 100 percent contraction. Feel the absence of tension. Now, contract these same muscles, but at half the full intensity. Hold the tension, keep holding; and now relax again. Feel how relaxed these muscles are. Compare this feeling of relaxation with what you felt at 50 percent intensity. Once again, contract the same muscles, but with only a 5 percent contraction—just the acknowledgement that these muscles can contract. Now hold it, keep holding, and relax. Release any remaining tension so that the muscles are completely loose and relaxed. Sense how relaxed the muscles are. To enhance this feeling of relaxation, take a comfortably slow, deep breath.

3.   *Neck.* Concentrate on the muscles of your neck and isolate them from surrounding head and shoulder muscles. Take a moment to feel the muscles of your neck. Notice any tension. (The neck muscles can harbor a lot of undetected muscle tension.) Now consciously tense the muscles of your neck really tight, as tight as you can, and hold it, even tighter, and hold it. Now release the tension and completely relax these muscles. Sense the tension disappear completely. Become aware of the difference

between how these muscles feel now compared to how they felt at 100 percent contraction. Once again, contract these same muscles, but at 50 percent contraction. Hold this level of tension, keep holding, and now relax again. Feel how relaxed your neck muscles are. Compare this feeling of relaxation with what you felt at half intensity. Now, finally, contract these same muscles at only 5 percent, a very slight twinge up and down the sides of the neck with no motion whatsoever. Hold it, keep holding, and relax. Release any remaining tension so that the muscles are completely relaxed. Feel just how relaxed these muscles are. To enhance the feeling of relaxation, take a comfortably slow, deep breath and sense how relaxed your neck muscles have become.

4.   *Shoulders.* Concentrate on the muscles of your shoulders and isolate these from surrounding neck and upper arm muscles. Take a moment to sense the muscles of the deltoid region. Notice any degree of residual tension. (The shoulder muscles can also harbor a lot of undetected muscle tension, resulting in stiffness. Quite literally, your shoulders carry the weight of all your thoughts, the weight of your world.) Now, consciously tense the muscles of your shoulders really tight, as tight as you can, and hold it, even tighter, and hold it (Fig. 24.3). Now relax these muscles and sense the tension disappear completely. Sense the difference between how these muscles feel now and how they felt during contraction. Once again, contract these same muscles, but this time at half the intensity. Hold the tension, keep holding; and now completely relax these muscles. Sense how relaxed your shoulder muscles are. Compare this feeling with what you felt at 50 percent intensity. Finally, contract these same muscles at only 5 percent, only just sensing clothing touching your shoulder muscles. Hold it, keep holding, and relax. Release any remaining tension so that these muscles are completely loose and relaxed. Feel just how relaxed these muscles are. To enhance this feeling of relaxation, take a comfortably slow, deep breath and sense how relaxed your shoulder muscles have become.

Figure 24.3 Shoulder stretch.

5. *Upper chest.* Concentrate on the muscles of your upper chest. Try to isolate these from the muscles of your neck, shoulders, and upper arms. Take a moment to feel these upper chest muscles. Sense the slightest tension these muscles may hold. Now, consciously tense your upper chest muscles really tight, as tight as you can, and hold it, even tighter, and hold it. Now, completely relax these muscles and sense the tension disappear completely. Sense the difference between how loose these muscles feel now compared with what you just experienced at 100 percent contraction. Contract these same muscles, but at half the full intensity. Hold the tension, keep holding, and now relax again. Feel an even greater sense of relaxation in these muscles. Compare this feeling of relaxation with what you felt at 50 percent intensity. Finally, contract these same muscles at only 5 percent, merely feeling the fabric of clothing over these muscles. Now hold it, keep holding, and relax. Release any remaining tension so that the chest muscles hold absolutely no tension whatsoever. Feel how relaxed these muscles have become. To enhance the feeling, take a comfortably slow, deep breath.

6. *Hands and forearms.* Concentrate on the muscles of your hands and forearms. Take a moment to feel these muscles, including your fingers, palms, and wrists. Notice the slightest bit of tension. Now consciously tense the muscles of each hand and forearm really tight by making a fist, as tight as you can, and hold it as if you were hanging on for dear life. Make it even tighter, and hold it. Now release the tension and relax these muscles. Sense the tension disappear completely. Open the palm of each hand slowly, extend your fingers, and let them recoil just a bit. Sense the difference between how relaxed these muscles feel now compared with what you just experienced at 100 percent contraction. They should feel very relaxed. Now contract these same muscles at a 50 percent contraction. Hold the tension, keep holding, and relax again. Sense how relaxed these muscles are. Compare this feeling of relaxation with what you just felt. Now,

contract these same muscles at only 5 percent, like holding an empty egg shell in the palm of your hand. Now hold it, keep holding, and relax. Release any remaining tension so that these muscles are completely relaxed. Feel just how relaxed these muscles have become. To enhance this feeling of relaxation, take a comfortably slow, deep breath and sense how relaxed your forearm and hand muscles have become.

7. *Abdominals.* Really focus your attention on your abdominal muscles. Take a moment to sense any residual tension in these muscles or the organs they protect. Now, consciously tense your abdominal muscles really tight, as if you have an intense stomach cramp. Contract as tight as you can and hold it, even tighter, and hold it. Now relax these muscles and sense the tension disappear completely. Feel the complete absence of tension. Compare the difference between how these muscles feel now with what you just experienced at 100 percent contraction. Once again, contract the same muscles, this time at half the full intensity. Hold the tension, keep holding, and now relax again. Feel how relaxed these muscles are. Compare this feeling of relaxation with what you felt at half intensity. When you compare the difference between tension levels and states of relaxation, a greater sense of relaxation will follow. Finally, contract these same muscles at only 5 percent, so that you barely feel the clothing over your stomach area. Just acknowledge that these muscles can contract. Now hold it, keep holding, and relax. Release any remaining tension so that the muscles are completely relaxed. Sense just how relaxed these muscles have become. Take a comfortably slow, deep breath and sense how relaxed your abdominal region has become.

8. *Lower back.* Isolate the muscles of your lower back. These muscles can get quite tense and cause much pain. Now, consciously tense these muscles by trying to press your lower back to the floor. Maintain this posture and hold really tight, as tight as you can, and hold it. Now, relax these muscles, allowing your back to curve naturally, and sense the tension

disappear completely. Sense how relaxed these muscles feel now and compare this with what you just experienced at 100 percent contraction. Once again, contract the same muscles, but at half the intensity. Hold the tension, keep holding, and now relax again. Feel how relaxed these muscles have become. Compare this feeling of relaxation with what you felt at 50 percent intensity. Once again, contract these same muscles, but this time at only 5 percent, a very slight twinge. Now hold it, keep holding, and relax. Release any remaining tension so that these muscles are completely loose and relaxed. Feel just how relaxed your lower back has become. Now, take a comfortably slow, deep breath.

9. *Buttocks.* Concentrate on your buttock muscles. Notice any residual tension and release it. Now, consciously tense these muscles really tight, as tight as you can and hold it, even tighter, and hold it. Now, release the tension, relax the muscles, and sense the tension disappear completely. Compare the difference between how these muscles feel now and what you just experienced at 100 percent contraction. Now contract these same muscles at a 50 percent contraction. Hold the tension, keep holding, and now relax again. Feel how relaxed these muscles are. Compare this feeling of relaxation with what you felt at half intensity. Now, finally, contract these same muscles at only 5 percent, showing no motion whatsoever. Now hold it, keep holding, and relax. Release any remaining tension so that these muscles are completely relaxed. Feel just how relaxed these muscles are. To enhance the feeling of

relaxation, take a slow, deep breath and sense how relaxed these muscles have become.

10. *Thighs.* Concentrate on the muscles of your left and right thigh. Try not to involve your abdominal or buttock muscles. Take a moment to sense just the muscles of your thighs. Notice any residual tension that might be there and release it. Now, consciously contract these muscles as tight as you can and hold it, even tighter, and hold it. Now relax these muscles and sense the tension disappear completely. Sense the difference between how these muscles feel now and what you just experienced. Once again, contract these same muscles, but at half the intensity. Hold the tension, keep holding, and now relax again. Feel how relaxed these muscles are. Compare this feeling of relaxation with what you felt at 50 percent intensity. Finally, contract these same muscles at only 5 percent. Now hold it, keep holding, and relax. Release any remaining tension so that these muscles are completely relaxed. Feel just how relaxed these muscles have become. Take a comfortably slow, deep breath.

11. *Calves.* Locate and sense the calf muscles of both legs and isolate these from all other leg muscles. Take a moment to sense your calf muscles. Notice if they have any residual tension. (These can be the tightest of all leg muscles.) Now, consciously tense these muscles really tight by pointing your toes (Fig. 24.4). (If they should begin to cramp, release the tension by pulling your toes toward your knees.) Contract as tight as you can, and hold it, tighter. Now relax these muscles and sense the tension disappear. Make a comparison between how relaxed these muscles now feel with the tension you just experienced at 100 percent contraction. Once again, contract these same muscles, but at a 50 percent contraction, like tip-toeing on a cold wood floor. Hold the tension, keep holding, and now relax again. Feel how relaxed these muscles are. Compare this feeling of relaxation with what you felt before. Now, contract these same muscles at only 5 percent, a very slight twinge with no motion whatsoever. Now hold it, keep holding, and relax. Release any remaining tension so

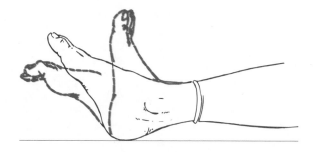

Figure 24.4 Pointing the toes to tighten calf muscles.

that these muscles are completely relaxed. Feel just how relaxed your calf muscles are. To enhance this feeling of relaxation, take a comfortably slow, deep breath and sense how relaxed your calves have become.

12. *Feet.* Focus your attention on muscles of your right and left feet. (Typically, the muscles of the feet are not tense, but when standing they can produce a lot of tension. In addition, in the confinement of shoes, they can become less than relaxed.) Now, consciously contract the muscles of your feet by scrunching your toes really tight, as tight as you can. Hold it, even tighter, and hold it. Now relax these muscles and sense the tension disappear completely. (You may even feel your feet become warm as they relax.) Feel the difference between how these muscles feel now and what you just experienced at 100 percent contraction. Once again, contract these same muscles at half the intensity. Hold the tension, keep holding, and now relax again. Feel how relaxed these muscles are. Compare this feeling of relaxation with the tension you felt at 50 percent intensity. Now, contract these same muscles at only 5 percent, a very slight twinge. Now hold it, keep holding, and relax. Release any remaining tension so that these muscles are completely relaxed. Sense how relaxed these muscles are. Finally, take a comfortably slow, deep breath and sense how relaxed your whole body is.

Your face and jaw muscles, your neck, shoulders, upper chest, arms and hands, your stomach and lower back, and your legs and feet—your whole body feels completely relaxed and calm. Now lie still, and enjoy the feeling of complete relaxation.

Best Application of Progressive Muscular Relaxation

Although Jacobson's technique was originally developed as a means to prevent the cumulative effects of stress, progressive muscular relaxation can also be used as an intervention technique when the body initiates the fight-or-flight response. As variations of PMR began to emerge, so too did the concept that this technique had the potential to reduce tension on the spot, in the midst of confronting a stressor, such as getting caught in traffic or standing in long shopping lines. As a preventive technique, however, the entire body must be systematically relaxed by progression through all the muscle groups, which may take up to thirty minutes. As an intervention technique, rather than going through the entire sequence of muscle groups, contract the hands or neck and shoulders—whatever muscle groups are tight—instead. This technique should be practiced not only in the morning or evening, but often during short (five–minute) PMR breaks over the course of a day.

Perhaps anger elicits the greatest response of unconscious muscle tension. Research shows that the suppression of anger can manifest itself in tension headaches and TMJ. And conventional wisdom suggests that PMR is one of the best relaxation techniques to deal with symptoms of anger.

There are some cautions to be noted with this technique. The isometric muscle tension used in PMR increases both systolic and diastolic blood pressure, even with contractions of short duration. Individuals with hypertension (elevated systolic and/or diastolic blood pressure) should refrain from using this technique, as it will certainly aggravate one's condition.

Summary

- Muscle tension is the most common symptom of stress. This is so because the initial neural response to stress initiates muscular excitation in order to prepare the body to move for its physical survival.
- Muscles can contract in one of three ways: concentrically (shortening), eccentrically (lengthening), and isometrically (no visible change in length). Muscle tension produced through the stress response is primarily isometric in that there is very little, if any, noticeable change. Yet over time, muscles contracted isometrically begin to show signs of shortening.
- In the early twentieth century, Jacobson recognized that virtually all his patients shared the same symptom regardless of illness: muscle tension. He concluded that if people could reduce muscular tension, their susceptibility to disease would decrease.
- The relaxation technique he created, called progressive muscular relaxation, involves systematically tensing and relaxing the body's musculature, from the feet to the head.
- PMR was quickly accepted by the medical community in the United States as the best way to promote relaxation. Today there are several versions of this technique, all showing similar positive results.
- Research, specifically biofeedback using electromyography, has proved that this technique indeed helps reduce muscular tension.

Concepts and Terms

Concentric contraction

Eccentric contraction

Isometric contraction

Progressive muscular relaxation

Residual tension

Zero firing threshold

References and Resources

Allen, R. *Human Stress: Its Nature and Control.* Burgess, Minneapolis, MN, 1983.

Allen, K. and Shriver, M. Enhanced Performance Feedback to Strengthen Biofeedback Treatment Outcomes with Childhood Migraine, *Headache* 37:169–173, 1997.

Belar, C. and Cohen, J. The Use of EMG Feedback and Progressive Muscular Relaxation in the Treatment of a Woman with Chronic Back Pain, *Biofeedback and Self-Regulation* 4:345–353, 1979.

Berkovec, T. D. and Fowles, D. C. Controlled Investigation of the Effects of Progressive and Hypnotic Relaxation on Insomnia, *Journal of Abnormal Psychology* 82:153–158, 1973.

Bernstein, D. and Berkovec, T. *Progressive Relaxation Training: A Manual for the Helping Professions.* Research Press, Champaign, IL, 1973.

Charlesworth, E. and Nathan, R. *Stress Management: A Comprehensive Guide to Wellness.* Ballantine, New York, 1984.

Curtis, J. and Detert, R. *How to Relax.* Mayfield, Mountain View, CA, 1981.

Gard, C. How Biofeedback May Help You Chill Out, *Current Health* 2(24):30–32, 1998.

Gellhorn, E. The Influence of Baroreceptor Reflexes on the Reactivity of the Autonomic Nervous System, *Experientia* 12:259–260, 1957.

Gellhorn, E. The Physiological Basis of Neuromuscular Relaxation, *Archives of Internal Medicine* 102:392–399, 1958.

Girdano, D. and Everly, G. *Controlling Stress and Tension: A Holistic Approach.* Prentice-Hall, Englewood Cliffs, NJ, 1990.

Greenberg, J. *Comprehensive Stress Management,* 4th ed. Brown, Dubuque, IA, 1999.

Hayes, S. N. Electromyographical Biofeedback and Relaxation Instructions in the Treatment of Muscle Contraction Headaches, *Behavior Therapy* 6:672–678, 1975.

Herman, C. et. al. Biofeedback Treatment for Pediatric Migraine: Prediction of Outcomes, *Journal of Consulting Psychological,* 65(4):611–616, 1997.

Jacobson, E. *Modern Treatment of Tense Patients.* Thomas, Springfield, IL, 1970.

Jacobson, E. *Progressive Relaxation.* University of Chicago Press, Chicago, 1929.

Jacobson, E. *You Must Relax.* McGraw-Hill, New York, 1978.

Marcus, A. and Smith, S.C. Biofeedback Helps Heart: A Successful Treatment for Chronic Heart Failure, *Prevention* 50:149–150, 1998.

Miller, E. *Letting Go of Stress.* Newman Communications, Albuquerque, NM, 1980. (Audio tape, CD)

Mitchell, K. and Mitchell, D. Migraine: An Exploratory Treatment, Application of Programmed Behavior Therapy Techniques, *Journal of Psychosomatic Research* 15: 137–57, 1978.

Rice, P. *Stress and Health,* 2nd ed. Brooks/Cole, Pacific Grove, CA, 1992.

Steinhaus, A. H. and Norris, J. E. *Teaching Neuromuscular Relaxation.* George Williams College, Chicago, IL, 1964.

Walker, C. E. *Learn to Relax: Thirteen Ways to Reduce Tension.* Prentice-Hall, Englewood Cliffs, NJ, 1975.

Chapter 25 Autogenic Training

Open your mind to the

power of self-suggestion.

—Johannes Schultz

The word *autogenic* means self-regulation or self-generation. It can also refer to a procedure or action that is self-produced. Specifically, it implies that individuals have the ability to regulate their physiological systems—the power to actually control various bodily functions. This is a novel concept, because for centuries internal functions of the human body like breathing and blood distribution were thought to operate independently of self-directed thoughts. Instead, most of these functions were thought to be totally regulated by the autonomic nervous system, a self-regulating mechanism ensuring the functioning of vital organs during both conscious and unconscious states.

During physical arousal heart rate, blood pressure, ventilations, and muscle tension can all increase in an effort to prepare the body to fight or flee. While this aroused state is greatly appreciated under the threat of physical harm, it becomes a liability when the threats are to the ego and identity. So when mental, emotional, or spiritual concerns threaten the psyche or ego, the body's responses need to be "retrained." By reprogramming the body's responses through self-generated thoughts or passive commands, physical effects are lessened considerably. We now know that mind-body integration is so profound that the antiquated survival mechanism can be overridden, much to our advantage, by conscious thoughts. Thus, the purpose of **autogenic training** is to reprogram the mind so as to override the stress response when physical arousal is not appropriate.

Historical Perspective

Beliefs regarding the regulation of bodily functions began to change in the nineteenth century, when Europeans traveled the globe and returned recounting stories of human feats in far-off lands. Visitors to the Himalayas reported yogi masters who showed a remarkable ability to control their breathing, heart rate, and blood flow, to the point where they could be mistaken for dead. In a state of profound relaxation produced by meditation, these individuals exhibited incredible control over their body's physiological functions. These yogis appeared to have no magic powers. Rather, they employed exceptional concentration skills to send internal messages from the conscious mind to specific body parts to alter their physiological function. In essence, by believing in the possibility of control, they induced a self-hypnotic state that then produced deep relaxation. (These observations were later documented at the Menninger Clinic by Elmer Green, Ph.D., in 1970 with the Hindu yogi Swami Rama.)

Meanwhile, on another continent at the turn of the twentieth century, self-hypnosis was being explored by a European brain physiologist, Oskar Vogt. Hypnosis, a trancelike state of consciousness, was already commonly practiced by doctors to better understand the relationship between the conscious and unconscious mind in their emotionally disturbed patients. But while working with several of his clients, Vogt discovered that if they were relaxed, some individuals could put themselves into this trancelike state. Vogt called this autohypnosis (Greenberg, 1999).

Building on this concept, the relaxation technique of autogenic training was introduced by two European physicians, Johannes Schultz and his protégé Wolfgang Luthe, in 1932. Although it was originally designed to calm the mind, patients often remarked on two other distinct physical sensations. The first was increased warmth of the extremities (the arms, hands, and feet). The second, which seemed to accompany the first, was an increased sense of heaviness in the extremities. Schultz speculated that both phenomena were due to vasodilation of blood vessels to localized musculature. It was this vasodilation that caused a change in the distribution of blood flow, bringing with it warmth from the body's core and a subtle but noticeable perception of heaviness. Although it seems that anyone can reap the benefits of self-hypnosis, Schultz and Luthe discovered several conditions that enhance this autogenic process. In addition, the term *training* was added when it was acknowledged that, like other skills, the more the technique was practiced, the better one's command over it, and the greater the relaxation response.

In their work with patients who mastered the autogenic technique, Schultz and Luthe (1959) concluded that it is most effective when the following factors are taken into consideration:

1. *The individual should be highly motivated and receptive to instructions and suggestions.* To master this technique, one must maintain a strong degree of self-confidence, faith, and willpower, knowing that the thoughts suggested in the conscious state will be passed from the mind through the body to produce the desired relaxation. Schultz and Luthe called this *passive concentration*.

2. *The individual should possess a strong sense of self-direction and control.* When practicing this technique, suggestions must be self-generated. In other words, one must take command or ownership of these thoughts to promote relaxation. Thus, the individual needs to take the initiative to organize thoughts and feed them systematically as the relaxation session unfolds. Individuals can be guided through the process with a series of directions, but ultimately the choice to follow these directions is in the mind of each individual.

3. *The individual should position himself or herself comfortably.* It was noted by Schultz and Luthe that body position is very important to achieve success with this technique. From their observations, they advocated two positions. The most beneficial is lying on one's back on a carpeted surface, with arms resting by the sides and palms facing up. This position is most conducive to feeling the heaviness effects. If this position is not possible, then a comfortably seated position is the best alternative.

4. *The individual should maintain a strong sense of concentration and body awareness.* Loss of mental focus or concentration will impede the

Figure 25.1 A person visualizing the flow of blood to the extremities.

flow of messages from the mind to the body. The effectiveness of this technique is enhanced by using both an alert conscious state and imaginative thought processes from the unconscious to focus on specific body regions. Complete attention, like that used by yogis in Nepal, promotes a greater sense of mental control and state of relaxation.

5. *The individual should minimize sensory reception.* Sensory information through the eyes, ears, nose, mouth, and body surface can and will compete for attention at the conscious level. By learning to tune out information from these sources (e. g., closing the eyes), the mind can focus on internal sensations, making them more effective.

6. *The individual should focus on internal physiological processes.* Because the conscious mind normally allows the autonomic nervous system to operate vital body functions, initially the ability to tune into these is embryonic at best. With practice, though, a keen sense of internal physiological processes will develop. Repeated suggestions received by the deeper levels of the mind will eventually transfer to the body through neurobiochemical reactions associated with the relaxation response.

Schultz and Luthe strongly believed that when these conditions are met, the stage is set for internal influences of both the conscious and unconscious mind to return the body to homeostasis through a balance of conscious mind-body awareness.

Unlike progressive muscular relaxation, in autogenic training there is no conscious, active effort to relax the muscles. Instead, emphasis is placed on making specific body regions warm and heavy through passive self-suggestions. In addition, greater degrees of body awareness and concentration are required to produce the desired relaxation effect. But because a passive attitude is adopted, you are in complete control and are able to stop at any time.

Psychological and Physiological Responses

The autogenic technique uses what is called *selected awareness* (Allen, 1983). Selected awareness refers to the receptivity of the conscious mind to acknowledgment and receipt of specific thoughts or messages. Ideally in the selected awareness process, the censorship role of the ego is eliminated and thoughts can travel freely from the conscious to the unconscious. Lack of censorship can improve dramatically the mind's ability to change or alter desired physiological functions. In a state of receptivity, too, sensations of pain are reduced, and sometimes eliminated altogether. In fact, there are volumes of anecdotal stories in newspapers around the world of people who have undergone incredible experiences, which under normal conditions would be impossible. For example, one runner reportedly ran the entire Boston Marathon feeling some pain in his leg, only to cross the finish line and collapse with a broken femur. Although barely understood scientifically, the powerful integration of conscious and unconscious thoughts allows for a greater state of psychic and physiological homeostasis.

Luthe (1969) also suggested that because the barriers between the conscious and unconscious mind are dismantled, there may be what he referred to as autogenic discharge, physical sensations such as muscle twitches, numbness, and emotional responses (e. g., crying), all triggered by the release of unconscious thoughts. These are said to be natural and healthy.

In its most characteristic sensations, warmth and heaviness, this technique can be compared to a muscle massage, although in this case, the muscles are massaged internally rather than on the surface of the skin. As mentioned in Chapter 2, the body's muscles are connected to a multitude of nerve cells that regularly release catecholamines at their synaptic junctions to produce minimal tension, or optimal tonus. Under hypnosis, however, the muscles become saturated with blood in a resting state, so the tension decreases and a message is sent back to the brain via the afferent nervous system to stop neural firing. It's a win-win situation for both the muscles, as they are allowed to relax, and the brain, which has less neurochemical work to do. The overall effect can be quite profound.

Several clinical tests measuring the effectiveness of this technique have revealed that a redistribution of blood flow indeed occurs in autogenic training, as well as many other changes. Decreases in heart rate, respiration, and muscle tension; increases in hemispheric alpha waves indicative of mental calmness; and even decreases in serum cholesterol levels have been clinically observed (Greenberg, 1999). Since its introduction, the autogenic relaxation technique has been used successfully in the treatment of several manifestations of physical stress including insomnia (Coates, 1978), migraines (Blanchard, 1985), muscle tension, Ray-

naud's syndrome (Keefe, 1980), a chronic condition of poor blood supply to the hands and feet, and perhaps most notably, hypertension (Silver, 1979).

But clinical laboratories and counseling centers are not the only sites where this technique has been employed. Houdini and several other magicians are known to have used the autogenic technique to "inflate" the size of their hands and wrists when handcuffed and locked up in a chest, then to reverse the process to escape the trap. National biathlon champion Kari Swenson, who was abducted by two men near Bozeman, Montana, in 1985 used this as a survival technique in an effort to minimize blood loss from her gunshot wound. In his book *Peace, Love, and Healing,* cancer surgeon Bernie Siegel wrote about the use of this technique with his patients during surgical procedures for which they were anesthetized. After giving them a clear understanding of the powers of the conscious and unconscious mind, Dr. Siegel asked his patients to shunt the flow of blood away from the operating site. After surgery he asked for their cooperation in healing the site. Siegel found that, when relaxed, patients can decrease blood flow in the area of the incision. Moreover, he noted that patients who are receptive to this power of suggestion tend to recover much more quickly from their surgery. Siegel also recounted an episode where a patient showed signs of cardiac arrhythmia immediately following surgery. Siegel whispered in the patient's ear to sense his heart contracting in a relaxed rhythm, like a swing moving back and forth on a swing set. Sure enough, the dysrhythmia disappeared.

Since its acceptance as a bona fide relaxation technique, autogenic training has been utilized in many clinical settings and helped a number of patients with a host of stress-related physical problems. As a result of its widespread use, many variations have surfaced in the past fifty years, including its combination with complementary techniques such as diaphragmatic breathing and mental imagery.

Steps to Initiate Autogenic Training
Body Position

As Schultz and Luthe suggested, there are two recommended positions (Fig. 25.2). The preferred position is lying on your back on a carpeted floor or bed, with your arms by your sides, palms facing up, and legs straight, heels resting evenly on the surface. Thin pillows or cushions may be used behind the head and knees for

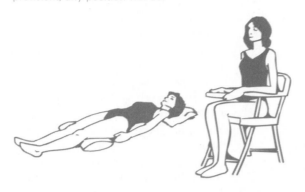

Figure 25.2 The two suggested body positions are (1) lying on your back on a comfortable floor surface, or if this is not possible, (2) sitting comfortably in a chair. Once you are proficient, any position will do.

support as long as the body remains in comfortable vertebral alignment. If circumstances do not permit lying down, then a seated position in a chair is recommended. While seated, keep your head aligned over your body, with your arms either on your lap or supported by the frame of the chair. It is important to have your limbs supported so that they don't compete with the force of gravity and negate the effects you are trying to produce. Luthe suggests that if your head becomes too heavy, let it hang comfortably. Because several postural muscles are called upon when seated, it may be less effective than the reclining position. With practice, however, sitting will also produce the desired relaxation. It is also recommended to remove jewelry and loosen any restrictive clothing. Perhaps most important, refrain from eating a big meal before practicing this technique. This will compromise its effectiveness because when food is digested, blood concentrates in the gastrointestinal area and this will compete with the blood flow to the extremities.

Concentration and Awareness

Under normal conditions, attention is easily distracted by interruptions, from phone calls to random thoughts roaming the interiors of our minds. To minimize external distractions, find a quiet place and designate it as your relaxation space. By training your relaxation skills in the same location each time, a comfort pattern is created for both mind and body. Next, control this environment by unplugging the phone, closing the door, and making other necessary adjustments such as closing the window or blinds.

Now you can focus internally. When first trying this technique, you may find your mind drifting toward what seems like more important thoughts. But autogenic concentration concerns only the "here and now," specifically, the present state of your body. If at first you find other thoughts competing for your attention, simply acknowledge them and then redirect your flow of consciousness back to your body. With practice, the frequency of competing thoughts will decrease and concentration will improve.

The concentration for relaxation skills is different from that required for driving a car, listening to a lecture, or watching a movie. Often those events require judgment and analysis. By contrast, during a state of relaxation, particularly autogenic training, concentration involves the right cerebral hemisphere's ability to receive and accept thoughts without judgment. In this technique, you must allow yourself to become open to suggestion and adopt a passive—but not defensive—frame of mind.

Other Suggestions

The principles of autogenic training can be learned quite quickly, and short-term effects are often experienced immediately. However, it may take a few weeks of practice to feel the cumulative effects. When learning and practicing this technique, try to practice twice a day for fifteen minutes each time so that a training effect does occur.

There are two general approaches to the autogenic relaxation technique. The first is the indirect approach, wherein you simply suggest to yourself that certain body regions become warm and heavy. The second is a more direct approach, wherein you employ a greater sense of mental imagery by making reference to the specific physiological systems responsible for the sensations of warmth and heaviness.

Indirect Approach

The indirect approach involves very general instructions to follow regarding body awareness. There is little detail and internal visual imagery involved. The phases of these instructions are a feeling of heaviness, a feeling of warmth, a calmness of the heart, a calmness of breathing, and even a coolness of the forehead. Attention to each phase should continue for about one minute by repeating the instructions until the desired sensation is felt. This whole progression of phases should take approximately fifteen minutes. When you are done, remain in position and try to lock the feeling of relaxation into your memory bank so you can recall it during times of stress and tension.

First, take a slow, deep breath and feel the sense of relaxation as you exhale. Do this once more, making the breath even slower and deeper than the last. Then say the following thoughts to yourself:

Phase 1: *Heaviness*
+ My arms and hands feel heavy.
+ My legs and feet feel heavy.
+ My arms and legs feel heavy.

Phase 2: *Warmth*
+ My arms and hands feel warm.
+ My legs and feet feel warm.
+ My arms and legs feel warm.

Phase 3: *Heart*
+ My heart is calm and relaxed.
+ My heartbeat is slow and relaxed.

Phase 4: *Breathing*
+ My breathing is slow and relaxed.
+ My breathing is calm and comfortable.

Phase 5: *Solar Plexus*
+ My stomach area is calm and relaxed.

Phase 6: *Forehead*
+ My forehead is cool.
+ My forehead is calm and relaxed.
+ My entire body is calm and relaxed.

Direct Approach

The direct approach is a more detailed visual interpretation of the general instructions just listed. It is a slight variation on the original technique offering added instructions for those who need more understanding of how the physiological changes occur. In the direct approach, the specific mechanisms involved in warmth and heaviness are focused on to initiate a stronger sense of relaxation. Here, you start out with diaphragmatic breathing to induce relaxation. When mind and body become relaxed through this technique, the mind becomes more receptive to additional thoughts (warmth and heaviness), and thus the selected awareness process is enhanced. The length of time required for this approach will vary. To begin, you may want to work on only one body region such as the arms and hands. With proficiency, you can add to the duration of each session. The following instructions can be read prior to your session, or they can be read to you by a friend while you are performing this technique.

1. First, concentrate on your breathing. Feel the air come in through your nose or mouth, down into your lungs, and feel your stomach rise and then fall as you exhale the air though your mouth.

2. Take a comfortably slow, deep breath, feeling the air enter the lower chambers of your lungs. Feel your stomach rise slowly with the intake of air, and then slowly descend as the air leaves your lungs. Repeat this, making the breath even slower and deeper. With each exhalation, feel how relaxed your body has become.

3. Focus on your heartbeat. Listen to and feel your heart beating in your chest. As you concentrate on this, allow a longer pause after each heartbeat. Just by allowing the thought of your heart relaxing, you can make it do so. Allow a longer pause after each beat. Now, to help relax the heart muscle, take one more slow, deep breath and as you exhale feel how relaxed your heart has become. Again consciously choose to place a longer pause after each heartbeat.

4. Take a moment to realize that in the resting state you are now in, your body's core receives the greatest percentage (80 percent) of blood, most of it going to the gastrointestinal tract. While the body's core is receiving a great supply of blood, the periphery—arms and legs—receive only a maintenance supply.

5. Be aware that when your muscles are saturated with blood, they become very relaxed and pliable, like a wet sponge. Now, think to yourself that you would like to recreate that feeling of relaxation in the muscles of your arms and hands.

6. Allow the blood to move from the body's core up to your shoulders and down toward your arms and hands. As you think and desire this, you will begin to constrict the blood vessels of your stomach area while at the same time dilating those of your arms and hands (Fig. 25.3).

7. With each breath you take, with each beat of your heart, allow the flow of blood to move from your stomach area to your arms and hands.

8. You will begin to notice that as you allow this movement of blood from your core to your arms and hands, they begin to feel slightly heavy. They feel heavy because they are not quite used to the sensation of additional blood flow to this region. You will also notice that your arms and particularly your hands feel warm, especially

your palms and fingers, since they have the greatest number of temperature receptors.

9. With each breath and each beat of your heart, allow the blood to continue to move from your stomach area toward your arms and hands. Feel how comfortable your arms and hands have become. They feel warm and heavy, and very relaxed. As the muscles become saturated with blood, stiffness dissipates and relaxation ensues.

10. Soon you will notice that your arms feel increasingly heavy, so much so that should you want to move them you couldn't because they feel immobilized. You feel as if they are making indentations in the floor or chair frame. Your arms and hands feel so relaxed they just don't want to move.

11. With each breath and each beat of your heart, continue to send the flow of blood to your arms and hands. Feel the warmth spread from your arms all the way down to your palms and fingers.

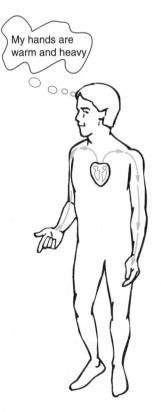

Figure 25.3 Visualizing blood flow to the arms and hands. the breath even slower and deeper. With each exhalation, feel how relaxed your body has become.

12. Take a long, slow, deep breath and gauge how relaxed your whole body feels as you exhale. Sense how relaxed your arms and hands feel.

13. Now, take one more slow, deep breath, and as you exhale allow the flow of blood to return back to your stomach area. Reverse the flow of blood from your arms and hands back to your body's core. By thinking this, you now allow the blood vessels of the arms and hands to constrict, shunting the blood back to the GI tract. At the same time, you allow the blood vessels of the stomach area to dilate and receive the flow of blood you have sent to it.

14. As the blood returns, you may notice that your arms begin to feel a little lighter, but the sensation of warmth still lingers.

15. With each breath you take, with each beat of your heart, allow the flow of blood to return to where it came from.

16. Again, concentrate on your breathing. Feel the air come in through your nose or mouth, down into your lungs, and feel your stomach rise and then descend as you exhale the air through your mouth.

17. Now, take a comfortably slow, deep breath and feel the air enter the lower chambers of your lungs. Feel your stomach rise slowly with the intake of air, and slowly descend as the air leaves your lungs. Do this again, making the breath even slower and deeper. With each exhalation, become more aware of how relaxed your body has become.

18. Next, focus again on the beat of your heart. Listen to and feel your heart beating in your chest. As you concentrate on this, allow a longer pause between heartbeats. Just by allowing the thought of your heart relaxing you can make it do so. Think to allow a longer pause between beats. To help relax the heart muscle, take one more slow, deep breath, and feel how relaxed your heart has become as you exhale. Again, place a longer pause after each heartbeat.

19. Again, take a moment to realize that in the resting state you are now in, your body's core contains the greatest percentage of your blood supply, roughly 80 percent.

20. Think to yourself that when your muscles are saturated with blood, they become very relaxed and pliable like a wet sponge. Now become

consciously aware that you desire to recreate that feeling of relaxation in the muscles of your legs and feet.

21. Allow the blood from your stomach area to move down toward your legs and feet. As you think and desire this, the blood vessels of your stomach area will begin to constrict, while at the same time those of your legs and feet will begin to dilate. This constriction process in your body's core will begin to shunt blood to your thighs, hamstrings, calves, and feet, where the dilating vessels will be able to receive more blood (Fig. 25.4).

22. With each breath you take, with each beat of your heart, allow the flow of blood to move from your stomach area down toward your legs and feet.

23. You will begin to notice that as you allow this movement of blood from your body's core to your legs and feet, both your legs and feet begin to feel slightly heavy. This heaviness increases with each breath and each heartbeat. They feel very heavy because muscles in this region are not used to the sensation of additional blood flow. You will also notice that your legs and particularly your feet feel warm, especially the heels of your feet and your toes, as they have the greatest number of temperature receptors.

24. With each breath and each beat of your heart, allow the blood to continue to move from your stomach area to your legs and feet. Feel how comfortable your thighs and calves are. They feel warm, comfortably heavy, and very relaxed. As the muscles become saturated with blood, stiffness dissipates and relaxation ensues.

25. Be aware that your legs now feel increasingly heavy, so much so that you want to move them but they feel immobilized. You feel as if each leg has sunk under its weight into the floor. Your legs and feet feel so relaxed they don't want to move.

26. With each breath and each beat of your heart, continue to send the flow of blood to legs and feet. Feel the warmth spread from your stomach area all the way down to your toes.

27. Take a long, slow, deep breath and gauge how relaxed your whole body feels as you exhale. Feel how relaxed your legs and feet feel.

28. Now, take one more slow, deep breath and as you exhale, allow the flow of blood to return to your stomach area. Reverse the flow of blood from your legs and feet back to your body's core. By thinking this, you allow the blood vessels of the legs and feet to constrict, shunting the blood back to the GI tract. At the same time, you allow the blood vessels of the stomach area to dilate and receive the flow of blood you are sending to it.

29. As the blood returns, you will notice that your legs are beginning to feel a little lighter, but the sensations of warmth linger, especially in your feet and toes.

30. With each breath you take, with each beat of your heart, allow the flow of blood to return to where it came from.

31. As your body returns to a resting state, feel the sensation of relaxation throughout. Although you feel relaxed, you don't feel tired or sleepy. You feel alert and energized.

32. When you feel ready, open your eyes and stretch the muscles of your arms, shoulders, and legs.

Visualizing blood flow to the legs and feet

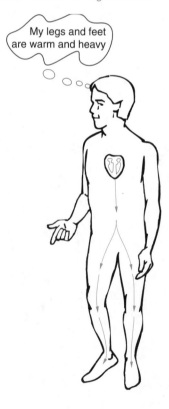

My legs and feet are warm and heavy

Figure 25.4

Adding Mental Imagery

As Aristotle once said, "The soul never thinks without a picture." When imagery is combined with autogenic training, it can produce profound physiological effects on the body. As explained in Chapter 20, imagery consisting of pictures or symbols that parallel and represent actual physiological responses seems to affect the body's functions in ways that words alone cannot. A host of stories shared in the medical community lend credence to this concept. Hypertensive patients who use mental imagery have shown significant decreases in blood pressure. For example, one client of mine used the image of a bottleneck traffic jam on a highway. By working to clear the jam in his mind and then visualizing only his car on the road, he was able to reduce his resting blood pressure to the point where he was taken off medication by his physician. This phenomenon can be explained through the specific cognitive functions of the right and left hemispheres of the brain. The left hemisphere, which controls verbal skills, is thought to communicate to the body in words. The right hemisphere, which is quite poor in verbal ability, but proficient with symbolic images, appears to communicate to the body visually. The combination of words and pictures seems to have a more profound effect on the body's physiology than do words alone.

Best Application of Autogenic Training

In its original design, autogenic training was created to be thorough in its attempt to relax the entire body. Sessions would last twenty to forty minutes and could be done at any time of the day. Today, stress-management instructors advocate relaxing all body regions for the entire duration of each session to achieve full effectiveness. With proficiency, however, the ability to relax upon suggestion of warmth and heaviness can be immediate, which is especially useful in situations that trigger the stress response. The autogenic technique is as portable as the thoughts that create it. Some health care professionals even suggest periodic short "autogenic breaks" in the course of a busy day as a preventive approach to the cumulative effects of stress. The jury is still out on whether this technique is more advantageous for reducing anxiety or anger. It appears to be effective with both emotional responses, depending on the individual and circumstances. It's best to try it for yourself and find out how it can best work for you.

Stress With a Human Face

A GOOD MAGICIAN NEVER REVEALS HIS OR her secrets, which is why going to a magic show can be as frustrating as it is entertaining. Trick after trick, you think to yourself, "How did he do that?" And the more amazing the stunt, the more baffled you become.

I once went to a magic show in college. The performer was renowned as an escape artist, and he announced that in the second half of the show he would escape from handcuffs and a locked trunk submerged in water. My friends and I were intrigued, to say the least.

After an amazing first act, I left my seat to stretch my legs. To my surprise, I met the star performer face to face as I walked outside the rear exit of the auditorium. I extended my hand to greet the magician and express my gratitude for a great show. As our hands clasped, I noticed that his palms and fingers were incredibly swollen, as if he had an acute case of poison ivy. After we exchanged polite comments, he went back to his dressing room and I went back to my seat.

I couldn't get over the feel of that handshake. It was like holding a balloon full of water. The escape act was very impressive and ended with thunderous applause. Walking home that night, I was still perplexed about how he got out of those handcuffs, but I was sure his spongy hands had something to do with it.

Years later, I learned that Houdini practiced a technique similar to autogenic training to effect his escapes. He was not only a master escape artist but apparently a master of relaxation as well. ◆

Summary

♦ The term *autogenic training* refers to the body's ability to regulate specific physiological functions through conscious suggestion. This term is often used synonymously with the clinical term *self-regulation*.

♦ This relaxation technique was created by two German physicians, Schultz and Luthe, after learning that some of their patients could hypnotize themselves to a profound state of relaxation. The primary effect was in peripheral body regions, which became warm and heavy. This effect is thought to be the result of changes in blood flow.

♦ Schultz and Luthe outlined six conditions they felt necessary for this technique to be effective. Among these are receptiveness to the self-suggestion to relax, positioning oneself comfortably, the ability to concentrate, and focusing on internal physiological processes.

♦ *Selective awareness* is a term used to explain how the mind focuses attention on the self-suggestion and receptivity that produce a sense of relaxation.

♦ Autogenic discharge refers to various sensory sensations and emotional responses triggered by this technique.

♦ The autogenic technique has been used in hospitals where patients have shunted blood away from surgical sites. It has also been reported to hasten recovery from surgery.

♦ There are two general approaches to this technique. In the direct method, the person consciously moves blood to the extremities where warmth and heaviness are desired. In the indirect method, the person focuses only on warmth and heaviness, not blood flow.

Concepts and Terms

Autogenic discharge

Autogenic training

Autonomic control

Direct approach

Indirect approach

Passive concentration

Selective awareness

Self-regulation

References and Resources

Allen, R. *Human Stress: Its Nature and Control.* Burgess Press, Minneapolis, MN, 1983.

Anderson, N., Lawrence, P., and Olson, T. Within-Subject Analysis of Autogenic Training and Cognitive Coping Training in the Treatment of Tension Headache Pain, *Journal of Behavioral Therapy and Experimental Psychiatry* 12:219–223, 1981.

Blanchard, E. B. et al. Biofeedback and Relaxation Treatments for Headaches in the Elderly: A Caution and a Challenge, *Biofeedback and Self-Regulation* 10(1):68–73, 1985.

Carruthers, M. Autogenic Training, *Journal of Psychosomatic Research* 23:437–440, 1979.

Coates, T. J. and Thoreson, C. E. What to Use Instead of Sleeping Pills, *Journal of the American Medical Association* 240:2311–2312, 1978.

Gorton, B. Autogenic Training, *American Journal of Clinical Hypnosis* 2:31–41, 1959.

Green, E. and Green, A. *Beyond Biofeedback.* Delacorte Press, New York, 1977.

Green, E., Green, A., and Walters, E. D. Voluntary Control of Intense States: Psychological and Physiological, *Journal of Transpersonal Psychology* 26:1–26, 1970.

Greenberg, J. *Comprehensive Stress Management,* 6th ed. Brown, Dubuque, IA, 1999.

Keefe, J. F., Surwit, R. S., and Pilon, R. N. Biofeedback, Autogenic Training, and Progressive Muscular Relaxation in the Treatment of Raynaud's Disease: A Comparative Study, *Journal of Applied Behavior Analysis* 13:3–11, 1980.

Luthe, W. *Autogenic Theory.* Grune and Stratton, New York, 1969.

Luthe, W. Method, Research, and Applications of Autogenic Training, *American Journal of Clinical Hypnosis* 5:17–23, 1962.

Miller, E. *Letting Go of Stress.* Newman Communications, Albuquerque, NM, 1980.

Pellitier, K. *Mind as Healer, Mind as Slayer.* Dell, New York, 1977.

Porter, G. and Norris, P. *Why Me?: Harnessing the Healing Power of the Human Spirit.* Stillpoint Press, Walpole, NH, 1985.

Schultz, J. *Das Autogene Training.* Geerg-Thieme, Verlag, Leipzig, Germany, 1932.

Schultz, J. and Luthe, W. *Autogenic Training: A Psychophysiological Approach to Psychotherapy.* Grune and Stratton, New York, 1959.

Siegel, B. *Peace, Love, and Healing.* Perennial Press, New York, 1990.

Silver, B. V. Temperature Biofeedback and Regulation Training in the Treatment of Migraine Headaches, *Biofeedback and Self-Regulation* 4:359–366, 1979.

Chapter 26 Clinical Biofeedback

I sing the body electric.

—Walt Whitman

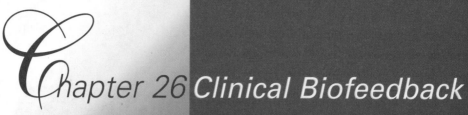

Picture this: wires taped to the forehead and scalp; electrode pads affixed to the clavicles, chest, and lower ribs; temperature pads stuck to the palms and fingers. Is it a scene from the latest version of Mary Shelley's *Frankenstein?* No, it's biofeedback—the newest scientific relaxation technique, which combines high technology and the ancient practice of meditation and body awareness. In simple terms, biofeedback is any information we observe and process about our bodies. Counting the number of times you breathe per minute is a type of biofeedback. Checking your pulse or target heart rate during an aerobics class is also a simple type of biofeedback. Even taking your temperature is considered a type of biofeedback. When information is accessed through clinical instrumentation, it is referred to as **clinical biofeedback.**

What Is Clinical Biofeedback?

Clinical biofeedback can be defined as the use of monitoring instruments to amplify the electrochemical energy produced by body organs. Normally individuals are not aware of producing this energy, but through biofeedback they can use information to gain voluntary control over various physiological processes. For example, let us say that you have just learned from your dentist that you apparently grind your teeth at night. Being unaware that your jaw muscles are clenched while you sleep makes the problem difficult to resolve. But the use of instrumentation to measure your physiological responses could show you the tension you produce in your jaw muscles while awake and thus teach you how to reduce it—and eliminate the wear and tear on your teeth.

What distinguishes clinical biofeedback from other techniques is that it allows a person to increase awareness of his or her own physiological responses (breathing, muscle tension, blood pressure, heart rate, and/or body temperature) by learning to monitor them through data gathered by a particular instrument. Through biofeedback training, a person can also learn to recondition the thought processes associated with increased autonomic nervous activity in order to relax. Some stressors are very obvious, as are our reactions to them. But others are more subtle, so much so that we condition ourselves to ignore the effects they produce throughout our bodies. Clinical biofeedback has the advantage of magnifying a biolog-

ical function to give you immediate evidence of changes in it, which in turn allows you to gain mastery over it as it is happening. And whereas most relaxation techniques are meant to have a general, overall effect, biofeedback is usually specific to one physiological parameter you want to target (e.g., tension in your jaw muscles).

Clinical biofeedback typically employs sophisticated technological equipment in combination with one or more other relaxation techniques, including meditation, diaphragmatic breathing, mental imagery, autogenic training, and progressive muscular relaxation. When these relaxation techniques are performed in conjunction with data from an instrument revealing what the autonomic nervous system is really doing, the person gains a stronger "feel" for how to relax that body region.

Stress management is not the only area facilitated by this technique. Clinical biofeedback is also used in several types of psychotherapy (e.g., gestalt therapy) and some cases of physical rehabilitation of knee, lower back, and shoulder joints.

Once again, this technique emphasizes the importance of a strong mind-body-spirit connection. Clinical biofeedback is currently used in the treatment of migraine and tension headaches, ulcers, hypertension, bruxism, Raynaud's disease, and a host of other stress-related illnesses. Dr. Edward Blanchard of the Center for Stress and Anxiety Disorders in Albany, New York, has conducted numerous scientific investigations demonstrating the beneficial effects of biofeedback on several different maladies, substantiating the validity of this technique. His work is well respected throughout the allied health fields. But despite the fact that biofeedback is known to be effective in gaining control over specific biological functions, the exact mechanisms involved are as yet not completely understood.

Historical Perspective

The term *biofeedback* was coined in the late 1960s at the first annual meeting of the Biofeedback Research Society to describe biological feedback through electrical instrumentation. This includes information on any physiological parameter that can be electronically detected, amplified, and converted into visual or auditory stimuli. An individual can observe and interpret these stimuli, and thereby make appropriate changes to enhance his or her health. While the name is rather new, the concepts of biofeedback date back to the classical conditioning theory of Pavlov (every stimulus produces a response through association) and operant conditioning theory of Thorndike (behaviors can be changed by redirected thought processes). Until 1960 it was strongly believed that the autonomic nervous system was reflexive in nature, influenced only by classical conditioning, not conscious thought. Like an autopilot computer program, the autonomic nervous system was thought to be under complete control of the lower brain centers. Basic physiological functions were called "involuntary," because it was believed that they could not be intentionally influenced or manipulated by the individual.

As discussed in the chapters on hatha yoga (Chapter 19) and autogenic training (Chapter 25), clinical investigations with the yogi Swami Rama, conducted at the Menninger Clinic, as well as other studies by Miller (1968) began to show that conscious thought really can influence the physiological functions of the autonomic nervous system. In addition to significantly lowering his resting heart rate and breathing well below "normal homeostatic levels," Swami Rama was able to shift blood flow to various regions of his body. Similar studies showed that some people had the ability to change their brain waves at will. In fact, people who were taught autogenic training proved that with practice almost anyone could control these "involuntary" functions. And the more they practiced, the more control they seemed to exhibit. Biofeedback training is now considered a type of operant conditioning wherein, with the help of a trained therapist, an individual can learn to control specific physiological functions by changing the thoughts and perceptions that produced them.

In his book *Mind as Healer, Mind as Slayer,* stress researcher Kenneth Pelletier states that biofeedback is comprised of three principles: (1) information can be obtained about specific organ activity, meaning that a machine can distinguish electrical conduction of heart muscle from that of brain and skeletal muscles; (2) every physiological change is paralleled by a change in attitude or consciousness, just as a change in feelings will produce a change in some biological function; and (3) people can be taught to control their autonomic nervous systems to influence these physiological changes directly. He also added that individu-

als must accept responsibility for their own health status; in this case, by learning to recondition thoughts and behaviors away from disease and toward health. This principle is closely related to Rotter's concept of locus of control, where a person learns to shift the focus of control from an external source (a stressor) to an internal source (his or her thoughts) to take control of physical health.

Purpose of Biofeedback

To get an idea of our physical appearance, we gaze into a mirror at our hair, our complexion, and the clothing we wear. Mirrors offer a clear reflection of our physical exterior. The many physiological functions which take place inside our bodies are much more difficult to observe yet equally necessitate our attention. For example, an estimated 20 percent of the United States population has hypertension, but blood pressure *cannot* be detected by physical appearance or by simply taking one's pulse. It must be monitored with a blood-pressure cuff, sphygmomanometer, and stethoscope. It is physiological functions we cannot see, involving the nervous, endocrine, and immune systems, that are so strongly activated during the stress response. While some people show the ability to scan their bodies and bring certain functions under control without the aid of a machine, most people need the additional help of biofeedback to do so. With enough practice, these people, too, attain the ability to perceive and regulate their internal functions without the use of machines.

Although the technology of clinical biofeedback may seem complex, the concept behind it is quite simple. Biofeedback is a *closed-loop feedback system,* where information taken from the system (the human body) is translated into a language understood by the five senses (Fig. 26.1). Biofeedback is like a horse-race track where the starting and finishing points are the same. In this case, the loop begins with the body, which is connected by wires to some type of electronic machine. The wires receive energy and send it to the machine, where it is converted to recognizable stimuli and then relayed back to the individual through one of the five senses. More technically, biochemical impulses generated by specific body organ tissue are transmitted via one or more electrodes attached to that body region and sent to an electronic receiver that converts the impulses to either visual or auditory

Figure 26.1 The biofeedback loop (Girdano/Everly/Dusek, *Controlling Stress and Tension*, 6e, © 2000, p. 253. Reprinted by permission of Allyn & Bacon, Boston)

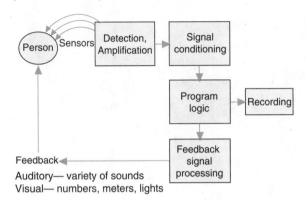

stimuli. These stimuli can be in the form of colored lights, sounds, and/or parts such as needle pens that chart the data. In one instance of biofeedback for children, Rice (1992) reported that a toy train wired to a machine provided feedback by moving only when subjects were completely relaxed.

Biofeedback has been called an educational tool because it teaches people how to monitor and change the frequency and amplitude of the electronic signals by controlling (relaxing) the body region to which the electrodes are attached. The purpose of biofeedback, therefore, is to teach people how to "tune in" to their bodies so that they may regulate those physiological functions that are susceptible to increased metabolic activity due to stress.

There are three distinct phases of biofeedback:

1. *Awareness of physiological response.* As mentioned before, the sensory stimulation deciphered by the biofeedback machine and decoded by one of the five senses helps one increase awareness of physiological adaptations to stress. Operating the instrument is a certified therapist who teaches the patient to interpret the amplified signals and thereby form an association between the flashing lights or beeping sounds and the body's current state of arousal.
2. *Control of physiological response.* The therapist guides the person through several types of relaxation techniques—meditation, mental

imagery, and autogenic training, among others. At the same time, the person attempts to consciously manipulate his or her physiological response to bring a particular body organ or reaction to a state of homeostatis.

3. *Application of reconditioned response in everyday routines.* After much practice with biofeedback instrumentation, the individual then transfers the new skill to the office, home, car, or wherever he or she experiences the sensations of stress, by practicing the relaxation technique without using the equipment. This, of course, is the real test of the effectiveness of biofeedback training sessions.

Types of Biofeedback

There are many types of biofeedback equipment. Some are so small you can hold them in your hand, and others involve large (expensive) instrumentation in a wall unit. Different machines have been designed to receive the electrical signals from the heart, brain, muscles, skin, back, and so forth. The use of biofeedback is specific to the symptom(s) the patient exhibits in a particular body region. In general, though, instrumentation falls into two categories: binary and proportional. Binary equipment provides information that lets someone know only whether he or she is controlling a physiological function. An example would be a light that is off when someone's systolic blood pressure is above 130 mm Hg, and goes on when blood pressure goes below that number. Proportional biofeedback, by contrast, reveals the *amount of change* occurring during a session. An example is a machine that changes the pitch of a sound as a person becomes more relaxed. Because it provides more information to the patient, proportional biofeedback is thought to be more effective as a teaching tool. Regardless of instrumentation, biofeedback is effective because it is accurate and reliable.

Electromyographic (EMG) Biofeedback

This biofeedback modality monitors electrical impulses produced by muscle tissue (Fig. 26.2). Electrodes are placed on the skin over specific muscles that are prone to tension such as the jaw, lower back, neck, and/or shoulders. For overall relaxation, the frontalis muscle on the forehead is used, as this muscle

EMG biofeedback instruments.

Figure 26.2

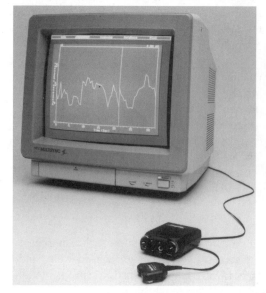

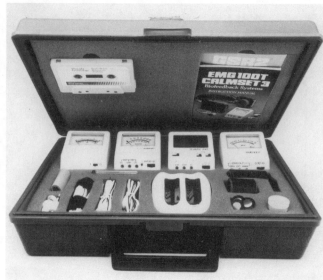

has no direct connection to bone. Through the EMG, the patient first becomes aware of the current level of muscle tension by watching visual feedback or hearing auditory feedback. With the aid of the therapist, the subject is then taught to relax the muscles that are diagnosed as tense, and to sense the difference between tension and relaxation, while monitoring visual and/or auditory data produced by the machine. EMG biofeedback is most commonly used for tension headaches and bruxism, or TMJ.

Electroencephalographic (EEG) Biofeedback

Like the heart and muscles, the brain also produces electrical impulses. In 1924, Hans Berger created an instrument to detect and monitor brain waves, which he called the electroencephalogram (EEG) (Fig. 26.3). An EEG is recorded by applying electrodes to designated points on the scalp, which monitor electrical activity close to the surface of the brain. Through the use of EEG, it has been observed that the human brain produces different electrical rhythms during various states of consciousness. These brain waves are grouped and characterized by oscillations per second and amplitude. The four groups are beta waves (> than 15 cycles per second), which are associated with normal or waking consciousness; alpha waves (7–14 cycles per sec-

EEG biofeedback equipment.

Figure 26.3

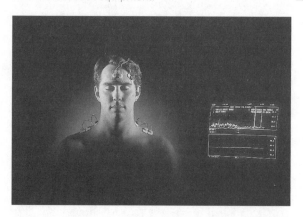

ond), which are produced in an altered or relaxed state of consciousness; and theta (4–7 cycles per second) and delta (between .5 and 4 cycles per second) waves, which are observed in unconscious and sleeping states. Each type of brain wave is represented by a specific sound or pitch from the EEG. For the purpose of relaxation, the patient is taught to decrease the pitch associated with beta waves and increase the alpha sound. The primary purpose of this type of biofeedback is to alleviate the cognitive arousal observed in insomnia. So far, it seems to be of very little help in relieving tension headaches or other stress symptomology.

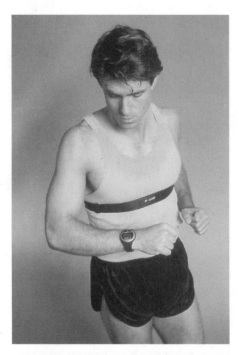

Figure 26.4 A heart rate monitor.

Cardiovascular (EKG) Biofeedback

Because there appears to be such a strong relationship between stress and coronary heart disease, cardiovascular biofeedback is often used to augment a patient's ability to control resting heart rate and blood pressure (Fig. 26.4). Portable equipment is now available for cardiac patients so that they may monitor their heart rate on a regular basis. Portable blood pressure kits are also available for people with hypertension. In either case, patients are taught to employ relaxation skills when the biofeedback machine indicates that cardiovascular parameters are above pre-set resting levels.

But cardiovascular biofeedback is not used solely by people at risk for cardiac disease. Many Olympic and professional athletes also use portable heart-rate monitors to aid their training. Several of these consist of a belt worn around the upper chest and a receiver worn on the wrist like a watch. The receiver is set to a target heart-rate range and if the athlete goes below or above this zone, the watch beeps, signifying that cardiovascular workload needs to be increased or decreased, respectively. In some cases, the receiver records heart rate for up to an hour, and these data can be retrieved and logged into a training diary.

Another type of cardiovascular monitor measures temperature. Thermal biofeedback, as it is called, monitors the flow of blood to a specific area by the heat it gives off. Temperature receptors are applied to specific body parts (e.g., fingers and toes) so that changes in blood flow can be detected as changes in temperature. Thermal biofeedback is most often used in the treatment of migraine headaches and Raynaud's disease.

Electrodermal (EDR) Biofeedback

Electrodermal (EDR) biofeedback, also known as galvanic skin response or GSR, is used to measure electrical conduction in the skin itself (Fig. 26.5). The hands and fingers produce beads of sweat under stress, and the fact that water is a good conductor of electricity is the basis of the operation of the EDR instrument. The premise behind EDR is that electrical impulses produced by the skin are activated by the sympathetic nervous system. In this type of biofeedback, electrodes are lubricated with a conductance gel and placed on the skin, usually the index and ring fingers of the left hand. As in other forms of biofeedback, the patient is then taught to decrease sympathetic activation through relaxation techniques. EDR is employed primarily to detect nervousness, and repeated use can help people learn to decrease anxiety. The same technology, incidentally, is used in polygraph (lie detector) tests.

Best Application of Clinical Biofeedback

Clinical biofeedback, like muscle massage, is a technique that requires the assistance of a qualified instructor or therapist. The primary organization that certifies therapists in clinical biofeedback training is the Biofeedback Certificate Institute of America (BCIA). Since 1980, all therapists practicing biofeedback have required certification by one of these organizations. If you are interested in this mode of relaxation therapy because of recurring health problems, contact your primary care physician, local hospital, or psychological counseling center. You may also contact the Association for Psychophysiology and Biofeedback at www.apb.org. When you meet with a biofeedback therapist, he or she will determine how this treatment can alleviate your stress-related symptoms and which type of biofeedback is best

EDR, or GSR, electrodes are applied to the fingers to detect nervousness, or used in conjunction with tapes to decrease anxiety.

Figure 26.5

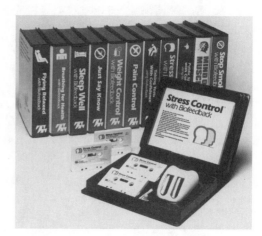

suited to do this. The number of therapy sessions required depends on the type and severity of the symptoms. Once you are familiar with the technique, you will then be given "homework" assignments in which you are to practice the biofeedback therapy on your own for a specified length of time.

Occasionally there is concern about dependency on the biofeedback equipment to obtain a complete state of relaxation. If the therapist is good at instruction and you are conscientious about practicing your relaxation techniques, there really is no danger of biofeedback dependence.

When biofeedback was first introduced into the world of clinical medicine, it was hailed as the most effective relaxation technique. Since that time, experts have learned that this technique holds no superiority over any other relaxation strategies or coping techniques. In many cases, it is effective for people with serious stress-related symptoms whom meditation or mental imagery alone does not seem to help. In any case, research has shown what many health practitioners and Eastern mystics already knew: that we do indeed have conscious control of the autonomic nervous system, and that this control can affect health and well-being.

Summary

- Biofeedback is a process of gathering information about specific physiological functions such as heart rate, respiration, and body temperature. Clinical biofeedback uses sophisticated instrumentation to amplify and measure these functions so that they are easier to detect and interpret.
- The purpose of biofeedback is to teach people with stress-related disorders to recondition their responses so that they gain control over the physiological system responsible for their symptoms.
- Clinical biofeedback combines sophisticated technology and various other forms of relaxation, including diaphragmatic breathing, auto-

genic training, progressive muscular relaxation, and mental imagery, to strengthen the conditioned response.
- There are several types of clinical biofeedback, each monitoring a specific physiological system. These are electromyography (EMG), electroencephalography (EEG), electrocardiography (EKG), electrodermal (EDR), and thermal biofeedback.
- The research conducted on various aspects of clinical biofeedback has produced promising results. Biofeedback is now recognized as one of the most effective methods of relaxation.

Concepts and Terms

Binary biofeedback

Cardiovascular (EKG) biofeedback

Clinical biofeedback

Closed-loop feedback system

Conditioned response

Electrodermal (EDR) biofeedback

Electroencephalographic (EEG) biofeedback

Electromyographic (EMG) biofeedback

Proportional biofeedback

Thermal biofeedback

References and Resources

Allen, R. *Human Stress: Its Nature and Control.* Burgess Press, Minneapolis, MN, 1983.

Basmanjian, J. *Biofeedback: Principles and Practice for Clinicians.* Williams & Wilkins, New York, 1989.

Beech, H. R., Burns, L. E., and Sheffield, B. F. *A Behavioral Approach to the Management of Stress: A Practical Guide to Techniques.* Wiley, Chichester, England, 1982.

Blanchard, E. B. and Haynes, M. R. Biofeedback Treatment of a Case of Raynaud's Disease, *Journal of Behavioral Therapy and Experimental Psychiatry* 6:230–234, 1975.

Blanchard, E. B. et al. Biofeedback and Relaxation Training with Three Kinds of Headaches: Treatment Effects and Their Predictions, *Journal of Consulting and Clinical Psychology* 50:562–575, 1982.

Brown, B. B. *Stress and the Art of Biofeedback.* Harper & Row, New York, 1977.

Budzynski, T. and Stoyva, J. Biofeedback Methods in the Treatment of Anxiety and Stress. In *Principles and Practices of Stress Management,* eds. R. Wolfolk and D. Lehrer. Guilford Press, New York, 1984.

Burish, T. G. EMG Biofeedback Transfer of Teaching and Coping with Stress, *Psychosomatic Research* 24(2):85–96, 1980.

Carrol, D. *Biofeedback in Practice.* Longman, New York, 1984.

Danskin, D. G. and Crow, M. *Biofeedback: An Introduction and Guide.* Mayfield, Palo Alto, CA, 1981.

DiCara, L. V. Learning in the Autonomic Nervous System, *Scientific American* 222(1):30–39, 1970.

Everly, G. *A Clinical Guide to the Treatment of the Human Stress Response.* Grosset & Dunlap, New York, 1976.

Fisher-Williams, M. *A Textbook of Biological Feedback.* Human Sciences Press, New York, 1986.

Fuller, G. D. *Biofeedback: Methods and Procedures in Clinical Practice.* Biofeedback Press, San Francisco, 1977.

Gaarder, K. and Montgomery, P. *Clinical Biofeedback: A Procedural Manual.* Williams & Wilkins, Baltimore, MD, 1977.

Green, E., and Green, A. *Beyond Biofeedback.* Delacorte Press, New York, 1977.

Green, E., Green, A., and Walters, E. D. Voluntary Control of Intense States: Psychological and Physiological, *Journal of Transpersonal Psychology* 2:1–26, 1970.

Marcer, D. *Biofeedback and Related Therapies in Clinical Practice.* Croom Helm, London, 1986.

Miller, N. E. Rx: Biofeedback, *Psychology Today,* February:54–59, 1985.

Miller, N. E. Visceral Learning and Other Additional Facts Potentially Applicable to Psychotherapy, *International Psychiatry Clinics* 5:294–312, 1968.

Miller, N. E. What Biofeedback Does (and Does Not Do), *Psychology Today,* November:22–24, 1989.

Pelletier, K. R. *Mind as Healer, Mind as Slayer.* Dell, New York, 1977.

Rice, R. L. *Stress and Health: Principles and Practices for Coping and Wellness,* 2nd ed. Brooks/Cole, Pacific Grove, CA, 1992.

Rosenbaum, L. *Biofeedback Frontiers: Self-Regulation of Stress Reactivity.* AMS Press, New York, 1988.

Runick, B. *Biofeedback—Issues in Treatment Assessment.* National Institutes of Mental Health, Rockville, MD, 1980.

Schwartz, M. S. *Biofeedback: A Practitioner's Guide.* Guilford Press, New York, 1987.

Turk, D. G., Meichenbaum, D. H., and Berman W. H. Application of Biofeedback for the Regulation of Pain: A Critical Review, *Psychological Bulletin* 86:1322–1338, 1979.

Wall, S.E. An Overview of Biofeedback: Philosophy of Biofeedback and Consciousness (on-line). Available at http://www.7hz.com/Loverview.html.

Whitman, W. *Leaves of Grass.* Signet Books, 2000.

Yates, A. J. *Biofeedback and the Modification of Behavior.* Plenum Press, New York, 1980.

Chapter 27 Nutrition and Stress

"Fortunately or unfortunately, we live in a world that tempts us with a great variety and abundance of food, and many of us eat not to satisfy physical hunger, but to allay anxiety, depression, and boredom, to provide a substitute for emotional nourishment, or to try to fill an inner void."

—Andy Weil, M.D.
Spontaneous Healing

Not long ago I went to a matinee to see one of the summer's blockbuster movies. It was advertised as a thriller and, indeed, it had people sitting on the edge of their chairs. Being somewhat detached from the theme (this is not my favorite kind of movie), I began to look around the theater to see what people's reaction would be to two hours of self-induced stress. People were engrossed in the film, but at the same time many were stuffing their mouths with popcorn and candy. In fact, it was the sound of jaws munching on popcorn that distracted my attention from the movie. It comes as no surprise that people tend to eat when they are stressed—a prime example of food acting as a pacifier. Days later in a conversation with the theater manager, my suspicions were confirmed. He told me it's a well-known fact that people eat more popcorn and candy during suspense movies than during any other type of motion picture.

Unfortunately, this habit of eating under stress goes well beyond the movie theater into real life. Imagine what it's like every day with bigger-than-life stressors that rival any Hollywood script. Food becomes a pacifier on many fronts, and the connection between food and our emotions is undeniably strong. Eating is definitely a relaxation technique, for when food enters the stomach, a sense of calm ensues. Yet, for many people, eating as a coping technique is often abused. We eat to celebrate, we eat to relax, we eat out of frustration and boredom, and we eat to satisfy our hunger. Food and mood go together like peanut butter and jelly.

It is impossible to talk about proper nutrition without addressing the issue of stress. The two are inextricably linked. For that matter, it is impossible to talk about proper nutrition and ignore the issue of politics of special interest groups and the power of the Food and Drug Administration, which work so diligently to control the dissemination of information leading to much inconsistent factual reporting and, thus, to even more stress for the consumer who tries to make sense of it all. One day there is a study reporting a particular finding, and the next day another study refutes the findings of the first study. It's no exaggeration to say that many people are confused and frustrated about the controversies in the field of nutrition—not to mention the ever-increasing number of popular diets, which itself can prove stressful, especially in our weight-conscious culture. This chapter will attempt to clarify some of the concepts regarding sound nutritional habits, how stress affects diet, how diet affects stress and mood, and nutritional concerns for women. In addition, this chapter contains information on herbs and an Eastern approach to eating called spiritual nutrition. Let's begin with the basics.

Aspects of Nutrition and Diet

Nutrition is a complex subject consisting of five aspects: nutrients, digestion, absorption, metabolism, and elimination. The focus is often placed on the first aspect, nutrients, but the other four are equally important. For if the nutrients are not digested, absorbed, and metabolized, and waste products are not eliminated properly, then there is a real problem with one's state of well-being. This section will deal primarily with the focus of nutrients, but keep the other factors in mind as well.

In simplest terms, the body needs six basic nutrients for optimal health: carbohydrates, fats, proteins, vitamins, minerals, and water. Water is cited as the most important of the six, for without water one would die of dehydration in a few days, but all nutrients are considered essential for optimal health. A food that has a high percentage of nutrients per gram is said to have high **nutrient density** when compared to fast food or junk food. Healthy nutrition encourages us to eat nutrient-dense foods. Following is a brief overview of the six nutrients and an explanation of their importance to optimal health.

Carbohydrates

Because energy is so important to the body, and because the role of carbohydrates is to provide energy, this nutrient is extremely important. Carbohydrates are classified into two categories: complex and simple sugars. Complex sugars are also known as starches. They are found in wheat, potatoes, rice, and several vegetables. The role of carbohydrates in the diet is to provide energy and fuel for performing daily body functions, as well as quick energy for fast movements. Carbohydrates are converted to glucose, and glucose is the body's "gasoline." Simple sugars (refined or processed sugars) are referred to as empty calories because they have been stripped of their nutritional value in the refining process. Simple sugars are found in candy, jams, table sugar, honey, and soft drinks.

Figure 27.1

The food guide pyramid was established to educate people about the types and numbers of servings per day for an optimally healthy diet. It is recommended that an individual consume six to eleven servings from the base group: breads, cereal, rice, and pasta; three to five servings from the vegetable group; two to four servings from the fruit group; two to three servings from the dairy group; two to three servings from the meat, poultry, and fish group; and little, if any, from the fats, oils, and sweets group at the top of the pyramid. Source: U.S. Department of Agriculture and U.S. Department of Health and Human Services.

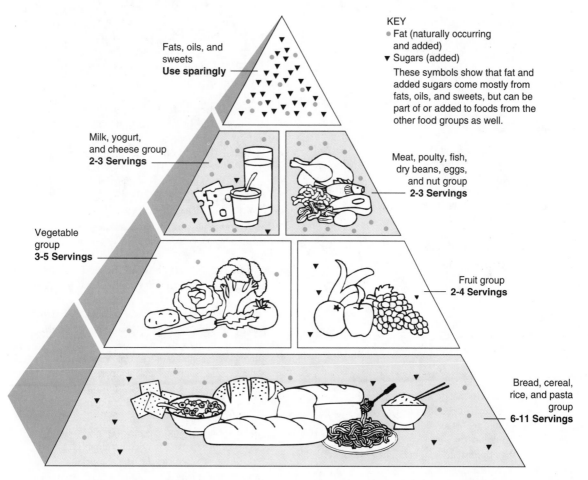

KEY
● Fat (naturally occurring and added)
▼ Sugars (added)
These symbols show that fat and added sugars come mostly from fats, oils, and sweets, but can be part of or added to foods from the other food groups as well.

Fats, oils, and sweets
Use sparingly

Milk, yogurt, and cheese group
2-3 Servings

Meat, poulty, fish, dry beans, eggs, and nut group
2-3 Servings

Vegetable group
3-5 Servings

Fruit group
2-4 Servings

Bread, cereal, rice, and pasta group
6-11 Servings

Complex carbohydrates include breads, pasta, and potatoes. As a rule, Americans consume too many simple sugars and not enough complex carbohydrates. When ingesting a meal consisting primarily of carbohydrates (e.g., pancakes, and syrup), blood sugar levels rise dramatically. Insulin is secreted from the pancreas to assist glucose into various cells and return blood sugar levels to normal. But in many cases, soon after eating a high-carbohydrate meal, blood sugar levels drop below normal, causing a sense of drowsiness and fatigue.

Fats

Fats are comprised of fatty acids and a substance known as *glycerol*. The metabolism of fats accomplishes two functions. First, fats are a concentrated supply of energy for prolonged, moderately intense activity. Fats typically contain twice as much energy as carbohydrates and are the preferred food source for aerobic exercise. Second, each cell membrane utilizes fat in its structure to help regulate the membrane transport system. Fat deposits are found around vital organs and act as protective cushions.

Andy Weil's Healthy Diet Recommendations

Box 27.1

Andy Weil, M.D., is a highly respected physician who advocates a holistic approach to health, including a proper, healthy, and balanced diet. In his much-acclaimed book, *Spontaneous Healing,* Weil outlines several suggestions for optimal health through healthy nutritional habits. Following are the highlights from the chapter entitled "A Healing Diet."

◆ *Cut total fat* by eliminating deep-fried foods; moderating consumption of chips, nuts, avocados, butter, cheese, and other high-fat foods; and learning to modify recipes to reduce fat content of favorite dishes. Read labels of products you buy to determine fat content, and try to keep your fat intake in the range of twenty to thirty percent of total calories.

◆ *Make a special effort to cut saturated fat in your diet* by cutting down substantially on meat, unskinned poultry, whole milk and whole milk products, butter, margarine, vegetable shortening, and all products made with tropical oils and partially hydrogenated oils.

◆ *Eliminate polyunsaturated vegetable oils from your diet,* avoiding safflower, sunflower, corn, soy, peanut, and cottonseed oils and products made from them.

◆ *Learn to rely on olive oil as your principal fat,* preferably a flavorful brand of extra-virgin olive oil.

◆ *Learn to identify and avoid all sources of hazardous **transfatty acids:*** margarine, solid vegetable shortening, and all products made with partially hydrogenated oils of any kind.

◆ *Increase consumption of omega–3 fatty acids* by eating the appropriate fish, hemp or flax oil, or flax meal regularly.

◆ *Eat less protein.* Learn to recognize sources of protein in your diet and to cut down on them. Practice making meals that do not revolve around large servings of dense protein foods.

◆ *Begin to replace animal protein in the diet with fish and soy protein.* By doing so you will both reduce your exposure to toxins and other harmful elements in meats, poultry, and milk and gain the benefits of health-promoting components of fish and soybeans.

◆ *Try to eat fewer calories* by eliminating high-fat foods and modifying recipes for favorite dishes by cutting fat content. Also experiment with periodic fasting or restricted dieting.

◆ *Cut down appreciably on saturated fat* by eating fewer foods of animal origin and none containing palm or coconut oils, margarine, vegetable shortening, or partially hydrogenated oils.

◆ *Do not use polyunsaturated vegetable oils for cooking.* Use only good-quality olive oil.

◆ *Eat more fruits and vegetables of all kinds.*

◆ *Eat more whole grains and products made from whole grains.*

◆ At breakfast: Take 1,000–2,000 milligrams of vitamin C and 25,000 IU of natural beta carotene.

◆ At lunch: Take 400–800 IU of natural vitamin E and 200–300 micrograms of selenium.

◆ At dinner: Take 1,000–2,000 milligrams of vitamin C.

◆ At bedtime (if convenient): Take another 1,000–2,000 milligrams of vitamin C.

◆ *Inform yourself about the source of your drinking water* and what contaminants it might contain.

◆ *Install a reverse osmosis filtration system in your kitchen.*

◆ *If you use bottled water,* buy only brands in glass or clear plastic containers from bottlers who are able to provide an analysis or certification of purity.

◆ *Do not drink water that tastes of chlorine.* When you travel, order bottled water or take a portable carbon filter with you.

◆ *Minimize consumption of foods known to contain natural toxins,* such as black pepper, celery, alfalfa sprouts, peanuts, and white button mushrooms.

◆ *Eat a varied diet* rather than eating the same items every day.

◆ *Always wash fruits and vegetables* (even though that will not remove many contaminants).

◆ *Peel fruits and vegetables if possible,* especially if they are not organically produced.

◆ *Try to buy only organically produced* apples, peaches, grapes, raisins, oranges, strawberries, lettuce, celery, carrots, green beans, potatoes, and wheat flour.

◆ *Look for sources of organic produce,* join cooperatives and buying clubs that distribute it, and let store managers know that you want it.

◆ *Reduce consumption of processed foods* and try to avoid those containing chemical dyes and artificial sweeteners.

Fat is essential to the body! Dietary fats can be found in red meats, butter, cheese, mayonnaise, eggs, cooking oils, and whole milk. There are two types of fats: saturated and unsaturated. Saturated fats, associated with cholesterol, are typically solid at room temperature, while unsaturated fats are liquid in the same environment. A national concern today is the overconsumption of fats, particularly saturated fats in animal products. Additionally, caution is now being expressed for unnatural sources of saturated fats with **partially hydrogenated oils,** such as margarine and vegetable shortening present in processed foods.

A new danger is **transfatty acids (TFAs),** formed from polyunsaturated oils (e.g., safflower oil, sunflower oil), a chemically unstable molecule. TFAs are known to compromise the integrity of the cell wall; damage DNA; and promote cancer, inflammation, and coronary heart disease.

Another caveat: most people don't know that two fats are considered essential, because the body cannot produce them, and most people don't consume enough of them. They are *linoleic acid* (also know as Omega-6 fatty acid, found in vegetable oils, seeds, and nuts) and *linolenic acid* (also known as Omega-3 acid, typically found in cold-water fish such as salmon).

Proteins

Proteins are the body's building blocks. They provide the cell structure to bones, muscles, skin, and all organ tissue, as well as constituting the building blocks of hormones and enzymes. The function of proteins is primarily to construct and to refurbish body cells. Proteins are broken down into amino acids, eight of which cannot be manufactured in the body and must be consumed naturally through various foods. Sources of proteins include red meats, fish, poultry, milk, legumes, nuts, seeds, beans, and some grains and cereals. Proteins are not used for energy production unless the sources of carbohydrates and fats are depleted. America, still a meat-and-potato culture, is thought to consume an excessive amount of proteins at the expense of complex carbohydrates. Proteins not used to refurbish cells are converted and stored as fat.

Vitamins and Minerals

Vitamins are divided into two categories: fat soluble vitamins (A, D, E, K) and water soluble vitamins (B complex and C). Taken in large doses, fat-soluble vitamins can become toxic, whereas high doses of water-soluble vitamins are excreted in the urine. The purpose of vitamins is to assist with a wide range of metabolic functions—from acting as **antioxidants** (Vitamin A, C, and E) and improving calcium absorption to aiding in blood clotting and boosting the immune system. Vitamins themselves are not a source of energy, but they do aid in the release of glucose and fatty acids for energy production. Deficiencies in any one vitamin can lead to a number of health-related problems.

Minerals also fall into two categories: major minerals (e.g., calcium, chloride, magnesium, phosphorus, potassium, sodium, and sulfur) and trace minerals (e.g., iodine, iron, zinc, copper, selenium, floride, and chromium). The most common mineral in the body is calcium, which constitutes bone tissue. Like vitamins, minerals—both major and trace—assist in a host of metabolic processes, including maintaining sodium-potassium balance refurbishing red blood cells, and disposing of damaging free radicals. Many minerals are found in dark, leafy green vegetables, beans, and fish. Mineral deficiency can lead to a host of problems, from anemia to an irregular heartbeat.

Water

Water is said to be the most important nutrient because, above all, one cannot survive without water. Water is critical to the optimal functioning of every cell in the body. It not only acts as a means of transportation of essential nutrients to all cells, but is involved in a host of chemical reactions, as well as maintenance of the body's temperature. As a rule, people don't drink enough water and, consequently, are less than fully hydrated, which can lead to a feeling of fatigue. Experts suggest eight glasses of water per day for optimal health.

These six nutrients comprise the ideal diet, but few people consume an ideal diet due to busy lifestyles, acquired habits, social customs, and laziness.

What Goes in Must Come Out

There is an old saying that if you want to get a good measure of how your body is functioning, monitor your bowel movements and your rate of excretion. There is truth to this adage. The average person eats three large meals per day, but typically has only one bowel movement, suggesting there is a problem with the digestion/absorption process. Any certified nutritionist will tell you there should be one bowel movement for each significant meal eaten, (assuming that there is an adequate intake of fiber). Why do so many people miss the quota?

There may be one of several reasons. First, the gastrointestinal (GI) tract is very sensitive to stress. The physiological response to stress is to slow down digestion and absorption so that blood may be redirected to the large muscle groups for movement (fight or flight). Even if you sit behind a desk for eight hours, the GI tract is influenced by the stress response. In fact, many stress problems show up first in the GI tract in the form of cramps, gas, diarrhea, ulcers, and hemorrhoids. Second, toxic residue (from years of eating toxic and junk food) may build up in the mucosal lining of the small intestine and colon. The result not only produces a sludge, inhibiting the digesting and absorption process (bio-availability), but it also creates a path of obstruction that slows the progression of chyme (partially digested food) through the GI tract. A third reason may be a lack of physical exercise. Cardiovascular exercise is known to help keep the digestive system regular, meaning a regular and healthy number of bowel movements per day. If you are not meeting your quota of daily excretions it is most likely an indication that there are some serious matters to become aware of. Careful consideration should be given to your diet and exercise habits (see Chapter 28), as well as your stress levels.

Diet for a Stressed Planet

Because of the global economy and trade among nations, the choices of foods available today are unparalleled. At a grocery store it is not uncommon to see strawberries, grapes, and a whole host of vegetables available year around, not to mention a selection of meats, fish, and other foods imported from states and countries thousands of miles away. Quantities of food are abundant as well, but this does not necessarily mean the quality of food is superior to that of our grandparents. Across the planet, there is an alarming concern that the soil used to grow crops is severely depleted of its nutrients, resulting in a loss of nutrient density in foods and people experiencing the effects of malnourishment, even though the caloric intake is much greater than in the days of our grandparents.

The biggest nutrition problem in the United States is overconsumption, yet overconsumption does not necessarily mean an overabundance of the various nutrients that the body requires for optimal functioning. Foods high in fat and simple sugars and empty calories tend to rob the body of essential nutrients. Consequently, the body is operating under a nutritional deficiency, not nutritional abundance. Under these conditions, the body is stressed to maintain its integrity for metabolic functioning. Over time, one or more physiological systems may go into a state of dysfunction. In addition, it is no secret that when people are stressed, their eating habits are greatly compromised, perpetuating an already negative condition. Stated simply, a person under stress is extremely vulnerable to nutritional deficiency.

Under the most optimal conditions, stress can cause problems with the body's ability to digest and absorb nutrients, thus impeding the availability of the essential nutrients, particularly the vitamins and minerals. As you will see, the physiological system most seriously affected by a poor nutritional state is the immune system. Following is a description of how stress affects our absorption of these essential nutrients and, ultimately, our susceptibility to a wide range of illnesses.

Stress and Mineral Depletion

Research conducted by the U.S. Department of Agriculture (Sizer & Whitney, 2000) has revealed that, despite what appeared to be an adequate dietary intake, several levels of minerals have decreased as much as 33 percent in the past twenty years throughout various age ranges of people. A depletion of minerals decreases the integrity of the immune system, making one more susceptible to disease and illness. The following minerals are in deficit under conditions of chronic stress: magnesium, chromium, copper, iron, and zinc.

Stress and Vitamin Depletion

Four vitamins are also known to be greatly affected by chronic stress: the antioxidants vitamin A, C, and E, and the vitamin B-complex.

The Antioxidants. The body encounters many environmental stressors in the course of a day, including particles known as free radicals. Free radicals are highly reactive oxygen particles most commonly found in air pollution, tobacco smoke, radiation, herbicides, and rancid fatty foods. Free radicals are also produced in the body under normal metabolic functioning. Left

Stress With a Human Face

JANIE GREW UP IN THE MIDWEST, WHERE THE words *hearty* and *healthy* were synonymous. These are her own words describing her journey through the countless land mines of weight loss and dieting:

"I was never obese, but chubby enough to be self-conscious and ridiculed by other kids. I began dieting when I was pretty young. When I was twelve, I began taking laxatives and diet pills to lose weight. It never worked. Being over-weight affected me in so many ways. My self-esteem was non-existent. I married at age twenty-three, then divorced less than two years later. My weight was up to 180 pounds. At first when I tried to diet, I was under the assumption that if a low-fat diet was good, a no-fat diet was better. It never occurred to me that my body needed some fat to function normally. I am now twenty-seven and it's taken me fifteen years to realize that there are no shortcuts to health. I have begun to pay attention to my body. I have begun choosing foods that will benefit my body, rather than comfort foods. I exercise regularly, which has helped my depression immensely. I am beginning to see and feel results. I feel like a different person."

Janie doesn't refer to her diet now as a weight loss program. Instead, she calls it "my life change." Rather than counting fat calories, she focuses her attention on making sound nutritional choices, ensuring the bio-availabilty of foods, consuming a healthy balance of essential fatty acids (omega-3s and 6s), avoiding alcohol and toxic residues on foods as well as supplementing her emotional and spiritual health—her new agenda for maintaining optimal wellness. The smile on her face tells the whole story. ✦

---

uncontrolled, free radicals will destroy various constituents of cells they come in contact with, including:

✦ The cell membrane: Free radicals change the permeability of the cell membrane, disturbing the transportation of essential nutrients into the cell as well as by-products out of the cell.

✦ The mitochondria: Free radicals destroy the constituents of the mitochondria (where cell respiration occurs) and compromising the energy capabilities of the cell.

✦ The DNA: Free radicals attach to the DNA structure and inhibit the genetic code process that regulates cell reproduction and function.

✦ RNA: Free radicals distort the ability of the RNA to transmit messages throughout the CNS.

Under normal healthy conditions, free radicals are removed (metabolized by beta carotene and vitamins C and E). But, under bouts of chronic stress these vitamins are depleted or, in many cases, not even absorbed into the body, so that free radicals are not destroyed. It has been noted that free radicals are often associated with the development of several diseases, including coronary heart disease and cancer.

Vitamin C.   In addition to acting as an antioxidant, Vitamin C is known to aid in the integrity of the immune system to battle colds and flu. Current estimates are that it takes about 200 mg of vitamin C to maintain the integrity of the immune system under stressful conditions. As a rule, people consume less than half that amount (about 60 mg per day, which is the Dietary Reference Intake [DRI]).

The Vitamin B Complex.   Vitamin B requirements are known to increase during prolonged bouts of stress because they aid primarily in the function of the central nervous system, which (as mentioned in Chapter 2) is in a high state of arousal during periods of stress. The vitamin B complex includes thiamin (B_1), riboflavin (B_2), niacin (B_3), B_6, folate, biotin, pantothenic acid, and B_{12}. According to studies at Loma Linda University in California, decreases in B_6 vitamin levels correlate with decreased immune function.

A Word about Supplements

Years ago when the soil used to grow crops was rich in nutrients, supplements were not necessary. Those who took them were looking for quick cures, weight loss or, in many cases, taking them in place of regular meals. For the average person, though, it was widely believed that if you ate well-balanced meals, there really was no need to take supplements. The same cannot be said today! Because of soil depletion, combined with the rushed pace of life leading to greatly compromised dietary habits, taking supplements is not only recommended, it is often required to maintain optimal health. Some facts to be aware of when choosing dietary supplements include the following:

✦   Not all vitamin supplements are created equal. Vitamin sources are either extracted from their original food sources or chemically synthesized. In the act of processing, vitamins may be *synthesized, crystallized, or lyophilized (freeze-dried)*. In the first two processes, extreme heat is used and, as a result, any beneficial qualities once present are most likely lost. In addition, the substance used in the process of binding the vitamins in a tablet is so strong that the body's enzymes cannot dissolve it. Consequently, the tablet is passed through the GI tract without ever being absorbed. Therefore, it is recommended that any vitamin supplement taken be lyophilized and that it be in the form of a powdered substance in a gel capsule for easy digestion and absorption.

✦   Taken in concentrated form, vitamin, mineral and protein supplements can actually block the absorption rate (decrease bioavailability) of other essential nutrients (other vitamins and minerals), thereby negating any positive effect. Consult a certified nutritionist about taking supplements.

The best source of vitamins is unprocessed food. Vitamin supplements are recommended for people who may not get essential nutrients, but vitamins should not be taken in place of a meal.

Figure 27.2

✦   In large doses, the fat-soluble vitamins (A, D, E, and K) are toxic. Because vitamins B and C are water soluble, excess amounts of them will be excreted—making for very expensive urine.

Additional Stress and Nutritional Factors to Consider

Nutrition plays a crucial role in both minimizing and increasing the physiological arousal of the stress response. The stress response increases the rate of metabolism by activating the mobilization of carbohydrates and fats into the bloodstream for energy production. Additionally, several substances, when ingested, tend to mimic or induce the stress response or decrease the efficiency of the body's metabolic pathways, thus setting the stage for a more pronounced physiological reaction to stress. Likewise, the stress response can deplete necessary nutrients, vitamins, and minerals, creating a cyclical process of poor health. The relationship between stress and nutrition is profound for many reasons, including the following:

✦   Stress increases the production of coritsol which, in turn, increases the production of the chemical neuropeptide Y (NPY) in the brain. NPY is thought to be responsible for the cravings of carbohydrate-rich foods, particularly sweets (possibly a reason for weight gain). NPY levels are normally high in the morning. This, coupled with a stress-filled day, can create the urge for sweets all day long. Eating a good breakfast is believed to help maintain levels of NPY and keep them in balance.

+ According to nutritionist Elizabeth Sommer (1995), a low-fat diet stimulates the immune system, whereas a high-fat diet increases the risk of illness. Therefore, eating foods with high fat content may be convenient during a long working day, but the long-term effects are quite detrimental to optimal health.

+ An excess of simple sugars tends to deplete vitamin stores, particularly the vitamin B complex (niacin, thiamin, riboflavin, and B_6 and B_{12}). White sugar (even bleached flour), flushed of its vitamin and mineral content, requires additional B-complex vitamins to be metabolized. These and other vitamins are crucial for the optimal functioning of the central nervous system. A depletion of the B-complex vitamins may manifest itself in fatigue, anxiety, and irritability. In addition, increased amounts of ingested simple sugars may cause major fluctuations in blood glucose levels, resulting in pronounced fatigue, headaches, and general irritability.

+ Caffeine is a stimulant that arouses the sympathetic nervous system—most likely the reason people drink coffee in the morning to help wake up and get a start on the day. Caffeine is quickly absorbed in the bloodstream and delivered to all parts of the body, with a direct effect on the brain. It is a well-known fact that caffeine is a diuretic. Also eliminated are various minerals such as calcium and magnesium. Food sources with caffeine that trigger the sympathetic nervous system are referred to as *sympathomimetic agents.* The substance in caffeine responsible for this effect is called **methylated xanthine.** This chemical stimulant with amphetamine-like characteristics triggers the sympathetic nervous system for a heightened state of arousal, as well as stimulating the release of several stress hormones. The result is a heightened state of alertness, which makes the individual more

susceptible to perceived stress. Caffeine is found in many foods, including chocolate, coffee, tea, and several types of soft drinks. According to current estimates, the average American consumes three six-ounce cups of coffee per day. A six-ounce cup of caffeinated coffee contains approximately 250 milligrams of caffeine, half the amount necessary to evoke an adverse arousal of the central nervous system.

+ Chronic stress can cause a depletion of several vitamins necessary for energy metabolism, as well as a depletion of constituents required by the stress response itself. The synthesis of cortisol requires the presence of vitamins. The stress response activates several hormones responsible for mobilizing and metabolizing fats and carbohydrates for energy production. The breakdown of fats and carbohydrates requires the involvement of vitamins, specifically vitamin C and B-complex vitamins. An inadequate supply of these vitamins may affect mental alertness and promote depression and insomnia. Stress is also associated with a depletion of calcium and the inability of bones to absorb calcium properly. This sets the stage for the development of osteoporosis, the demineralization of bone tissue. Vitamin supplementation is a controversial issue. When a balanced diet is consumed, there is typically an adequate supply of vitamins and nutrients for energy metabolism. However, a balanced diet is not the rule for the majority of Americans. Vitamin supplements may be recommended for individuals who are prone to excessive stress.

+ It seems that Americans have a love affair with salt. Many people add salt to their food without even tasting it. High sodium intake is associated with high blood pressure, because sodium acts to increase water retention. As water volume increases in a closed system, blood pressure increases. If this condition persists, it may contribute to hypertension.

+ The excessive consumption of alcohol is thought to suppress the immune system by depleting water-soluble vitamins and minerals (primarily potassium, magnesium, calcium, and zinc), which are involved in the synthesis of components for the immune system. What is excess consumption of alcohol? While this may vary from person to person, nutritionists suggest that more than one drink per day is excessive.

◆ For years scientists have warned against the dangers of eating too many foods with cholesterol and saturated fat, but the choices of foods that are offered as substitutes are proving to be no better and, in some cases, perhaps, worse. Margarine is a processed form of corn oil; it is produced by changing the molecular structure through *hydrogenation,* in which the empty bonds are filled in order to turn the liquid oil into a solid at room temperature. Recently scientists have observed an association between the hydrogenation process and the loss of integrity of the cell wall (through free radicals), setting the stage for the development of cancer and coronary heart disease.

◆ People who are constantly on the go rarely have time to prepare their own meals, and may not eat regularly. On average, many people eat one or two meals a day outside the home, which frequently leads to some rather unhealthy eating habits that will, over time, be the cause of stress. If you tend to eat out frequently—whether as a matter of convenience or social habit—you should be aware of these facts. Food prepared in restaurants is generally high in sodium and sugar, and is particularly high in saturated fats. People like fatty foods because they taste good, and many of the selections on a menu are created with this in mind. Appetizers that are fried, salad dressings made with heavy oils, and rich desserts with heavy creams are where the fat calories are hidden. Fast food is even higher in fat, sodium, and sugars. If you must eat out, make a habit of skipping appetizers, soft drinks, and salad dressings; choosing fresh fruits and vegetables over fried foods; and passing on dessert.

A Word about Genetically Altered Foods

Research into various hybrids of plant species, such as peas, oranges, and lettuce, has been conducted for centuries, in the hopes of making more delicious and nutritious food. The line between science and science fiction became rather fuzzy in 2000 when it was reported that food scientists were splicing a unique gene from flounder (salt-water fish) into the DNA of tomatoes, and the genes of Brazil nuts into the DNA of corn. Scientists proceeded to alter the genetic makeup of corn by splicing genes of Roundup, a synthetic pesticide, into the DNA of corn, which resulted in the mysterious death of thousands of migrating monarch butterflies (Teitel and Wilson 1999). In the fall of 2000, corn taco shells were recalled from Taco John restaurants and corn flakes were recalled from grocery store shelves by Kellogg Corporation because of consumer alarm over genetically modified organisms (GMOs) or what some have labeled as "Frankenfood." Over 65% of foods found in the grocery store are genetically modified. Commerical foods and food products may not be labeled as containing "genetically altered" ingredients. Because of the possibility of severe allergic reactions to such foods, it is best to avoid them and choose whole foods with "certified organic" labels.

Nutritional Needs for Women

Because of the dynamics of the reproductive system, women need to pay specific attention to several aspects of their nutritional habits. The following are important factors to consider when constructing your diet and considering your nutritional needs.

Benign Breast Pain. Breast pain (*cyclic mastalgia*) is one of the most common reasons why women see their gynecologists. Breast pain can be caused by too much estrogen in the body, excessive caffeine consumption, and constant stress, as well as by fluid retention, benign breast lumps, and normal breast thickening. The following changes in dietary habits can help minimize the symptoms of cyclic mastalgia:

◆ Reduce or eliminate dairy products. Dairy products—specifically milk and cheese—contain steroids (estrogen). Ingesting excess amounts of dairy products can increase pain.

◆ Eliminate caffeine, including coffee, tea, sodas, chocolate, and even decaffeinated (caffeine-reduced) coffee.

◆ Take a multivitamin supplement. Women who have breast pain are known to be helped by taking the antioxidant combination of vitamin E (400–800 IU per day), vitamin A (5,000–10,000 IU per day), and the mineral selenium (100–200 mcg per day).

◆ Consume adequate amounts of gamma linoleic acid. Sources include flax seed oil, black currant oil, and evening primose oil. These oils can be added to soups, salads, and grains.

◆ Use an iodine supplement. Iodine changes the way estrogen binds to breast tissue. Iodine may be obtained as a prescription supplement, and is also found in sea vegetables including wakame, kombu, and hiijiki.

Birth Defects. If you are pregnant or are considering becoming pregnant, you will want to include adequate amounts of folic acid in your diet, because the presence of this B vitamin lowers the risk of spina bifida. Many gynecologists suggest taking a preconception supplement to ensure adequate amounts of folic acid. Natural sources include dark green, leafy vegetables, beans, and wheat germ.

Cancer. Breast cancer, cervical cancer, and colorectal cancer are very prominent in the female population, and diet is believed to play an integral role in reducing the risk for these types of cancers. Many vegetables—including broccoli, cauliflower, cabbage, brussels sprouts, kale, and spinach—contain the compound indole-3-carbinol, a substance believed to alter the metabolic processes of estrogen. Low levels of vitamins A and B-complex are associated with cervical cancer. Increasing your intake of dark green and deep orange fruits and vegetables, whole grains, wheat germ, and tuna fish are thought to be beneficial. It has also been noted (Northrup, 1995) that in women who developed cervical cancer while on oral contraceptives (which tend to lower blood levels of vitamin B), high doses of folic acid helped reverse cervical cancer. A diet high in fiber (25 grams per day) is recommended to prevent the incidence of colorectal cancer. Fiber-rich sources include whole grain breads, pasta, cereals, apples, peaches, celery, beans, and potatoes with the skin.

Osteoporosis. Aside from eating a well-balanced diet with a rich supply of calcium, avoid diet sodas, which contain phosphorus. In large quantities, phosphorus depletes calcium stores from bone tissue, resulting in demineralization. High levels of protein also cause this to occur, as calcium is released from the bones to buffer the blood. Note also that a diet high in fat prevents calcium absorption into the blood. Include natural sources of calcium such as fish, legumes, and dark green leafy vegetables in your diet. Sources low in calcium are also noted with low levels of magnesium. Excellent sources of magnesium include tofu, unrefined grains, and dark green, leafy vegetables.

Yeast Infections. Yeast infections (commonly called candida) can occur as a result of a deficit of the intestinal bacteria lactobacillus acidopholus, which is often killed when taking antibiotics. Stress is also associated with increased levels of yeast in the intestines, which then spread to the vaginal area. Yogurt is recommended, as well as a supplement of acidopholus.

Premenstrual Disturbances. It is suggested that caffeine and alcohol be eliminated from the diet to prevent mood swings associated with PMS. Caffeine and alcohol affect blood sugar levels, and alcohol interferes with the phase of sleep known as rapid eye movement (REM). This, in turn, interferes with quality sleep, resulting in higher stress levels during the waking hours. If you have a craving for sweets, try fruit juices (which have greater nutrient density, vitamins, minerals, and fiber than do candy or soda).

According to Christiane Northrup, M.D., food becomes an emotional issue because women tend to eat as a means to deal with their problems. The author of the acclaimed *Women's Bodies, Women's Wisdom*, Northrup offers these suggestions to lend balance for women living a rushed lifestyle:

◆ *Eat only when you are hungry.* Paying attention to feelings of hunger is a lost art in an age when we are constantly receiving media messages to consume various products. Northrup suggests determining your hunger level on a scale of one to eight with one being extremely hungry and eight being full or not hungry. If you feel you are at a level 1 or 2, sit down and eat something. If you feel somewhere between levels 3 and 8, wait until your hunger level reaches 1 or 2 before snacking or sitting down to a meal. Furthermore, don't feel pressured to eat something just because someone provides food (perhaps an office snack) or invites you to a restaurant for lunch or dinner.

◆ *Don't eat on your feet.* Excessive calories can be consumed on the run. Make it a point to sit down when you eat.

✦ *Focus on each meal.* Many people eat while watching TV or reading. Few people actually taste the food they are eating. By focusing on the food you are eating, you can also pay attention to your eating behaviors, such as eating too fast, chewing your food, and tasting the food. Many people who are engaged in other activities while eating tend to ignore the sensation of fullness and to overeat. By focusing on the food you are eating, you have a more accurate perception of when you are full.

✦ *Listen to and learn to curb your cravings.* Many cravings are associated with emotional outlets. The next time you have a craving for something like cookies, ice cream, or chocolate, evaluate what is happening to your body. Northrup says that what is happening to your body can be translated into an emotion. By dealing with the emotion, you can learn to prevent overeating and bingeing.

✦ *Keep a food diary.* If you really want to analyze your dietary habits, keep track of food as you eat it. You will begin to take note of not only calories, but the types of foods you eat and even emotions and behaviors associated with certain foods.

✦ *Fine tune your meals.* We are accustomed in our culture to eating three meals a day, but this may not suit your body every day. If you are not hungry during the noon hour, don't sit down and eat a meal. You may be the kind of person who would rather snack several times a day than eat three big meals. Learn to recognize how many meals are best for you, and then eat accordingly.

Spiritual Nutrition

What does nutrition have to do with spirituality? On the surface, perhaps not much; but with closer examination we learn that some aspects of nutrition have a very strong spiritual and energy component. For instance, in the Eastern culture it is believed that there are several energy centers (called *chakras*), which run from the top of the head to the base of the spine. Each of the seven energy centers is associated with a color: red (base of spine), orange (navel), yellow (spleen), green (heart), aqua-blue (throat), indigo blue (fore-head), and violet (crown). The Ayurvedic principles from India suggest that people eat foods, specifically fruits and vegetables, that correspond to the colors of the energy centers. New research into light and color therapy suggests that every color has a vibrational frequency, and that when people or animals are denied full-spectrum lighting, the effects are evident in the functions of various organs. Eating foods that contain a specific frequency may, indeed, replenish what is not available through exposure to natural light.

The Taoist philosophy of the Chinese culture also advocates finding balance in the foods we eat, specifically in terms of acid (yin) and alkaline (yang) substances. Grains and animal foods (acids) should be balanced with seeds, vegetables, and salt (alkalines). According to this approach, the correct alkaline/acid balance is 80/20. The Chinese believe that a diet comprised of food heavy in acids creates an energy disturbance, resulting in poor health and disease.

In his book *Spiritual Nutrition and the Rainbow Diet*, Gabriel Cousens, M.D., highlights several ways to make our nutrition and eating habits more conducive to healthy living and more harmonious with the planet. His suggestions include:

1. Eat a great variety (full spectrum) of foods, noting color (outside), to nurture the care of specific organs associated with each chakra area.
2. Avoid eating big meals prior to meditation, since the stomach and the brain compete for blood flow, and when the stomach is full more blood is needed for digestion. As a rule, undereat.
3. Drink plenty of water to cleanse the body of nutrients and toxins no longer needed.
4. In addition to digesting quality foods, good nutrition includes adequate sunlight (vitamin D), plenty of fresh air (oxygen), and plenty of fresh water to drink.
5. Learn what foods are associated with the acid/alkaline balance and make an effort to achieve this balance in your daily diet.
6. Learn to concentrate on the foods you are eating, noting the taste, texture, and temperature, and even the origin. According to the Eastern tradition, being mindful (mindfulness) of the food we eat is a spiritual experience.

The Psychological Effect of Food

It would be a simple world if eating were done solely to meet nutritional needs, but this is not the case. Often the act of eating, as so eloquently stated in the opening quote by Andy Weil, is done for emotional reasons that have nothing to do with nutritional demands of the body. Food is often used as a means to pacify our minds and hearts, a behavior learned from day one at a mother's breast or bottle. This pattern continues from infancy well into adulthood as we stuff our faces in an attempt to stuff our feelings or control them at some level. The consequences are serious, if not fatal. Experts in dietary behaviors will tell you that the problem of being overweight may look like a problem of overconsumption, but a closer examination reveals that there are some serious emotional issues under the surface. Likewise, eating disorders such as anorexia and bulimia may appear to suggest a problem with malnutrition, but the truth is that eating disorders are symptoms of much more serious unresolved emotional problems. As discussed in Chapter 5, eating can be an outlet for unresolved anger (for example, guilt: the self-punisher or even the underhander who eats and drinks on an employer's expense account to seek revenge for working extra hours). But anger alone is not the cause of eating problems. In addition, boredom, loneliness, procrastination, anxiety, and poor willpower also contribute to the blend of psychological and physiological interactions. In essence, food becomes a tranquilizer that calms nerves.

Cravings

The average person tends to gravitate toward one or more foods when feeling depressed or lonely. Food can become a friend when there are no other friends around. If at first we become acquainted with a particular food at a low point, we can become conditioned to return to that type of food when the condition arises again. Chocolate, french fries, diet sodas, potato chips, candy bars, popcorn, and ice cream are some foods people crave in times of stress. If you are like most people, you also crave a particular food or foods when you are stuck at the end of your emotional spectrum. What is your particular craving? What specific food calms your nerves or gives you a lift when things are not going as expected? While it is acceptable to seek simple pleasures in food, problems arise

when the occasional craving becomes a habit. An occasional craving is not bad, but it can become self-destructive if the behavior is not stopped or if help is not sought to regain emotional balance.

Eating Disorders

There is no simple solution to eating disorders because they involve various eating habits, perceptions of foods, personal history, social pressures, and personality—all of which add up to the monumental task of aligning these factors long enough to make some positive changes. Three of the most common eating disorders are anorexia, bulimia, and overeating.

Anorexia.   Anorexics are classified into two groups: the individual who restricts food intake and starves herself and the bulimic who runs through cycles of gorging and then starving. Typically anorexics are described as well-educated females with a middle- to upper-class background. The issue of starvation is centered around control—there is something the anorexic feels helpless about and self-starvation is a way to appease this condition, however remote or tangential. Anorexics have a very distorted body image, often seeing themselves as fat when they have little or no body fat. Aside from the obvious characteristic of extreme weight loss, anorexics are prone to insomnia, obsessive-compulsive disorder, stoicism, perfectionism, introversion, and frequently, emotional inhibition. Statistics reveal that one out of every one hundred adolescent girls are diagnosed with this condition (Levenkron 2000, Gordon 2000).

Bulimia.   In the American culture, thinness is an obsession. This fact is validated by the plethora of women's magazines that feature thin models on the covers and convey the subliminal message that, unless you look like this, you are not pretty. Women who fall prey to the whims of these marketing attempts and social mores are often confronted with a dilemma, and food becomes the vehicle to control feelings of self-image, self-worth, and self-esteem. In an effort to control body weight, bulimics binge on an assortment of foods (typically junk food) and then purge (either by vomiting or using laxatives) in an attempt to satisfy the need to eat and also satisfy the need to control their weight. Bingeing efforts can be quite extreme: eating a whole gallon of ice cream or consuming an entire pizza or an entire box of cookies. The result of such behavior is the loss of control over caloric balance and the beginning of a cycle of bingeing and purging that frequently leads to malnutrition. Continued bulimia may result in tooth enamel erosion (from vomiting), bowel problems, constipation, irregular menstruation, electrolyte imbalance, and rips and tears in the GI tract.

Overeating. Excessive overeating may be a result of many factors, including guilt, loneliness, or nervousness. The use of food as a pacifier to calm the nerves becomes ingrained in the daily lifestyle. Overeating can also be a means to create a protective shell in order to keep people at a distance. This is often the case with people who were sexually abused or violently attacked as children. In many cases of overeating, low self-esteem is observed.

Is there a physiological explanation for eating disorders? Perhaps not, but there are links between eating and personality that can lead to a better understanding of how to deal with the problem. As the theme of this book suggests, all things connect and there is a direct link between the mind and the body, as evidenced by the hypothalamus. The hypothalamus, which registers emotional feelings, also controls appetite—the desire to eat and consume food. When food is placed in the stomach, a calming message is sent to the hypothalamus to decrease the intensity of neural stimulation throughout the rest of the body. There is a profound connection between food and stress. Eating to pacify the nerves is such a common behavior that it is often overlooked in the field of stress management. But what is considered normal is not necessarily healthy. Take note (perhaps in a journal) of your eating behaviors in times of stress. From there, ask yourself whether eating is something you feel you have control over, or whether eating is something that is controlling you.

Recommendations for Healthy Eating Habits

Experts agree that the following dietary practices can minimize the body's arousal to stress and enhance optimal functioning.

Eat a Well-Balanced Diet. The typical American consumes too many fats and proteins and, frequently, not enough carbohydrates, specifically complex carbo-

hydrates. An unbalanced diet leads to poor physical performance. At a young age it can retard the physical growth process. During the college years both men and women seem to function at an acceptable level. But if habits are not corrected, the foundation is laid for a series of health-related problems later in life. Following is a comparison of the typical American diet and federal-government-recommended daily allowances:

Typical American Diet	U.S. DRI Suggested Diet
Carbohydrates: 30–40%	Carbohydrates: 55–70%
Fats: 40–50%	Fats: 20–30%
Proteins: 20–30%	Proteins: 15–20%

Eat a Good Breakfast and Space Meals Evenly Throughout the Day. Americans typically skip breakfast, with college students being the worst offenders. The body operates on carbohydrates, and this is usually what breakfast foods consist of: breads, cereals, and fruits. When the body is not refueled after eight to ten hours of sleep, it doesn't function well. Symptoms of shortened attention span, early fatigue, and depression are common. When the mind is not alert, the body does not respond well to stress—it typically overreacts. Poor cognitive functioning can result in poor decision making, which can perpetuate the stress cycle. There is a new theory that humans should eat six small meals a day rather than three large ones for better metabolism. Regardless of the number, meals should be spaced evenly throughout the day. An irregular eating schedule interrupts the body's natural rhythms.

Avoid or Minimize the Consumption of Caffeine and Sugar. Overconsumption of caffeine is unhealthy on many fronts. In the short term it can cause headaches, irritability, nervousness, sleeplessness, and in some cases gastrointestinal irritation. Caffeine should be avoided when you know you may encounter a stressor, and caffeine consumption is not recommended when performing relaxation techniques. Refined sugar can also lead to problems. Research (Sizer & Whitney, 2000) indicates that individuals consume their body weight in refined sugar each year. For reasons explained earlier, this is extremely unhealthy. Efforts should be made to decrease consumption of refined sugar.

Eat a Diet That Provides Adequate Levels of Vitamins and Minerals That Are Potentially Vulnerable to Stress. Vitamins are classified as either fat soluble (A, D, E, and K) or water soluble (B complex and C). It is the water-soluble vitamins that tend to be targeted for destruction during the stress response. A well-balanced diet should exceed the minimum requirements of all of these vitamins, as well as the RDA of essential minerals. Poor nutritional habits compounded by chronic physical stress set the stage for vitamin depletion and defi-

ciency. Caution is advised with vitamin supplementation. An overabundance of fat-soluble vitamins can lead to vitamin toxicity, while an excess of vitamins C and B complex is usually excreted, making for very expensive urine. Eat a well-balanced diet with whole and fresh foods and add a quality vitamin supplement.

Unlike third-world nations that strive to feed their citizens, the United States is perhaps the only country in the world with a problem of overconsumption. According to federal government sources, we as a nation overconsume calories in general and specifically fats, simple sugars, salt, and alcohol. These trends in the American diet are closely associated with six of the ten leading causes of death in this country, including coronary heart disease and cancer. Based on a review of these national eating behaviors, the following list of dietary guidelines was established by the U.S. Department of Agriculture and Health and Human Services.

1. Aim for a healthy weight.
2. Be physically active each day.
3. Let the Pyramid guide your food choices.
4. Choose a variety of grains daily, especially whole grains.
5. Choose a variety of fruits and vegetables daily.
6. Keep foods safe to eat.
7. Choose a diet that is low in saturated fat and cholesterol and moderate in total fat.
8. Choose beverages and foods to moderate your intake of sugars.
9. Choose and prepare foods with less salt.
10. If you drink alcoholic beverages, do so in moderation.

Herbal Therapies

Appreciating the connection between food and health, it is important to recognize how some food sources—specifically herbs—are known to boost the immune system to combat the ill effects of stress-related illnesses. Long before Western science was able to synthesize a host of medicinal agents for curing disease and illness, healers and shamans from all cultures and geographic locations used herbs for the same purpose, and their knowledge is founded on thousands of years of experience. Two of the oldest forms of recorded **herbal therapies** are Ayurvedic medicine and Chinese

---

Box 27.2

Food Label Warning

The following items have been noted to be a danger to your health and should be minimized or completely avoided in your diet.

Hydrogenated oils (transfatty acids)

Partially hydrogenated oils (transfatty acids)

Aspartame

Saturated fats

Sodium

Monosodium glutamate (MSG)

Caffeine

Red and blue dyes

Food prepared with more than 30 percent simple sugars

Homogenized milk (contains hormones and steroids)

Nitrites

Nitrates

Steroids in meats and chicken

Olestra

Any artificial flavor or coloring

Any artificial preservative

 ✦ If you cannot pronounce it, you probably shouldn't eat it.

medicine, which date back to antiquity. Current research reveals that over 80 percent of these herbal medicines prove effective against the cause of illness they are intended to treat. Over one-half of the medicines prescribed today are derived from plant or synthetic analogs. Although Western-trained specialists demand more clinical studies to prove efficacy, common wisdom prevails in the mind of the average person: the natural form of medicine—in this case herbs—is far more effective than a chemically synthesized version of it.

One reason for the great controversy over the use of herbs is that the Food and Drug Administration (FDA) is heavily lobbied by the nation's leading pharmaceutical companies, who are against the use of herbal remedies. Rob McCaleb, President of the Herb Research Foundation, states that the reason for the heavy politicking is that, unlike synthesized drugs, herbs cannot be patented, which means lower revenues for the pharmaceutical companies. But the tide is slowly changing as alternative medicine becomes mainstreamed into the American culture. Based on his book, *The Encyclopedia of Popular Herbs* (McCaleb 2000), the following is a look at various herbs and their medicinal properties with regard to stress, disease, and nutrition.

Astragalus. Astragalus, first introduced through Chinese medicine over 4,000 years ago, is known as an immunoenhancer due to its ability to increase white blood cell count. Recent studies at the University of Texas M.D. Anderson Cancer Center revealed the clinical efficacy of astragalus as an immunoenhancer.

Echinacea. Noted for centuries in the American Indian culture as an immunostimulant, echinacea is best known as a natural treatment for colds and flu, particularly at the onset of cold or flu-like symptoms. The agent found in echinacea is known to have an effect on the thymus gland, the master gland of the immune system, which feeds white blood cells into circulation. By binding to the surface of T-cells, this agent increases the production of *interferon,* a natural antiviral substance. In addition, *inulin,* a substrate found in echinacea, is responsible for activating the body's resistance to infection. Echinacea is also known to increase the production and release of *properdin,* a protein found in blood, which provides natural resistance to foreign antigens.

Feverfew. Feverfew is an herb that affects the physiological hormones that trigger migraine headaches,

so that the pain and severity of discomfort are dramatically reduced.

Garlic. For medicinal purposes, this herb is known as a cardiovascular enhancer. It has the ability to decrease cholesterol levels, sometimes below pre-meal levels.

Ginger. Known to most people as a spice, ginger root can help relieve stomach cramps, motion sickness, and problems associated with the gastrointestinal tract. The effects of ginger have been proven to the extent that it is now being used to reduce chemotherapy's side effect, vomiting, and as a treatment for postoperative nausea. Ginger is also thought to have some antioxidant properties.

Ginkgo. The most popular herb taken in Europe, ginkgo is a neurostimulator. Its use is associated with increased blood flow to the brain and its effect is increased memory function, particularly in people over the age of fifty.

Ginseng. Ginseng, a staple in Chinese medicine, is known in the Western world as a cardiovascular enhancer. Recent studies have proven its efficacy in lowering cholesterol levels by improving the ratio of LDLs to HDLs. It is also known to increase the stamina and endurance of athletes, and is thought by sports physiologists to increase mental and physical performance. It is interesting to note that the only area in which its benefits have not been proven is the Chinese claim that it is an aphrodisiac.

Goldenseal. Like echinacea, goldenseal is regarded as a natural healing agent for colds and flu. Goldenseal is known to increase the supply of blood to the spleen which, in turn, releases the spleen's immune-stimulating compounds. The primary agent in goldenseal is berberine, which stimulates the production of macrophages, the immune system's defense against viruses, bacteria, and tumor cells. Echinacea and goldenseal are often used in combination, and the combination of these two herbs often shows immediate results when taken at the onset of a cold or flu.

Hawthorn Berry. This herb is also known as an antiarrhythmia agent and is used extensively in Europe for congestive heart problems.

Licorice. Licorice is thought to be good for pain associated with ulcers.

Milk Thistle.   Milk thistle is known as an antitoxin, which acts like an antioxidant, specifically against ailments associated with the liver. Research reveals that milk thistle helps remove free radicals found in air pollution, chemical toxins, solvents, and alcohol. And due to the nature of several pain relievers with toxic side effects, milk thistle is known to help combat this toxicity on the liver as well.

St. John's Wort.   This herb is widely known as a natural antidepressant for people with mild to moderate depression.

Saw Palmetto.   This herb is highly regarded for its ability to alleviate problems with the prostate gland.

Valerian.   Valerian, a root extract, is known as a natural sedative used to treat insomnia. Unlike synthesized sedatives, it has no synergistic effect with alcohol.

As research continues on the effects of herbs on health status, we will gain a clearer perspective on these natural remedies. What we do know is that, because of their natural composition, herbs show fewer or none of the side effects of drugs synthesized in their molecular likeness. It is very important to note that herbs, like standard medical prescriptions, should be used only when needed to reestablish normal immune function or reestablish metabolic balance in the body. They are not recommended for use on an ongoing basis.

Additional Tips for Healthy Eating

Many of our eating habits were formed years ago and have become ingrained. When it comes to nutrition, there is no shortage of ideas and suggestions to follow to get back on the right track to eating better. Here are some additional tips:

- Thoroughly wash all pesticides from fruits and vegetables before eating. Studies show that individually, these pesticides are not harmful, but no studies have looked at the cumulative effects of various pesticides. It's a good idea to rinse all produce well.

- Avoid canned fruits and vegetables when possible because, by the time they are eaten, vitamins and minerals have been absorbed into the water used to package the goods and are often discarded in preparation.

- Avoid nutritional supplements that advertise "time released." This phrase is a marketing gimmick that does not hold up under the constraints of human physiology.

- Consider alternative options for healthier meals when you are away from home. It is just as easy to go to a grocery store and pick up some produce as it is to pull into a fast food restaurant.

- If you do choose to take a nutritional supplement, take it with food and water, not on an empty stomach.

- Eating a high-carbohydrate meal can make your blood glucose levels soar, only to fall down below resting levels soon thereafter. Eat some protein with the carbohydrates so that fatigue will not set in.

- If you are in the habit of eating while watching TV and you are hoping to lose weight, make a new habit to eat only in the kitchen area. TV commercials often send a message to eat even when you are not hungry. Hold fast to this rule: No eating in front of the TV.

- DRIs were designed to inform the general public about nutritional needs, yet these recommendations were not established for the optimal levels. Rather, what is listed are average amounts. Without pushing the limits of toxicity, you should consider increasing your levels of nutrients, specifically the vitamins and minerals.

- Switch from diet drinks that contain aspartame and caffeine to caffeine-free herbal teas when looking for a beverage and rehydration.

- If you are having problems sleeping at night, be careful to avoid foods that contain caffeine, and avoid eating a meal or snack before bedtime.

- Don't try to make several dietary changes all at once. Try making one change at a time (perhaps one each week) until you are at a level where it is comfortable to adopt a new eating behavior.

- While there are few known interactions between herbs and pharmaceutical prescriptions, please check with your physician to avoid any undesired side effects.

Summary

◆ Optimal nutrition involves five aspects: nutrients, digestion, absorption, metabolism, and elimination.

◆ There are six food nutrients that should be included in every diet: carbohydrates, fats, proteins, vitamins, minerals, and water.

◆ *Nutrient density* is a term used to describe the nutritional value (energy, vitamins, and mineral content) of a food substance. An apple has a greater nutrient density than a Twinkie®.

◆ Nutritionists recommend that you follow guidelines regarding adequacy (of essential nutrients), moderation (limited sugar, fat, and salt), balance (of nutrients), caloric control, and variety.

◆ Because of the global condition of soil depletion, even a healthy diet is considered deficient of the essential vitamins and minerals, so that supplementation is encouraged.

◆ A malnourished diet—one that is deficient of essential amino acids, essential fats, vitamins, and minerals—is itself a stressor on the body.

◆ Although the primary purpose of food is as a source of nutrients, many people use food as a means to fill an emotional void created by stress.

◆ Research has shown that some foods actually induce a state of stress. Excess amounts of sugar, caffeine, salt, and foods poor in vitamins and minerals weaken the body's resistance to the stress response, and may ultimately make a person more vulnerable to disease and illness.

◆ Not all supplements are created equal. Check to see that the processing does not destroy what it is intended to promote. Taken in excess, supplements can do more harm than good by inhibiting the proper digestion and absorption of essential nutrients.

◆ For optimal health, there should be one bowel movement for each meal eaten.

◆ Women should pay specific attention to their nutritional needs regarding the relationship between food substances and breast soreness, breast cancer, cervical cancer, colorectal cancer, premenstrual problems, and osteoporosis.

◆ Food affects not only the physical body, but the mental, emotional, and spiritual aspects as well. The concept of spiritual nutrition suggests eating a wide variety of fruits, vegetables, and grains that nurture the health of the seven primary chakras. In addition, spiritual nutrition suggests ensuring a balance in all aspects of food, including the acid/base balance.

◆ Eating disorders are emotionally rather than physiologically based, ranging from bulimia and anorexia to overeating—all of which have serious consequences if not resolved.

◆ Herbal therapies are considered an essential aspect of nutrition. Several herbs are used to enhance the immune system (astragalus, echinacea, goldenseal) and the cardiovascular system (garlic, ginsing, and hawthorn berry), as well as to aid in the health of various organs and physiological systems.

◆ Several herbal remedies are used to boost the immune system during times of stress when symptoms of colds or flu appear. Herbs should be taken only on these occasions, unlike vitamins, which should be consumed on a daily basis.

◆ Change various aspects of your diet, including reducing or eliminating the consumption of caffeine, refined sugar, sodium, and fats, to reduce the risk of stress-related problems.

Concepts and Terms

Absorption
Antioxidants
Aspartame
Astragalus
Bioavailability
Carbohydrates
Digestion
Echinacea
Elimination
Fats
Fat-soluble vitamins

Feverfew
Free radicals
Ginger
Ginkgo
Ginseng
Goldenseal
Green leafy vegetables
Herbal therapies
Methalated xanthines
Milk thistle
Mineral deficiency

Monosodium glutamate (MSG)
Nutrient density
Partially-hydrogenated oils
Proteins
Saw palmetto
Spiritual nutrition
Transfatty acids
Valerian
Vitamin supplements
Water-soluble vitamins

The association between nutrition and stress is a very important one. The following questions will increase your awareness about the kinds of foods you eat and the stress behaviors associated with eating.

1. **Do you regularly consume caffeine?**   Yes   No

2. **List the foods you ingest that contain caffeine and the estimated amounts you consume (coffee, tea, sodas, chocolate, etc.).**

   Types of food with caffeine   Amount per day

   1. _____   _____

   2. _____   _____

   3. _____   _____

   4. _____   _____

   5. _____   _____

   6. _____   _____

3. **Do you take vitamin supplements?**   Yes   No   If so, what kinds? _____

   _____

4. **Do you frequently use table salt?**   Yes   No

5. **Do you eat one or more meals that are prepared outside the home daily?**   Yes   No

6. **Do you consume junk food (from vending machines, etc.) regularly?**   Yes   No

7. **Do you eat cereals containing sugar?**   Yes   No

8. **Do you drink a lot of soft drinks?**   Yes   No

9. **Do you find that when you are stressed, you tend to eat more?**   Yes   No

10. **Do you find that when you are angry, you tend to snack more?**   Yes   No

11. **Do you eat a wide variety of fruits and vegetables?**   Yes   No

12. **Do you eat foods (fish and nuts) with the essential oils (Omega 3 and 6)?**   Yes   No

13. **Do you eat quickly?**   Yes   No

14. **Describe any other eating habits that you associate with a stressed lifestyle.**

   _____

   _____

   _____

   _____

References and Resources

Aronson, V. and Fitzgerald, B. *Guidebook for Nutrition Counselors.* Prentice Hall, Upper Saddle River, NJ 1990.

Blackburn, G. Nutritional Medicine: Eating Under Stress, *Prevention* 43(6):104, 1991.

Blaylock, R. *Excitotoxins: The Taste That Kills.* Health Press, Santa Fe, NM, 1994.

Cousens, G. *Spiritual Nutrition and the Rainbow Diet.* Cassandra Press, San Rafael, CA, 1986.

Dotson, G. Food in Treatment: Education for Self-Nurturance of the Body/Mind/Spirit, *Journal of Traditional Acupuncture,* Summer: 35–38, 1986.

Gershoff, S. *The Tufts University Guide to Total Nutrition,* 2nd edition. HarperPerennial, New York, 1996.

Husband, A. J. and Bryden, W. L. Nutrition, Stress and Immune Activities *Proceedings of the Nutrition Society of Australia,* 20:60–70, 1996.

Gordon, R. *Eating Disorders: Anatomy of A Social Epidemic.* Blackwell Publishing, New York, 2000.

Kesten, D. *Feeding the Body, Nourishing the Soul: Essentials of Eating for Physical, Emotional and Spiritual Wellbeing.* Conari Press, Berkeley, CA, 1997.

Kirby, J. Eat to Beat Stress. *American Health* Dec:81, 1997.

Langer, S. Stressless: Natural Strategies to Help You Cope, *Better Nutrition* 60(11):38, 1998.

Lappe, F. M. *Diet For a Small Planet.* Ballantine Books, New York, 1975.

Levenkron, S. *Anatomy of Anorexia.* WW Norton & Company, New York, 2000.

Levinstein, H. *Paradox a Plenty.* Oxford University Press, New York, 1993.

McCaleb, R. et al. *The Encyclopedia of Popular Herbs.* Prima Publishing, Roseville, CA, 2000.

McCaleb, R. *Nutrition and Herbs.* Lecture Presentation at the University of Colorado, Department of Kinesiology, November 12, 1995.

Mindell, E. *Earl Mindell's Herb Bible.* Fireside Books, New York, 1992.

Northrop, C. *Healing Foods for Women.* Philips Publishing, Inc., Potomac, MD, 1995.

Northrup, C. *Women's Bodies, Women's Wisdom.* Bantam Books, New York, 1994.

Robbins, J. *Diet For a New America.* Stillpoint Press, Walpole, NH, 1986.

Rubin, R. Eating Against the Grain, *U.S. News and World Report,* June 3: 62–63, 1996.

Simone, C. *Cancer and Nutrition: A Ten-Point Plan to Reduce Your Risk of Getting Cancer.* Avery Books, New York, 1994 (revised edition).

Sizer, F. and Whitney, E. *Hamilton and Whitney's Nutrition; Concepts and Controversies,* 6th edition. Wadsworth/Thomson Learning, Belmont, CA, 2000.

Smith, L. *Dr. Lendon Smith's Low-Stress Diet.* McGraw-Hill, New York, 1985.

Sommer, E. *Food and Mood.* Henry Holt and Company, Inc., New York, 1995.

Steinman, D. *Diet for a Posioned Planet.* Random House, New York, 1990.

Teitel, M. and Wilson, K. *Genetically Engineered Food: Changing the Nature of Nature.* Park Street Press, Rochesker, VT, 1999.

Townsen Newsletter for Doctors and Patients. Pt. Townsend, WA 98368, http://www.tldp.com.

Waterman, R. *Nutrition and Stress.* http://www.umanitoba.ca/outreach/manitoba_womens_health/nstress.htm

Weil, A. *Eating Well for Optimal Health: The Essential Guide to Food, Diet and Nutrition.* Knopf, New York, 2000.

Weil, A. *Spontaneous Healing.* Fawcett Books, New York, 1995.

Weiner, M. and Weiner, J. *Herbs That Heal.* Quantum Books, Mill Valley, CA, 1994.

Weiss, R. *Herbal Medicine.* Medicine Biologica, Portland, OR, 1988.

Chapter 28 Physical Exercise

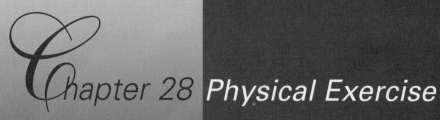

A sound mind

in a sound body.

—Juvenal

Years ago, actress Sally Field starred in a movie in which she portrayed a West Coast college student living at home. At the age of breaking away, she was in constant conflict with her controlling parents. Her way of reducing stress was to take out her aggression in the backyard pool by doing laps. Much to her parents' chagrin, she would hop in for a swim in the middle of the elaborate parties they frequently hosted outdoors. But when she got out of the water, she had calmed down considerably. For many people, physical exercise is a tranquilizer, and this is why it has become perhaps the most popular and effective means to reduce stress. It is also literally one of the most natural means to express the manifestation of the stress response.

In Chapter 1, we described how the ancient fight-or-flight response prepares the body for immediate physical movement. An increase in heart rate and blood pressure redistribute blood from the abdominal region to the large-muscle groups. Increased ventilation and circulation provide a greater supply of oxygen to the working muscles. The release of catecholamines and stress hormones activates the processes for metabolism of fats and carbohydrates, and these remain elevated long enough to ensure that muscles have adequate energy for contraction. Physical exercise strengthens the integrity of the body's physiological systems. Just as Selye observed physical deterioration from chronic distress, researchers in the field of exercise physiology have observed physical improvement from habitual exercise. There is adaptation to good stress as well as to bad stress.

The human body is a fantastic and complex phenomenon. In Chapter 2, we saw that there are several back-up systems in the fight-or-flight response to ensure the best chance of physical survival. For example, there are at least four hormones responsible for increasing blood pressure to shunt blood from the body's core to the periphery. In addition, conversion of proteins to glucose substrates occurs to meet the body's energy demands.

Even though exercise perpetuates the stress response while one is in motion, when physical activity ceases, the body returns to homeostasis. In a well-trained individual, the rate of return is not only quicker, but also the degree of homeostasis attained is more complete than before the individual began to exercise. It seems that the body's natural inclination, when confronted with stress, is to move, be active, or exercise. To remain inactive results in an incredible strain on internal systems. When the body stays still, various organ tissues go into metabolic overdrive, like "flooring it" with the car in Park for hours at a time. As a case in point, a study by Porter and Allsen (1978) showed that head basketball coaches had heart rates well above resting levels during games, in some cases as much as 253 percent (162 beats/min) above resting pregame levels—for a ninety-minute period.

In the past thirty years, since the recognition of coronary heart disease as America's number one cause of death and the factors putting one at risk, the effects of physical exercise on human anatomy and physiology have been studied feverishly. The overwhelming conclusion is that physical exercise is not only good, it is a virtual necessity to maintain proper function of major physiological systems. Just as the body requires a state of calmness or homeostasis, it equally demands physical stimulation or it will go into dysfunction. In other words, use it or lose it. Given what we now know, it is obvious that there must be a balance between physical arousal (activity) and homeostasis (rest) for optimal wellness.

Types of Physical Exercise

There are six components of fitness: cardiovascular endurance, muscular strength and endurance, flexibility, agility, power, and balance. (Some people include body composition as a seventh.) Cardiovascular endurance is the ability of the heart, lungs, and blood vessels to transport oxygenated blood to the working muscles for energy metabolism. Muscular strength is the ability to exert maximal force against a resistance, and muscular endurance is the ability to sustain repeated contractions over a prolonged period of time. Flexibility is defined as the ability to use a muscle group throughout its entire range of motion. These are thought to be the three most important components of fitness. Agility refers to maneuverability and coordination of fine and gross motor movements. Power is defined as force times distance over time; and balance is the ability to maintain equilibrium in motion. Agility, power, and balance supplement the first three components. Some or all of these components are used in every type of physical activity.

Although there are many kinds of exercise (Table 28.1)—from swimming, to weightlifting, to golf—exercise physiologists classify all physical activity in two categories: anaerobic or aerobic. These two types of physical exertion nicely parallel the two aspects of the fight-or-flight response as well as the emotions they elicit.

Anaerobic Activities

Anaerobic exercise is defined as a physical motion intense in power and strength, yet short in duration. Theoretically speaking, anaerobic activity is the type of movement or exercise used in the "fight" response. When expression of anger comes to mind, it is associated with power and strength. That is, when someone becomes angry and attempts to defend self or territory, it had better be forceful, quick, and decisive. Without these qualities, this half of the stress response proves ineffective for survival.

The word *anaerobic* means "without oxygen." There are two anaerobic energy systems: the adenosine-triphosphate-creatine system (ATP-PC), which lasts only one to ten seconds, and anaerobic glycolysis, or the lactic acid system, which continues after the ATP-PC system for approximately five to six minutes. At this point, activity is either suspended due to extreme fatigue, or the aerobic energy system kicks in. Lactic acid has an incredibly fatiguing effect on muscle contraction. Because the full redistribution of blood takes four to six minutes, depending on the condition of the individual, initial oxygen supply is minimal at best. This means that the muscles required to do the work must metabolize energy sources (carbohydrates) using oxygen already stored in muscle cell tissue. Thus, anaerobic exercise involves only short bursts of energy. Weightlifting is perhaps the most common example of this type of activity. Sprints and some calisthenics also fall into this category. Anaerobic exercise employs the muscular strength and power (force over distance) components of fitness.

Aerobic Activities

Running, swimming, cycling, cross-country skiing, rhythmic dancing, and walking are examples of aerobic activities. **Aerobic exercise,** or cardiovascular-endurance activities, are described as rhythmic or continuous in nature. They involve an equal supply and demand of oxygen in the working muscles. Aerobic work involves moderate intensity, but for a prolonged

Sport	Calories Burned
Swimming (free style)	249 kcal
Jogging	400 kcal
Golf	129 kcal
Raquetball	348 kcal
Aerobic dance	201 kcal

Table 28.1

Calories burned during 30 minutes of various activities in a person weighing approximately 140 pounds.

duration. Intensity is typically measured by heart rate (beats/min) or volume of oxygen consumed (liters/min). Aerobic exercise is the "flight" of the fight-or-flight response, and its primary energy source consists of fats. Theoretically speaking, aerobic exercise, as the flight response, is stimulated by fear and anxiety. These emotions make a person want to run for the hills, literally.

The word *aerobic* was coined many years ago to describe biological reactions using oxygen for metabolism. The term was adapted by the fitness industry in the early 1970s by physician Kenneth Cooper, whose research on fitness-training effects (primarily running) set the national standard for fitness programming. Also in the 1970s, with the inspiration of Jackie Sorenson, originator of aerobic dance, the term *aerobics* started being used to describe a new activity, rhythmic (aerobic) dancing. Aerobic dancing soon became a popular alternative to jogging for men and women alike. Since then, *aerobics* has become a household word, not only across America, but also around the world.

Whereas anaerobic exercise stimulates muscular strength (hypertrophy of muscle fibers), aerobic exercise challenges the cardiovascular and pulmonary systems to increase endurance (and to some extent muscular endurance, depending on the nature of the activity). Volumes of research support the theory that cardiovascular-endurance exercise helps reduce the risk of heart disease by modifying several risk factors. These include (1) a reduction of blood pressure, (2) reduction of cholesterol, specifically low-density lipoproteins (LDLs), (3) significant decreases in percentage of body fat, and (4) decreased physical arousal due to stress. For this reason, aerobic exercise tends to receive more favorable attention than anaerobic exercise. If it is true that epinephrine, the hormone associated with fear, is released three times as much and lasts much longer than norepinephrine, then perhaps the best technique to deal with fear is aerobic exercise. Note that aerobic exercise provides a great release for all shades of anger as well as anxiety.

The 1990 position statement by the American College of Sports Medicine stated that for a fitness program to be effective it must integrate all primary components of fitness. Thus, a well-balanced exercise program should incorporate both anaerobic and aerobic exercise, as well as flexibility in the training regime.

Physiological Effects of Physical Exercise

Exercise, like money in the bank, can be considered an investment in health. Unfortunately, unlike money, it accrues very little, if any, tangible interest. It is a pay-as-you-go plan. The short-term effects (neural and hormonal) of a single bout of exercise last approximately thirty-six hours. There are also incredible long-term benefits, but one must continue training to keep them. Studies of inactive astronauts in space (Vailus, 1992), deconditioned runners (Coyle et al., 1984), and bed-rest patients (Lenzt, 1981) have shown that when a physical training program is interrupted or discontinued for longer than two weeks, approximately 10 percent of cardiovascular gains can be lost. In some cases, up to 40 percent is lost after a month's time, depending on the nature of the inactivity.

On the other hand, clinical studies by Davies and Knibbs (1971) and Shephard (1968) indicate that significant physiological changes begin to become evident between the sixth and eighth week of training. And the gains from cardiovascular exercise are quite impressive; they read like a list of who's who in physiological homeostasis. Cardiovascular efficiency can be equated with better health status. The following are some of its benefits:

1. Decreased resting heart rate
2. Decreased resting blood pressure
3. Decreased muscle tension
4. Better quality sleep
5. Increased resistance to colds and illness
6. Decreased cholesterol and triglyceride levels

The following are additional benefits from habitual cardiovascular exercise:

1. Decreased body fat, improved body composition
2. Increased efficiency of heart
3. Decreased bone demineralization
4. Decreased rate of aging (several aspects)
5. Increased tolerance of heat and cold through acclimatization

In general, cardiovascular-endurance exercise acts as a catalyst to keep the body's physiological systems in balance. Through the multitude of mechanisms involved in energy metabolism, hormones, enzymes, and food substrates are used for their intended purpose. That is, minerals like calcium are absorbed by bone tissue where they are needed. But in a state of imbalance, other organs, like the lining of blood vessels, or in some cases mammary glands, begin to absorb these trace minerals and then show signs of dysfunction. Just how this unique balance is maintained is still under scientific investigation.

Regarding the relationship between physical exercise and the relaxation response, one important concept to remember is **parasympathetic rebound.** In anticipation of movement, seconds before exercise begins, epinephrine and norepinephrine are released by order of the central nervous system. The level of catecholamines remains elevated throughout the duration of the activity. Upon completion of physical movement, the secretion of epinephrine and norepinephrine is inhibited by the parasympathetic nervous system, which initiates a calming response. In studies comparing stress-induced arousal (physical exercise) in athletically trained individuals versus sedentary ones, the trained subjects returned to their resting heart-rate and serum catecholamine levels sooner than did their nonactive counterparts. In addition, the same values continued to decrease *below* prearousal levels in the conditioned individuals. These results indicate a very efficient calming mechanism by the parasympathetic nervous system indeed.

Based on the work of Bellet et al. (1969), Davies and Few (1974), Galbo and colleagues (1977), Sutton (1978), Tharp (1975), and Winder et al. (1973, 1982), the following conclusions have been drawn regarding the immediate, short-term, and long-term effects of cardiovascular exercise as a relaxation technique. First, it appears that a single bout of aerobic exercise "burns off" existing catecholamines and stress hormones by directing them toward their intended metabolic functions, rather than allowing them to linger in the body to undermine the integrity of vital organs and the immune system. This in itself can be considered a constructive intervention technique to counter daily stressors. Second, the training effect of aerobic exercise appears to prepare the body for future stressful episodes by decreasing the level of hormonal secretions when feelings of anger or fear manifest themselves. In effect, exercise can be used as a preventive measure, as it tends to minimize or neutralize physical arousal to nonphysical threats. Third, the long-term effect of exercise appears to be prolonged, efficient function of several organ systems, including the heart, lungs, blood vessels, kidneys, muscle, and skeletal tissue. Many researchers are of the opinion that while exercise training is not a panacea for the multitude of diseases and illnesses, nor is it the Fountain of Youth, its cumulative effects do appear to add to both the quality and quantity of life.

Theories of Athletic Conditioning

Numerous studies have been conducted to determine the minimal amount of exercise needed to maintain its benefits. The studies have investigated the intensity, frequency, and duration of aerobic exercise, specifically, as aerobic activity has the greatest effect on reducing the risks of heart disease. At this point in the high-technology age, where machines now do in minutes what men and women used to take hours to accomplish, sedentary lifestyles are no longer the exception; they are the norm. So every possible variable and permutation thereof has been examined, and a formula now accepted by the American College of Sports Medicine (ACSM) has set the standard for exercise programs for virtually all individuals. This is sometimes referred to as the all-or-none conditioning principle.

All-or-None Conditioning Principle

As stated in the ACSM guidelines, four major factors make up the **all-or-none conditioning principle:** intensity, frequency, duration, and mode of exercise.

Intensity. Intensity refers to the challenge (stress) placed on a specific physiological system involved in an activity. In the case of the cardiovascular system, intensity is measured in terms of heart rate, the num-

Figure 28.

The target heart-rate zone, or intensity of work needed to challenge the heart muscle for a more efficient cardiovascular system. Your exercise heart rate should be maintained for the duration of the workout. (From Edlin, G., and E. Golanty: *Health and Wellness.* Fourth Edition. © 1992 Boston: Jones and Bartlett Publishers. Reprinted by permission.)

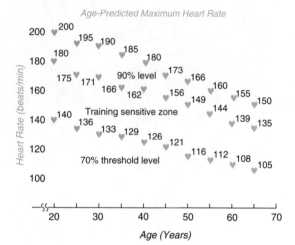

ber of beats per minute, and should vary with age (Fig. 28.1). In a cardiovascular fitness program, the suggested range is between 65 and 85 percent of maximal intensity, with an average intensity of 75 percent for healthy individuals. This is often called the target heart rate or target zone. Target heart rate is the range of numbers of heart beats one expects to "hit" or reach during exercise. This can be calculated using the following formula (Karvonen, 1959):

Target Heart Rate Formula

Maximal heart rate

= 220 (A constant used by everyone under 30)

− _____ (Age)

= _____ (Predicted maximal heart rate)

− _____ (Resting heart rate)

× .75 (75% intensity of workload)

= _____ (Heart-rate reserve)

= _____ (Your resting heart rate)

+ _____ (Target heart rate)

= _____ (× 6 for a 10-second count)

Data collected by Dr. Kenneth Cooper and highlighted in his book *The New Aerobics* indicates that this is the desired intensity for cardiovascular benefits. If a person goes beyond an intensity of 80 to 85 percent (depending on fitness level), he or she begins to phase out of the aerobic energy system, because the supply of oxygen can no longer meet the demand. Then the anaerobic energy system kicks in, but because of lactic acid production, exercise using this energy system cannot last long due to muscle fatigue. Note that for sedentary or non-physically active individuals, as well as those with coronary heart disease, a target heart rate of 65 percent of maximal heart rate is suggested. Note, too, that when the musculoskeletal system is challenged, as in weight training, intensity is measured in terms of pounds or kilograms, repetitions, and sets instead of heart rate.

Frequency. Frequency is the number of exercise sessions per week. The minimum number recommended is three. When first starting a fitness program, however, it is advisable to follow a day of aerobic exercise with a day of rest. This allows the body time to recover, preventing too much strain on muscles, tendons, and ligaments. Overuse can result in several types of injuries, from shin splints to tendonitis. After the third or fourth week of exercising every other day, additional days may be added, but three days per week is the frequency needed to maintain one's level of fitness.

Duration. In addition to level of intensity, what really distinguishes aerobic and anaerobic exercise is the length of time involved with the activity. The elevated heart rate of aerobic activity is continuous for the entire duration. Conversely, there are several pauses and fluctuations in heart rate during anaerobic exercise, since the individual exerts power or strength for a short period and is then forced to relax due to muscle fatigue. The minimum duration, or number of minutes per exercise session, is suggested to be twenty to thirty minutes. Less than twenty minutes does not guarantee any benefits.

Mode of Exercise. This refers to the type of activity chosen to challenge a particular physiological system. Walking, running, and swimming, for example, are types of aerobic exercise that adequately challenge the cardiovascular system. Weight training, on the other hand, taxes the anaerobic energy system, despite claims by several manufacturers of weight training equipment to the contrary. Only an Olympic-trained athlete could achieve cardiovascular benefits from a circuit-weight training program. Likewise, running will tone and define muscles, but muscle hypertrophy is not of any benefit to cardiovascular endurance, so running is not considered superior to other forms of aerobic work.

Progressive Overload Principle

The general adaptation syndrome theorized by Hans Selye has direct implications for the effects of physical exercise. It appears that adaptations occur as a result of eustress as well as distress. During physical exercise, adaptations take place in muscle fiber and skeletal tissue, and include many changes at the subcellular level (e.g., an increase in the size and number of mitochondria in muscle tissue). When ACSM exercise guidelines are followed, the positive adaptations that occur will increase the efficiency of all the physiological systems involved. In other words, when the body meets the resistance of exercise, whether this resistance is measured in time, speed, distance, or weight, and is able to overcome it, then new physiological adaptations result. These may include muscle hypertrophy, increased bone density, decreased body fat, and increased cardiac contractility, to name just a few. But remember: these adaptations revert back to untrained levels when exercise-induced resistance (stress) is discontinued, and this deconditioning can occur within weeks.

Phases of a Workout

Just as there is a formula for calculating maximum cardiovascular benefits of exercise, there is also a formula for ensuring safe workouts. The components are a proper warm-up, stimulus or conditioning period, and cool-down.

Warm-Up Period. The warm-up is the preparation for exercise. It usually lasts approximately five to ten minutes. The purpose of the warm-up is to slowly increase heart rate and allow working muscles to become saturated with oxygenated blood. Muscles are like sponges: when they are dry, they are difficult to stretch. In this state, they are prone to microtears. When saturated with blood, though, they are very pliable, and this ensures efficient contractility and less susceptibility to injury. Redistribution of blood flow takes several minutes. But because of long-term adaptations, an athlete who is in fine cardiovascular shape will warm up much more quickly than a person leading a sedentary life.

To initiate the warm-up period properly, any activity can be performed at a low intensity. Walking, slow jogging, and calisthenics are examples. Once the body is warmed up, stretching the muscles can begin. Flexibility is an important component of fitness and should not be neglected, especially as one ages, because elasticity decreases over time. Warm-ups used to be advocated as a necessary step to avoid muscle and joint injuries. In studies to determine whether exercise-related injuries decreased with a proper warm-up, however, it was learned that the presence or absence of a warm-up made no significant difference in reducing the rate of injuries. To the contrary, many injuries take place during the warm-up phase—if there is inadequate redistribution of blood flow. In other words, people frequently overstretch prior to adequate heart-rate increase. Stretching prior to the redistribution of blood flow is not a good idea; it can lead to tendon and tissue damage.

Stimulus Period.   The stimulus period is the "meat" of the workout. This is the period of intensity for the various physiological systems. The stimulus period should be a minimum of twenty minutes, regardless of which energy system—aerobic or anaerobic—is used (Fig. 28.2). After the first eight weeks of training, you may wish to add to the duration of this phase of the workout.

Cool-Down Period.   No workout should end without adequate time for the body to return to a natural resting state. In fact, the cool-down period is described by some exercise physiologists as the most important part of the workout. The purpose of the cool-down is to decrease the signs and symptoms of the stress response: heart rate, blood pressure, ventilations, and so forth. If an activity ceases at high intensity, then blood pools in the extremities because the working muscles are no longer acting as pumps to send it back to the heart. The heart must now work even harder, requiring even more oxygenated blood, to circulate blood and eliminate metabolic by-products. In a young heart, this extra burden may not be noticeable. With age, however, the taxing effort can cause damage to the entire cardiovascular system. This is why most exercise fatalities occur during or shortly after an inadequate cool-down. The cool-down phase should consist of five to ten minutes of, first, decreasing intensity of activity (e.g., running, to jogging, to walking), then a few moments of stretching the muscles used in the activity.

Figure 28.2

Of the three phases of a workout—warm-up, stimulus and cool-down—the stimulus phase is when your target heart rate should remain elevated. The more efficient your cardiovascular system, the sooner your heart rate will return to resting level during cool-down.

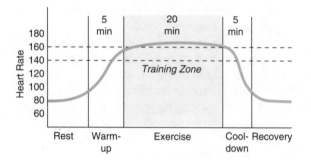

Psychological Effects of Physical Exercise

When the fitness movement mushroomed in the late 1970s, the complexity of the many benefits reported caught some in the field of clinical medicine off guard. At the time, the most frequently prescribed drug in the country was the tranquilizer Valium. The Rolling Stones even wrote a hit song, "Mother's Little Helper," satirizing its widespread use.

But as people initiated running programs, they began to talk less and less about muscle soreness, weather conditions, and rude drivers; these concerns seemed to have relatively little importance. Instead, thoughts began to turn inward, and running began to take on a Zen-like quality. Moreover, it became a private time to sort out problems, resolve issues, and reflect about life in general, relationships, and the purpose of life. Running became a time for self-reflection and meditation. Many people stopped taking prescribed sedatives and tranquilizers; and some people even stopped going to their therapists. In time, members of the medical community also took up running. And some psychologists even changed counseling styles, taking their patients off the office couch and onto the sidewalk or high-school track.

As an investigative eye was kept on this national activity, reports soon filtered in that running could have an addictive quality. Specifically, it was learned that when running routines were interrupted for more than a few days, some individuals showed signs of withdrawal similar to those observed with chemical addictions. For his book *Positive Addiction,* William Glasser interviewed over 700 long-distance runners to gain a better understanding of this phenomenon. His analysis revealed six important criteria for a physical activity to take on this addictive nature:

1. The activity must be done for at least an hour per day.
2. The activity must be done on a regular basis.
3. The activity must have a base of six months of training.
4. The activity must be well liked by the person doing it.
5. The activity must be noncompetitive.
6. The activity must be done alone, or perhaps with one other person.

Just when Glasser was conducting his research, other scientists were investigating the same concept from a physiological approach. In the early 1980s, a new human neuropeptide was discovered, and it showed remarkable morphinelike qualities. Beta-endorphin was soon hailed as the body's own natural opiate. In minute quantities, it significantly reduced sensations of pain and seemed to promote feelings of euphoria and exhilaration. And like various other chemical substances, beta-endorphin had an addictive quality; many people showed signs of depression after days of inactivity. What's more, this neuropeptide was released by other locations as well as the brain during physical activity, most notably running. Not everyone who ran, however, experienced this effect, perhaps because of the training effect.

While to date no songs have been written about runner's high, this phenomenon is now commonly accepted as perhaps the greatest psychological effect of exercise. But as it turns out, running is not the only physical activity during which beta-endorphin is released. Many other types of cardiovascular-endurance exercises, such as swimming and walking, potentially produce the same effect. What is necessary, regardless of the activity, is that the exercise be egoless, or noncompetitive.

Speculation now has it that activities with rhythmic, repetitive motion, such as swimming, running, walking, or cycling, offer a meditative form of conscious awareness. As discussed in Chapter 18, it has been suggested that such rhythmic activities may shift hemispheric dominance from the left to the right

brain. Several long-distance runners interviewed by Fixx (1977) and Glasser (1976) stated that running heightened mental receptivity, resulting in greater imagination and creativity to apply to problem solving. Between this discovery and the other positive effects, psychologists took a new interest in cardiovascular exercise as a coping technique to reduce the psychological fallout from stress. Among the thousands of investigators to delve into the relationship between exercise and emotional health were Berger (1982, 1983), Dishman (1981), Folkins (1981), Ismail (1977), and Morgan (1987, 1980, and 1982). The conclusion drawn from all this research is that athletic training or exercise is viable as both a relaxation technique and a coping technique to deal with stress. The following are the reported psychological benefits of habitual exercise (particularly from jogging):

1. Improved self-esteem
2. Improved sense of self-reliance, self-efficacy
3. Improved mental alertness, perception, and information processing
4. Increased perceptions of acceptance by others
5. Decreased feelings of depression and anxiety
6. Decreased overall sense of stress and tension

Steps to Initiate a Fitness Training Program

While physical exercise is now praised as the wonder technique for stress reduction, it also poses a threat to physical well-being if not done correctly. The typical way many people approach something can be summarized in four words: too much too soon. Individuals get caught up in the whirlwind of excitement, and as a result often go overboard, thinking that if some is good, more is better. The result is burnout. When too-much-too-soon behavior is applied to physical exercise, it can result in injury, particularly muscle and tendon damage.

Let there be no doubt: exercise is demanding work. And after cranking out for eight to ten hours at the office, shop, or other place of business, the last thing a person wants is to go out and do more work. Motivation can be rather elusive at the end of the day. Because the effects of exercise don't occur overnight, people can become quite disenchanted with the whole concepts of muscle fatigue and sweat. In fact, motivation peaks about three to seven days after the start of a fitness program and then rapidly declines. Without internal as

Stress With a Human Face

THERE ARE BASICALLY TWO TYPES OF SUMMER jobs where I come from: waiting tables or lifeguarding. I grew up doing the latter to finance my college education, and I also taught swimming lessons and coached several swim teams over the years. But when I chose a career in academia, lifeguarding and swim lessons became a distant memory—or so I thought. One day on campus, I was introduced to a nationally-known figure, and soon found myself agreeing to give swim lessons once again.

At first Dan (not his real name) said his primary goal of getting in shape was to lose weight. Due to a back injury, running and biking were out of the question, so he chose swimming. But after he had progressed from blowing bubbles to swimming a quarter-mile, he confided that getting in shape was really secondary to clearing his mind and coping with stress. He needed not only physical conditioning, but some time alone to think and get his head straight, sort out problems, and access his intuition and creativity on a daily basis. But his fast-paced job in the nation's capital wasn't doing him any good, nor were his coronary risk factors (mainly hypertension). He knew there was only one solution: to take out his aggressions and anxieties in the pool.

Dan is up to a mile a day now, and his physical shape is superseded only by the smile on his face as he gets out of the water and heads for the showers. The risk factors are minimized, and he feels like a new man every day. On numerous occasions he has said that I literally saved his life. I know better than that. How does the expression go? You can lead a horse to water, but . . . ✦

well as external reinforcement, most exercise programs peter out before real physiological changes occur.

Exercise specialists and health educators have begun to incorporate goal setting into the design and prescription of exercise programming as a means to maintain motivation during this crucial period. Scientific research has unequivocally proven that physical exercise is necessary for optimal health. It should become a habit in everyone's lifestyle. The following are some suggestions regarding cardiovascular (aerobic) fitness to help guide you through the transition period. Table 28.2 is a suggested program of jogging and walking for those who are so inclined.

1. *Start cautiously and progress moderately with your program.* The American College of Sports Medicine suggests that every person, particularly those over the age of thirty-five get a physical examination for medical clearance prior to starting a fitness program. As a part of the physical evaluation, you should be assessed for your fitness capacity and given an exercise prescription. The prescription includes a target heart rate, a mode of exercise, a selected intensity, frequency and duration, as well as a review of the components of a workout and the design of health and fitness goals. Sometimes it helps to see physical exercise as a process, not an outcome. People who experience a natural high from exercise are in a sense detached from the physical sensations and immediate rewards (e.g., losing weight). One rule of thumb to go by when working out is this: If you can't hold a conversation while exercising, you are pushing too hard. The no pain-no gain approach was discredited a long time ago.

2. *Pick an activity you really enjoy.* Not everyone is a jogger. If you have tried jogging and found it too difficult or displeasing, there are plenty of other aerobic activities to choose from. Perhaps the most underrated exercise is walking. Walking provides the same benefits as running if an adequate heart rate is maintained. Likewise, swimming is one of the best choices as it is cited as not only improving

Table 28.2 Suggested Walking/Jogging Program

	Warm-Up	Target Zone Exercise*	Cool-Down	Total Time
Week 1				
Session 1	Slow walk, limber up 5 min.	Walk 10 min. (try not to stop.)	Slow walk 5 min.	20 minutes
Session 2	Repeat above schedule after a day or two of rest.			
Session 3	Repeat above schedule again after a day or two of rest. (Try to maintain three exercise sessions per week.)			
Week 2				
Session 1–3	Slow walk, limber up 5 min.	Walk 5 min., jog 1 min., walk 5 min.	Slow walk 4 min, stretch 3 min.	23 minutes
Week 3				
Sessions 1–3	Slow walk, limber up 5 min.	Walk 4 min., jog 3 min., walk 6 min.	Slow walk 3 min., stretch 3 min.	25 minutes
Week 4				
Sessions 1–3	Slow walk, limber up 5 min.	Walk 4 min., jog 5 min., walk 4 min., jog 5 min.	Slow walk 3 min., stretch 3 min.	29 minutes
Week 5				
Sessions 1–3	Slow walk, limber up 5 min.	Walk 4 min., jog 5 min., walk 4 min., jog 6 min.	Slow walk 3 min., stretch 3 min.	30 minutes
Week 6				
Sessions 1–3	Slow walk, limber up 5 min.	Walk 4 min., jog 5–6 min., walk 4 min., jog 5–6 min.	Slow walk 3 min., stretch 4 min.	30–32 minutes
Week 7				
Sessions 1–3	Slow walk, limber up 5 min.	Walk 4 mins., jog 6–7 min., walk 4 min., jog 6–7 min.	Slow walk 3 min., stretch 4 min.	32–34 minutes
Week 8				
Sessions 1–3	Slow walk, limber up 5 min.	Walk 4 min., jog 7–8 min., walk 4 min., jog 7–8 min.	Slow walk 3 min., stretch 4 min.	34–36 minutes

*CHECK your pulse periodically to see if you are exercising within your target zone. As you become more fit, gradually increase your jogging time from eight to twenty-five minutes.

Figure 28.3

cathy® **by Cathy Guisewite**

cardiovascular endurance, muscular endurance, and flexibility, but is least likely to result in overuse injuries to muscle tissue and joints. Sometimes alternating activities is a great way to avoid burnout or staleness from the same sport. Most important, pick an activity that is non-ego-involved and noncompetitive. Many people find that when the ego gets involved, the activity promotes, rather than reduces, feelings of stress.

3. *Select a time of day to exercise.* Make a commitment to allocate a special time each day just for this purpose, and make this time yours and yours alone, with no other responsibilities and commitments to take this time away from you. Mornings before work or school are often the easiest times to schedule exercise, and the immediate physiological effects certainly help meet the challenges of the day. Sometimes early morning workouts mean sacrificing badly needed sleep; in this case, afternoon or evening is a good option. After a long and perhaps busy day, exercise is a great way to unwind and literally release pent-up energy. If neither of these options is workable, the lunch hour (the new executive recess) is always an alternative. And to be realistic, if you are like many people with busy schedules and no two days alike, the time for exercise may have to vary from day to day. Remember, you only need three days a week, half an hour each day to achieve and maintain the benefits of exercise. That is a total of one and a half hours per week.

4. *Exercise using the right clothes and equipment.* Perhaps the most important piece of equipment is a good pair of athletic shoes. The cost may be rather high, but quality shoes serve as a good insurance policy against injuries to the lower back, shins, ankles, feet, and most notably, knees. The knees are the weakest joint in the body. Poor shoes can decrease the stability of the tendons and ligaments supporting the knee, resulting in chronic knee pain known as chondromalacia. Also, cardiovascular exercise tends to significantly increase body-core temperature, so clothing should be layered so that it can be "peeled off" if you get overheated in the cool months.

5. *Initiate a support group.* Although exercise is not always considered miserable, at times it does love company. There may be times when you would like nothing better than to exercise alone, but a companion certainly serves as a motivator for those days when the thought of exercising is not appealing.

6. *Set personal fitness goals for yourself.* Do you want to lose weight? Would you like to decrease your cholesterol levels? Would you like to have a "washboard" stomach? Do you want to reduce your resting blood pressure? Would you like to run a 10K road race? These are some commonly heard goals.

Figure 28.4 Noncompetitive exercising with a group of people serves as a great motivation factor to continue the activity.

Progression toward and accomplishment of health and fitness goals can be wonderful means of motivation. It is easy to see the progress you have made when you keep track of it. The most popular method for doing so is jotting a short note on a calendar. The companion to goal setting is reward: When you accomplish a goal, treat yourself to something special.

7. *Care and prevention of injuries.* The best way to treat an injury is to prevent it, but if you encounter pain along the way, treat the injury immediately. The most common injuries occur to joints, where tendons begin to pull away from bone. If you feel pain in a joint, you should stop the activity and put ice on the joint as soon as possible. Some injuries, if caught early, may not need immediate medical attention. If pain persists after a day or two, however, see a physician. Not long ago, physicians knew very little about sports medicine, but today it is easier to find qualified care in this area. Please don't take an injury lightly.

These are some of the basic guidelines to follow when initiating a personal fitness program. But above all, use common sense. If you would like assistance in developing your personal fitness program, health clubs, community recreation centers, and YMCAs and YWCAs have qualified personnel to help you design a safe, quality program. Good luck and have fun!

Best Application of Physical Exercise

To get the most benefits from physical exercise, there must be the right intensity, frequency, and duration as well as the best mode of exercise for the individual involved. Physical activity of any type is best used as a postponed response to stress, unless the situation is right to put on your exercise clothes and run out the door. Exercise—both aerobic and anaerobic—provides a wonderful catharsis of emotional frustrations. This includes both anger and anxiety. It is best to schedule a time to work out, and stick to it. Because injury or burnout can occur with a once-favorite activity, it is a good idea to have a backup sport.

Summary

- Physical exercise is a form of stress: the enactment of all the physiological systems that the fight-or-flight response triggers for physical survival.
- Physical exercise is classified as either anaerobic (fight) or aerobic (flight). Anaerobic (without oxygen) is short, intense, and powerful activity, whereas aerobic exercise (with oxygen) is moderately intense activity for a prolonged period of time. Aerobic exercise is the better type to promote relaxation.
- The body adapts, either negatively or positively, to the stress placed upon it. Proper physical exercise will cause many adaptations that in the long term are thought to be effective in reducing the deleterious effects of stress by returning the body to a profound state of homeostasis. Physical exercise allows the body to use stress hormones for their intended purposes, detoxifying the body of stress hormones by utilizing them constructively.
- To get the benefits of physical exercise, four criteria must be met: intensity, duration, frequency of training, and mode of exercise. Together they are called the all-or-none principle, meaning that without meeting all four requirements few if any benefits will be gained. It takes between six and eight weeks to see significant benefits in the body.
- The positive effects of physical exercise are lowering resting heart rate, resting blood pressure, and muscle tension, and a host of other functions that help maintain or regain physiological calmness.
- Exercise evokes not only physiological changes but various psychological changes (e.g., runner's high) as well, again suggesting that mind and body act as one entity. Habitual physical exercise produces both physiological homeostasis and mental homeostasis. Individuals who engage in regular physical exercise report higher levels of self-esteem and lower incidences of depression and anxiety.

Concepts and Terms

Adenosine-triphosphate-creatine (ATP)
Aerobic exercise
Agility
All-or-none conditioning principle
Anaerobic exercise
Balance
Cardiovascular endurance
Chondromalacia

Cool-down period
Duration of exercise
Flexibility
Frequency of exercise
Intensity of exercise
Karvonen's heart rate equation
Lactic acid
Mode of activity
Muscular endurance
Muscular strength

Parasympathetic rebound
Phases of a workout
Power
Progressive overload principle
Runner's high
Stimulus period
Target heart rate
Warm-up period
Water-soluble vitamins

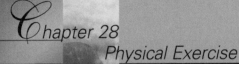

Self-Assessment

1. What type of physical exercise do you enjoy most to reduce stress? Explain why.

   _____

   _____

2. Describe your physical exercise routine in terms of intensity, frequency, and duration.

Intensity	Frequency	Duration
_____	_____	_____
_____	_____	_____
_____	_____	_____
_____	_____	_____

3. Do you tend to exercise alone or with friends? Why?

   _____

   _____

   _____

   _____

4. If you incur an injury during your exercise routine, do you have a second activity that you could do in its place?   Yes   No

   If so, what is it? _____

   _____

5. Have you ever experienced runner's high?   Yes   No

   If so (even if it was swimming, riding, or some other activity), what did it feel like?

   _____

   _____

   _____

   _____

References and Resources

American College of Sports Medicine. *Guidelines for Exercise Testing and Prescription,* 4th ed. Lea and Febiger, Philadelphia, 1990.

American College of Sports Medicine. *Recommended Quantity and Quality of Exercise for Developing and Maintaining Cardiovascular and Muscular Fitness in Healthy Adults.* ACSM, Indianapolis, IN, April, 1990.

Artal, M. and Sherman, C. Exercise and Depression, Physician and Sports Medicine, October: 55–60, 1998.

Bartholomew, J.B. Stress Reactivity after Maximal Exercise: The Effect of Manipulated Performance Feedback in Endurance Athletes, *Journal of Sports Science* 18(11):893, 2000.

Bein-Ari, E.T. Take Two Exercise Sessions and Call Me in the Morning, *BioScience* 50(1):96, 2000.

Bellet, S. et al. Effect of Physical Exercise on Adrenocortical Excretion, *Metabolism* 18:484–487, 1969.

Berger, B. et al. Comparison of Jogging, the Relaxation Response and Group Interaction for Stress Reduction, *Journal of Sport and Exercise Psychology* 10(4):431–447, 1988.

Berger, B. G. Facts and Fancy: Mood Alteration through Exercise, *Journal of Physical Education, Recreation, and Dance* 53(9):47–48, 1982.

Berger, B. G. Stress Reduction through Exercise: The Mind-Body Connection, *Motor Skills: Theory into Practice* 7(2):31–46, 1983.

Collingwood, T. The Effects of Physical Training upon Behavior and Self-Attitudes, *Journal of Clinical Psychology* 28:583–585, 1971.

Colt, E., Wardlaw, S. L., and Franz, A. G. Effect of Running on Plasma B-Endorphin, *Life Science* 28:1637–1640, 1984.

Cooper, K. *The Aerobics Program for Total Wellbeing.* Bantam Books, New York, 1983.

Cooper, K. *The New Aerobics.* Evans, New York, 1970.

Coyle, E .G. et al. Time Course of Loss of Adaptations after Stopping Prolonged Intense Endurance Training, *Journal of Applied Physiology* 57(6):1857–1864, 1984.

Davies, C. and Few, J. D. Effects of Exercise on Adrenocortical Function, *Journal of Applied Physiology* 35:887–891, 1974.

Davies, C. and Knibbs, A. The Training Stimulus: The Effects of Intensity, Duration, and Frequency of Effort on Maximum Aerobic Power Output, *Int Z Angew. Physiology* 29:299–305, 1971.

DeBenedette, V. Getting Fit for Life: Can Exercise Reduce Stress? *The Physician and Sports Medicine* 16:185–200, 1988.

Dishman, R. K. Biological Influences on Exercise Adherence, *Research Quarterly for Exercise and Sport* 52(2):143–159, 1981.

Dishman, R. K., Ickes, W., and Morgan, W. P. Self-Motivation and Adherence to Habitual Physical Activity, *Journal of Applied Social Psychology* 1:115–125, 1980.

Farrell, P. A. Exercise, and Endorphins: Male Responses, *Medicine and Science in Sports and Exercise* 17:89–92, 1985.

Fixx, J. *The Complete Book of Running.* Random House, New York, 1977.

Folkins, C. H. Psychological Fitness as a Function of Physical Fitness, *Archives of Physical Medicine and Rehabilitation* 53:503–508, 1972.

Folkins, C. H. and Sime, W. E. Physical Fitness Training and Mental Health, *American Psychologist* 36:373–389, 1981.

Galbo, H. et al. Diminished Hormonal Responses to Exercise in Trained Rats, *Journal of Applied Physiology* 43:953–958, 1977.

Getchel, B. *Physical Fitness: A Way of Life.* Wiley, New York, 1983.

Glasser, W. *Positive Addiction.* Harper & Row, New York, 1976.

Grossman, A. Endorphins: Opiates for the Masses, *Medicine and Science in Sport and Exercise* 17:74–80, 1985.

Ismail, A. H. and Young, R. J. Effect of Chronic Exercise on the Personality of Adults, *Annals of the New York Academy of Sciences* 301:958–969, 1977.

Karvonen, M. J. Effects of Vigorous Exercise on the Heart. In *Work and the Heart*, eds. F. F. Rosenbaum and R. Kriegel. Hoeber, New York, 1959.

Kozak, D. Keep Moving—Stay Happy, *Prevention* 53(2):39, 2001.

Lamb, D. *Physiology of Exercise*. Macmillan, New York, 1984.

Lenzt, M. Selected Aspects of Deconditioning Secondary to Immobilization, *Nursing Clinics of North America* 16(4):729–737, 1981.

Lyon, L. S. Psychological Effects of Jogging: A Preliminary Study, *Perceptual and Motor Skills* 47:1215–1218, 1978.

McCaleb, R. Research and Reviews, HerbalGram 29:19–22, 1993.

Mikevic, P. Anxiety, Depression, and Exercise, *Quest* 33(1):140–153, 1982.

Mobily, K. Using Physical Activity and Recreation to Cope with Stress and Anxiety: A Review, *American Corrective Therapy Journal* 36(3):77–81, 1982.

Morgan, W. P. Psychological Effects of Exercise, *Behavioral Medicine Update* 4:25–30, 1982.

Morgan, W. and Goldstein, S., eds. *Exercise and Mental Health*. Hemisphere, New York, 1987.

Morgan, W. P. et al. Exercise as a Relaxation Technique, *Primary Cardiology* 6:48–57, 1980.

National Dairy Council. *Statement of Dietary Goals for the United States Submitted to the Select Committee on Nutrition and Human Needs, U.S. Senate*. The Council, Rosemont, IL, 1977.

Nieman, D.C. *The Exercise–Health Connection*. Human Kinetics, Champaign, IL, 1997.

Pizzorno, J. Pow! Supercharge your Immune System, *Natural Health*, Sept/Oct. 81–85, 1994.

Porter, D. T. and Allsen, P. E. Heart Rates of Basketball Coaches, *Physician and Sports Medicine*, October: 84–90, 1978.

President's Council on Physical Fitness and Sports. *Introduction to Running: One Step at a Time*. PCPFS, Washington, DC, 1980.

Sachs, M. and Buffone, G., eds. *Running as Therapy: An Integrated Approach*. University of Nebraska Press, Lincoln, NE, 1984.

Sharkey, B. J. *Physiology of Fitness: Prescribing Exercise for Fitness, Weight Control, and Health*, 2nd ed. Human Kinetics, Champaign, IL, 1984.

Shephard, R. *Exercise Physiology*. Decker, Toronto, 1987.

Shephard, R. Intensity, Duration, and Frequency of Exercise as Determinants of the Response to a Training Regimen, *Int Z, Angew. Physiology* 26: 272–278, 1968.

Snelling, A., Meholick, B., and Seaward, B. L. Counseling Fitness, *Fitness Management* 5(1):40–41, 1990.

Sorenson, J. *Aerobic Dancing*. Rawson-Wade, New York, 1979.

Stamford, B. The Adrenaline Rush, *Physician and Sports Medicine* 15:205–212, 1987.

Sutton, J. R. Hormonal and Metabolic Responses to Exercise in Subjects of High and Low Work Capacity, *Medicine and Science in Sport* 10:1–6, 1978.

Tharp, G. D. The Role of Glucocorticoids in Exercise, *Medicine and Science in Sports* 7:6–11, 1975.

Vailus, A. Effects of Weightlessness on Aerobic and Anaerobic Capacity, unpublished paper, Dept. of Health Fitness, American University, Washington, D.C., 1992.

Watson, T. and Wu, C. Are You Too Fat? *U.S. News and World Report* 120(1):52–61, 1996.

Wilson, V., Morley, N., and Bird, E. Mood Profiles of Marathon Runners, Joggers, and Nonexercisers, *Perceptual and Motor Skills* 50:117–118, 1980.

Winder, W. W., Beattie, M. A., and Holman, R. T. Endurance Training Attenuates Stress-Hormone Responses to Exercise in Fasted Rats, *American Journal of Physiology* 243: R179–R184, 1982.

Winder, W. W. and Heinger, R. W. Effect of Exercise on Degradation of Thyroxine in the Rat, *American Journal of Physiology* 224:572–575, 1973.

Epilogue

Creating Your Own Stress-Management Program

Human beings are like tea bags.
You don't know your strength until
you're put in hot water.

—*Bruce Laingen*
Former Chargé D'affaires,
American Embassy in Iran

Creating a stress-management program is a very individual undertaking. There is no set formula or series of dogmatic guidelines, only suggestions. If there is a secret to successful stress management, it is to cultivate and utilize your inner resources. Just like Dorothy, who all along had the ability to leave Oz and return home, you have the power of your inner resources. Inner resources are those abstract qualities and characteristics that become a tangible bridge over the chasm of chaos. These include, among others, intuition, creativity, willpower, faith, humor, love, courage, self-reliance, and optimism.

Once these are nurtured, how does one access inner resources? The answer begins with awareness and the desire to grow. From this desire comes a greater consciousness of yourself and the events and circumstances in your environment. Ultimately, these circumstances contribute to your growth and maturation. Awareness and desire serve as catalysts for positive change.

No one relaxation technique works for everyone. Neither is one coping strategy applicable in every stressful situation. They hold a wide range of functions. Exposure to an array of coping strategies and relaxation techniques allows you to pick and choose those that are most appropriate and will ensure the greatest returns. The initial purpose of this book was to do just that: to provide as great an exposure as possible. Now, knowledge can certainly be gained by reading a book such as this; and our educational system is based on this premise. But it has been demonstrated time and time again that people are less likely to forget something once they have experienced it for themselves. Thus, putting the concepts in this book into practice is where the real learning will take place.

The following are my best suggestions for constructing a personal stress-management program:

1. *Make a habit of spending some quality time each day to get to know yourself.* Take perhaps a half hour every day for self-exploration, whether in the form of journal writing, art therapy, music therapy, exercise, or something else. Be selfish. Believe that you deserve this time, and you will find it takes priority in your life. Time management is one of the major cornerstones of a successful stress-management program; allocate time for this self-development. Keep in mind that there is a fixed amount of time in a day and that when a new activity is planned an old one must be edited out of the daily agenda. Survey your daily routine to note where you can squeeze in a block of time for this purpose. If half an hour seems too long, start with five minutes and build from there. And remember that the occasion when you feel you do not have time for self-exploration is when you need it most.

2. *Make a habit of reading your emotional barometer.* Recognize the times when you feel angry, frustrated, anxious, and guilty. When you catch yourself feeling a certain emotion, ask yourself, What triggered this response? Why did this emotion surface? What is the most appropriate action or behavior to resolve the feeling? Emotional well-being is the ability to feel and express the full range of emotions, but it also means being able to control these emotions. On average, people laugh fifteen times a day. Make sure you fill this quota.

3. *Practice the art of unconditional love.* Self-esteem is so critical to effective stress management that it should be given top priority in the design of your stress-management program. Focus on your positive attributes, not what you perceive to be your negative ones, and work to enhance these. Don't just think of yourself as a physical entity; appreciate your intellectual, emotional, and spiritual aspects as well. Self-esteem is the seed of unconditional love. To say hello, to smile, to share a song, to give positive feedback, these are all expressions of love. And when these behaviors are practiced, they seem to double our own sense of self-esteem and self-love.

4. *Nurture your creativity skills.* Creativity is second in importance only to self-esteem as a means to manage stress. Creativity plays a direct role in problem solving and an indirect role in distracting attention from stressful episodes during moments of "play." Don't let childhood memories suffocate your creative abilities.

5. *Balance all components of your well-being and take time to nurture them.* Stress is often expressed in terms of things being out of balance. In physiological terms, this is called lack of homeostasis. But our mental, emotional, and spiritual components can also lack homeostasis. Search out and practice ways to help you achieve mental homeostasis by learning how to either stimulate or desensitize your intellect, depending on its current state. Be attentive to your emotional component as well, by being aware of emotional states as they arise. Learn to express, not suppress, your emotions, but do it in a way that is both therapeutic and diplomatic. Take good care of your body. Exercise it regularly. Feed it good nutrients, and get adequate amounts of sleep. Finally, give attention to your spirit by taking steps to enhance the maturation of your higher consciousness. Practice centering, emptying, grounding, and connecting on a regular basis. Search for and fulfill your purpose in life.

6. *Be like a child.* Children, like adults, experience acute stress, but they have not yet learned to be self-conscious about giggling, or to suppress their tears. Before children are taught to conform to adult expectations, they are rich in curiosity, imagination, and creativity. These and other characteristics of young children can be relearned if we take the time to do so.

Designing and implementing your own stress-management program may not seem easy at first, but it doesn't have to be difficult. It just takes a little desire, some discipline, and the realization that you are worth the effort. Most important, you don't have to be hit with an avalanche of stressors to begin the process of creating a sense of calm in your life. You can begin right now, gradually, one step at a time.

The following strategic plan is comprised of insights and wisdom from the previous chapters in the book. As you take yourself through the progression of steps, feel free to embellish this plan to make it as personable for your situation as possible.

Step 1: Identify Your Stressors. List your top five stressors (from most stressful to least stressful) and explain each with a sentence. The purpose of this exercise is to identify the problem, which is the first step in resolving it.

1.

2.

3.

4.

5.

Step 2: Interventions. Now, look at your list of stressors. Ask yourself which problems trigger a sense of fear and mark these with an *F.* Next, ask yourself which of these issues promote feelings of anger (and remember: anger can surface in a great many ways, from impatience to rage and hostility). Place an *A* next to all of these, and it's OK if one or more items on your list has both an *A* and an *F* by it. Remember, once you have identified the underlying emotion associated with the problem, it becomes easier to address and resolve it.

Step 3: Integration. Stress affects all aspects of our being: mind, emotions, body, and spirit.

✦ *Mind:* Do you feel overwhelmed or bored with your problems? If you feel overwhelmed, this is a sign that there is too much on your plate; some things need to be edited out or eliminated. If you feel bored, your threshold of stimulation probably is not being reached, and you might want to consider changing or adding something to find this balance. Mental well-being also involves attitudes and perceptions.

Describe one thing you can do to find mental balance. _____

_____

✦ *Emotions:* The spectrum of stress-based emotions is rather wide, yet each emotion can be traced to some element of fear or anger. In the course of your day, ask yourself how you feel (not think, but feel). If you find that stress emotions occupy more than 50 percent of your time on a regular basis, this indicates an emotional imbalance.

Describe one thing you can do to find emotional balance. _____

_____

✦ *Body:* As you have learned throughout this book, stress can and will affect physical wellbeing. Do you have any health problems that you can associate with stress?

Describe one thing you can do to find physical balance. _____

_____

✦ *Spirit:* Take a look at your current list of stressors. How many of your stressors involve relationships, values (or value conflicts) and a meaningful purpose in life? Spiritual balance can be attained in a great many ways, from time spent alone in meditation to support groups or prayer.

Describe one thing you can do to find spiritual balance. _____

_____

Self-esteem is a part of spiritual well-being. Low self-esteem sets the stage for a bad hair day to the day from hell.

List one thing you can do to give your self-esteem a boost. _____

_____

Step 4: Your Personal Stress Management Strategy. *Coping skills* are mental and emotional skills that help

you change a threatening perception to a non-threatening perception. Humor, reframing, time management, creativity, prayer, and social engineering are just a few examples of coping skills.

Take a look at the list of stressors that you completed in Step 1. Try to match at least three effective coping skills with each stressor.

Skills you are now utilizing:

1.

2.

3.

4.

5.

6.

Skills you would like to incorporate:

1.

2.

3.

4.

5.

6.

Relaxation skills include any and all activities that return you to a sense of calm and tranquillity.

Skills that you are now using:

1.

2.

3.

4.

5.

6.

Skills that you would like to incorporate:

1.

2.

3.

4.

5.

6.

Time management plays a huge role in putting stress management strategies to work, especially relaxation techniques. Here is an important question to ask yourself: Where can I find a block of time (15 to 30 minutes) to sit or lay down comfortably and relax?

References

Carlson, R. *Don't Sweat the Small Stuff.* Hyperion Books, New York, 1998.

Kirsta, A. *The Book Of Stress Survival: How to Relax and Live Positively.* Simon and Schuster, 1987.

Seaward, B.L. The Art of Calm: Relaxation through the Five Senses. Health Communications, Inc., Deerfield Beach, FL., 1999.

My Mandala Action Plan

In the circle, label each of the four quadrants (mind, body, spirit, and emotions). Then write in four ideas you have to engage in each area to deal with stress. If you wish, take some colored pens and bring your mandala to life. Then cut out this page and post the mandala in a place where you will see it regularly (e.g., on the fridge, bathroom mirror, cork board, or alongside your computer screen) as a reminder to find peace each day.

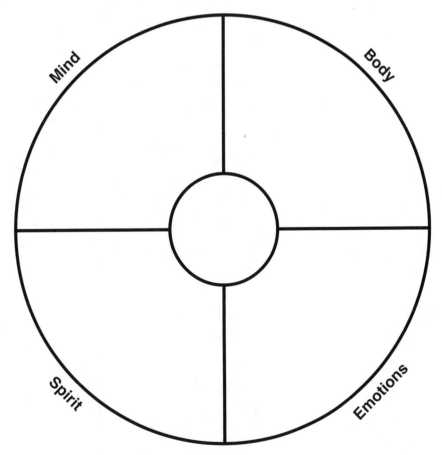

Glossary

Acetylcholine (ACh): A neurochemical substance released by neural endings through the parasympathetic nervous system to promote homeostasis and relaxation.

ACTH axis: A physiological pathway whereby a message is sent from the hypothalamus to the pituitary, then on to the adrenal gland to secrete a flood of stress hormones for fight or flight.

Active imagination: A term coined by Carl Jung describing a mental imagery process where, in a lucid dream state or relaxed state, you consciously imagine (and resolve) the end of a recurring dream. Active imagination is a form of visualization.

Acute stress: Stress that is intense in nature but short in duration.

Adrenal gland: The adrenal gland sits on top of the kidney. It is often called the stress gland because it secretes several stress hormones. The adrenal medulla secretes epinephrine and norepinephrine; the adrenal cortex secretes cortisol and aldosterone.

Aerobic exercise: Rhythmic physical work using a steady supply of oxygen delivered to working muscles for a continuous period of not less than twenty minutes.

All-or-none conditioning principle: A principle of exercise that states that to benefit from physical training, you must have the right intensity, frequency, and duration for each component of fitness challenged.

Anaerobic exercise: Physical work done in the absence of oxygen; activity that is powerful and quick but does not last more than a few minutes.

Art therapy: A coping technique of self-expression and self-awareness employing various media to describe feelings and thoughts in ways that verbal language cannot.

Arteriosclerosis: The third and final stage of coronary heart disease, wherein the arteries become hardened by cholesterol buildup, calcium deposits, and loss of elasticity.

Atherogenesis: The first stage of coronary heart disease, wherein a fat streak appears on the inner lining of artery walls.

Atherosclerosis: The second stage of coronary heart disease, wherein artery walls slowly become occluded by cholesterol-plaque buildup.

Autogenic training: Introduced by Schultz and Luthe; a relaxation technique where the individual gives conscious messages to various body parts to feel warm and heavy; effects are thought to result from vasodilation to the specified body regions intended for warmth and heaviness.

Autonomic dysregulation: Increased sensitivity to perceived threats resulting from heightened neural (sympathetic) responses speeding up the metabolic rate of one or more organs.

Autonomic nervous system: Often referred to as the automatic nervous system, the ANS is comprised of the sympathetic (arousal) and parasympathetic (relaxed) nervous systems. This part of the central nervous system requires no conscious thought: actions such as breathing and heart rate are programmed to function automatically.

Behavior modification: A coping strategy; in stress management, the adoption of assertive behaviors to increase self-esteem and decrease the likelihood of perceived stress.

Black humor: Humor about death and dying; thought to decrease fear of death.

Catharsis: Emotional release through crying, yelling, laughing, and the like.

Chakras: Chakra (pronounced shock-ra) is a Sanskrit word for spinning wheel. Chakras are part of the subtle anatomy. The seven major chakras align from the crown of the head to the base of the spine and connect to various endocrine glands. Each major chakra is directly associated with various aspects of the mind-body-spirit dynamic. When a specific chakra is closed, distorted, or congested, the perception of stress, disease, or illness may ensue.

Chronic stress: Stress that is not as intense as acute stress but that lingers for a prolonged period of time.

Clinical biofeedback: A process using one or more specially designed machines to amplify body signals (e.g., heart rate, muscle tension) and display these signals in a way that can be interpreted so that their intensity can be changed for the health of the individual.

Codependency: A stress-prone personality with many traits and behaviors that seem to increase the likelihood of perceived stress and the inability to cope effectively with it; addictive in nature; based on the need to make others dependent to receive self-validation.

Cognitive restructuring: A coping technique; substituting negative, self-defeating thoughts with positive, affirming thoughts that change perceptions of stressors from threatening to nonthreatening.

Collective unconscious: Coined by psychologist Carl Jung; the deepest level of consciousness, which connects all people together as one; divine consciousness.

Corticosteroids: Stress hormones released by the adrenal cortex; e.g., cortisol and cortisone.

Cortisol: A stress hormone released by the adrenal cortex.

Creative problem solving: A coping technique; utilizing creative abilities to describe a problem, generate ideas, select and refine a solution, implement the solution, and evaluate its effectiveness.

Defense mechanisms: Described by Sigmund Freud; unconscious thinking patterns to either decrease pain or increase pleasure to the ego.

Diaphragmatic breathing: The most basic relaxation technique; breathing from the lower stomach or diaphragm rather than the thoracic area.

Distant Healing: A term used to describe the healing effects of prayer where the person who consciously submits an intention for healing, who may in fact be thousands of miles away, has an effect on the person being prayed for.

Emotional well-being: The ability to feel and express the full range of human emotions and to control these feelings, not be controlled by them.

Enabler: A term coined in the alcohol recovery movement, referring to a person who enables spouse, parent, or child to continue either a substance or process addiction.

Entrainment: In physics, the mutual phase locking of like oscillations; in human physiology, organs or organisms giving off strong vibrations influencing organs or organisms with weeker vibrations to match the stronger rate of oscillation; thought to conserve energy.

Epinephrine: A stress hormone released by both the neural endings throughout the body and the adrenal medulla.

Eustress: Good stress; any stressor that motivates an individual toward an optimal level of performance or health.

Exploder: A person exhibiting a mismanaged anger style by exploding and intimidating others in a means to control them.

Fear: of failure: Anxious feelings of not meeting your own expectations. *of rejection:* Anxious feeling of not meeting the expectations of others. *of unknown:* Anxious feelings about uncertainty and future events. *of death:* Anxious feelings about death and the dying process. *of isolation:* Anxious feelings of being left alone. *of loss of self-dominance:* Anxious feelings of losing control of your life.

Fight-or-flight response: Coined by Walter Cannon; the instinctive physiological responses preparing the body, when confronted with a threat, to either fight or flee; an ancient survival mechanism.

General adaptation syndrome: Coined by Hans Selye; the three distinct physiological phases in reaction to chronic stress: the alarm phase, the resistance phase, and the exhaustion phase.

Genetically Modified Organisms (GMO's): The DNA of foods such as tomatoes, corn and soy beans have been genetically altered with genes from other species to produce super foods, the results of which are not fully known, but possibly dangerous to human consumption (e.g., anaphalatic shock).

Hardy personality: Coined by Maddi and Kobasa; personality characteristics that, in combination, seem to buffer against stress: control, commitment, and challenge.

Hatha yoga: A relaxation technique originating in Asia; a series of stretching postures to promote balance between body, mind, and spirit.

Homeostasis: A physiological state of complete calmness or rest; markers include resting heart rate, blood pressure, and ventilation.

Humor therapy: A coping technique; the use of humor or comedy to relieve a stressful situation; self-parody is thought to be the most effective.

Hypothalamus: Often called the "seat of the emotions," the hypothalamus is involved with emotional processing. When a thought is perceived as a threat, the hypothalamus secretes a substance called corticotrophin releasing factor to the pituitary to activate the fight-or-flight response.

Immune dysregulation: An immune system wherein various functions are suppressed; now believed to be affected by emotional negativity.

Inclusive meditation: A form of meditation where all thoughts are invited into awareness without emotional evaluation, judgment, or analysis. Zen meditation is an example.

Individuation: A term coined by Carl Jung to describe the self-realization process, a process leading to wholeness.

Ineffability: Experiences that cannot be expressed verbally; especially common during meditation.

Information seeking: A common coping technique; searching for detailed information to increase awareness about a situation that has become a perceived threat.

Journal writing: A coping technique; expression of thoughts, feelings, memories, and ideas in written form, either prose or poetry, to increase self-awareness.

Kirlian photography: A technique developed by Russian Semyon Kirlian enabling the viewer to see the electromagnetic energy given off by an object such as the leaf of a tree or human hand. This technique is one of several technologies that substantiates the human energy field.

Leftover guilt: A term coined by psychologist Wayne Dyer explaining the ill effects of unresolved guilt left over from an early childhood experience.

Locus of control: A sense of who or what is in control of one's life; people with internal locus of control take responsibility for their actions; those with external locus of control place responsibility on external factors like luck or the weather; the latter is associated with the helpless-hopeless personality, a stress-prone personality.

Logotherapy: A term coined by psychologist Viktor Frankl describing the search for meaning in one's life.

Mantra: A vehicle of concentration for meditation, typically a spoken word, such as "OM," "peace," "love," or "one."

Massage therapy: A relaxation technique; the manipulation of skin, muscles, ligaments, and connective tissue for the purpose of releasing muscle tension and increasing physical comfort of musculature and surrounding joints.

Mental imagery: Using the imagination to observe, in the first-person, images created by the unconscious mind; falls into three categories: (1) images that replicate peaceful scenes to promote relaxation, (2) images that substitute a less desirable behavior with a more healthy one, and (3) images that help to heal damaged body tissue.

Mental well-being: The ability to gather, process, recall, and communicate information.

Methylated Xanthines: The active ingredient in caffeine which triggers a sympathetic response.

Mindfulness meditation: A type of meditation where all senses concentrate on the activity being performed during the present moment, like eating an apple or washing the dishes.

Music therapy: Experiencing an altered state of physical arousal and consequent mood through processing a pleasing progression of musical notes of varying tone, rhythm, and instrumentation.

Non-Local Mind: A term given to consciousness which resides outside the brain (possibly outside the human energy field) which may explain premonitions, distant healing and prayer.

Noo-dynamics: A term coined by Viktor Frankl describing a state of tension, a spiritual dynamic, that motivates one to find meaning in life. The absence of Noo-dynamics is an existential vacuum.

Norepinephrine: A stress hormone released by both the neural endings throughout the body and the adrenal medulla.

Nutrients: There are thought to be six major nutitrients derived from food. They include: carbohydrates, fats, proteins, vitamins, minerals and water. (not included, but equally important: oxygen and sunlight.

Opening-up meditation: *See* Inclusive meditation.

Paradigm shift: Moving from one perspective of reality to another.

Parasympathetic Nervous System: The branch of the Central Nervous System which specifically calms the body through the parasympathetic response.

Parasympathetic rebound: The parasympathetic effect of relaxation (homeostasis) after physical exercise. Typically the response is such that parameters such as heart rate and blood pressure dip below pre-exercise levels.

Parasympathetic response: A calming or relaxation effect throughout the body brought about by release of neurotransmitters from neural endings.

Partially Hydrogenated Oils: A synthetically-altered lipid used in processed foods to prolong the shelf-life of food products to avoid rancidity, however these synthetically altered oils are though to be dangerous to the integrity of human physiology and possibly related to cancer and coronary heat disease.

Physical well-being: The optimal functioning of the body's eight physiological systems (respiratory, skeletal, etc.)

Pituitary gland: An endocrine gland located below the hypothalamus which, upon command from the hypothalamus, releases ACTH and then commands the adrenal glands to secrete their stress hormones.

Process addiction: The addiction to a behavioral process such as shopping, intercourse, gambling, television watching, and codependent behaviors.

Progressive muscular relaxation: A relaxation technique; tensing then relaxing the body's muscle groups in a systematic and progressive fashion to decrease muscle tension.

Psychic equilibrium: A term coined by Carl Jung to describe the balance of thought (and subsequent health-wholeness) between the conscious and unconscious minds, by having the conscious mind become multilingual to the many languages of the unconscious mind.

Psychoneuroimmunology: Specifically, the study of the effects of stress on disease; treats the mind, central nervous system, and immune system as one interrelated unit.

Restrictive (exclusive) meditation: A form of meditation wherein concentration is focused on one object (e.g., mantra, *tratek*) to the exclusion of all other thoughts, to increase self-awareness and promote relaxation.

Self-esteem: The sense of underpinning self-values, self-acceptance, and self-love; thought to be a powerful buffer against perceived threats.

Self-imposed guilt: A term coined by psychologist Wayne Dyer to describe the guilt one places on oneself when a personal value has been compromised or violated.

Self-punisher: A person exhibiting a mismanaged anger style by denying a proper outlet of anger, replacing it with guilt. Self-punishers punish themselves by excessive eating, exercise, sleeping, or even shopping.

Self-talk: The perpetual conversation heard in the mind, usually negative and coming from the critical (ego), which rarely has anything good to say.

Social engineering: A coping technique; either (1) changing stress-producing factors in the environment, or (2) changing the entire stress-producing environment; the path of least resistance (as distinguished from avoidance).

Social support: A coping technique; those groups of friends, family members, and others whose company acts to buffer against and dissipate the negative effects of stress.

Somatizer: A person exhibiting an anger style by suppressing rather than expressing feelings of anger. *Soma* means body, and when anger is suppressed, unresolved anger issues appear as symptoms of disease and illness.

Spiritual health: A term coined by the author to describe the use of our inner resources to help us cope with stress and dismantle the roadblocks on the path of life.

Spiritual potential: A term coined by the author to describe the potential we all have as humans to cope with stress through the use of our inner resources (e.g., humor, compassion, patience, tolerance, imagination, and creativity).

Spiritual well-being: The state of mature higher consciousness deriving from insightful relationships with oneself and others, a strong value system, and a meaningful purpose in life.

Stress: The experience of a perceived or real threat to mental, physical, emotional, and spiritual wellbeing resulting from a series of physiological responses and adaptations.

Subtle energy: A series of layers of energy that surround and permeate the body; thought to be associated with layers of consciousness comprising the human energy field.

Sympathetic Nervous System: The branch of the Central Nervous System which is triggers the fight or flight response when some element of threat is present.

Sympathetic response: Also known as the stress response; the release of epinephrine and norepinephrine to prepare various organs and tissues for fight or flight.

Synchronicity: A term coined by Carl Jung to explain the significance of two seemingly unrelated events that, when brought together, have a significant meaning.

Systematic desensitization: A term coined by psychologist Joseph Wolpe to describe a process of progressive tolerance to stress by gaining a greater sense of comfort with the unknown through repeated exposure and visualization.

T'ai Chi ch'uan: A relaxation technique originating among the Chinese; a succession of movements to bring the body into harmony with the universal energy (*chi*); a moving meditation.

Target organ: Any organ or tissue receiving excess neural or hormonal stimulation that increases metabolic function or abnormal cell growth; results in eventual dysfunction of the organ.

Technostress: A term used to define the result of a fast paced life dependent on various means of technology including computers, cell phones, palm computers, faxes, and email—all of which was supposed to give people more leisure time, but instead, people have become slaves, addicted to the constant use of these devices.

Time management: The prioritization, scheduling, and execution of daily responsibilities to a level of personal satisfaction. Effective time management does not mean you have more time; it means you make better use of the time you have.

Time mapping: A time-management technique; breaking down the day into fifteen- to thirty-minute segments and assigning a task or responsibility to each segment.

Tragic optimism: A term coined by psychologist Victor Frankl to explain the mindset of someone who can find value and meaning in the worst situation.

Transfatty Acids: The result of the hydrogenation process where CIS formation of a fatty acid is converted to a TRANs formation making a liquid fat solid at room temperature.

Tratek: A visual type mantra, such as a seashell, a colorfully designed mandala, or any object which is used by the eyes to focus attention and ignore distracting thoughts.

Type A behavior: The hurry sickness; the collection of stress-producing or -promoting characteristics reflecting low self-esteem, and including time urgency, rapid speech patterns, super-competitiveness, and hostile aggression.

Underhander: A person exhibiting a mismanaged anger style by seeking revenge and retaliation. This passive-aggressive anger style is a means to control others, but in a very subtle way.

Visualization: A directed exercise in mental imagery; consciously creating images of success, healing, or relaxation for the purpose of self-improvement.

Wellness paradigm: The integration, balance, and harmony of mental, physical, emotional, and spiritual well-being through taking responsibility for one's own health; posits that the whole is greater than the sum of the parts.

X-factor: A term coined by psychologist Leo Buscaglia to describe that special quality that makes each one of us unique. By focusing on our X-factor and not our faults and foibles, we enhance our self-esteem.

Yerkes-Dodson principle: The theory that some stress (eustress) is necessary for health and performance but that beyond an optimal amount both will deteriorate as distress increases.

Zen meditation: A form of meditation wherein one learns to detach from one's emotional thoughts by becoming the observer of those thoughts.

Index